Integrated media and you

Communication and You also features a full integrated media program designed to enhance the self-assessment and learning experiences.

■ ■ ■ ■ ■

LearningCurve

An online learning tool that adapts to what students already know and helps them learn what they don't yet understand, LearningCurve ensures that each student receives as much targeted instruction and practice as they need. Integrated call-outs at the end of each major section and at the beginning and end of each chapter prompt students to visit the book's LearningCurve Web site and take adaptive review quizzes, testing their knowledge of the material. Access to LearningCurve comes with every new copy of *Communication and You*.

Video

New copies of *Communication and You* also come with access to more than 300 short video clips illustrating key concepts from the book. There are also numerous public speaking clips and full-length student and professional speeches. See the last page of the book for a complete list of videos, and the inside back cover for log-in information.

For more information about *Communication and You*, please visit **bedfordstmartins.com/commandyou/catalog.**

Communication and You

AN INTRODUCTION

Dan O'Hair
University of Kentucky

Mary Wiemann
Emeritus, Santa Barbara City College

WITH

Dorothy Imrich Mullin
University of California, Santa Barbara

Jason J. Teven
California State University, Fullerton

Bedford/St. Martin's
Boston • New York

For Bedford/St. Martin's

Publisher for Communication: Erika Gutierrez
Developmental Editor: Jesse Hassenger
Senior Production Editor: Harold Chester
Assistant Production Manager: Joe Ford
Marketing Manager: Stacey Propps
Editorial Assistant: Caitlin Crandell
Copy Editor: Mary Lou Wilshaw-Watts
Indexer: Kirsten Kite
Photo Researcher: Julie Tesser
Permissions Manager: Kalina K. Ingham
Art Director: Lucy Krikorian
Text Design: Jerilyn Bockorick
Cover Design: Billy Boardman
Cover Photos: Getty Images
Composition: Cenveo Publisher Services
Printing and Binding: RRD Harrisonburg

President, Bedford/St. Martin's: Denise B. Wydra
Director of Development: Erica T. Appel
Director of Marketing: Karen R. Soeltz
Production Director: Susan W. Brown
Director of Rights and Permissions: Hilary Newman

Manufactured in the United States of America.

8 7 6
f e d c b

For information, write: Bedford/St. Martin's, 75 Arlington Street, Boston, MA 02116
(617-399-4000)

ISBN 978-1-4576-3891-6 (Student Edition)
ISBN 978-1-4576-6369-7 (Loose-leaf Edition)

Acknowledgments

} Preface

When we first wrote our book *Real Communication*, our goal was to capture the dynamic and evolving nature of the human communication discipline while engaging students' own experiences and drawing connections between topics in a wide-ranging course. As instructors, we know that making these connections clear to students can be a challenge in a course that requires diverse coverage in a relatively short period. We felt, and still feel, that communication instruction should reflect the real world that students live in. The success we experienced with *Real Communication* was gratifying, as we've heard from so many instructors and students that our friendly, familiar, and scholarly approach helps them teach and study modern communication.

The experience of writing for this course was also instructive for us, as we listened to those instructors and students talk about what approaches to communication—inside the classroom and out—work best for them. As teachers, we realize that there is no one-size-fits-all book for the human communication course, and that some students would benefit from a more streamlined, personal approach. We saw a place for another book: one just as comprehensive in its treatment of human communication, but focusing even more closely on what students want and need—and how those wants and needs relate to the communication processes.

Communication and You is the result, and writing this book began with those simple questions: What do students want? What do students need? We've found that many students are interested in the self,

which is why *Communication and You* has a uniquely personal vision of communication—a human approach to a human subject. The book covers the full spectrum of communication—interpersonal, nonverbal, group, public speaking, mass communication—while zeroing in on self-assessment and self-reflection across all of those topics, weaving them together through the students' experiences. To this end, each chapter includes prominent "What About You?" self-assessment quizzes, an enjoyable way for students to interact with the material they've just learned. This interaction continues online: *Communication and You* comes with LearningCurve, an integrated media program that allows students to take adaptive online review quizzes, assessing their progress in the course.

Many students also want to see how communication skills can be applied in the real world. We've received great encouragement about the engaging and relatable examples we use in our books, and we've built on those real-life connections for *Communication and You*. In addition to examples from real-life students, instructors, and professionals, *Communication and You* features "And You" boxes throughout each chapter that prompt students to consider their own experiences as they relate to culture, technology, and ethics; and "Things to Try" boxes that offer students activities for applying their communication skills.

Finally, communication students want to succeed in their human communication courses, and our book gives them the tools they need for that success. With its program of self-assessment, self-reflection, and online practice, *Communication and You* allows students to interact and engage with the material and, by emphasizing the application of communication skills, it prepares students to excel both in the course and in their real-life communication. We hope that having a lower price than many other human communication books will allow *Communication and You* to be accessible to students and instructors seeking an affordable option for their classrooms.

Teachers and students using the focused yet comprehensive pedagogy and accompanying digital resources of *Communication and You* should find that the human communication course becomes more manageable and easier to understand. We're excited for students to connect the study of communication with the study of their own lives.

Features of *Communication and You*: A Closer Look

A focus on skills and their application. *Communication and You* delivers everything students need in an introduction to human communication text, in an accessible and relevant voice, and offers plenty of opportunities for students to apply the material to their own lives. Throughout the book students are prompted to reexamine and reinforce concepts like perception, cognition, intercultural communication, nonverbal messages, and group roles through their own experiences.

"What About You?" self-assessment quizzes. These quizzes, appearing toward the end of each chapter, use a variety of formats, all prompting students to examine their own communication techniques, tendencies, and skills. By answering questions about themselves, readers can see the way the chapter's concepts apply to their daily interactions.

"And You" boxes. Throughout each chapter, short boxes pose thought-provoking, self-examining questions related to culture, technology, and ethics in communication. These questions, drawing on readers' experiences, infuse these three core topics with real-world

resonance. They also make great prompts for classroom discussion or quick response assignments.

"Things to Try" activities. Each chapter also includes activities that provide more involved writing and research assignments. The "Things to Try" boxes maintain the book's self-reflection focus, with activities that blend the book's concepts with personal application.

Adaptive learning and integrated self-assessment with LearningCurve. An online learning tool that adapts to what students already know and helps them practice what they don't yet understand, LearningCurve ensures that students receive as much targeted instruction and practice as they need. The goal of the program is learning, not proving what has been learned, and the practice it offers in understanding and applying communication skills helps students gain the confidence they need in their courses. At the end of major headings, as well as at the beginning and end of each chapter, integrated call-outs prompt students to visit the book's LearningCurve Web site and take adaptive review quizzes, testing their knowledge of the material. Free access to LearningCurve comes with every new copy of *Communication and You*.

Video resources. New copies of *Communication and You* also come with access to *VideoCentral: Human Communication*, an online resource featuring hundreds of short video clips illustrating the most important terms from the text.

Print and Digital Formats

For more information on these formats, please visit the online catalog at **bedfordstmartins.com/commandyou/catalog**.

The loose-leaf edition of *Communication and You* features the same print text in a convenient, budget-priced format, designed to fit into any three-ring binder.

The Bedford e-Book to Go for *Communication and You* includes the same content as the print book and provides an affordable, tech-savvy PDF e-book option for students. Instructors can customize the e-book by adding their own content and deleting or rearranging chapters. Learn more about custom Bedford e-Books to Go and about other e-book versions of *Communication and You* in a variety of formats at **bedfordstmartins.com/ebooks**.

Coming soon! The *Bedford x-Book for Communication and You* reimagines what a text can do online, integrating video and social tools that let instructors and students get into the book in a whole new way. Assignments are organized into a clear road map so that students can focus on what they need, detailed reports give instructors insight into what students have read and how they've performed on assigned activities, and handy course links let instructors upload or link to important course resources. Instructors can also customize the x-book, changing the table of contents or embedding their own materials. Learn more at **bedfordstmartins.com/catalog/ebooks**.

Launchpad for *Communication and you* is designed to support students in all aspects of the introduction to communication course. It's fully loaded with the x-book, hundreds of video clips, and opportunities for students to assess their learning. Launchpad makes it easy to upload and annotate video, embed YouTube clips, and create video assignments.

Resources for Students

For more information on these resources or to learn about package options, please visit the online catalog at **bedfordstmartins.com/commandyou/catalog**.

Integrated media for *Communication and You*. Every new copy of *Communication and You* comes with access to LearningCurve, an adaptive online learning tool that helps students study, practice, and apply their communication skills. At the end of major headings, prompts refer students to the book's LearningCurve Web site, where they can answer questions about the material in each chapter. New copies of *Communication and You* also come with access to *VideoCentral: Human Communication*, an online resource of short video clips that define important terms from the text (see last page of book for a list). Finally, the book has a companion Web site with free and open access to a host of resources and study tools, including chapter outlines and review quizzes, activities, and more.

***The Essential Guide to Intercultural Communication* by Jennifer Willis-Rivera (University of Wisconsin, River Falls).** This useful guide offers an overview of key communication areas, including perception, verbal and nonverbal communication, interpersonal relationships, and organizations, from a uniquely intercultural perspective. Enhancing the discussion are contemporary and fun examples drawn from real life as well as an entire chapter devoted to intercultural communication in popular culture.

***The Essential Guide to Rhetoric* by William M. Keith (University of Wisconsin, Milwaukee) and Christian O. Lundberg (University of North Carolina, Chapel Hill).** This handy guide is a powerful addition to the public speaking portion of the human communication course, providing an accessible and balanced overview of key historical and contemporary rhetorical theories. Written by two leaders in the field, this brief introduction uses concrete, relevant examples and jargon-free language to bring concepts to life.

***The Essential Guide to Presentation Software* by Allison Ainsworth (Gainesville State College) and Rob Patterson (University of Virginia).** This guide shows students how presentation software can be used to support but not overtake their speeches. Sample screens and practical advice make this an indispensable resource for students preparing electronic visual aids.

Outlining and Organizing Your Speech by Merry Buchanan (University of Central Oklahoma). This student workbook provides step-by-step guidance for preparing informative, persuasive, and professional presentations and gives students the opportunity to practice the critical skills of conducting audience analysis, dealing with communication apprehension, selecting a speech topic and purpose, researching support materials, organizing and outlining, developing introductions and conclusions, enhancing language and delivery, and preparing and using presentation aids.

Media Career Guide: Preparing for Jobs in the 21st Century, Ninth Edition, by Sherri Hope Culver (Temple University) and James Seguin (Robert Morris University). Practical and student-friendly, this guide includes a comprehensive directory of media jobs, practical tips, and career guidance for students considering a major in communication studies and mass media.

Research and Documentation in the Electronic Age, Fifth Edition, by Diana Hacker (late, of Prince George's Community College) and Barbara Fister (Gustavus Adolphus College). This handy booklet covers everything students need for college research assignments at the library and on the Internet, including advice for finding and evaluating Internet sources.

Resources for Instructors

For more information or to order or download these resources, please visit the online catalog at bedfordstmartins.com/commandyou/catalog.

Instructor's Resource Manual. This manual contains helpful tips and teaching assistance for new and seasoned instructors alike. Content includes learning objectives, lecture outlines, general classroom activities, and review questions as well as suggestions for setting up a syllabus, tips on managing your classroom, and general notes on teaching the course.

ESL Students in the Public Speaking Classroom: A Guide for Teachers by Robbin Crabtree (Fairfield University) and Robert Weissberg (New Mexico State University). As the United States increasingly becomes a nation of non-native speakers, instructors must find new pedagogical tools to aid students for whom English is a second language. This guide specifically addresses the needs of ESL students in the public speaking arena and offers instructors valuable advice for helping students deal successfully with the unique challenges they face. Free to adopters.

Professional and student speeches. Available on DVD, volume 19 of the esteemed Great Speeches series offers dynamic professional speeches for today's classroom, featuring such compelling speakers as Bill Clinton, Christopher Reeve, and the Dalai Lama. Additional professional videos are available from the Bedford/St. Martin's Video Library. In addition, three recordings of student speeches (featuring students of varying abilities from Texas Tech and the University of Oklahoma) provide models for study and analysis. These professional and student speech resources are free to qualified adopters. Please contact your sales representative for more information.

Coordinating the Communication Course: A Guidebook by Deanna L. Fassett and John T. Warren. This guidebook offers the most practical advice on every topic central to the coordinator/director role. Starting with setting a strong foundation, this professional resource continues on with thoughtful guidance, tips, and best practices on crucial topics such as creating community across multiple sections, orchestrating meaningful assessment, hiring and training instructors, and more. Model course materials, recommended readings, and insights from successful coordinators make this resource a must-have for anyone directing a course in communication.

Acknowledgments

First and foremost, we owe a great deal of gratitude to our families and friends who supported us and listened to us as we worked through ideas for the book, who made us laugh during bouts of writer's block, and who were understanding when we had to cancel plans to meet deadlines. So thank you, Mary, John, Erica, and Jonathan, as well as John, Molly, Chad, William, Jackson, John, and Andrea. You will always remain our litmus tests for just how real our communication is across its many applications. In addition, we both wish to credit and thank Gus Friedrich and John Wiemann, whose contributions to this book and our discipline are far too many to list. Thanks also to John O'Loughlin of HR Capital Partners and vice president of Global Human Resources at SkinIt, for consulting on and reviewing the Interviewing Appendix. And, of course, we must thank our students—including Daniel Bernard, Cory Cunningham, Vanessa Gonzales, Cynthia Inda, Michel Haigh, and Kim Potts, among countless others—who continue to inspire us as teachers. We're grateful for the frank discussions that have opened our eyes to many of the challenges of this course from your point of view, and we are grateful for your helpful and thoughtful suggestions for examples.

We would also like to thank everyone at Bedford/St. Martin's who helped make this book possible, including President Denise Wydra, Director of Development Erica Appel, and Director of Production Sue Brown. We owe a particular debt of gratitude to our editorial colleagues at Bedford: Publisher Erika Gutierrez for her leadership and passion for education; Senior Development Editor Karen Schultz Moore and Development Editor Jesse Hassenger for their creativity, feedback, and vision to create a book that truly reaches students; Editorial Assistant Caitlin Crandell for her artistic eye in organizing and executing our art program; and Media Editor Tom Kane for managing all of the video material with professionalism and grace. Without the production staff at Bedford, this manuscript would be nothing more than black words on white paper fresh from our printers (with quite a few typos to boot!). So we thank Managing Editor Shuli Traub for her leadership; Senior Project Editor Harold Chester for his dedication and superior organizational skills; and Associate Director, Production, Elise S. Kaiser for making a seemingly impossible schedule actually happen. Also, we credit our copy editor, Mary Lou Wilshaw-Watts; our proofreaders, Jennifer Brett Greenstein and Dorothy Hoffman; Art Director Lucy Krikorian; cover designer Billy Boardman; the designer of this beautiful book, Jerilyn Bockorick of Cenveo © Publisher Services; our permissions specialist, Linda Winters; and our capable photo researcher, Julie Tesser. Finally, we wish to thank Bedford's extraordinary marketing staff for their incredible commitment and excitement about our book—and their willingness to share that excitement with others: Director of Marketing Karen R. Soeltz, Marketing Manager Stacey Propps, Senior Market Development Manager Sally Constable, and Marketing Assistants Allyson Russell and Kate George.

ABOUT THE AUTHORS

Dan O'Hair is dean of the University of Kentucky College of Communications and Information Studies. He is past presidential professor in the Department of Communication at the University of Oklahoma and past president of the National Communication Association. He is coauthor or coeditor of fifteen communication texts and scholarly volumes and has published more than eighty research articles and chapters in dozens of communication, psychology, and health journals and books. He is a frequent presenter at national and international communication conferences, is on the editorial boards of various journals, and has served on numerous committees and task forces for regional and national communication associations.

Mary Wiemann is professor emeritus in the Department of Communication at Santa Barbara City College in California. Her books, book chapters, journal articles, student and instructor manuals, and online instructional materials all reflect her commitment to making effective communication real and accessible for students. A recipient of awards for outstanding teaching, she is also a communication laboratory innovator and has directed classroom research projects in the community college setting. She serves on the editorial board of the *Journal of Literacy and Technology*, is a frequent presenter at the National Communication Association convention, and has held a number of offices in the Human Communication and Technology Division of that organization.

Dorothy "Dolly" Imrich Mullin is a continuing lecturer in the Department of Communication at the University of California, Santa Barbara. Her published research is in the area of media policy and effects. Her current focus is on teaching communication to undergraduates. She specializes in large introductory communication courses, including research methods and theory, and has been recognized for her efforts with a Distinguished Teaching Award. She also trains and supervises the graduate student teaching assistants, working to develop and promote excellent teaching skills among the professors of the future.

Jason J. Teven, an award-winning scholar and teacher, is professor of Human Communication Studies and the basic course coordinator at California State University, Fullerton. He has published widely in academic journals and is devoted to programmatic research and the social scientific approach to human communication, with research relating to credibility, caring, and social influence within instructional, interpersonal, and organizational communication contexts. His most recent scholarly activities include the examination of superior-subordinate relationships within organizations; communication competence; and the impact of personality traits on communication within the workplace and interpersonal relationships.

Brief Contents

} Contents

2 Perceiving the Self and Others 29

3 Communication and Culture 51

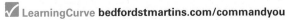

4 Verbal Communication 75

5 **Nonverbal Communication** 97

6 **Listening** 119

PART TWO **Interpersonal Communication**

7 Developing and Maintaining Relationships 141

8 Managing Conflict in Relationships 167

PART FOUR   Public Speaking

11 Preparing and Researching Presentations 233

12 Organizing, Writing, and Outlining Presentations 259

13 Delivering Presentations   287

14 Informative Speaking   309

15 Persuasive Speaking   335

Appendix A: Competent Interviewing 361

Appendix B: Understanding Mass and Mediated Communication 387

Communication and You

AN INTRODUCTION

✓ Look for **LearningCurve** throughout the chapter to help you review.
bedfordstmartins.com/commandyou

1 } Communication: Essential Human Behavior

I t was the very definition of a catastrophe: eleven men were killed on April 20, 2010, when an explosion rocked the BP drilling rig *Deepwater Horizon*, sparking a fire that was visible for more than thirty miles and burned for two days before the entire rig sank to the bottom of the Gulf of Mexico. Afterward, millions of gallons of oil gushed from the blown-out rig, assaulting wildlife, beaches, and the livelihoods of Gulf Coast residents still reeling from Hurricane Katrina. Attempts to stop the leak failed. Americans were further horrified when, on May 31, BP chief executive Tony Hayward told reporters, "We're sorry for the massive disruption it's caused. . . . There's no one who wants this over more than I do. I would like my life back"

(Mouawad & Krauss, 2010, p. A1). When the embattled CEO spent a day watching his yacht compete in a big race the following month—with oil still spilling into the Gulf of Mexico at an alarming rate—one Alabama senator commented on Hayward's activity as the "height of arrogance" (Robbins, 2010, p. A20).

Fingers were pointed in many directions. Some blamed BP; BP blamed Transocean (the company from which it rented the rig); others blamed the government agencies that had failed to enforce safety regulations (Barstow, Dodd, Glanz, Saul, & Urbina, 2010). Amid all the accusations, a generation of Gulf Coast residents braced themselves for an even more uncertain future.

After you have finished reading this chapter, you will be able to

Define the communication process.

Describe the functions of communication.

Assess the quality (communicative value) of communication by examining its six characteristics.

Define what communication scholars consider to be competent communication.

Describe the visual representations, or models, of communication.

Describe why communication is vital to everyone.

Communication is the process by which we use symbols, signs, and behaviors to exchange information. That process is so crucial that communication is described as "the process through which the social fabric of relationships, groups, organizations, societies, and world order—and disorder—is created and maintained" (Ruben, 2005, pp. 294–295). Successful communication allows us to satisfy our most basic needs, from finding food and shelter to functioning in our communities and developing meaningful relationships. Because communication is such a natural part of our daily lives, we often take it for granted. Yet every day, communication failures lead to failed plans, isolation, misunderstandings, hurt feelings—and disasters like the BP oil spill.

Communication challenges exist in every profession and every personal relationship. For example, communication professor (and reserve police officer) Howard Giles claims that 97 percent of law enforcement practices involve communication skills (Giles et al., 2006). But police academies usually spend little time teaching those skills. Most citizens lack these crucial skills as well. One professor who teaches college-level communication classes to prisoners notes that "the vast majority of [his] imprisoned students have been caged, in large part, because of their communicative illiteracy" (Hartnett, 2010, p. 68).

Effective communicators understand how their communication choices affect *others* and why *others'* communication choices affect *them* as they do. So in this chapter, we look at why we communicate, how we communicate, and what it means to communicate well. Then we examine ways of visualizing the communication process and consider the history of this rich discipline.

We Must Communicate: The Functional Perspective

We communicate from the moment we're born. A baby's cry lets everyone within earshot know that something isn't right: he's hungry, cold, or has a painful ear infection. Throughout our lives, we dedicate a huge amount of time to communicating with others to ensure that our needs are met—though in more sophisticated ways than we did as infants. We talk, listen, smile, and nod; we write up résumés and go on dates. In these ways, we learn, express ourselves, form relationships, and gain employment. This **functional perspective** of communication examines how our communication helps (or doesn't help) us accomplish our goals in personal, group, organizational, or public situations.

Technology and You
Many technologies that you may think of as having fun or leisure uses also have a functional side. Do you use technology like text messaging, Facebook updates, or Twitter posts for fun, function, or both?

All communication "works" (or not) within the context of **relationships**—the interconnections between

---

Box 1.1 Communication Is Not Just Common Sense

Everyone has ideas about what constitutes good communication. But just how correct are those ideas? Do your personal theories of communication match what social science tells us about the way we communicate? Consider the following questions:

- **Does talking equal effective communication?** Have you ever sat through a lecture only to find that your instructor was boring, unclear, disorganized, or even offensive? Talking is one way of giving information, but it isn't always effective on its own. To communicate effectively, we also need to be thoughtful and to use silence, listening skills, and symbols other than words.

- **Do body movements (often called "body language") constitute a language?** As you will learn in Chapter 5, nonverbal communication is important and useful, but there is no direct translation for what body movements mean. Because nonverbal communication can be interpreted in many different ways, it is not a true language.

- **Is more control necessarily better in communication?** While we admire people who can articulate their point of view, if we think they are trying to trick us or force us, we often resist what they are saying. Your father may stay on topic and clearly state his case against your choice of a major, for example, but he still can't make you do what he wants.

- **Are most communication behaviors inborn and entirely natural?** No. Although we are certainly born with some ability to communicate, most of the skills we need to communicate must be learned—otherwise we'd go through life crying whenever we needed something. The best communicators never stop learning.

- **Is speaking well more important than listening?** If you talk and nobody listens, has communication taken place? No. Communication is a two-way street, and listening is a crucial part of the process.

---

people that function to achieve some goal. Our relationships involve **interdependence**, meaning that our actions affect one another. For example, Jamie flips burgers to get a paycheck to help pay for college—that's her goal. Her boss depends on Jamie to do her job well and keep the business profitable. The customers, who want an inexpensive and quick lunch, depend on both of them. Jamie, the boss, and the lunch customers are interdependent.

A long line of research conducted in a variety of contexts—including work groups, families, and friendships—has found that virtually all communication behavior serves one or more primary functions, such as expressing affiliation, achieving goals, or influencing others (Wiemann & Krueger, 1980). Let's consider each of these functions, keeping in mind that they are often intertwined.

Expressing Affiliation

Affiliation is the feelings you have for others. You show how much you want to be connected to or associated with someone by expressing liking, love, or respect—or alternatively, dislike, hatred, or disrespect (Wiemann, 2009). This love-hate continuum works to establish and maintain relationships happily (or unhappily).

Obviously, it feels good to be loved, liked, and respected. But affiliation may also meet practical needs, as when you marry someone you believe can offer you stability and security. Other times affiliation fulfills emotional needs, offering companionship or intellectual stimulation (or both).

Affiliation can be expressed in many different ways—verbally (by saying "I love you") and nonverbally (with a big hug) and through face-to-face or

⭕ All communication relationships, whether fleeting or enduring, involve interdependence.

mediated (like when sending text messages or using social-networking sites) channels. In fact, we are increasingly using media technologies to develop and maintain a positive affiliation with each other (Walther & Ramirez, 2009), especially with people who are physically far away. A "U can do it!" text message from Mom can help you go into your midterm exam with confidence. A simple click of the "Like" thumbs-up icon on Facebook can show that you enjoy something a friend posted.

Achieving Goals

To reach our goals, we must communicate. Without communication, such things as becoming educated,

> **Technology and You**
>
> Can you think of a recent situation in which you expressed or received a positive affiliation through Facebook or other social media? What was the situation, and what technology was involved?

getting a job, and completing tasks like opening a bank account or making dinner for a large group would be impossible. We need communication to accomplish particular objectives, a function we call **goal achievement**.

> Without communication, such things as becoming educated, getting a job, and completing tasks like opening a bank account or making dinner for a large group would be impossible.

There are usually multiple goals at play in any given situation. For example, you may want to host Thanksgiving this year to illustrate your adult status in the family, but your mother-in-law may insist on keeping the holiday at her home out of tradition. If you and she are interdependent, both of you will likely try to accomplish your individual goal without losing any affection for each other. In addition, goals may change during a communication encounter. For instance, you initially think you want to host Thanksgiving but then realize you don't want that responsibility once you recognize how much work is involved. We achieve our goals in a variety of ways too. To illustrate, you might simply ask your sister to help you host Thanksgiving. You might try to bully her into it. Or you might hint at what you want or suggest that she's lazy if she doesn't help you host.

📍 Contestants in demanding competitions, such as on the show *Hell's Kitchen*, know that it would be impossible to achieve goals without clear communication.

Influencing Others

Most communication is influential in one way or another. Some influence is intentional: a politician uses gestures strategically during a press conference to shape how voters perceive her. Other influence is unintentional; Michaela's lack of eye contact during an after-class meeting gives her professor the sense that she lacks confidence, but she's really just having trouble with her contact lenses.

The ability of one person, group, or organization to influence others, and the manner in which their relationships are conducted, is called **control**. Unlike affection, which you can give and receive infinitely, control is finite: the more control one person has in a relationship, the less the others in the relationship have. Distribution of control is worked out between the relational partners through communication—by how they talk with each other, what they say, and when they interact. This negotiation of control may seem like a power struggle at times.[1] But it is a necessary aspect of every type of relationship: between family members, friends, romantic partners, colleagues, doctors and patients, teachers and students, and advertisers and consumers.

The amount of control you have over others or that they have over you varies, depending on the

Culture and You

In your family's culture and relationships, are there members who tend to have greater control than others? If so, who are they, and why do you think that is? Have you noticed different distributions of control in other families or groups of friends?

---

[1]Some scholars use *dominance* as a synonym for *control*. See, for example, Dillard, Solomon, and Palmer (1999).

What About You?

Assessing Your Control Needs
Answer these questions to understand how you negotiate control in certain situations.

1. You are unhappy with your roommate because you feel that he does not do his share of cleanup in the kitchen. You
   A. continuously point out when it is his turn to clean up.
   B. tell him to forget it and do it yourself.
   C. give him the silent treatment until he realizes you're upset.
   D. ask why he doesn't do the chores and consider reassigning tasks.

2. Your family is planning a summer reunion. You
   A. push to have it when and where you want.
   B. take over the planning yourself.
   C. leave it to other family members to haggle over the annoying details.
   D. participate in the decision process, volunteering to do your share.

3. You're assigned to a group project in class. You
   A. take leadership early, telling others what to do to get an A.
   B. give up trying to get everyone to cooperate and just do the work yourself.
   C. sit back and let others take leadership roles.
   D. help distribute tasks and work on a time line with others.

4. You are reviewing an employee's performance. You
   A. speak to the employee about his or her strengths and weaknesses and outline a plan to meet goals.
   B. deliver a written evaluation without a face-to-face meeting.
   C. avoid any formal evaluation and hope the employee figures things out.
   D. ask the employee for a self-evaluation and respond to it.

If you responded A to most items: You are comfortable exerting a lot of control, though you should express affiliation (respect, liking) so that others know you care about and respect them.

If you responded B to most items: You have a tendency to take control because you don't have much confidence in others. Instead, try having confidence in your ability to influence others so you don't end up doing everything yourself.

If you responded C to most items: You have a low control need. This often helps you avoid confrontation, but you're probably not getting your needs met in a number of areas.

If you responded D to most items: You are more willing to share control in relationships, making you more likely to accomplish goals with the cooperation of others.

◉ In most learning environments, teachers should have more control than students in the classroom.

THINGS TO TRY

Keep a log of all the different channels (face to face, written, computer mediated, telephonic, and others) you use to communicate during the course of one morning or afternoon. Do you regularly communicate with a particular person via a specific channel (for example, stay in touch with your mother mostly over the phone, with your romantic partner through text messages, and with your childhood best friend via Facebook postings)? What channels do you prefer to use when sending different types of messages (a long or a short message, a positive or a negative message, a business or a personal message, and so on)?

situation and each person's status. Sometimes control shifts from one party to another. For example, as a new bank employee, Manny looks to his manager, Alexis, for direction and advice about how to do his job well. The unequal control distribution is appropriate and meets Manny's and Alexis's expectations of their job responsibilities. But as Manny becomes more comfortable in the job, he will likely take more control, and Alexis will let him work more independently. This redistribution of control is a natural process.

LearningCurve
bedfordstmartins.com/commandyou

How We Communicate

It's 8:45 A.M. in New York City. A woman walks up to a street vendor's cart, smiles and nods quickly at the vendor, and says, "Regular." The man promptly prepares her a small coffee with milk and two sugars. He hands her the coffee; she hands him a dollar, says, "Thanks," and continues on her way.

With only two words spoken, an entire business transaction has been carried out to the satisfaction of both parties. But what exactly occurred? The characteristics of communication can explain.

Characteristics of Communication

Communication has six defining characteristics: the extent to which the message is *symbolic*, the extent to which the *code is shared*, the degree to which the message is *culturally bound*, the sender's perceived *intentionality*, the presence of a *channel*, and the degree to which the encoding and decoding of messages are *transactional*. That's quite a mouthful, so let's look at each characteristic more closely.

◉ Orchestra conductors communicate with dozens of musicians without speaking a word, conveying their meaning through body movements and facial expression.

Communication Is Symbolic. Communication relies on the use of **symbols**—arbitrary constructions (usually language or behaviors) that refer to objects: people, things, and ideas. The stronger the connection between symbol and object, the clearer the intended meaning, and vice versa. For example, in the scenario presented earlier, our customer greeted the street vendor with a smile and a nod—behaviors clearly indicating the idea of "greeting."

A symbol can take on a new meaning if at least two people agree that it will have that meaning for them. A romantic couple, for example, might use the phrase "I'm sleepy" to indicate interest in lovemaking. Social groups, such as fraternities and sororities or sports teams, might use a handshake, a password, or an article of clothing to set themselves apart from others. We cover verbal and nonverbal symbols more deeply in Chapters 4 and 5.

Communication Requires a Shared Code. A **code** is a set of symbols that are joined to create a meaningful message. For communication to take place, the participants must share the code to encode and decode messages. **Encoding** is the process of mentally constructing a message. **Decoding** is the process of interpreting and assigning meaning to a message. If the relational partners are using the same code, they are more likely to encode and decode messages accurately and arrive at the shared meaning they want to communicate.

Speaking a common language is the most obvious example of sharing a communication code, though it is certainly not the only one. Baseball teams, for example, develop elaborate codes for various pitches and plays, which players communicate through hand gestures and body movements (for example, by removing a baseball cap, holding up three fingers, and shaking them twice). Similarly, consider the emoticons and texting and chat-room shorthand we use when communicating online—especially when we're in a hurry.

Communication Is Linked to Culture. If you've ever traveled abroad, or even through the different neighborhoods of a large city, you know that communication is linked to culture. **Culture** refers to the shared beliefs, values, and practices of a group of people. A group's culture includes the language (or languages) and other symbols used by group members as well as the norms and rules about appropriate behavior.

Most people are members of several co-cultures simultaneously. **Co-cultures** are smaller groups of people within a larger culture who are distinguished by features such as race, religion, age, generation, political affiliation, gender, sexual orientation, economic status, educational level, occupation, and a host of other factors.

> **Culture and You**
>
> Can you name several co-cultures that you belong to? How have these different co-cultures affected your communication? Are there people in your life who are easier to communicate with because of shared culture? Do you have friends or family who you communicate with differently because of differing cultures or co-cultures?

Consider Anna, who identifies with a number of co-cultures: she is an American, an African American, a midwesterner, a married lawyer with two children, a person with an income over $100,000 a year, a Democrat, and a Baptist. Each of these co-cultures carries different meanings for Anna and affects her communication—including the languages she speaks, how she presents herself to others, and how she interprets others' behavior (Chen & Starosta, 1996). Cultural identities can even form around interests and hobbies. For example, a music critic at *Blender* magazine might distinguish among rock, soul, and hip-hop and might even break those styles down further, using terms like *old-school, freestyle, classic, punk, techno,* and *R & B*. For someone less involved or less interested in the music scene, such distinctions might seem unimportant—it's all just popular music.

Communication Can Be Unintentional. Some communication is *intentional*, such as IM-ing a friend to let her know you'll be away from your computer and using a mutually understood code (BRB! ☺). Other

> { **The most successful communicators are sensitive to the fact that both intended and unintended messages exert an impact on the people around them.** }

communication is *spontaneous* and therefore unintentional (Buck, 1988; Motley, 1990). For example, you communicate a message when you blush, even though blushing is an involuntary action. The distinction between the two types of communication can be described as the difference between *giving* information and *giving off* information (Goffman, 1967).

These distinctions are important: we tend to see involuntary messages as more honest and reliable because the person giving off the information doesn't have the opportunity to censor it. However, most spontaneous messages are ambiguous: Are you blushing because you're embarrassed? Because you're angry? Because you've had a hot cup of tea? Because you just ran up six flights of stairs? To interpret information that someone else gives off, we generally attend to other surrounding cues, but even then, our final assessment can be questionable. The most successful communicators are sensitive to the fact that both intended and unintended messages exert an impact on the people around them.

> **Technology and You**
>
> Have you ever had an online communication—a Facebook comment, a blog post, a Twitter entry—misinterpreted by people you know (or even by strangers)? Did that misunderstanding affect the way you use these technological tools?

Communication Occurs Through Various Channels. Once, the only means of communication—the only channel—was face-to-face contact. But as society became more sophisticated, other channels emerged. Smoke signals, handwritten correspondence, telegraph, telephone, e-mail, and text messaging are all examples. A **channel** is simply the method through which communication occurs. We must have a channel to communicate.

Most people in technologically advanced societies use many channels to communicate, though they are not always proficient at adapting communication for the channel being used. Do you have a friend who leaves five-minute voice-mail messages on your cell phone as though speaking directly with you? Or do you have a cousin who shares deeply private information with all six hundred of her Facebook "friends"? We all need to identify the channel that will work best for certain messages, at certain points in our relationships with certain people, and then adapt our messages to that medium.

> **Ethics and You**
>
> What might be some ethical dangers when using so many different technological channels to communicate? How does the privacy, or sometimes lack thereof, involved in communicating through a medium like Facebook affect your decision making?

Communication Is Transactional. You may recall the 2009 MTV Video Music Awards for one reason: rapper Kanye West jumped on stage during Taylor Swift's acceptance speech for best female music video to declare that Beyoncé had been robbed of that award. West later expressed regrets about his behavior and offered apologies on talk shows like *The View* and *The Tonight Show with Jay Leno*. Yet no amount of apologizing could change what West had done, how Swift had reacted, or how audiences worldwide perceived the incident. That's because communication is a **transactional** process: it involves two or more people acting in both *sender* and *receiver* roles, and their messages are interdependent—influenced by those of their partner. Once a message has been sent (intentionally or not) and received, it *cannot* be

Table 1.1 Communication Characteristics: Anatomy of a Coffee Sale

The simple coffee sale in New York City described in the text is clearly communicative because it has all six defining characteristics.

Characteristic	Behavior
Communication is symbolic.	Both parties understand the meaning of "regular." Both parties understand the smile and nod greeting.
Communication requires a shared code.	Both parties speak English.
Communication is linked to culture.	Both parties are New Yorkers.
Communication can be unintentional.	The customer uses gestures and facial expressions.
Communication occurs through various channels.	The woman uses both words and gestures; they are not ambiguous to the street vendor.
Communication is transactional.	The woman understands the message she is giving, and the vendor understands the message he is receiving.

reversed, nor can it be repeated in precisely the same way. This ongoing process can be immediate (as in a real-time conversation) or delayed (as in the case of a text-message exchange).

As we illustrate throughout this book, whenever you communicate with others, you try to influence them in some way. Equally important, you are influenced by others. Who has the most influence, however, depends on the communication situation. For example, in close friendships or romantic relationships, each party tends to exert influence equally. But during a formal presentation, the speaker is usually seen as attempting to influence the audience.

Assessing Communicative Value

To understand communication more fully, you assess the quality, or communicative value, of your communication. You do this by examining the degree to which the communication demonstrates the six characteristics discussed earlier. If it is definitely symbolic, with a shared code, and definitely intentional, it has high communicative value, and misunderstandings are less likely.

For example, recall the coffee sale described at the beginning of this section. The woman and the

street vendor share a clear, if unwritten, code: in New York City, "regular" coffee means coffee with milk and two sugars. The code has a cultural meaning unique to New York. Even within the city, it is somewhat specialized, limited to street vendors and delicatessens. Had she said the same word to the counterperson at a Seattle's Best coffee shop on the West Coast—or even at the Starbucks just down the street—she might have gotten a perplexed stare in reply. See Table 1.1 for a more detailed breakdown of this transaction.

LearningCurve
bedfordstmartins.com/commandyou

Communicating Competently

Communicating is inherently complex because people and situations vary. For example, in the classic film *Walk the Line*, singer-songwriter Johnny Cash is thoroughly at ease in front of an audience but falls apart when communicating at home. Cash's relationship with his wife Vivian seems marked by a lack of

⬦ While Johnny Cash (played by Joaquin Phoenix in the film *Walk the Line*) had a great connection and rapport with his fans, his first marriage lacked those communication qualities and was unsuccessful.

understanding, dishonesty, and an inability to connect on a personal level. The Academy Award–winning film reveals that Johnny Cash has a set of useful and unique talents but that he must adapt them to suit the needs of different people and situations. He does this in his personal life in his successful second marriage to June Carter Cash.

In studying communication, our goal is to become competent communicators. By competent, we do not mean merely adequate. Indeed, communication scholars use the term **competent communication** to describe communication that is effective and appropriate for a given situation and in which the communicators evaluate and reassess their own communication process (Wiemann & Backlund, 1980). We examine each of these aspects of competent communication in the following sections.

Competent Communication Is Process Oriented

An old sports adage says, "It's not whether you win or lose; it's how you play the game." This means that the *process* (how you play) is more important than the *outcome* (whether you win or lose). In communication,

an **outcome** has to do with the product of an interchange. In a negotiation, for example, the outcome may be that you get a good deal on a product or get a contract signed. Competent communication is also concerned with **process**—the means by which participants arrive at an outcome. Although outcomes obviously still play a role in a communication process, *what* is said and *how* it is said have great significance.

When it comes to process, communicators who strive to create mutually satisfying outcomes are the most competent (Wiemann, 1977). A study of fathers and daughters, for example, found that the most satisfactory relationships involved a matching of needs and a balancing of control (Punyanunt-Carter, 2005). Asif, for example, hoped his daughter Laila would attend his alma mater. In the summer before Laila's senior year of high school, the two visited that university as well as several others. They worked together on her college applications and debated the merits of each school. Both Asif and Laila describe their relationship

📍 Jon Stewart and Stephen Colbert's Rally to Restore Sanity was described by the organizers as a "call to reasonableness" in a time of polarized, vitriolic, and often unethical exchanges between Democrats and Republicans.

as satisfying and note that the process of searching for the right school made them closer, even though Laila ultimately chose another school.

Ethical considerations are a crucial part of the communication process. **Ethics** is the study of morals, specifically the moral choices individuals make in their relationships with others. Your personal values, along with your culture's values, provide guidance on how to appropriately construct your messages and how to analyze messages directed toward you (Casmir, 1997; Christians & Traber, 1997). Ethical concerns arise whenever standards of right and wrong significantly affect our communication behavior (Johannesen, 1996). For example, a political spokes-

> ### Ethics and You
> Have you witnessed ethical lapses in communication? What was the situation, and what was the eventual outcome? How would you have handled the situation differently if you had been in charge of the communication process?

person who lies or twists the truth to get a bump in the polls for a candidate is unethical, manipulative, and exploitive—hardly the characteristics of a competent communicator.

Box 1.2 National Communication Association Credo for Ethical Communication

Questions of right and wrong arise whenever people communicate. Ethical communication is fundamental to responsible thinking, decision-making, and the development of relationships and communities within and across contexts, cultures, channels, and media. Moreover, ethical communication enhances human worth and dignity by fostering truthfulness, fairness, responsibility, personal integrity, and respect for self and others. We believe that unethical communication threatens the quality of all communication and consequently the well-being of individuals and the society in which we live. Therefore we, the members of the National Communication Association, endorse and are committed to practicing the following principles of ethical communication:

- We advocate truthfulness, accuracy, honesty, and reason as essential to the integrity of communication.

- We endorse freedom of expression, diversity of perspective, and tolerance of dissent to achieve the informed and responsible decision-making fundamental to a civil society.

- We strive to understand and respect other communicators before evaluating and responding to their messages.

- We promote access to communication resources and opportunities as necessary to fulfill human potential and contribute to the well-being of families, communities, and society.

- We promote communication climates of caring and mutual understanding that respect the unique needs and characteristics of individual communicators.

- We condemn communication that degrades individuals and humanity through distortion, intimidation, coercion, and violence and through the expression of intolerance and hatred.

- We are committed to the courageous expression of personal convictions in pursuit of fairness and justice.

- We advocate sharing information, opinions, and feelings when facing significant choices while also respecting privacy and confidentiality.

- We accept responsibility for the short- and long-term consequences for our own communication and expect the same of others.

Competent Communication Is Appropriate and Effective

The fictional doctor Temperance Brennan on the television show *Bones* believes in communicating clearly, without nuance, sarcasm, or self-censorship. Her commitment to absolute scientific objectivity means that she will describe a sexual encounter with the same precision that she might describe a body she is examining and with the same detached language that someone else might use to describe a block of wood. Her communication, though clear, is largely inappropriate. It is also ineffective because, although meant to inform her colleagues with as little ambiguity as possible, it tends to amuse or embarrass them instead.

If you've ever laughed or cringed at an inappropriate outburst coming from someone else, you already understand that for communication to be competent it needs to be both effective and appropriate. You would not speak to your grandmother the same way you talk to your friends; nor would a lawyer ask her husband to complete a task the same way she would ask her office receptionist. Competent, successful communicators adjust their behavior to suit particular individuals and situations.

Appropriate Behavior. When Congressman Joe Wilson (R-S.C.) shouted, "You lie!" during the 2009 State of the Union address, few people were amused. Although many Americans may have been dissatisfied with President Barack Obama's policies, and most Americans cherish their right to free speech, Wilson's outburst was widely regarded as inappropriate. Even Senator John McCain, Wilson's fellow Republican from Arizona, called the outburst "totally disrespectful" and maintained that Wilson "should apologize immediately" (Reaction, 2009).

Communication is appropriate when it meets the demands of the situation as well as the expectations of others present. In almost all situations, cultural norms and rules set the standards for expectations. Had Wilson called the president a liar in a newspaper interview or even during debate on the House floor, the incident would have received less press. But the State of the Union is a nationally televised address

◊ On *Bones*, Dr. Temperance Brennan's commitment to scientific objectivity doesn't always result in appropriate or effective communication.

and a very formal affair. During the address, members of Congress traditionally defer to a code of etiquette that demands respect for the presidency and all that it represents, regardless of who is in office at the time. Wilson's outburst was considered inappropriate because of the particular setting in which he said it.

Ethics and You

What is the difference between inappropriate communication and unethical communication? Can you think of examples of each you've encountered in your own life?

Cultural norms affect individual behaviors in a similar way. For example, research shows that women tend to feel more comfortable expressing emotional caring to one another, often outright (using words of sympathy and comforting gestures), whereas men often feel they should show caring in less open ways (Burleson, Holmstrom, & Gilstrap, 2005). Thus, when comforting their friend Joe after the loss of his partner, Eva sat and held Joe's hand, while Dave got on the phone to help Joe manage details for the funeral.

Describe two communication situations, one in which the communication was appropriate but not effective and one in which the communication was effective but not very appropriate. Analyze these situations, considering the situational and relational contexts involved.

Successful communicators know what is and isn't appropriate in a variety of situations. Moreover, they have **behavioral flexibility**: the ability to use a number of different behaviors depending on the situation. So although you might love to talk about politics or your grades when you're with your friends, you might decide that these topics aren't appropriate during Passover dinner at your aunt's house.

Culture and You

Think back to the co-cultures you belong to. If these co-cultures were presented with the same situation, would they handle it differently? Do you have examples of these differences from your own experiences?

Effective Behavior. Behaving appropriately is not enough in itself. Competent communication must also be effective—it must help you meet your goals. This can be challenging because it's not always easy to know what messages will work best—and you may have more than one goal (Canary, Cody, & Smith, 1994). For example, Travis and his fiancée, Leah, are arguing over whose family they will visit at Thanksgiving. Travis has conflicting goals: he wants to see his family for the holiday, but he also wants Leah to be happy.

If you have some knowledge of your communication partner's expectations, you can more easily determine which messages will be more effective than others. If Travis knows that Leah would like to spend Thanksgiving with her family because she wants to see her elderly grandmother, he might suggest that they spend the four-day Thanksgiving weekend with his family but the longer Christmas–New Year holiday with hers. In addition, prioritizing your goals can help you construct effective messages. If Leah knows that her grandmother is ailing, she may decide that going home for Thanksgiving is a more important goal than pleasing Travis. She can then tell him that she's sorry to let him down but that she absolutely must return home.

Communication behavior that is effective in one setting might not be appropriate in others. For example, many students feel that their best teachers are those who are organized and logical (Kramer & Pier, 1999). But if your roommate handed you a detailed schedule of what you should do every day in your apartment during the upcoming semester, you might find this behavior annoying.

Competent Communication Involves Communication Skills

Having exemplary skills in one area does not make someone competent overall: your mechanic may work wonders on your car, but that doesn't mean he can fix your computer. The same idea is true for great communicators: a politician who delivers a great speech may falter during a debate, a press conference, or an interview. A social worker who conveys instructions clearly to her staff may have trouble clarifying her points during a meeting with the hospital board.

Communication skills are behavioral routines used to achieve particular goals (such as asking for a raise, maintaining a relationship, or working on a team). People who are judged as incompetent in some situations often don't know that they are unskilled; their inflated image of themselves seems to block their awareness (Dunning & Kruger, 1999). For example, suppose you see yourself as a great team player. During the evaluation at the end of a class project, you're surprised to learn that your teammates see you as "bossy." This feedback suggests that although you may be good at leading a team, you're less adept at working alongside others as an equal. The lesson? You may need to master some new communication skills to be a competent group member. In fact, having a number of skills increases your behavioral options, thereby boosting your odds of success in communicating with others.

Competent Communication Involves Using Technology

Communicating competently in face-to-face situations is complex. Adding technology to the mix can present even more interesting opportunities as well as challenges (Cupach & Spitzberg, 2011). Can you measure the effectiveness and appropriateness of communication when you are on the phone or using a social-networking site in the same way as when you are communicating face to face? Research indicates that the answer is yes *and* no.

As we've seen, competent communication must meet the goals of the communicators and be effective and appropriate for the situation. But our goals can sometimes be enhanced by the simultaneous use of more than one technology. For example, while chatting online or on the phone, many people surf the Web to locate information to back up their arguments (Walther, Van Der Heide, Ton, Carr, & Atkin, 2010). If they were talking face to face with someone, surfing the Web might be considered rude.

> ### Technology and You
> A number of communication methods are available to you because of technology. Have these methods changed in your lifetime? Are there technologies you would not have used four or five years ago for certain types of communication that you might consider appropriate today?

The technologies you use can also change others' perceptions of your communication competence. Texting a "thank you" might be an appropriate way to thank a friend for a compliment, but it probably won't impress your grandmother after she gives you a generous graduation gift. She'll likely be expecting a low-tech, handwritten thank-you note.

Finally, research shows that if you are comfortable with a particular technology, you will see yourself as more competent with that technology and use it to accomplish your goals more often (Keaten & Kelly, 2008). For example, you may feel comfortable applying for jobs online; you are familiar with the technologies involved and are willing to wait for an electronic response. You would likely describe yourself as competent with these technologies (Bakke, 2010), whereas your parents may question your use of them for job hunting if they are less familiar with them.

LearningCurve
bedfordstmartins.com/commandyou

Modeling Communication

As we've stated, the communication process is infinitely complex. For this reason, scholars have generated different models, or visual representations, of the process to help deepen our understanding of communication. Let's look at three models: linear, interaction, and competent.

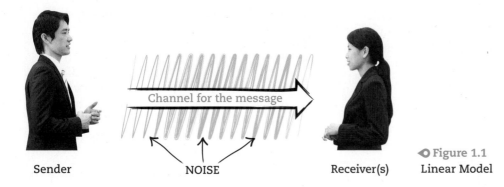

Sender   NOISE   Receiver(s)

◐ **Figure 1.1**
Linear Model

The Linear Model

In the **linear model** of communication (see **Figure 1.1**), a **sender** originates communication with words or action constituting the **message**. The message is carried through a *channel* (via sound waves, in written or visual form, over telephone lines, cables, or by electronic transmissions). Along the way, some interference, called **noise**, occurs. Because of the noise, the message arrives at the **receiver** changed in some way from the original (Shannon & Weaver, 1949).

The linear model has limitations. For example, it depicts communication as occurring in only one direction: from sender to receiver. Moreover, it offers no information on whether (or how) the message was received by anyone. This model helps

illustrate how television and radio transmit electronic signals to the public, but it does not show the receiver's active role in interpreting meaning. For this reason, the linear model is not useful for understanding most kinds of communication, particularly interactive forms. However, the model's basic concepts can help us build more complex models of communication.

The Interaction Model

The **interaction model** shows communication as a two-directional process that incorporates feedback into communication between sender and receiver (see **Figure 1.2**). **Feedback** is a message from the

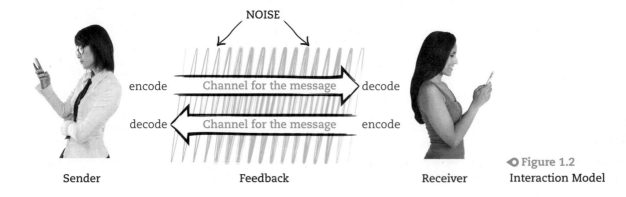

Sender   Feedback   Receiver

◐ **Figure 1.2**
Interaction Model

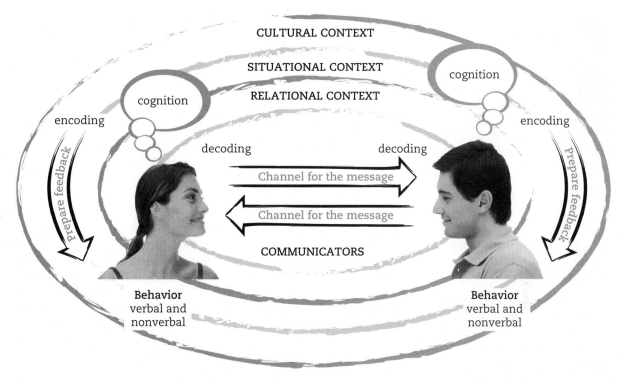

🜄 Figure 1.3 **Competent Communication Model**

receiver to the sender that illustrates responses that occur when two or more people communicate. As with the linear model, noise occurs along the way.

Feedback can be a verbal message (your friend invites you to a party on Friday night, and you reply, "About nine?"), a nonverbal message (your roommate asks if you enjoyed the dinner, and you look up, smile, and nod), or both (you frown while saying, "I don't think I understand"). Through feedback, communicators in the interaction model take turns sending and receiving messages.

The Competent Communication Model

Though the linear and interaction models help illustrate the communication process, neither captures the complex process of competent communication that we talked about in the preceding section (Wiemann & Backlund, 1980).

To illustrate this complex process, we developed a model of communication that shows effective and appropriate communication (see **Figure 1.3**). This **competent communication model** is *transactional*: the individuals (or groups or organizations) communicate *simultaneously*, sending and receiving messages (verbally and nonverbally) at the same moment—and all this takes place within three contexts: relational, situational, and cultural.[2]

---

[2]The competent communication model is based on the research of John Wiemann (1977) and the Wiemann Competence Model (Wiemann & Wiemann, 1992).

In this model, arrows show the links between communication behaviors by representing messages being sent and received. In face-to-face communication, the behaviors of both communicators influence each individual at the same time. For example, Cliff smiles and nods at Jalissa without saying anything as Jalissa talks about the meeting she hosted for her book club. Through these behaviors, Cliff is sending messages of encouragement while receiving her verbal messages. Jalissa is sending all sorts of messages about the book she chose for that week's discussion, as well as the foods she selected and the way she prepared for the get-together. But she is also receiving messages from Cliff that she interprets as positive interest. Both Cliff and Jalissa are simultaneously encoding (sending) and simultaneously decoding (receiving) communication behavior.

This transaction changes slightly with different types of communication. For example, in a mediated form of communication—a Facebook wall posting or texting, for example—the sending and receiving of messages may not be simultaneous. In such cases, the communicators are more likely to take turns or time may elapse between messages. In mass media such as TV or radio, feedback may be even more limited and delayed—audience reactions to a TV show are typically gauged only by Nielsen ratings (how many people watched) or by comments posted by fans on blogs or Twitter.

The competent communication model takes into account not only the transactional nature of communication but also the role of communicators themselves—their internal thoughts and influences as well as the various contexts in which they operate. There are four main spheres of influence at play in the competent communication model:

- The *communicators*. Two individuals are shown in Figure 1.3, but many variations are possible: an individual speaking to a live audience, multiple individuals in a group communicating, and so on.
- The *relationships* among the communicators.
- The *situation* in which the communication occurs.
- The *cultural setting* that frames the interaction.

Let's take a closer look at each of these influences.

The Communicators. The most obvious elements in any communication are the communicators themselves. When sending and receiving messages, each communicator is influenced by **cognitions**, the thoughts they have about themselves and others, including their understanding and awareness of who they are (smart, funny, compassionate, and so on), how well they like who they are, and how successful they think they are. We discuss this process in much more depth in Chapter 2. But for now, understand that your cognitions influence your behavior when you communicate. **Behavior** is observable communication, including verbal messages (the words you use) and nonverbal messages (facial expressions, body movements, clothing, gestures). So your cognitions inform your behavior—the messages you encode and send—which are then received and decoded by your communication partner. Your partner's own cognitions influence how he or she interprets the message, prepares feedback, and encodes a new verbal or nonverbal message that is sent to you.

This constant cycle can be seen in the following example. Devon knows that he's a good student, but he struggles with math, chemistry, and physics. This embarrasses him because his mother is a doctor and his brother is an engineer. He rarely feels like he will succeed in these areas. He tells his friend Kayla that he can't figure out why he failed his recent physics test since he studied for days beforehand. When he says this, his eyes are downcast and he looks angry. Kayla likes to think that she's a good listener and prides herself on the fact that she rarely responds emotionally to delicate situations. She receives and decodes Devon's message, prepares feedback, and encodes and sends a message of her own: she calmly asks whether Devon contacted his physics professor or an academic tutor for extra help. Devon receives and decodes Kayla's message in light of his own cognitions about being a poor science student and feeling like he's always struggling with physics. He notices that Kayla made very direct eye contact, that she didn't smile, and that her message didn't include any words of sympathy. He concludes that she is accusing him of not working hard enough. He prepares feedback and sends another message—his eyes are large and his arms are crossed and he loudly and sarcastically states, "Right, yeah, I guess I was just too dumb to think about that."

Because communication situations have so many "moving parts," they can vary greatly. Moreover, successful communicators usually have a high degree of cognitive complexity. That is, they can consider multiple scenarios, formulate multiple theories, and make multiple interpretations when encoding and decoding messages. In this case, Kayla might have considered that Devon really just needed some friendly reassurance rather than advice; Devon might have realized that Kayla was just trying to offer a helpful suggestion.

Ethics and You

Recall a communication situation in which you felt uncomfortable. What were your thoughts (cognitions) about yourself? About your partner? What could you say or do to clarify the situation?

Relationships Among the Communicators. All communication, from mundane business transactions to intimate discussions, occurs within the context of the relationship you have with the person or persons with whom you are interacting. This relational context is represented by the inner sphere in the competent communication model. A kiss, for example, has a different meaning when bestowed on your mother than it does when shared with your spouse or romantic partner. When you make a new

acquaintance, saying "Let's be friends" can be an exciting invitation to get to know someone new, but the same message shared with someone you've been dating for a year shuts down intimacy. The relationship itself is influenced by its past history as well as both parties' expectations for the current situation and for the future.

A **relational history** is the sum of the shared experiences of the individuals involved in the relationship. References to this common history (such as inside jokes) can be important in defining a relationship, both for the participants and for the participants' associates. That's because such references indicate to you, your partner, and others that there is something special about this relationship. Your relational history may also affect what is appropriate in a particular circumstance. For example, you may give advice to a sibling or close friend without worrying about politeness, but you might be more hesitant or more indirect with an acquaintance you haven't known for very long. Relational history can complicate matters when you're communicating on social-networking sites like Facebook. Your "friends" probably include those who are currently very close to you as well as those who are distant (for example, former high school classmates). Even if you direct your message to one friend in particular, all your friends can see it, so you might be letting those in distant relationships in on a private joke (or be making them feel left out).

Our communication is also shaped by our expectations and goals for the relationship. Expectations and goals can be quite different. For example, high school sweethearts may want their relationship to continue (a goal) but at the same time anticipate that going to college in different states could lead to a breakup (an expectation). With expectations and goals in mind, you formulate your behavior in the current conversation, and you interpret what your partner says in light of these same considerations. Clearly, our expectations and goals differ according to each relationship. They can and do change during the course of conversations, and they certainly change over the life span of a relationship.

⬭ The meaning of a kiss changes depending on context. A kiss between mother and child doesn't have the same meaning as a kiss between romantic partners.

The Situation. The **situational context** (represented by the middle sphere in the competent communication model) includes the social environment (a loud, boisterous party versus an intimate dinner for two), the physical place (at home in the kitchen versus at Chicago's O'Hare International Airport), specific events and situations (a wedding versus a funeral), and even a specific mediated place (a private message versus a Facebook status update). Situation also includes where you live and work, your home or office decorations, the time of day or night, and the current events in the particular environment at the time.

For example, if Kevin gets home from work and asks Rhiannon what's for dinner and Rhiannon shrieks, Kevin might conclude that she is mad at him. But if he considers the situational context, he might reinterpret her response. Looking around, he might see that his wife is still in her suit, meaning that she only just got home from a long day at work. He might notice that the kitchen sink is clogged, the dog has gotten sick on the living-room rug, and the laundry (his chore) is still sitting, unfolded, on the couch because he didn't get around to finishing it. By considering the context, Kevin is able to ascertain

that Rhiannon is upset because of these situational factors, rather than because of anything he has said or done.

The Cultural Setting. Finally, we must discuss the fact that all communication takes place within the powerful context of the surrounding culture (represented by the outermost sphere of the competent communication model). Culture is the backdrop for the situational context, the relational context, and the communicators themselves. As discussed earlier, culture helps determine which messages are considered appropriate and effective, and it strongly affects our cognitions. For example, Hannah comes from a culture that shows respect for elders by not questioning their authority and by cherishing possessions that have been passed down in the family for generations. Cole, by contrast, was raised in a culture that encourages him to talk back to and question elders and that values new possessions over old ones. Both Hannah and Cole view their own behaviors as natural—their cognitions about elders and possessions have been influenced by their culture. But when each looks at the other's behavior, it might seem odd or unnatural. If Hannah and Cole are to become friends, colleagues, or romantic partners, each would benefit from becoming sensitive to the other's cultural background.

> ### Culture and You
> What cultural contexts are influencing you as you read this book? Consider your gender, ethnicity, academic or socioeconomic background, and other factors. What expectations and goals do you have for this book and this course, and how are they affected by your cultural context?

Cultural identity—how individuals view themselves as members of a specific culture—influences the communication choices people make and how they interpret the messages they receive from others (Lindsley, 1999). Cultural identity is reinforced by the messages people receive from those in similar cultures. In our example, both Hannah's and Cole's cognitions have been reinforced by their respective friends and family, who share their cultural identity.

LearningCurve
bedfordstmartins.com/commandyou

The Study of Communication

If you've never studied communication before, right now you might feel like you know more about messages and relationships and communication contexts than you ever thought you'd need to know! But there is still so much more to study that can profoundly affect your friendships, romantic relationships, group memberships, career, and overall success in life.

You've seen that communicating well—effectively, appropriately, and ethically—is not an innate ability; it is a process we can all improve on throughout our lives.

So what's behind this discipline? What do communication scholars (like those of us who wrote this book) do? Well, in democracies from ancient Greece to the United States, scholars realized early on that communication was crucial to helping people participate in the government and civic life. Public speaking, for example, was taught in America's first universities, partly to reinforce the powerful effect that speaking out can have on society (Dues & Brown, 2004). A similar concern for the public's welfare lay behind the addition of professional journalism courses to university curricula early in the twentieth century. At that time, the sensationalistic excesses of the "penny press" highlighted the need for newspeople who were trained in both the technical aspects of reporting and the ethical responsibilities of journalists in a free society.

Today, communication continues to be a dynamic and multifaceted discipline focused on improving interactions and relationships, including those between two individuals, between individuals of different cultures, between speakers and audiences, within small groups, in large organizations, and among nations and international organizations. (Table 1.2 illustrates some of the major areas of specialization and the focus of each.) The research in our field draws clear connections between these assorted types of relationships. Furthermore, the principles of communication laid out in this chapter can be successfully applied to various communication situations and contexts. For example, as technology advances, communication becomes more complicated, expansive, and sometimes unclear. For most of human existence, an interpersonal

{ **Communicating well is not an innate ability; it is a process we can all improve on throughout our lives.** }

Table 1.2 **Common Areas of Specialization in Communication Research Today**

Area of Study	Focus of Study
Rhetorical theory and criticism	The analysis of speeches and other public messages
Argumentation and debate	Persuasion, reasoning, logic, and presentation
Interpersonal communication	Basic two-person (dyadic) processes
Intergroup communication	Ways in which communication within and between groups affects social relationships
Relational communication	Interpersonal communication in close relationships such as romances, families, and friendships
Small group communication	The function, dynamics, and performance of group members
Organizational communication	Communication efficiency and effectiveness in businesses and other organizations
Mass communication and media studies	The design and production of media messages and the identification and evaluation of media effects
Political communication	The study of politicians, voters, and audiences and their impact on one another
Public relations	The production of messages designed to improve the image of individuals and organizations
Intercultural communication	Communication rules and values across cultures and co-cultures
Family communication	Communication between parents and children and between generations
Health communication	The communication messages of health care providers and patients
Conflict management	The reduction of adversarial messages in personal, organizational, and community contexts
Nonverbal communication	Nonlanguage codes that communicate
Communication technology and telecommunication studies	Development and application of new technologies in all communication situations

relationship was limited to face-to-face interactions, later enhanced by mediated communication via the written word and the telephone. But today, individuals strike up personal and business relationships through e-mail, social-networking groups, and phone contact across the globe, often without ever meeting in person.

Throughout this book, we'll explore how communication skills, concepts, and theories apply to various communication situations and offer scholarship from four distinct areas of the discipline:

- **Basic communication processes.** All communication involves the basic processes of perception, intercultural interaction, verbal communication, nonverbal communication, and listening. Skills that we develop in these areas inform the way we handle communication in a variety of contexts, from talking with friends to making presentations in front of a class or a large public audience. In the remainder of Part 1 of this book, you will learn how these basic processes affect every communication situation.

- **Interpersonal communication.** As social animals, we human beings cannot avoid forming interpersonal relationships and interacting with other individuals. Interpersonal communication is the study of communication between **dyads**, or pairs of individuals. Most students find this study particularly relevant to their lives as they negotiate their friendships, romantic relationships, and family relationships. We investigate the exciting, nerve-racking, fun, confusing, tumultuous, and rewarding world of relationships and conflict in Part 2 of this book. An in-depth analysis of interviewing—one of the most

daunting and important types of interpersonal communication—is offered in Appendix A at the back of the book.

- **Group and organizational communication.** If you've ever tried to run a professional meeting, manage a class or work group, or plan a day trip for a bunch of friends, you know that as the number of people involved in a conversation, an activity, or a project increases, communication becomes more complicated. By studying interactions in groups and organizations, communication scholars help create strategies for managing the flow of information and interactions among individuals in groups. We'll explore this in Part 3 of the book.

- **Public speaking.** Don't panic! We're going to provide a lot of help and guidance to assist you as you become a competent public speaker. Even if you've never had to speak in front of a group before, in Part 4 you'll learn not only how to research and develop a presentation but also how to connect with your audience on a personal level. We also offer tips on becoming a more critical audience member, whether you are engaged with a speaker in a lecture hall, at a protest rally, or at a professional conference.

We are confident that this book will provide you with an enjoyable reading experience as well as help you improve your communication. As a result, your life, your work, your relationships, and your ability to speak out will all be enhanced.

LearningCurve
bedfordstmartins.com/commandyou

The Gulf Oil Spill

Back to }

At the beginning of this chapter, we talked about BP's failure to communicate competently in the wake of the *Deepwater Horizon* explosion. Let's consider the spill and reactions to it in light of what you've learned in this chapter.

- Communication disasters in the Gulf were many: public-relations gaffes, lack of coordination, confusion over who was in control, and avoidance of responsibility. These communication failures had real economic consequences: fishing and tourism are crucial to the Gulf Coast economy, and many people lost their livelihoods as the oil spill killed marine life and fouled beaches. Deepwater drilling is also vital to the Gulf Coast economy; a Louisiana oil industry group estimated that each rig in the Gulf of Mexico represented monthly wages of at least $165 million (Zeller, 2010).

- BP executive Tony Hayward's comments and activity in the days and weeks that followed the spill showed that he failed to consider the situational context. Hayward's words and behavior (enjoying a yacht race as oil gushed into the Gulf) displayed that he didn't appreciate the needs and distress of the Gulf Coast community still suffering the economic and social effects of Hurricane Katrina.

- In the end, Hayward's apology largely fell flat because of the transactional nature of communication. He might have been able to utter apologetic words for his statements and behavior, but nothing could ultimately erase listeners' memories. Once a communication transaction occurs, it cannot be reversed.

- Consider also the effectiveness of the corporate messages. While the media focused on the vastness of the devastation, offering insights from locals and showing detailed, twenty-four-hour coverage of the spill itself, messages from BP seemed more concerned with protecting the company than with conveying clear and accurate information. Thus, the messages were not appropriate for the situation, nor were they effective in helping the company's PR image.

Your Reference }

A Study Tool

Now that you have finished reading this chapter, you can:

Define the communication process:

- **Communication** is the process by which individuals use symbols, signs, and behaviors to exchange information (p. 4).
- Communication requires more than "common sense" (p. 5).

Describe the functions of communication:

- The **functional perspective** examines how communication behaviors work (or don't work) to accomplish goals (p. 4).
- **Relationships** are the interconnections, or interdependence, between two or more people that function to achieve some goal (pp. 4–5).
- Relationship **interdependence** means that what we do affects others and vice versa (p. 5).
- There are three primary functions in communication:
  - expressing **affiliation**, or feelings for others (p. 5).
  - relying on communication to accomplish particular objectives, or **goal achievement** (p. 6); and
  - negotiating **control**, the influence one individual, group, or organization has over others (p. 7).

Assess the quality (communicative value) of communication by examining its six characteristics:

- Communication relies on **symbols**, arbitrary constructions related to the people, things, or concepts to which they refer (p. 10).
- Communication requires a shared **code**, or a set of symbols that create a meaningful message; **encoding** is the process of producing and sending a message, and **decoding** is the process of receiving it and making sense of it (p. 10).
- Communication is linked to **culture**, the shared beliefs, values, and practices of a group of people, and **co-cultures**, smaller groups within a culture (p. 10).
- Communication may be intentional or spontaneous (pp. 10–11).
- Communication requires a **channel** ⊙, the method through which it occurs (p. 11).
- Communication is a **transactional** process: you influence others while they influence you (p. 11).

Define what communication scholars consider to be competent communication:

- **Competent communication** is more **process** than **outcome** focused (p. 13).
- Competent communication is **ethical** (p. 14).

- Communication is appropriate when it meets the demands of the situation (p. 15).
- **Behavioral flexibility** involves knowing and using a number of different behaviors to achieve that appropriateness (p. 16).
- Communication is effective when it achieves desired goals (pp. 16–17).
  - **Communication skills** are behaviors that help communicators achieve their goals (p. 17).

Describe the visual representations, or models, of communication:

- In the **linear model**, a **sender** originates the **message**, which is carried through a channel—where it is perhaps interfered with by **noise** ⊙—to the **receiver** (p. 18).
- The **interaction model** expands on the linear model by including **feedback** between the receiver and the sender (pp. 18–19).
- The **competent communication model** is a transactional model incorporating three contextual spheres in which individuals communicate (pp. 19–23).
  - *Communicators:* **Cognitions**, thoughts that communicators have about themselves, influence **behavior**, observable communication, and how the message is interpreted before preparing feedback (pp. 20–21).
  - *Relational context:* Communication occurs within the context of a relationship and is influenced by the relational history (p. 21).
  - *Situational context:* The circumstances surrounding communication, including social environment and physical place, influence communication (p. 22).
  - *Cultural context:* Cultural identity, how individuals view themselves as a member of a specific culture, influences communication choices (pp. 22–23).

Describe why communication is vital to everyone:

- The discipline of communication grew out of the need to have informed citizens aware of the power of speaking out (p. 23).
- The discipline focuses on improving interactions and relationships between **dyads**, groups, organizations, and speakers and audiences (p. 25).

✓ Look for LearningCurve throughout
the chapter to help you review.
bedfordstmartins.com/commandyou

2 } Perceiving the Self and Others

When Susan Boyle took the stage at the *Britain's Got Talent* competition in 2009 and told the audience and judges that she wanted to be a professional singer, she was met mostly with eye rolls, barely muffled giggles, and at least one ironic whistle. In a society that equates youth, beauty, and glamour with talent, people didn't expect much from a middle-aged, overweight, never-been-kissed cat lady from Scotland. As the music to "I Dreamed a Dream" from *Les Misérables* cued up over the sound system, viewers steeled themselves for what they thought would be a cringe-worthy performance.

But by the time Boyle had belted out the first bar, those derisive expressions had melted away. During her pitch-perfect performance, cameras scanned the audience, capturing tears welling up in eyes that had been cynically rolling just a few minutes prior. As she headed into the bridge of the song and audience members leaped to their feet, television presenter Anthony McPartlin joyfully chided viewers watching at home: "You didn't expect that, did you? Did you? No!" Judge Piers Morgan told Boyle, "Without a doubt, that was the biggest surprise I've had in three years of this show. . . . Everyone was laughing at you. No one is laughing now."

Within hours, footage of Boyle's performance was on YouTube, snatching upward of two million hits in less than three days; today, it remains one of the most watched YouTube videos ever. Boyle would go on to live the dream she dreamed with a new look, a successful debut album and tour, and popularity that continues to this day.

After you have finished reading this chapter, you will be able to

Describe how our personal perspective on the world influences our communication.

Explain how we use and misuse schemas when communicating with others.

Define the attributions we use to explain behavior.

Describe how cultural differences influence perception.

Identify how our self-concept—who we think we are—influences communication.

Describe how our cognitions about ourselves and our behavior affect our communication with others.

ost people know that the ability to sing has little to do with one's appearance. So why were audiences stunned by Susan Boyle's performance on *Britain's Got Talent*? The answer lies in perception.

We all have unique ways of perceiving ourselves, others, and the world around us, and we communicate based on those perceptions. **Perception** is a cognitive process through which we interpret our experiences and form our own unique understandings. Those thoughts, or cognitions, influence how and what we communicate to others. They also affect how we interpret others' behaviors and messages. Thus, understanding the role that perception plays in communication is crucial to our success as communicators. In this chapter, we explore how we see ourselves, how we see others, and how culture affects these perceptions.

Perception: Making Sense of Your World

It's eight o'clock on a Wednesday night, and a roomful of singles are gathered at an Atlanta hot spot for an interesting event: over the next hour and a half, each woman will be introduced to no fewer than twenty eligible men. The problem: she'll have only three minutes with each. Every pair will divulge their first names, perhaps their occupations, where they're from, and why they're there.

Speed dating has become popular in many metropolitan areas.[1] Organized by upstart companies that promise to screen applicants and put together large groups of potentially compatible singles, the event is arranged so that each person meets anywhere from ten to twenty potential mates. They spend usually less than ten minutes with each to see if there is any "chemistry." But how much can one person learn about another in just a few minutes?

Actually, first impressions can generate quite a bit of information. Irina might tell Adam that she's thirty-one, is a public-relations executive, was born in Milwaukee but has lived in Atlanta for nine years, and has a passion for film noir. Adam might hear all this but also notice that Irina is tall and attractive, that she makes steady eye contact, and that she has assertive mannerisms. This information might lead him to draw conclusions: for example, "She's probably more successful than I am." Adam might also notice that Irina is what he considers a "funky" dresser— she wears lots of brightly colored bead jewelry along with her conservative business suit. This, and her mention of film noir, puts him off a bit; he wonders if she's an "artsy" type. His last girlfriend was into art and was always dragging him to gallery openings that he found painfully boring and pretentious. He feels a little intimidated by Irina and decides that they probably aren't compatible.

---

[1]This speed-dating trend is found in the United States but is popular in England and India as well (Doshi, 2005, p. 60).

Even during brief encounters—like Adam's meeting with Irina—we get bombarded with information: the other person's words, tone of voice, facial expressions, degree of eye contact. Through **communication processing**, we gather, organize, and evaluate all this information. Although we receive information through our senses, this is just the beginning of the process. How we interpret that information is unique to each of us, influenced by how we select and organize it.

Selecting Information

If you've ever listened to testimony at a trial (or seen a trial on TV), you may have been struck by how one witness will remember the exact time of an accident or the color and make of the cars involved, while another will describe the scene and note the sequence of events. They both saw the same accident but selected different parts of it to remember. In any situation, we encounter a great deal of information, which we must sift through to determine what is important. In our speed-dating example, Adam takes in some of the information Irina provides: what she says, how she says it, what she looks like, and how she presents herself. But other information escapes his notice. For example, the next man Irina meets, Ben, might note that she has a warm smile and that she laughs easily (at his bad jokes, no less). Of course,

it's possible that Ben and Adam were exposed to different information: perhaps Irina was more comfortable with Ben. But often people can come to vastly different conclusions even under the exact same circumstances. This is because we each organize our perceptions in existing memory bases called *schemas*.

> ### Culture and You
>
> Do you think your cultural background affects the way you select and process information in communications? Can you think of examples from your experiences?

Schemas: Organizing Perceptions

As you receive information, you strive to make sense of it. To do so, you consider the new information but also how it fits with information you already have. For example, in evaluating Irina, speed dater Adam makes associations with his own experience and his own feelings. He compares Irina to his old girlfriend ("artsy") and to himself, guessing about her professional success. Adam is making sense of the interaction's many inputs through **schemas**, mental structures that put together related bits of information (Fiske & Taylor, 1991) (see **Figure 2.1**). Once put together, these

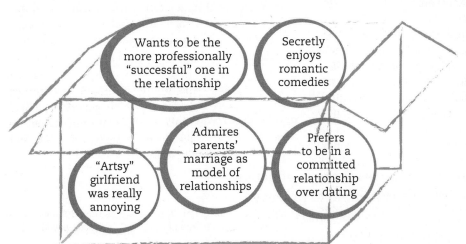

◁ **Figure 2.1 Adam's Schema About Dating and Relationships.** This box represents pieces of information from various sources in Adam's life.

chunks of information form patterns that we use to create meaning.

The Function of Schemas. Your schemas help you understand how things work or should work. Communicators retrieve schemas from memory and interpret new information, people, and situations in accordance with those schemas. For example, imagine that during your walk across campus, a classmate approaches and says, "Hey, what's up?" An existing schema (memory of past encounters) tells you that you will exchange hellos and then, after some small talk, go your separate ways. When you recognize one component of a schema, the entire schema is activated and tells you what will most probably happen next.

As you go through life, you continually perceive new bits of information that help you make sense of different situations. Your schemas change through this process. Consider the popular *Harry Potter* books, in which author J. K. Rowling creates a world that continually challenges readers' (and Harry's) preconceived schemas. When young Harry first arrives at Hogwarts, he is surprised and delighted by his new environment: candles float, broomsticks fly, chess pieces move by themselves. These events don't fit Harry's existing schemas of how things work. Yet during his seven years at Hogwarts, his schemas evolve: things that surprised him in year one no longer raise an eyebrow in year seven.

Challenges with Schemas and Perception. To send and receive messages that are effective and appropriate, you must be able to process information in a way that makes sense to you but that also is accurately perceived by others. Schemas can help you do all of this. However, sometimes schemas can make you a less perceptive communicator; they may cloud your

◊ Seeing "Mad-Eye Moody" use the unforgivable curses in Defense Against the Dark Arts in *Harry Potter and the Goblet of Fire* shocked Harry and made him feel uncomfortable. However, by the seventh book, witnessing these curses no longer seems jarring to him.

judgment or cause you to rely on stereotypes (discussed later in this chapter) or misinformation. Communication researchers note that schemas present three key challenges to competent communication: mindlessness, selective perception, and undue influence.

Mindlessness. To communicate competently, you must focus on the task at hand, a process called **mindfulness**. Schemas, however, may make you a less critical processor of information by producing a state of **mindlessness**, during which you process information passively. Mindlessness helps you handle some transactions automatically; for example, you don't have to consciously think about how to

{ To send and receive messages that are effective and appropriate, you must be able to process information in a way that makes sense to you but that also is accurately perceived by others. }

place an order every time you go to a restaurant. But mindlessness can create problems too—including reduced cognitive activity, inaccurate recall, and uncritical evaluation (Roloff, 1980). Reduced cognitive activity means that when your schemas take effect, you have fewer thoughts; it is like being fatigued. An example of inaccurate recall of information is when your friend asks for directions to a store you've shopped at and you can't remember how, exactly, you got there. Uncritical evaluation means that you don't question the information you're receiving, which is problematic if it's wrong or incomplete.

Selective perception. Whereas mindlessness is passive, **selective perception**—that is, biased perception—constitutes active thought. If a group of five people watches a televised debate between two political candidates, they will likely have five different interpretations of what took place and what was important. The person who is keenly interested in economics will likely focus on what the candidates said about the federal budget. The one who's most concerned about foreign affairs will probably pay closer attention to the candidates' opinions about that topic.

Undue influence. When you give greater credibility or importance to something shown or said than should be the case, you are falling victim to **undue influence**. For example, some people tend to give undue influence to male friends when discussing sports. The media can also be a source of undue influence. For instance, people who have been exposed to local media coverage of crimes are much more likely to perceive defendants in a trial as guilty (Wright & Ross, 1997).

> **Ethics and You**
> Think of an individual whom you hold in high regard, such as a parent, a mentor, or a close friend, and how he or she might influence you. How might you make sure that this person doesn't hold undue influence over your decisions or opinions?

Attributions: Interpreting Your Perceptions

When perceiving others, we often try to explain why they said something or acted in a certain way, especially if their behavior does not fit our schema. Personal characteristics that we use to explain behavior are known as **attributions** (Jones, 1990). Consider the following exchange:

EMMA   I'm heading over to Mark's place to help him study for our midterm. He has really been struggling this semester.

CALEB   Well, he was never exactly a rocket scientist.

📍 Graphic news stories of muggings, murders, and brutal assaults might make you more likely to lock the doors and look repeatedly over your shoulder when you're out alone.

Analyze the text of a presidential speech online at www.whitehouse.gov. After reading the complete speech, consider how the speech is characterized in various sources (blogs, liberal and conservative news sources, late-night comedy and satires). How do perceptions of the speech change from one source to another? Does your perception of the speech change as you consider these various sources' viewpoints? If so, how?

Emma might attribute Caleb's comment to his personality ("Caleb is mean!") or to the situation ("Wow, something has put Caleb in a bad mood"). When we attribute behavior to someone's personality (or something within the person's control), we call that an *internal* attribution. When we attribute it to the situation (something outside the person's control), that's an *external* attribution. How do we decide? If Emma thinks Caleb is not usually so blunt or harsh about other people, she will likely attribute his behavior to the situation, not to his personality.

The attributions we make can create problems, as the **fundamental attribution error** illustrates (McLeod, Detenber, & Eveland, 2001; Ross & Nisbett, 1991). The fundamental attribution error causes us to overemphasize internal and underestimate external causes of behaviors we observe in others. (For example, "Carla failed the midterm because she was too lazy to study.") The error works in the opposite way when we make attributions about ourselves. Owing to the **self-serving bias**, we usually attribute our own successes to internal factors ("I got an A because I'm smart") and attribute our failures to external effects ("I failed the midterm because my professor stinks").

We make attributions all the time, and they powerfully shape our communication. However, our attributions are not necessarily set in stone. Unexpected events or simply the passage of time can change them. For example, Mel Gibson, once considered a megastar, morphed into box-office poison after tapes of his violent, bigoted, and sexist rants became public.

Interaction appearance theory helps explain how people change their attributions of someone, particularly their physical attractiveness, the more they interact (Albada, Knapp, & Theune, 2002). Audiences' perceptions of Gibson adjusted as they witnessed more and more of his behavior. We do the same in our relationships: people become more or less attractive to us as we get to know them better. For example, perhaps you find someone more attractive after you discover her quirky sense of humor.

Improving Your Perceptions

Making accurate perceptions can be challenging. For example, in the classic basketball film *Hoosiers*, Gene Hackman plays Hickory High basketball coach Norman Dale. Dale's small-town players are intimidated by the cavernous arena where they'll be playing for the Indiana state championship. Though they know the court is regulation size, it looks enormous to them. Dale uses a tape measure to confirm the height of the basket and the distance from the foul line. Only then do they believe that the court is the same size as the one they play on in their gym. This restores their confidence.

The following suggestions can help you improve your perception abilities and thus become a better communicator.

- **Verify your perceptions.** It's natural to jump to some conclusions—to depend too much on your existing schemas—but take some time to confirm (or debunk) your conclusions. For instance, if you see a mother yell at a small child in the park and grab his arm, you might conclude that she's harsh or even abusive. But look more closely: the child may have been about to reach for a razor-sharp piece of broken glass on the ground.

- **Be thoughtful when you seek explanations.** Look beyond the most obvious explanation for what you observe. For example, scuffles occasionally break out among players in college and professional sports. You might assume that the person who threw the first punch instigated the fight. Frequently, however, a fight starts when someone else says or does something that the fans cannot easily perceive: a hockey player might have thrown his stick high in the face of another player or may have said something insulting. In seeking explanations for what caused an event, consider whether something unseen might have provoked what you observed.

- **Look beyond first impressions.** Don't rely completely on your first impressions; these often lead to inaccurate conclusions. Consider Meghan, who frequently comes off as gregarious and loud when people first meet her. Meghan is actually quite thoughtful and kind—she just loves meeting new people and enthusiastically asks questions while getting to know them. Hold off forming a judgment until you can make further perceptions.

LearningCurve
bedfordstmartins.com/commandyou

Perception in a Diverse World

A few generations ago, people may have gone months without coming into contact with someone from a different village or neighborhood. A wheelchair-bound child may have been unable to attend public schools. And in parts of this country, white and black Americans were not permitted to sit at the same lunch counter. Today, people from all walks of life learn, work, and play together. And through technology, we can communicate with others across vast distances. A student in Louisville, Kentucky, can chat online with a student from Bangladesh. A salesperson in Omaha, Nebraska, may work full time with clients in Tokyo. Such diversity is inextricably linked to our perceptions.

The Cultural Context

If you love soccer—or football, as most of the world calls the game—you probably followed the World Cup in 2010. If so, you heard the monotone buzzing sound emanating from the crowds, as tens of thousands of fans blew on long plastic horns called *vuvuzelas*. But how you perceived the noise depended significantly on your cultural background. For American broadcasters, the buzzing was a nuisance and a technological hurdle; for some international players, it was an annoying distraction. But for South African fans, it was part of the game. As one commentator put it, the vuvuzela is the "recognized sound of football in South Africa . . . [and] absolutely essential for an authentic South African footballing experience" (Mungazi, 2009).

Culture profoundly shapes how we perceive ourselves and the people around us. It's why something seen as delightful by South African fans could seem inappropriate and irritating to fans from other cultures.

> **Culture and You**
> Have you ever seen a part of your own culture that you enjoy deemed inappropriate or irritating by others? How did you attempt to resolve that difference?

Think back to the competent communication model you saw in Chapter 1. The ring representing the cultural context consists of variables that make our perceptions unique: race, ethnicity, religion, politics, gender, sexual orientation, age, education, role, occupation, abilities/disabilities, geography, and so on. These differences constitute *diversity* (Loden & Rosener, 1991). To communicate effectively and appropriately today, you must appreciate that people from other cultures may perceive things differently than you do and that your own background affects your perceptions.

Perceptual Barriers

Karl Krayer is a communication consultant who does diversity training for corporations, schools, and other organizations. Based on his experience, Krayer notes that successful intercultural communication requires mindfulness, respect for others, and accurate perceptions of situations. "Resistance to cultural diversity usually boils down to ignorance," he says. "Once people understand other cultural groups better, it doesn't take long to see . . . people working cooperatively together for a common cause" (personal communication, May 19, 2004). In our diverse world, perceptual challenges, including narrow perspectives and stereotyping, can present barriers to competent communication.

A Narrow Perspective. When Hurricane Katrina devastated New Orleans in 2005, leaving countless residents trapped on rooftops or huddled in the Super-dome for shelter, many Americans wondered why New Orleans residents didn't just get into their cars and leave the city when the flood warnings were announced. For many upper- and middle-class Americans, the idea never crossed their minds that a family might not own a car, might not have enough money to stay in an out-of-town hotel, or might fear that their abandoned home would be looted. Their own experiences clouded their perception of other people's reality. Individuals who fail to consider other cultural perspectives in this manner have **cultural myopia**, a form of nearsightedness grounded in the belief that one's own culture is appropriate and relevant in all situations and to all people (Loden & Rosener, 1991). Cultural myopia is especially danger-ous when members of the dominant group in a soci-ety are unaware of or insensitive to the needs and values of other members of the society.

Stereotyping and Prejudice. Schemas can be dan-gerous in a diverse society if we overrely on them to make generalizations about people. For example, **stereotyping** is using an impression so fixed or set that you apply your perceptions of an entire group to each individual from that group.

Stereotypes may be positive, negative, or neutral; they may be about a group to which you belong or one that is different from your own. If you have a negative stereotype about corporate executives, for example, you may think that they are all greedy and unethical, even though many (if not most) are hardworking, hon-est men and women who have climbed the corporate ladder. On the other hand, a positive stereotype might blind you to bad behaviors that don't conform to your ideas.

Stereotypes lead to **prejudice**, a deep-seated feel-ing of unkindness and ill will toward particular groups, usually based on negative stereotypes and feelings of superiority over those groups. In its most extreme form, prejudice can lead to a belief that the lives of some people are worth less than those of others. In-deed, the institution of slavery in the United States flourished based on this belief. Even today, the cul-tural landscape of almost every nation is dotted with groups who advocate the notion of racial superiority.

Prejudice is not limited to groups either. We might have preconceived ideas about an individual based on limited experience. If Shayla was feeling ill on the day that Clark met her, he might conclude that she is grumpy all the time. This snap judgment colors his perception of her in future communica-tion. Clark has made the fundamental attribution er-ror discussed earlier in this chapter. Making that same kind of error based on judgments about a per-son's race, culture, or ethnicity is a common trap. We'll discuss these perceptual errors further—and ways to remove them—in Chapter 3.

LearningCurve
bedfordstmartins.com/commandyou

⚲ In Shakespeare's famous play, Romeo and Juliet (portrayed here by Leonardo DiCaprio and Claire Danes) look beyond the feuding of their families, the Montagues and the Capulets, to find true love.

Cognition: Perceiving Ourselves

Imagine spending the first nineteen years of your life without an official first name. That's what "Baby Boy" Pauson did. His father disappeared and his mother never got around to picking a name for his birth certificate. People referred to him as Max (after his mother, Maxine), yet his official records still noted his legal name as "Baby Boy." Tormented, teased, and bounced around for years, Pauson perceived himself as an outcast and escaped through comic books, animation, and fantasy. It wasn't until he entered San Francisco's School of the Arts that he discovered that others valued his creativity and nonconformity. He finally found a lawyer who helped him create an official identity with the weighty name he had imagined for himself as a child—Maximus Julius Pauson (Eckholm, 2010).

For most of us, our name (or nickname) is an important element in our *cognitions*, or thoughts about ourselves. For example, many women who marry debate whether to change their last names: some worry that losing the last name they were born with might signify the loss of a personal identity; others see changing their name as a way to communicate their relationship status or signify a new beginning.

To become a competent communicator, you need to understand everything that influences your cognitions. In this section, we examine three such important influences: self-concept, self-esteem, and self-efficacy (see **Figure 2.2** on p. 40).

Self-Concept: Who You Think You Are

Who are you? You may describe yourself to others as a college student, a Latino male, a white female, a heterosexual, a biology major, an uncle, a parent, or a friend. But who you are involves much more. Your awareness and understanding of who you are—as interpreted and influenced by your thoughts, actions, abilities, values, goals, and ideals, as discussed in Chapter 1—is your **self-concept**. You develop a self-concept by thinking about your strengths and weaknesses, observing your behavior in a wide variety of situations, witnessing your own reactions to situations, and watching others' reactions to you (Snyder, 1979). You form views about yourself as active and scattered, as conservative but funny, as plain and popular—the list goes on and on. These are your cognitions. Remember from the model in Chapter 1 that both cognition and behavior make a communicator. In Chapter 1, we focused on cognitions about other people, places, media, and so on. But cognitions about self matter too.

> ## Culture and You
>
> Think about characteristics that describe your self-concept and define who you are. How did you come to believe such things about yourself? What type of direct and indirect evidence led you to believe such things about yourself? Do you think other members of your culture share similar self-concepts?

Your self-concept powerfully shapes your communication with others. It can affect what you think of other people because your perception of others is related to how you view yourself (Edwards, 1990). If attributes like honesty and wit are important to you, you will consider them important traits in other people. If you think that swearing makes you appear cheap and vulgar, you will likely think the same of others when they use foul language. When you interact with others, your self-concept comes into play as well. It can affect how apprehensive you get in certain communication situations (McCroskey, 1997), whether you're even willing to interact with others (Cegala, 1981), and how you approach someone with a request (timidly or confidently). People whose self-concept includes pride in their ability to communicate well often

> { **For most of us, our name (or nickname) is an important element in our *cognitions*, or thoughts about ourselves.** }

place themselves in situations where they can use their skills most effectively. Barbara Walters and Conan O'Brien didn't become TV-show hosts by accident! Similarly, people whose self-concept contains a less favorable view of their communication skills may shy away from opportunities where such skills (or lack of them) would be in the spotlight—such as seeking out a romantic partner or a new friendship.

So while your self-concept strongly influences how and when you communicate with others, the reverse is also true: when you interact with other people, you get impressions from them that reveal how they evaluate you as a person and as a communicator. This information gets woven into your self-concept. In fact, many researchers believe that social interaction is key to developing one's self-concept. Why? When you communicate with others, you receive evidence that you can then use to develop, confirm, or change your self-concept. *Direct evidence* comes in the form of compliments, insults, support, or negative remarks. For example, if a professor you admire tells you that you have great potential as a manager because you possess excellent leadership skills, you would probably incorporate this information into your self-concept. *Indirect evidence* that influences your self-concept might be revealed through innuendo, gossip, subtle nonverbal cues, or a lack of communication. For instance, if you ask a friend to evaluate your promise as a contestant on *American Idol* and he changes the subject, you might get the impression that you might not be as talented a singer as you'd hoped.

Other people with whom you interact also influence your self-concept. We all tend to compare ourselves to others as we develop ideas about ourselves. Explained by **social comparison theory** (Bishop, 2000; Festinger, 1954), this tendency can influence how we think about ourselves and what we're willing to do to close the unavoidable gap created by such comparison. For example, if you make a lot less money than all your friends, you may feel as though you are poor. But given the same income in a circle of less fortunate friends, you might consider yourself well-off. Images in the media—including those conveying ideas about beauty, wealth, and happiness—can affect your

> ### Technology and You
> Have you ever used technology, such as Facebook statuses, blog posts, or e-mails from friends, to compare yourself to others? Have these comparisons been more positive, more negative, or a mixture of the two?

self-concept in a similar way. Body-image issues and eating disorders, for example, have been linked to individuals' perceptions of beauty and health formed from images of perfection exhibited in the media (Bishop, 2000; Hendriks, 2002).

Barbara Walters and Conan O'Brien have honed their confident and charismatic personalities to build successful television careers.

Clearly, our self-concept exerts a powerful influence on our lives, our relationships, and our communication. Struggles with self-concept—the way we see ourselves—are closely related to the way we feel about ourselves. Let's look at how these feelings relate to communication.

Self-Esteem: How You Feel About Yourself

Self-esteem refers to how you feel about yourself, usually in a particular situation. Self-esteem consists of attitudes that people hold about their own emotions, thoughts, abilities, skills, behavior, and beliefs. These attitudes fluctuate according to the situation. Self-concept and self-esteem are closely related: people need to know themselves before they can have attitudes about themselves. Consequently, many researchers believe that the self-concept forms first, and self-esteem emerges later (Greenwalk, Bellezza, & Banaji, 1988).

You have probably noticed that people with high self-esteem have confidence in what they do, how they think, and how they perform. That's partly because these individuals are better able to incorporate their successes into their self-concept. This projection of confidence led the Italian high-end clothing company Canali to make Yankee baseball pitcher Mariano Rivera the first sports star in its advertising campaign history (Araton, 2010). Rivera's self-assurance and self-control add to the perception of Canali's elegant clothing.

Research shows that people with high self-esteem are more confident in their interpersonal relationships too—perhaps because they tend to believe that being friendly will cause others to be friendly in return (Baldwin & Keelan, 1999). Research also shows that perceived commitment from a romantic partner enhances self-esteem (Rill, Baiocchi, Hopper, Denker, & Olson, 2009). So, individuals with high self-esteem may not feel a strong need for public displays of affection. By contrast, people with low self-esteem might press their romantic partners to show affection in public, so others get their message that "someone loves me!"

Research suggests that some people have low self-esteem, or a poor view of themselves, because they lack accurate information or mistrust the knowledge they do possess. For example, you may feel that you are a poor student because you have to study constantly to keep up your grades in German class. Your German professor, on the other hand, might find that your efforts and the improvement you've made over the semester reveal that you are a good, hardworking student. Low self-esteem may also result from an *inconsistent* view of oneself (Campbell, 1990). Some people who think they possess shortcomings or negative traits may ignore them so that they can maintain a positive self-esteem. This kind of denial is demonstrated by the characters in the satire *It's Always Sunny in Philadelphia*. In that show, siblings Dennis and Dee each exhibit some of the most unlikable characteristics imaginable. They are at once ignorant, smug, prejudiced, and childish. Yet each remains convinced of his or her own superiority—believing himself or herself to be highly attractive and intellectually enlightened. And each ignores any evidence that contradicts this view.

Each member of the *It's Always Sunny in Philadelphia* crew is so blinded by his or her own ego that butting heads is an almost constant occurrence among the pals.

Self-Efficacy: Assessing Your Own Abilities

The cosmetic industry typically relies on flawless models to sell its products. So how did Lauren Luke—a plain Englishwoman—become a celebrity stylist? Luke began selling cosmetics for a modest profit on eBay. Instead of showing just products, she used them on herself and took photos. Soon she began posting videos on YouTube that she'd taped from her bedroom and was logging more than fifty million views. Luke may not have possessed the star quality of cosmetics spokeswomen like Queen Latifah and Eva Longoria, but she did have confidence in herself and her skills as a makeup artist. She was soon a celebrity in her own right, striking a deal with Sephora and being hailed by *Allure* magazine as a 2010 "Influencer" (La Ferla, 2009).

Luke's experiences reveal the power of self-efficacy, which is the third factor influencing our cognitions. Like Luke, you have an overall view of all aspects of yourself (self-concept), as well as an evaluation of how you feel about yourself in a particular area at any given moment in time (self-esteem). Based on this information, you approach a communication situation with an eye toward the *likelihood* of presenting yourself effectively. According to Albert Bandura (1982), this ability to predict actual success from self-concept and self-esteem is **self-efficacy**. Your perceptions of self-efficacy guide your ultimate choice of communication situations, making you much more likely to avoid situations where you believe your self-efficacy to be low. Indeed, many people who worry about their ability or inability to make a good impression choose computer-mediated communication (CMC) over face-to-face interactions. Sugitani (2007) found that because CMC (such as e-mail) lacks the nonverbal cues that often reveal our nervousness, we can feel more confident in and better control how we present ourselves through text alone.

Even though a person's lack of effort is most often caused by perceptions of low efficacy, Bandura (1982) has observed that people with very high levels of self-efficacy sometimes become overconfident. Defending Olympic men's figure-skating champion Evgeni Plushenko bragged to media that winning the gold in 2010 would be easy; he even held up both index fingers when he finished, as if to say, "Was there any question?" But his overconfidence may have cost him the gold, which went to U.S. skater Evan Lysacek. Bandura recommends that people maintain a high level of self-efficacy with just enough uncertainty to cause them to anticipate the situation accurately and prepare accordingly. To illustrate, a professional athlete might review footage of an opponent's best plays to keep her competitive edge sharp.

Interpreting Events. Self-efficacy also affects our ability to cope with failure and stress. For instance, feelings of low efficacy may cause you to dwell on your shortcomings. A snowball effect occurs when you already feel inadequate and then fail at something: the failure takes a toll on your self-esteem, causing you to experience stress and negative feelings about yourself. These emotions then bring your self-esteem down even more, which in turn sends your self-efficacy level even lower. For example, Jessie is job hunting but worries that she does not do well in interviews. Every time she goes to an interview and then doesn't get a job offer, her self-efficacy drops. She lowers her expectations for herself, and her interview performance worsens as well.

By contrast, people with high self-efficacy are less emotionally battered by failures because they usually chalk up disappointments to a "bad day" or some other external factor. When Erin doesn't get a job she interviewed for, for example, she concludes that she'd stumbled on her words this time because

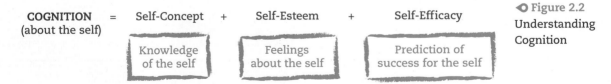

COGNITION (about the self) = Self-Concept + Self-Esteem + Self-Efficacy

Knowledge of the self | Feelings about the self | Prediction of success for the self

○ Figure 2.2 Understanding Cognition

she wasn't as well prepared as she usually is. Rather than dwelling on the failure, she simply vows to be better prepared for the next interview.

Self-Fulfilling Prophecies. Inaccurate self-efficacy may lead to a **self-fulfilling prophecy**—a prediction that causes you to change your behavior in a way that makes the prediction more likely to occur. If you go to a party believing that others don't enjoy your company, for example, you'll probably stand in a corner, not talking to anyone and making no effort to be friendly. Others won't like you, so your prophecy gets fulfilled. But your problem began before you even reached the party. You had anticipated that the party might turn out poorly for you based on your understanding of your likability.

Self-efficacy and self-fulfilling prophecy are therefore related. When you cannot avoid situations where you experience low efficacy, you are less likely to make an effort to prepare or participate than you would for situations in which you are comfortable and have high efficacy. When you do not prepare for or participate in a situation (such as the party), your behavior causes the prediction to come true, creating a self-fulfilling prophecy (see **Figure 2.3**).

Self-fulfilling prophecies don't always produce negative results. If you announce plans to improve your grades after a lackluster semester and then work harder than usual to accomplish your goal, your prediction may result in an improved report card. But even the simple act of announcing your goals to others—for example, tweeting your intention to quit

SELF-FULFILLING PROPHECY (SFP)

○ **Figure 2.3** The Self-Fulfilling Prophecy

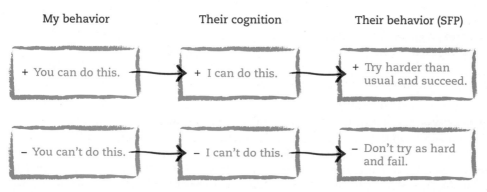

smoking or to finish a marathon—can create the commitment to make a positive self-fulfilling prophecy come true (Willard & Gramzow, 2008).

Assessing Our Perceptions of Self

Whenever you communicate, you assess your strengths and weaknesses. These assessments of self are important before, during, and after you have communicated, particularly when you've received feedback from other people. You evaluate your expectations, execution, and outcomes in three ways: through self-actualization, through self-adequacy, and through self-denigration.

Self-Actualization. The most positive evaluation you can make about your competence level is referred to as **self-actualization**—the feelings and thoughts you get when you know that you have negotiated a communication situation as well as you possibly could. At times like these, you have a sense of fulfillment and satisfaction. For example, Shari, a school psychologist, was having problems with the third-grade teacher of one of the students she counsels. The teacher seemed uninterested in the student's performance, would not return Shari's phone calls or e-mails, and seemed curt and aloof when they did speak. Shari finally decided to confront the teacher. Although she was nervous at first about saying the right thing, she later felt very good about the experience. The teacher had seemed shocked at the criticism but offered an apology. At the end of the meeting, Shari was quite content that she had been honest and assertive, as well as fair and understanding. This positive assessment of her behavior led to a higher level of self-esteem. When Shari needs to confront someone in the future, she will likely feel more confident about doing so.

Self-Adequacy. At times you may think that your communication performance was not stellar, but it was good enough. When you assess your communication competence as sufficient or acceptable, you feel a sense of **self-adequacy**, which is less intensely positive than self-actualization. Feelings of self-adequacy

can lead you in two directions: to contentment or to a desire for self-improvement.

Suppose that Phil has been working hard to improve his public speaking abilities and does a satisfactory job when he speaks to his fraternity about its goals for charitable work in the coming year. He might feel very satisfied about his speech, but he realizes that with a little more effort and practice, he could have been even more persuasive. In this case, Phil's reaction is one of *self-improvement*. He tells himself that he wants to be more competent in his communication, regardless of his current level.

While self-improvement is a good motivation, in some circumstances being satisfied or content with your self-adequacy is sufficient. For example, Lilia has a long history of communication difficulties with her mother. Their relationship is characterized by sarcastic and unkind comments and interactions. But during her last visit home, Lilia and her mother managed not to get into an argument. So Lilia felt good about her communication with her mom. The two didn't become best friends or resolve all their old problems, but Lilia thought she communicated well under the circumstances. She was content with her self-adequacy.

Self-Denigration. The most negative assessment you can make about a communication experience is **self-denigration**: criticizing or attacking yourself. This occurs most often when communicators overemphasize their weaknesses or shortcomings ("I knew I'd end up fumbling over my words and repeating myself—I am such a klutz!"). Most self-denigration is unnecessary and unwarranted. Even more important, it prevents real improvement. Hunter, for example, thinks that he can't talk to his sister; he perceives her as stubborn and judgmental. Hunter says, "I know my sister won't listen. In her opinion, I can't do anything right." Hunter needs to assess his communication behaviors: what specific words and nonverbal behaviors (like tone of voice) does he use with his sister? He must avoid self-denigration by focusing on times when he has had positive communication with his sister. He can also plan for communication improvement ("Next time, I will listen to my sister until she is finished talking before I say

COMPETENCE ASSESSMENT

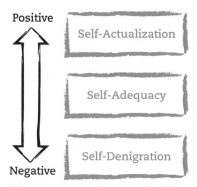

Positive

Self-Actualization

Self-Adequacy

Self-Denigration

Negative

⬧ Figure 2.4 **Assessing Our Perceptions of Self**

anything back to her"). Thus our assessments of our competence run from self-actualization on the positive end of the spectrum to self-denigration on the negative end (see **Figure 2.4**).

LearningCurve
bedfordstmartins.com/commandyou

Behavior: Managing Our Identities

As you've learned, you define yourself through your self-concept and your ideas about self-esteem and self-efficacy. But you also make decisions about how to share these internal viewpoints with others. This is manifested in your verbal and nonverbal behaviors.

We all have aspects of ourselves that we want to share and aspects that we would rather keep private. Many of the choices we make in our communication behavior, from the clothes we wear to the way we speak, are determined by how we want others to perceive us. In this section, we consider how we let the world know who we think we are and how our communication with others can shape their perceptions of us.

{ We all have aspects of ourselves that we want to share and aspects that we would rather keep private. }

Let's examine the process illustrated in **Figure 2.5**. At the core of this process is the self. The self has cognitions (about the self) that consist of self-concept (knowing and understanding the self), self-esteem (evaluating the self), and self-efficacy (predicting success)—all of which we discussed earlier. These cognitions influence our verbal and nonverbal behavior, which consist of self-presentation and self-disclosure, two terms we explain in this section. Our behavior generates feedback from others, which leads to our assessments of self-actualization, self-adequacy, and self-denigration. These judgments of our performance then affect our cognitions. As you read about self-presentation, self-disclosure, and feedback in the coming pages, refer to this illustration to remind yourself of the roles these play in your interactions with others.

Self-Presentation

You let others know about yourself through **self-presentation**—intentional communication designed to show elements of self for strategic purposes. For example, if you want to create the impression among your coworkers that you are competent at your job as an editor, you might mention during conversations the names of popular authors you've worked with or tell stories about hilariously terrible errors you've found in manuscripts you've worked on.

We all tend to focus on self-presentation when our social identity is being evaluated, formally or informally, by others (Canary & Cody, 1993). For example, you probably behave very differently when you are meeting your significant other's parents for the first time than when you're hanging out with your friends or your family.

Self-presentation can take many forms. You can present yourself through face-to-face conversation, through e-mail or text messaging, and on social-networking sites like Twitter and Facebook. You may

○ **Figure 2.5 The Self.** The self is composed of our cognitions, our behavior, and our self-assessments. These factors work together to affect our communication.

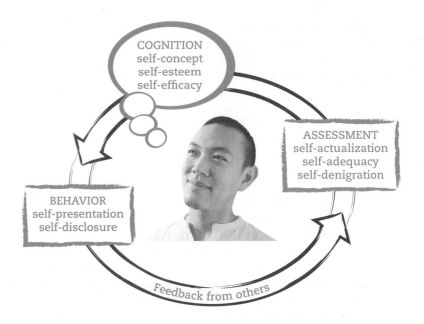

even have a preference for one of these channels of communication when self-presenting. For example, many people use asynchronous channels (e-mail, text messages, cards) when they are unsure of the reaction they will get from the recipient (O'Sullivan, 2000). For example, after a heated argument with her boyfriend, Lance, Julie wants to apologize. Because she's uncomfortable making this self-presentation to Lance over the phone or in person, she chooses to send him a text message when she knows he'll have his phone turned off. In fact, the most common reasons for choosing e-mail or a text message over face-to-face interaction is the ability to carefully construct

our messages and "shield" ourselves from any immediate negative feedback that might come from the other person (Riordan & Kreuz, 2010).

To figure out how to present yourself in the best way, you have to pay attention to your own and others' behavior. **Self-monitoring** is your ability to watch your environment and others in it for cues about how to present yourself in a particular situation (Snyder, 1974). High-self-monitoring individuals try to portray themselves as "the right person in the right place at the right time." These people watch others for hints on how to be successful in social situations. And they try to demonstrate the verbal and nonverbal behaviors that seem most appropriate. You may know someone who is a high-self-monitoring communicator. During class, this person always sits in a certain strategic position, gets involved in discussions when others do so, gestures in a manner similar to others, and when it is time to let others talk, is very strategic with silence. These "sufficiently skilled actors" can display situation-appropriate communication behaviors (Snyder, 1974).

Low-self-monitoring individuals are not nearly as sensitive to situational cues that prescribe communication behavior. They communicate according

Technology and You

You have probably encountered situations where you chose to engage in either face-to-face communication or mediated communication. Why did you choose a particular channel? If you chose a mediated channel, did you feel safer from an unknown reaction, as the research suggests? Why or why not?

to their deep-seated values or beliefs. They do not feel the need to adapt to situations or people; rather, they feel that people and situations must take them the way they are, at face value. If low self-monitors anticipate a communication situation that is different from their own self-presentation style, they will either avoid the situation or accept the fact that their communication may not please all the parties involved.

Communicating successfully involves finding the appropriate level of self-monitoring for the situation and the people involved. It might seem like high self-monitors are the winners in social interaction, but this isn't always the case. High self-monitors can drive themselves to distraction by focusing on every little thing that they say and do (Wright, Holloway, & Roloff, 2007). By contrast, competent communicators will monitor their self-presentation just enough to present themselves effectively but without forgetting that communication involves others. They also know that they can't control what *others* do that may affect their efforts to present themselves effectively—including what friends post on their Facebook wall!

📍 Places of worship often have dress codes, whether they are explicitly stated or not. People may feel that you are being disrespectful and inappropriate if you ignore the rules and do things your own way.

THINGS TO TRY

Describe how you managed an impression of yourself in a face-to-face interaction and a mediated one. Describe what you did to prepare for this impression management and what the outcome was. What contributed to your successful or unsuccessful management of self? Were the impression-management strategies you employed in the face-to-face interaction different from the mediated situation?

Self-Disclosure

Angelica is a stylish dresser; has a lovely apartment in Austin, Texas; regularly eats out at nice restaurants; and drives a new car. But she has a secret: she is drowning in debt, barely keeping up with her minimum credit card payments. She looks around at her friends, all the same age as she and living similar lifestyles. She wonders if they make more money than she does or if they, too, are over their heads in debt. One night while she's having coffee with her best friend, Shawna, Angelica comes clean about her situation: she can't go on their upcoming trip to Cozumel, she tells Shawna, because her credit cards are maxed out.

When you reveal yourself to others by sharing information about yourself—as Angelica has done with Shawna—you engage in **self-disclosure**. To count as self-disclosure in a relationship, the disclosure must be important. (Telling someone that you like snacking on raw vegetables is not self-disclosure, but explaining to them why you became a vegetarian is.) The disclosure must be not easily known by others. Finally, it must be voluntary.

Self-disclosure can help you confirm your self-concept or improve your self-esteem; it can also enable you to obtain reassurance or comfort from a trusted friend (Miller, Cooke, Tsang, & Morgan, 1992). For example, Angelica might suspect that Shawna is also living on credit; if Shawna discloses that she is, her confession might reassure Angelica that it's OK to buy things she can't afford on credit because everyone else is doing it. However, if Shawna reveals that she makes more money than Angelica, or that she manages her money more wisely, Angelica's self-concept may incur some damage. As you may remember from Chapter 1, information you receive about yourself is termed feedback. The feedback Angelica receives from Shawna will be in response to her self-disclosure. That

same feedback—and how she interprets it—will also influence Angelica's perception of herself.

How you incorporate feedback into the self depends on several factors. One of the most important factors is your *sensitivity level* to feedback. Research

What About You? }

Self-Monitoring Test

To test your own perceived level of self-monitoring, complete the following items, being careful to answer them as accurately and truthfully as possible. Use a 5-point scale for your answers: 5 = strongly agree; 4 = agree; 3 = neither agree nor disagree; 2 = disagree; and 1 = strongly disagree.

_____ 1. I am concerned about acting appropriately in social situations.

_____ 2. I find it hard to imitate the behavior of others.

_____ 3. I have good self-control of my behavior. I can play many roles.

_____ 4. I am not very good at learning what is socially appropriate in new situations.

_____ 5. I often appear to lack deep emotions.

_____ 6. In a group of people, I am rarely the center of attention.

_____ 7. I may deceive people by being friendly when I really dislike them.

_____ 8. Even if I am not enjoying myself, I often pretend to be having a good time.

_____ 9. I have good self-control of my emotional expression. I can use it to create the impression I want.

_____ 10. I can argue only for ideas that I already believe in.

_____ 11. I openly express my true feelings, attitudes, and beliefs.

_____ 12. I'm not always the person I appear to be.

Add up your scores on items 1, 3, 5, 7, 8, 9, and 12. Now reverse the scoring on items 2, 4, 6, 10, and 11 (5 = 1, 4 = 2, 2 = 4, 1 = 5). Finally, add these scores to the sum you calculated from the first set of items. If you scored 43–60, you are a high self-monitor; if you scored 30–42, you are an average self-monitor; and if your score was 12–29, you are a low self-monitor.

Source: Adapted from Snyder (1974).

demonstrates that some individuals are highly sensitive, whereas others are largely unaffected by the feedback they receive (Edwards, 1990). Presumably, people who are more sensitive to feedback are susceptible and receptive to information about their abilities, knowledge, and talents. Less sensitive people would be less responsive to such information. For example, when Olympic short-track skater Apolo Ohno bombed at the Olympic trials in 1998, he wasn't interested in hearing that his efforts weren't sufficient. He was demonstrating a low sensitivity level to the advice and feedback from his coach, friends, and family. Ohno's father sent him to a secluded cabin for eight days to contemplate his career. After that, Ohno decided that he was ready to receive the feedback that he needed to improve his game. He developed a higher sensitivity to feedback, and won eight Olympic medals at the 2010 Vancouver games (Bishop, 2010). Figure 2.6 illustrates how self-presentation and self-disclosure constitute the behavior segment of "The Self," seen in Figure 2.5 (p. 44).

Technology: Managing the Self and Perceptions

If you're wondering how your friend Ned is doing, all you need to do is check out his Facebook profile—right? There you see photographs of his recent visit with his longtime girlfriend's family in Texas. You read funny status updates about his apartment hunt. And you see that others wrote on his wall to congratulate him on his recent promotion. Life is going well for Ned, so you send him a private message to let him know that you're glad for him. Would you be surprised if Ned responded to share that he is considering a breakup with his girlfriend, that he hates his job, and that he can't afford a decent apartment because

> ### Technology and You
> Select five of your Facebook friends and visit their profiles. What type of impression does each profile make on you? How would you describe these individuals based on their profiles? Do you believe your friends are presenting themselves accurately?

his student loans are crushing him? How is this possible (you wonder) when Ned's profile seems to indicate that his life is fulfilling and happy?

This is possible because in blogs, in chat rooms, and on dating and social-networking sites we can control the presentation of self far more carefully than in face-to-face encounters. When you manage the self online, you can much more easily choose what to reveal and what to conceal. You can decide whether you will reveal your gender, ethnicity, and race, as well as your religious or political preferences. What's more, you can edit, revise, and organize the information you disclose before the message goes out. In this way, you can present an image that is smart, charming, and eloquent, even if you tend to be nervous or timid in face-to-face communication. In Ned's case, he chose to present a self that is carefree and happy—even though his current situation is quite the opposite. Among adolescents in particular, the Internet presents an appealing opportunity to experiment with identity. Sherry Turkle, a technology researcher, notes that the online environment offers young people a virtual "identity workshop" where they can try on different identities with little risk. "Things get too hot, you log off," Turkle notes, "while in time and space, you have consequences" (quoted in Wallis, 2006).

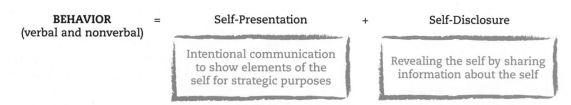

BEHAVIOR (verbal and nonverbal) = Self-Presentation + Self-Disclosure

Intentional communication to show elements of the self for strategic purposes

Revealing the self by sharing information about the self

◊ Figure 2.6 **Understanding Behavior**

On the other hand, how *you* present yourself online may not be the only factor in how you come across to others. Statements made by your friends on Facebook, for example, can significantly affect people's impressions of you. A study by Walther, Van Der Heide, Kim, Westerman, and Tong (2008) found that when people post on their friend's wall positive statements about their friend's behavior, their friend's credibility and "social attractiveness" increase, compared to negative statements (for example, about excessive drunkenness or sexual behavior). Even the number and type of friends you have on Facebook can have an influence—if you have "too few" or "too many" friends, your reputation could suffer (Tong, Van Der Heide, Langwell, & Walther, 2008). The attractiveness of your friends can also affect perceptions of your own attractiveness (Walther, Van Der Heide, Kim, Westerman, & Tong, 2008).

LearningCurve
bedfordstmartins.com/commandyou

Back to } *Britain's Got Talent*

At the beginning of this chapter, we asked why audiences were so stunned—and intrigued—by Susan Boyle's performance on *Britain's Got Talent*. Let's reconsider Boyle's performance—and people's reactions to it—in light of what we've learned about perception.

- When people looked at Susan Boyle, they quickly formed an assessment of her based on their own schemas. What they heard and saw from Boyle surprised and delighted them because she was not what they expected—her voice and her poise did not conform to the perceptions they had about her based on her age, appearance, and demeanor.

- Audiences' schemas were informed by more than just stereotypes. Shows like *Britain's Got Talent* and *American Idol* often feature auditions by performers who lack real musical gifts. Indeed, many who clicked on links to Boyle's clip on YouTube were probably expecting something more laughable. (Think of *American Idol*'s William Hung, whose performance of "She Bangs" ironically made him a star a few years back.) The assumptions they had about Boyle were based on their experiences with these types of shows.

- There have been a great many wonderful performances from a variety of singers on YouTube in the years before and since Boyle's performance. But none have generated the same intensity of buzz that Susan Boyle's first clip generated. That's because people were moved by the reactions of the audience members as well as the judges. As one writer noted, "Part of the joy of watching her performance was seeing the obnoxious, smarmy grimaces disappear from the faces of Simon Cowell and Piers Morgan, two of the show's judges, and seeing the audience shift, in an instant, from tittering condescension to open-mouthed admiration" (Lyall, 2009).

- Interaction appearance theory also plays a role here: as we get to know people better through positive interactions, we find them more socially attractive, which then leads to greater physical attraction. The more the audience heard Susan Boyle's amazing voice, the less dowdy she appeared to them. In fact, when Boyle underwent a makeover a few weeks later, some of her newfound fans were disappointed that she hadn't kept her original look.

- While the audience clearly saw Susan Boyle as a frumpy old lady who was about to make a fool of herself, she saw herself as someone with the potential to be a professional singer. When it came to self-efficacy, Boyle's assessment of her abilities was more accurate than anyone expected.

Your Reference }

Describe how our personal perspective on the world influences our communication:

- **Perception** is the cognitive process that helps us make sense of the world (p. 30).
- **Communication processing** is the means by which we gather, organize, and evaluate the information we receive (p. 31).
- Because we are constantly bombarded with information in any situation, we must sift through it to determine what is important and what to remember (p. 31).

Explain how we use and misuse schemas when communicating with others:

- **Schemas** are mental structures we use to connect bits of information (p. 31).
- Schemas help us understand how things work and decide how to act; they evolve as we encounter new information and situations. **Mindfulness** helps us focus on the task at hand (p. 32).
- Schemas present three challenges that derail good communication: **mindlessness**, responding passively to information; **selective perception**, allowing bias to influence our thoughts; and **undue influence**, giving other sources too much say (pp. 32–33).

Define the attributions we use to explain behavior:

- When we need to explain why someone says or does something in a manner that does not fit into our schemas, we look to **attributions** ◉ (p. 33).
- The **fundamental attribution error** explains our tendency to assume that another person's wrong behavior stems from an internal flaw, while the **self-serving bias** attributes our own failures to external causes (p. 34).
- **Interaction appearance theory** explains how people change their perception of someone else as they spend more time together (p. 34).

Describe how cultural differences influence perception:

- Effective communication depends on understanding how diversity, the variables that make us unique, affects perception (p. 35).

- The failure to see beyond our own beliefs and circumstances, or **cultural myopia**, blinds us to alternative points of view (p. 36).
- **Stereotyping**, or generalizing about people, limits our ability to see the individual and can lead to **prejudice**, ill will toward a particular group and a sense of one's own superiority (p. 36).

Identify how our self-concept—who we think we are—influences communication:

- We are more willing to interact in situations where we feel we have strengths and where our self-concept is confirmed or changed by responses from others (pp. 37–38).
- We compare ourselves against idealized images in the media, according to **social comparison theory** ◉, often to our own disadvantage (p. 38).
- **Self-esteem** relates to self-concept and is how we feel about ourselves in a particular situation (p. 39).
- **Self-efficacy** is the ability to predict, based on self-concept and self-esteem, our effectiveness in a communication situation. Inaccurate self-efficacy may lead to a **self-fulfilling prophecy** ◉, whereby we change our behavior in ways that make our prediction more likely to come true (pp. 40–42).
- We assess our communication effectiveness through the lenses of **self-actualization** (positive feelings about a highly successful performance), **self-adequacy** (satisfied or determined feelings about an adequate performance), and **self-denigration** (negative and destructive feelings about a poor performance) (pp. 42–43).

Describe how our cognitions about ourselves and our behavior affect our communication:

- **Self-presentation** is intentional communication designed to show elements of self for strategic purposes; it's how we let others know about ourselves (pp. 43–44).
- The tendency to watch our environment and others in it for cues as to how to present ourselves in particular situations is called **self-monitoring** ◉ (pp. 44–45).
- Sharing important information about ourselves, such as with a close friend, is **self-disclosure** ◉ (pp. 45–47).
- We can more easily control presentation of self online than in face-to-face encounters (pp. 47–48).

 Look for **LearningCurve** throughout the chapter to help you review.
bedfordstmartins.com/commandyou

3 } Communication and Culture

I f you were trying to imagine a group that clearly reflects the diversity of the United States, it might look a bit like the cast of *Glee*. And in case you don't catch the differences in race, ethnicity, religion, sexual preference, or physical abilities represented by the fictional William McKinley High School show choir, the politically incorrect cheerleading coach, Sue Sylvester, will be happy to point them out to you.

Glee debuted in May 2009 to rave reviews and an immediate audience following. It is at once a scathing satire of high school life and a joyful celebration of music. It is also a charming—and often troubling—exploration of intercultural and co-cultural communication and relationships. The diverse characters conform to stereotypes in many ways—Finn represents the not-so-intelligent jock; Rachel, the ambitious diva. But the show also deals with real communication issues and challenges in almost every episode, including bullying and teen

pregnancy, as well as the way differences in religious beliefs, personal lifestyles, and social status affect group bonding.

There's no doubt that individuals from different co-cultures respond well to seeing people like them represented on television. But *Glee* is not a sweet take on multiculturalism: Sue Sylvester doesn't merely point out the differences between team members—she openly mocks them. Her mean-spiritedness not only provides the show with zinging laughs and a definable "bad guy" but also acknowledges the real struggles with which teens from just about every co-culture must deal.

While Sue Sylvester considers glee club members the lowest form of high school life, Jane Lynch (the actress who plays her) has a clear sense of why the show's celebration of outcasts and misfits has struck such a chord. "No matter who you are or how different you are from the 'norm,' you're going to get supported in this glee club," says Lynch (McLean, 2011).

After you have finished reading this chapter, you will be able to

Define and explain culture and its impact on your communication.

Delineate seven ways that cultural variables affect communication.

Describe the communicative power of group affiliations.

Explain key barriers to competent intercultural communication.

Demonstrate skills and behaviors that contribute to intercultural competence.

A s episodes of *Glee* demonstrate, communication among individuals of different races, sexes, religions, and so on can be messy—but it can also be exciting, challenging, enlightening, and enjoyable. To be part of any team, or to be a good neighbor and an informed citizen, you need to understand this essential communication process. Whether you're looking to learn how to better communicate with your older relatives, understand the way your roommate's faith plays out in her communication, or contemplate current national debates surrounding issues like immigration and religious tolerance, this chapter aims to help you better understand cultural differences *and* similarities to increase your competence in intercultural encounters. We begin with an overview of culture. Then we explore cultural variations and group affiliations as well as the challenges and opportunities that intercultural communication offers.

Understanding Culture

As you'll recall from the communication competence model (Chapter 1), your encounters with others occur within overlapping relational, situational, and cultural contexts. **Culture** is a learned system of thought and behavior that belongs to and typifies a relatively large group of people; it is the composite of their shared beliefs, values, and practices. Although we might commonly think of culture as a person's nationality, it applies to any broadly shared group identity. In this section, we investigate how culture is learned, how it affects our communication, and why learning how to communicate with members of different cultures is so important.

Culture Is Learned

Culture is not something you're born with; it is something you learn through communication. As children, you observe the behaviors of your parents, siblings, and extended family members. For example, they teach you how to greet guests in your home, whether to make direct eye contact with others, and what words are polite rather than inconsiderate. Later you observe the behaviors of your teachers and your peer groups. You learn what types of conversational topics are appropriate to discuss with peers rather than with adults; you learn the nuances of interacting with members of the same and the opposite sex. You also listen to and observe television, movies, and various forms of advertising that reflect what your culture values and admires.

Through these processes, you acquire an understanding of what constitutes appropriate behavior. This is the framework through which you interpret the world and the people in it—your **worldview**

> ### Culture and You
>
> Consider a time when a friend, coworker, classmate, or even a family member behaved in a manner that seemed unnatural or uncomfortable to you. Is it possible that your different behavioral expectations could have been due to a cultural difference, as noted in the example about eye contact? Explain your answer.

(Schelbert, 2009). Much of your worldview is not obvious. For example, many of your nonverbal behaviors (like gestures, eye contact, and tone of voice) occur at an unconscious level (Hall, 1976). You have learned these behaviors so well that you don't even notice them until someone else behaves in a manner that doesn't meet your expectations. For example, you may not realize that you routinely make eye contact during conversation until someone fails to meet your gaze.

Your use of language carries more obvious cultural cues: speaking Italian in Italy enables you to fully participate in and understand the Italian way of life (Nicholas, 2009). Language can also teach you the traditions of your culture as evidenced by prayers of your faith, folk songs of your grandparents, or patriotic oaths you make (such as the Pledge of Allegiance).

Culture Affects Communication

Just as we learn culture *through* communication, we also use communication to *express* our culture. Our worldview affects which topics we discuss in personal and professional settings, as well as how we communicate nonverbally. It also affects the way we perceive others' communication.

In the United States, a popular worldview often equates thinness with feminine beauty; this perception is reflected in the mass media and personal messages we communicate. After tabloids mocked actress and singer Jessica Simpson for her supposed weight gain, she journeyed around the world with two friends to understand diverse notions of beauty. They discovered that people in other cultures have different worldviews and, consequently, different ideas about physical attractiveness. Their experiences in Japan, Thailand, France, Brazil, Uganda, Morocco, and India aired in 2010 as VH1's series *The Price of Beauty* (Hinckley, 2010). Simpson and her friends were surprised to find that in Uganda, where larger women are considered desirable, women prepare for marriage in a "fattening hut." While their findings are merely observations, they exposed young teens to the widely differing views of what is and isn't attractive and the ways these views are expressed through cultural practices.

Technology and You
Technology has, in essence, made the world smaller. We can go online and be connected with individuals around the globe. Do you believe this easy access to other cultures' perceptions of beauty and physical attractiveness has informed your own worldview? Why or why not?

Intercultural Communication Matters

People from different cultures have correspondingly different worldviews. This can lead to misunderstandings, anger, hurt feelings, and other challenges when individuals from various backgrounds interact. In an attempt to avoid such negative outcomes, communication scholars invest a great deal of time and effort to study and write about **intercultural communication**, the communication between people from different cultures who have different worldviews. Communication is considered intercultural when the differences between communicators are so substantial that they can create different interpretations and expectations (Lustig & Koester, 1993).

The answer to addressing intercultural misunderstanding isn't to interact only with those you perceive as *exactly like you*. You live in a diverse and mobile society, and you study, play, and work with people who are different from you on a number of levels. Let's consider why studying intercultural communication matters so much.

A Diverse Society. The United States is a diverse country, with a population that reflects a range of ethnic, racial, and religious backgrounds. Different regions of the country (and sometimes different neighborhoods in the same city) have distinct cultures as well (see **Figure 3.1**). You have a unique cultural background and communication style that differ in some ways from those of others. So, to function as a member of such a diverse society, you need to be able to communicate appropriately and effectively

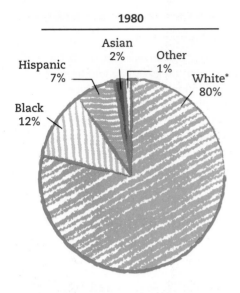

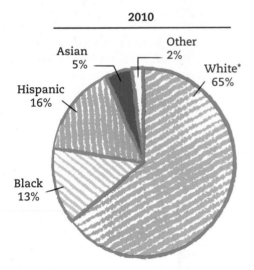

* Non-Hispanic

◊ **Figure 3.1** **U.S. Census Data Indicating Increased Diversity in the Nation**

Source: U. S. Census Bureau; numbers have been rounded

with a wide variety of individuals. Two key parts of this process are understanding your own cultural expectations for communication and respecting those of others.

Mobility. More than six in ten adults have moved to a new community at least once in their lives, and more than one in five say the place they are living now is not "home" (Taylor, Morin, Cohn, & Wang, 2008). Therefore, you must be ready to address cultural differences—not just between nations but also between regions, states, and cities. Even if you don't plan on ever leaving your hometown, you will almost certainly communicate at some time or another with people from outside of it, face to face and through a variety of media.

> **Culture and You**
>
> How long have you lived in your current location? Are people where you reside treated differently based on their status as new or established members of the community? How does their status change based on their level of involvement in the community?

Mediated Interaction. Clearly, mediated communication is changing the way we experience the world and broadening the range of people and groups with whom we regularly interact. In the United States today, some 66 percent of American adults have broadband access at home (Smith, 2010a). In addition, 40 percent of adults access the Internet via mobile devices. Thus, we communicate electronically more and more each year (Smith, 2010b). Through the Internet and other technology, we connect not only with far-off family and friends but also with individuals from around the country—or around the world—when we participate in online gaming, post our thoughts on online forums, or read others' personal blogs.

Even among Americans who do not have access to these technologies, more traditional media enable exposure and interaction with people from different cultures. Calls to customer-service centers are answered in other parts of the country or on the other side of the world. Radio stations bring international music and news right to your car. Newspapers carry

Technology and You

Are you part of any online groups or discussion forums that allow you to interact with individuals in other cities, states, or nations? If so, have you encountered any specific intercultural communication issues? (This may be something seemingly small—like confusion over the meaning of a phrase—or something more significant—like different levels of directness in communication.) If so, how did you handle the situation to increase the effectiveness of communication?

stories from correspondents across the globe. And television offers glimpses of cultures we might not be a part of—through broadcasts of British situation comedies on PBS, soccer games from South America, and foreign films on the Sundance Channel. American TV programs also have increasingly diverse casts.

Diverse Organizations. Any job you take will involve some degree of intercultural communication. A teacher may have students whose families are from different parts of the country or from other countries entirely; an entrepreneur must understand how different groups respond to her product and her marketing campaigns. Being aware of how culture affects communication is especially crucial to business communication across borders (Busch, 2009). During negotiations, for instance, you may need to know how hard to push a client to commit and when to be silent.

Clearly, intercultural communication is important in your life as a student, a citizen, and a professional. The culture in which you live (or were raised) has particular ways of communicating in the world. We illustrate these by examining the following seven cultural variations.

LearningCurve
bedfordstmartins.com/commandyou

Communication and Cultural Variations

Scholars have identified seven major communication variations[1] across cultures: high and low context, collectivist and individualist orientations, comfort with uncertainty, masculine and feminine orientations, approaches to power distance, time orientation, and value of emotional expression (Hall, 1976; Hofstede, 1984, 2001; Matsumoto, 1989).

These seven variations may seem like opposites, and you may think that your culture must be one or the other. However, these variations play out along a spectrum: your culture may be masculine in some

---

[1] Geert Hofstede (1984) referred to these variations as cultural *dimensions*—largely psychological value constructs that affect the way people think about and perform communication behaviors.

ways and feminine in others. Also, within any culture, there is great variance among different groups in terms of where they fall on the spectrum. Finally, there are always some people who reject the thinking and behaviors associated with their dominant culture. With these caveats in mind, let's consider each variation more closely.

High- and Low-Context Cultures

Our culture strongly affects how direct we are in our use of language and how much we rely on other, nonverbal ways to communicate. Individuals in **high-context cultures** (including those of Japan, Korea, China, and many Latin American and African countries) use contextual cues—such as time, place, relationship, and situation—to interpret meaning and send subtle messages (Hall, 1976; Hall & Hall, 1990). A Chinese person who disagrees with someone, for example, may not say anything; the communication partner must look for clues of disagreement in the context. These clues may include the amount of time that passes before a response or the nonverbal behaviors that occur or don't occur. People from a high-context culture also tend to attribute a communication partner's behavior to factors related to the situation rather than to an individual's personality. For instance, instead of assuming that someone who remains

silent is rude, they might think that the individual didn't respond because the situation called for restraint and politeness.

A **low-context culture**, by contrast, uses very direct language and relies less on situational factors to communicate. The United States, Canada, Australia, and most northern European countries tend to have a low-context style. In the United States, for example, it would seem normal for someone to say, "Alex, I need a list of twenty items for the Allan project from you by five o'clock today." Someone from a high-context culture would more likely say, "We are starting the project," and would assume that Alex would have the list ready on time because Alex understands the situation as the speaker does. If Alex did not get the list completed on time, a boss in a low-context culture would blame it on Alex's laziness or incompetence, whereas a manager in a high-context culture would blame it on situational constraints, such as Alex having too many projects to work on. Table 3.1 compares high- and low-context styles.

Collectivist and Individualist Orientations

Differences in the value of personal space and independence versus belonging and group loyalty illustrate our second cultural value: collectivist and individualist orientations.

Table 3.1 **A Comparison of High- and Low-Context Cultures**

High-Context Cultures	Low-Context Cultures
■ Rely on contextual cues for communication	■ Rely on direct language for communication
■ Avoid speaking in a way that causes individuals to stand out from others	■ Value self-expression
■ Avoid intruding on others	■ Construct explicit messages
■ Avoid saying *no* directly, preferring to talk around the point	■ State opinions and desires directly
■ Usually express opinions indirectly	■ Persuade others by speaking clearly and eloquently
■ Usually express disagreement by saying nothing	■ Usually express disagreement clearly
■ Tend to find explanations for behaviors in the situation	
■ Admire relationship harmony	

> **Ethics and You**
> Whose responsibility is it to clarify communication misunderstandings that might occur among individuals from high- and low-context cultures? Do both parties have an equal responsibility? What other factors (including age, status, and so on) might influence your thoughts on this question?

> **Culture and You**
> To what degree do you identify with individualist or collectivist cultures? How might the answer to this question be complicated if the family you grew up with identifies strongly with one dimension but the larger culture in which you were raised strongly identifies with the other?

Individuals from **collectivist cultures** perceive themselves first and foremost as members of a group—and they communicate from that perspective (Triandis, 1986, 1988, 2000). Collectivist cultures (including many Arab and Latin American cultures as well as several Asian cultures, such as found in China and Japan) emphasize cooperation and group harmony, group decision making, and long-term, stable friendships. Communication in such cultures is governed by a clear notion of status and hierarchy, and loyalty to the group and the honor of one's family are more important than individual needs or desires (Wang & Liu, 2010). In addition, collectivist communicators are generally concerned with relational support; they avoid hurting others' feelings, apologize, and make efforts to help others maintain the group's reputation and position of respect (Han & Cai, 2010). For example, if an individual attending a business meeting discovers a financial error, she will not likely mention who made the error, nor will she call attention to her own success in discovering it. Instead, she will emphasize the group's success in correcting the error before it became a problem for the company.

Conversely, people from **individualist cultures** value autonomy and privacy and pay relatively little attention to status and hierarchy based on age or family connections. In such cultures, individual initiative and achievement are rewarded, and individual credit and blame are assigned. Thus, an individual who notes an error—even one by her superiors—will probably be rewarded or respected for her keen observation (as long as she presents it sensitively). The United States is a highly individualist culture—American heroes are usually those celebrated for "pulling themselves up by their bootstraps" to achieve great things or change the world. Other Western cultures, such as those of Great Britain, Australia, and Germany, are also at the high end of the individualism scale.

Comfort with Uncertainty

Cultures also differ in the degree of anxiety that individual members tend to feel about the unknown. All cultures, to some degree, adapt their behaviors to reduce uncertainty and risk, a process called **uncertainty avoidance**. Cultures that are more anxious about the unknown are said to be *high uncertainty avoidance cultures;* people from these cultures strive to minimize risk and uncertainty. In high uncertainty avoidance cultures (such as those of Greece, Peru, and Japan), communication is usually governed by formal rules to satisfy a need for absolute truth and stability, with little tolerance for differences of opinion. By following social rules and minimizing dissent, they reduce uncertainty and anxiety in prescribed communication situations (Gudykunst, 1993).

On the other hand, cultures with a higher tolerance for risk and ambiguity (like those found in Denmark, Ireland, and the United States) are considered *low uncertainty avoidance cultures* (Samovar, Porter, & McDaniel, 2009). Their lower level of anxiety about the unknown means that these cultures are comfortable with a variety of communication styles, are more tolerant of differences of opinion, and have fewer formal rules for behavior (Hoeken et al., 2003) (see **Figure 3.2**).

Masculine and Feminine Orientations

The masculinity or femininity of a culture refers to the way an entire culture (including both men and women within the culture) values and reflects characteristics that are traditionally associated with one sex or the other. Thus, a **masculine culture**—sometimes referred to as an *achievement culture*—places value on assertiveness, achievement, ambition, and competitiveness (Samovar, Porter, & McDaniel, 2009). Men and women in such cultures also usually make clear distinctions between the sexes, such as expecting more aggressiveness in men and more passiveness in women.

Highly **feminine cultures**—sometimes referred to as *nurturing cultures*—place value on relationships and quality of life. Rather than assertiveness, such cultures prize affection, friendliness, and social support among people. Scandinavian cultures (such as those of Sweden and Norway), as well as the cultures of Chile and Portugal, tend to rank high in femininity, whereas Mexico, Japan, and Italy tend to have cultures high in masculinity.

When discussing masculine and feminine orientation, remember that individual men and women *within* each culture vary in their valuing of masculinity and femininity (Tripathy, 2010). For example,

Japan ranks as a highly masculine culture, yet in recent years many Japanese men have been embracing a less restrictive view of masculinity. Analysts note that these men may communicate in ways that are gentle, shy, and sensitive (Faiola, 2005).

Approaches to Power Distance

The movie *Slumdog Millionaire* is about Jamal, a Mumbai teen who grows up in the city slums and becomes a contestant on the Indian version of *Who Wants to Be a Millionaire?* Jamal endures brutal police interrogation on suspicion of cheating because the show's producers cannot imagine that he could know so much. This may seem shocking to some people in the United States, where upward mobility is a value and underdogs become folk heroes. Why?

It has to do with a culture's ideas about the division of power among individuals, a concept known as **power distance**. In India, social status is far more stratified than in the United States. The caste system—formally outlawed in 1950 but still lingering in India's culture—placed individuals, families, and entire groups into distinct social strata. That meant that the family you were born into determined who you could associate with and marry and what job you

▶ Figure 3.2 **Communication and Cultural Variation**

Source: Adapted from Hofstede, 1984, 2001.

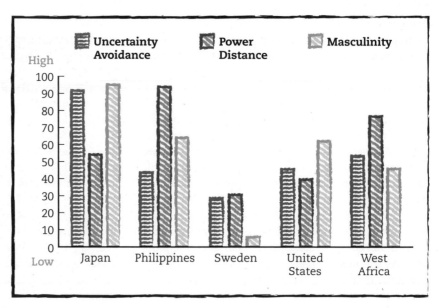

could hold. Those born into the lowest tier (the untouchables) were considered subhuman, even contagious, and were ignored by higher castes of people. Individuals generally accepted their place in the caste system. Today, the idea that one's social status is set in stone lingers (Bayly, 1999).

Status differences in a culture result in some groups or individuals having more power than others. But a person's position in the cultural hierarchy can come from sources besides social class, including age, job title, or even birth order. In *high power distance cultures* (like those in India, China, and Japan), people with less power accept their lower position as a basic fact of life. They experience more anxiety when they communicate with those of higher status. And they tend to accept coercion as normal and avoid challenging authority. People in *low power distance cultures* (such as in the United States, Canada, Germany, and Australia) tolerate less difference in power between people and communicate with those higher in status with less anxiety. They are more likely to challenge the status quo, consider multiple options or possibilities for action, and resist coercion.

Time Orientation

Time orientation, or the way cultures communicate about and with time, is an important—yet frequently overlooked—cultural dimension (Hall, 1959).

Many Western cultures (such as those in the United States and Great Britain) are extremely time conscious. Every portion of the day is oriented around time—including time for meals, sleep, meetings, and classes. Even sayings express the importance of time: *time is money, no time to lose, wasting time* (Mast, 2002). But in many Latin American and Asian cultures, time is fluid and the pace of life is slower. Arriving two hours late for an invitation is perfectly acceptable. An American businessperson might get frustrated and give up after spending six months working on a deal with a Japanese company, whereas the Japanese might be wondering why the American quit so soon when they were all just getting to know each other!

A key cultural distinction operating here is whether cultures are monochronic or polychronic (Gudykunst & Ting-Toomey, 1988; Hall, 1976; Victor, 1992). **Monochronic cultures** treat time as a limited resource. Such cultures (including those found in the United States, Germany, Canada, and the United Kingdom) use time to structure activities and focus on attending to one person or task at a time; they value concentration and stick to schedules. In monochronic cultures, people line up to wait their "turn"—to see a professor at office hours, to check out at the grocery store, to buy tickets for a concert. **Polychronic cultures** are comfortable dealing with multiple people and tasks at the same time. Seven or eight people all crowding around a stall and shouting out their needs at a mercado in Mexico is expected, not rude. Polychronic cultures (such as those found in Mexico, India, and the Philippines) are also less concerned with making every moment count. They don't adhere as closely to schedules, are less likely to make or attend appointments, and change plans often and easily.

📍 Though this market may seem like utter chaos to a British or American tourist visiting Bangkok, native Thai people are more comfortable with the busy multitasking nature of their polychronic culture.

Even Web-based communication can be affected by such differences in the perception of time. One study found that people from polychronic cultures were less bothered by download delays than were people from monochronic cultures (Rose, Evaristo, & Straub, 2003).

Value of Emotional Expression

One thing that people from all cultures share is the ability to *experience* emotion. But *expressing* emotions (including which emotions and under what circumstances) varies greatly. In some cultures, emotional expression is associated with strength, while in others it is associated with weakness. Sometimes emotional expression is seen as chaos and other times as identifying and processing of problems (Lutz, 1996).

Many collectivistic cultures (for example, Arab cultures) often use **hyperbole**—vivid, colorful language with great emotional intensity (and often exaggeration). Individualistic cultures (particularly those of English-speaking people) tend toward **understatement**, language that downplays (often with use of euphemisms) the emotional intensity or importance of events (Wierzbicka, 2006). Consider, for example, the difference between describing a military battle by saying "the river ran red with the blood of the slaughtered" versus "there were a number of casualties."

Communication in different cultures varies along continuums in seven key ways. Yet within these broadly defined cultures, we all vary our communication in many more specific ways based on the many groups to which we belong or with which we

identify, as we outline in the next section on group affiliation.

Understanding Group Affiliations

Ellen DeGeneres is an American, a woman, and a baby boomer. She is white. She is a Californian, but also a southerner. She is a lesbian, a vegan, an animal rights activist, and an environmentalist. She is also a successful entertainer and is very wealthy. All of these characteristics—and many others—form DeGeneres's unique identity. These attributes also make her a member of various groups. Some of these groups might be formal (as expressed by her affiliations with various animal rights groups). However, most are informal, reflecting the more general ways in which we group ourselves and others based on particular characteristics. Thus, Ellen is a member of the white community, the southern community, the wealthy community, the entertainment community, and so on.

You too have multiple aspects to your identity, including the many groups to which you belong. These group affiliations powerfully shape your communication and affect how others communicate with and about you. In this section, we'll consider these facts by examining co-cultural communication as well as social identity theory and intergroup communication.

What About You?

Discovering Your Cultural Values

Consider each of the following statements and mark SA (strongly agree), A (agree), N (neither agree nor disagree), D (disagree), or SD (strongly disagree).

Value Statements	SA	A	N	D	SD
People who work hard are to be admired.	☐	☐	☐	☐	☐
People should take care of family before themselves.	☐	☐	☐	☐	☐
It is important to plan carefully for the future.	☐	☐	☐	☐	☐
It is important to show respect to your elders.	☐	☐	☐	☐	☐
Risk taking is dangerous; people should follow the rules.	☐	☐	☐	☐	☐
It is important to be on time to appointments.	☐	☐	☐	☐	☐
People should share their emotions with one another.	☐	☐	☐	☐	☐
People should clearly and directly say what they think.	☐	☐	☐	☐	☐
Competition is beneficial for society.	☐	☐	☐	☐	☐
Change is a necessary and good part of life.	☐	☐	☐	☐	☐

There is no official scale to help you grade this self-assessment; since cultural values occur on a continuum (and are not polar opposites), you will likely discover your cultural variation as you contemplate each question. Try to assess your answers according to the cultural value variations detailed in this chapter.

Co-cultural Communication

As we discussed in Chapter 1, **co-cultures** are groups whose members share at least some of the general culture's system of thought and behavior but who also have distinct characteristics or attitudes that unify them and distinguish them from the general culture. As you saw in our example about Ellen and as **Figure 3.3** shows, ethnic heritage, race (or races), gender, religion, socioeconomic status, and age form just a few of these co-cultures. But other factors come into play as well: some co-cultures are defined by interest, activities, opinions, or membership in particular organizations (for example, "I am a Republican" or "I am a foodie").

Our communication is intrinsically tied to our co-cultural experience. For example, a **generation** is a group of people who were born during a specific time frame and whose attitudes and behavior were shaped by that time frame's events and social

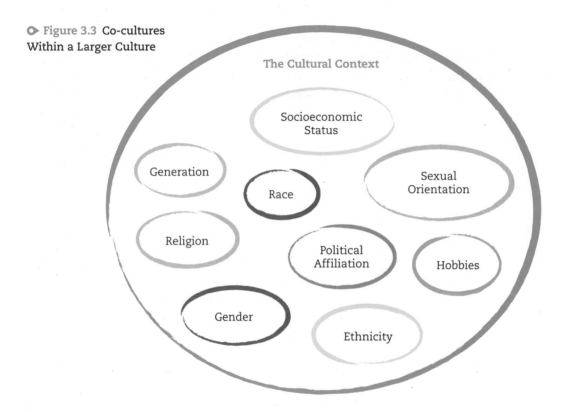

◐ Figure 3.3 **Co-cultures Within a Larger Culture**

The Cultural Context

Socioeconomic Status

Generation

Race

Sexual Orientation

Religion

Political Affiliation

Hobbies

Gender

Ethnicity

📍 Ellen DeGeneres belongs to a variety of co-cultures.

changes. Generations develop different ideas about how relationships work, ideas that affect communication within and between generations (Howe & Strauss, 1992). For example, Americans who lived through the Second World War share common memories (the bombing of Pearl Harbor, military experience, home-front rationing) that have shaped their worldviews in somewhat similar—though not identical—ways. This shared experience affects how they communicate, as shown in **Table 3.2.**

Similarly, the interplay between our sex and our gender exerts a powerful influence on our communication. *Sex* refers to the biological characteristics (that is, reproductive organs) that make us male or female. **Gender** refers to the behavioral and cultural traits assigned to the sexes; it is determined by the way members of a particular culture define notions of masculinity and femininity (Wood, 2008, 2011).

Table 3.2 **Generation as Co-culture**

Generation	Year Born	Characteristics Affecting Communication
Matures	Before 1946	Born before the end of the Second World War, these are the generations that lived through the Great Depression and the war. They are largely conformist, with strong civic instincts.
Baby Boomers	1946–1964	The largest generation, products of an increase in births that began after the Second World War and ended with the introduction of the birth control pill. In their youths, they were antiestablishment and optimistic about the future, but recent surveys show they are more pessimistic today than any other age group.
Generation X	1965–1980	Savvy, entrepreneurial, and independent, this generation witnessed the fall of the Berlin Wall and the rise of home computing.
Millennials	1981–2000	The first generation of the new millennium, this includes people under thirty; the first group to fully integrate computers into their everyday communication.

Source: Taylor & Keeter, 2010.

For example, according to linguistics professor Deborah Tannen, men tend to communicate in a "report" style that is assertive, focused on outcomes, and competitive; men also tend to avoid many other nonverbal behaviors, including touching, gesturing, and using vocalizations (fillers such as "uh-huh") when communicating with others (Tannen, 1992; Wood, 2009). On the other hand, Tannen noted that many women communicate in a "rapport" style that is collaborative and focused on others' feelings and needs. This style also tends to include many nonverbal behaviors, such as touching communication partners and giving vocal, facial, and gestural indications that the partner is being heard (Tannen, 1992; Wood, 2009).[2]

---

[2] Scholars have long debated whether these communication differences are based on nature (inherent differences between men and women), nurture (the ways in which men and women are encouraged to have, and are rewarded for having, different styles), or some combination of the two. We cannot possibly do justice to the nuances of this debate in the confines of this chapter, but we will discuss these issues related to verbal and nonverbal communication in Chapters 4 and 5.

Technology and You
Knowing what research states about gender, sex, and communication styles, do you believe the same holds true for online communication? Do you believe you can tell if someone who comments on your favorite blog is male or female based on the words they use? Why or why not? (If possible, test your beliefs.)

So, are we destined to live our lives bound by the communication norms and expectations for our sex or gender, our generation, our profession, our hobbies, and our other co-cultures? Hardly. Recall the concept of *behavioral flexibility* discussed in Chapter 1. This concept notes that competent communicators adapt their communication skills to a variety of life situations. There are contexts and relationships that call for individuals of both sexes to adhere to a more feminine mode of communication (for example,

{ **So, are we destined to live our lives bound by the communication norms and expectations for . . . our generation, our profession, our hobbies, and our other co-cultures? Hardly.** }

may not communicate in the exact same style simply because they are both women, they were born in the same year, or they were both college graduates who became high-school English teachers.

Similarly, the group typically defined as African Americans includes Americans with a variety of cultural and national heritages. For some, their story stretches back to colonial times; others are more recent immigrants from Africa, the Caribbean, and elsewhere ("Census," 2010). Christians include a wealth of different denominations that practice various aspects of the larger faith differently. Christians also hail from different races and ethnicities, socio-economic statuses, regions, political views, and so on. All of these intersecting factors affect communication within any given co-culture.

Ethics and You

Have you witnessed others communicating in ways that do not conform to their culture or co-culture (for example, by using masculine or feminine language unexpectedly)? What was the outcome? Did you perceive that communication partner differently? Have you exhibited such behavioral flexibility in your own life? How do you feel you were perceived?

Social Identity and Intergroup Communication

Clearly, our group memberships strongly influence our communication. This point is further illustrated and clarified by two concepts: social identity theory and intergroup communication. According to **social identity theory**, you have a *personal identity*, which is your sense of your unique individual personality, and you have a *social identity*, the part of your self-concept that comes from your group memberships (Tajfel & Turner, 1986). We divide ourselves into "us" and "them" partly based on our affiliations with various co-cultures. The groups with which we identify and to which we feel we belong are our **ingroups**; those we define as "others" are **outgroups**. We want "us" to be distinct and better than "them," so we continually compare our co-cultures to others in the hope that we are part of the "winning" teams.

comforting a distraught family member), while other contexts and relationships require them to communicate in a more masculine way (for example, using direct and confident words when negotiating for a higher salary). Similarly, a teenager who feels most comfortable communicating with others via text messaging or Facebook might do well to send his grandma a handwritten thank-you note for his graduation gift.

In addition, there is a great diversity of communication behaviors within co-cultures (as well as diversity within larger cultures). For example, your grandmother and your best friend's grandmother

Studies in **intergroup communication**, a branch of the discipline that focuses on how communication within and between groups affects relationships, find that these comparisons powerfully affect our communication (Giles, Reid, & Harwood, 2010; Pagotto, Voci, & Maculan, 2010). For example, group members

Ethics and You

Have you encountered a situation in which someone made assumptions about you or your beliefs based on some aspect of your culture or co-cultures? How did you handle this situation? What was the outcome?

often use specialized language and nonverbal behaviors to reveal group membership status to others (Bourhis, 1985). So, a doctor might use a lot of technical medical terms when with nurses to assert her authority as a doctor. The Chicago Bears fan proudly wears her team jersey on game day, while her husband and children proudly don their Dallas Cowboys T-shirts.

Our group identification and communication shift depending on which group membership is made **salient**—or brought to mind—at a given moment. For example, students often consider themselves ingroup members with fellow students and outgroup members with nonstudents. However, students from different schools might also identify themselves in smaller units: for example, community college students might consider themselves outgroups from students attending a four-year university. At the same time, if all of these students discovered that they're rabid fans of the *Hunger Games* trilogy or that they volunteered for Habitat for Humanity, they might see each other as ingroup members in relation to these interests and experiences.

In addition, your group memberships are not all equally salient for you at any given time, and your

THINGS TO TRY

On a blank piece of paper, begin listing all the co-cultures to which you belong. How many can you come up with? How do they overlap? If someone asked you to identify yourself by using only one of them, could you do it? Try ranking them in order of importance to you.

Technology and You

Do you believe that the issue of salience is more, less, or equally important in online interactions? Under what circumstances might one of your group memberships become particularly salient in an online environment?

📍 John Boehner's tearful response upon becoming Speaker of the House in 2011 gained him much media airtime, perhaps because we are prone to criticize open displays of emotion from men.

communication reflects this. For instance, suppose you are a Latina Catholic from a middle-class family and a straight-A student with a love of languages and a passion for outdoor adventure sports. When displaying who "you" are, you may emphasize your "studentness" (by wearing your college insignia) and sports enthusiasm (by participating actively in sporting events). Your race, religion, and socioeconomic status don't come as much to the forefront. But remember that other people treat you based on the groups *they* think you belong to. So someone else might focus on other aspects of how you look or talk and see you primarily as "a woman," "a Catholic," or "a Latina."

The ways in which others perceive our social identity influence communication on many levels. In the 1960s, Rock Hudson was a Hollywood heartthrob who kept his identity as a gay man a secret. At that time, audiences would likely not have accepted him in heterosexual romantic roles if they had known he was not interested in women. Today, straight actors take on gay and lesbian roles (as Heath Ledger and Jake Gyllenhaal did in *Brokeback Mountain*). But it isn't certain whether audiences will accept gay and lesbian actors in straight roles. To be sure, the openly gay Neil Patrick Harris has no problem playing the womanizing Barney Stinson on *How I Met Your Mother*. But some actors, including Rupert Everett and Richard Chamberlain, have noted that coming out hurt their careers irreparably, and they have advised young gay actors to maintain their privacy in regard to their sexuality (Connelly, 2009; Voss, 2010).

> **LearningCurve**
> bedfordstmartins.com/commandyou

Intercultural Communication Challenges

With all the cultural variations in society, along with the individual and overlapping co-cultures to which each person belongs, it is understandable that communication difficulties sometimes arise. Even with people you know well who are like you in many ways, you can sometimes experience difficulties during communication. Let's look at three of the more pressing intercultural challenges that communicators experience when interacting with others: anxiety, ethnocentrism, and discrimination.

Anxiety

"What if I say something offensive?" "What if I don't know how to behave?" "What if I embarrass myself?" These are just a few of the worries that people sometimes have as they approach intercultural communication encounters. Consider the experience of Allison Goodrich, an American student at Georgetown University about to set off on a semester abroad in China:

> Here I was, standing in the check-out line of the Chinese market in Rockville, Maryland, listening to the cashier yell at me with an incomprehensible stream of syllables. This was after a rather harrowing attempt to find groceries in the overcrowded store. A year of Chinese wasn't helping me as I stood in front of an entire display of green vegetables, trying to figure out which sign would lead me to my desired product. During all of this, my accompanying friend turned to me and said, "This is how crowded it will be wherever you go in China." (Goodrich, 2007, para. 1)

You can probably imagine Allison's anxiety as she considered her upcoming adventure: if she felt uncomfortable navigating the market just a few miles from her dorm, how would she be able to communicate effectively several thousand miles away?

But for most of us, the more positive experiences we have with those who are different from us, the less intimidated we feel about communicating with someone from another culture. And the less intimidated we feel, the more competent our communication becomes. In fact, a 2009 study found that American students who took the risk and studied abroad perceived themselves as being more proficient, approachable, and open to intercultural communication than those who lacked overseas experience (Clarke, Flaherty, Wright, & McMillen, 2009). Even

○ Positive experiences with those who differ from us—like these girls learning a new musical instrument—reduce feelings of intimidation over communicating with someone from another culture.

online interactions across cultures tend to ease anxiety and foster understanding. Users of the online virtual may be physically isolated, but they engage in virtual travels and interactions with other users around the world. These encounters encourage the use of multiple languages, cross-cultural encounters and friendships, greater awareness of cultural perspectives, and openness toward new viewpoints (Diehl & Prins, 2008).

> **Culture and You**
>
> Most people experience some degree of anxiety in new communication situations. What types of intercultural communication encounters make you anxious? Speaking with members of the opposite sex? Communicating in other than your native language? Why?

While anxiety may be a natural part of any new experience or interaction, it would be unfortunate to allow it to prevent you from experiencing the clear benefits and enrichment gained from intercultural experiences.

Ethnocentrism

In the fashion world, the gowns worn by prominent trendsetters are always big news. So, when Michelle Obama wore a stunning Naeem Kahn sheath to a state dinner in 2009, newspapers and bloggers were bound to comment. But the buzz the following morning was not over what she wore but on how to explain the color of the gown. The gown, described by its designer as "a sterling-silver sequin, abstract floral, nude strapless gown," was a color somewhere between peach and sand. The Associated Press initially described it as "flesh-colored," but changed it to "champagne" when one editor questioned, "Whose flesh? Not hers" (Phanor-Faury, 2010).

Using "flesh-colored" is a simple and common example of **ethnocentrism**, the belief in the superiority of your own culture or group and the tendency to view other cultures through the lens of your own. Ethnocentrism can make communication biased: we tend to communicate from the perspective of our own group without acknowledging other perspectives. The offense is unintended, which further reveals that we sometimes behave in ways that "normalize" one group and marginalize another—without even realizing it. Describing a peach-colored dress as "flesh" colored, for example, insinuates that light-colored skin is the default standard and that darker skin tones are therefore something "other" or different from the norm. It's also unclear. "While beige may be 'nude' for most white women," noted one commentator, "'nude' for me would be brown" (Phanor-Faury, 2010).

Ethnocentrism is not the same thing as ethnic or cultural pride. It's a wonderful and uniquely human experience to express feelings of patriotism or to experience deep respect for your religion or ethnic heritage. Ethnocentrism arises when you express a bias on behalf of your own co-cultures—when your outlook leads you to treat others as inferior or inconsequential or to ignore them altogether. Carlos, for example, is a proud Catholic for whom the Christmas holidays have great religious meaning. He decorates his home with a nativity scene and sends Christmas cards to family and fellow Christians as December 25 draws near. But he also sends a separate set of "season's greetings" cards to his friends who do not celebrate Christmas. He thus shows respect for their traditions while still sharing his wishes for peace and goodwill with them.

Discrimination

Ethnocentrism can lead to **discrimination**—behavior toward a person or group based solely on their membership in a particular group, class, or category. Discrimination arises when attitudes about the supposed superiority of one culture lead to rules and behaviors that favor that group and harm another.

Recall from Chapter 2 that *stereotypes* about and *prejudice* toward a particular cultural group may result in discrimination, preventing individuals from understanding and adapting to others (Cargile &

Giles, 1996). Yet seemingly positive stereotypes can have similarly discriminatory effects. For example, consider the "model minority" stereotype of Asian Americans that characterizes them as quiet, hard-working, studious, and productive. As Suzuki (2002) points out, these beliefs have led some employers to dismiss Asian Americans' complaints about discrimination in the workplace and have made government agencies and nonprofit organizations less inclined to support programs that assist lower-income Asian Americans because Asian communities seemed largely self-sufficient.

Discrimination can be explained in part by research on intergroup communication. Studies show that we have a biased tendency to treat fellow ingroup members better than we treat members of outgroups (Giles, Reid, & Harwood, 2010). In fact, we even *interpret* ingroup behaviors more favorably than outgroup behaviors. For example, if you discovered that someone in your sorority was caught cheating on an exam, you would likely explain the behavior as an unusual situation brought on by challenging circumstances. On the other hand, if you heard about someone from another sorority (an outgroup) cheating, you would be more likely to attach a personal explanation, such as that the cheater is dishonest.

On a related note, **behavioral affirmation** is seeing or hearing what you want to see or hear in the communication of assorted group members. In other words, if you think teenagers are lazy, then regardless of how hard your fourteen-year-old cousin studies, you don't see the effort. Instead, you notice his eye rolling or slumped shoulders, so you still perceive him as unmotivated. **Behavioral confirmation** is when we act in a way that makes our expectations about a group come true (Snyder & Klein, 2005). Again, if you think your teenage cousin (like all teens) is lazy, you'll more likely give him tasks that do not require much effort. When he, in turn, fails to put in a great deal of effort, you confirm to yourself, "See? I knew he wouldn't try very hard."

LearningCurve
bedfordstmartins.com/commandyou

Improving Intercultural Communication

As with many worthwhile things in life, you can improve your intercultural communication with effort. Training programs can help you become more mindful and considerate in your interactions across cultures and lead to positive changes in your thinking, feelings, and behavior (Landis, Bennett, & Bennett, 2004). Intercultural training generally focuses on three areas:

- **Changing thinking (or cognition).** Our thinking changes when we increase our knowledge about cultures and co-cultures and develop more complex (rather than simplistic) ways of thinking about a culture. These moves reduce negative stereotypes and help individuals appreciate other points of view.

- **Changing feelings (or affect).** When we experience greater enjoyment and less anxiety in our intercultural interactions, we feel more comfortable and positive about intercultural exchanges.

- **Changing behavior.** When our thoughts and feelings are altered, our behavior changes too. We develop better interpersonal relationships in work groups and perform our jobs better when we know what to say and not say—what to do and not do. We thus act with greater ease and effectiveness in accomplishing goals.

You don't need to attend a special program or hire a professional intercultural trainer to improve your intercultural communication. You simply need to consider some important points as you communicate with people from other generations, faiths, ethnicities, and so on: be mindful, desire to learn, overcome intergroup biases, accommodate appropriately, and practice your skills.

Be Mindful

As you learned in Chapter 2, being *mindful* means being aware of your behavior and others' behavior. To be mindful, you must know that many of your

> You don't need to attend a special program or hire a professional intercultural trainer to improve your intercultural communication. You simply need to . . . be mindful, desire to learn, overcome intergroup biases, accommodate appropriately, and practice your skills.

communication attitudes and behaviors are so rooted in your own culture that they are unconscious. When someone stands a bit too close to you, you might just sense "something funny." Or you might interpret someone's very direct eye contact as a sign of hostility rather than merely a cultural difference. Of course, not all uncomfortable interactions stem from cultural differences, but being mindful of the possibility gives you a wider range of effective ways to respond.

You should also ask yourself whether you might be interpreting another person's behaviors negatively or positively based on whether the individual shares your group memberships. Part of this mindfulness is practicing **intercultural sensitivity**, or mindfulness of behaviors that may offend others (Bennett & Bennett, 2004). When Caroline, a Jew, married Luke, a Catholic, his mother insisted that the family pictures be taken in front of the church altar or in front of religious statues in the garden outside. This was insensitive to the Jewish side of Caroline's family. Had Luke's mother reflected on how she would have felt if her own religious beliefs had been disregarded in this manner, she might have behaved very differently. Being sensitive doesn't mean giving up your own beliefs and practices, but it does mean not blindly forcing them on others.

Desire to Learn

Learning culture-specific information can be a useful starting point in intercultural communication; knowledge of general interaction patterns common for a particular group can increase your awareness of other ways of communicating. It can also prepare you to adapt—or to decide not to adapt—as you consider the many factors influencing an intercultural interaction.

Technology and You

In what ways might technology and mediated communication help you learn about another culture? Have you used such means to learn about another culture in the past? What did you find most and least helpful about this approach?

But *how* do you go about learning about another culture or co-culture and its members' communication preferences? Is it OK to ask group members questions or to seek clarification? Do you have to visit a foreign country to learn about that nation's culture? Do you need a close friend within a given co-culture to help you understand aspects of that co-culture's communication? We encourage you to ask respectful and earnest questions and to experience other cultures in whatever way you are able—whether that means trying foods from outside your own culture, studying the scriptures of another faith, or deciding to study abroad.

Overcome Intergroup Biases

Learning about other cultures is a great start to improving intercultural communication. But many scholars also recommend spending time with members of other cultures and co-cultures, both virtually and face to face.

Intergroup contact theory is one prominent idea for addressing intercultural challenges (Allport, 1954). According to this theory, interaction between members of different social groups generates a possibility for more positive attitudes to emerge (Pettigrew &

Many mainstream films in the United States are based on foreign-language films from other cultures, such as *The Departed* (2006, based on *Infernal Affairs,* 2002, from Hong Kong), *The Tourist* (2010, based on the French film *Anthony Zimmer,* 2005), and *Let Me In* (2010, based on Sweden's *Let the Right One In,* 2008). Watch one such film, as well as the original foreign-language movie that inspired it. What cultural changes to the story can you detect? How do the nonverbal behaviors of the actors differ?

Tropp, 2006). In other words, if you have contact with people who are different from you, you realize that the expectations you had about them might be incorrect, and this helps you better understand others. By getting to know others across the ocean or across the street, you will have *reduced uncertainty* about what is likely to happen in encounters with them. You will become more confident, more knowledgeable about how to behave, more decisive, more able to predict behavior, and thus more likely to understand one another (Gudykunst, 2004).

Although contact theory has some support, researchers also find that mindlessly getting people from different groups together can actually backfire and reinforce cultural stereotypes (Paolini, Harwood, & Rubin, 2010). This happened in many U.S. cities during the 1970s and 1980s, when there was a highly controversial effort to racially integrate schools by busing children to schools in other neighborhoods, which were sometimes on faraway sides of their cities. Even staunch proponents of the plan admitted that racial tensions became worse, not better (Frum, 2000).

So, how do we make successful intergroup interactions more likely? First, intergroup researchers argue that we must have *good quality contact* with outgroup members because negative contact can increase the perception of differences (Paolini, Harwood, & Rubin, 2010). But good contact is not enough because it is easy to explain away such positive

interactions as unique to the individual or the situation. For example, if you believe that fraternity brothers are simply party boys and you wind up in a study group with a particularly hardworking member of Phi Sigma Phi, you can mentally create excuses: "Ben is the exception to the rule." Researchers argue that we must have good contact *with people we think are "typical" of their group* (Giles, Reid, & Harwood, 2010). If you attended a few fraternity events and got to see Ben and several of his brothers more regularly in their fraternity setting, you might learn that many of them are serious students and that a few of them aren't even into the party scene. We all need to be aware of our *own* behaviors and biased perceptions when interacting with members of other cultures and groups so that we do not simply confirm our existing expectations.

Accommodate Appropriately

Another way to improve intercultural communication is to adapt your language and nonverbal behaviors, a process called **accommodation.** On a simple level, you do this when you squat down to get good eye contact and use basic vocabulary when talking to a child; police officers also do this when they adopt the street slang or foreign phrases commonly used in the neighborhoods they patrol. When speakers shift their language or nonverbal behaviors *toward* each other's way of communicating, they are engaging in **convergence.** We typically converge to gain approval from others and to show solidarity (Gallois, Franklyn-Stokes, Giles, & Coupland, 1988). Convergence usually results in positive reactions; if I behave like you, it is a way of saying "I am similar to you."

Accommodation is not an absolute, all-or-nothing goal: usually, it involves making small efforts to show that you respect others' cultural and communication behaviors and that you appreciate their efforts to communicate with you. Ramon makes efforts to speak English when he greets his customers at the restaurant where he works, even though it is not his native language and he struggles with it at times. Conversely, many of his regular customers who do not speak Spanish will greet him with the

⬥ When visiting Japan, President Obama accommodates to Japanese traditions and bows to Emperor Akihito in a show of respect.

Spanish words they do know ("Hola, Ramon! Buenos días!") or when thanking him for their meal ("Gracias!").

However, it is important to be careful not to **overaccommodate**, which means to go too far changing your language or to change it based on an incorrect or a stereotypical notion of another group

(Harwood & Giles, 2005). For example, senior citizens often find it patronizing and insulting when younger people speak "down" to them (slow down, increase volume, and use childish words) (Harwood, 2000). If his customers were to speak slowly and loudly or in mangled attempts to communicate in Spanish, Ramon might think they were making fun of him.

Practice Your Skills

Communicators need to use verbal and nonverbal behaviors effectively and appropriately to attain goals and get along in intercultural situations. Sometimes this means literally using the language of another culture well enough to communicate effectively. Sometimes it simply means communicating your interest and appreciation for another person's life experiences and point of view (Chen & Starosta, 1996). Communicators with fewer social skills have more difficulty managing the "different" interactions that intercultural situations demand, so it is important to develop the following skills (Arasaratnam, 2007).

- **Listen effectively.** You can't be mindful unless you listen to what people say (and what they

📍 Whereas squatting to speak at eye level with a child is an appropriate accommodation, a senior adult may perceive this behavior as patronizing. Sitting may be more respectful.

don't say). For example, health practitioners first need to listen to what cultural groups say about themselves and their beliefs about what will make them healthy. Then health practitioners need to shape health messages for these specific audiences (Larkey & Hecht, 2010). Knowing when to talk and when to be quiet (so you can listen) is crucial to intercultural encounters.

- **Think before you speak or act.** When someone communicates in a way that seems strange to you—not meeting your gaze, for example, or speaking very directly—take a moment to think about whether his or her behavior is a cultural difference rather than evasion or hostility.

- **Be empathic.** *Empathy* is the ability to picture yourself in someone else's place in an attempt to understand that person's experience. When you develop empathy, you can change your perceptions and improve your understanding of the ways in which another person's culture affects his or her communication.

- **Do the right thing.** Stand up for someone who is being mocked for his or her race, religion, or sexual orientation. Fight for those who don't have a voice. You don't need to be wealthy, established, or powerful to do this. When a friend makes a remark that you see as culturally insensitive, respond with a simple reminder ("That's a rude statement" or "Oh, man, don't talk like that"). You'll send a powerful message without chiding or berating your friend.

 LearningCurve
bedfordstmartins.com/commandyou

Back to } *Glee*

At the beginning of the chapter, we talked about the hit musical comedy *Glee*, which depicts the complexity within and between co-cultures with a satirical take on high school life. Let's revisit *Glee*, and see how the show relates to and reflects some of the concepts described in this chapter.

- *Glee* reflects culture in the United States in terms of the diversity of the cast as well as in the overarching themes. The members of the McKinley glee club are underdogs not only at their school but also among the other show choirs with whom they compete. As part of an individualist, low power distance, and masculine culture, Americans tend to believe that with a level playing field and a lot of hard work anyone can be successful. *Glee* taps into this sentiment, following a long tradition of underdog stories.

- *Glee* also explores the ways in which cultural differences can threaten, but not necessarily damage, relationships. Kurt and Mercedes may be best friends, but their different views about faith pose challenges that threaten their friendship:

Mercedes is a devout Christian, while Kurt, a young gay man, has an extremely negative reaction to religion. Through exploration and discussion, the two learn to respect each other's views, even though they do not agree.

- **Think about social identity.** The first impression most people get of Puck is that he is a jock, but he also identifies closely with his Jewish heritage. Artie, who uses a wheelchair, is often seen as "different," but when popular cheerleader Brittany finds him attractive, others come to view him as a "normal" teen. In addition, members of the football team (ingroup) and cheerleading squad (ingroup) who also participate in glee club (outgroup) try to balance expectations of themselves.

Your Reference }

Define and explain culture and its impact on your communication:

- **Culture** is a learned system of thought and behavior that reflects a group's shared beliefs, values, and practices (p. 52).
- We learn culture through communication with others and, in turn, express our culture through communication (p. 52).
- Your **worldview** is the framework through which you interpret the world and the people in it (pp. 52–53).
- **Intercultural communication** is the communication between people from different cultures who have different worldviews (p. 53).

Delineate seven ways that cultural variables affect communication:

- Individuals in **high-context cultures** use contextual cues to interpret meaning and send subtle messages; in **low-context cultures**, language is much more direct (p. 56).
- In **collectivist cultures**, people perceive themselves primarily as members of a group and communicate from that perspective; in **individualist cultures**, people value individuality, communicate with autonomy, and prefer privacy (pp. 56–57).
- Our comfort/discomfort with the unknown (**uncertainty avoidance**) varies with culture (p. 57).
- **Masculine cultures** tend to place value on assertiveness, achievement, ambition, and competitiveness; **feminine cultures** tend to value nurturance, relationships, and quality of life (p. 58).
- **Power distance** is the degree to which cultures accept the division of power among individuals (p. 58).
- **Time orientation** is the way that cultures communicate about and with time. In **monochronic cultures**, time is a valuable resource that is not to be wasted. **Polychronic cultures** have a more fluid approach to time (pp. 59–60).
- Cultures differ in their expression of emotion. Collectivist cultures often use **hyperbole**; individualist ones use more **understatement** (p. 60).

Describe the communicative power of group affiliations:

- **Co-cultures** are groups whose members share some of the general culture's system of thought and behavior but have distinct characteristics (p. 61).

- A **generation** is a group of people born into a specific time frame (pp. 61–62).
- **Gender** refers to the behavioral and cultural traits associated with biological sex (p. 62).
- **Social identity theory** notes that you have a *personal identity* as well as a *social identity*. Our social identity shifts depending on which group membership is most **salient** at a given moment (pp. 64–65).
- **Intergroup communication** finds that we communicate differently with people in **ingroups** versus **outgroups** (p. 64).

Explain key barriers to competent intercultural communication:

- Anxiety may cause us to worry about embarrassing ourselves in an intercultural interaction (pp. 66–67).
- **Ethnocentrism** is the belief in the superiority of your own culture or group (p. 67).
- **Discrimination** is behavior toward a person or group based on their membership in a group, class, or category. We often discriminate based on *stereotypes* and *prejudiced* views of other groups (pp. 67–68).
- **Behavioral affirmation** is seeing or hearing what you want to see or hear in the communication of assorted group members (p. 68).
- **Behavioral confirmation** is when we act in a way that makes our expectations about a group come true (p. 68).

Demonstrate skills and behaviors that contribute to intercultural competence:

- You can improve intercultural communication by being mindful of cultural differences and developing **intercultural sensitivity**, an awareness of behaviors that might offend others (pp. 68–69).
- **Intergroup contact theory** holds that interaction between members of different social groups generates more positive attitudes (pp. 69–70).
- Research supports the importance of **accommodation**, adapting and adjusting your language and nonverbal behaviors. This can lead to **convergence**, or adapting communication to be more like another individual's. If you **overaccommodate**, however, the interaction can be perceived of negatively (pp. 70–71).

✓ Look for **LearningCurve** throughout the chapter to help you review.
bedfordstmartins.com/commandyou

4 } Verbal Communication

Anne Kerry was walking to the bank in her San Francisco neighborhood when she suddenly ran into Scott, an old college friend, accompanied by another young man. "Anne," he said warmly, "I want you to meet my partner, Bryan." Anne was surprised—she hadn't realized that Scott was gay. She asked, "How long have you two been together?" Both men looked at her quizzically before they realized what she was thinking. "No," said Scott, "I became a police officer. Bryan and I work patrol together." "I was embarrassed," said Anne. "I didn't mean to misunderstand their relationship. I just figured that 'partner' meant love interest" (A. Kerry, personal communication, March 7, 2008).

Like many words in the English language, *partner* has a variety of definitions: it can mean anything from "an associate" to "a dancing companion" to "a group of two or more symbiotically associated organisms." But like Anne, many of us immediately jump to another definition: "half of a couple who live together or who are habitual companions." Indeed, *partner* is widely used by gays and lesbians seeking a label for their loved one. Some heterosexual couples have also embraced the term to reveal their committed state, particularly when they feel they've outgrown the term *boyfriend* or *girlfriend* or are unwilling to use the terms *husband* and *wife*.

The term *partner* can create ambiguity: Is the person you introduce with this term a business colleague, someone you play tennis with, or your "significant other"? That ambiguity makes it difficult for others to grasp your intended meaning. Perhaps that's why some Massachusetts gays and lesbians who wed after the commonwealth ratified same-sex marriage avoid the term *partner*. Bob Buckley felt the power of such labels when his partner, Marty Scott, needed medical treatment. When hospital administrators asked his relationship to the patient, Buckley replied "husband" and was allowed to stay with Scott, since spouses have this privilege but partners do not (Jones, 2005).

Describe the power of language—the system of symbols we use to think about and communicate our experiences and feelings.

Identify the ways language works to help people communicate—the five functional communication competencies.

Label communication problems with language and discuss how to address them.

Describe how language reflects, builds on, and determines context.

The Nature of Language

In 1970, a "wild child" was discovered in California. Thirteen-year-old "Genie" had been chained in a small room with no toys and little food for nearly her entire life. Her abusive father gave her no hugs, no loving words, and no conversation. As a result, Genie never developed language. Medical doctors, linguists, and psychologists worked intensely with her for over seven years, hoping to give the girl a chance at life in a community with others. But despite their efforts, Genie never learned more than a few hundred words and was never able to form sentences of more than two or three words (Pines, 1997; "Secret," 1997). Genie's sad story highlights the complex nature of language: someone with her background will never fully grasp that language is symbolic, has multiple meanings, is informed by thought, and is shaped by grammar and context. We explore these points here.

As our opening vignette shows, the names used to describe our connections with others have power. This is true for all kinds of relationships. For example, calling your father "Dad" reveals less formality in your relationship than calling him "Father" would. In a stepfamily situation, calling your father's wife "Mom" indicates more closeness than using her first name would. Choosing words can get complicated. That's why we dedicate this chapter to studying verbal communication, the way we communicate with language. **Language** is the system of symbols (words) that we use to think about and communicate experiences and feelings. Language is also governed by grammatical rules and is influenced by contexts.

Of course, nonverbal behaviors—pauses, tone of voice, and body movements—accompany the words we speak. Thus they are an integral part of our communication. We look at nonverbal communication in Chapter 5. But first let's examine the nature of language, its functions, some problems with it, and contexts that influence our use of it.

Language Is Symbolic

What comes to mind when you see the word *cat*? A furry childhood best friend? Fits of sneezing from allergies? Either way, the word evokes a response because it is a *symbol*, a sign representing a person, an idea, or a thing. Words in each language evoke particular responses because speakers of that language agree that they do. Thus, we can use words to communicate ideas and thoughts about particular subjects. Moreover, using words as symbols is a uniquely human ability (Wade, 2010).

Words Have Multiple Meanings

As you saw in the opening vignette, a single word can have a lot of meanings. A dictionary can help you find the **denotative meaning** of a word—its basic, consistently accepted definition. But to be a competent communicator, you'll also need to consider a word's **connotative meaning**, people's emotional or attitudinal response to it. Consider the word *school*. The noun has several denotative meanings, including a building where education takes place and a large

⬥ The noun *school* has multiple denotative meanings: it is the place where students learn and it is a group of fish.

group of fish. But the word can also carry strong connotative meanings based on your attitudes toward and experiences with school: it might bring back happy memories of class birthday parties in second grade, or it might make you feel anxious about final exams.

When you use a word, you must make sure the denotative meaning is clear. For example, you wouldn't use the word *ostentatious* with a bunch of six-year-olds; they simply won't understand it. You also have to be aware of a word's possible connotative meanings (Hample, 1987). For instance, for some people, the term *wife* might imply a woman who does not work outside the home, who cooks all her husband's meals, and who does all the household chores.

Culture and You

Can you think of a word, phrase, or piece of slang that may have a different meaning within your culture than it does in other cultures? Has using it ever caused confusion in communication between you and someone else?

Thought Informs Language

Jamal Henderson is preparing to apply to colleges. He keeps his father, Michael, involved in the process because he values his opinion. They both agree that Jamal should attend a "good college." But Michael feels hurt when Jamal starts talking seriously about urban universities in another state. He thinks his son has ruled out his own alma mater, the local campus of the state university system. Jamal and Michael have different thoughts about what a "good college" is. Their language and thoughts are related in their own minds, and each thinks he is using the term appropriately.

Your **cognitive language** is the system of symbols you use to describe people, things, and situations in your mind. It influences your language (Giles & Wiemann, 1987) and is related to your thoughts, attitudes, and co-cultures and the society in which you live (Bradac & Giles, 2005). Michael may think a "good college" is close to home, is involved in the local community, and offers small class sizes. Meanwhile, Jamal may think a "good college" presents the opportunity to live in a new city and to study with people from other countries.

Our thinking affects the language we use. But our language also influences our thoughts. If you tell yourself that a coworker is an "idiot," the word may influence your future impressions of him. To illustrate, if he's quiet during a meeting, you might conclude that he knows nothing about the subject under discussion. As another example, a study of women who stayed in violent romantic relationships found that they often crafted dark narratives to explain why the abuse was their fault or how it somehow expressed caring ("He's in a great mood now—it must have been the alcohol. He really wants the best for me. I should try to please him more—not 'push his buttons'") (Boonzaier, 2008; Olson, 2004).

Language Is Ruled by Grammar

In Alice Walker's Pulitzer Prize–winning novel *The Color Purple* (1982), Celie, who is black, struggles with learning to read from a primer written for white children. She grows frustrated being corrected repeatedly. She says, "Look like to me only a fool would want you to talk in a way that feel peculiar to your mind" (p. 184). Is it necessary for Celie to master standard grammatical English in order to communicate well? That is, does good grammar equal good communication?

The answer to these questions is yes, *to some extent*. **Grammar**—the system of rules for creating words, phrases, and sentences in a particular language—is important. Using correct grammar helps you communicate clearly. For example, if you pronounce the word *tomato* "tommy-toe," other people probably won't understand that you are referring to the red fruit that tastes really good on a hamburger. That's because grammar has *phonological rules* governing how words should be pronounced.

Similarly, grammar has *syntactic rules* guiding the placement of words in a sentence. For instance, suppose you shuffle the words in "I ran to the store to buy some milk" to "Store I to milk to ran the buy some." The meaning becomes unclear. Understanding a language's grammar can also help us learn other languages. Native speakers of English, for example, must remember that the grammar of Romance languages (such as French and Spanish) requires a different syntax. For example, in English, adjectives typically precede a noun ("I have an intelligent dog"), whereas in Spanish,

adjectives usually follow the noun ("*Tengo un perro inteligente,*" literally translated as "I have a dog intelligent"). To communicate clearly in Spanish, an English speaker must adjust.

Nonetheless, excellent grammar will not automatically make you an outstanding communicator. Telling your professor in perfect English that her style of dress is a sorry flashback to the 1980s is still offensive and inappropriate. That's because competent communicators also consider the situational, relational, and cultural context whenever they use language.

Language Is Bound by Context

Imagine a scenario in which your cousin prattles on and on about her wild spring break in Miami—how much she drank, how many parties she went to, and so on. Now imagine that she's talking to your seventy-year-old grandmother . . . at your niece's fifth birthday party . . . in front of a group of conservative, devoutly religious family members. These contrasting scenarios suggest that language is bound by contexts such as our relationship with the people we're with, the situation we're in, and the cultural factors at play. Does Grandma really want to hear about your cousin's behavior? Is it really OK to talk about this at a little kid's party? What about respecting the beliefs and sensibilities of your family members? We examine relational, situational, and cultural context later in this chapter. But for now, keep in mind that communicating competently involves understanding context as well as grammar.

LearningCurve
bedfordstmartins.com/commandyou

The Functions of Language

One of the first phrases that eighteen-month-old Josie learned to use was "thank you." Had this toddler already mastered the rules of etiquette? Was she just picking up a habit from her parents? Or was she learning that certain phrases would help her get things she wants: a compliment, a smile, a cookie?

We all learn isolated words and grammar as we acquire language. Josie, for example, probably picked up the expression "thank you" from her parents, her older brother, or her babysitter. But to become a competent communicator, she must learn to use this and other symbols appropriately. If Josie uses "thank you" as the name for her stuffed bear, she's not using it appropriately, so she's not communicating effectively. **Communication acquisition** requires that we learn individual words in a language but also how to use that language *appropriately* and *effectively* in various contexts. And just as Josie gets a smile from her parents for saying "thank you," we must use language competently to achieve our goals.

Researchers have identified five competencies (Wood, 1982) focusing on how language behaviors function for people: controlling, informing, feeling, imagining, and ritualizing. We all develop these competencies when we're young, by interacting with family and peers and observing television and other media. These competencies remain important throughout our lives. For that reason, in the following section we look at them more closely.

Using Language as a Means of Control

Language is used as an instrument of *control*, to influence ourselves, others, and our environment. Josie's use of the phrase "thank you" impresses her mother, who reassures her that using the term makes her a "good girl." Such appropriate use of language can make children seem cute, smart, or polite, giving them the ability to present themselves in a positive light. Recall from Chapter 1 that *control* is actually a neutral term; it is a crucial social skill whether used in a positive or negative way. As an adult, Josie will be able to use language to control her environment by, for example, persuading others to vote against land development in her community, negotiating a pay

> { **For anyone who has been the victim of hurtful language and actions, speaking out . . . can actually restore a sense of control.** }

raise, and bargaining with a car dealer. However, she will also need to avoid negative control strategies, such as whining, ridiculing, insulting, threatening, or belittling, as these do not contribute to productive, successful communication.

For anyone who has been the victim of hurtful language and actions, speaking out—harnessing the power of language—can actually restore a sense of control. Tens of thousands of women have been brutally raped in the Congo, and their shame has kept them silent. Cultural taboos about gender and sexual behavior have also prevented them from sharing their stories. However, local and international aid groups have recently organized open forums to help victims talk about the atrocities, connect with others, and regain control of their lives.

📍 We've all been there: a tourist asks you for directions and you mutter, "Um, yeah, you go a little bit up this way, and turn around that way . . ."

Words about such experiences are certainly hard to speak, but once they are out, they can empower the speaker (Gettleman, 2008).

Using Language to Share Information

Have you ever asked a sick child to tell you "where it hurts" only to receive a vague and unhelpful answer? This is because young children are still developing the next functional competency, **informing**—using language to give and receive information. As an adult, if you've ever been asked for directions, you know that providing people with information that they can understand and being able to understand the information they convey to you are equally important skills.

There are four important aspects of informing: questioning, describing, reinforcing, and withholding.

- **Questioning** is something we learn at a young age and use throughout our lives. Young children hungry for information about their world quickly learn the power of the simple, one-word question "Why?"

- **Describing** helps us communicate our world to others. Parents and teachers may ask children to repeat directions to their school or their home or to detail the specifics of a story they've heard.

- **Reinforcing** information can help us become competent listeners. We might take notes or simply repeat the information (to ourselves or to the other person) to confirm our comprehension.

- **Withholding** information or opinions may be the right thing to do in some situations. For example, you may choose not to express your opposition to your manager's plan because you want to keep your job. Or you may elect not to reveal a piece of information that might embarrass a friend.

Using Language to Express Feelings

Poets, writers, and lyricists are celebrated for using language to capture and express emotions. But most expressions of feelings are less elaborately composed

> **Technology and You**
> What kinds of technical words and phrases have become part of your everyday language? Would you think it odd if you had to explain the meaning of the verb *Google* to someone in a conversation, for example?

than a Shakespearean sonnet or an angry protest song. In everyday conversation and correspondence, we use language to send messages to others expressing how we feel about ourselves, them, or the situation. Young children can say, "I'm sad," and cry or laugh to communicate feelings. As we mature, we learn how to express a more complex set of emotions: liking, love, respect, empathy, hostility, and pride. The functional competency of expressing **feeling** is primarily relational: we let people know how much we do, or don't, value them by the emotions we express.

We all use language to express our feelings, but to be competent at this, we must do so appropriately and effectively. Many people don't communicate well when it comes to their own emotions. For example, Elliot expresses his frustration with his staff by yelling at them; his staff responds by mocking Elliot at a local pub after work. Instead of yelling, Elliot could have said, "I'm *worried* that we're not going to make the deadline on this project"; someone on his staff could have said, "I'm feeling *tense* about making the deadline, too, but I'm also *confused* about why you yelled at me." Sometimes, appropriate and effective communication means avoiding expressing feelings that we consider inappropriate or risky in a given situation (Burleson, Holmstrom, & Gilstrap, 2005). For example, when Abby's boyfriend suggests sharing an apartment next semester, Abby changes the subject to avoid admitting that she's uncomfortable taking that step.

Using Language to Express Creativity

What do Edward Cullen, Wolverine, Madea, and Sheldon Cooper have in common? Each is the product of the imagination of a writer or storyteller. And regardless of whether they were conceptualized as part of a novel, comic book, or screenplay, each character and his or her story was expressed primarily through language.

Imagining is probably the most complex functional competency. It is the ability to think, play, and be creative in communication. Children imagine, for example, by pretending to be a superhero. Adults imagine too. The way a song is worded, the way a play is scripted, and the way special effects coordinate with the message delivered in a film—these all stem from imagination. On the job, imagining is manifested by the ability to use language to convey to your coworkers the vision for a project (such as an architect would use words to explain blueprints and models). In a debate, imagining enables you to think ahead of your opponent, to put words to each side of an argument, and to use language in logical and convincing ways.

Using Language as Ritual

When little Josie says "thank you" for her cookie, it's a sign that she has learned the fifth functional competency: ritualizing. **Ritualizing** involves learning the rules for managing conversations and relationships. We begin learning these rules as children: peekaboo games require us to learn turn taking in conversations. When we learn to say "hi" or "bye-bye" or "please," we internalize politeness rituals. Later, teasing, joke telling, and even gossiping may present early lessons on how to manage relationships.

In adulthood, ritualizing effectively means saying and doing the "right" thing at weddings, funerals, dinners, athletic events, and other social gatherings. Simple exchanges, like telling a bride and groom "congratulations" or offering condolences to a grieving friend, are some ways we ritualize language. However, our ritualizing is not always that formal, nor is it limited to big events.

LearningCurve
bedfordstmartins.com/commandyou

Problems with Language

"I think we're still in a muddle with our language, because once you get words and a spoken language it gets harder to communicate" (Ewalt, 2005, para.1). The famous primatologist Jane Goodall made this point when explaining why chimpanzees resolve disputes much faster than humans. They strike out at each other and then offer each other reassuring pats or embraces, and *voilà*, argument over. Not so with people: words can be hard to forget.

As you've probably experienced, words can lead to confusion, hurt feelings, misunderstandings, and anger when we blurt things out before considering their effects carefully (Miller & Roloff, 2007). We sometimes speak too vaguely and fail to consider the timing of our words. We sometimes use labels in ways others don't appreciate, reveal bias through our words, or use offensive, coarse language. And when we put such hastily chosen words in e-mails or post them on Twitter or Facebook, they become "permanent," and we may have great difficulty taking back what we have said (Riordan & Kreuz, 2010).

Abstraction and Meaning

Language operates at many levels of abstraction, meaning that it can range from being very vague to very specific. You might talk in such broad, vague terms that no one knows what you are staying ("Stuff is cool!"), or you can speak so specifically that people may think you are keeping notes for a court case against them: "I saw you at 10:32 P.M. on Friday, January 29, at the right-hand corner table of Harry's Bar with a six-foot-tall, brown-haired man wearing black jeans, boots, and a powder-blue T-shirt."

The famous linguist S. I. Hayakawa (1964) illustrated the specific versus the general levels of abstraction by constructing an **abstraction ladder** (see **Figure 4.1**). The top rungs of the ladder are high-level abstractions: these are the most general and vague. Lower-level abstractions are more specific and can help you understand more precisely what people mean. "Request something interesting from Netflix" is a high abstraction that allows a wide range of

Higher

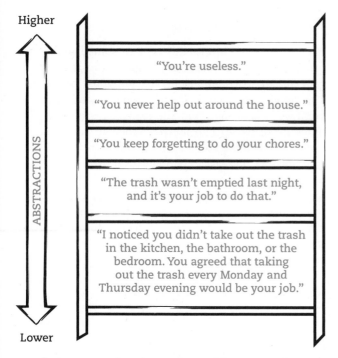

ABSTRACTIONS

"You're useless."

"You never help out around the house."

"You keep forgetting to do your chores."

"The trash wasn't emptied last night, and it's your job to do that."

"I noticed you didn't take out the trash in the kitchen, the bathroom, or the bedroom. You agreed that taking out the trash every Monday and Thursday evening would be your job."

Lower

◊ Figure 4.1 **The Abstraction Ladder**

choices (and the possibility of some really bad movies). Saying "I'd like to watch an action film tonight" (lower abstraction) is more likely to get you something you'll enjoy, but naming the exact movie ("Get *The Avengers*") ensures satisfaction.

But even though lower abstractions ensure clarity, high abstractions can accomplish certain communication goals. Here are a few examples:

- **Evasion.** Through **evasion**, we avoid providing specific details. A teenager might tell her parents that she is "going out with some friends." Her parents might counter by demanding less abstract answers: "Where exactly are you going to be? Which particular friends are you going with?"

- **Equivocation.** Through **equivocation**, we use words that have unclear or misleading definitions. Equivocation can help us get out of an uncomfortable situation, as when a friend asks what you think of her new sweater—which you think is hideous—and you reply, "It's ... *colorful*."

- **Euphemisms.** Sometimes we use **euphemisms**, inoffensive words or phrases that substitute for terms that might be perceived as upsetting. For example, you might say that your uncle "passed on" rather than "died" or that your mother had a "procedure" rather than an "operation."

Finally, abstract language can offer information about your affiliations and memberships. For example, **slang** is language that is informal, nonstandard, and usually particular to a specific group; it operates as a high-level abstraction because meanings of slang are known only by a particular group of people during a specific time in history. A rock concert might be described as "groovy," "totally awesome," or "off the hook"—each expression places the speaker in a particular time or place in the world. Teenagers might alert each other online that they've "GTG" (got to go) because of "POS" (parent over shoulder), and their parents are none the wiser.

> **Culture and You**
> What kinds of slang do you regularly use? How did you become familiar with these terms, and how would you go about explaining them to someone unfamiliar with them?

Related to slang is **jargon**, technical language that is specific to members of a given profession or interest group or people who share a hobby. Jargon may seem abstract and vague to those outside the group but conveys clear and precise meanings to those within the group. For example, when a fan of the model game Warhammer 40K speaks of "kit bashing," other fans understand that the speaker is taking parts from two different models and mixing them together. The rest of us, however, would probably just stare blankly.

Situation and Meaning

Imagine a three-year-old child sitting in a house of worship with his parents. He's having a great time

♀ Gamer jargon—words like "noob" and "pwned"—have developed to describe the people, scenarios, and experiences exclusive to the world of gaming.

THINGS TO TRY

Look at a piece of writing you've produced (an essay, your résumé, or an e-mail to a friend). Do you use high or low levels of abstraction? Is your choice of language appropriate for the communication contexts involved? (For example, is your essay written in a way that is mindful of your relationship with your professor and the context of the academic setting?)

banging his stuffed toys around until his mother grabs them away during a silent part of the service. Clearly upset, the child calls her a nasty name. Mom's face turns bright red, and she escorts her little one out to the car.

Semantics involves the relationship among symbols, objects, people, and concepts and refers to the *meaning* that words have for people, either because of their definitions or because of their placement in a sentence's structure (syntax). Our little friend in the example understood the relationship between the word he used and the concept of being unhappy; he was upset about losing his toys, so he uttered the same word he had probably heard a family member use when unhappy. He may have also observed strong responses from others to that word, so he thought it would help him get what he wanted. What he had not learned was **pragmatics**,

the ability to use his culture's symbol systems appropriately. He may have gotten a few laughs by using the curse word in front of his family at home, but he hadn't yet learned that it's inappropriate to use the word outside the home. When you acquire language, you learn semantics, but when you learn *how* to use the verbal symbols of a culture, you learn pragmatics.

The Limits of Labeling

Labels can be at the same time all-encompassing and limiting, depending on the cultural connotations associated with them. For example, the literal definition of *feminist* is "a person who advocates equal social, political, and all other rights for women and men." But who are these people who label themselves feminists? In our years of teaching undergraduates, we've heard plenty of students note that feminists are women who hate men and care only about professional success. But as the communication professor Andrea McClanahan (2006) points out, "There is no way to tell what a feminist 'looks' like. Feminists are young, old, women, men, feminine or masculine, and of varying ethnicities" (para. 5).

Feminists also hail from different religious backgrounds, causing some interesting discussions about the labels believers choose regarding their feminist viewpoints. When a group of Spanish Muslims approached city officials in Barcelona, Spain, about sponsoring a conference on Islamic

{ **When you acquire language, you learn semantics, but when you learn *how* to use the verbal symbols of culture, you learn pragmatics.** }

83

What About You?

How Vague Are You?
Circle the response you'd most likely give in each of the following situations:

1. A friend asks what you'd like to do tonight.
   A. "Oh, whatever you want."
   B. "I heard about a party on Garden Street."
   C. "I'd like to watch *The Dark Knight Rises* and make Indian food."

2. You have to evaluate an employee who has frequently been late.
   A. "We have guidelines around here, you know."
   B. "I need you to try harder to be on time."
   C. "I want you to be here at 8:55 each morning."

3. A member of a group you belong to suggests that everyone contribute $50 for a wedding present for another member.
   A. "Wow, that's pretty generous!"
   B. "What are we going to buy?"
   C. "I'm willing to contribute $25 for a gift certificate to his favorite restaurant."

4. You're asked to give a speech about your athletic success to a high school sports team.
   A. "I'm no good at that sort of thing."
   B. "What goal do you have in mind?"
   C. "I can't commit to speaking this fall."

5. Your father asks if you'll be coming home for the holidays this year.
   A. "I have a life, you know."
   B. "I'll do the best I can."
   C. "I can visit for three days, December 27–29."

If you responded A to most items: Vague language (high abstraction) is your specialty. In addition, you put the responsibility for communicating on others rather than taking it on yourself.

If you responded B to most items: You avoid being too vague or specific but use a question to avoid a specific answer.

If you responded C to most items: You are good at specific, low-abstraction language, and you take responsibility for your actions in your language.

⬥ What does a feminist look like? Stereotypes may cause you to believe that the professional woman on the left is a feminist. But the woman on the right, Mukhtar Mai, is a feminist too. A devout Muslim, she also supports and champions Pakistani rape victims.

feminism, one official responded with shock, noting that "Islamic feminism" must surely be a contradiction or an oxymoron (Nomani, 2005). Similarly, the evangelical organization Christians for Biblical Equality, which is committed to the equality of men and women in the home, the workplace, and the church, surveyed members about whether they label themselves feminists. Fred Gingrich noted his dilemma: "I consider myself a Christian feminist, though I am cautious about the contexts in which I share that. Not because I am ashamed of the label, but because I don't want it to be a stumbling block to dialogue" (quoted in Greulich, 2005, para. 2). Others have eschewed the feminist label entirely because of its connection to liberal politics. Recently, prominent conservative female politicians have donned the label

"mama grizzly" to express the fierceness of pro-life, limited-government-espousing women (Torregrosa, 2010).

These examples reveal that the labels we choose for our beliefs affect how we communicate them to others (and how others respond). When we place gender, ethnic, class, occupation, and role labels on others, we sometimes ignore individual differences (Sarich & Miele, 2004). So if you think all feminists are liberal, secular, career-oriented women, you may miss out on the opportunity to understand the feminist views of your aunt who is a stay-at-home mom or your male neighbor who is a Conservative Jew.

Sometimes our use of labels goes beyond ignoring individual differences and moves into the realm of bias. Derogatory labels, such as racial and ethnic slurs, demean and disenfranchise entire groups of people. To empower themselves, however, members of a particular group or co-culture may adopt these labels *within* the group. Consider, for example, the evolution of the word *queer*. Its literal definition means "strange, odd, or suspicious," and it has a history of being used as a derogatory term for gay, lesbian, and transgendered people. But recently, the word has been "taken back," for example, as when used to distinguish the discipline "queer studies." This reappropriation has helped legitimize LGBT (lesbian, gay, bisexual, and transgender) studies in academia.

The Dangers of Biased Language

Some labels are easily identifiable as derogatory. Others, however, are infused with more subtle meanings that influence our perceptions about the subject. This is known as **biased language**. For example, referring to an older person as "sweetie" or "dear" (even if kindly intended) can belittle him or her (Leland, 2008). In particular, older individuals struggling with dementia are sensitive to language that implies that they are childlike ("Did you eat your dinner like a good girl?") because they are struggling to maintain their dignity (Williams, Herman, Gajewski, & Wilson, 2009).

When language openly excludes certain groups or implies something negative about them, we often attempt to replace the biased language with more neutral terms, employing what is known as **politically correct language**. For example, the terms *firefighter*, *police officer*, and *chairperson* replaced the sexist terms *fireman*, *policeman*, and *chairman*, reflecting and perhaps influencing the fact that these once male-dominated positions are now open to women as well. In other cases, politically correct terms evolve around group preferences, with groups redefining the ways they want to be described or labeled: terms such as *physically challenged* or *differently abled* have largely replaced the term *handicapped*.

Ethics and You

Has anyone ever labeled you in a way that truly offended you? What terms did they use? How might you consider addressing biased language that may seep into conversations among your friends, family, or coworkers?

Critics of political correctness, however, argue that attempts at sensitivity and neutrality can undermine communication. They note that political correctness focuses attention on rhetorical arguments rather than real issues underlying language. They also maintain that it substitutes euphemisms for clarity when dealing with difficult subjects and that it makes communication more difficult by placing certain words and phrases off-limits. But others note that there is value in always trying to be sensitive—and accurate—when we make choices regarding language.

Profanity, Rudeness, and Civility

When CBS picked up the Twitter-based sitcom $#*! My Dad Says and adapted it for television, the network faced one crucial challenge: how to express on television the somewhat raunchy language that over a million Twitter fans had embraced and found funny. Recent years have seen an increase in swearing and other rude language in real life as well as in media. Indeed, perceptions about what terms are acceptable and appropriate for broadcast are continually changing. For example, media reviewer Edward Wyatt noted that the word *douche*, once considered inappropriate, had been used at least seventy-six times in 2009 on twenty-six prime-time network series like *The Vampire Diaries* and *Grey's Anatomy*. Wyatt claimed that several curse words seldom heard on television just ten years ago had, by 2009, become "passé from overuse" (2009, p. A1). In fact, some critics believe that public outrage over sex, violence, and profanity seems to have waned in recent decades (Steinberg, 2010).

Profanity includes words or expressions considered insulting, rude, vulgar, or disrespectful. The words get their social and emotional impact from the culture's language conventions. For example, swearing can be a powerful expression of emotion, especially anger and frustration, but the perception of swearing as offensive depends on the context and the relationship (Jay & Janschewitz, 2008). For instance, Jet Blue flight attendant Steven Slater gained national fame in August 2010 when he responded to a barrage of insults from a passenger with his own colorful language (as he quit his job by jumping down the plane's emergency chute). While we don't advocate responding to profanity with profanity, many people viewed Slater's response as "reasonably hostile." Tracy (2008) argues that language attacking people who are exhibiting bad behavior in local governance meetings is viewed the same way.

Whether our language is viewed as rude or "reasonably hostile" also depends on the culture and times. What language does have to do is meet some standards of **civility**, the social norm for appropriate behavior. Crude, offensive, vulgar, and profane language can create uncomfortable and unproductive relationships and work environments. Communication business specialists Rod Troester and Cathy Mester (2007) offer five guidelines for using more civil language in the workplace—but most of them are applicable outside the business context too:

- Use no words rather than offensive ones.
- Use words appropriate to your specific listener.
- Choose temperate and accurate words over inflammatory ones when commenting on ideas, issues, or persons.
- Use objective, respectful, nondiscriminatory language.
- Use clean language at all times when at work.

LearningCurve
bedfordstmartins.com/commandyou

Language in Context

You learned about the importance of context in Chapter 1 as part of our model of communication competence. Context is particularly important to our study of language in three ways: language reflects, builds on, and determines context.

- **Language reflects context.** The language we use reflects who we're around, where we are, and what sort of cultural factors are at play—that is, the context we're in. In fact, we each have sets of complex language behaviors or "files" of language possibilities called **speech repertoires**. We call on different speech repertoires to find the most effective and appropriate language to meet the demands of a given relationship, situation, or cultural environment.

- **Language builds on context.** At the beginning of this chapter, we wondered about the difference between calling your stepmother "Mom" versus calling her by her first name. It's an example of language building on context. If your stepmother raised you and is your primary maternal figure, you might well want to call her "Mom." But if your relationship with her is strained, you are close to your own biological or adopted mother, or your stepmother entered your life once you were an adult, you may well prefer to call her by her name. As you develop relationships, you learn how people prefer to be addressed (and how you are comfortable addressing them), and you adjust your language accordingly.

- **Language determines context.** We can also *create* context by the language we use. If your professor says, "Call me Veronica," one context is created (informal, first-name basis, more equal). If she says, "I'm Dr. Esquivel," you will likely have expectations for a more formal context (less personal, less equal). This context will then influence your choice of speech repertoires—you're more likely to tell "Veronica" about your weekend plans than you are to tell "Dr. Esquivel."

With these points in mind, let's consider how language works within our relationships, our situations, and our cultures, as well as in mediated settings.

The Relational Context

Kathryn Stockett's bestseller *The Help* (2009) and its 2011 film adaptation are fascinating representations of the relationships between black domestic servants and their white employers in Mississippi in the early 1960s. The dialogues (told in different voices) ring true because they reflect the relationships between and among women of different races, social classes, and experiences. We all choose different language to communicate in different relationships: you don't speak to your grandmother the way you speak to your best friend, and college professors don't speak to students the same way they speak to colleagues. That's because language both reflects and creates the relational context. Let's consider some examples.

Michelle and Chris have been dating for a few weeks. After a movie one night, they run into one of Chris's colleagues. When Chris introduces Michelle as his *girlfriend*, Michelle is surprised. She hadn't thought of their relationship as being that serious yet. The English language allows us to communicate the status of many of our relationships quite clearly: mother, brother, aunt, grandfather, daughter, and so on. But as with the word *partner*, the language we use when communicating about other types of relationships can be confusing. Chris and Michelle are in the somewhat undefined state of "dating." When Chris uses the term *girlfriend* as a label for Michelle, this implies a more defined level of intimacy that Michelle isn't yet sure she feels. Chris certainly had other options, but each has its own issues. For example, if Chris had said that Michelle is a *friend*, it might have implied a lack of romantic interest (and might have hurt Michelle's feelings). The fact is, the English language has very few terms to describe the different levels of intimacy we have with friends and romantic partners (Bradac, 1983; Stollen & White, 2004).

Labels can also confer status and create understandings between and among individuals. If you say, "I'd like you to meet my boss, Mr. Edward Sanchez," you are describing both Mr. Sanchez's status and the professional relationship that you have with him. The introduction of Mr. Sanchez as your boss notes that he has a degree of power over you, so it tells others what language is appropriate in front of him. (For example, you wouldn't tell stories about your boss that would be professionally embarrassing.) Similarly, you might introduce a coworker by saying "Grace and I work together" to avoid implications of superiority or inferiority.

The Situational Context

As with the relational context, different situations (being at a job interview, in a court of law, or at your uncle Fred's sixtieth birthday party) call for different speech repertoires. Sometimes situational context determines the language you speak (English, Spanish, Japanese). For instance, you might speak English in the classroom or on the job but use another language at home because it creates a special bond between family members (Bourhis, 1985; Gudykunst, 2004).

Language can also reflect how comfortable we are in a given situation. For example, we use **high language**—a more formal, polite, or "mainstream" language—in business contexts, in the classroom, and in formal social gatherings (as when trying to impress the parents of our new romantic interest). We use the more informal, easygoing **low language** (often involving slang) when we're in more comfortable environments—such as when watching a football game at a sports bar or enjoying movie night in a basement rec room.

Moreover, our sex and gender can interact with our situation to affect our language use. For example, women and men adapt their language use to same-sex versus mixed-sex situations. When women speak with other women, they tend to discuss relationships and use words that are more affection oriented (concerned with feelings, values, and attitudes). Men chatting with other men use more instrumentally oriented language (concerned with doing things and accomplishing tasks) (Reis, 1998). Socially constructed gender also comes into play in workplace situations. Occupations that have been traditionally defined as "masculine" or "feminine" often develop a job culture and language that follow suit. Male nursery-school teachers (in a job traditionally considered "feminine") and fathers doing primary child care may use feminine language at work; female police officers (in a job traditionally considered "masculine") may adopt more masculine language while on patrol (Winter & Pauwels, 2006).

But as we've learned, competent communicators use the most effective and appropriate ways of interacting in a given situation. That may mean putting aside gendered speech "appropriate" for our sex. For instance, a successful male manager uses language that reflects liking and respect when building relationships in the workplace, and a successful female manager uses direct language to clarify instructions for completing an important task (Bates, 1988).

📍 The formal, high language that this young woman employs while at work with her colleagues will differ from the more casual, low language that she probably uses when relaxing at home or socializing with friends.

The Cultural Context

Throughout this book, we remind you about the relationship between culture and communication (particularly in Chapter 3). In this section, we examine particular aspects of how cultural context shapes our language, including the relationship among culture, words, and thoughts; the relationship between gender and language; the impact of our region (where we grew up or where we live now); and the ways we accommodate others through our verbal communication choices.

Culture, Words, and Thought. As we have seen, our language use can affect our thoughts. Consider the study of the Pirahã tribe of Brazil (Gordon, 2004) that shows that the Pirahã language does not have words for numbers above two; anything above two is simply called "many." When researchers laid a random number of familiar objects (like sticks and nuts) in a row and asked the Pirahã to lay out the same number of objects in their own pile, tribe members were able to match the pile if there were three or fewer objects. But for numbers above three, they would only approximately match the pile, becoming less and less accurate as the number of objects increased. In addition, when researchers asked them to copy taps on the floor, the Pirahã did not copy the behavior beyond three taps. Researchers concluded that the limitation of words for numbers above two prevented the Pirahã from perceiving larger numbers (Biever, 2004).

The study's findings support the **Sapir-Whorf hypothesis**, which holds that the words a culture uses (or doesn't use) influence the thinking of people from that culture (Sapir & Whorf, 1956). In other words, if a culture lacks a word for something (as the Pirahã lack words for higher numbers), members of that culture will have few thoughts about that thing or concept. Two ideas, linguistic determinism and linguistic relativity, are related to the Sapir-Whorf hypothesis. **Linguistic determinism** posits that language influences how we see the world around us. **Linguistic relativity** holds that speakers of different languages have different views of the world.

For example, some languages (like Spanish, French, and German) assign a gender to objects. This is a foreign concept to many native speakers of English because English is gender neutral; English speakers simply say *the shoe* whereas a Spanish speaker marks the word as masculine (*el zapato, el* being the masculine article); a French speaker marks the word as feminine (*la chaussure, la* being the feminine article). Some researchers wondered if marking an object as masculine or feminine changes a speaker's mental picture of the object. To test this, they asked German and Spanish speakers to describe a key (*key* is a masculine word in German and a feminine word in Spanish). The German speakers described the object in traditionally masculine terms (*hard, heavy, jagged, metal, serrated,* and *useful*), whereas the Spanish speakers used traditionally feminine terms (*golden, intricate, little, lovely, shiny,* and *tiny*) (Cook, 2002; Moran, 2003; Wasserman & Weseley, 2009).

Gender and Language. Cultural and situational factors deeply affect our thinking and perception of gender roles. Gender roles, in turn, are often inscribed with "different languages" for the masculine and the feminine (Gudykunst & Ting-Toomey, 1988). The idea that men and women speak entirely different languages is popular fodder for comedy, talk shows, and pop psychologists, so let's identify what actual differences have contributed to that view.

In Deborah Tannen's classic 1992 analysis of men and women in conversation, she found that women primarily saw conversations as negotiations for closeness and connection with others, but men experienced talk more as a struggle for control, independence, and hierarchy.

Indeed, social expectations for masculinity and femininity might play out in men's and women's conversation styles, particularly when people are negotiating who has more control in a given relationship. We may use powerful, controlling language to define limits, authority, and relationships. We may use less controlling language to express affection. Let's look at a few examples.

- **Interruptions.** The situation and the status of the speakers can affect who interrupts whom (Pearson, Turner, & Todd-Mancillas, 1991). For example, female professors can be expected to interrupt male students more often than those male students interrupt the professors, owing to the difference in power and status. But when status and situation are neutral, men tend to interrupt women considerably more often than women interrupt men (Ivy & Backlund, 2004).

- **Intensifiers.** Women's speech patterns, compared with men's, contain more words that heighten or intensify topics: ("*hot pink,*" "*so excited,*" "*very happy*") (Yaguchi, Iyeiri, & Baba, 2010). Consider the intensity level of "I'm upset" versus "I'm *really* upset." Attaching *totally* to a number of verbs and adjectives is a popular way to express intensity ("She's *totally* kidding" or "He's *totally* awesome!").

- **Qualifiers, hedges, and disclaimers.** Language that sounds hesitant or uncertain is often perceived as being less powerful—and such hesitations are often associated with women's speech. *Qualifiers* include terms like *kind of, sort of, maybe, perhaps, could be,* and *possibly. Hedges* involve expressions such as "I think," "I feel," or "I guess." *Disclaimers* discount what you are about to say and can head off confrontation or avoid embarrassment: "It's probably nothing, but I think . . ." or "I'm likely imagining things, but I thought I saw . . ." (Palomares, 2009).

Culture and You

What are your personal thoughts on sex, gender, and language? Do you think men and women speak different languages, or do you feel that we all speak more similarly than differently? Do you have experiences that support this opinion?

■ **Tag questions.** Another sign of hesitancy or uncertainty associated with feminine speech is the *tag question*, as in "That was a beautiful sunset, wasn't it?" or "That waitress was obnoxious, wasn't she?" Tag questions attempt to get your conversational partner to agree with you, establishing a connection based on similar opinions. They can also come across as threats (Ivy & Backlund, 2004): for example, "You're not going to smoke another cigarette, *are you?*"

■ **Resistance messages.** Differences in the way men and women express resistance can have serious consequences. Specifically, date rape awareness programs advise women to use the word *no* when a male partner or friend makes an unwanted sexual advance. But a woman might instead say, "I don't have protection," choosing vague or evasive language over the direct *no* to avoid a scene or hurt feelings. Men, however, sometimes perceive an indirect denial as a *yes*. Women's use of clear messages, coupled with men's increased understanding of women's preference for more indirect resistance messages, can lead to more competent communication in this crucial area (Lim & Roloff, 1999; Motley & Reeder, 1995).

In summary, research has corroborated some differences in communication style due to sex (Kiesling, 1998), but many of those differences pale when we consider context, role, and task (Ewald, 2010; Mulac, Wiemann, Widenmann, & Gibson, 1988; Newman, Groom, Handelman, & Pennebaker, 2008). The lesson? While a person's sex may influence his or her communication style, gender—the cultural meaning of sex—has far more influence. Furthermore, some studies have found that conversational topic, age, setting or situation, and the sex composition of groups have just as much influence on language usage as gender (Palomares, 2008). As Mary Crawford (1995) noted, studying language from a sex-difference approach can be misleading because it treats women (and men) as a homogenous "global category," paying little attention to differences in ethnicity, religion, sexuality, and economic status.

In fact, in more recent work, Tannen (2009, 2010) focuses on how we present our "face" in interaction and how language choices are more about negotiating influence (power, hierarchy), solidarity (connection, intimacy), value formation, and identity rather than about sex (Tannen, Kendall, & Gorgon, 2007). Through decades of research, Tannen and others have shown that we are less bound by our sex than we are by the language choices we make. Thus, regardless of whether we are male or female, we can choose to use language that gives us more influence or creates more connection—or both.

Geography and Language. Our editor from New Jersey assures us that, even in such a small state, it makes a big difference if you are from North Jersey or South Jersey. (The status of people from the middle part of the state remains unclear, at least to us!) People in North Jersey eat subs (sandwiches that you buy at 7-Eleven or QuickChek) and Italian ice (a frozen dessert). The night before Halloween, when shaving cream and toilet paper abound, is Goosey Night or Cabbage Night. And "the city" is, of course, New York City. People from South Jersey eat hoagies (typically from a convenience store called Wawa) and water ice. The night before Halloween is Mischief Night. And going to "the city" means taking a trip to Philadelphia.

Culture and You

Think about where you grew up. Are there terms that you use that would cause confusion to others who grew up in different areas but still speak your native tongue? Have you ever been in a situation where you've used a regional term that caused an embarrassing miscommunication?

As this example illustrates, even for speakers of the same language who grow up just fifty miles apart, culture affects their language and their understanding of the world. Other examples are more extreme. Consider our friend Ada, who kindly shared an embarrassing moment with us (and who is allowing us to tell you). When she came to the United States from Hong Kong, she knew she had to give up some of her Britishisms to communicate more effectively with her American-born classmates at Wesleyan University. This was never more apparent than when she asked a classmate for a rubber (to correct some mistakes in her notebook). She wanted an eraser; he thought she was asking for a condom. Needless to say, she was a bit perplexed by his response: "Maybe after class?"

Accommodation. *Accommodation*—changing our communication behavior to adapt to the other person—can help us communicate with individuals from different cultures or co-cultures (Giles & Smith, 1979). **Code switching** and **style switching** are types of accommodation in which communicators change their regular language and slang, as well as their tonality, pitch, rhythm, and inflection, to fit into a particular group. These language accommodations may be ways to survive, to manage defensiveness, to manage identity, or to signal power or status (Bourhis, 1985). As mentioned, police officers use this type of accommodation when they adopt the street slang or foreign phrases used by citizens in the neighborhoods they patrol and when they use more formal, bureaucratic language when interacting with superiors, filling out reports, or testifying in court.

Mediated Contexts

Have you ever sent an e-mail or a text message that was misunderstood by the recipient? It has happened to all of us—often because our e-mails, text messages, tweets, and wall postings lack the nonverbal cues and hints that we provide in face-to-face conversation. So if you text your spouse to say that you both have to spend Friday night with your slightly quirky aunt Ethel, and he texts you back "Great," is he really excited? Is he being sarcastic? "Great" could mean either thing, but you can't see his nonverbal reaction to know if he's smiling or grimacing and rolling his eyes. That's why communication in mediated contexts must be extra clear to be effective (Walther, 2004).

Other characteristics of our online language can make a difference as well. For example, people in computer-mediated groups who use powerful language, such as direct statements of their personal goals, are seen as more credible, attractive, and persuasive than those who use tentative language (hedges, disclaimers, and tag questions) (Adkins & Brashers, 1995). However, in a recent study of an international adolescent online forum, students who were elected as "leaders" (Cassell, Huffaker, Tversky, & Ferriman, 2006) made references to group goals and synthesized other students' posts. This group-oriented language was seen as more persuasive and effective than language pushing personal goals.

Interestingly, sex and gender can influence the language you use with technology. In computer-mediated games, for example, people who were assigned avatars of their own gender were more likely to use gender-typical language (more emotional expressions, apologies, tentative language if assigned a feminine avatar) than those assigned mismatched avatars (Palomares & Lee, 2010). Another study found that people infer a person's sex from language cues online (such as amount of self-disclosure or expression of emotion) and conform

> Our e-mails, text messages, tweets, and wall postings lack the nonverbal cues and hints that we provide in face-to-face conversation.

Technology and You

Have you ever participated in an online forum or discussion group for school, work, or fun? Did you notice that the group dynamics were different form those that might have occurred in person? Do you ever find yourself saying things differently in an online communication? For example, you might take more care with your articulation— or you might give in to your impulses more readily.

Examine the language you use in computer-mediated communication. How do you and your communication partners negotiate influence and create connectedness? Are any language choices related to sex or gender? How does the language you use in mediated contexts differ from the language you use in face-to-face contexts?

more to computer-mediated partners whom they believe are male (Lee, 2007).

But technology affects language use in broader ways as well, including the proliferation of English as the language of the Internet. Individuals in Salt Lake City, São Paulo, and Stockholm can all communicate digitally, often in English. Critics often claim that because English dominates the mass media industries, English speakers' values and thinking are being imposed on the non-English-speaking world. Nevertheless, many non-Western countries have benefited from this proliferation, with countless jobs being relocated to places like India and Hong Kong (Friedman, 2007). The fact is, every day brings increasing language diversity to the Internet, and Internet-based translators make it much easier to translate material into innumerable languages (Danet & Herring, 2007).

Despite the controversies surrounding English and the Internet and mass media, technology has, in some sense, created a language of its own. The language of text messaging and chat rooms frequently relies on acronyms (IMO for "in my opinion," LOL for "laughing out loud") that people use in other contexts now. Acronyms are useful in texting because they enable rapid keystroking. However, it's important to keep text language in its appropriate context. If your professor writes you an e-mail asking about your recent absences from class, it's probably not a good idea to respond with "NOYB, IMHO" ("none of your business, in my humble opinion"). That would show not only a lack of respect for your instructor but also a lack of understanding regarding context. E-mail etiquette calls for more complete sentences.

LearningCurve
bedfordstmartins.com/commandyou

Back to } Our Partners

Our discussion of the word *partner* and its various meanings showed that the labels we choose are powerful—and can complicate our communication.

- The word *partner* has several denotative meanings, as we discussed earlier. But it can also have powerful connotative meanings. Let's look at romantic couples who choose the term *partner*. When some people hear an individual refer to his or her "partner," they may assume the individual is gay or lesbian. And they may have positive, negative, or neutral reactions based on their cultural background. Others may wonder if the individual is trying to hide his or her marital or legal status. Still others may see *partner* as a term that marks equality in romantic relationships.

- Abstraction plays an important role in the use of the term *partner*. "This is my boyfriend" or "This is my business partner" is a low-level abstraction, offering others a clear definition of your status. But the term *partner* is a high-level abstraction, keeping your status and relationship considerably more vague.

- Considering the relational, situational, and cultural context is one way to make the term *partner* less abstract and vague. If you let your chemistry professor know that your "partner" needs some help with an experiment, the instructor understands that you mean your lab partner rather than your romantic partner or the person you play tennis with. Similarly, when introducing the love of your life to your elderly great-aunt, you might want to use a less ambiguous term. Your aunt may be of a generation that did not use the term *partner* for a love interest.

Your Reference } A Study Tool

Now that you have finished reading this chapter, you can:

Describe the power of language—the system of symbols we use to think about and communicate experiences and feelings:

- Words are symbols that have meanings agreed to by speakers of a language (p. 76).
- A **denotative meaning** ⓘ is the accepted definition of a word; its **connotative meaning** ⓘ is the emotional or attitudinal response to it (p. 76).
- **Cognitive language** is what you use to describe people, things, and situations in your mind (p. 77).
- Correct **grammar**, the rules of a language, helps ensure clarity (p. 78).
- Learning words and how to use them effectively is the process of **communication acquisition** (p. 79).

Identify the ways language works to help people communicate—the five functional communication competencies:

- As an instrument of control (p. 79).
- For **informing**, including four aspects: questioning, describing, reinforcing, and withholding (p. 80).
- For expressing **feelings** to let people know how we value them (p. 80).
- For **imagining**, communicating a creative idea (p. 81).
- For **ritualizing**, managing conversations and relationships (p. 81).

Label communication problems with language and discuss how to address them:

- The **abstraction ladder** ranks communication from specific, which ensures clarity, to general and vague (pp. 81–82).
- Some communication situations may call for abstractions: **evasion** ⓘ, avoiding specifics; **equivocation** ⓘ, using unclear terms; or **euphemism** ⓘ, using substitutions for possibly upsetting terms (p. 82).
- **Slang** is a group's informal language; **jargon** is a group's technical language (p. 82).
- **Semantics** refers to the meaning that words have; **pragmatics** refers to the ability to use them appropriately (p. 83).

- We ignore individual differences when we place gender, ethnic, or other role labels on people (pp. 83–86).
- **Biased language** has subtle meanings that influence perception (p. 86); using **politically correct language** is an attempt at neutrality (p. 86).
- **Profanity** includes words or expressions that are considered insulting, rude, vulgar, or disrespectful whereas **civility** involves language that meets socially appropriate norms (pp. 86–87).

Describe how language reflects, builds on, and determines context:

- We use different **speech repertoires** to find the most effective language for a given situation (p. 87).
- We use language to create or reflect the context of a relationship (p. 88).
- Some situations call for formal language, or **high language**; in more comfortable environments, **low language**, often including slang, is appropriate (p. 88).
- The **Sapir-Whorf hypothesis** suggests that our words influence our thinking (p. 89).
- **Linguistic determinism** is the idea that language influences how we see the world; **linguistic relativity** holds that speakers of different languages have different views of the world (pp. 89–90).
- Assuming gender differences in communication can be misleading, yet some differences in masculine and feminine language exist. The use of interruptions, intensifiers, qualifiers, hedges, disclaimers, and tag questions are linked with feminine versus masculine speech patterns (pp. 90–91).
- The culture of the geographical area affects language (pp. 91–92).
- **Code switching** and **style switching**, changing language use as well as tone and rhythm, are two types of *accommodation*, whereby we modify our language to adapt to another person's communication style (p. 92).
- Communication technology has made English the dominant world language and has created a global society. But the Internet also continues to create a language of its own (pp. 92–93).

 Look for LearningCurve throughout the chapter to help you review.
bedfordstmartins.com/commandyou

5 } Nonverbal Communication

Can you tell a compelling, believable, and heartwarming love story in just four minutes—without using any words? Pixar's Academy Award–nominated *Up* (2009) does just that (Docter & Peterson, 2009). After opening with a simple meet-cute between young, quiet Carl and adventurous, talkative Ellie, the sequence that follows offers a montage of life moments, explained simply and graphically: Carl and Ellie express affection by holding hands and devotion by the cross-my-heart gesture of their childhood. Their dreams of children are symbolized in visions of baby-shaped clouds, and as those dreams are crushed, their grief is conveyed by Ellie's silent sobs and Carl's quiet gestures of comfort. As the years go by, their plans to travel are shown with paintings and brochures; their financial struggles, through vignettes detailing home repairs, car troubles, and medical bills. Relying entirely on nonverbal behaviors and set to a mesmerizing musical score, the sequence clearly conveys the events and emotions that shaped these characters' decades-long romance, as well as Carl's loneliness and isolation after Ellie's death—without a word of dialogue.

The filmmakers at Pixar were no strangers to near "silent" films. One previous offering, the equally stunning *WALL-E* (2008), included virtually no dialogue for the first forty minutes, in what the British newspaper the *Independent* called "a masterclass in non-verbal communication" (Quinn, 2008, para. 7). During those scenes, the film created compelling characters out of a pair of robots and a lone, unspeaking cockroach. It also presented in a simple, accessible way a fairly complicated story line of environmental devastation.

After you have finished reading this chapter, you will be able to

Describe the power of nonverbal communication.

Outline the functions of nonverbal communication.

Describe the set of communication symbols that are nonverbal codes.

Illustrate the influences culture, technology, and situation have on our nonverbal behavior.

Telling a story on screen is complicated because filmmaking encompasses nonverbal performances (be they by actors or by animations). These performances include the visual choices made by the artists and directors, from colors used in a scene's background to the characters' clothing. For animators like the team at Pixar, the challenge is even more daunting. They must make objects—whether computer-generated "people" like Carl and Ellie or robots (or fish or toys or insects)—into believable, humanlike characters who can effectively communicate complex information and emotions.

Likewise, in real life, we communicate with many tools other than language. In this chapter, we examine **nonverbal communication**—the process of intentionally or unintentionally signaling meaning through behavior rather than words (Knapp & Hall, 2010). This definition encompasses a variety of actions, such as gestures, tone of voice, and eye behavior, as well as all aspects of physical appearance. We begin by examining the nature and functions of nonverbal communication. Then we move to the nonverbal codes that convey messages.

The Nature of Nonverbal Communication

A deaf woman signs a message to a companion. A colleague writes a note to you on a pad of paper during a boring meeting. A man taps his watch to signal to a friend that it's almost time for lunch. In all three instances, communication occurs without a word being spoken. But not all of these examples are actually nonverbal communication. Studying the essential nature of nonverbal communication reveals why.

Nonverbal Behavior Is Communicative

You communicate nonverbally when you convey a message without using any words. But you also communicate nonverbally when you use nonverbal behaviors in *addition* to words: when you smile, frown, or gesture as you speak or when you use a particular tone or volume while talking. For example, as a kid, maybe you knew when your parents were angry with you because they called you by your full name while using "that tone."

Consider the examples we just gave. American Sign Language (ASL), a visual language with its own grammatical structure used by hearing-impaired individuals in the United States and English-speaking Canada, is still verbal communication. It is *nonvocal* because the communicators don't use their voices. However, it is still a language because it uses gestures (rather than spoken words) as symbols and it has grammar rules. Likewise, the note that your colleague writes to you uses words, so it too is a form of verbal communication. Only the third example is nonverbal communication—tapping a watch signals meaning without use of linguistic symbols. Yet this example reminds us that nonverbal behavior and verbal communication are connected. Had the friends not made a verbal agreement to meet for lunch, the act of tapping the watch might be confusing.

⬧ Giving someone a big hug is an example of nonverbal communication, but communicating with someone using American Sign Language is not.

Nonverbal Communication Is Often Spontaneous and Unintentional

The best poker players think a great deal about nonverbal communication. They know how to bluff, or convince their opponents that they are holding a better (or worse) hand than is actually the case. A player who figures out an opponent's "tell"—a nonverbal signal indicating a good or bad hand—can profit from this knowledge if he, quite literally, plays his cards right. Mike Caro, a poker professional and author of *The Body Language of Poker*, warns players not to look at the cards as they are laid out on the table. Players who look away from "the flop" have a strong hand, he explains. Those who stare at it—or at their cards— have a weak one. He also advises players to memorize their hand so opponents won't see them looking at their cards and glean cues from this action (Zimbushka, 2008).

Like poker players, we often send nonverbal messages unintentionally—we roll our eyes, laugh, slouch, or blush without meaning to. And our nonverbal behaviors can send powerful, unintended messages. Great poker players know that they can't completely eliminate such behaviors. That's why many of them wear sunglasses while playing: they want to mask their eyes so their opponents can't pick up subtle and unintentional cues from their eye movements.

Nonverbal Communication Is Ambiguous

Professional players like Caro might have a system for reading nonverbal behaviors, but even they know that it's more of an art than a science. That's because nonverbal communication is often ambiguous. Blinking, stammering, or hesitations in speech can indicate deception. But they can also indicate anxiety or uncertainty. In many cases, you can pick up clues about the meaning of behavior from the situational context. If your friend is sighing deeply and blinking rapidly as she heads off to her biochemistry final exam, she's probably anxious. But you can't know for sure. Perhaps her boyfriend broke up with her twenty minutes ago and she just doesn't feel like talking about it. For this reason, it's best to regard nonverbal behavior (and poker "tells") as cues to be checked out rather than as facts.

Record a new episode of your favorite scripted television show. Try watching it with the sound turned all the way down (and closed captions turned off). Can you guess what's going on in terms of plot? How about in terms of what the characters are feeling? Now watch it again with the sound on. How accurate were your interpretations of the nonverbal behaviors shown? How successful do you think you would have been if it were an unfamiliar show, one with characters you didn't know as well?

Nonverbal Communication Is More Believable Than Verbal Communication

Imagine you're grabbing lunch with your brother, talking a mile a minute about your exciting plans for after graduation. He's staring off into space. You wonder if you're boring him. But when you look closer, you notice that his face is ashen, he isn't making eye contact with you, and he hasn't shaved in a few days. You pause and ask, "Hey, is everything OK with you? You seem . . . not yourself." Your brother looks up somewhat startled, tries to smile, and says, "What? Oh! Yes, everything's great."

You've just experienced **channel discrepancy**, a situation in which one set of behaviors says one thing and another set says something different. In this case, your brother's verbal communication says he is fine, but his nonverbal communication says he is not fine at all. So which message do you believe? In most cases, you'll believe the nonverbal message.

Ethics and You

How certain should you be when deciding to believe a nonverbal message that contradicts a verbal message? When faced with this decision, do you consult with others or confront the person making the mixed communication?

Like most of us, you assume your brother has less control over his nonverbal behaviors, so they are more reliable indicators of truth. Research supports your assumption.

Studies show that nonverbal behavior carries more importance than verbal behavior when we

- express spontaneous feelings (such as crying) (Burgoon & Hoobler, 2002),
- assess others' motives and self-presentation (as with deception),
- express rapport with others (such as showing liking), and
- figure out others' meanings when there are few other behaviors to observe (Grahe & Bernieri, 1999; Knapp & Hall, 2010).

However, just because we tend to place more stock in nonverbal communication doesn't mean we always interpret that communication accurately. Your brother might be fine, just as he says he is. Perhaps he is growing a "play-off beard" along with the rest of his hockey team and is thinking about the next day's game rather than listening to you talk about your

⬥ Though this poker player might be smiling now, his ability to mask emotion and maintain a "poker face" is what brought about the victory that makes him so visibly happy now.

plans. Even when we know someone very well, we sometimes fail to detect deception or read their non-verbal behaviors accurately (Knapp & Hall, 2010; Manusov & Patterson, 2006).

LearningCurve
bedfordstmartins.com/commandyou

Functions of Nonverbal Communication

It's impossible to discuss every purpose that non-verbal behaviors serve. Nevertheless, in this section we highlight the most important ways that nonverbal behaviors work on their own—and in combination with verbal behaviors—to affect communication.

Reinforcing Verbal Messages

Nonverbal behavior often serves to clarify meaning by reinforcing verbal messages. It does so in three ways: by repeating, by complementing, and by accenting. **Repeating** mirrors the verbal message, offering a clear nonverbal cue that repeats it. For example, you hold up three fingers while saying "three" or shake your head at a toddler while saying "no." You can also reinforce verbal messages with **complementing**, non-verbal behavior that matches (without actually mir-roring) the verbal message it accompanies. For exam-ple, when you pat a friend on the back while saying, "You did a great job," you reinforce the message that your friend has done well.

Nonverbal behaviors are also used for **accenting**, or clarifying and emphasizing specific information in a verbal message. For example, suppose you want your friend to meet you at a local pub at 6 P.M. You can make eye contact as you talk (indicating that you are monitoring your friend's attention level) and touch the friend lightly on the forearm as you mention the pub on State Street (to verify "Do you know the one I mean?").

Substituting Verbal Messages

Nonverbal cues can also be used for **substituting** or replacing words. For example, a traffic officer's raised palm substitutes for the word *stop*, and wagging a fin-ger at a toddler can indicate "no" without your saying anything. Substituting is common in situations where words are unavailable, as when you're communicat-ing with someone who speaks a different language from yours. It's also common when words are inap-propriate (such as situations that call for silence) or unintelligible (such as noisy situations like a party, where you might signal your partner that you're ready to leave). Substitution can also signal informa-tion you'd rather not say aloud. For example, you raise your eyebrows at a friend seated across the table from you when the other friend you're dining with mentions (for the tenth time) that his current intern-ship is paying him *really* well.

Contradicting Verbal Messages

When a person's verbal and nonverbal messages seem at odds, why are we more likely to trust the nonverbal cues? It's because nonverbal communication also functions as **contradicting** behavior to convey meaning that is the opposite of the verbal message. Sometimes this is unintentional, as when you clearly look upset but say that nothing's wrong, and you don't realize your nonverbal behavior is giving you away. Other times, contradicting behavior is inten-tional. For instance, Caroline sighs deeply to get Andy to ask, "What's wrong?" She can keep the attention coming by refusing to answer or by tersely stating, "Nothing." He responds, "No, really, I'm worried. Tell me what's up." Although such tactics can get another person's attention, they're somewhat deceptive because they take advantage of the person's concern in order to serve selfish purposes.

{ **When a person's verbal and nonverbal messages seem at odds, why are we more likely to trust the nonverbal cues?** }

Contradicting behavior is also part of what makes joking around, teasing, and the use of sarcasm (cutting remarks) so powerful. When you roll your eyes and say, "Wow, that was a captivating lecture," you let your classmate know that, despite your words, you found listening to your professor about as interesting as vacuuming. Contradicting behavior can work positively as well. For instance, your friend calls to your beloved dog, "Come here, you smelly, ugly little monster!" Your friend's smile, high pitch, and open arms reveal that your friend really thinks your dog is adorable.

Technology and You

Have you ever experienced (or been responsible for) a failed attempt at sarcasm or teasing via a text message or social-network posting? What caused the communication breakdown? How might it have been avoided?

Regulating Interactions

Nonverbal cues are also used in **regulating** or coordinating verbal interaction; they help us navigate the back-and-forth of communication. For example, if you pause after saying "Hello" when answering your phone, you are offering the person on the other end a chance to self-identify and explain the purpose of the call. Face to face, you may hold your hand up while speaking to signal that you don't want to be interrupted. Raising your hand in a face-to-face classroom setting lets your professor know that you have a question or information to share. Slouching or sitting back may indicate that you don't want to speak or are waiting for someone else to contribute before you get involved.

If conversational regulation doesn't go smoothly, there can be negative consequences. For example, if you successfully interrupt others when they are speaking, you may gain influence, but they may like you less. This is particularly true for women who interrupt, as social conventions hold that they should be polite and meek in conversation. On the other hand, if you allow interruptions, others may perceive you as less influential (Farley, 2008). Naturally, the situational context plays a role. It's a more serious infraction to interrupt (or to be interrupted) during a debate or a business meeting, whereas some interruption is acceptable during casual conversation with friends.

Creating Immediacy

Nonverbal communication can also create **immediacy**, a feeling of closeness, involvement, and warmth between people (Prager, 2000). Such behaviors include sitting or standing somewhat close to another person, turning and leaning toward the individual, smiling, making eye contact, and giving an appropriate touch. Even adding "smiley face" icons to your e-mail messages can be helpful: they have been found to increase perceptions of immediacy and liking (Yoo, 2007).

In addition to the classic immediacy behaviors just described, mimicry is sometimes used to enhance immediacy. **Mimicry** is the synchronized and usually unconscious pattern of imitating or matching gestures, body position, tone, and facial expressions to create social connections with others (Carey, 2008). To illustrate, if your younger brother is upset about his grade in algebra and tells you about it with downcast eyes, a frown, and a sober tone of voice, you would likely respond with similar nonverbal behavior to let him know that you care.

Imagine how challenging it must be to create these close connections with others if you lack the ability to reproduce a range of nonverbal behaviors. This is precisely what Kathleen Bogart is experiencing. She suffers from Moebius syndrome, a rare congenital condition that causes facial paralysis. She can recognize others' expressions, but she can't produce them herself (Carey, 2010). She thus cannot express joy, sorrow, or frustration—nor can she mimic these important emotions to support her relational partners. Kathleen relies on eye contact, hand gestures, posture, and vocal tone to create the connection and warmth of immediacy.

Immediacy behaviors help you form and manage impressions, particularly if you want to have more social influence. The implications for interpersonal relationships are clear: physical contact, eye contact, smiling, and other gestures tell your romantic partner, family members, and close friends that you love and care for them and that you want to be near them. Regarding the professional world, one study found that physicians who engage in immediacy behaviors usually have patients who are less fearful of them and more satisfied with their medical care (Richmond, Smith, Heisel, & McCroskey, 2001).

Deceiving Others

If we're honest, most of us will admit to occasionally engaging in **deception**—the attempt to convince others of something that is false (O'Hair & Cody, 1994). Sometimes we deceive others to protect them, as when you tell your friend that no one noticed her torn slacks. Other times, we deceive out of fear, as when victims of abuse blame their injuries on falls or accidents. However, deception can have malicious and self-serving motives. Our neighbor Barbara received a phone call from a friendly guy who claimed to be "with the government." Saying he wanted to make sure that everything was correct in her "file" so she could receive retirement benefits the next year, he asked for her Social Security number and other personal information. Realizing later that she'd been a victim of identity theft, Barbara confided, "I feel so stupid . . . I can't believe I fell for it. But he sounded so sincere" (B. Smith, personal communication, January 8, 2010).

Like many of us, Barbara was drawn in by the sound of a warm, friendly voice. Most of us look for the opposite type of behavior to sniff out a liar (Canary, Cody, & Manusov, 2008). People who appear or sound anxious, who avoid making eye contact, who blink frequently, or who have frequent and awkward body movements seem deceptive (Leal & Vrij, 2008). We also suspect people who have dilated pupils and who raise their vocal pitch. Because these nonverbal behaviors are less under conscious control, they seem more believable than words or other, more controllable nonverbal behaviors (Burgoon, Buller, & Woodall, 1989; Goss & O'Hair, 1988). Research supports the idea that nonverbal behaviors can help us detect lying and deception, but this is not always the case. As Canary, Cody, and Manusov (2008) note, "A liar may appear anxious only if he or she is concerned about the lie or about getting caught. If the lie is unimportant, a communicator may instead be relaxed and controlled. Further, someone who is accused of lying but is in fact telling the truth may show signs of anxiety" (pp. 82–83).

The ultimate deception? Stockbroker and investment adviser Bernie Madoff executed the largest Ponzi scheme in history, defrauding his clients of billions of dollars over a period of more than twenty years.

Ethics and You

When attempting to deceive others, are you aware of your nonverbal messages? Do you alter your tone of voice or change your eye contact? What types of nonverbal indications do you look for in others to figure out if they're being honest with you?

This doesn't mean we're destined to be tricked by those seeking to deceive us. We can still use verbal messages to evaluate someone's honesty. Barbara could have realized that someone from "the government" would probably have a more official title and would already know her Social Security number. We can also consider the relational and situational context of our interaction. For instance, if you suspect that your partner is lying to you and you have caught him or her lying in the past, you might have more reason to be suspicious.

LearningCurve
bedfordstmartins.com/commandyou

Nonverbal Communication Codes

In this section, we examine **nonverbal codes**, symbols we use to send messages without, or in addition to, words. Although we divide these codes into categories for simplicity and clarity, nonverbal behaviors seldom communicate meaning in isolation. Usually, clusters of nonverbal behaviors convey a message—for example, raising your eyebrows and gasping show surprise or shock, with or without any words. The codes we examine here are gestures and body movements, facial expressions, eye behavior, voice, physical appearance, space and environment, touch, and time.

Gestures and Body Movements

On the television show *Lie to Me*, the character Dr. Cal Lightman claims to be able to "read" nonverbal behaviors—"body language"—to detect when someone is lying. But the way you move your body is not a language at all: for example, shaking your leg while you're sitting has no specific, consistently understood definition. Such behavior is called **kinesics**—the aspects of gestures and body movements that send nonverbal messages. When Eva turns her body

to include Jane in a conversation, or Rodney walks into an interview standing tall to project confidence, for example, you are witnessing kinesic behaviors. And research shows that we're fairly good at deciphering others' emotions from their gestures and movements (Montepare, Koff, Zaitchik, & Alberet, 1999).

There are five main categories of body movements that convey meaning (Ekman & Friesen, 1969):

- **Emblems** have a direct verbal translation in a particular group or culture. They substitute for verbal messages. During his inauguration parade, Barack Obama greeted the marching band from his old high school with a shaka sign—a pinkie and thumb salute that is a common form of greeting in Hawaii. Though it has no direct translation, the shaka sign is widely regarded as a representation of the Hawaiian "aloha spirit." Depending on context, it can be interpreted as hello, good-bye, praise, or a call to "hang loose." Emblems don't always translate from one culture to another.

- **Illustrators** reinforce verbal messages and help visually explain what is being said. Holding your hands two feet apart while saying, "The fish was *this* big!" is an illustrator. Illustrators can also be used to increase influence in relationships, as when we emphasize our words with pointing or sketching a thought in the air (Dunbar & Burgoon, 2005).

- **Regulators** help us manage our interactions. Raising your hand and lifting your head, for example, indicate that you want to speak. Raising your eyebrows usually indicates you want information from others (Flecha-García, 2010).

- **Adaptors** satisfy some physical or psychological need, such as rubbing your eyes when you're tired or twisting your hair when you're nervous or bored. Adaptors are not conscious behaviors; they are used to reduce bodily tension, often in response to heightened emotional stimulation. They may be more frequent when someone is stressed, impatient, or bored and are often interpreted as indicators of negative feelings (Goss & O'Hair, 1988).

■ **Affect displays** are nonverbal behaviors that convey feelings, moods, and reactions. They are often unintentional, reflecting the sender's emotions: slumping in a chair may indicate fatigue or boredom; a fist thrust high in the air indicates joy when your team scores a touchdown. That's not to say they're *always* unintentional, though: you may purposely set your jaw and hit your fist on the table to indicate your anger or frustration.

Facial Expressions

We're wired to use our faces to indicate emotions. Although the reasons behind our facial expressions might be difficult to ascertain, several specific expressions are common across all cultures (Ekman & Friesen, 1971). A smile, for example, usually indicates happiness; a frown, sadness; raised eyebrows, surprise; and wrinkled eyebrows, concern (see **Figure 5.1**). Irenaus Eibl-Eibesfeldt (1973) observed that blind children, who cannot learn to mimic facial movements through sight, exhibited sadness, anger, disgust, fear, interest, surprise, and happiness in the same way that sighted people exhibit these feelings. Eibl-Eibesfeldt concluded that these seven primary facial expressions are inborn, whereas most other expressions are learned from our culture. (See also Gagnon, Gosselin, Hudon-ven der Buhs, Larocque, & Milliard, 2010). Recent evidence also suggests that pride may be a universally recognized emotion (Tracy & Robins, 2008).

Though we're fairly adept at deciphering these common expressions of emotion, we're not necessarily experts at decoding all facial expressions. That's because the human face can produce more than a thousand different expressions (and as many as

Sadness   Anger   Disgust

Fear   Interest   Surprise   Happiness

⬦ Figure 5.1 **Cross-Cultural Primary Facial Expressions.** Research shows that these seven expressions of emotion exist in all cultures and are inborn.

twenty thousand if you take into account all the combinations of different facial areas) (Ekman, Friesen, & Ellsworth, 1972; Harrigan & Taing, 1997). Moreover, our emotions can be concealed by facial management techniques, conscious manipulation of our faces to convey a particular expression. One common facial management technique is **masking**, replacing an expression that shows true feeling with an expression that shows appropriate feeling for a given interaction. Actors use masking all the time. But you also use it when you smile at customers at the restaurant where you work even though you're in a horrible mood and wish they'd leave (Richmond, McCroskey, & Payne, 1991).

Eye Behavior

The film *Harry Potter and the Deathly Hallows, Part I* (2010), finds Harry and his friends Ron and Hermione hidden away from the evil Voldemort as they attempt to complete a quest in a time of all-out war. We never doubt what the characters are feeling. We clearly see the soft eyes of love between Ron and Hermione, and we can't miss Harry's terrified glances as he wonders what has become of his loved ones back at Hogwarts and beyond. **Oculesics** is the study of the use of the eyes to communicate.

Researchers found that newborn infants (two to five days old) stared significantly longer at faces offering a direct gaze rather than an averted one. The babies also oriented themselves more often toward the face that made eye contact with them. Previous studies also confirmed that babies as young as three months old would smile less when adults averted their gaze, though the smiling returned when adults resumed eye contact (Farroni, Csibra, Simion, & Johnson, 2002).

There are some cultural variations in gaze with children. For example, European American parents gaze more at their children; this is particularly true between mothers and sons. Mexican American parents, on the other hand, spend less time making eye contact with children. In return, children gaze more directly at fathers in European American homes than in Mexican American homes (Schofield, Parke,

Castañeda, & Coltrane, 2008). Perhaps children in Mexican American homes gaze less directly at fathers as a sign of respect or because of the cultural hierarchy of the family.

The human gaze remains important beyond childhood. You might make direct eye contact with a hiring manager in a job interview in the United States to make a stronger impression. And you will likely use eye behavior to send messages in more personal relationships. For example, the way you look at a friend is likely not the same way you look at your significant other and certainly not the way you look at someone you dislike immensely. Each glance can send a message of liking, loving, attraction, or contempt (see Table 5.1 on p. 107).

> **Culture and You**
>
> In what situations do you feel comfortable making eye contact? In what situations is it easy to do so? When is it difficult?

Voice

When Roger Ebert lost the ability to speak due to complications from thyroid cancer, family, friends, and fans of the legendary film critic thought they'd never hear his voice again. He was able to communicate using a computer equipped with text-to-speech technology, but of course it didn't sound like him. A company in Scotland approached him, saying it could create a customized voice for his computer by using the many hours of audio commentary Ebert had recorded over the years. When he unveiled his new "voice" to his wife, she was moved to tears: although the voice still had the stilted speech pattern that typifies computerized speech, it sounded like Ebert, whom she had not heard speak for more than three years (Hare, 2010).

The vocalized sounds that accompany our words are nonverbal behaviors called **paralanguage**. Text-to-speech programs try to mimic human speech. Indeed, the program developed for Roger Ebert can

Table 5.1 **The Power of Eye Contact**

Function of Eye Contact	Example
Influences attitude change	Looking at someone to get the person to trust you or comply with your wishes
Indicates a degree of arousal	Glancing across a crowded room to signal attraction or interest; looking at a customer attentively in the interest of receiving positive evaluations—and sales (Ford, 1999)
Expresses emotion	Soft eyes of loving looks; frightened eyes of a startled person; hard eyes of an angry person
Regulates interaction	Looking more at a conversational partner when listening; regulating eye contact to assume or give up the speaking role (Wiemann & Knapp, 1999)
Indicates power	Direct, prolonged gaze to convey dominance; avoidance of eye contact to signal submissiveness
Forms impressions	Making eye contact with an audience to communicate confidence and sincerity

Source: Leathers (1986). Adapted with permission.

replicate certain aspects of his paralanguage—specifically, the pitch, tone, and volume of his real voice. **Pitch** in language involves variations in the voice that give prominence to certain words or syllables. Vocal **tone** is a modulation of the voice, usually expressing a particular feeling or mood; you may notice your friend sounds "down" or hear the excitement in your teammate's revelry about your win. Vocal **volume** is how loud or soft the voice is—as in the softness of a whisper or the thunder of an angry shout.

In addition to pitch, tone, and volume, paralanguage also involves behaviors like pauses, vocal quality, and the rate and rhythm of speech. It exhibits qualities like hoarseness, smoothness, or deepness, and it may sound precise, clipped, slurred, or shrill. We all have preferences about which voices are most attractive—and while individual tastes vary, research points to some general preferences. For example, we find angry, demanding voices annoying and whiny

voices *really* annoying (Sokol, Webster, Thompson, & Stevens, 2005). Look no further than your favorite radio DJs or newscasters to examine the vocal qualities people enjoy the most. These individuals tend to have smooth voices and find a middle ground between precise and fluid speech. Pronunciation matters too; it can identify individuals as having come from another country or region. Thus, people in Texas talk about the city of "*Hew*-ston," while New Yorkers might point to "*How*-ston" Street, even though both locations are spelled "Houston."

Meanwhile, **vocalizations** are paralinguistic cues that give information about our emotional or physical state, such as laughing, crying, sighing, yawning, or moaning. Other vocalizations simply replace words or create nonword fillers in conversations. You might clear your throat to get someone's attention or use "Shhhh" to quiet a crowd, and most of us tend to insert "umms" and "ahs" into conversation

⬦ Almost four years after losing the ability to speak owing to complications from thyroid cancer, Roger Ebert found his voice once again with the aid of a customized text-to-speech computer program. He continued communicating right up until days before his passing in 2013.

when we're taking a moment to think. Sometimes such **back-channel cues** signal when we want to talk versus when we're encouraging others to continue talking.

Physical Appearance

Reality television's *What Not to Wear* stylists Clinton Kelly and Stacy London are experts at redoing the appearance of people who have been nominated by their friends and family for makeovers. What you wear—or the way you fix your hair or makeup—doesn't really speak to your abilities or define you as a person, but it communicates a message about you nonetheless. In fact, the initial impression your appearance makes may affect your future interactions with others (Burgoon, Buller, & Woodall, 1989; DeKay, 2009).

Research shows that attractiveness gives people certain advantages. For instance, attractive students receive more interaction from their teachers (Richmond, McCroskey, & Payne, 1991), and "good-looking" job candidates have a greater chance of being hired (Molloy, 1983; Shannon & Stark, 2003). Jurors find attractive defendants innocent more often (Efran, 1974), although discussion and deliberation can mitigate this bias (Patry, 2008). Appearance affects not only perceptions of attractiveness but also judgments about a person's background, character, personality, status, and future behavior (Guerrero & Floyd, 2006). In fact, the psychologist Nancy Etcoff (1999) claims that all cultures pursue and value attractiveness as a matter of survival.

Perceptions about appearance and attractiveness are inferred from not only physical characteristics like body shape and size, facial features, skin color, height, and hair color but also from clothing, which can reveal a lot about your status, economic level, social background, goals, and satisfaction (Crane, 2000; Sybers & Roach, 1962). For example, many uniforms are often associated with lower-status jobs, such as working in a fast-food restaurant. More formal attire (business suits) and certain uniforms (doctors' coats, judges' robes) are associated with higher-status occupations.

We also infer a great deal of meaning from **artifacts**—accessories carried or used on the body for decoration or identification. For example, the expensive Rolex watch that your uncle wears sends a very different message about wealth and status than a ten-dollar watch would. Other artifacts, such as briefcases, tattoos, earrings, nose rings, nail polish, and engagement and wedding rings, also convey messages about your relational status, your gender, and even how willing you are to defy conventions.

Space and Environment

You also send nonverbal messages by the spaces that surround you and your communication partners. We examine three such factors here: proxemics, territoriality, and environment.

What About You?

}

You and Your Artifacts

Take a look at the following list of artifacts. Do you make use of or wear any of these items? If so, what does the artifact mean to you, personally, about your identity? What messages might the artifact send to others?

Artifact Type	What Does It Mean to Me?	What Does It Say About Me?
Jewelry (necklaces, rings, watches, cuff links)		
Perfume or cologne		
Body piercings (tongue rings, nose rings, eyebrow piercings)		
Tattoos		
Specific hairstyles (Mohawk, shaved, braided, long, disheveled)		
Clothing labels or logos		
Eyewear (sunglasses, eyeglasses versus contact lenses)		
Other accessories (scarves, belts, high-heeled shoes)		

Proxemics. **Proxemics** is the study of the way we use and communicate with space. Professor Edward Hall (1959) identified four specific spatial zones that carry communication messages (see **Figure 5.2**).

- **Intimate** (0 to 18 inches). We often send intimate messages in this zone, which is usually reserved for spouses or romantic partners, very close friends, and close family members.
- **Personal** (18 inches to 4 feet). In the personal zone, we communicate with friends, relatives, and occasionally colleagues.
- **Social** (4 to 12 feet). The social zone is most comfortable for communicating in professional settings, such as business meetings or teacher-student conferences.
- **Public** (12 feet and beyond). The public zone allows for distance between the interactants, such as public speaking events or performances.

Your personal space needs may vary from these space categories. They vary according to culture too; Hall "normed" these zones for different cultures around the world. How close or distant you want to be from someone depends on whom you're dealing with, the situation, and your comfort level. You might enjoy being physically close to your boyfriend or girlfriend while taking a walk together, but you probably don't hold hands or embrace during class. Gender also plays a role. Research shows that groups of men walking together will walk faster than men walking alone, and typically leave more space between themselves and others (Costa, 2010). But regardless of your personal preferences, violations of space are almost always uncomfortable and awkward and can cause relational problems.

Proxemic messages are not limited to the real world. In the online virtual world *Second Life*, you create your own space, in which you and your avatar

Shake up your clothing and artifacts today. Wear something completely out of character for you, and consider how people react. If you normally dress very casually, try wearing a suit, or if you're normally quite put together, try going out wearing sweatpants, sneakers, or a T-shirt. If you're normally a clean-shaven man, try growing a beard for a week, or if you're a woman who never wears makeup, try wearing lipstick and eyeliner. Do you get treated differently by friends? By strangers (such as store clerks) or professionals (such as doctors or mechanics) with whom you interact?

Technology and You

How else might you experience proxemics messages in the virtual world? Do you find that there are online equivalents of intimate, personal, social, and public "space"?

move. Avatars use proxemic cues to send relational messages and structure interaction, much as people do in real life (Antonijevic, 2008; Gillath, McCall, Shaver, & Blascovich, 2008).

Territoriality. **Territoriality** is the claiming of an area, with or without legal basis, through continuous occupation. Your home, your car, and your office are personal territories. But territories also encompass implied ownership of space, such as a seat in a class-room, a parking space, or a table in a restaurant. Few people like their territory encroached on. If you're a fan of *The Big Bang Theory*, then you know never (ever) to take Sheldon Cooper's seat on the couch, as you will be subjected to a haughty lecture.

Territoriality operates in mediated contexts as well. Just as we do with physical spaces in the real world, we claim our Twitter and Facebook pages by

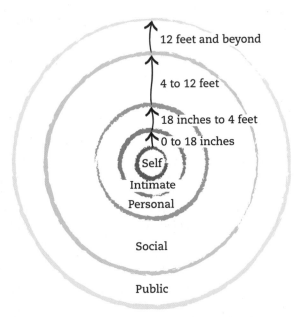

○ **Figure 5.2 Zones of Personal Space.** The four zones of personal space described by Edward Hall indicate ranges that generally apply across cultures.

○ Sheldon Cooper's seat on the couch is the throne of his kingdom (or apartment, which even has its own flag). The *Big Bang Theory* character has established his regular spot as personal—and strictly guarded—territory.

{ **The layout and decoration of your home, your office, and any other space you occupy tell others something about you.** }

naming them, decorating them with our "stuff," allowing certain people ("friends") access, and "cleaning up" by deleting or hiding comments. Research shows that young people are more adept than their parents are at managing space on Facebook (Madden & Smith, 2010). Some clean up their wall regularly, deleting status updates and wall posts as often as they make them. Others use what has become known as a "super logoff": they deactivate their accounts when they are not online so "friends" cannot see their wall, post anything on it, or tag them in photos while they're metaphorically not around (Boyd, 2010).

Environment. Any home designer or architect knows that humans use space to express themselves. The layout and decoration of your home, your office, and any other space you occupy tell others something about you. For example, the way you arrange your furniture can encourage interaction or discourage it; the décor, lighting, and cleanliness of the space all send messages about how you want interactions to proceed. The environment's power to affect communication may explain, in part, the success of shows like *Extreme Makeover: Home Edition* and *Clean House*. Episodes often show a dreary or cluttered space transformed into a warm and vibrant room that everyone wants to be in. The best makeovers reflect not only a family's practical needs but also its unique personalities and interests. That's because the designers understand that our environment communicates who we are to others.

Touch

Touch is the first communication we experience in life. A newborn baby is soothed in the arms of her parents; she begins learning about herself and others while reaching out to explore her environment. The study of touch is termed **haptics**. We hug our loved ones in happy and sad times, we reassure others with a pat on the back, and we experience intimacy with the caress of a spouse.

There are as many different types of touches as there are thoughts about and reactions to being touched. Scholar Richard Heslin's (1974) intimacy continuum provides insights into how our use of touch reflects our relationship with a communication partner:

- **Functional-professional touch** is used to perform a job. How would your dentist perform your root canal if he or she didn't touch you?
- **Social-polite touch** is often a polite acknowledgment of the other person, such as a handshake.
- **Friendship-warmth touch** conveys liking and affection between people who know each other well. Examples might be hugging your friends or offering your brother a pat on the back.
- **Love-intimacy touch** is used by romantic partners, parents and children, and even very close friends and family members. Examples include kissing (whether on the mouth or on the cheek), embracing, and caressing.
- **Sexual-arousal touch** is an intense form of touch that plays an important part in sexual relationships. It often reveals intimacy—as between spouses or romantic partners—but is also used in nonintimate sexual relationships.

Another classification system for touch distinguishes among a dozen different kinds of body contact (Morris, 1977). Table 5.2 illustrates these types of contact in connection with Heslin's intimacy continuum.

Clearly, touch powerfully affects our relationships. In fact, it is one factor related to liking and sustaining liking in healthy marriages (Hinkle, 1999). Our reassuring touch also lets our friends know that we care and serves to regulate social interactions, as when beginning or ending an interaction with a handshake. However, not all touch is positive. Bullying behaviors like kicking, punching, hitting, and poking are inappropriate forms of touch, unless inside a boxing ring.

Table 5.2 **How People Touch**

Type of Contact	Purpose	Intimacy Type
Handshake	Forming relational ties	Social-polite
Body guide	A substitute for pointing	Social-polite
Pat	A congratulatory gesture but sometimes meant as a condescending or sexual one	Social-polite or sexual-arousal
Arm link	Used for support or to indicate a close relationship	Friendship-warmth
Shoulder embrace	Signifies friendship; can also signify romantic connectiveness	Friendship-warmth
Full embrace	Shows emotional response or relational closeness	Friendship-warmth
Hand in hand	Equality in an adult relationship	Friendship-warmth
Mock attack	An aggressive behavior performed in a nonaggressive manner, such as a pinch meant to convey playfulness	Friendship-warmth
Waist embrace	Indicates intimacy	Love-intimacy
Kiss	Signals a degree of closeness or the desire for closeness	Love-intimacy or sexual-arousal
Caress	Normally used by romantic partners; signals intimacy	Love-intimacy or sexual-arousal
Body support	Touching used as physical support	Love-intimacy

Culture and You

Are you accustomed to touches from strangers or colleagues? Does it depend on the situation? How do you think your upbringing or co-cultures explain your feelings about touch communication?

touch, but someone who wants "too much" (such as constant hand-holding) can be perceived as needy or clingy. Withholding touch communicates a message of disinterest or even dislike, which can damage a relationship, whether with a friend, a romantic partner, or a colleague. Obviously, it's important to adjust touch to individual expectations and needs (and culture, as we explain later in the chapter).

Time Orientation

Imagine you're late for a job interview. If you are the interviewee, you've probably lost the job before you

Gauging the appropriate amount of touch for a given situation or relationship is also critical for communication. For example, dating partners usually expect

have a chance to say a word—your lateness sends a message to the employer that you don't value punctuality and his or her time. If you are the interviewer, however, it's completely acceptable for you to keep the interviewee waiting. In fact, by making the person wait, you assert your status by clearly conveying that you have control.

Your use of time is a form of nonverbal communication because it sends a message without a single word. A person's *time orientation*—his or her personal associations with the use of time—determines the importance that person ascribes to conversation content, the length of the interaction, the urgency of the interaction, and punctuality (Burgoon, Buller, & Woodall, 1989). For example, when you are invited to someone's home for dinner, it is normal to arrive about ten minutes after the time suggested (in the United States, anyway—lateness norms vary considerably across cultures). It shows consideration for your host not to arrive too early or too late (and possibly ruin the dinner!). Similarly, spending time with others communicates concern and interest. For example, good friends will make plans to spend time together even when it's inconvenient.

Using time to send a message can be confusing, however. How long do you wait to text or call someone you met at a party to see if he or she might want to grab a meal with you? Right after you've left the party may seem too eager, but a week later may suggest you're not really interested. Research shows that we do use people's response rate (how quickly they return e-mails, texts, etc.) as an indication of interest and immediacy, but the situation and context also make a difference (Döring & Pöschl, 2009; Ledbetter, 2008).

LearningCurve
bedfordstmartins.com/commandyou

Influences on Nonverbal Communication

Pick any individual nonverbal code—let's say a kiss. A kiss can mean lots of different things in different places and between different people in different situations.

A kiss is a friendly manner of greeting between the sexes and with friends of the same sex throughout much of southern Europe and Latin America. This is not necessarily the case in the United States and Canada, where kissing tends to be reserved for immediate family, romantic partners, or very close friends. You might kiss your romantic partner differently in front of your family members than you would when you're alone. And if you're sending an e-mail to your eight-year-old niece, you might end it with a big wet kiss, signaled by the emoticon :-X. Clearly, culture, technology, and the situation all serve as powerful influences on our nonverbal behavior.

Culture and Nonverbal Communication

Hold up one hand, with your thumb and two middle fingers folded in, and wave it at a crowd of people. That's what then president George W. Bush and members of his family did before cameras during inaugural festivities. The next day, newspapers in Norway ran photos of a smiling Jenna Bush holding her hand in the "Hook 'em Horns" salute to the University of Texas Longhorns (her alma mater), with a headline reading "Shock Greeting from Bush Daughter" (Douglass, 2005). Why all the fuss over a gesture of support for a college football team? Because in Norway (and indeed, in heavy-metal co-cultures around the world) the gesture is commonly understood as a satanic salute.

As this example illustrates, nonverbal communication is highly influenced by culture. What may be an innocent gesture in one group, context, region, or country can convey a different and possibly offensive message elsewhere. Culture affects everything from eye behavior to touch to facial expressions and includes time orientation and notions of physical attractiveness, both of which we explained earlier. For example, in the United States, people tend to make direct eye contact when speaking to someone, whether a colleague, a supervisor, or a professor. Similarly, in the Middle East, engaging in long and direct eye contact with your speaking partner shows interest and helps you assess the sincerity and truth of the other person's words (Samovar, Porter, & Stefani, 1998). However, in Latin America, Japan, and the Caribbean, such eye behavior is a sign of disrespect.

Similarly, culture affects touch. Some cultures are **contact cultures** (for example, that of Italy) (Williams & Hughes, 2005) and depend on touch as an important form of communication. Other cultures are **noncontact cultures** and are touch sensitive or even tend to avoid touch. Latin American, Mediterranean, and Eastern European cultures, for example, rely on touch much more than Scandinavian cultures do. Public touch, linked to the type of interpersonal relationship that exists and the culture in which it occurs, affects both the amount of touch and the area of the body that is appropriate to touch (Avtgis & Rancer, 2003; McDaniel & Andersen, 1998). Social-polite touch, for example, involves a handshake between American men but a kiss between Arabic men. And some religions prohibit opposite-sex touch between unmarried or unrelated individuals.

Sex and gender also influence nonverbal communication. Women usually pay more attention to both verbal and nonverbal cues when evaluating their partners and deciding how much of themselves they should reveal to those partners, whereas men attend more to verbal information (Gore, 2009). Women also engage in more eye contact than men, initiate touch more often, and smile more (Hall, 1998; Stewart, Cooper, & Steward, 2003).

Such differences are not necessarily biologically based. For example, mothers may use more varied facial expressions with their daughters because they believe that women are more expressive (or are supposed to be more expressive) than men. A more emotionally expressive and varied environment in childhood may present women with more opportunities to develop nonverbal skills (Hall, Carter, & Hogan, 2000). Adult gender roles may also play a part. Since women are expected to look out for the welfare of others, smiling—as well as other affirming nonverbal behaviors—may help women meet situational, gendered expectations (Hall, Carter, & Hogan; 2000).

This may also help explain why women exhibit greater sensitivity to nonverbal messages. They tend to exhibit more signs of interest (such as head tilts and paralinguistic encouragers like "uh-huh" and "ah") and also decode others' nonverbal behaviors more accurately, particularly those involving the face (Burgoon & Bacue, 2003).

Mediated Nonverbal Communication

At a conference, a colleague told an interesting story about nonverbal communication and e-mail—a story that you may have experienced from both sides. She asked her students to submit their assignments via e-mail by midnight on the date they were due. At 1:00 A.M., she received a frantic e-mail from one of her students, Aaron, explaining that laptop malfunctions had prevented him from sending his speech outline until then. As Aaron typically provided quality work and never missed deadlines, our colleague was not concerned and did not intend to penalize him. So she simply wrote back "Got it" to let him know she had received his outline. When she later saw Aaron in class, she was shocked to learn that her e-mail worried him. He took her short response as a sign of annoyance for his lateness; she meant the response as a quick assurance. In the end, Aaron noted, "If you had used a smiley face, I would have known what you meant."

When you speak with someone face to face, you've got a number of nonverbal codes at your disposal. Even on the telephone, where you have no visual cues, you can use *paralinguistic cues* (vocal tone, rate, pitch, volume, sighs) to offer information. But when you write a letter or send an e-mail, an IM, or a text message, many of the nonverbal channels you rely on (eye contact, paralanguage, and so on) are unavailable. However, people have developed a series of creative substitutions for nonverbal cues: capital

> **Punctuation (or the lack of it) can help readers "hear" the intonation of what is being said (many people say that they "hear" their friend's e-mails in that friend's "voice").**

letters to indicate shouting; creative use of font sizes, colors, and typefaces to provide emphasis; random punctuation (#@*&!) to substitute for obscenities; and animations, figures, diagrams, and pictures to add visuals to messages. Punctuation (or the lack of it) can help readers "hear" the intonation of what is being said (many people say that they "hear" their friend's e-mails in that friend's "voice").

As Aaron noted in our example, some individuals expect others to use emoticons in mediated texts to help clarify meaning—whether to express emotion or to signal that something is a joke. Emoticons can also strengthen the intensity of a message, add ambiguity (was that *really* a joke?), or indicate sarcasm (Derks, Bos, & von Grumbkow, 2008). One study in Japan even found that college students use positive emoticons as a "flame deterrent" to try to prevent emotional misunderstandings that might upset others (Kato, Kato, & Scott, 2009). Since we can't hear voice inflection or see facial expressions in many mediated situations, effective use of the keyboard and computer graphics can help create a sense of nonverbal immediacy (O'Sullivan, Hunt, & Lippert, 2004).

As technology becomes more widely available and affordable, our electronic communication will

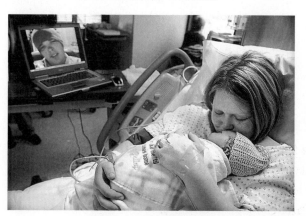

📍 Technology has become so advanced that a father stationed overseas is now able to witness his child's birth in the United States via webcam!

THINGS TO TRY

Play with text-to-speech features on your computer. Compare the way the machine reads a passage of text to the way you would read it. Do you have a choice of voices to use, and is there one you prefer? Would you rather listen to an audiobook performance by a noted actor or a computer-generated voice reading the same material?

likely become open to more nonverbal channels. Skype and similar services, for example, allow us to have visual, as well as audio and text, contact.

The Situational Context

Dancing at a funeral. Raising your Starbucks cup to toast your professor. Making long, steady, somewhat flirtatious eye contact with your doctor. Wearing a business suit to a rock concert. Do these situations sound strange or potentially uncomfortable? The situational context has a powerful impact on nonverbal communication. Recall from our model of competent communication in Chapter 1 that the situational context includes spheres like the place you are, your comfort level, the event, current events, and the social environment.

Now imagine dancing at a wedding, toasting your friend's accomplishment, flirting with an attractive friend, or wearing a business suit to a job interview. In each instance, the situational context has changed from those in the examples presented earlier.

Ethics and You

To what degree do you feel it ethical to present a particular image that's incongruous with how you see yourself, particularly in a situation like a job interview? Would you remove a piercing or cover a tattoo for this purpose? Do you think it's possible to render these things less important through your verbal communication skills?

Situational context determines the rules of behavior and the roles people must play under different conditions. Competent communicators will always consider the appropriateness and effectiveness of nonverbal communication in a given context.

Two of the primary factors involved in situational context are the public-private dimension and the informal-formal dimension. The **public-private dimension** is the physical space that affects our nonverbal communication. For example, you might touch or caress your partner's hand while chatting over dinner at your kitchen table, but you would be much less likely to do that at your brother's kitchen table or during a meeting at city hall. The **informal-formal dimension** is more psychological, dealing with our perceptions of personal versus impersonal situations. The formality of a situation is signaled by various nonverbal cues, such as the environment (your local pub versus a five-star restaurant), the event (a child's first birthday party or a funeral), the level of touch (a business handshake as contrasted with a warm embrace from your aunt), or even the punctuality expected (a wedding beginning promptly at 2:00 P.M. or a barbecue at your friend Nari's house going from 6:00 P.M. to whenever) (Burgoon & Bacue, 2003). Competently assessing the formality or informality of the situation affects your use of nonverbal communication—you might wear flip-flops and shorts to hang out at Nari's, but you probably wouldn't wear them to a wedding and certainly wouldn't wear them on a job interview.

If your nonverbal communication does not appropriately fit the public-private and formal-informal dimensions, you'll likely be met with some nonverbal indications that you are not being appropriate or effective (tight smiles, restless body movements, gaze aversion, and vocal tension).

LearningCurve
bedfordstmartins.com/commandyou

Back to } Pixar Animation Studios

At the beginning of this chapter, we considered how animators at Pixar use elements of nonverbal communication to tell elaborate stories in films like *Up* and *WALL-E*. Let's reconsider some of the ways nonverbal codes operate in these and other films.

- The directors of *Up* used simple visual cues to highlight the characters so their appearance provides insights into their personalities. Carl is very squarish in appearance, so he's perceived as boxed in, in both his house and his life. Eight-year-old Explorer Scout Russell is round and bouncy—like Carl's balloons, reflecting his optimistic, energetic personality. These nonverbal elements carry subtle yet influential messages.

- Animators study human kinesics to make decisions about how their animated characters should move. To animate the aged Carl, they studied their own parents and grandparents and watched footage of the Senior Olympics. If Carl moved like eight-year-old Russell, the credibility of the film would be compromised.

- It takes talented voice actors to bring a script to life. The veteran actor Ed Asner breathed life into Carl, delivering not only his lines but also believable vocal cues—grunts, sighs, speaking through clenched teeth—that made those lines more human and real. But for the roles of young Ellie and Russell, the directors chose nonactors who would give genuine, unpolished performances full of childish energy—the goal was for them to sound more like real children than like actors reading from a script.

Your Reference } A Study Tool

Now that you have finished reading this chapter, you can:

Describe the power of nonverbal communication:

- **Nonverbal communication** is the process of signaling meaning through behavior rather than words. It is often spontaneous and unintentional, and its meaning may be ambiguous (pp. 98–99).
- When **channel discrepancy** occurs, words and actions don't match, and nonverbal behaviors are more likely to be believed than verbal ones (p. 100).

Outline the functions of nonverbal communication:

- Nonverbal communication reinforces verbal communication in three ways: **repeating** (mirroring the verbal message), **complementing** (reinforcing the verbal message), and **accenting** (emphasizing a part of the verbal message) (p. 101).
- Nonverbal cues can be used for **substituting** or replacing words (p. 101).
- Nonverbal communication also functions as **contradicting** behavior, conveying the opposite of your verbal message (pp. 101–102).
- Nonverbal cues are used in **regulating** or coordinating verbal interaction (p. 102).
- A feeling of closeness, or **immediacy**, can be created with nonverbal behaviors. **Mimicry** can enhance immediacy if perceived as sincere (p. 102).
- Individuals with good nonverbal communication skills may practice **deception**, with good or bad intentions, when they attempt to use nonverbal behaviors to convince others of something that is false (p. 103).

Describe the set of communication symbols that are nonverbal codes:

- **Kinesics** ⊙, the way gestures and body movements send various messages, includes **emblems** ⊙ (movements with direct verbal translations in a specific group or culture), **illustrators** ⊙ (visually reinforcing behaviors), **regulators** ⊙ (interaction management cues), **adaptors** ⊙ (unconscious release of bodily tension), and **affect displays** ⊙ (indications of emotion) (pp. 104–105).
- **Masking** is a facial management technique whereby we replace an expression of true feeling with one appropriate for a given interaction (p. 106).
- **Oculesics** is the study of the use of the eyes in communication settings (p. 106).

- How we pause, the speed and volume of our speech, and the inflections we use are vocalized nonverbal messages called **paralanguage** ⊙ (pp. 106–108), including **pitch** (vocal variation that gives prominence to certain words or syllables), **tone** (vocal modulation that expresses feelings or moods), **volume** (how loud or soft words are spoken), and a variety of other factors.
- **Vocalizations** are paralinguistic cues that give information about the speaker's emotional or physical state, such as laughing, crying, or sighing (pp. 107–108).
- **Back-channel cues** are vocalizations that signal vocally but nonverbally that you do or don't want to talk (p. 108).
- **Artifacts**, accessories used for decoration and identification, offer clues to who we are (p. 108).
- **Proxemics** ⊙, the study of the way we use and communicate with space, depends on the cultural environment and is defined by four specific spatial zones: intimate, personal, social, and public (pp. 109–110).
- **Territoriality** is the claiming of an area, with or without legal basis, by regular occupation of the area (pp. 110–111).
- The study of touch as a form of communication is known as **haptics** ⊙; what a touch means depends on the relationship with the communication partner (p. 111).
- **Time orientation** determines the importance a person ascribes to content, length, urgency, and punctuality of communication (pp. 112–113).

Illustrate the influences culture, technology, and situation have on our nonverbal behavior:

- **Contact cultures** are more likely to communicate through touch whereas **noncontact cultures** may even tend to avoid touch (p. 114).
- Gender influences communication, with behaviors traditionally associated with femininity, such as smiling, often perceived as weak (p. 114).
- In mediated communication, capitalization, boldfaced terms, and emoticons are used as nonverbal cues (pp. 114–115).
- Competent nonverbal communication relates to the situation; the **public-private dimension** is the physical space that affects our nonverbal communication, and the **informal-formal dimension** is more psychological (pp. 115–116).

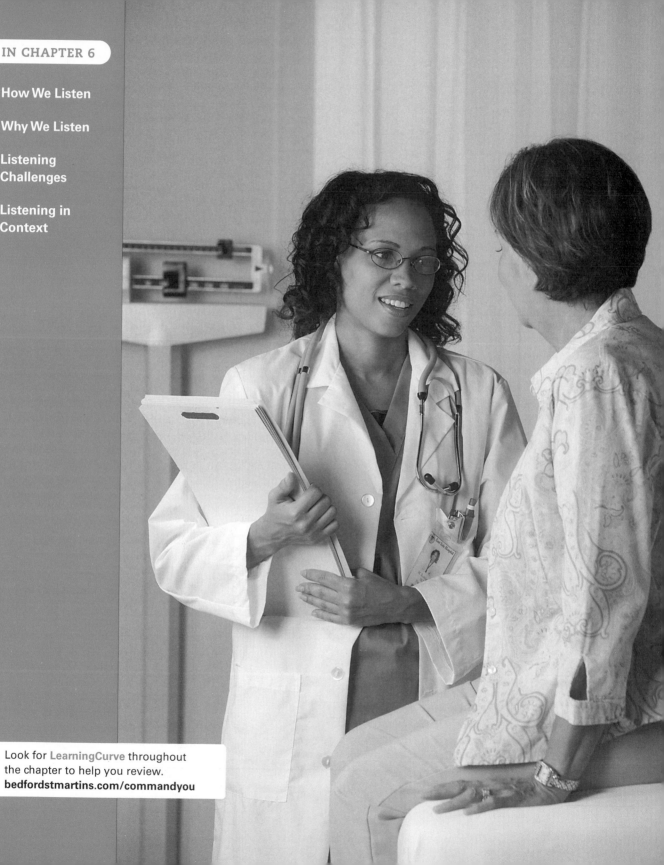

Look for **LearningCurve** throughout the chapter to help you review.
bedfordstmartins.com/commandyou

6 } Listening

Erno Daniel looks for "stealth germs." As a physician and author of *Stealth Germs in Your Body* (2008), he's on the lookout for conditions caused by bacteria, viruses, and other microbes that can go undiagnosed and untreated until they manifest themselves as something serious later. Although his clinical medical experience helps him diagnose hidden, chronic, or low-grade infections, he can't run hundreds of tests on every patient. He can, however, listen to them.

Unfortunately, not all physicians listen effectively. One study found that, on average, doctors interrupt patients only eighteen seconds after they begin to speak (Appleby, 1996). They try to jump to a diagnosis, relying on familiar technical knowledge, and fail to hear the patient's whole story. Financial pressures in the health care industry often limit the amount of time doctors can spend with their patients. Consequently, many don't gather the full details of conditions afflicting patients, which may be more relevant than the first symptom patients disclose.

But Daniel asks patients to tell him when their symptoms started; he asks them where they've traveled, what they've eaten, when the symptoms became more acute, and what else is going on in their lives. Early in his career he used this strategy to discover that an infectious organism in the water of a small community was causing many people to have ulcerlike symptoms. At the time, it was thought that all these symptoms were due to stress, but Daniel's listening skills led him to find the treatable infectious cause.

After you have finished reading this chapter, you will be able to

Outline the listening process and styles of listening.

List the reasons we listen.

Identify challenges to good listening and their remedies.

Identify attitudinal and ethical factors that inhibit listening.

Describe how contexts affect listening.

O n elementary school report cards, "Listens well" and "Follows directions" are high praise for young children (Edwards & Edwards, 2009). But somewhere in the years that follow, we stop thinking about listening as a crucial skill. "I listen well" probably isn't a line on your résumé, like being able to speak German or knowing the ins and outs of JavaScript. Yet professors, employers, and medical professionals often define effective listening as a crucial skill. In fact, listening pioneer Ralph Nichols claimed that listening helps us achieve our most basic human need: to understand and be understood (Beall, 2006; Floyd, 2006; Nichols, 2006; Purdy, 2006; Wolvin, 2006).

In this chapter, we examine the nature of listening—how we hear, process, come to understand, and then respond to others' communication. We learn why listening is so important and why we so often fail to listen effectively. And we describe tools and techniques you can use every day to become a more effective and competent listener.

How We Listen

How many times have you had the radio on, only to realize you weren't listening to it? You know you heard the music, and you may have sung along. But just moments after it ends, you can't recall the name of the song or how the DJ introduced it. You were thinking about something else or not paying enough attention to retain what you heard.

Although the two are often confused, hearing and listening are not the same thing. **Hearing** is the physiological process of perceiving sound, the process through which sound waves are picked up by the ears and transmitted to the brain. Unless there is a physical reason hearing does not take place, it is an involuntary process—you can't turn it on or off. But you can, to some degree, decide what sounds you're going to notice. This is where listening comes in.

Listening is the process of recognizing, understanding, accurately interpreting, and responding effectively to the messages you hear. It is much more than just hearing words or being able to recall information (Janusik, 2005; Todd & Levine, 1996). Listening involves *processing* what others say and do, paying attention, understanding (Thomas & Levine, 1994), and *creating* messages that respond to the speaker and are directed toward achieving goals (Janusik, 2005; Wiemann, Takai, Ota, & Wiemann, 1997). In this section, we examine how this crucial process works.

The Listening Process

The listening process occurs so quickly that we may think of it as automatic. However, listening involves a

> **Unless there is a physical reason hearing does not take place, it is an involuntary process— you can't turn it on or off. But you can, to some degree, decide what sounds you're going to notice.**

🔹 There's a big difference between hearing a song on the radio and listening to a friend express concern about a personal issue.

complex web of skills. We can develop and improve those skills by focusing on the voluntary parts of the process, as detailed in the following sequence of steps:

1. **Selecting.** Since hearing is involuntary, we cannot choose what we hear. In the face of competing stimuli—the television in the next room, the dishwasher running, and your roommate Brett complaining about his economics midterm—you must choose one sound over the others. This process is called **selecting**.

2. **Attending.** Through **attending**, you elect to *focus attention* on someone else's presence and communication. If you select Brett's voice (deciding that it's more interesting than the sound of the running dishwasher), you then attend actively to his words and message. It's important to be aware of attending, as this step is not always easily achieved. If your other roommate Elton has the TV tuned to your favorite show, attending to Brett's message may be difficult. Being silent can help; research shows that this improves listening effectiveness (Johnson, Pearce, Tuten, & Sinclair, 2003).

3. **Understanding.** While talking about his midterm, Brett mentions a disagreement he had with his professor over the wording of an essay question. He throws around phrases like "aggregate supply" and "reciprocal demand." You've never studied economics, so you barely understand a word he's saying. **Understanding**—interpreting and making sense of messages—is a crucial step in the listening process because it enables you to interpret meaning. When you don't understand something, you need to listen more actively. For example, you might ask Brett questions to learn more about his situation (Husband, 2009).

4. **Remembering.** As a student, you know it's important to recall information from class during an exam and in real-life situations. **Remembering**, or recalling information, contributes to perceptions of competence in interactions far beyond the classroom (Muntigl & Choi, 2010). If you don't recall what happened in your conversation with Brett, he might be annoyed later when he tells you about how his dilemma turned out.

5. **Responding. Responding** involves generating feedback or reactions that let others know

you've received and understood their message. So when Brett wonders if he should talk to his professor and you say, "That sounds like the best course of action given the importance of this exam for your grade," it lets him know that you fully comprehend his concern.

Though these steps may seem to happen without much conscious thought, they result from a series of quick decisions we make when communicating with others. Through **active listening**, we make choices about selecting, attending, and so on. A failure to make such choices is called **passive listening**. Passive listeners often need information and instructions repeated for them; they may misinterpret messages or ignore them altogether. And they are often seen as less competent by the people around them. After all, you probably wouldn't pour your heart out to someone who seems more interested in watching TV than in listening to you.

The goal, then, is **listening fidelity**, by which our thoughts and another person's thoughts and intentions match following communication (Fitch-Hauser, Powers, O'Brien, & Hanson, 2007; Mulanax & Powers, 2001). Active listening can play an important role in achieving this goal.

> ### Technology and You
> Are there times when technology enhanced your ability to listen? Are there times when it hindered that ability? Give examples from your life.

Personal Listening Preferences

Each day, you spend a lot of time listening to your professors, other students, family members, and friends—more time than you spend reading or writing (as shown in Figure 6.1). Use of communication technologies can fuse these categories; for example, when you're reading a post that your friend wrote on your Facebook wall, you're also "listening" to the

message your friend is conveying.[1] Clearly, listening will remain a vital communication skill no matter how technology continues to evolve (Janusik & Wolvin, 2009).

But how, exactly, are you listening? Four distinct preferences, or styles, emerge when it comes to listening—regardless of whether the communication is face to face or mediated through the use of technology (Barker & Watson, 2000; Watson, Barker, & Weaver, 1995):

- **People-oriented listeners** listen with relationships in mind. They tend to be most concerned with other people's feelings, are usually good at assessing others' moods, and can listen without judging.
- **Action-oriented listeners** usually focus on tasks; they organize the information they hear into concise and relevant themes. They tend to keep the discourse on track, so they're often valuable in meetings and as members of teams and organizations.
- **Content-oriented listeners** carefully evaluate what they hear. They usually prefer to listen to information from sources they feel are credible and to critically examine the information they receive from a variety of angles. They can be particularly effective when information is complex, detailed, and challenging.
- **Time-oriented listeners** are most concerned with efficiency. They prefer information that is clear and to the point and have little patience for speakers who talk too much or wander off topic. They prefer time limitations on the listening interaction.

Though some people show a clear preference for one style over another, about 40 percent of people score high on two or more listening styles; thus, they can adapt their listening styles to different situations

---

[1]The time you spend communicating on social-networking sites and cell phones hasn't yet been worked into listening research at this time.

TIME COMMUNICATING

Listening
24%

Speaking
20%

Radio
2%

Internet use
13%

Listening
to music
4%

E-mail
5%

Writing
9%

Phone
use
7%

TV
watching
8%

Reading
8%

○ **Figure 6.1 Time Communicating.**
Time spent by college students in
communication activity, including
personal computer time, multitasking, weekday and weekend time with
work, family, friends, and school. Listening to mediated communication
channels occupies the most time.
Source: Janusik & Wolvin, 2009

(Barker & Watson, 2000). For example, you may be
more content oriented while listening to a political
debate so you can analyze the information and make
a judgment. But you might be more people oriented
when consoling a friend because you care about
maintaining the relationship. Meanwhile, you might
favor action-oriented listening during a meeting on a
group project or time-oriented listening when you're
working under a tight deadline.

Culture and You

Consider the examples of different listening
styles here; in addition to individual
preferences, styles may differ across cultures.
Are you able to adopt different styles when
listening to different groups of friends,
acquaintances, family, or coworkers?

LearningCurve
bedfordstmartins.com/commandyou

Why We Listen

A court stenographer depends on specialized listening skills to record court proceedings accurately. But
is he listening differently than, say, the judge or the
jury? Does he listen the same way when he is watching a movie, reading Twitter posts, or chatting with
friends? Probably not. In this section, we discuss the
different ways in which we listen, as well as the benefits of listening well.

Meeting Listening Goals

There are many reasons you want others to listen to
you—and many reasons for listening to others. In
some situations, you need to listen for information;
in others, you must listen for ideas, emotions, or enjoyment. You listen to comprehend, to evaluate, to
communicate empathy, and to appreciate (Steil,
Barker, & Watson, 1983). And sometimes you listen
with all these goals in mind.

Informational Listening. When you listen to a
weather report on the radio, attend a lecture, or hear

When *Modern Family* parents Claire and Phil Dunphy sit their children down for a family meeting or lecture, Haley, Alex, and Luke must listen more attentively than they would during casual, everyday interactions with Mom and Dad.

the details of your significant other's day at work, your primary goal is to understand what's being said. Through this process of **informational listening** (sometimes referred to as *comprehensive listening*), you seek to understand a message. As a student, you use informational listening extensively to understand concepts and information your instructors are presenting to you. When someone gives you directions, provides instructions, or tells a story, it requires informational listening from you.

Questions are important aids to informational as well as other types of listening. Through *questioning techniques*, you coordinate what the speaker is saying with what you are hearing. Asking such questions signals that you *are* listening; it also indicates to the speaker that you are tuned in and interested. Questions can also help a speaker become more effective by getting to the points that will do the listener the most good.

Critical Listening. Most listening is informational, but we sometimes need to go a step further—to make a judgment about a message we're hearing. When you evaluate or analyze information, evidence, ideas, or opinions, you engage in **critical listening** (sometimes called *evaluative listening*). This type of listening is valuable when you cannot take a message at face value. Most of us probably need to employ this type of listening when considering a big financial purchase, like a car. Don bought his last car from a friend of a friend and failed to ask enough questions about the vehicle's history. If he'd listened more critically, he would have learned the car had been in two accidents.

Critical thinking is a necessary component of critical listening. When you think critically, you assess the speaker's motivation, credibility, accuracy (Has she presented all the facts? Is the research current?), and ethics (What does she stand to gain from this?). Four tips can help you improve your critical listening abilities:

- **Determine the thesis or main point of the speaker's message.** This isn't always easy, particularly if the speaker is rambling on and on without making a point. But you can watch for key words and phrases like "What I'm trying to say . . ." or "The issue is . . ." or "OK, here's the deal . . . ."

- **Focus your efforts.** Listening is sometimes hard work. You might need to store up energy. For example, don't head into your three-hour large group lecture after working out or frantically finishing a paper. You may also need to concentrate and avoid distractions.

- **Decode nonverbal cues.** As you learned in Chapter 5, nonverbal behavior communicates volumes of information. Your friend might reveal sadness or anger in ways that don't come across in his verbal message; your professor might hint at information that will be on a test by sharing it slowly and loudly or by repeating it.

- **Use your memory.** If you're in a lecture or on a job interview, note-taking can help jog your memory of what was said. If you're listening to a classmate share concerns about a group project, note-taking might be awkward, so try to make mental associations with her words. For example, if she says, "Benjamin's too controlling," you might think "bossy Benjamin" to remember her complaint.

Empathic Listening. When we engage in **empathic listening**, we try to know how another person feels. This kind of listening requires openness, sensitivity, and caring. Through empathic listening, we can provide emotional support for someone in need or comfort someone when tragedy or disappointment has struck. This is particularly important in medical situations. Doctors, nurses, and other health care providers must listen compassionately to the seriously ill. They need to determine the mental and emotional state of patients and their families to decide how much information to disclose to them and when. Empathic listening helps manage the emotions of people confronting adverse events and can help uncover erroneous assumptions contributing to their anxieties (Iedema, Jorm, Wakefield, Ryan, & Sorensen, 2009; Rehling, 2008).

When you listen empathically, it's helpful to **paraphrase** the thoughts and feelings being expressed. This involves *guessing* at feelings and rephrasing what you think the speaker has said. Empathic listening is person-centered (Burleson, 1994). It recognizes and elaborates on others' feelings, giving them some degree of legitimacy. The empathic listener reflects the speaker's feelings and thoughts without suggesting an answer or a solution (Fent & MacGeorge, 2006; Shotter, 2009). Effective listeners don't overdo paraphrasing because overdoing makes for an awkward conversation and may cause the other person to feel ridiculed (Weger, Castle, & Emmett, 2010).

> { **Empathic listening involves *guessing* at feelings and rephrasing what you think the speaker has said.** }

Appreciative Listening. We use **appreciative listening** to take pleasure in sounds. Listening to music, poetry, narrations, comedy routines, plays, movies, and television shows are all appreciative listening situations (Christenson, 1994). Some people find this type of listening so important that they schedule time to do it—that's why they buy tickets to concerts and other performances or tell family members not to bother them when *America's Got Talent* is on. Appreciative listening can also help relieve stress, unclutter the mind, and refresh the senses.

Table 6.1 offers ideas for accomplishing each of the four listening goals discussed in this section.

The Value of Listening Well

Listening affects more than your ability to communicate: it enables you to live a productive, satisfying, and healthy life.

Effective Listening Helps Your Career. Effective listening is greatly valued and rewarded professionally. Employers report that effective listening is related to job satisfaction, performance, and achievement of the organization's goals (Cooper, 1997; Gray, 2010). Surveys of *Fortune* 500 company personnel reveal that listening is one of the most important skills that a college graduate can possess (Wolvin & Coakley, 1991). In the professional world, employees who are good listeners are seen as alert, confident, mature, and judicious. Employers also value employees who can listen effectively in diverse contexts. For example, a manager expects her assistant to listen carefully

Table 6.1 **Listening Goals**

Type	Description	Strategies
Informational	Listening to understand, learn, realize, or recognize	Listen for main ideas or details; take speaker's perspective; use memory effectively
Critical	Listening to judge, analyze, or evaluate	Determine speaker's goal; evaluate source of message; question logic, reasoning, and evidence of message
Empathic	Listening to provide therapy, comfort, and sympathy	Focus on speaker's perspective; give supportive feedback; show caring; demonstrate patience; avoid judgment; focus on speaker's goal
Appreciative	Listening for enjoyment of what is being presented	Remove physical and time distractions; know more about originator (author, artist, composer); explore new appreciative listening opportunities

to instructions for a project but also to listen for irritation or confusion in an e-mail from a customer. Similarly, employees must listen carefully to others during teleconferences and WebEx meetings, despite distractions like background noise or malfunctioning equipment (Bentley, 2000).

Moreover, to be strong leaders, established professionals need to listen to others, make them feel heard, and respond effectively to them (Stillion Southard & Wolvin, 2009). The CBS reality series *Undercover Boss* features CEOs who go "undercover" in their companies. Unrecognized by employees, they listen more than anything—by asking questions, hearing about the reality of work life for people at all levels of the organization, and probing for insights into what works and what doesn't. In most instances, the CEO returns to make positive changes in the

📍 On *Undercover Boss*, executives at companies like Comfort Inn must listen carefully and take directions from veteran lower-level employees.

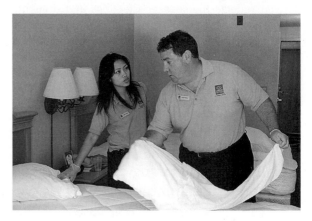

company's operations and to improve communication with employees as well.

Effective Listening Saves Time and Money. One reason that professionals value listening skills so much is that good listeners save time by acting quickly and accurately on information presented to them. You comprehend more when you listen well (Rubin, Hafer, & Arata, 2000), so if you actively listen to your instructor's remarks about an upcoming exam, you can save time by studying more effectively. If you listen carefully when someone gives you driving directions, you'll be more likely to arrive at your destination on time.

Businesses lose millions of dollars each year because of listening mistakes alone (Rappaport, 2010; Steil, Summerfield, & de Mare, 1983). Repeated or duplicated tasks, missed opportunities, lost clients, botched orders, misunderstood instructions, and forgotten appointments can cost companies money—as can failing to listen to customers. In 2009, the makers of Tropicana orange juice changed its product packaging, and loyal customers deluged the company with irate letters and e-mails. Company officials quickly responded and reverted to the recognizable label (an orange with a straw protruding from it), but they could have avoided the costly fiasco if they had listened to their customers in the first place (Wiesenfeld, Bush, & Sikdar, 2010).

Effective Listening Creates Opportunities. Good listeners don't just avoid mistakes; they find opportunities that others might miss. A real estate agent who listens to what a young couple is looking for in their first home and comprehends their financial constraints will more likely find them the right home. An entrepreneur who listens to fellow diners at a

◊ How will your real estate agent help you find your dream home if he doesn't listen to and comprehend your desire for high ceilings and hardwood floors?

popular restaurant complain that no place in town serves vegetarian fare might find an opportunity for a new business. Even writing a textbook like the one you are reading involves listening. As authors, we must listen to our peers, who help us decide what topics and scholarship to include in the book. We must listen to the students who have reviewed our manuscript to find out what kinds of examples and issues will be most relevant to them. And we must listen to our editors, who help us make the material more clear and engaging.

Effective Listening Strengthens Relationships. Have you ever had a friend who just talked about himself or herself without ever allowing you to share your own thoughts or concerns? Does your roommate or a colleague send text messages or update Facebook while you're talking? They may be hearing, but they're almost certainly

{ **Repeated or duplicated tasks, missed opportunities, lost clients, botched orders, misunderstood instructions, and forgotten appointments can cost companies money— as can failing to listen to customers.** }

not listening. And your relationship may be suffering as a result.

In new relationships, the partners must listen competently to learn more about each other; failure to do this usually results in less attraction and more negative emotions (Knobloch & Solomon, 2002). As your relationships progress, listening remains a top priority. For example, you probably won't continue making self-disclosures to a friend who doesn't listen to you. Similarly, you can significantly reduce your partner's stress in a challenging situation by letting him or her talk through difficult events while you listen (Lewis & Manusov, 2009).

LearningCurve
bedfordstmartins.com/commandyou

Listening Challenges

Despite the tremendous benefits of listening well, we all fail to listen effectively at times. We may find ourselves unable to listen to material (or a speaker) that we find boring. We may have trouble focusing when we have a lot on our mind, are in a rush, or are coming down with a cold. In this section, we discuss **listening barriers**, factors that interfere with our ability to comprehend information and respond appropriately. We also offer advice for overcoming these barriers (Nichols, Brown, & Keller, 2006).

Environmental Factors

Loud noise, such as what we experience at sporting events and rock concerts or when working around heavy equipment, is only one environmental factor impairing our ability to listen (and sometimes hear). Large groups present another difficulty, as they involve more people competing for your attention (Beatty & Payne, 1984). Distractions in your environment—a television on, a baby crying, a train rumbling by your house—can also impair listening. Indeed, local transit systems can be as loud as a rock concert (around 120 decibels) (Childs, 2009). Even the temperature or

air quality in a room can be distracting enough to affect listening.

If you know ahead of time that environmental factors will distract you from a listening situation, you can take steps to eliminate distractions. For example, if there's a classroom on your campus that's always cold, even when it's 90 degrees outside, bring a sweater or jacket to that class. Avoid busy public places when meeting for an intimate conversation. And if you must attend a lecture with a lot of rowdy individuals, get to it early and pick a seat closer to the speaker.

> ### Technology and You
> What kinds of activities and technologies distract you and affect your ability to listen? Are there any tasks you feel you can do without them affecting your listening ability?

Hearing and Processing Challenges

Sometimes difficulty with listening lies not in the environment but in a physical or medical issue. For example, our hearing ability declines with age, affecting our ability to hear words as well as speech tone, pitch, and range (Bellis & Wilber, 2001; Villaume & Brown, 1999). Stereotypes of older adults portray them as unable to engage in normal conversation because of cognitive decline, but often the real problem is that they have to work harder to distinguish sounds (Murphy, Daneman, & Schneider, 2006). Accidents, diseases, stress and anxiety, and physical differences can also cause varying degrees of hearing impairment for anyone, not just elderly people (Roup & Chiasson, 2010).

Still, hearing loss (even total hearing loss) does not mean that an individual cannot listen competently. Deaf individuals often speak of "listening with their eyes," and research notes that those who cannot hear physically are quite competent at decoding nonverbal behaviors revealing a speaker's emotions (Grossman & Kegl, 2007). In addition, individuals who use American Sign Language as a primary language also listen to each other and encode and decode messages visually, as do any individuals speaking the same vocal language.

Even someone with perfect hearing can face listening challenges. For instance, a person with *attention deficit disorder* (ADD) may have difficulty focusing on information and tasks, which can make listening challenging. People with *auditory processing disorder*, a learning disability that makes it difficult to process information they hear, must use strategies to focus on and understand spoken information; they might adjust their environment, for example, by always sitting in the front of the classroom or always studying in the quietest section of the library. They might rely more heavily on written or visual cues when learning new information, use paraphrasing to confirm that they've received and processed messages correctly, and focus on only one listening task at a time.

Multitasking

Listening well can be nearly impossible when your attention is divided among many important tasks. **Multitasking**—attending to several things at once—is often considered an unavoidable part of modern life. We routinely drive, walk, cook, or tidy up while listening to music, talking on the phone, communicating on social-networking sites, or watching television.

We may believe we're giving fair attention to each task, but research shows that our ability to attend to more complicated chores suffers when we multitask. That's because our ability to focus is limited—we end up shifting our attention between various tasks,

◊ Listening is not reserved for those with the ability to hear. These two friends are sharing ideas through sign language.

which decreases our efficiency and accuracy (Wallis, 2006). If you grew up surrounded by television, PlayStations, and iPods, you may be able to multitask better than people who grew up without such distractions. But regardless of age or experience, the brain cannot process as much information during multitasking as it can when focusing on one task (Wallis, 2006).

So what are realistic remedies for this listening barrier? One remedy is discipline: vow to silence your cell phone, log out of Facebook, and refrain from texting for a specified period. Another remedy is to be mindful and considerate of others. You may think it's no big deal to text a friend during a classmate's presentation in your human communication course, but if the roles were reversed, you might take offense or wonder if you were boring your listeners (Mello, 2009; Stephens & Davis, 2009). This point goes for interpersonal interactions too—if you're texting Rodney or playing Words with Friends with Denise while having lunch with Alex, you might be sending Alex an unintended message that you don't value his company.

Culture and You

Taking into account your culture and co-cultures, do you find multitasking behaviors—such as updating Twitter while a friend is talking—rude or acceptable? How do you think your answer might change if you were older, younger, or from a different region of the world?

Boredom and Overexcitement

It can be hard to listen to a speaker whose voice lulls you to sleep or whose presentation is lifeless. It can be equally hard to listen to a perfectly competent speaker who is giving a presentation on a boring topic. When something (or someone) seems overwhelmingly dull, we can wind up daydreaming. There are so many more interesting things to think about: weekend plans, that interesting person you met at a party, what you want to do after graduation. Nonetheless, boring information may still be important enough to warrant your attention.

On the flip side, overexcitement can distract you from listening effectively, even if the speaker is saying something you might normally find engaging. If you're consumed by plans for an upcoming vacation, for instance, you may have difficulty listening to a class lecture.

You can still improve your listening skills in situations in which you're experiencing boredom or overexcitement. First, become more conscious about the situation. Think about how *you* would deliver the information being discussed and how you would restructure it or give examples. As you do this, you may find yourself listening more attentively. Second, avoid daydreaming by taking notes. Third, relate information to your own life. To illustrate, if you're sick of listening to a friend complain for the hundredth time about her problems with a professor, imagine how you'd feel in the same situation. Your interest in your friend's problem may perk up.

Attitudes About Listening

Few people spend much time analyzing their attitudes about listening. Yet sometimes our attitudes are precisely what cause us to struggle when communicating with others. Let's examine three examples here.

Talking Seems More Powerful Than Listening. In many Western societies, people tend to think that talking is powerful, so *not* talking must be weak. Because we fail to value the power of listening, we tend to neglect it. Michael listens to his wife

◊ Your ability to accomplish tasks would undoubtedly be stretched too thin if you attempted to write a paper, browse Web sites, and carry on a phone conversation simultaneously.

only to plan what he's going to say next; he's not interested in what his wife has to say, only in making *her* listen to *him*. Katrina thinks she already knows what others will say; when her sister is speaking to her, she nods quickly and says, "Yeah, yeah, I know." Michael and Katrina would likely be better communicators and experience healthier relationships if they remembered that listening actually empowers us.

Many people assume that a key to listening well is simply to stop talking. But that's easier said than done; you have to raise your awareness of your listening versus talking time. If a desire to dominate a conversation creeps up on you, remind yourself that through the act of listening you empower your communication partners to reveal their thoughts, insights, fears, values, and beliefs (Fletcher, 1999). Equally important, you free yourself to comprehend multiple concepts and make more connections between ideas (Dipper, Black, & Bryan, 2005). In the long run, you may even exert more influence in your relationships. As people feel more confident about your caring for them, they will *give* you more influence.

Overconfidence and Laziness. Randall walked into a status meeting certain that he knew everything that was going to be said. As he confidently sat through the meeting only half listening to his colleagues tossing ideas around, his boss began asking him questions that he was unprepared to answer. The root of Randall's problem lies in overconfidence—he assumed that he didn't need to pay attention because he thought he already knew everything. Overconfidence frequently leads to laziness—we use our high estimations of ourselves as an excuse not to prepare or plan for or pay attention during an encounter.

Listening Apprehension. **Listening apprehension** (also called *receiver apprehension*) is a state of uneasiness, anxiety, fear, or dread associated with a listening opportunity. Listening to your boss reprimand you about your job performance, listening to someone else's personal problems, or listening to highly detailed or statistical information can trigger listening apprehension, which compromises your ability to concentrate on or remember what is said (Ayres, Wilcox, & Ayres, 1995).

Students with high listening anxiety have lower motivation to process information in the classroom, which can affect their overall academic performance (Schrodt, Wheeless, & Ptacek, 2000). Confident individuals usually understand information better than their less confident peers (Clark, 1989). So it is important to assess your ability to listen effectively and to spend time developing your listening confidence. What do you think about your own listening apprehension? You may have a better idea after you complete the self-assessment on page 132.

Unethical Listening Behaviors

We may all be guilty of unethical listening behaviors from time to time (Beard, 2009; Lipari, 2009). These include defensive listening, selective listening, selfish listening, hurtful listening, and pseudolistening, all discussed in this section. Such behaviors will not benefit you in any way personally or professionally. But with careful attention and the development of positive listening behaviors, you can overcome them.

Defensive Listening. If you've ever read the *Harry Potter* series of books or seen the movies, you know that Harry Potter can't stand Professor Snape and that Professor Snape despises Harry. To some extent, the mutual dislike is earned: Snape often singles Harry out for punishment, and Harry frequently disrespects Snape. Throughout the series, their preconceived notions of one another hamper their communication. When Snape tries to teach Harry a crucial skill, Harry refuses to listen to the valuable advice and corrections. In Harry's eyes, Snape is picking on him yet again, trying to make him feel like a failure, so he

Harry Potter and Professor Snape may have their issues, but Harry's defensive listening isn't going to help him learn Occlumency.

What About You?

Your Listening Apprehension

Lawrence Wheeless has developed a test that identifies listening areas that can cause apprehension. Some of these areas are listed below. Answer the following questions to get an idea of your listening-apprehension level.

Score your answers to the following questions according to whether you strongly agree (1), agree (2), are undecided (3), disagree (4), or strongly disagree (5).

_____ 1. I am not afraid to listen as a member of an audience.

_____ 2. I feel relaxed when I am listening to new ideas.

_____ 3. I generally feel rattled when others are speaking to me.

_____ 4. I often feel uncomfortable when I am listening to others.

_____ 5. I often have difficulty concentrating on what is being said.

_____ 6. I look for opportunities to listen to new ideas.

_____ 7. Receiving new information makes me nervous.

_____ 8. I have no difficulty concentrating on instructions given to me.

_____ 9. People who try to change my mind make me anxious.

_____ 10. I always feel relaxed when listening to others.

Scoring: Add up your scores for items 1, 2, 6, 8, and 10. Now add up your scores for items 3, 4, 5, 7, and 9. Subtract the total of the second set of answers from the first total to get a composite score. If your final score is positive, you have a tendency toward listener apprehension; the higher the score, the more apprehension you report. If your final score is negative, you have little or no apprehension.

Source: Wheeless (1975). Adapted with permission.

simply shuts down and responds with anger. Snape, on the other hand, refuses to acknowledge any talent or hard work on Harry's part. Both characters, because of their mutual dislike and distrust, are guilty of **defensive listening**, responding with aggression and arguing with the speaker without fully listening to the message.

We've all been in situations in which someone seems to be confronting us about an unpleasant topic. But if you respond with aggressiveness and argue before completely listening to the speaker, you'll experience more anxiety, probably because you'll anticipate not being effective in the listening encounter (Schrodt & Wheeless, 2001). If you find yourself listening defensively, consider the tips shown in **Table 6.2**.

Selective Listening. When you zero in only on bits of information that interest you, disregarding other messages or parts of messages, you are engaging in **selective listening**. Selective listening is common in situations where you are feeling defensive or insecure. For example, if you really hate working on a group project with your classmate Lara, you may only pay attention to the disagreeable or negative things that she says. If she says, "I can't make it to the meeting on Thursday at eight," you shut off, placing another check in the "Lara is lazy" column of proof. However, you might miss the rest of Lara's message—perhaps she has a good reason for missing the meeting or maybe she's suggesting that you reschedule.

Selective listening can work with positive messages and impressions as well, although it is equally unethical in such situations. Imagine that you're a manager at a small company. Four of your five employees were in place when you took your job, but you were the one who hired Micah. Since hiring well makes you look good as a manager, you might tend to focus on Micah's accomplishments and the feedback from others in the organization about Micah's performance. He may be a great employee, but you should listen to compliments about other employees as well, particularly when making decisions about promotions.

To improve our communication, particularly when we're feeling apprehensive or defensive, we must take care not to avoid particular messages or close our ears to communication that makes us uncomfortable. Being mindful of our tendency to behave in this manner is the first step in addressing this common communication pitfall.

Selfish Listening. Selfish listeners hear only the information that they find useful for achieving specific goals. For example, your colleague Lucia may seem really engaged in your discussion about some negative interactions you've had with Ryan, your boyfriend. But if she's only listening because she's

Table 6.2 Steps to Avoid Defensive Listening

Tip	Example
Hear the speaker out	Don't rush into an argument without knowing the other person's position. Wait for the speaker to finish before constructing your own arguments.
Consider the speaker's motivations	Think of the speaker's reasons for saying what is being said. The person may be tired, ill, or frustrated. Don't take it personally.
Use nonverbal communication	Take a deep breath and smile slightly (but sincerely) at the speaker. Your disarming behavior may be enough to force the speaker to speak more reasonably.
Provide calm feedback	After the speaker finishes, repeat what you think was said and ask if you understood the message correctly. Often a speaker on the offensive will back away from an aggressive stance when confronted with an attempt at understanding.

interested in Ryan and wants to get a sense of your relationship's vulnerability, then she's listening selfishly.

Selfish listening can also be **monopolistic listening**, or listening to control the communication interaction. We're all guilty of this to some degree—particularly when we're engaged in conflict situations. Suppose your grades declined last semester. Your father says, "I really think you need to focus more on school. I'm not sure I want to shell out more money for tuition next semester if your grades get worse." You may not take his advice seriously if all you're doing while he's talking is plotting a response that will persuade him to pay next semester's tuition.

Hurtful Listening. Hurtful listening also focuses on the self, but it's more direct—and perhaps even more unethical—than selfish listening. *Attacking* is a response to someone else's message with negative evaluations ("That was a stupid thing to say!"). *Ambushing* is more strategic. An ambusher listens specifically to find weaknesses in others—things they're sensitive about—and pulls those weaknesses out at strategic or embarrassing times. So if Mai cries to Scott about failing her calculus final and Scott is later looking for a way to discredit Mai, he might say something like, "I'm not sure you're the right person to help us draw up a budget, Mai. Math isn't exactly your strong suit, is it?"

At other times, we don't intend our listening to be hurtful, but we still end up offending others or being inconsiderate of their feelings. **Insensitive listening** occurs when we fail to pay attention to the emotional content of someone's message, instead taking it at face value. Your friend Adam calls to tell you that he got rejected from Duke Law School. Adam had mentioned to you that his LSAT scores made Duke a long shot, so you accept his message for what it appears to be: a factual statement about a situation. But you fail to hear the disappointment in his voice—even if Duke was a long shot, it was his top choice as well as a chance to be geographically closer to his partner, who lives in North Carolina. Had you paid attention to Adam's nonverbal cues, you might have known that he needed some comforting words.

> **Ethics and You**
>
> Do you know any people who engage in the unethical listening behaviors described? Is that behavior frequent or a rare slip? How do these tendencies affect your interactions with these people? Do you ever find yourself engaging in such unethical behaviors?

Pseudolistening. When you become impatient or bored with someone's communication messages, you may find yourself engaging in **pseudolistening**—pretending to listen by nodding or saying "uh-huh" when you're really not paying attention at all. One of the many downsides of pseudolistening is that you can actually miss important information or offend your communication partner and damage the relationship. Pseudolistening is a common trope in television sitcoms—when Homer Simpson nods absently (daydreaming about food or some other inappropriate topic) even though he hasn't listened to a word his boss has said, we find it funny and perhaps a little familiar. But in real life, implying that we have listened when we have not can have disastrous consequences: we miss instructions, neglect tasks that we have implied we would complete, and fail to meet others' needs.

LearningCurve
bedfordstmartins.com/commandyou

Listening in Context

Chances are, you've recognized bits of yourself or your friends scattered throughout this chapter. We have all, at one time or another, felt defensive, nervous, bored, or lazy and found that we were less effective listeners because of it. But you probably don't feel that way all the time. You might find yourself to be a great listener in certain situations and weak in others. That's because, as with every other part of communication, our listening skills and abilities are affected by context (Bommelje, Houston, & Smither, 2003). In this section, we examine the ways in which the context of communication influences listening.

The Relational and Situational Listening Contexts

Imagine that you're a shy, introverted person, standing in a crowd of people at a party or a conference. You positively hate events like this, vastly preferring interpersonal or very small group activities. Your friend Yvonne asked you to come here, but as usual, she is late. (You've stopped going to the movies with Yvonne since it's pointless to pay $12 for a ticket when you'll miss the first half hour of the film.) Suddenly, Yvonne calls you on your cell phone and begins a hasty explanation: "I'm sorry I'm late, but . . ." You may hear Yvonne's excuse, but are you listening?

The situation we're in and the relationship we have with other communicators at any given time have a profound effect on our communication. When you're in an unfamiliar or uncomfortable place or at a formal event (such as a funeral, a wedding, or a professional conference), you may experience the sort of listening apprehension that we discussed earlier. And in some situations, such as a party, background noise can make it hard for you to listen. You've most likely been in a situation where so many people were talking or music was playing so loudly that you literally had to scream to be heard. In cases like this, it feels as if it takes all your energy and concentration just to make out a conversational partner's words. Clearly, this kind of situational context can make communication more challenging.

The relational context can also create problems. Take your friend Yvonne. As great a friend as she is, you perceive her chronic lateness as a sign that she doesn't value your time or friendship. So when she tries to explain why she's late for this particular event, you hardly pay attention. You offer no empathy, and you don't think deeply about her message. Perhaps it's another excuse about car trouble or running into an old friend on her way to meet you. But maybe it isn't—and there's something far more serious going on with Yvonne. The only way to find out is to listen actively.

MATT GROENING

⬦ What might Mr. Burns have just said? Homer Simpson doesn't know because he was pseudolistening.

The Cultural Listening Context

In various parts of the United States and abroad, you will encounter listening behaviors different from your own. As you travel or do business across the country or the world, you'll likely find it necessary to understand and adapt to listening differences.

When you think about traits and habits that make someone a "good" listener or a "bad" listener, you're often thinking about how your culture judges listening ability. For example, indirect styles of communication, common in Eastern cultures like those of China and Japan, require listener-responsible communication that saves face for the speaker. So a listener would be expected not to question the speaker directly, to construct meaning and understanding from the context of the situation, and to accommodate the speaker's needs more than the listener's (Lustig & Koester, 2006). Speaker-responsible listening, common in Western cultures like those found in the United States and

Canada, is more direct; the speaker usually tells the listener what he or she wants the listener to know. The listener can ask direct questions without offending the speaker, and both speaker and listener may be assertive without threatening the relationship or making the situation uncomfortable.

In addition to actual listening behaviors themselves, *perceptions* of appropriate listening vary among cultures. One study of competence and listening found that U.S. Caucasians are perceived as expressive listeners who exhibit nonverbal facilitators (like nodding, saying "mmm-hmmm," and the like). Caucasians are also seen as using more questioning techniques to clarify and comprehend the speaker's message. Latinos and Asian Americans are perceived as somewhat less expressive than whites, and African Americans are perceived as the least expressive listeners among these groups (Dillon & McKenzie, 1998). If you are comfortable or aware of only the preferred listening style of your own culture, miscommunication can occur. So Jennifer, a Colombian American, speaking with Jonathan, an African American colleague,

might judge Jonathan as an ineffective listener if he is less expressive than she would hope as she complains about their mutual boss. She needs to remember that culture—including gender—is at play in this situation.

In traveling around the globe, you will also find that expressiveness is viewed very differently in different cultures. Whereas many Westerners consider deep feelings private (or to be shared only with intimate relational partners), other cultures, including that of Hindus in Fiji and the Ommura in New Guinea, do not regard private feelings as sacrosanct; they communicate a variety of emotions to others to build shared experiences (Brenneis, 1990). Table 6.3 shows suggestions for communicating with people of different cultures.

A discussion of culture would not be complete without thinking about how your concepts of masculinity and femininity affect your perceptions of listening competence. For example, men in the United States are usually discouraged from expressing intense emotions in public (Brody, 2000). This reluctance to react emotionally to information may give the appearance that men are not listening. Expectations about

Table 6.3 **Tips for Communicating Across Cultures**

Tactic	Explanation	Example
Recognize cultural differences	When communicating with someone from a different culture, keep in mind that factors such as country of origin, religion, gender, educational level, and socioeconomic status all play into our values and beliefs about communication. If you can, learn about the person's background, and ask questions.	If your future mother-in-law is a devout Catholic from France and you are a nonreligious person from St. Louis, you might want to learn more about French culture and Catholicism; you might ask your significant other questions about how to get to know Mom.
Clarify behaviors as appropriate	Pay attention to the cultural needs of the listener. If you find that cultural differences are preventing good communication, tell the speaker or be silent to observe context and nonverbal behaviors.	"I don't think I'm understanding you correctly. Can you say that in another way for me, please?"
Adjust to differences	Ask more questions if necessary; ask the speaker to work with you to bridge the gap between cultural differences.	"I'm sure I'm not getting the complete picture. Can you give me an example of the problem to help me understand it better?"

appropriate feminine behavior encourage women to exhibit *more* verbal and nonverbal feedback when listening, such as nodding and smiling more and using more encouraging filler words ("Really?" "Oh, wow," "Right"). Most research indicates that an individual's role (being a parent, for example) accounts for more listening differences than the sex of the listener does (Duncan & Fiske, 1977; Johnston, Weaver, Watson, & Barker, 2000). Nonetheless, listening stereotypes are still powerful and make their way into entertainment and advertising at every level. In the episode "I Am Peter, Hear Me Roar," *Family Guy*'s Peter decides to get in touch with his feminine side and calls his buddy Quagmire "just to talk." He wants to listen to what's going on with his friend and have his friend listen to him in turn. Quagmire is so uncomfortable with this situation that he slams down the phone!

⬧ The gang from *Family Guy* believes that listening— and the verbal and nonverbal expressions that accompany it—is for women only!

> **Culture and You**
>
> Have you ever felt stereotyped in terms of how you were expected to listen to a friend, coworker, or family member? If so, what were the other person's expectations, and how do you think they were formed?

Such differences are not necessarily biologically based, however. Listener behavior is not consistent in all situations. For example, in brief debates, South African men engaged in more of these supportive verbal and nonverbal cues when they addressed female audiences, indicating that situational and relational context may be more powerful than gendered expectations (Dixon & Foster, 1998).

The Technology Listening Context

Anish Patel could have walked across campus to attend his microeconomics course in person. But why bother, when the lecture is streaming live over the campus network? Instead of listening with his classmates in a crowded lecture hall, he watches on his laptop in the comfort of his own apartment (Gabriel, 2010).

Russell Hampton is both a father and the president of a book and magazine publishing unit of Walt Disney Company. When he was driving his daughter and her teenage friends to a play, he listened to their conversation about an actor in a Disney movie and tried to join in the conversation. Suddenly, the girls became very quiet. Russell could see his daughter texting in the rearview mirror and chided her for being rude and ignoring her friends. He later discovered that all three teens were texting each other so that they could listen to one another without Russell listening to them (Holson, 2008).

As these two examples illustrate, technology can be both helpful and hurtful to the listening process. Anish Patel might listen more effectively in a classroom with the energy of live interaction where questions can be asked and notes compared. But he might also be able to process the lecture more effectively by rewinding and listening again to sections of the lecture without distraction. Russell Hampton might be hurt that his daughter and her friends shut him out of their conversation, but their texts give them a powerful way of listening to one another.

Listening to messages in various technological contexts requires a lot more effort than other forms of communication. For example, when you talk on the phone, you rely on verbal messages as well as vocal nonverbal messages (tone of voice, speaking rate, silences, and so on) because you lack other nonverbal cues such as body movement and eye behavior. But when you read your mom's e-mail or you text your significant other, you often lack both components.

Practice listening with your eyes as discussed in this chapter. When you go to your next class, observe your instructor or whoever is speaking. Form an overall impression of the speaker from nonverbal cues such as body movements, eye behavior, and gestures. What emotions do they suggest? Do they match the verbal message being conveyed?

For this reason, you must be sure to listen actively to the cues you do have at your disposal. When your friend Sheila capitalizes a word in an e-mail, she's giving emphasis to a particular point; you can show her that you've listened by making sure to address that particular point. In general, you show your communication partners that you've listened to their e-mails when you respond to all the questions or concerns that they raised. You're not listening competently if you respond to your father's questions about when you're coming home next with an e-mail that details what you had for lunch. Similarly, you listen well when you enter a chat room and read the sequence of comments before responding (rather than blurting out a response to the first post you see).

Technology and You

What technologies, if any, do you prefer for listening? Do you enjoy talking on the phone, or do you miss the presence of body language when communicating that way? Do you prefer chatting online or via text message, or do you like the immediacy of in-person listening? Can you tell when people are listening to you when you communicate using technology? How?

And of course, using technology competently also means taking into account the receiver of your message. Consider how your friend Eddie in Milwaukee would want to hear the news that you've broken up with his cousin whom you've been dating for two years: Through a text message? On Twitter? Over the phone? You'll want to choose the channel that is the most effective and appropriate for the occasion.

LearningCurve
bedfordstmartins.com/commandyou

Back to } Stealth Listening

We started this chapter with a discussion of the role listening plays in doctors' diagnoses of illness and disease. Let's consider the ways that listening skills and barriers affect the doctor-patient interaction and health care in general.

- Effective listening involves thoughtful and intelligent *active* interactions with patients, not just a smiling bedside manner. For doctors like Erno Daniel, active listening means engaging patients, carefully assessing what they say, and inviting them to say more, a form of informational listening. On another level, Daniel's diagnoses involve critical listening — a constant mental process of testing and refining alternate hypotheses that might explain the symptoms and findings at hand (Lawson & Daniel, 2010).

- It's not just the doctor who has listening responsibilities. Daniel (2008) provides worksheets

to help patients inform their doctors about their symptoms and their lives. Patients should also come prepared to ask questions—What causes are possible? What tests could give clues? What multiple processes or conditions might be at work in my case?—and to carefully listen to the responses.

- Listening apprehension is a huge barrier for many patients. They may be concerned or preoccupied with anxiety about their health, with fears that their concerns will sound foolish, or with feelings of embarrassment or modesty during a medical exam. Such situational and environmental concerns often intensify listening apprehension.

Your Reference

} A Study Tool
Now that you have finished reading this chapter, you can:

Outline the listening process and styles of listening:

- **Hearing** is the physiological process of perceiving sound; **listening** is the process of recognizing, understanding, and interpreting the message (p. 120).
- We improve listening skills by focusing on the voluntary parts of the process: **selecting**, choosing one sound over others; **attending**, focusing on the message or sound; **understanding**, making sense of the message; **remembering**, recalling information; and **responding**, giving feedback (pp. 121–122).
- **Active listening** involves making choices about selecting, attending, and so on, and is more competent than **passive listening** (p. 122). **Listening fidelity** is the degree to which the thoughts of the listener agree with the intentions of the source of the message following their communication (p. 122).
- **People-oriented listeners** listen with relationships in mind (p. 122).
- **Action-oriented listeners** focus on tasks (p. 122).
- **Content-oriented listeners** ⊙ carefully evaluate what they hear (p. 122).
- **Time-oriented listeners** ⊙ prefer information that is clear and to the point (p. 122).
- Most people develop multiple listening preferences (pp. 122–123).

List the reasons we listen:

- **Informational listening** is used to understand a message (pp. 123–124).
- In **critical listening,** you evaluate or analyze information, evidence, ideas, or opinions and use critical thinking (pp. 124–125).
- **Empathic listening** is an attempt to know how another person feels, often using **paraphrasing** to recognize and elaborate on the other's feelings (p. 125).
- **Appreciative listening** is used when the goal is simply to appreciate the sounds, such as music (p. 125).

Identify challenges to good listening and their remedies:

- **Listening barriers** are factors that interfere with our ability to comprehend information and respond appropriately (p. 128).
- Distractions such as suffering from allergies and the sound of crying babies are examples of environmental factors that impair our ability to listen (p. 128).
- Hearing loss challenges can be overcome with understanding of nonverbal behaviors (pp. 128–129). Auditory processing challenges (for example, ADD) are faced by many who have normal hearing (p. 129).
- **Multitasking**, attending to several things at once, limits focus on any one task (p. 129).
- A boring speaker or topic can be hard to follow, and on the flip side, overexcitement can be distracting (p. 130).
- Talking may be regarded as more powerful than listening (pp. 130–131).
- Overconfidence may cause us to not pay careful attention during communication (p. 131).
- **Listening apprehension**, anxiety or dread associated with listening, may hinder concentration (p. 131).

Identify attitudinal and ethical factors that inhibit listening:

- **Defensive listening** ⊙ is responding with aggression and arguing with the speaker without fully listening to the message (pp. 131–133).
- **Selective listening** ⊙ is zeroing in on bits of information that interest you, disregarding other messages or parts of messages (p. 133).
- Selfish listeners listen for their own needs and may practice **monopolistic listening**, or listening in order to control the communication interaction (pp. 133–134).
- **Insensitive listening** occurs when we fail to pay attention to the emotional content of someone's message and just take it at face value (p. 134).
- **Pseudolistening** is pretending to listen while not really paying attention (p. 134).

Describe how contexts affect listening:

- Different situations (a crowded party, a professional conference) create different listening challenges (p. 135).
- The dynamics of the relationship between communicators can also change how you listen (p. 135).
- As in all aspects of communication, the cultural context affects listening behavior (pp. 135–137).
- It may seem that we don't listen when we communicate electronically, but technology is an important context for listening (pp. 137–138).

✓ Look for **LearningCurve** throughout
the chapter to help you review.
bedfordstmartins.com/commandyou

7 } Developing and Maintaining Relationships

Mary Marquez is a U.S. Army wife. She's strong; she has to be. For a good part of the year, she manages her job, two teenage sons, their house, and her relationships, all while missing—and worrying about—her husband, Justin. When Justin is home, Mary obviously wants to spend time with him. But as soon as she's feeling comfortable, he's sent off to some other part of the world and she's on her own again.

Mary and Justin are like many other families whose military-related separations put a strain on their communication and relationships. Justin and Mary often don't know when and where Justin will deploy, and this uncertainty strains every member of the family as they struggle between the independence they must have and the connectedness they desire (Merolla, 2010b). Some military spouses

deal with it by not dealing with it at all, engaging in arguments or shutting down communication completely. But Mary and Justin work on their communication. They hide notes for one another around the house while he is home. When he is away, they plan times when they can connect online, and during those conversations they try to focus on "normal" things like talking about their days or discussing a book they are both reading. Mary said these behaviors "made it feel more routine and made it feel like he wasn't so far away" (Sahlstein, Maguire, & Timmerman, 2009, p. 431).

The distance and time zone differences are still difficult; when family members miss a connection, it can lead to hard feelings and misunderstandings. For example, one of Mary's friends described how disgruntled her husband became when she and the kids weren't at home waiting for his call.

After you have finished reading this chapter, you will be able to

Explain key aspects of interpersonal relationships.

Describe how and why we form relationships.

List the advantages and disadvantages of relationships.

Describe the factors that influence self-disclosure.

Outline the predictable stages of most relationships.

between two people who have a relationship and are influenced by the partner's messages. You engage in interpersonal communication in your most intimate relationships—when you sit down to a heartfelt conversation with your significant other or when you catch up with your best friend. But you also engage in interpersonal communication when you talk with your professor about your midterm grade and when you chat with your waiter at Chili's. Even though your relationship with your friends or significant other is probably more important to you than your relationship with a waiter, competent communication allows you to meet personal needs, whether it's support after a hard day's work or getting the right dinner order.

Let's take a closer look at interpersonal relationships and the communication that takes place in them by examining the types of relationships we form, why and how we do so, and what happens once we're in them.

A s you learned in Chapter 1, people need to be in relationships with other people: relationships help us meet our needs for companionship and intellectual stimulation and also help us meet our physical needs. Could Frodo of *The Lord of the Rings* have survived without his friend Samwise Gamgee helping stave off the evil effects of the ring? Of course not! The military families we described here are no different; their relationships are important to their survival too.

In this chapter, we focus on **interpersonal relationships**, the interconnections and interdependence between two individuals. To understand these relationships, we need to be aware of the role communication plays in them. **Interpersonal communication** is the exchange of verbal and nonverbal messages

Types of Interpersonal Relationships

Martin asks Pete, "Do you know my friend Jake?" Pete responds, "I've met him once or twice. He seems OK." In two short sentences, we gain information about the relationships at play: to Martin, Jake is a friend; to Pete, he's just an acquaintance. We're all involved in multiple relationships, and we distinguish between them in countless ways: acquaintances, colleagues, friends, close friends, family members, romantic partners, virtual strangers we see all the time (like a Starbucks barista), and so on. Every person has a complex **relational network** or web of relationships that connect

> Even though your relationship with your friends or significant other is probably more important to you than your relationship with a waiter, competent communication allows you to meet personal needs, whether it's support after a hard day's work or getting the right dinner order.

individuals to one another. In this section, we focus on family relationships, friendships, and romantic partnerships, as well as online relationships.

Family

For some people, the term *family* refers to immediate relatives who live in the same household. For others, it means a more extended family that includes grandparents, aunts, uncles, and cousins. Still others use the term to describe groups of people whom they are intimately connected and committed to, even without blood or civil ties, like some fraternal organizations or religious communities. But for our purposes, a **family** is a small social group bound by ties of blood, civil contract (such as marriage, civil union, or adoption), and a commitment to care for and be responsible for one another, usually in a shared household.

Our first and most basic relationships are with family. From them, we learn communication skills and develop characteristics that affect how we

Culture and You

What characteristics do you consider most important in family relationships? Do your family members meet those expectations? How do your friends' family relationships and communications differ from yours? How are they similar?

interact with other people throughout our lives. TLC's reality series *Little People, Big World* revolves around the daily family life of the Roloffs, led by parents Matt and Amy, who are both dwarfs (little people), and their four children. What's truly endearing about the show are the relationships and communication between the family members as they face living in a world where everything is built for taller people. How does Zach, who is also little, relate to his average-height twin, who is nearly two feet

📍 *Little People, Big World* depicts struggles and triumphs that any family can relate to while also representing dwarfism in mainstream media.

Table 7.1 **Family Communication Qualities**

Communication Standard	Examples
Openness	• Being able to talk when something is wrong • Talking about sensitive issues like sex or drugs • Sharing feelings
Structural stability	• Having at least one person in the family whom everyone listens to and obeys • Dealing with emotional issues only when everyone can handle them
Affection	• Being loving and affectionate with one another • Saying affectionate things like "I love you"
Emotional and instrumental support	• Helping each other • Being able to count on each other • Knowing support will be there
Mind reading	• Knowing what's going on with each other without asking • Understanding how the other feels without discussing it
Politeness	• Never being rude or inconsiderate • Not talking back
Discipline	• Having clear rules for family members • Knowing that there are consequences for breaking family rules
Humor or sarcasm	• Being able to tease other family members • Poking fun at each other
Regular routine interaction	• Meeting regularly to discuss things • Setting aside time to communicate
Avoidance	• Avoiding topics that are too personal • Agreeing to skirt issues that are painful

Dr. John Caughlin at the University of Illinois conducted three studies of 1,023 undergraduate students and found that people generally agree that these ten qualities constitute "excellent family communication" (2003).

taller than he is? How do idealistic dreamer Matt and logical planner Amy communicate about important family decisions? Through all the mishaps around their Oregon farm, the Roloffs deal with one another with openness, affection, discipline, and humor—qualities that reveal strong family communication (see Table 7.1). Moreover, Matt and Amy teach their children the beliefs, values, and communication skills they need to face life's challenges, to feel loved and secure, and to achieve success both professionally and personally (Ducharme, Doyle, & Markiewicz, 2002). These communications are essential for enriching family life and positively developing younger family members (Canary & Dainton, 2003; Guerrero, Andersen, & Afifi, 2007; Mansson, Myers, & Turner, 2010).

Friendship

As individuals grow and interact with people outside their families, they establish new, nonfamily relationships. **Friendship** is a close and caring relationship between two people that is perceived as mutually satisfying and beneficial. Friendship benefits include emotional support, companionship, and help coping with major life stressors (Rawlins, 1992, 2008). Children who form successful friendships with others perform better academically and demonstrate fewer aggressive tendencies than those who do not (Doll, 1996; Hartup & Stevens, 1997; Newcomb & Bagwell, 1995; Rawlins, 1994; Weisz & Wood, 2005). And secure, stable friendships and family relationships serve to enhance children's ability to process communication behaviors (Dwyer et al., 2010).

Although everyone has a personal opinion as to what qualities a friend should possess, research finds agreement on six important characteristics of friendship (Pearson & Spitzberg, 1990):

- **Availability:** making time for one another
- **Caring:** feelings of concern for the happiness and well-being of each other
- **Honesty:** being open and truthful with each other, even if that means saying things that are hard to hear (Shuangyue & Merolla, 2006)
- **Trust:** being honest and maintaining confidentiality
- **Loyalty:** maintaining relationships despite disagreements and framing differences as positives (Baxter, Foley, & Thatcher, 2008)
- **Empathy:** communicating the ability to feel what each other is feeling and experiencing

The extent to which you and your friend share these characteristics helps build the relational context of your relationship, as you learned in Chapter 1. The amount of trust, loyalty, honesty, and other characteristics that you experience together affects you as you construct and decode messages.

Romantic Relationships

What ideas, thoughts, and feelings come to mind when you think about romantic relationships? Do you think of romantic dinners, jealousy, butterflies in your stomach? Perhaps you think about sex or about commitment and love (Tierney, 2007).

Love can be used to describe feelings other than romantic ones, including our feelings for our families, friends, pets, or anything that evokes strong feelings of like or appreciation (as in "I love the Philadelphia Eagles" or "I love burritos"). But we typically define **love** within the context of relationships as a deep affection

---

📍 Kate Winslet and Leonardo DiCaprio first starred together as lovers in *Titanic* and have played other romantic pairs over the years, but they reap the benefits of a close and supportive friendship rather than a romantic relationship off screen.

for and attachment to another person involving emotional ties, with varying degrees of passion, commitment, and **intimacy**, or closeness, and understanding of the relational partner (Sternberg, 1988). There are many types of love that can characterize different relationships—or even the same relationship at different times. For example, the love between Anna and Mario, married for fifty-seven years, is probably not the same as when they were first wed. Studies involving hundreds of people revealed six categories of love: *eros* (erotic, sexual love), *ludus* (playful, casual love), *storge* (love that lacks passion), *pragma* (committed, practical love), *mania* (intense, romantic love), and *agape* (selfless, romantic love) (Hendrick & Hendrick, 1992; Lee, 1973). These types of love are explained in detail in Table 7.2. Some relationships may be characterized by only one of these types, while others may move through two or more types over time.

The complexities of romantic love can be astounding, but the desire to attain it is as universal as it is timeless. In fact, the value of relationships and the characteristics associated with love and commitment between two people are fairly consistent regardless of culture, though in countries where marriage is voluntary and divorce is accessible, there are more positive associations with marriage than in countries where less freedom exists (Fowers, Fışıloğlu, & Procacci, 2008). Studies also show that relational harmony has both physical and psychological benefits, as you can see in Figure 7.1 (Parker-Pope, 2010a). Same-sex couples in long-term, committed relationships share the same benefits of meaningful commitment (such as life satisfaction and general well-being) as other romantic couples (Kurdek, 1989; Lipman, 1986), and cohabiting unmarried couples enjoy greater well-being than single people (though not as much as married couples) (Brown, 2000; Horwitz & White, 1998).

Perceptions of love and romance are also somewhat consistent across cultures: one study found that

Table 7.2 **Types of Love**

Type	Description	Explanation
Eros	Beauty and sexuality	Sex is the most important aspect of erotic love. This type of relationship is quite intense, both emotionally and physically, focusing on beauty and attractiveness.
Ludus	Entertainment and excitement	*Ludus* means "play" in Latin, and the ludic lover views love as a game. Ludic love does not require great commitment.
Storge	Peacefulness and slowness	*Storge* is a type of love that lacks passion and excitement. Storgic lovers often share common interests but rarely disclose any feelings about their relationship.
Pragma	Deed, task, work	In Greek, *pragma* means "life work." Pragmatic lovers are extremely logical and practical. They want a long-term relationship with someone who shares their goals in life.
Mania	Elation and depression	This is the love that is often referred to as "romantic love." It exhibits extreme feelings and is full of intense excitement, but it reaches a peak and then quickly fades away.
Agape	Compassion and selflessness	In this type of love, the individual gives willingly and expects nothing in return. This type of lover can care for others without close ties; a deep relationship is not necessary for agapic love to develop.

Psychological Health
Fewer mood swings
Less risk of depression
Lowered levels of stress
  hormones

Physical Health
Lowered risk of diseases
  like diabetes and heart
  disease

Healing
Stronger immune system
  and quicker healing

○ **Figure 7.1 Effects of Relational Harmony.**
Drawing on research from Parker-Pope (2010a)
on marital discord, this figure represents
some of the benefits that people in happy
relationships might expect.
Source: Parker-Pope (2010a)

📍 Romantic couples, regardless of sexual orientation, age, race, or ethnicity, all enjoy
similar benefits of being in a relationship: intimacy and commitment.

among Americans, Chinese, Japanese, and Koreans, differences in notions of love were not pronounced, and respondents from all four countries reported that happiness and warmth were associated with love (Kline, Horton, & Zhang, 2005).

Online Relationships

Holly and Delia's friendship began long before they met face to face. As regular readers of a blog, the two women began posting in the site's comments section. Over time, they developed a friendly conversation that led to direct texting correspondence. When Holly found herself traveling on business to Delia's hometown of Phoenix, the two finally met.

Technology and You

Do you have any relationships that began online and eventually moved to in-person communication? How did the way these relationships developed compare to relationships that began face to face? Do you consider technology helpful in or more of a barrier to fostering new friendships? Why?

For years, online relationships were considered impersonal, lacking the richness of nonverbal cues found in face-to-face relationships (Tidwell & Walther, 2002). But Joe Walther (1996) found that mediated communicators often took advantage of the lack of these cues to gain greater control over both their messages and their presentation of self. His **social information processing theory** (SIP) (1996; Walther & Parks, 2002) argues that communicators use unique language and stylistic cues in their online messages to develop relationships that are just as close as those that develop face to face—but using text takes more time to become intimate. Online communicators often even develop what Walther (1996) calls **hyperpersonal communication**, communication that is even *more* personal and intimate than face-to-face interaction. Freed from the less-controllable nonverbal cues (such as appearances or nervous fidgeting),

online communicators can carefully craft their messages and cultivate idealized perceptions of each other (see Walther & Ramirez, 2009). Indeed, relational partners often feel less constrained in the online environment (Caplan, 2001). As we saw with Holly and Delia above, they can develop rich and meaningful relationships both online and off (Anderson & Emmers-Sommer, 2006; Antheunis, Valkenburg, & Peter, 2010; Parks & Roberts, 1998; Pauley & Emmers-Sommer, 2007).

In a similar manner, romances can also bud and be maintained through the use of electronic media. Many couples today first "meet" online through a dating site like Match.com or eHarmony, and their initial interactions are entirely electronic; they only meet face to face after a series of messages, e-mails, and perhaps phone calls. Established couples maintain long-distance relationships by using e-mail, video chat, texts, Facebook, and phone calls to communicate feelings. As with friend relationships, such couples tend to communicate greater intimacy than geographically close partners; they are more likely to avoid conflict and problematic topics when using these media (Stafford, 2010). On the other hand, their online communication may avoid the very behaviors that are necessary to manage the future of the relationship face to face.

In all types of relationships, online communication enables us to maintain intimacy with others over great distances. Sharing photos, videos, and stories on Facebook, Twitter, or blogs allows us to share our lives with family and friends in other states and countries. And regular texting, video chats, phone calls, and e-mail messages keep partners close and aware of each other's lives (Bergen, 2010; Maguire, 2007; Maguire & Kinney, 2010; Mansson, Myers, & Turner, 2010; Merolla, 2010a; Stafford, 2005). So whereas once a group graduating from college or leaving the military would scatter around the country or region and gradually lose touch, today these individuals can much more easily remain parts of one another's daily lives if they choose to make use of all or some of the available media.

Other online relationships include online communication that is merely part of the larger relationship.

Technology and You

Do you have any relationships that exist only online and that have never moved to in-person communication? Do you consider these relationships different from other ones in your life? Are they more intimate or less so?

For example, work colleagues frequently e-mail each other or video chat throughout the day. However, they still see each other in the hallways or in meetings. In fact, some married and cohabiting couples report that they will use computer-mediated communication to discuss their conflicts, even though they could handle it face to face, because it helps them remain less emotionally involved and defensive (Quenqua, 2010). Perhaps this is because e-mail or Facebook messages do not require immediate responses, allowing the communication partners time to formulate appropriate and thoughtful messages.

LearningCurve
bedfordstmartins.com/commandyou

Why We Form Relationships

We've already established that romantic relationships are a universal desire, but you might also expect that collectivist cultures (like the Japanese culture) would place more importance on other types of relationships than fiercely individualistic cultures such as we find in the United States. But research fails to demonstrate large differences between these culture types, revealing instead that individuals in all cultures value their relationships (Diener & Diener, 1995; Endo, Heine, & Lehman, 2000; Landsford, Antonucci, Akiyama, & Takahashi, 2005). In this section, we examine why everyone forms relationships and which factors influence how they're formed.

Functions of Relationships

In U.S. prisons today, more than twenty-five thousand inmates are serving their time in solitary confinement—removed from the general prison population, isolated in small cells with little human contact (Sullivan, 2006). Prison officials consider this necessary to maintain order, but some activists worry about the harshness of the measure. They hold that human beings form and maintain relationships in order to satisfy basic human needs—for companionship, for stimulation, for achieving goals—and it is cruel to deny those needs (Ramirez, Sunnafrank, & Goei, 2010).

Companionship. Humans feel a natural need for companionship and **inclusion**—to involve others in their lives and to be involved in the lives of others. Thus loneliness can be a major motivation behind some people's desire for a relationship. In fact, psychological problems such as anxiety, stress, depression, alcoholism, drug abuse, and poor health have all been tied to loneliness (Canary & Spitzberg, 1993; Segrin & Passalacqua, 2010). Depriving prisoners of companionship may be an effective form of punishment, but it may also be damaging to them on a psychological level, dashing any hopes for eventual rehabilitation.

Stimulation. People have a need for intellectual, emotional, and physical stimulation (Krcmar & Greene, 1999; Rubin, Perse, & Powell, 1985). Nobody enjoys being bored! So we seek out diversions like television or music. But interaction with another person occurs on a personal, unique level and frequently provides multiple types of stimulation at once. In fact, the emotional communication we receive when our partners are involved with us contributes to our relational satisfaction (Guerrero, Farinelli, & McEwan, 2009).

Consider some of the communication relationships you have with various people over the course of a day. You might chat with your roommates or your family in the morning about nerves over an upcoming exam. You see your professor at office hours

◊ Senator John McCain cites communication with fellow prisoners of war, even if fleeting, as one of the factors that helped him survive solitary confinement in Vietnam: "Even if it's only a wave or a wink . . . it makes all the difference" (2008, para. 1).

help you. This is the argument that is made to justify solitary confinement. When particularly dangerous prisoners are kept in isolation, they are unable to form relationships that might help them accomplish dangerous goals (such as gang membership or terrorist networking) (Sullivan, 2006).

> **Ethics and You**
> When you enter into a relationship primarily as a means of achieving a goal, how aware should the other person be of your reasons? Would you feel comfortable if the other person thought the relationship had more of a companionship or stimulation function, even if you considered it more practical and goal related?

to share an interesting story related to your class. You check up on your old high school buddies on Facebook. And then you meet up with your significant other, who greets you with a warm hug after a long day.

These innate needs for stimulation are why many people feel that solitary confinement is unethical and immoral.

Achieving Goals. Some people enter into relationships to achieve particular goals. Sometimes the goal is simply satisfying the needs we have discussed earlier: to alleviate loneliness or to provide stimulation. Other goals are more practical: if you have dreamed all your life about working in finance, you might seek relationships with influential people in that field through networking via your college alumni group or through an internship.

Often your initial motivation for developing a relationship is to see how a particular individual can

Interpersonal Attraction

Hollywood movies often deal with troubled relationships, but the movie *Julie and Julia* is different. It revolves around a young blogger attempting to find purpose in her life by cooking her way through Julia Child's famous cookbook, but this story plays against the reality of Child's life: her love of cooking and her marriage to Paul Child are the refreshing background for the rest of the film (Parker-Pope, 2010b). It depicts not only the exciting beginning of relationships but also the possibility of happy, easy, fun, interesting relationships in which people can remain attracted to one another for a lifetime.

As discussed previously, we seek relationships to meet basic needs for companionship, stimulation, and goal achievement. But our reasons for forming specific relationships are as individual and complex as we are and rooted in unique needs and motivations, which develop and change over our lives (Westmyer, DiCioccio, & Rubin, 1998). Let's examine how proximity, physical attraction, and similarity influence our likelihood of establishing particular relationships.

⬦ Julie and Julia's depiction of Julia Child's supportive and stimulating marriage to husband Paul is a look at the best of what interpersonal attraction can become: deep, lifelong companionship.

Proximity. As practical and unromantic as it sounds, one of the first criteria of relationship formation is simple **proximity**, or nearness. Think about how many of your friends you got to know because they sat next to you in elementary school, lived on the same dorm floor, or worked with you at Starbucks. Proximity is not just something we need in order to meet other people—it's what enables us to interact in ways that form and develop relationships.

Physical proximity was once the most important factor in determining and maintaining relationships. If you were to move away from a neighborhood, switch schools, or change jobs, you would likely lose touch with old friends and eventually make new friends in your new surroundings. But as noted earlier, modern technology allows us to redefine proximity: in addition to physical proximity, we have virtual proximity with those whom we are able to interact with regularly through mediated channels, even if they are physically quite far away. Nonetheless, if persons are not in physical proximity and fail to establish and maintain virtual proximity—for example, if they avoid social networking or don't have access to a computer—the chances of forming or maintaining relationships dwindle.

Physical Attraction. If you've ever watched a makeover show like *What Not to Wear* or *The Biggest Loser*, you've no doubt seen at least one client or contestant who expressed a belief that an improved physical appearance would enhance his or her prospects for love and career success. And as you've learned in earlier chapters, your physical appearance does indeed play an important role in attracting others, especially in the very early stages of a relationship, when first impressions are formed. People who are considered beautiful or attractive are often perceived as kinder, warmer, more intelligent, and more honest than unattractive people, and they have earlier opportunities for dating and marriage (Canary, Cody, & Manusov, 2008).

But before you focus only on physical attractiveness, remember two things. First, beauty is largely in the eye of the beholder, and individual tastes vary due to factors too numerous to discuss here, as well as cultural standards. For example, among the Padaung tribe of Southeast Asia, women wrap rings around their necks to push down their collarbones and upper ribs, giving them the illusion of having extremely long necks, considered a sign of beauty and wealth. Second, our communication affects perceptions of beauty. For example, Levinger (as cited in Canary, Cody, & Manusov, 2008) notes that "initial impressions of a beautiful person are outweighed by subsequent interaction" with the person. So your ability to use verbal and nonverbal messages appropriately and effectively probably has a lot more to do with your attractiveness than the perfection of your smile or the size of your jeans.

Similarity. The notion that "opposites attract" is so common in popular culture that many people take it as an undeniable truth. But despite the popularity of the concept, research shows that attraction is often based on the degree of *similarity* we have with another person, whether through shared hobbies, personality traits, backgrounds, appearances, or values (Gonzaga, Campos, & Bradbury, 2007). For example, consider close friends Liza and Cheryl. Liza is an African American student from Denver, a literature major, and a tomboy who loves the Broncos. Cheryl is a white student from Boston, majoring in engineering; she hates sports but follows fashion and rarely steps out of her dorm room without makeup. To an outsider, they seem like a mismatched pair. But ask either of them what they have in common and they'll roll off a list of similarities: both grew up in urban neighborhoods, attended all-girl Catholic high schools, love indie rock, and take great pride in their ability to quote J. R. R. Tolkien. So long as the relational partners feel that they have much in common, as Liza and Cheryl do, they feel similar and attracted to one another.

> **Culture and You**
>
> Consider someone with whom you share a very close relationship. In what ways are you culturally similar to this person? Are those similarities what attracted you in the first place?

Communication researchers have several ideas to explain how the degree of similarity works in relationships: attraction-similarity, matching, and genetic similarity (Amodio & Showers, 2005; Berscheid, 1985; Byrne, 1971; Fehr, 2001; Morry, 2005; Rushton, 1990). The **attraction-similarity hypothesis** suggests we project ourselves onto another person based on the attraction we feel for that person. Greater attraction to an individual leads to perceptions of greater similarity. The **matching hypothesis** also deals with attraction, positing that we seek relationships with

others who have comparable levels of attractiveness. Finally, the **genetic-similarity hypothesis** argues that two individuals who hail from the same ethnic group are more genetically similar than two individuals from different ethnic groups. According to this hypothesis, the impact on our behavior is that we tend to help, favor, and form relationships with people from our own ethnic groups (Rushton, 1980). Nonetheless, physical and social attraction coupled with more societal acceptance is contributing to more pervasive intercultural relationships (Balaji & Worawongs, 2010; McClintock, 2010). And as people from various cultures interact more and more, they have opportunities to practice relational skills (like self-disclosure and empathic listening) and see similarities in each other (Jin & Oh, 2010).

LearningCurve
bedfordstmartins.com/commandyou

Managing Relationship Dynamics

When it comes to relationship advice, you don't need to look far for what seems like "expertise." The self-help and magazine aisles at bookstores are brimming with advice on managing and maintaining healthy relationships. While Dr. Phil pontificates on TV and Candace Bushnell (the real-life counterpart of *Sex and the City*'s Carrie Bradshaw) offers insights on dating, communication scholars explore the way we manage relationships in a far more scientific way. In this section, we explore the dynamics of relationships on the assumption that our connections to others are constantly changing, growing, and evolving throughout our lives (Conville, 1991; John-Steiner, 1997; Knapp & Vangelisti, 2008).

Costs and Rewards

Every relationship has advantages and disadvantages for the parties involved. A close friendship may offer

What About You?

Determining Your Own Costs and Rewards

Consider the following list of traits and behaviors, and decide which you consider rewards and which costs in a romantic relationship. Write R1 next to rewards that you feel you must have from your partner and R2 next to those you see as less important. Write C1 next to costs that you simply couldn't tolerate from your partner and C2 next to costs that you could live with.

_____ Laughs at my jokes

_____ Is physically attractive

_____ Fits in with my family

_____ Dislikes sharing emotions

_____ Is career oriented

_____ Has views about religion different from mine

_____ Has an exciting personality

_____ Has annoying friends

_____ Is likely to be financially successful

_____ Comes from a close-knit family

_____ Is affectionate

_____ Fits in with my friends

_____ Makes inappropriate jokes or comments

_____ Ignores my feelings

_____ Wears clothes I dislike

_____ Has views about children similar to mine

_____ Overlooks my shortcomings

_____ Shares similar dreams for the future

_____ Enjoys very different hobbies and activities

_____ Is of a different race or from a different culture

There is no official grading scale for this self-assessment; its purpose is to help you clarify your goals for and desires in a relationship. Now think of a romantic relationship that you have been in or are currently in. How well does your partner meet your expectations regarding costs and rewards? Just for fun, retake the quiz with friendship rather than romance in mind, and see whether or not your evaluation of rewards and costs changes.

companionship and intimacy, but you will also need to accept your friend's negative personality characteristics and invest time in working through difficult situations together. **Social exchange theory** explains this process of balancing the advantages and disadvantages of a relationship (Cook, 1987). Relationships begin, grow, and deteriorate based on an exchange of rewards and costs.

Rewards are the elements of a relationship that you feel good about—things about the person or your relationship that benefit you in some way. There are

extrinsic rewards, the external advantages you gain from association with another person (such as social status or professional connections); _instrumental rewards_, the resources and favors that partners give to one another (for example, living together to save money); and _intrinsic rewards_, the personally satisfying rewards that result from an exchange of intimacy (for instance, intellectual stimulation or feelings of safety) (Rempel, Holmes, & Zanna, 1985). **Costs**, by contrast, are the things that upset or annoy you, cause you stress, or damage your own self-image or lifestyle. If you find your relationship too costly (for example, there is a lot of conflict, jealousy, or infidelity), you may decide to engage in negative behaviors or end the relationship (Dainton & Gross, 2008; Guerrero, La Valley, & Farinelli, 2008).

> ### Ethics and You
> Have you ever had a relationship where the costs began to outnumber the rewards? Did you attempt to repair the relationship? If so, what repair tactics did you use? If you haven't been in that situation, how do you think you would handle it?

The social exchange of costs and benefits is inherently complicated. You might wonder, for example, why *The Good Wife*'s Alicia Florrick (or any of the real-world political wives who inspired the character) would stand by her husband after he humiliated her with an affair that became public. But the benefits of her marriage (including the love and the history she shares with her husband and the stability the marriage provides for her children) might outweigh the costs (such as her personal humiliation or her subsequent distrust of her husband).

Reducing Uncertainty

We begin to weigh the costs and rewards in the early stages of a relationship. Uncertainty creates excitement at the prospect of a new friendship to enjoy or romance to explore, but it's also uncomfortable. That's why we need to use a variety of techniques to get to know one another.

According to **uncertainty reduction theory**, when two people meet, their main focus is on decreasing the uncertainty about each other (Berger & Calabrese, 1975). The less sure you are of the person's qualities, the way the person will behave, or what will happen, the higher the degree of uncertainty. Thus, reducing uncertainty increases your ability to predict that person's behavior. As two people—college roommates, coworkers, romantic partners—reduce uncertainty between them, they uncover similarities, become

◊ *The Good Wife's* Alicia Florrick must carefully weigh the costs and benefits of remaining with her husband after discovering his affair and enduring a public scandal.

better at predicting what the other will do or say, and thus develop more comfort.

In order to reduce uncertainty and increase the likelihood of a closer relationship, you must obtain information about your new relational partner. If you're a fan of the *Twilight* series, you know that upon first noticing each other at school, Edward and Bella each used several strategies to find out more information about the other. Bella asked her classmates about Edward; she watched how he behaved and made observations about how he presented himself. Eventually, she questioned him directly. Edward, finding his ability to read minds useless on Bella, was forced to employ similar strategies. Unless you too can read minds, you've likely employed those same strategies yourself. Depending on the situation, three types of strategies may work well: passive strategies, active strategies, and interactive strategies.

Passive Strategies. Most college students who live on campus are faced with the prospect of sharing a small space with a complete stranger. When Shawna heard about her new roommate, Ramona, she entered her name and hometown into Google. She quickly found Ramona on Facebook and learned that she is a concert pianist and an avid knitter who sometimes sells her creations through Etsy.com (see Antheunis, Valkenburg, & Peter, 2010).

Shawna engaged in a passive uncertainty reduction strategy. **Passive strategies** involve observing others in communication situations without actually interacting with them. You may also analyze their interactions with others when you believe they are not under a lot of pressure to conform to social roles. Without Ramona knowing it, Shawna had already found out quite a bit about her. Social networking allows us to monitor others with relative ease, but we also use passive strategies whenever we observe others going about their day-to-day business.

Active Strategies. **Active strategies** let you obtain information about a person more directly, by seeking information from a third party. For example, Shawna may discover (via Facebook) that she and Ramona have one friend in common. In that case, Shawna might contact this individual to see how much she knows about Ramona. Does she party a lot? Is she neat or messy? Does she snore?

Active strategies can be particularly useful when the information you are seeking could be awkward to bring up in a new relationship. For example, Shawna might wonder if Ramona would be uncomfortable having significant others spend the night in their dorm room. Thus, she might chat with the mutual friend to get a sense of Ramona's feelings in order to be prepared to discuss it when they arrive on campus.

Interactive Strategies. Sometimes you will need to find out important information about a relational partner via **interactive strategies**, or speaking directly with them rather than observing or asking others for

information. When they "meet" for the first time (be it in person or virtually), Shawna might ask Ramona what kind of music she likes, what major she is pursuing, and why she chose this particular school. Although direct questioning reduces some uncertainty, it also entails risks. If you ask questions that are perceived as too forward or inappropriate (for example, "What are your religious beliefs?"), you might do more harm than good.

Dialectical Tensions

Weighing costs against benefits and reducing uncertainty are not the only challenges we face in developing relationships. In any relationship, it is common to experience contradictions or opposing feelings about your relational partner and about the relationship itself (Baxter & Erbert, 1999; Pawlowski, 1998). When a love relationship becomes serious, for example, one or both partners might find themselves mourning their old, single lifestyle, despite the benefits of commitment.

Relational dialectics theory holds that **dialectical tensions** are contradictory feelings that tug at us in every relationship. These tensions can be external (between the partners and the people they interact with) or internal (within their relationship). Of the many possible types, we focus on three internal tensions that dominate research: *autonomy* versus *connection*, *openness* versus *closedness*, and *predictability* versus *novelty* (Baxter & Simon, 1993). Note that dialectics exist along a continuum; they are not all-or-nothing trade-offs but rather ranges of options that need to be continually negotiated and adjusted (Baxter, Braithwaite, Bryant, & Wagner, 2004). Also, these tensions are natural and normal—experiencing them does not indicate that your relationship is falling apart!

Autonomy Versus Connection. Identical twins Teresa and Marie have always done everything together—from their first breaths of air right on through their college educations. As they grew older, loosening these bonds was a real struggle. Marie remembers bursting into tears at her bridal shower and explaining, "It's just that I've never had a party all to myself before" (Hazel, Wongprasert, & Ayres, 2006).

In all close personal relationships—family connections, romantic relationships, and friendships—there is a tension between independence (autonomy) and dependence (connection). In other words, we struggle because we want to be our own person while also being a part of something else: a couple, a family, or a group. This tension can result in hurt feelings. Attempts to express autonomy can be easily misunderstood—children's attempts to express their own identities are often seen as acts of rebellion, while romantic partners risk alienating their loved ones when they pursue certain interests alone. On the other hand, we can be seen as nagging when we try to force connectedness on our relational partner: if we drag our partners off to yoga class or a sporting event in which they have no interest, we're more likely to alienate them than to bring them closer.

Openness Versus Closedness. Every superhero from Batman to Superman knows about this tension. To become close, individuals must share information with their relational partners. However, by disclosing information, they reveal a part of their private selves that then becomes vulnerable. The tension comes as partners strive to find a balance between sharing information (openness) and a desire to keep some things private (closedness). This can be seen in superhero comics and movies, when a character like Bruce Wayne wants to maintain close relationships with various love interests but cannot tell any of them about his secret life as Batman. The tension between Batman's duty to Gotham City and duty to his loved ones takes a toll on those relationships.

Without the excuses of double lives, most people need to disclose some private information to those with whom they have relationships in order to facilitate a perception of involvement and deep understanding. Even when we take into account cultural differences (see Chapter 3), relational intimacy is consistently advanced by self-disclosure (as we develop more fully in the following section) (Chen & Nakazawa, 2009). But it is not always a good idea to reveal your every thought to your partner. Contrary to the notion that there should be "no secrets between us," relational dialectics researchers argue that much information might be better left unsaid. The comparison you make in your mind between your current romantic partner and an attractive celebrity is a good example.

Predictability Versus Novelty. Which is more important to you, safety and security or excitement and novelty? This third dialectical tension assumes that most people have a simultaneous need for stability through predictable relational interaction as well as a need for new and exciting experiences in personal relationships. On the one hand, partners seek stable patterns of interaction: Colin and Casey, for example, enjoy the comfort of their evening routine of dinner and television, as well as their usual Friday night at the movies. At the same time, every relationship needs some degree of spontaneity and novelty. This is why Colin and Casey have made plans to travel to Japan next summer and why they find enjoyment in shaking up their routine with odd projects—such as building their own computer or learning to cook Thai food.

📍 *The Dark Knight's* Bruce Wayne searches for the proper balance of openness and closedness in his relationships: can he reveal his secret identity?

LearningCurve
bedfordstmartins.com/commandyou

Self-Disclosure and Interpersonal Relationships

Do you remember Angelica from Chapter 2 (p. 45)? You may recall her heavy debt due to her lifestyle (expensive vacations, a new car, a nice apartment, and so on). When she divulges her personal financial mishaps to a friend, she is self-disclosing, revealing very personal information. As you've likely experienced in your own life, self-disclosure has a powerful impact on the development of interpersonal relationships (Samter, 2003). The process of choosing what information to disclose to others and when has long fascinated communication scholars. In this section, we look at the ways in which we choose to divulge or withhold personal information and how those decisions affect relationships.

Social Penetration Theory

In many relationships, a primary goal is to increase intimacy, or relational closeness. **Social penetration theory** (SPT) explains how partners move from superficial levels to greater intimacy (Altman & Taylor, 1973). SPT uses an onion as a metaphor to describe how relationships move through various stages: just as you might peel off layers of an onion in an attempt to reach the core or center, a relational partner attempts to reach the most intimate thoughts and feelings at the other partner's "core."

According to SPT, each layer contains information that is increasingly more private and therefore more risky to divulge to someone else. The outer layer represents aspects of the self that are obvious and observable, such as appearance and nonverbal behavior. Successive layers become more private as partners assess the costs and benefits of the relationship and of disclosing information to each other. If costs exceed rewards, it is unlikely that the partners will move inward toward the more deeply concealed layers. Upon getting to know Jorge, for example, you might find that despite his boisterous exterior, he sometimes suffers from serious

bouts of depression, which he manages with medication. But Jorge must choose to reveal this information: it is a part of him that only his closest, most trusted friends know, and he's likely to reveal it only as a relationship becomes more intimate.

Communication Privacy Management

Communication privacy management (CPM) **theory** helps explain how people perceive the information they hold about themselves and whether they will disclose or protect it (Petronio, 2000, 2002). CPM explains why Celeste, for example, will boldly share her religious beliefs, whereas Eddie will keep his faith intensely private. CPM theory presumes that people believe they own their private information and need to set up boundaries to control the potential risk that may make them vulnerable (Petronio, 2004).

Two key features of relationships are central to privacy management. First, privacy management can be affected by dialectical tensions such as openness versus closedness, discussed earlier in the chapter. You want to share information in order to increase intimacy with your partner, but it may be risky to do so, and maintaining private information is a worthy

> You want to share information in order to increase intimacy with your partner, but it may be risky to do so, and maintaining private information is a worthy goal in its own right.

goal in its own right. Second, privacy management requires cultural, situational, and relational rules or expectations by which people must be willing to abide. For example, it would likely be considered impolite for you to ask your boss about his medical condition because that topic is far too private for a work context in many cultures, and you are unlikely to have that level of personal intimacy with your manager. Yet that type of disclosure is expected in close relationships (Derlega, Winstead, Mathews, & Braitman, 2008).

Ethics and You

Can you think of examples of unethical privacy management in a workplace? Have you experienced any examples of this yourself? If so, how did you resolve the situation?

If there is a threat to your privacy boundaries (for example, your trusted friend told your secret to someone else), you experience **boundary turbulence** and must readjust your need for privacy against your need for self-disclosure and connection (Guerrero, Andersen, & Afifi, 2007; Theiss, Knobloch, Checton, & Magsamen-Conrad, 2009). Boundary turbulence occurs in mediated situations too. If you have personal information about someone else, do you have the right to post it on Facebook? What about inside jokes or pictures taken at a party—do you have the right to share them with others? Judgments can be made based on your "friends" on Facebook, so you can see how complex privacy management becomes in mediated situations (Walther, Van Der Heide, Kim, Westerman, & Tong, 2008).

Technology and You

Do you post any personal information on social-networking sites? What kind of information are you willing to reveal? What kind of information do you consider too private to share in mediated contexts?

Strategic Topic Avoidance

Certain topics are simply too sensitive for some people to confront openly. One or both relational partners can use **strategic topic avoidance** to maneuver the conversation away from potentially embarrassing, vulnerable, or otherwise undesirable topics (Dailey & Palomares, 2004). As we touched on in our discussion of communication privacy management, there are also topics we avoid because we are culturally trained to do so. For example, prior relationships, negative information, dating experiences, money issues, and sexual experiences are largely considered inappropriate for public communication (Baxter & Wilmot, 1985; Dailey & Palomares, 2004; Guerrero & Afifi, 1995). So if a colleague at the office asks about the size of your recent bonus, you could say that it's none of his business, but research shows that you'd be better off using a less direct avoidance tactic, such as keeping silent, deflecting, giving an unrelated response, lying, or simply ending the conversation (Dailey & Palomares, 2004).

Like other issues related to self-disclosure, there are ethical considerations regarding pursuing and avoiding topics. Is it appropriate for parents to disclose the private details of their impending divorce to their children? They may mean well (for example, they may want to reduce uncertainty for their children), but they may use such strategies unethically (such as if each parent offers his or her own side of the story in order to be viewed in a better light). In addition, adolescent children may suffer emotionally and view the disclosures as inappropriate (Afifi, McManus, Hutchinson, & Baker, 2007). Every relationship is unique, and as we have discussed, relational partners may experience different degrees of comfort with self-disclosure at various points.

Research into strategic topic avoidance illustrates both benefits and detriments. Most people in healthy relationships, for example, report that topic avoidance seems to work best when partners are sensitive to each other's concerns and when accommodating strategies are used (Dailey & Palomares, 2004). In other words, the divorcing parents' relationships with their children might remain positive if they allow the kids to bring up the divorce in their own time. You may find that some of your relational partners are more comfortable disclosing personal history, especially about sensitive issues such as childhood abuse, money, or health problems, at a slow rate.

LearningCurve
bedfordstmartins.com/commandyou

Stages of a Relationship

Although every relationship is unique, several scholars argue that relationships go through somewhat predictable stages (Knapp & Vangelisti, 2000). Communication differs during each stage as relational partners select messages that are individualized for the stage they perceive themselves to be in (Avtgis, West, & Anderson, 1998). Not every relationship will experience every stage—our assessments of costs and rewards will determine how the relationship will change, deepen, or possibly end. A number of interpersonal researchers have outlined relational stages and they all have in common the stages we develop in this section (see **Figure 7.2**).

Initiating Stage

In the **initiating stage** of a relationship, you make contact with another person, saying hello or asking for a name. If you think about the number of new people you initiate with on a given day, you won't be surprised to learn that most relationships don't move beyond this stage. Just because you say "Good morning" to the woman who sold you a bagel doesn't mean the two of you will be chatting on the phone later today. But you will likely use your first impression of a person to gauge whether or not you're interested in moving forward with the relationship (Canary, Cody, & Manusov, 2008).

Exploratory Stage

In the **exploratory stage**, you are seeking relatively superficial information from your partner. You make small talk, asking things like "Do you watch *The Walking Dead?*" or "How many brothers and sisters do you have?" You're not likely to reveal anything too deep or personal; you're still testing the waters, so to speak. There are also a number of monitoring strategies at work to reduce uncertainty in this stage. In addition to the small-talk questioning we mentioned, you're likely to observe your partner closely in order to learn more about his or her attitudes and behaviors. As in the initiating stage, you'll want to invest further in the relationship if the rewards seem high.

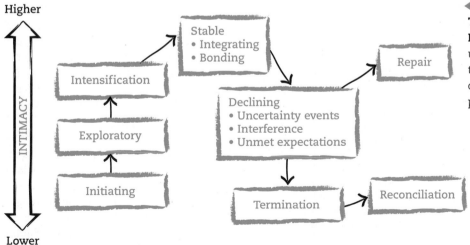

⟡ **Figure 7.2**

Typical Stages of a Relationship. Most of us will move between these eight stages over time in our interpersonal relationships.

Technology and You
How might you use technology like cell phones, e-mail, or social-networking sites in the exploratory stage of a new relationship?

💧 Superstars Jay-Z and Beyoncé epitomize the stable stage of a relationship: love, familiarity, comfort—and they prove that it's possible to reach this stage even as a Hollywood couple!

Intensification Stage

The **intensification stage** occurs when relational partners become increasingly intimate and move their communication toward more personal self-disclosures. This stage includes the use of informal address or pet names ("honey," "darling") as well as "we" talk ("We're going to the concert on Friday night, right?" "Where are we going for your birthday next week?"). Relational partners in this stage also understand each other's nonverbal communication to a greater degree and often share their affection with one another ("What would I do without you!") (Knapp & Vangelisti, 2000).

Stable Stage

By the time partners reach the **stable stage**, their relationship is no longer volatile or temporary. They now have a great deal of knowledge about one another, their expectations are realistic, and they feel comfortable with their motives for being in the relationship. According to Goss and O'Hair (1988), relationships reach the stable stage when uncertainty reduces to the point where partners feel comfortable understanding each other's preferences and goals. That doesn't mean, however, that stable relationships are set in stone, as the partners and their goals can still change.

Knapp and Vangelisti (2000) note two substages that occur during the stable stage. First, we see relational partners **integrating** or "becoming one." You and your roommate Dana now cultivate common friends, develop joint opinions, and may share property. People also treat you as a pair—one of you would never be invited to a party without also inviting the other one. If the relationship progresses beyond integrating, **bonding** takes place, the stage of the relationship when two partners share formal symbolic messages with the world that their relationship is important and cherished. Becoming engaged, getting married, joining in civil union, and entering into legal contracts (such as buying a house together) are common ways to distinguish that a romantic couple has bonded.

Life's challenges inevitably arise for partners in a stable relationship, so each individual will need to determine if the benefits of the relationship (such as intimacy or companionship) outweigh the costs that these challenges represent. The relationship can evolve to meet those challenges and remain stable. This is why Marge puts up with Homer's antics on *The Simpsons*. However, if one or both partners feel that the costs outweigh the benefits, the relationship may go into decline. For a few tips on developing and maintaining stable relationships, see Table 7.3.

Declining Stage

Have you noticed your partner criticizing you more often, refusing to talk about issues important to you,

Table 7.3 **Strategies for Managing Stable Relationships**

Strategy	Examples
Remember what made you interested in the relationship in the first place.	▪ Share inside jokes. ▪ Visit favorite places (for instance, a coffeehouse where you used to meet).
Spend quality time together.	▪ Share your day-to-day activities. ▪ Explore new hobbies and interests. ▪ Take part in activities like going to the movies or to sporting events.
Be understanding.	▪ Empathize with your partner's concerns, dreams, fears, and so on. ▪ Avoid unnecessary judgments. ▪ Try to see conflict-causing situations from your partner's point of view.
Express affection.	▪ Proclaim how important your partner is ("You're a great friend" or "I love you"). ▪ Do something nice or unexpected for your partner without being asked.
Have realistic expectations.	▪ Don't compare your relationship to others. ▪ Accept your partner's strengths *and* weaknesses.
Work on intimacy.	▪ Maintain a trusting, open environment where self-disclosure is possible. ▪ Offer supportive, positive messages, particularly during stressful times. ▪ Reveal your commitment by showing and sharing that you are invested in the relationship.

Sources: Dindi & Timmerman (2003); Gilbertson, Dindi, & Allen (1998); Goffman (1971); Harvey, Weber, & Orbuch (1990); Stafford (2003); Vangelisti & Banski (1993).

getting defensive, or speaking with contempt? If these behaviors are occurring more often than positive behaviors in your relationship, it is probably in the **declining stage**, when the relationship begins to come apart (Gottman & Silver, 1999). Three factors typically lead to this stage: uncertainty events, interference (concerning family, work, timing, money, or the like), and unmet expectations.

Uncertainty Events. Events or behavioral patterns that cause uncertainty in a relationship are called **uncertainty events.** They may be caused by competing relationships (romantic or platonic), deception or betrayal of confidence, fluctuations in closeness, and sudden or unexplained changes in sexual behavior,

personality, or values (Planalp & Honeycutt, 1985). One or both partners are left wondering about the cause of the events and their significance for the relationship. Imagine how you would feel if your romantic partner suddenly started withholding information from you or if a close friend began engaging in activities that you found offensive. Uncertainty events may be sudden and very noticeable (betrayal of confidence, for example) or they may be subtle and escape immediate attention (your sister stops returning your phone calls).

Interference. When Patrick becomes involved in a serious romantic relationship, his best friend, Dennis, feels abandoned. Jason wants to get married, but

Norah is not ready. Emma and Leigh find that financial troubles are straining their relationship.

These are just some of the many obstacles that may pop up in a relationship and interfere with its growth. Timing, the family or friends of one or both partners, and problems with work or money can all contribute to the decline of a relationship. For example, a *Money* magazine study of one thousand spouses found that 84 percent of married couples reported money as a culprit in marital distress ("Money," 2006). Romantic partners or even friends often view money differently because of upbringing, spending habits, and gender (Blumstein & Schwartz, 1983).

Unmet Expectations. Whenever people enter into a relationship, they form ideas about what they think will or should happen; these expectations influence how we (and our partners) send and receive messages. Unrealistic expectations can create problems in a relationship: if Hannah believes that true love means never arguing, she might interpret her boyfriend Liam's criticism of her messy apartment as a sign that they're not meant to be together. Realistic expectations, by contrast, can increase relational satisfaction and improve interpersonal communication (Alexander, 2008). Luisa, for example, has learned that her friend Emily is never going to remember her birthday. It's not a sign that Emily doesn't care; she just isn't good with dates. Instead, Luisa focuses on all the kind things that Emily does for her, like sending her funny postcards from her business travel or watching the dogs when Luisa had to leave town for a funeral.

Relationship Repair

A relationship in decline is not necessarily doomed to failure: partners may attempt to save or repair their relationship by changing their behavior, interactions, or expectations. If you have a strong commitment to someone else, particularly in a romantic relationship, you often perceive problems as less severe, so you are more likely to reduce conflict and potentially repair the relationship (Miczo, 2008). **Repair tactics** should include improving communication, focusing on the positive aspects of each partner and of the relationship

itself, reinterpreting behaviors with a more balanced view, reevaluating the alternatives to the relationship, and enlisting the support of others to hold the relationship together (Brandau-Brown & Ragsdale, 2008; Duck, 1984).

In short, partners hoping to repair a relationship must focus on the benefits of their relationship rather than the source of a particular argument (see Table 7.3, p. 161; many tips for managing stable relationships also apply to repairing them). Relational partners should listen to each other, take into account each other's perspective, and remind themselves about the attractive qualities that sparked the relationship in the first place (for example, how Talia can make Greg laugh and how Greg can make Talia feel at ease with her emotions). Partners may also try to increase their intimacy by offering more self-disclosures and spending quality time together (Blumstein & Schwartz, 1983). If a relationship is in serious decline, however, and seems beyond repair, the partners may need to seek professional help or outside support.

Termination Stage

Try as they might, not all relational partners stay together. (Hence the existence of sad songs and heartbroken poetry.) The **termination stage**, or end of a relationship, usually comes about in one of two ways (Davis, 1973). The first is *passing away*, which is characterized by a gradual fade as the relationship loses its vitality, perhaps because of outside interference or because partners don't make the effort to maintain it. Also, if partners spend less time together as a couple, communication and intimacy may decline, leading to dissatisfaction and a perception of different attitudes. This is why romances and friendships sometimes deteriorate when one partner moves away or why marriages and outside friendships change when kids come into the picture. The second way relationships often end is in *sudden death*—the abrupt, and for at least one partner, unexpected termination of a relationship. This might happen if a spouse or romantic partner has an affair or if someone can no longer tolerate a friend's emotionally manipulative behavior. Communicating the desire to end a relationship can be difficult; some messages useful for terminating romantic relationships in particular are listed in Table 7.4.

Reconciliation

Is there any hope for a terminated relationship? Soap operas and sitcoms say so—but it's true in real life as well. **Reconciliation** is a repair strategy for rekindling an extinguished relationship. Attempting reconciliation entails a lot of risk—one partner might find that the other partner is not interested, or both partners might find that the problems that pushed them apart remain or have intensified. But research reveals that

Table 7.4 **Termination Strategies for Romantic Relationships**

Strategy	Tactics	Examples
Positive-tone messages	Fairness	"It wouldn't be right to go on pretending I'm in love with you when I know I'm not!"
	Compromise	"I still care about you. We can still see each other occasionally."
	Fatalism	"We both know this relationship is doomed."
De-escalation	Promise of friendship	"We can still be friends."
	Implied possible reconciliation	"We need time apart; maybe that will rekindle our feelings for each other."
	Blaming the relationship	"It's not your fault, but this relationship is bogging us down."
	Appeal to independence	"We don't need to be tied down right now."
Withdrawal or avoidance	Avoid contact with the person as much as possible	"I don't think I'll be able to see you this weekend."
Justification	Emphasize positive consequences of disengaging	"It's better for you and me to see other people since we've changed so much."
	Emphasize negative consequences of not disengaging	"We will miss too many opportunities if we don't see other people."
Negative identity management	Emphasize enjoyment of life	"Life is too short to spend with just one person right now."
	Nonnegotiation	"I need to see other people—period!"

Source: Canary, Cody, & Manusov (2008), pp. 278–286. Adapted with permission.

there are a few tactics that can help the partners mend the relationship (O'Hair & Krayer, 1987; Patterson & O'Hair, 1992):

- **Spontaneous development.** The partners wind up spending more time together. Perhaps a divorced couple is involved in their son's school or two ex-friends find themselves helping a mutual friend.

- **Third-party mediation.** The partners have a friend or family member mediate the reconciliation.

- **High affect.** The partners resolve to be nice and polite to one another and possibly remind each other of what they found attractive about the other in the first place.

- **Tacit persistence.** One or both partners refuse to give up on the relationship.

- **Mutual interaction.** The partners begin talking more often following the dissolution, perhaps remaining friends after their breakup.

- **Avoidance.** The partners avoid spending time together and begin to miss each other.

If you think about couples in popular culture who have broken up and gotten back together—Ross and Rachel on *Friends*, for instance—you can clearly see some of these strategies at work.

 LearningCurve
bedfordstmartins.com/commandyou

 **Back to** }

Mary and Justin

At the beginning of this chapter, we met Mary and Justin, a couple struggling to maintain a close and functional family life during Justin's regular military deployment. Let's consider how they deal with the strains of time, distance, and uncertainty in light of what we've learned in this chapter.

- Military spouses often take on the role of single parents, making new rules and routines for interaction with the children when their partners are gone. When the soldier returns, his or her unfamiliarity with these behaviors may strain communication. When Justin is home, he and Mary talk a lot about how they should guide and discipline their sons, so that the boys feel consistency—and so that they manage the dialectical tension of autonomy-connection.

- Technology can help some military families keep abreast of one another's lives. Depending on what technologies are available (and when), families can talk every day or regularly. They can also engage in activities together, even though they are far apart. Mary and Justin like to choose a book that they read independently and then discuss when they have time together. They also pray together at an agreed-upon time, even though they are not connected physically or electronically. These simple but meaningful activities help them feel a sense of closeness despite the distance.

- Sharing family news—whether big ("Doug made the basketball team") or small ("Daniel was home from school today with a bit of a cold")—helps keep Justin involved in the family's day-to-day activities. Mary and Justin's discussions of their daily lives help them increase feelings of intimacy.

- Sahlstein, Maguire, and Timmerman (2009) urge military couples to develop better communication skills to handle separations and reunions. For example, Justin worries that if he self-discloses his emotions (particularly negative ones) about his experiences, he may be seen as weak, but he also knows that talking about them with Mary (who shows support without judgment) helps him deal with his experiences (another example of the openness-closedness dialectic).

Your Reference }

A Study Tool

Now that you have finished reading this chapter, you can

Explain key aspects of interpersonal relationships:

- **Interpersonal relationships**, the interconnections between two individuals, are influenced by **interpersonal communication**, the exchange of verbal and nonverbal messages between two people who are influenced by their partner's messages (p. 142).
- We all have a complex **relational network** or web of relationships. We have **family** relationships, **friendships**, and romantic partners, in addition to acquaintances, colleagues, and others (pp. 142–145).
- **Love** is a deep affection for another person with varying degrees of passion, commitment, and **intimacy**, or closeness and understanding—and it is important to romantic relationships (pp. 145–148).
- **Social information processing theory** explains that virtual relationships develop much like those that grow from face-to-face contact but that the process often takes longer to become more intimate. Online relationships have the potential to become even more personal and intimate than face-to-face relationships, a phenomenon known as **hyperpersonal communication** (p. 148).

Describe how and why we form relationships:

- Humans have a natural need for companionship and **inclusion**—a need to share our lives with others (p. 149).
- Relationship formation involves a number of types of attraction. For attraction to occur, a relationship requires **proximity**, or nearness (p. 151).
- Research shows that similarity influences attraction; supporting evidence includes the **attraction-similarity hypothesis**, the **matching hypothesis**, and the **genetic-similarity hypothesis** (p. 152).

List the advantages and disadvantages of relationships:

- **Social exchange theory** explains how we balance the advantages and disadvantages in our relationships (p. 153).
- **Rewards** are what make you feel good about the relationship and may be extrinsic, instrumental, or intrinsic. **Costs** are aspects of the relationship that upset you (pp. 153–154).
- According to **uncertainty reduction theory** ▶, a relationship priority is to decrease the uncertainty between partners through the use of **passive strategies** (which involve observing others without actually

interacting—pp. 154–155), **active strategies** (which involve seeking information from a third party—p. 155), and **interactive strategies** (which involve communicating directly with the person—p. 155).
- **Relational dialectics theory** holds that **dialectical tensions** ▶ arise when opposing or conflicting goals exist in a relationship (p. 155).
- Individuals may struggle to find a balance between independence (autonomy) and dependence (connection), openness and closedness, and predictability and novelty (pp. 155–156).

Describe the factors that influence self-disclosure:

- **Social penetration theory** explains how relational partners move toward intimacy, the primary goal of many relationships (p. 157).
- **Communication privacy management theory** helps explain how people perceive the information they hold about themselves and how they disclose it (p. 157). **Boundary turbulence** arises when violations occur in a relationship that make it necessary to readjust the need for disclosure versus privacy (p. 158).
- **Strategic topic avoidance** is used to maneuver the conversation away from topics that make people feel vulnerable (p. 158).

Outline the predictable stages of most relationships:

- The **initiating stage** is the first contact (p. 159).
- In the **exploratory stage**, there is superficial communication (p. 159).
- More self-disclosure occurs in the **intensification stage** (p. 160).
- In the **stable stage**, expectations are accurate and realistic. We see partners **integrating** ▶, or becoming one, and **bonding** ▶, sharing messages about their relationship with the world (p. 160).
- In the **declining stage**, **uncertainty events**, interference from outside the relationship, and unmet expectations take a toll, though **repair tactics** may reverse the decline (pp. 160–162).
- In the **termination stage**, the relationship fades (passing away) or is unexpectedly terminated by one partner (sudden death) (pp. 162–163).
- **Reconciliation** is a repair strategy for rekindling an extinguished relationship (pp. 163–164).

Look for **LearningCurve** throughout the chapter to help you review.
bedfordstmartins.com/commandyou

8 } Managing Conflict in Relationships

I If you believe the story detailed in the (fiction) film *The Social Network*, Mark Zuckerberg invented Facebook as revenge (O'Brian, 2010). Feeling angry because he got dumped, Zuckerberg begins posting nasty things about his ex on his personal blog and then goes on to develop the site that will eventually become the most ubiquitous (and profitable) social-networking site on the Internet.

The story was exaggerated for dramatic effect in the film, but his invention can nonetheless be a blunt weapon for individuals seeking to air grievances. Facebook, like Twitter and blogs, provides a forum for communication, including users voicing opinions and complaints to everyone they know—and plenty of people they don't. Slamming celebrities, talking smack about sports teams, deriding government policies, and maligning social groups are common practices on Facebook. Confrontational posts are often met with confrontational comments, and online bullying is not unusual. Chances are you've witnessed or even become embroiled in a Facebook conflict yourself.

What starts out as a complaint or an observation can quickly develop into a nasty conflict or even an investigation. Just ask Joe Lipari, who in 2010 posted a paraphrased line from the film *Fight Club* regarding his experience at a local Apple Store. A Facebook "friend"—more likely an acquaintance unfamiliar with Lipari's sarcastic sense of humor—misread his post as a threat against the store and alerted authorities. A few hours after Lipari posted what he intended as a funny complaint on Facebook, police were knocking on his door, searching his apartment, and questioning him as a suspected terrorist (Calhoun, 2010).

After you have finished reading this chapter, you will be able to

Describe the factors that lead to productive conflict.

Identify conflict triggers in yourself and others.

Explain the forces that influence how people handle conflict.

Evaluate and employ strategies for managing conflict in different situations.

Compare levels of resolution in conflict outcomes.

D ealing with conflict—be it with a romantic partner, a family member, a colleague, a classmate, or an institution—can be hard. Some avoid it altogether, while others lash out aggressively, in person or on Facebook. But there is also a middle ground that falls between covering our ears and posting aggressive comments in a public forum. There are also lots of ways in which we can not only manage conflict but also grow and learn from it. In this chapter, we'll take a look at some of the root causes of conflict and examine the ways in which we engage in it with others. We'll then consider productive ways to manage conflict in our relationships as well as conflict outcomes.

Understanding Conflict

You've undoubtedly had countless conflicts in your life. But just what is conflict, anyway? **Conflict** is not simply an argument or a struggle: it's a negative interaction, rooted in some actual or perceived disagreement, between two or more interdependent people.

Scholars like to distinguish between conflict—which is inevitable and sometimes cannot be resolved—and **conflict management**, which refers to the way that we engage in conflict and address disagreements with our relational partners. For example, consider Lisa and Steven Bradley, a couple who seemed to have it all: a beautiful home, four expensive cars, designer clothes, dinner out (or ordered in) every night. But they had a secret: Lisa spent lavishly without consulting Steven, and Steven stewed about it without ever confronting Lisa. Like countless Americans today, even the relatively well-off Bradleys were spending more than they earned, essentially living on credit. Though they rarely fought about it, Lisa and Steven were struggling to keep up with their bills and were on the brink of divorce (Greenhouse, 2006; Oprah .com, 2008).

For Lisa and Steven, the conflict was rooted in differing ideas about money, credit, and financial priorities. And they chose to manage their conflict by avoiding discussion and confrontation, which in this case wasn't particularly helpful. As the Bradleys eventually discovered—and as you'll see throughout this chapter—conflict can be managed productively or unproductively. Let's examine these two approaches to conflict and consider the costs and benefits of each one.

Unproductive Conflict

If you haven't already guessed, Lisa and Steven's approach to managing their conflict over money was an unproductive one. **Unproductive conflict** is conflict that is managed poorly and has a negative impact on the individuals and relationships involved.

In many respects, our relationships—including those with family, friends, colleagues, and romantic partners—are defined by how we manage conflict. But the damage of unproductive conflict isn't always limited to relationships. Researchers have discovered

🌢 Even with matters as simple as making plans for a Friday night, we may be uncompromising and create unproductive conflict or discuss the options, reach an agreement, and act on it.

that when conflict is handled poorly those involved can experience medical problems, including emotional distress (Davies, Sturge-Apple, Cicchetti, & Cummings, 2008), mood disorders (Segrin, Hanzal, & Domschke, 2009), heart disease, and immune deficiency (Canary, 2003).

Productive Conflict

Not all conflict is negative, though. In fact, conflict can be as valuable as it is inevitable! Conflict that is managed effectively is called **productive conflict**. We don't always notice the conflicts that we handle productively, as when two people quickly reach a compromise over some issue on which they disagree (like whether to eat at the Olive Garden or

Pizza Hut), without argument or confrontation. But productive conflict can also follow unproductive conflict, as when Lisa and Steven, fed up with debt and aware that their marriage was in jeopardy, began to confront and work on their financial and relationship problems, cutting their budgets and taking on additional work for more income. By addressing the problem collaboratively—facing the reality of their debt, agreeing on their financial priorities, setting a budget, and making decisions about money together—the couple began both resolving their financial problems and healing their relationship.

Productive conflict does not necessarily mean a successful resolution of conflict, but even without resolution, productive conflict can still benefit both parties. Let's look at a few examples.

Productive Conflict Fosters Healthy Debate. To believe that conflict can be productive rather than destructive, you have to actively engage in it. There is no greater intellectual exercise than exploring and testing ideas with another person. And like a sport, it can get competitive, as evidenced by the popularity of debate teams in schools and the media fanfare surrounding political debates during major elections. In fact, active and lively debate allows us to exchange ideas, evaluate the merits of one another's claims, and continually refine and clarify each other's thinking about the issue under discussion; debates on the floors of Congress, for example, allow representatives to go on record with their opinions on bills being considered and to try to persuade their colleagues to consider their positions. When government leaders fail to engage in such debates—when they evade questions or block a bill from going to debate on the floor of the legislature—they are formally engaging in the same kind of unproductive conflict avoidance that individuals use when they refuse to discuss difficult subjects. Conflict and healthy debate can also be a useful part of everyday life, as when a couple discusses and evaluates the pros and cons of buying a new car.

{ **There is no greater intellectual exercise than exploring and testing ideas with another person.** }

Productive Conflict Leads to Better Decision Making. Healthy debate serves a real purpose in that it helps individuals and groups make smarter decisions. By skillfully working through conflicting ideas about how to solve a problem or reach a goal, we identify the best courses of action. That's because a productive conflict provides an arena in which we can test the soundness of proposed ideas. Suggested solutions that are logical and feasible will stand up to scrutiny during the decision-making process, whereas weaker solutions are likely to be exposed as flawed. So by engaging in productive discussion about your conflict, the real costs and impact of, say, a new hybrid car are revealed, and you are able to come up with a workable solution: you will continue driving the old car while sacrificing this year's vacation and dinners out to put an additional $350 every month into a special savings account toward the purchase of a second-hand hybrid car in one year.

Productive Conflict Spurs Relationship Growth. Differences of opinion and clashing goals are inevitable in any relationship. And that can be part of what keeps our relationships fun and interesting! But it's how the partners *handle* the disagreements that arise that determines whether their bond will grow stronger. As two individuals—be they romantic partners, friends, roommates, or colleagues—work through their disagreements productively, they build on the relationship (Dainton & Gross, 2008). To paraphrase the German philosopher Friedrich Nietzsche, that which does not kill a relationship can indeed make it stronger.

LearningCurve
bedfordstmartins.com/commandyou

Conflict Triggers

- "He was drinking from the milk carton again. I caught him. It's so disgusting—I have to use that milk too, you know!"

- "Is there any point to making lunch plans with Abby? She's always breaking them."

- "My boss is at it again. I swear, she would throw me underneath a truck if it would make her look good."

Do any of these scenarios seem familiar? Everyone has a trigger that drives him or her absolutely mad

📍 Behavior that bothers you, like your roommate drinking straight from the milk carton, could be a conflict trigger.

when it happens, and conflict often ensues. The fact is, conflicts arise for a number of reasons. People often have conflicting goals, beliefs, or ideas; we face competition for scarce resources, such as money or time. We experience misunderstandings, and unfortunately, we lose our tempers. And sometimes we encounter people who are deceitful or uncooperative or who intentionally undermine our efforts to achieve our goals. In this section, we'll examine a few common conflict triggers (Sanford, 2010).

Inaccurate Perceptions

Misunderstandings are a common—and regrettable—cause of conflict. For example, in the movie *The Break-Up*, partners Brooke and Gary fight over the give-and-take in their relationship. Brooke is frustrated that she frequently accompanies Gary to baseball games (which she does not particularly enjoy), but Gary never takes her to the ballet. Although it may seem that Gary is selfish and uninterested in Brooke's desires, Brooke does have a role in this conflict. Gary points out that Brooke never told him she dislikes baseball—he thought they were mutually enjoying the games—and she never shared her desire to attend a ballet. Had they communicated openly, they could have avoided these perceptual errors altogether and potentially saved their relationship.

Incompatible Goals

Since much communication is goal driven, conflicts are bound to arise when goals are perceived as incompatible (Canary, 2003). On one episode of *Grey's Anatomy*, for example, the happy and committed relationship between Callie and Arizona is shattered by their different ideas about children: Callie realizes that she wants to settle down and start a family, but Arizona is certain that she never wants to have children. When couples differ on such serious life decisions, it can be extremely difficult to resolve the conflict. But even among relational partners who are in agreement on big life decisions, other goals are likely to come into conflict. For example, couples who are committed to having a family have conflicts about the timing, number, and rearing of children.

Unbalanced Costs and Rewards

Your roommate is annoyed that you keep eating her food; you are annoyed that she doesn't clean the bathroom. Conflict often arises when we are struggling to get a share of some limited resource, such as money, time, or attention. According to some researchers, we treat our interpersonal relationships almost like financial exchanges; we tally up our *rewards* (what we're getting from a relationship) and compare these to our *costs* (what we're putting into the relationship). If we think our costs are outweighing the rewards, then conflict may likely be triggered.

Provocation

Of course, not every conflict arises out of natural differences between individuals' goals or perceptions. The hard truth is that people can be uncaring or even aggressive at times. While conflict is indeed a natural part of every relationship, a great many conflicts arise through **provocation**—the intentional instigation of conflict. Research by Dan Canary (2003) reveals a wide range of events that can spark intense negative emotions in a relationship:

- **Aggression.** Aggressive behaviors range from verbal intimidation to physical threats. Fear and defensiveness (along with even more aggression) are common responses to such behavior.

- **Identity management.** When someone insults you, it can threaten your identity. Threats to identity management range from mild insults ("Man, you have a messy car") to condescending remarks ("I'll go slowly so you can keep up") to attacks on one's values or religion and racial or ethnic slurs. The reverse is also true, as evidenced by a study revealing that those who feel entitled to admiration from others engage in high amounts of identity management. As such, their self-image goals cause conflict and hostility in their relationships (Moeller, Crocker, & Bushman, 2009).

- **Lack of fairness.** When someone uses more than a fair share of resources—in families, workplaces, or living situations, for example—it commonly leads to conflict.

- **Incompetence.** When someone you work with or depend on performs poorly, the person is in a sense provoking conflict. Feelings of anger and resentment occur when a lab partner fails to bring needed supplies or write her share of the lab report.

- **Relationship threats.** When a relationship comes under threat, conflict is likely to arise. If your romantic partner reveals things that suggest he or she has other interests, you feel jealousy, anger, or insecurity. But not all threats to relationships are so cut-and-dried: a young child can see a new baby as a threat to his relationship with his parents; you might see a new, talented coworker as a threat to your career.

You may have noticed that most provocations are closely related to strong, unpleasant emotions: conflict often springs out of fear, anger, frustration, sadness, or insecurity. But as you will see, the factors

---

Culture and You

Are there particular provocations that spark negative emotions in your relationships? If so, why do you think some of them bother you more than others? Has it always been this way, or have those factors changed as you've aged?

---

that influence all communication—situation, culture, gender, personality, and so on—also influence the way we handle conflict. We'll consider these and other factors in the next section.

LearningCurve
bedfordstmartins.com/commandyou

Factors Affecting Conflict

We've just looked at triggers that can cause a conflict to crop up between people. But once a conflict arises, several specific forces can influence how the people involved handle the conflict. We examine these forces next.

Power Dynamics

When one person has power over another, that dynamic can cause one or both of the people to handle conflict unproductively. Power dynamics are often at play in the workplace, where your boss determines the nature of your work and can fire, promote, or transfer you. If you and your boss disagree about some issue at work, your boss may pull rank, saying something like "I'm in charge here." But power dynamics also come into play in more intimate relationships. For example, if you are dependent on your parents for tuition, shelter, food, or anything else, they may use that power to control your behavior, perhaps pressuring you to choose a specific school or major or making bold declarations about how you should spend your time.

Dan Canary and his colleagues have studied the effects of power on romantic relationships. They note, for example, that unhealthy relationships are often characterized by too much dependence of one partner on the other, control of one partner, and an inability to communicate boundaries, among other things (Canary, Cody, & Manusov, 2003). You can imagine what happens when conflict enters such an unbalanced relationship. In some cases, the partner with more power may engage in activities that make the other partner fearful and compliant, such as bullying or intimidating. Let's say that Chris and Amy are considering purchasing their first home together and that Amy is just starting a freelance writing career. Amy now relies on Chris's full-time job for health insurance and a stable income. In a relationship where power is balanced and healthy, Chris would be supportive of Amy's new venture and would want to come to a mutual decision about the size and type of home they purchase. But if the balance of power is skewed in Chris's favor—either because he is domineering or because Amy refuses to voice her opinions—Chris may engage in some of the tactics we mentioned: such as saying, "Well, I'm the one *paying* for the house" or "Fine, I guess we'll just keep throwing away money on rent" if Amy suggests that perhaps Chris's top-choice house isn't what's best for them.

It's important to bear in mind that differences in power aren't limited to material resources. In any relationship, one person has power over another if he or she controls something that the other person values. For example, when you are angry with your best friend, you may ignore her, depriving her of the benefit of spending time with you. In fact, some people—even entire cultures—will shun individuals whose behavior they disapprove of. For example, old-order Amish communities in the United States and Canada may shun members who are baptized in the faith and transgress the moral order of the church (for example, by purchasing a car or marrying someone outside the community). Shunning may prevent community members from eating with the shunned individual or conducting business with him or her (Kraybill, 2007). Although this may seem a bizarre practice to outsiders, it is actually a reflection of the fact that the Amish actively seek a difference in power, valuing the authority of the church and the needs of the community over the power of individuals.

Attitudes Toward Conflict

Certain attitudes about conflict in general (for instance, "Conflict is always bad") or about specific disagreements can cause people to avoid dealing with it. For example, you might steer clear of conflict for any of the following reasons:

- You don't consider the particular disagreement important enough to merit discussion.
- You dislike arguing or debating issues.
- You fear that openly acknowledging and talking about a disagreement will destroy the relationship.
- You don't believe that the current time or place is appropriate for talking about a particular disagreement.

Another reason that some people avoid dealing with conflict is that they're reluctant to discuss certain topics with particular people, a behavior known as **communication boundary management** (Petronio, 2000). For instance, you might be unwilling to discuss your spouse's annoying habits with your brother, who is feeling anxious and upset about the fact that he hasn't been able to find a

> ### Culture and You
> Think of an attitude you have about conflict that makes it difficult for you to talk productively about disagreements. For example, do you believe that discussing conflict can destroy a relationship? What steps might you take to begin letting go of this attitude?

relationship since his divorce. Why? Because you not only want to be considerate of your brother but also want to prevent him from becoming more distant from you if he perceives you as insensitive or petty.

Communication Climate

Conflicts can stem from certain atmospheres, or feelings, surrounding different relationships. This is known as a **communication climate**. According to Folger, Poole, and Stutman (1997), climates represent the dominant temper, attitudes, and outlook of a group and provide continuity and coherence in mutual activities.

How might you determine what type of climate you may face when engaging in conflict with others? We suggest three likely possibilities: uncertain, defensive, and supportive (Gibb, 1961). In what follows, we use the AMC television series *The Walking Dead* to illustrate the ways different climates affect conflict management.

- **Uncertain climates** are those in which at least one of the people involved is unclear, vague, tentative, and awkward about the goals, expectations, and potential outcomes of the conflict situation. Many conditions can create uncertain climates, including unfamiliarity with the people, the surroundings, or the topic at hand. In uncertain climates, communicators are hesitant to take action, and conflict management can bog down. On *The Walking Dead*, a small group of individuals who escape a zombie epidemic outside of Atlanta manage to band together in order to survive. Clearly there are innumerable uncertainties in this postapocalyptic world: What if the zombies find their camp? How will they obtain necessary supplies? What if one of the group members is attacked? But this confusion is compounded by the overwhelming fear and hesitancy of many of the individual characters, who can't seem to decide on a clear course of action.
- **Defensive climates** are those in which the people involved feel threatened. It is an atmosphere of mistrust, suspicion, and apprehension. On *The*

Walking Dead, protagonist Rick Grimes is attacked and captured by a father, Morgan Jones, and his son who have survived the epidemic. Grimes awakens bound to a bed, and a suspicious, fearful Jones proceeds to interrogate him harshly about whether he has been exposed to the zombie virus—letting Grimes know that the wrong answer or move will lead to his demise.

- **Supportive climates** are ideal because they offer communicators a chance to honestly and considerately explore the issues involved in the conflict situation. Communicators are open to one another's ideas and feelings and together construct a reality that induces productive resolution of the problems that instigated the conflict in the first place. On *The Walking Dead*, supportive climates are hard to find. But individuals—friends, spouses, siblings, and even strangers—do work to manage problems among themselves by exploring issues and being sensitive to one another's feelings. For example, friends Dale and Andrea manage to share their sentiments about Andrea's decision to remain behind at the doomed Centers for Disease Control and Prevention facility and resolve their conflict with mutually beneficial results.

How do you move from a defensive or uncertain climate to a supportive one? Your first task is to make sure you know which climate you are experiencing. Your gut instincts can be a credible guide here, but you can also make some formal assessment of the climate situation. What are your past experiences with this topic, this person or group, or these conditions? How do you feel things turned out? Once you know the climate you are in, you can take steps to move toward a supportive one. **Figure 8.1** offers several communication steps to help you find your way to supportive conflict climates.

Culture and Conflict

Culture and conflict are clearly linked. If we consider how important culture is to our identities and

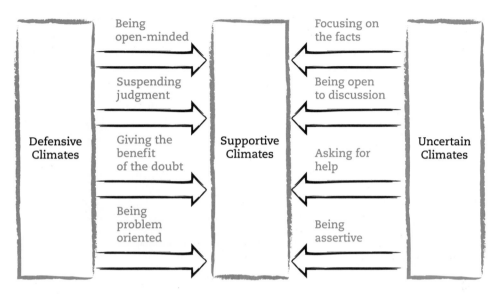

⬧ Figure 8.1 **Steps to Reaching a Supportive Climate**

how pervasive conflict is in our lives, we can begin to understand how culture influences and guides our conflict experiences. Differences in cultural values, beliefs, and attitudes can lead to conflict directly, and they can also affect how individuals perceive conflict, what their goals are for conflict, and how conflict is handled. Let's examine two of the innumerable cultural influences on conflict: individualist versus collectivist cultures and sex and gender.

Individualist Versus Collectivist Cultures. Research in the area of race, ethnicity, and conflict often examines differences between individualist, low-context cultures and collectivist, high-context cultures. As you learned in Chapter 3, *individualist cultures* emphasize personal needs, rights, and

{ **Culture and conflict are clearly linked.** }

identity over those of the collective or group, whereas *collectivist cultures* emphasize group identity and needs. In addition, you'll recall that people rely more on social norms and nonverbal communication than on what is actually said in *high-context cultures*. In *low-context cultures*, people are expected to say what they mean.

According to Ting-Toomey and her colleagues (2000), European Americans are individualist and low context, while Latinos and Asians are collectivist and high context. Thus, European Americans tend to view conflict as a necessary way to work out problems and feel that specific conflict issues should be worked out separately from relational issues. For Latinos and Asians, on the other hand, conflict is perceived as having a negative effect on relational harmony, and conflict issues cannot be divorced from relationships. Because conflict is viewed as damaging to relationships, Asians tend to avoid conflict and often use less direct communication than their more individualist American counterparts (Merkin, 2009).

When it comes to power in relationships, individualist, low-context cultures rely on and compete for tangible power resources. For example, people with power can reward and punish others; power is often asserted through threats and direct requests. In collectivist, high-context cultures, however, power is about gains or losses in reputation and is displayed subtly through indirect requests. Communication during conflict in individualist, low-context cultures is expected to be clear and direct, whereas in collectivist, high-context cultures, people are supposed to pick up on subtle cues and vague verbal messages. So whereas a Canadian parent might assert, "I'm angry with you because you used my car without asking," a Vietnamese parent may stare at his son or daughter, wait for an acknowledgment of wrongdoing, and then ask, "Why did you take the car without asking?" Understanding these very influential differences between cultures can help us understand how confusion, frustration, and miscommunication can happen when communicating across cultures.

> **Culture and You**
>
> The United States is home to people with a great variety of cultural backgrounds. Do you feel that your family comes from a more individualist culture or a more collectivist culture? Do you think it has always been that way, or have your family's cultural norms changed over time?

Sex and Gender. In the 2010 film *The Kids Are All Right*, mothers Jules and Nic are worried about

 In *The Kids Are All Right*, mothers Jules and Nic and adolescent son Laser play out the typical imbalance of communicativeness between females and males.

their teenaged son, Laser, who appears withdrawn. They ask him, over and over, if there's anything he wants to talk about. They complain that his friend Clay is a bad influence. They ask him why he sought out his biological father without telling them. But Laser simply does not want to talk. While such nagging female/noncommunicative male stereotypes are standard in fiction and film, there is some evidence to suggest that, in fact, women are more inclined to voice criticisms and complaints, and men tend to avoid engaging in such discussions.

Researcher John Gottman (1994) has studied marital conflict and the differences in conflict behaviors between men and women. He believes that four destructive behaviors are predictors of relationship dissolution: criticism and complaints, contempt, defensiveness, and stonewalling. Criticism is attacking your partner's character, especially when the criticism is weaved into the complaint; contempt is attacking your partner's sense of self-worth; defensiveness is making yourself the victim; stonewalling is refusing to engage in conflict and withdrawing from the interaction. Gottman (1994) found that women tend to criticize more than men and that men tend to stonewall more than women. Recent research also suggests that sex and gender influence satisfaction level with regard to certain conflict management strategies. Afifi, McManus, Steuber, and Coho (2009) found that when women perceived that their dating partner was engaging in conflict avoidance, their satisfaction level decreased, but avoidance did not cause the same dissatisfaction in men.

The outcome of such behavioral patterns does not mean inevitable doom for relationships. According to Gottman's Web site, gottman.com, one way of improving conflict is to focus on the bright side of the relationship and give five positive statements for every negative one. In other words, Veronica may well have reason to be upset that Brent continually stonewalls her when she attempts to bring up the topic of marriage. But while she seeks productive ways to address this area of conflict, she might do well to remember the reasons she's interested in

marrying him in the first place. Similarly, Brent might try to focus on Veronica's traits that bring joy to his life—her sense of humor, her ambition, and her adventurous nature—rather than constantly viewing her attempts to discuss "settling down" as a nagging criticism.

When we think of these aspects of conflict and culture, it is important to remember that assuming cultures are at one extreme or the other is dangerous because it can lead people to believe that differences in culture mean irreconcilable differences in conflict. It may be difficult to understand others' cultural values, and we may feel compelled to persuade others to see things the way we do, but competent communication in conflict means understanding and respecting differences while working to "expand the pie" for both parties. Even in the most uncomfortable and frustrating conflict situations, we can learn a great deal about others and ourselves through culture.

Communication Channel

In many communication situations, we don't think much about which available channel we should choose. Not so when it comes to conflict. If you've ever sent flowers as a way of apologizing, left a voice mail on a weekend to let an instructor or a colleague know you've missed a deadline, or delivered bad news via text message, chances are you chose that channel as a way of avoiding engaging in conflict face to face. But conflict and communication channels are often intertwined: conflict can arise from poor channel choices, as we perceive things differently depending on the channel used (see Chapter 2). But even more interesting is the powerful way that channel choice influences conflict management.

Of course, some practical considerations can influence which channel we select to communicate with someone else about a disagreement, such as whether a person lives close enough for you to talk about an issue in person. However, our reasons for choosing one channel over another are often rooted

◊ The cofounder of Wikipedia, Jim Wales, allegedly broke up with his girlfriend on his Wikipedia page. Perhaps that wasn't the best channel!

in emotions. If you're intimidated by someone you're in a conflict with, you may feel safer communicating with them by e-mail than over the phone or face to face. But beware: managing conflict with close friends or romantic partners through electronic channels can come across as insensitive and even cowardly. Just ask anyone who found out that a relationship was over via a changed "relationship status" on his or her significant other's Facebook page!

Online Anonymity and Conflict

On a related front, the relative anonymity of electronic communication has emerged as a new factor that influences conflict, particularly in the generation of heated and unproductive electronic exchanges in Internet forums, in e-mails, and through social-networking sites (Shachaf & Hara,

2010). Of course, people have long been able to provoke conflict anonymously, but the Internet has provided a vast arena for **flaming**—posting online messages that are deliberately hostile or insulting toward a particular individual. Such messages are usually intended only to provoke anger and can ignite flame wars between individuals when friendly, productive discussions give way to insults and aggression. In many cases, the root cause of these conflicts is not even a true disagreement but rather one person's misinterpretation of another's message (as with Joe Lipari's pseudothreat on the Apple Store detailed in the chapter opener).

Technology and You

Have you ever witnessed flaming or trolling in online messages? How do you tell them apart? Have you ever posted messages that were mistaken for flaming or trolling when that wasn't your intention? How do you make sure that your online messages are understood as you intend them to be?

Flaming should be distinguished from **trolling**, which is posting provocative or offensive messages to whole forums or discussion boards in order to elicit some type of general reaction (Morzy, 2009). Trolls often use their online anonymity to intentionally stir up conflict and create damage in an online community; research reveals that they are often motivated by boredom, a need for attention, and revenge (Shachaf & Hara, 2010).

Technological channels are also an arena for even more aggressive conflict behaviors, such as **cyberbullying**—multiple abusive attacks on individual targets conducted through electronic channels (Erdur-Baker, 2010). Social-networking sites like Facebook and Twitter offer an open forum for bullies. Sociologists and educators point out that traditional bullying, while highly unpleasant, is also extremely intimate; cyberbullying, by contrast, makes use of e-mails, instant messages, and text messages to deliver cruelty to its victims, often anonymously (Maag, 2007b). Among teens and pre-teens, the problem has serious consequences, as evidenced by the suicide of a thirteen-year-old Missouri girl, Megan Meier. Moments after receiving a message that "the world would be a better place without you" from a boy she'd connected with through MySpace, Megan ran to her closet and hanged herself with a belt. In the aftermath of her suicide, it was revealed that the boy Megan thought she was flirting with for months, and who then viciously turned on her, didn't really exist and was in fact the creation of the mother of a former friend of Megan's (Maag, 2007a).

> ### Ethics and You
> Does it seem ethical to use the anonymity of the Internet to pose as or create an alternate identity? Do social-media users also have the responsibility not to trust unfamiliar communications? How might you respond to an online communication from someone you're not sure you know?

In some cases, cyberbullies—so empowered by their anonymity—entirely disregard expectations surrounding particular situational contexts. After seventeen-year-old Alexis Pilkington took her own life, her friends and family set up a Facebook memorial page to remember Alexis and to share their mutual grief. Sadly, alongside messages honoring this young woman's life were lewd, hateful, and inappropriate messages indicating that Alexis "got what she deserved." A family friend summarized the bullies' attempt to create controversy and conflict in such an inappropriate time and space: "Children want to mourn their friend, and there are posts of photos

with nooses around her neck. It's disgusting and heartless" (Martinez, 2010, para. 6).

LearningCurve
bedfordstmartins.com/commandyou

Strategies for Managing Conflict

A number of strategies might be employed to manage any conflict. To get an initial sense of these strategies, let's consider a common, very simplistic scenario: Leslie is sitting with her twin sister, Kathy, at the dinner table after a family meal. There's one last piece of key lime pie, and both sisters want it.

In certain conflict situations, such as a competition for a piece of pie, the people involved can resolve the conflict—that is, bring it to an end—in just seconds. But when the conflict is more complex or when a seemingly simple disagreement is a symptom of a larger problem between people, resolving the situation will require more time and thought. If Leslie is growing resentful of always having to share everything with Kathy—her room, her friends, her laptop, her clothes—their conflict is bigger than a piece of pie. Resolving it may require a more involved approach, such as honest, lengthy dialogue about Leslie's resentments and possible ways for her to have more things she can call her own. The strategies we use for managing conflict, be they simple or complicated, generally fall into one of three basic categories: escapist, challenging, or cooperative (see Table 8.1).

Escapist Strategies

One way for Leslie to manage the conflict is to make a decision to avoid it and let Kathy have the

◊ Sometimes the competition for a lone piece of pie can mask larger emotional issues.

to steer clear of a confrontation because they're afraid a direct conflict would hurt the other person or the relationship. Or maybe they wish to postpone dealing with the conflict until a more convenient time, when they can talk at length about it with the other person. Another reason for selecting this type of strategy might be to force the other person to raise the issue instead of having to do so themselves.

In certain situations, escapist strategies can be harmless and practical, offering a quick resolution to issues that are relatively unimportant (like pie), and can help maintain relationships that might be damaged if conflict erupted over every little thing. Stafford (2010) found that couples in long-distance relationships engage in greater conflict avoidance than couples in geographically close relationships but notes that this strategy is effective for long-distance partners' relational maintenance because it minimizes differences and maximizes positive affect. But such strategies may be unproductive if they continually prevent people from dealing with issues that need addressing: if Leslie always defers to Kathy, for example, resentment is likely to brew between the sisters. The pie could become a tipping point for a larger issue. In fact, recent research has found that continual avoidance of conflict in

pie, even though she really wants it for herself. Through such **escapist strategies**, people try to prevent or avoid direct conflict. Perhaps they want

Table 8.1 Conflict Strategies: The Key Lime Pie Incident

Type	Description	Examples
Escapist	Conflict is avoided or prevented; goals may not be important; conflict is not seen as a viable alternative	▪ Relinquish the pie ("You can have the pie")
Challenging	Individual goals are pursued; relationship is threatened	▪ Take the pie ("That's my piece of pie") ▪ Fight for the pie ("Oh, no, it's not")
Cooperative	Pursuit of mutual interests; problem-solving approach emphasized; relationship is preserved	▪ Share the pie ▪ Flip a coin for the pie ▪ Broker a deal for the pie ("I'll do the dishes if you let me have the pie")

families negatively affects family strength and satisfaction (Schrodt, 2009).

Challenging Strategies

If Leslie decides that she wants the pie more than she wants to avoid fighting with Kathy, she might demand the entire piece for herself, at her sister's expense. Such **challenging strategies** promote the objectives of the individual who uses them, rather than the desires of the other person or the relationship. Challenging strategies are often referred to as assertiveness. Assertive people are generally effective at handling conflicts because they don't let negative emotions like anxiety, guilt, or embarrassment get in the way and they stand up for what they believe is right.

Challenging strategies may or may not strengthen the relationship of the people involved, depending on the situational context and how the strategy is employed. For example, if Leslie becomes aggressive with Kathy and rudely demands the last slice of pie, she's probably not doing much to be considerate of her sister or to strengthen their bond. However, research does reveal that challenging others can sometimes have positive benefits. For example, Canary, Cunningham, and Cody (1988) found that people tend to employ challenging strategies when they feel the need to defend themselves from a perceived threat. So, you would rightly be assertive when the friend you came to a party with attempts to get behind the wheel of a vehicle after consuming alcohol. Drunk driving is a threat to your, your friend's, and the public's well-being.

In some relationships, challenging strategies are accepted as part of a relational context that is generally open and forgiving. To illustrate, perhaps Leslie and Kathy are so close and feel so confident of their love for one another that Leslie knows a moment of selfish behavior on her part will be overlooked or forgiven by Kathy (and vice versa). Conversely, if the relationship is not really valued, challenging strategies can enable individuals to get what they want without any consequential losses, since maintaining the relationship is not a priority.

⬦ While Kieran might be sure he wants to join the Army, negotiating alternatives with his mother might allow him to explore his choices and uncover other options.

Cooperative Strategies

Of course, the most practical and fairest way for Leslie to manage this conflict is to propose a compromise, offering to split the last piece of pie with Kathy. If Leslie decides to share the pie, she is attempting to arrive at the best outcome for both partners in this relationship. Strategies that benefit the relationship, serve mutual rather than individual goals, and strive to produce solutions that benefit both parties are called **cooperative strategies** (Zacchilli, Hendrick, & Hendrick, 2009).

Whether the issue is pie or child custody decisions, several tactics are useful in cooperative conflict management. For example, let's consider a larger issue that is causing conflict within a family: twenty-year-old Kieran wants to drop out of college to join the Army. His mother is very upset and wants him to continue his education. A number of strategies can help them manage the conflict cooperatively.

Focus on Issues. With any issue, it's very important that the discussion remain centered on the matter at hand and steer clear of any personal attacks. If Kieran's mother boldly declares, "You are irrational and thoughtless. Who drops out of college with only one year left?" she's making the argument personal and isn't considering the fact that Kieran may well have thought through the ramifications of his decision. Such **verbal aggressiveness**—attacks on individuals rather than issues—is common, but it is also unproductive. Research by Roberto, Carlyle, Goodall, and Castle (2009) suggests that

What About You? }

Hitting Above and Below the Belt

The concepts of argumentativeness and verbal aggressiveness are important to the study of conflict management because the first is more likely to produce positive outcomes than the second. Examine the items below, and mark each one according to how you feel about most conflicts (1 = true, 2 = undecided, 3 = false).

_____ 1. Arguing over controversial issues improves my intelligence.

_____ 2. I really come down hard on people if they don't see things my way.

_____ 3. I am good about not losing my temper during conflict situations.

_____ 4. Some people need to be insulted if they are to see reason.

_____ 5. I prefer being with people who disagree with me.

_____ 6. It is exhilarating to get into a good conflict.

_____ 7. I have the ability to do well in conflict situations.

_____ 8. It is not hard for me to go for the throat if a person really deserves it.

_____ 9. I know how to construct effective arguments that can change people's minds.

_____ 10. I avoid getting into conflicts with people who know how to argue well.

_____ 11. I know how to find other people's personal weaknesses.

Scoring: Add your scores for items 1, 3, 5, 6, 7, and 9. Reverse your scores for items 2, 4, 8, 10, and 11 (1 = 3, 3 = 1); after converting the numbers, add these scores to your previous total. If you score between 11 and 18, you are prone to argumentativeness. If you score between 26 and 33, you are likely to be verbally aggressive when you are in conflict situations. If you score between 19 and 25, you are probably neither very argumentative nor very aggressive.

Source: From Infante (1988). Adapted with permission of the publisher.

parents' verbal aggression toward their children can have a negative impact on relationship satisfaction and is associated with nonsecure attachment styles among young adult children. Further, when verbal aggression is used by supervisors toward their subordinates in the workplace, it can negatively affect employee job satisfaction and commitment (Madlock & Kennedy-Lightsey, 2010).

Such personal attacks do little to foster cooperation and usually succeed only in putting the other person on the defensive and making the interaction more heated. So Kieran's mother would do better to keep the focus on his decision rather than on Kieran himself.

Debate and Argue. As noted earlier in this chapter, when we engage in conflict by debating the issue at hand, we exchange more ideas, reach better decisions, and foster stronger, healthier relationships. Healthy debate is, therefore, a cornerstone of cooperative conflict management. A number of tactics can help foster debate.

One is **probing**—asking questions that encourage specific and precise answers. If Kieran's mother asks probing questions ("Why do you want to join the Army now when you're so close to graduating?"), she'll get a better understanding of why and how he's come to this decision. Likewise, Kieran will get a better sense of his mother's feelings if he asks similar questions of her ("Why is it so important to you that I finish my degree now?").

Probing can help encourage either side of a conflict to consider both the positive and the negative aspects of an issue. Kieran, for example, might note that the job market for college graduates in his major is completely flat, and so he sees the Army as a solid employment opportunity. His mother might point out that he'll still have to pay back his college loans, with or without his degree, and that all that expenditure will have amounted to little if he doesn't finish. Kieran's mother might also play the role of **devil's advocate**—pointing out the worst-case scenarios ("There's a war going on. What if you get hurt or killed?")—to make sure her son has considered all possible

outcomes of his decision (and revealing her own fears in the process).

Consider Options and Alternatives. Offering—and potentially negotiating—alternatives is a useful tactic for cooperative conflict management. Kieran's mother might suggest, for example, that he join the Army Reserve instead, which would allow him to finish school while also serving his country and would ensure a career if he wants to go on active duty after graduation.

> **Ethics and You**
> Have you ever been caught in the middle of a conflict between family members, friends, or people in a romantic relationship? Did your involvement feel fair to you? How might you navigate this sort of conflict when it involves people who are close to you?

Consider the Importance of the Outcome. Obviously, a disagreement over a serious issue like quitting school to join the Army warrants serious debate. But many of the conflicts in which we find ourselves embroiled (like disputes over pie) don't seem all that important. Nevertheless, it's important to clarify that the issue will have consequences. For example, Kieran's mother might emphasize that the Army is not a job he can simply quit if he doesn't like it.

Reassure Your Partner. To resolve a conflict cooperatively, a straightforward explanation of your good intentions might be in order. When Kieran's

{ **Offering—and potentially negotiating—alternatives is a useful tactic for cooperative conflict management.** }

mother tells him, "Please, I just want to talk about this to make sure I understand your reasons before you make your decision," she's stating her desire to resolve the disagreement, showing him that she respects his feelings and intelligence, and reassuring him that she wants to engage in a discussion with him, not simply tell him what to do.

LearningCurve
bedfordstmartins.com/commandyou

Conflict Outcomes

As we noted earlier, conflict cannot always be resolved. But every conflict does, eventually, have an outcome. Regardless of how they engage in it, the conflict between twins Leslie and Kathy will produce some result: one or the other sister may get the pie, the two might share the pie, or neither might get any pie at all.[1] Conflict outcomes fall into several categories.

Compromise

You may buy into the idea that compromising is always the easiest and best way to resolve a conflict. Sometimes that may be true, as when a compromise involves sharing a piece of pie; other times, however, it may prove more challenging, as when you must set up a schedule for using a jointly owned computer or split the cost of some shared item with a roommate or neighbor. With most **compromises**, both sides give up a little to gain a little.

---

[1]Research on conflict types has been conducted in the communication field for many years, and many terms are given for the types you will read about in this section. An excellent source that describes these conflict types (using many different terms) is the comprehensive review by Oetzel and Ting-Toomey (2006).

Compromises can be arrived at through **trading**, whereby one partner offers something of equal value in return for something he or she wants. Separated parents who must navigate joint custody arrangements might strike compromises regarding time spent with their children: Maggie offers Sean extra weekends with their boys in the spring if he'll let her have them for Christmas for the second year in a row.

Other options might include **random selection** (for example, Maggie and Sean could flip a coin to decide who gets the kids for Christmas) or, when appropriate and practical, a vote (having the kids weigh in on where they want to go and when).

The advantage of compromise is that it lets you and the other person quickly resolve or avert a conflict by agreeing on a decision-making method. However, important relationships can suffer if the people involved are *always* making compromises. That's because compromising means giving up *some* of what you want, even though you're getting a little of something else in return. After a while, that can get tiresome. With romantic partners, close friends, and family members, it often feels better to come up with more creative, thoughtful approaches to ongoing conflicts that lead to "win-win" resolutions.

Win-Win

When both participants in a conflict discuss the situation and arrive at a solution that fully satisfies each of them, the conflict has been resolved in a win-win manner. Thinking back to the key lime pie incident, if sisters Leslie and Kathy use that conflict to work through their issue of having to share everything, they may be able to arrive at a variety of solutions to the problem and strengthen their relationship in the process. They might agree to pool their money for a second computer or come up with a system for sharing certain items of clothing while placing others off-limits. Through such "win-win" solutions, both parties can meet their own goals (unlimited computer access, a bigger wardrobe), help the other with her goals, and improve their relationship.

Lose-Lose

Of course, there are times when a conflict is resolved without either side getting what it wants. If Leslie decides that if she can't have the pie nobody can, and tosses it in the trash, she's resolved the conflict at hand, even though she didn't get what she wanted. While such outcomes seem childish, they are in fact relatively common. Individuals often stay in jobs they hate and do them poorly because they don't see the possibility for other outcomes; in such cases, both the individual and the employer lose, along with any customers or clients who depend on them.

Separation

By contrast, individuals who quit jobs opt for a different outcome: **separation**. Removing oneself from a situation or relationship is a clear way to end a conflict without necessarily creating clear wins or losses for either party. For example, suppose you're renting an apartment from a friend who, as the landlord, never repairs burst pipes or fixes the fridge when it breaks, even though you pay your rent on time every month. You've tried to reason with him; you've even tried to guilt him into reimbursing you for the money you've spent on repairs he should have paid for. But nothing has worked. In this case, the best resolution to this conflict may be to simply pack up your things and move.

THINGS TO TRY

This week, if you have a disagreement with a friend, roommate, romantic partner, family member, or boss, identify one change you could make to manage and resolve the conflict more productively. For example, could you suggest a compromise? Could you look for a broader range of promising solutions to your disagreement?

◊ Many people stay in jobs they hate because they fear the unknown. But this way, nobody wins: you're unhappy and you do your job poorly, which affects those who depend on you.

{ The advantage of compromise is that it lets you and the other person quickly resolve or avert a conflict by agreeing on a decision-making method. However, important relationships can suffer if the people involved are *always* making compromises. }

Allocation of Power

Yet another way to resolve conflict is to decide, with the other person, which of you will have the power to make certain decisions in the relationship. For example, in a couple, one individual may be dominant on one issue (such as finances) while the other makes the decisions on others (such as child rearing); in a work environment, several employees may split the responsibilities of a given project, with one member making financial decisions, another in charge of creative ones, and a third in charge of communicating all those decisions to others outside the group.

LearningCurve
bedfordstmartins.com/commandyou

Back to } *The Social Network*

At the beginning of this chapter, we talked about the film *The Social Network* and how in real life people often use Facebook status updates as a means of airing grievances and dealing with conflict. Let's consider how the concepts we've learned about in this chapter play into social-networking conflicts.

- When you're dealing with conflict, it's important to consider the forum, especially in mediated communication. Mark Zuckerberg's personal blog reveals that he did indeed insult a woman on the night he began working on SmashFace (the precursor to Facebook), though there is no evidence that he created the site as revenge. Regardless, Facebook, Twitter, and personal blogs turn complaints, which in a face-to-face setting would be a simple letting off of steam among a few friends, into something public and permanent, which can never be deleted.

- While some of the conflicts dramatized in the film *The Social Network* are fictional, others, including disputes over who actually conceptualized and owned Facebook, are matters of public record. Zuckerberg was initially hired by twins Cameron and Tyler Winklevoss and Divya Narendra to write code for a social network they were developing. He instead launched his own site, which they claim he stole from them. Though they tried to settle the matter in Harvard's Honor Court, they wound up suing Zuckerberg for a share in the company. In this type of dispute, avoiding conflict might have cost them millions—if not billions—of dollars.

- When using Facebook to vent about a conflict, it's important to be aware of your goals. Announcing one's divorce or changed relationship status on Facebook can be helpful if your goal is to inform your friends of what you're going through without having to detail or live through painful events all over again as you tell person after person what is going on. But using it as a forum to insult or complain about your ex is a less productive means of conflict management.

- It's also important to consider relational context when posting on Facebook. Will everyone in your friend list understand your references, your sense of humor, and your intentions? Joe Lipari's close friends probably got the joke when he paraphrased a violent threat from *Fight Club* in his status update, but someone took it seriously enough to alert authorities.

Your Reference }

A Study Tool
Now that you have finished reading this chapter, you can

Describe the factors that lead to productive conflict:

- **Conflict** is a negative interaction, rooted in disagreement, between interdependent people (p. 168).
- **Conflict management** refers to how relational partners address disagreements (p. 168).
- **Unproductive conflict** is conflict that is managed poorly and that has a negative impact (p. 168).
- **Productive conflict** is healthy and managed effectively. It fosters healthy debate, leads to better decision making, and spurs relationship growth (pp. 169–170).

Identify conflict triggers in yourself and others:

- Many conflicts are rooted in errors of perception (p. 171).
- Incompatible goals can spark conflict (p. 171).
- Conflicts arise when the costs of an interpersonal relationship outweigh the rewards (p. 171).
- **Provocation**, the intentional instigation of conflict, arises when one party demonstrates aggression, a person's identity feels threatened, fairness is lacking, someone you depend on is incompetent, or an important relationship is threatened (pp. 171–172).

Explain the forces that influence how people handle conflict:

- Power dynamics affect relationships in which there is an imbalance of power (pp. 172–173).
- Attitudes about conflict in general or about specific disagreements can cause people to avoid dealing with them (p. 173).
- People may be reluctant to discuss certain topics with particular people, a behavior known as **communication boundary management** (p. 173).
- **Communication climate** varies and may be **uncertain** ⊙, **defensive** ⊙, or **supportive** ⊙ (p. 174).
- Cultural issues, such as gender expectations, religious beliefs, and identification with an *individualist culture* or a *collectivist culture*, have a strong influence on conflict (pp. 174–177).

- Our reasons for choosing certain channels may be rooted in emotions or practical considerations (pp. 177–178).
- The Internet provides an arena for **flaming**, posting hostile online messages to an individual; **trolling**, posting hostile online messages to a more general group; and **cyberbullying**, sending multiple abusive attacks through electronic channels (pp. 178–179).

Evaluate and employ strategies for managing conflict in different situations:

- **Escapist strategies** avoid direct conflict and are good for quick resolutions but may leave issues unresolved (p. 180).
- **Challenging strategies** promote the interests of individuals who use assertiveness to get their way (p. 181).
- **Cooperative strategies** benefit both parties (p. 181).
- A focus on the issues avoids **verbal aggressiveness**, or personal attacks on individuals (pp. 181–183).
- **Probing**, asking questions that encourage precise answers, and playing **devil's advocate**, pointing out worst-case scenarios, are two techniques for healthy debate (p. 183).
- Other useful tactics include negotiating alternatives, clarifying the importance of the outcome, and reassuring your partner of your good intentions (pp. 183–184).

Compare levels of resolution in conflict outcomes:

- With **compromise**, which may involve **trading** or **random selection**, both parties give up something to gain something (p. 184).
- A solution that satisfies all parties is win-win; a lose-lose solution has no winner (pp. 184–185).
- **Separation**, removing oneself from the situation, is a form of resolution, as is making a decision to allocate power for certain decisions (pp. 185–186).

Look for **LearningCurve** throughout the chapter to help you review.
bedfordstmartins.com/commandyou

9 } Communicating in Groups

Curtis walks for his wife. Danielle walks for her mother. Lynette walks for herself. And Cindy walks for her young granddaughter in the hope that she'll never hear the four terrifying words that changed Cindy's life forever: "You have breast cancer."

Every year, the organization Susan G. Komen for the Cure plans "3-Day," sixty-mile walks all over the United States to raise funds for breast cancer. Individuals are required to raise a minimum of $2,300 to participate and must train mentally and physically for the challenge of the walk.

Even given the challenges, thousands of men and women (over 220,000 since 2003) gladly devote their time and effort to participate ("Susan G. Komen," 2011a). They plan money-raising events, from car washes to fashion shows. They prepare their bodies with virtual trainers and volunteer practice walks. Susan G. Komen for the Cure also hosts online forums so that participants have a virtual space to encourage and support one another, before and after the walk.

By the time the 3-Day for the Cure weekends arrive, participants know that they are members of a community—more powerful than any individual—that shares goals, drive, and quite often, the experience of being touched by breast cancer, either personally or through the struggle of a loved one. That sense of community certainly comes in handy when rain pours down, calves get sore, blisters form, and ice packs just aren't enough. In any direction a participant looks, there is a fellow teammate ready to point out their shared commitment: "Sixty miles. I can do that."

After you have finished reading this chapter, you will be able to

List the characteristics and types of groups and explain how groups develop.

Describe ways in which group size affects communication.

Identify the influence of networks in groups.

Define the roles individuals play in a group.

Identify key issues affecting group communication and effectiveness.

G iven the complexity of communication between two individuals (a dyad), as mentioned in earlier chapters, consider how much more complicated the process can become when you add more people! When three or more people come together, their interactions and relationships—and their communication—take on new characteristics, as you can see in our discussion of the 3-Day for the Cure walks. In this chapter, we'll learn more about group communication, how groups operate, and the factors that influence their communication.

Understanding Groups

Your family sitting down to dinner. A group of coworkers sitting down for a drink at the end of a shift. Six exasperated parents sitting in a doctor's office with sick kids. Each of these examples involves multiple people engaged in some activity—and most of us would probably say that these are examples of "groups of people." But are they really groups? We'll explore what it means to be in a group, in addition to what types of groups exist and how those groups develop.

Characteristics of Groups

For our purposes, a **group** is a collection of more than two people who share some kind of relationship, communicate in an interdependent fashion, and collaborate toward some shared purpose. When we break that definition down, we can identify three key characteristics that make a group something other than just a collection of individuals:

- **A shared identity.** Members of a group perceive themselves as a group. That is, they share a sense of identity: they recognize other members of the group, have specific feelings toward those individuals, and experience a sense of belonging. Thus, a variety of people who identify themselves as part of a group (political parties, for example, or fan organizations) are as much a group as a baseball team or a string quartet.

- **Common goals.** Members of a group usually identify with one another because they have one or more goals in common. Goals may be very specific—coming up with an ad campaign for a new project or organizing a mission trip for a congregation—or they might be quite general, such as socializing. In either case, a shared sense of purpose helps define a group, even when there is some disagreement about specific goals or ways of achieving them.

- **Interdependent relationships.** Members of a group are connected to one another and communicate in an interdependent way. Simply put, the behavior of each member affects the behavior of every other member. This interdependence is fostered by the way that group members adopt specific roles and collaborate to accomplish goals. These goals might be very specific (completing a specific task) or very general (socializing).

{ **Thus, a variety of people who identify themselves as part of a group (political parties, for example, or fan organizations) are as much a group as a baseball team or a string quartet.** }

Looking back at the examples that we opened this section with, you can probably guess that your family or a group of coworkers constitutes a group. You share an identity with the other members and have feelings about them (for better or worse); you likely have common goals, and you are interdependent—that is, you rely on them, and they on you, for love, friendship, or professional growth. This is not the case with the strangers in a pediatrician's office. They might share a goal (seeing the doctor), but they are not interdependent, and they do not share an identity.

Size and proximity were once major factors in group creation, but the ease with which modern technology allows individuals to communicate has diminished the relevance of those factors. Four friends chatting over coffee at your local Starbucks constitute a group; so do twenty individual photographers who've never met but who contribute to a group photo pool on Flickr. In both cases, the individuals are joined by shared goals, shared identity, and interdependence; these three key factors—not size or proximity—determine group status. Of course, not all groups are alike. Let's take a look at different types of groups.

Group Types

Groups can take many forms. The most common among them are called **primary groups**—long-lasting groups that form around the relationships that mean the most to their members. Your family constitutes one primary group to which you belong; your friends are another.

In addition to primary groups, there are groups defined by their specific functions (for instance, support groups, study groups, and social groups). However, any one of these groups can perform multiple functions. Alcoholics Anonymous (AA), for example, is primarily a **support group**—a set of individuals who come together to address personal problems while benefiting from the support of others with similar issues. But AA is also a **social group**, as membership in the group offers

◊ Bandmates, such as the members of TV on the Radio, must share a sense of identity, communicate interdependently, and collaborate to achieve their shared goal of creating music.

opportunities to form relationships with others. And finally, as a group with a specific mission—to help members manage their struggles with alcohol and addiction—AA is also a **problem-solving group**.

Culture and You

In Chapter 7, we talked about family interactions as an example of interpersonal relationships. Now think about your family as a group. What are your family's common goals? What do the members of your family see as the family's defining traits?

While all groups are to a degree social, some are more task oriented than others. **Study groups**, for example, are formed for the specific purpose of helping students prepare for exams. Perhaps the most task-oriented and goal-driven type of group is the **team**—a group that works together to carry out a project or to compete against other teams. Sports teams are obvious examples, but teams are also common in large organizations or as subsets of other groups: an Army unit might select a few members to form a reconnaissance team; a community group might nominate a team of individuals to take charge of its annual fundraiser.

One of the more noteworthy and common types of groups in today's organizations is the **self-directed work team**, a group of skilled workers who take responsibility for producing high-quality finished work (Douglas, 2002). In self-directed work teams, members bring complementary skills and experiences that enable the team to accomplish more than any individual member could achieve independently (Katzenbach & Smith, 1993).

In self-directed work teams, many typical management functions are completely controlled by the team members. For example, members arrange their own schedules, buy their own equipment, and set their own standards for productivity, quality, and costs. They conduct their own peer evaluations, bring in new members, and coordinate future plans with management. The theory is that when people have more control over their work, they have a more positive attitude and are more committed to the group.

Perhaps the most dramatic impact of self-directed teams is the improved performance and behavior of employees throughout the organization. In enterprises characterized by self-directed teams, the environment is marked by cooperation rather than competition.

Of course, the lessons of self-directed work teams extend far beyond work situations. Collaborative software programs (most commonly known as open-source pages or wikis) allow many individuals to collaborate on a written project, creating, editing, and linking content and reviewing the work of others.

Group Development

If you've ever become wrapped up in a reality TV show, such as *Survivor*, *The Biggest Loser*, or *Top Chef*, you know how fascinating and dramatic group interactions can be. In each of these shows, a season typically opens with the formation of a group: cast members start off as strangers but are quickly thrust into a group situation—sharing a living space and working together to accomplish certain tasks. As the season progresses, the group members bond, conflicts erupt, and alliances are forged. In fact, much of the drama in reality television stems from the tensions that arise between cast members as they struggle to work with—or against—one another. Of course, these "reality" shows are often manipulated—contestants are selected at least in part for their TV "presence," and scenes are edited to heighten the drama. But the shows do reflect some basic truths about how groups develop (Wheelan, 1994). Research shows that as a group progresses it goes through five specific stages, memorably called forming, storming, norming, performing, and adjourning (Tuckman, 1965). Using *Survivor* as an extended example, let's take a look at each stage.

Forming. When a group first comes together, its members are unsure how to act around one another, nervous about how others perceive them, and unclear on their roles. In this **forming** stage, group members try to negotiate who will be in charge and what the group's goals will be. The primary purpose of this stage is for group members to make friends, come to a point where they feel that they "fit in," and learn more about one another and the group's objectives. Once individuals feel accepted, they can begin to identify with the group (Moreland & Levine, 1994). On *Survivor*, contestants are initially divided into two groups, or "tribes." Contestants don't usually have much say regarding which tribe they'll become a part of: they might be randomly selected or assigned to a tribe based on factors like gender (seasons 6 and 9), age (season 21), or even race (season 13). Almost immediately, tribe members begin sizing up their competition—making judgments about one another's strengths, weaknesses, trustworthiness, and likability.

Storming. After forming, group members move into the **storming** stage, in which they inevitably begin experiencing conflicts over issues such as who will lead the group and what roles members will play. On *Survivor*, a tribe member who shows prowess in gathering food or making fires, for example, will become more valued than other members. This process is shown in harsh relief as tribe members continually assess each of their fellow contestants during periodic "tribal councils." Group members who are detrimental to the groups' goals—or who pose a threat to individual goals—are voted off.

Norming. During the **norming** stage, norms emerge among members that govern expected behavior. **Norms** are recurring patterns of behavior or thinking that come to be accepted in a group as the "usual" way of doing things (Scheerhorn & Geist, 1997). During this stage, group roles also solidify, and a leader emerges. On *Survivor*, some tribe members take on leadership roles or present themselves as likable heroes or ambitious villains; other contestants draw on specific strengths (such as physical prowess or fishing expertise) to make themselves invaluable to their fellow tribe members. In addition, group identity grows stronger as members begin to realize the importance of their roles within the group and the need to cooperate to accomplish goals.

Performing. Once the group has established norms, the action shifts to accomplishing tasks. During the **performing** stage, members combine their skills and knowledge to work toward the group's goals and overcome hurdles. On *Survivor*, tribemates work together on group challenges, such as building a shelter for the tribe. They might also endeavor to work together on physical challenges to earn rewards for the tribe.

Adjourning. Many groups—though clearly not all—eventually disband. For groups whose project or task has come to an end, there is an **adjourning** stage. The group members reflect on their accomplishments and failures as well as determine whether the group

📍 On *Survivor: Nicaragua*, Shannon quickly decides that teammate Jud is a "dumb blond" and dubs him "Fabio." The nickname sticks, but not the impression: "Fabio" is the last survivor standing and wins the million-dollar prize.

will disassemble or take on another project. Members may also opt to maintain friendships even if they will no longer be working together. On reality shows like *Survivor*, some or all contestants typically return for a reunion episode of the season, where they discuss the game. Some contestants' friendships endure long past the end of the show; others profess their dislike or use the reunion as an opportunity to make amends with tribemates with whom they had a conflict.

LearningCurve
bedfordstmartins.com/commandyou

Group Size and Communication

When you chat with an instructor in her office, you probably speak freely and informally. The two of you may exchange questions and comments rapidly, interrupt one another, and prompt each other for more information. But when you sit with that same professor in a classroom full of other students, the nature of your communication changes; you might be expected to raise your hand, defer to other students who are already speaking, or not ask questions at all.

What has changed? Why is the nature of your communication so different in the classroom compared to the way you converse in her office? In this section, we'll take a look at how group communication grows more complex as the number of individuals increases.

Size and Complexity

The basic logistics of communication—the need to take turns speaking and listening, for example—grow more complex the larger a group gets, creating the need for more structured exchanges among members. Specifically, the bigger the group, the more its communication takes on the following characteristics:

- **Interaction is more formal.** Group communication simply cannot work in the same kind of informal way that dyadic communication occurs, due to the need to include more communicators in the discourse. Individuals participating in a group may feel the need to obtain permission to speak, and they may also be reluctant to interrupt a speaker.

◍ When you're chatting with a professor during office hours, you are the focus of your professor's attention. However, in the classroom, you have to respect the fact that other students want to speak as well!

- **Each member has limited opportunities to contribute.** Participants may want or be required by a leader to share "floor time" with other group members. Such time constraints can inhibit the quality and quantity of their contributions. Even without a formal leader, in larger groups a few members tend to dominate much of the talk, while the less assertive members tend to remain quiet.

- **The communication becomes less intimate.** The greater the number of participants, the less comfortable participants feel self-disclosing or voicing controversial opinions.

- **The interaction consumes more time.** As more participants are invited to contribute or debate, the interaction takes longer to complete.

- **Relationships become more complex.** As more participants are added, the relationships become more complex. In the dyad, of course, there is only one relationship—that between person 1 and person 2.

As indicated by **Figure 9.1**, adding just one person to a dyad means that each of the three members of the new group must now deal with four potential relationships—one between persons 1 and 2; another between persons 1 and 3; a third between persons 2 and 3; and finally, the group relationship among all three participants. The number of relationships at play multiplies with each additional participant who joins a group: in a group of four, there are 11 potential relationships; in a group of five, there are 90; a six-member group involves 301 relationships; and so on.

Size and the Formation of Cliques

In the comedy series *The Big Bang Theory*, geniuses Leonard and Sheldon are roommates and close friends. Sheldon, the quirky theoretical physicist, is extremely socially awkward and rarely takes kindly to new people

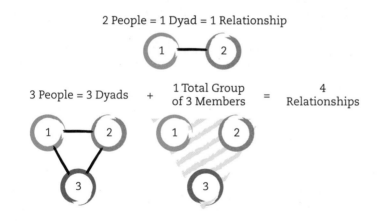

2 People = 1 Dyad = 1 Relationship

3 People = 3 Dyads + 1 Total Group of 3 Members = 4 Relationships

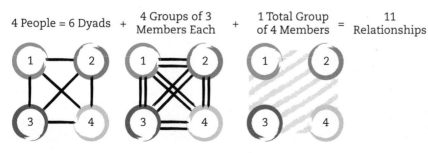

4 People = 6 Dyads + 4 Groups of 3 Members Each + 1 Total Group of 4 Members = 11 Relationships

◐ Figure 9.1 **Complexity of Group Relationships.** Each time a person is added to a group, the number of potential relationships increases substantially.

🔵 Leonard and Penny's relationship turns *The Big Bang Theory* into a big awkward-fest because best friend Sheldon fails to pick up on social cues and give the couple privacy.

or situations. Inevitably, when Leonard starts dating their neighbor Penny, Sheldon has a difficult time adapting to his friend's new time commitments. In fact, he even winds up trying to trail along on Leonard and Penny's dates and frequently interrupts them when they wish to enjoy time alone. Even if you've never behaved quite like Sheldon, perhaps you've felt like he does—you love hanging out with your best friend, but whenever her boyfriend is around, you feel like you might as well be invisible. That's because your presence has changed the nature of the communication from dyadic to group communication, but the other two people haven't adjusted their communication behavior. They've remained a dyad, forming a subgroup that leaves you the lone outsider.

As a group's size increases, similar problems arise. **Cliques** (or coalitions) emerge—small subgroups of individuals who have bonded together within a group (Wilmot, 1987). Cliques are a common part of group life—they're a fixture in middle and high schools. You have your marching band kids, your football players, the art students, and so on. Many people think that they will escape cliques once

high school ends, but this is usually not the case. In college, you might form cliques with people in your major, your dorm, or a particular organization. In office settings, members of cliques or coalitions typically sit next to each other in meetings, eat lunch together, and support one another's positions.

When cliques take shape in a group, communication becomes more challenging because members are no longer dealing only with other individual members. Rather, they must navigate relationships and figure out how to communicate with entire subgroups. In addition, **countercoalitions**, in which one subgroup positions itself against another on an issue, can leave anyone who isn't affiliated with a subgroup in a very awkward position.

Group Size and Social Loafing

On many education and learning blogs, you can find students and instructors complaining about one of the most dreaded assignments of all time: the group project. At first glance, doesn't it seem that group projects should be easier than working solo? There are more minds to share in the work and more people to try out ideas with. But what we all dread is having group members who don't pull their own weight. The fact is, the larger a group, the more prone members may become to **social loafing**—failing to invest the same level of effort in the group that they'd put in if they were working alone or with one other person. Even in cutthroat competitions like *Survivor*, there are always a few contestants who manage to make it through to the final simply by keeping their heads low and letting their teammates do most of the work.

> ### Ethics and You
>
> Are you comfortable pointing out social loafing in a group? How much responsibility do you feel to combat this problem in a group situation?

Clearly, social loafing affects both participation and communication in groups (Comer, 1998; Shultz,

1999). When a person fails to speak up because he or she feels shy around a lot of people, the person is engaging in social loafing. Social loafing also results from the feelings of anonymity that occur in large groups, where it is more difficult for an individual member's contributions to be evaluated. Thus, a member may put in less effort, believing that nobody will notice that he or she is slacking or, conversely, that he or she is working hard. Social loafing even occurs in large electronic networks: some members of an online discussion group, for example, may actively engage in the discourse by posting regular messages, while others—known as lurkers—may just read others' posts and contribute very little.

Group Networks

Just as a group's size strongly influences communication within the group, so do networks. **Networks** are patterns of interaction governing who speaks with whom in a group and about what. To understand the nature of networks, you must first consider two main positions within them. The first is *centrality*, or the degree to which an individual sends and receives messages from others in the group. The most central person in the group receives and sends the highest number of messages in a given time period. At the other end of the spectrum is *isolation*—a position from which a group member sends and receives fewer messages than other members.

A team leader or manager typically has the highest level of centrality in a formal group, but centrality is not necessarily related to status or power. The CEO of a company, for example, may be the end recipient of all information generated by teams below her, but in fact only a limited number of individuals within the organization are able to communicate directly with her. Her assistant, conversely, may have a higher degree of centrality in the network. As you might imagine, networks play a powerful role in any group's communication, whether the group is a family, a sports team, a civic organization, or a large corporation.

In some groups, all members speak with all others regularly about a wide range of topics. In others, perhaps only a few members are "allowed" to speak directly with the group's leader or longest-standing member about serious issues. In still other groups, some members may work alongside one another without communicating at all. There are several types of networks, including chain networks, all-channel networks, and wheel networks (see **Figure 9.2**) (Bavelous, 1950).

Chain Networks. In a **chain network**, information is passed from one member to the next rather than shared among members. Such networks can be practical for sharing written information: an e-mail forwarded from person to person along a chain, for example, allows each person to read the original information from prior recipients. But this form of group communication can lead to frustration and miscommunication when information is conveyed through ways that are easier to

◯ Figure 9.2 Group Communication Networks
Source: Scott (1981), p. 8. Adapted with permission.

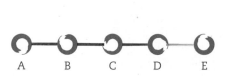

Chain

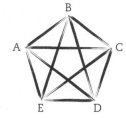

All-Channel

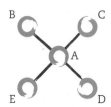

Wheel

distort, such as spoken words. Person A tells person B that their boss, Luis, had a fender bender on the way to work and will miss the 10:00 A.M. meeting. Person B tells person C that Luis was in an accident and will not be in the office today. Person C tells person D that Luis was injured in an accident; no one knows when he'll be in. You can imagine that Luis will be in a full-body cast by the time the message reaches person G!

All-Channel Networks. In an **all-channel network**, all members are an equal distance from one another, and all members interact with each other. When people talk about roundtable discussions, they're talking about all-channel groups: there is no leader, and all members operate at equal levels of centrality. Such networks can be useful for collaborative projects and for brainstorming ideas, but the lack of order can make it difficult for such groups to complete tasks. Imagine, for example, that you're trying to arrange a meeting with a group of friends. You send out a mass e-mail to all of them to determine days that will work, and you ask for suggestions about where to meet. Each recipient can simply hit "reply all" and share their response with the group. By using an all-channel network, the entire group learns that Friday is not good for anyone, but Saturday is; and while a few people have suggested favorite spots, there's no consensus on where to go. That's where wheel networks come in.

⦿ The copyediting team in a newsroom works as a wheel network. All of the copyeditors report to one copy chief, who regulates the copyediting style.

Wheel Networks. Wheel networks are a sensible alternative for situations in which individual members' activities and contributions must be culled and tracked in order to avoid duplicating efforts and to ensure that all tasks are being completed. In a **wheel network**, one individual acts as a touchstone for all the others in the group; all group members share their information with that one individual, who then shares the information with the rest of the group. Consider the preceding example: as the sender of the initial e-mail, you might take on a leadership role and ask everyone to reply just to you. Then you could follow up with a decision about a time and place to meet and send that out to everyone else. Wheel networks have the lowest shared centrality but are very efficient (Leavitt, 1951).

LearningCurve
bedfordstmartins.com/commandyou

Understanding Group Roles

Within the various groups we belong to, we all tend to fall into particular roles—and these roles influence group communication. There are three types of roles—task, social, and antigroup. Let's look at each of them in turn.

Task Roles

In some cases, a role is defined by a task that needs doing, and a person is asked or appointed to fill it (or he or she volunteers). Such **task roles** are concerned with the accomplishment of the group's goals—specifically, the activities that need to be carried out for the group to achieve its objectives. For example, your role on a committee charged with organizing a sorority rush party might be to post advertisements for the event in key locations around campus and in the campus newspaper.

Task roles can also be specifically related to the group's communication:

- An *information giver* offers facts, beliefs, personal experience, or other input during group discussions ("When the sisters of Chi Omega posted their ad in the student lounge, they had good attendance at their rush party").

- An *information seeker* asks for additional input or clarification of ideas or opinions that members have presented ("Jane, are you saying you're not comfortable with the party theme we're proposing?").

- An *elaborator* provides further clarification of points, often adding to what others have said ("I agree with Ellie about selecting Currier & Chives as our caterer; my friend works there, and she's a great cook").

- An *initiator* helps the group move toward its objective by proposing solutions, presenting new ideas, or suggesting new ways of looking at an issue the group is discussing ("How essential is it that we schedule the rush party for the last Friday of the month? If we moved it a week later, we'd have more time to find the right band").

- An *administrator* keeps the conversation on track ("OK, let's get back to the subject of when to schedule the party") and ensures that meetings begin and end on time ("We've got five minutes left; should we wind up?").

- In an online forum, the person who coordinates and sometimes screens the members' comments is called the *moderator* or *master*. An *elder* is the name given to an online group member who has participated a long time and whose authority is respected by the less experienced *newbies*.

Technology and You

Have you ever functioned as or interacted with an online moderator? How did it change your perception of online group dynamics?

Social Roles

Some group roles evolve to reflect individual members' personality traits and interests; such roles are called **social roles**. For example, a nurturing housemate might unofficially fill the role of "house parent"—baking cookies for everyone, listening compassionately to people's problems, and making everyone feel taken care of. Consider these additional examples of social roles (Anderson, Riddle, & Martin, 1999; Benne & Sheats, 1948; Salazar, 1996):

- A *harmonizer* seeks to smooth over tension in the group by settling differences among members ("OK, you both want the party to succeed; you just have different ideas about how to get there").

- A *gatekeeper* works to ensure that each member of the group contributes to discussions ("Tonya, we haven't heard from you yet on this question of when to schedule the party. What are your thoughts?").

- A *sensor* expresses group feelings, moods, or relationships in an effort to recognize the climate and capitalize on it or modify it for the better ("I'm registering a lot of frustration in the committee right now. Let's take a break and reconnect in half an hour").

Each member in a group can play task and social roles. For example, though Evelyn was appointed chairperson of the rush party committee, she also serves as the group's unofficial harmonizer because she has a knack for mitigating tensions between people. Members can also adopt a personal or task role if they believe the role is needed but no one else seems to be willing to fill it. To illustrate, by the end of the rush party committee's first meeting, Candace noticed an air of excitement infusing the gathering as ideas for the party theme began flying back and forth. At the end of the meeting, she took on the role of sensor to tell the other members, "I'm really excited about all the progress we made today. I think that with this kind of enthusiasm, we're going to throw the best rush party in our history!" The meeting ended on a high note, and members adjourned eager to dig into their tasks.

Antigroup Roles

Unlike task and social roles, **antigroup roles** create problems because they serve individual members' priorities at the expense of group needs. You've probably seen evidence of these antigroup roles in the groups you belong to:

- A *blocker* indulges in destructive communication, including opposing all ideas and stubbornly reintroducing an idea after the group has already rejected or bypassed it ("None of the dates any of you proposed will work for the party. It really needs to be five weeks from today, as I said earlier").

- An *avoider* refuses to engage in the group's proceedings by expressing cynicism or nonchalance toward ideas presented or by joking or changing the subject ("Well, whatever, I'm guessing it's not a big deal if this party doesn't even happen, right?").

- A *recognition seeker* calls attention to himself or herself by boasting or by going on and on about his or her qualifications or personal achievements ("I planned a gathering for a women's studies group last year, and it went really well. People still talk about it! So trust me on this one").

- A *distractor* goes off on tangents or tells irrelevant stories ("Does anyone know what happened on *Awkward* last night? I missed it").

- A *troll* is someone in an online group who intentionally inserts irrelevant and inflammatory comments into the discussion in order to stir up controversy.

To mitigate the impact of these antigroup roles, members can revisit the norms the group has established and make the changes needed to improve group communication (for example, "All ideas get a fair hearing"). People fulfilling certain task or social roles can also help. For instance, if you're a gatekeeper, you can prompt an avoider to contribute her opinion on a proposal that the group has been considering. Research also indicates that positive and proactive responses to avoiders and blockers can help establish individuals as leaders in their organizations (Garner & Poole, 2009).

Role Conflict

Imagine that you work at a local retail store and you've been promoted to store manager. As part of your new role, you will have to manage staff members who are working as individual contributors at the store. Several of them are also your close friends, and you all used to be at the same level in the store.

Role conflict arises in a group whenever expectations for a member's behavior are incompatible. The roles of manager and friend are inherently in conflict. After all, as a manager, you'll have to evaluate staff members' performance. And how can you give a good friend a poor performance review and still remain friends?

As you might imagine, role conflict can make group communication profoundly challenging, and there are no easy answers to this kind of dilemma. In the case of the retail store, you might decide not to give your friend a negative review in the interest of saving the friendship. Or perhaps you'll decide to give candid constructive feedback to your friend on his performance. But you'll try to constrain the damage to your friendship by saying something like "I hope you know I'm offering this feedback as a way to help you improve. As your friend and manager, I want to see you do well here."

LearningCurve
bedfordstmartins.com/commandyou

Additional Factors Affecting Group Communication

In addition to size and networks, numerous other factors affect communication within groups—most notably cohesion, groupthink, norms, clarity of goals, and individual differences. In this section, we explore each of these additional factors in more detail.

Cohesion

Cohesion is the degree to which group members have bonded, like each other, and consider themselves to be

⬥ Groups of coworkers who participate in challenges like Tough Mudder while outside of the workplace find that they experience greater cohesion when they return—having made it through electric shock fields, pools of freezing mud, and other physical obstacles together.

one entity. A cohesive group identifies itself as a single unit rather than a collection of individuals, which helps hold the group together in the face of adversity. In fact, cohesion is an important factor in generating a positive group temperament, or *climate*, in which members take pride in the group, treat each other with respect, feel confident about their abilities, and achieve higher success in accomplishing goals. Such positive climates can also foster optimism and confidence in the face of obstacles. A self-confident, cohesive group tends to minimize problems, eliminate barriers, and cope well with crises (Folger, Poole, & Stutman, 2001). In general, cohesive groups perform better than noncohesive groups on decision-making tasks (for example, selecting a course of action more quickly and making more informed choices) (Carless & DePaola, 2000). Nonverbal communication is also influenced by group cohesion; Yasui (2009) found that cohesive group members often repeat and build on one another's gestures.

You can determine group cohesion in two ways. First, take a look at how the participants feel about their own membership in the group. Members of a cohesive group are enthusiastic, identify with the purposes of the group, and tell outsiders about its activities. Even positive, constructive argumentation (as opposed to verbal aggressiveness) can be a sign of group cohesiveness (Anderson & Martin, 1999). Second, consider how well the group retains members. A cohesive group will retain more members than a noncohesive group. The more satisfaction and fulfillment members feel through their group participation, the more cohesive the group.

Gouran (2003) offers several practical suggestions for increasing cohesion and fostering a more positive group experience:

- Avoid dominating other group members.
- Stay focused on the tasks the group must accomplish.
- Be friendly.
- Show sensitivity to and respect for other members.
- Demonstrate that you value others' opinions.
- Cooperate with other members rather than compete with them.

Clearly, cohesive groups offer tremendous benefits, but too much cohesion can actually cause the group to be unproductive. For example, if you and the other members of your study group enjoy each other's company to the point that you never get your work done, then you'll be unlikely to achieve your goal: doing well on an exam! In addition, excessive cohesion can lead to groupthink, an important group factor that we discuss next.

> A cohesive group identifies itself as a single unit rather than a collection of individuals, which helps hold the group together in the face of adversity.

Groupthink

As you learned in Chapter 8, engaging in productive conflict fosters healthy debate and leads to better decision making. Unity and cohesion are important for groups to operate effectively, but if these qualities are taken to an extreme—that is, if they become more powerful than members' desire to evaluate alternative courses of action—the group can't generate enough diverse ideas to make smart decisions (Miller & Morrison, 2009; Park, 2000).

Consider the tragic explosion of the U.S. space shuttle *Challenger* in 1986. Prior to launch, there had been some concern among many engineers that certain fittings (called O-rings) might fail, but the shuttle launched in spite of these concerns. Eventually, those fittings were indeed found to be related to the explosion, but a large part of the blame for the disaster was laid on communication failures within NASA. Engineers later testified that the climate at NASA made them reluctant to voice their concerns if they couldn't back them up with a full set of data (McConnell, 1987). Indeed, the Rogers Commission (1986), which investigated the disaster, noted that if safety concerns had been more clearly articulated—and if NASA management had been more receptive to concerns raised by engineers from various departments—it is unlikely that *Challenger* would have launched that day.

The *Challenger* explosion is often pointed to as a classic example of **groupthink**—a situation in which group members strive to maintain cohesiveness and minimize conflict by refusing to critically examine ideas, analyze proposals, or test solutions (Janis, 1982). In a more receptive group climate, a productive conflict over the O-rings might have revealed the problems that the engineers sensed but couldn't quite put their fingers on. The following are some symptoms of groupthink that you should be aware of in all your group memberships:

- Participants reach outward consensus and avoid expressing disagreement so as not to hurt each other's feelings or appear disloyal.

⬦ Sometimes voicing dissent is more important than group unity. If the engineers at NASA had shared their concerns, the *Challenger* disaster might not have happened.

- Members who do express disagreement with the majority are pressured to conform to the majority view.
- Tough questions are ignored or discouraged.
- Members spend more effort justifying their decisions than testing them.

One important way to prevent groupthink is to encourage dissent among members and manage it productively (Klocke, 2007). In fact, some of the same practices for handling interpersonal conflict discussed in Chapter 8 can help you deal constructively with disagreements in a group. For example, frame conflicts as disagreements over issues or ideas, not as evidence of a weak character or some other personal shortcoming in particular members. To illustrate, when someone in the group expresses a dissenting viewpoint, don't say, "It's clear that you aren't as dedicated to our cause as I had hoped." Instead, say something like "It looks like we have some different ideas circulating about how to handle this new problem. Let's list these ideas and talk about the possible benefits and risks of each of them." A recent study by Aakhus and Rumsey (2010) supports this point by noting that

productive conflict can generate *more* supportive communication for members of an online cancer support community than simply expecting members to keep dissenting opinions private.

Norms

As you saw earlier in the chapter, over time a group will develop norms. Norms are determined by the group itself and are imposed by members on themselves and on each other; they direct the behavior of the group as a whole and affect the conduct of individual members. In a business environment, norms might dictate the kinds of topics that can be expressed in a meeting (Should non-task-related conversation be interjected? Are jokes appropriate?). In an online group, norms might evolve to govern the use of foul language, negative comments, or criticism. For example, a recent study showed that established members of an online anorexia support group allow new members to share pro-anorexic statements in order to establish that they are ill. In time, however, these members are initiated into the group norm that prohibits such unhealthy and negative statements (Stommel & Koole, 2010).

Some norms have a negative impact on communication. For example, suppose a group permits one member to dominate the conversation or allows members to dismiss an idea before discussing its pros and cons. A group with these norms will have difficulty generating enough diverse ideas to make informed decisions. If you find yourself in a group with unproductive norms like these, consider modifying them—this is possible if you approach the task diplomatically (Brilhart & Galanes, 1992). The following three-step process can help:

1. **Express your loyalty and dedication to the group, to show that you have the group's best interests at heart.** For instance, say something like "I've been a member of this school committee for two years now and have hung in there during the tough times as well as the good times. I want to see us be the best we can be."

2. **Cite specific examples of the behavior you find harmful to the group's effectiveness.** The following illustrates that method: "When we didn't take time to explore the pros and cons of the special-ed funding strategy that came up last month, we ended up making a decision that we regretted later."

3. **Ask other members for their opinions about the problem norm you've identified.** If others feel that the norm is still warranted, they may advocate keeping it ("Well, there are some situations where we don't have as much time as we'd like to consider the merits of an idea. During those moments, we need to be able to move ahead with a decision quickly").

With respectful, productive discussion, the group may decide to maintain the norm, change it under specific conditions ("We'll have someone play devil's advocate when time allows"), or abandon it entirely.

Clarity of Goals

Think of the worst group meeting you've ever attended. How would you describe that meeting? Was the conversation disorganized? Unproductive? Confusing? Did you leave the meeting with a bad feeling about working with the group again in the future? Often these reactions to a group's communication are caused by the lack of a clear goal. To communicate productively in any group, members need goal clarity; that is, they must understand what the group's purpose is, what goals will help the group achieve its purpose, how close the group is to achieving its goals, and whether the activities members are engaging in are helping the group move toward its goals.

Goals vary considerably from one group to another. For example, a team in one of your classes may have the simple goal of completing a fifteen-minute in-class exercise and reporting the results to the rest of the class. An urban beautification fund-raising committee may have the goal of collecting $4,000 for new landscaping at a neighborhood park.

The best way to make sure your group has clear goals is by encouraging the members to define them as a group. When members take part in establishing goals, they feel more committed to and excited about achieving those objectives. Research shows that a group is more likely to reach its goals when those goals are communicated in terms that are specific ("Raise $4,000 by the end of March"), inspiring ("Imagine our neighborhood becoming a community of choice for young families"), and prioritized ("We'll need to focus on this goal first and then this other one next") (O'Hair, Friedrich, & Dixon, 2002).

Groups are also more likely to reach their goals if members have some autonomy in deciding how to achieve them. For example, everyone on the urban beautification committee has agreed that the group wants to raise $4,000 by the end of March. But the committee chair decides not to dictate how the group should approach this task. Instead, he invites members to brainstorm ideas for reaching the goal. By encouraging people to come up with ways to achieve the goal, a group leader ensures that members produce a wide range of ideas. And the more ideas the group explores, the more likely its members will ultimately make an informed choice about how to move forward.

Here are some additional communication strategies for effectively setting group goals (O'Hair, Friedrich, & Dixon, 2002):

- **Define goals in terms of problems to be solved** (for example, "Our goal is to raise $4,000 to beautify Dixon Park"), not values to be embodied ("Our goal is to be good citizens of this community"). Value-based goals are vague, so it's difficult to know if and when you've achieved them.

- **Establish clear performance standards.** How will your group know when it has succeeded in reaching its goal? For example, "We will have $4,000 in our checking account by the last day of March."

- **Identify the resources your group will need to accomplish its goals.** Include such things as members' time, office space, funds, and equipment. By anticipating resources, you avoid getting into a situation where your worthy goal shrivels and dies because it never received sufficient funding or attention.

- **Recognize contingencies that may arise.** For instance, "Our goal is to have $4,000 in our account by the end of March, on the assumption that we have good weather for the fund-raising campaign we're planning to hold on the town common."
- **Determine how you will monitor and report progress toward your group's goals.** Will the group hold a weekly status meeting? Will members circulate daily e-mails to update one another?

Once your group begins working toward its goals, encourage members to talk regularly about decisions being made and actions being taken to ensure that these support progress toward the goals.

Individual Differences

Members of a particular group may share goals and an identity, but they each bring personal differences too that can strongly affect communication. Let's examine how cultural factors and communication apprehension—which vary by individual—affect our ability to communicate in groups.

Cultural Factors. As you've learned throughout this book, culture has a big impact on how we communicate. When a group has culturally diverse members, that diversity can have benefits (such as enabling the group to produce a wide array of viewpoints) as well as challenges (including misunderstandings between members).

As we noted earlier, cultures in nations such as the United States, Great Britain, and Canada are largely individualist, valuing personal

> **Culture and You**
> Have you ever misunderstood another member of a group you were involved in because of cultural differences? If so, how did you and the other person deal with the misunderstanding?

accomplishment and competition. As such, people in individualist cultures want their own opinions heard and appreciated, and so they may strive to have their ideas "win" within the group. In a collectivist culture, people value cooperation and group harmony. They allow group norms (rather than their own personal goals) to have the largest influence on their behaviors and thoughts (Triandis, Brislin, & Hul, 1988). Not surprisingly, this difference can present a challenge when members of these cultures are working together in groups. People from individualist cultures will likely more openly vocalize their disagreement with others and try to persuade each other, while the collectivists may feel "bulldozed" as they stifle their own objections for the good of the group.

Gender and sex differences can also affect group communication largely due to the social expectations of masculine and feminine individuals. For example, research shows that women are socially encouraged to focus on establishing relationships within a group, while men—who are socialized to focus on autonomy and success—tend to pay more attention to completing the task at hand (Baird, 1986). Moreover, masculine individuals seek to display signs of their power while communicating in groups (for example, pointing out

> People from individualist cultures will likely more openly vocalize their disagreement with others and try to persuade each other, while the collectivists may feel "bulldozed" as they stifle their own objections for the good of the group.

What About You?

How Well Do You Interact in a Group Setting?

To test how apprehensive you might be in a group setting, complete the following six items, which are based on the Personal Report of Communication Apprehension (PRCA-24). Use the following scale: 1 = strongly agree; 2 = agree; 3 = undecided; 4 = disagree; and 5 = strongly disagree.

_____ 1. I do not like to participate in group discussions.

_____ 2. Generally, I feel comfortable participating in group discussions.

_____ 3. I am tense and nervous while participating in group discussions.

_____ 4. I like to get involved in group discussions.

_____ 5. I get tense and nervous when I engage in a group discussion with new people.

_____ 6. I am calm and relaxed while participating in group discussions.

Scoring: Use the following formula, in which the numbers in parentheses represent your answers to the six items. (For example, if you answered "4" for item 1, then replace the "1" in the formula with a 4.)

$$18 - (1) + (2) - (3) + (4) - (5) + (6)$$

A score of 24 or above indicates a high level of communication apprehension for participation in group discussions; a score of 12 or below indicates a low level of communication apprehension for this situation.

Source: McCroskey (1982). Adapted with permission.

📍 Poor Lisa. She enjoys the camaraderie of other girls at school, but she wants to learn how to *do* math, not feel it!

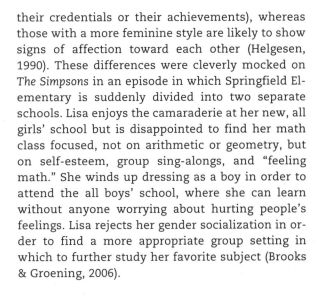

MATT GROENING

their credentials or their achievements), whereas those with a more feminine style are likely to show signs of affection toward each other (Helgesen, 1990). These differences were cleverly mocked on *The Simpsons* in an episode in which Springfield Elementary is suddenly divided into two separate schools. Lisa enjoys the camaraderie at her new, all girls' school but is disappointed to find her math class focused, not on arithmetic or geometry, but on self-esteem, group sing-alongs, and "feeling math." She winds up dressing as a boy in order to attend the all boys' school, where she can learn without anyone worrying about hurting people's feelings. Lisa rejects her gender socialization in order to find a more appropriate group setting in which to further study her favorite subject (Brooks & Groening, 2006).

Communication Apprehension. The next time you're sitting in your communication classroom or logging on to a discussion forum in your online course, take a peek around. Is there someone who never speaks up or raises a hand? Is there someone who rarely posts thoughts on a discussion board? Perhaps you're assuming that this person has nothing to say or that he or she is a social loafer. Maybe you're right. But it's also possible that this individual feels uncomfortable participating in group conversation even when his or her contribution would clearly help the group. What explains this communication apprehension? Scholars have identified several causes (Schullery & Gibson, 2001):

- **Lack of self-esteem.** When an individual doubts the worth of his contributions, he may decline to speak up in a group. Fear of being wrong, of being mocked, or of creating a bad impression can further lead to communication apprehension.

- **Status differences.** Group members who hold a relatively low position in the group's social or political hierarchy may avoid disagreeing with their superiors in the group because they fear retribution from the more powerful persons.

- **Unbalanced participation.** When a group member—or a small number of group members—dominates the conversation in a group, the less aggressive members may retreat from communicating. This strongly influences how decisions get made in the group.

> ### Technology and You
> Have you ever belonged to a group that used technology to address communication apprehension? If so, what technological tools did you use? How effective were they?

Some simple techniques can help a group address communication apprehension among members. For example, to ease self-esteem problems, consider

THINGS TO TRY

Read up on the history of some influential but now defunct music group (such as the Beatles, Nirvana, or Public Enemy). Did the group go through all the stages of group development outlined in this chapter? How did the group determine roles and establish norms? How did members deal with conflict? How did the eventual disbanding of the group play out?

starting a group meeting by having each member tell what he or she appreciates about the member to his or her left. To neutralize status differences, have members sit in a circle and invite lower-status members to speak before higher-status ones. To rebalance participation, suggest a norm that calls for everyone to weigh in on ideas presented in the group. Or look for members who are holding back and invite them specifically to contribute their views.

⬩ As the equitable group leader of Andy's toys in the *Toy Story* films, Woody takes particular care to hear the input of quieter and more apprehensive members of the group, such as Rex and Slinky Dog.

LearningCurve
bedfordstmartins.com/commandyou

Back to } The "3-Day" Walks

At the beginning of this chapter, we talked about the annual Susan G. Komen for the Cure's 3-Day, sixty-mile walks to raise funds for breast cancer—and the initiation of individual participants into a community that shares their goals, drive, and (quite often) life experiences. Consider the nature of the 3-day walks in light of what you've learned in this chapter.

- It may seem unbelievable that thousands of men and women—most of whom will not speak to each other in the process of the walk—could be considered a group. And yet they develop a shared identity (fighters, survivors, supporters), share common goals (to raise money in an effort to rid the world of the scourge of breast cancer), and develop interdependent relationships (supporting each other's fund-raising and training efforts).

- Participants in the 3-day walks fall into several group types. They are certainly examples of a support group: participants share and work through similar struggles and life experiences.

In addition, 3-day walk groups can be considered problem-solving groups (because they attempt to raise money for a cure) and even primary groups (many walkers go on to develop committed friendships with each other).

- As noted, Susan G. Komen for the Cure requires that each participant raise at least $2,300 and commit to training for the walk. While there are opportunities for group training and fund-raising, each individual member of the group is still held personally accountable for his or her efforts. This makes social loafing—common in large groups—much more difficult.

Your Reference } A Study Tool
Now that you have finished reading this chapter, you can

List the characteristics and types of groups and explain how groups develop:

- A **group** is a collection of more than two people who have a shared identity, have common goals, and are interdependent (p. 190).
- **Primary groups** are long-standing and meaningful groups, such as family groups (p. 191).
- Specific-function groups include **support groups**, **social groups**, **problem-solving groups**, and **study groups** (p. 191).
- A **team** is a task-oriented group, and a **self-directed work team** is a group with responsibility for producing high-quality finished work (p. 192).
- Groups develop through five specific stages: **forming** ⊙, **storming** ⊙, **norming** ⊙ (norms are recurring patterns of thought or behavior), **performing** ⊙, and **adjourning** ⊙ (pp. 192–194).

Describe ways in which group size affects communication:

- The bigger the group, the more the group interaction becomes formal, less intimate, more time-consuming, and complex and the less opportunity members have to contribute (pp. 194–195).
- The bigger the group, the more likely **cliques** (coalitions)—small subgroups—will emerge, making communication more challenging (pp. 195–196).
- A **countercoalition**—a subgroup positioned against another subgroup—may leave unaffiliated members in an awkward position (p. 196).
- The larger the group, the more members are prone to **social loafing**, or giving less effort (pp. 196–197).

Identify the influence of networks in groups:

- **Networks** are patterns of interaction governing who speaks with whom in a group (p. 197).
- The member who sends and receives the most messages has the highest degree of centrality; the other end of the spectrum is isolation (p. 197).

- In a **chain network**, information is passed from one member to the next rather than shared among members (pp. 197–198).
- In an **all-channel network**, all members are equidistant and all interact with each other (p. 198).
- In a **wheel network**, one individual is the touchstone for the others (p. 199).

Define the roles individuals play in a group:

- **Task roles** involve accomplishment of goals and include information giver, information seeker, elaborator, initiator, administrator, moderator, and elder (p. 199).
- **Social roles** evolve based on personality traits and members' interests and include harmonizer, gatekeeper, and sensor (p. 200).
- **Antigroup roles** put individual needs above group needs and include blocker, avoider, recognition seeker, distractor, and troll (p. 200).
- **Role conflict** arises when expectations for behavior are incompatible (p. 201).

Identify key issues affecting group communication and effectiveness:

- **Cohesion**, how tightly group members have bonded, helps hold the group together in the face of adversity and helps create a positive climate (pp. 201–202).
- **Groupthink** occurs when members minimize conflict by refusing to critically examine ideas and test solutions (p. 202).
- Norms direct the behavior of the group, sometimes negatively, and may require modification (pp. 203–204).
- Goals should be specific, arrived at by group decision, clearly defined, supported with the necessary resources, and able to be monitored (pp. 204–205).
- Individual differences—including cultural factors and varying levels of communication apprehension—can create communication challenges in groups (pp. 205–207).

 Look for **LearningCurve** throughout the chapter to help you review.
bedfordstmartins.com/commandyou

10 } Leadership and Decision Making in Groups

Parks and Recreation's Leslie Knope loves her job. As deputy director of the Department of Parks and Recreation in the small town of Pawnee, Indiana, she is a committed public servant who is quite simply thrilled to be a part of local government. And while she may seem naive or even delusional (she describes the citizens who scream at her during town meetings as "people caring loudly at [her]"), she is, in fact, an effective and essential leader.

The people she works with are decidedly less enthusiastic. Her boss, Ron, believes that the government should "do as little as possible," and once hired an assistant, April, to thwart any work that comes his way. (Want a meeting with Ron? April will happily pencil you in for Marchtember Oneteenth.) Colleague Tom seems preoccupied with the clothing–rental business he runs on the side.

But Leslie is always focused on her goals, whether it's building a park where there once was a pit or reviving the town's long-forgotten Harvest Festival. She also has a well-earned reputation for being kind, honest, and ethical, which proves to be an asset: when Leslie asks the Pawnee Police Department to provide security at the festival on a volunteer basis, the chief agrees, no questions asked. "Leslie Knope gets as many favors as she needs," he says, "because she's the kind of person who uses favors to help other people."

After you have finished reading this chapter, you will be able to

Describe the types of power that effective leaders employ.

Describe how leadership styles should be adapted to the situation.

Identify how culture affects appropriate leadership behavior.

List the forces that shape a group's decisions.

Explain the six-step group-decision process.

List behaviors to improve effective leadership in meetings.

Demonstrate three aspects of assessing group performance.

 hat makes a leader? Skills? Character? Power? An ability to make decisions? And is it possible for groups to exist, if not thrive, without someone like Leslie Knope taking on an effective and inspiring leadership role? In this chapter, we continue our discussion of group communication by examining two additional processes that often emerge in groups: leading and decision making. These two processes are tightly interrelated: a group's leader affects how the group makes decisions, and the decisions a group makes affect how the leader operates. When leadership and decision making work together in a constructive way, a group stands the best possible chance of achieving its goals. To understand how these processes influence a group's effectiveness, let's begin by taking a closer look at group leadership.

Understanding Group Leadership

It's a word that's constantly tossed about in political campaigns, highlighted on résumés, and used in book titles and biographies. But just what is *leadership*? Scholars have grappled with the task of defining leadership for many years.

Two key terms that show up in many definitions are *direction* and *influence*. That's because in its most essential form, **leadership** is the ability to direct or influence others' behaviors and thoughts toward a productive end (Nierenberg, 2009). This capacity for influence may stem from a person's power or simply from group members' admiration or respect for the individual. Because influence involves power over others, let's take a look at power—what it is and where it comes from.

Five Sources of Power

If you've ever seen the classic Steven Spielberg film *Jaws*, you know that it is, on the surface, the tale of a small coastal town being terrorized by a nasty, man-eating shark. But at the heart of the tale is the interaction among a group of men, each of whom bears or takes some responsibility for ridding the waters of the treacherous animal. First, there's the town's mayor, whose main priority is protecting the local economy. Second, there's the town's new chief of police, who's thrust into the story when the first body washes ashore. Also playing a role are Matt Hooper, a young marine biologist who studies sharks, and Quint, the war-scarred local shark hunter. Over the course of the film, each man demonstrates leadership that is firmly rooted in the nature of the power he possesses.

Researchers have identified five types of power—legitimate, coercive, reward, expert, and referent (French & Raven, 1959).

- **Legitimate power** comes from an individual's role or title. The president, your supervisor at

⬦ Quint, Chief Brody, and Matt Hooper each bring something different to the shark-hunting mission and derive their power from different sources.

work, and the coach of a team all possess legitimate power as elected or appointed leaders. In *Jaws*, the elected mayor of Amity Island, Larry Vaughn, has some degree of legitimate power, as does Martin Brody, the chief of police, though his power is subordinate to the mayor's.

- **Coercive power** stems from a person's ability to threaten or harm others. A harsh dictator who keeps his people under threat of violence or economic hardship holds such power, but so does a boss who threatens to dock or demote employees if they step out of line. In *Jaws*, the mayor—whose primary concern is protecting the town's tourist-dependent economy—uses this kind of power to influence or override decisions made by the police chief. He hired Chief Brody, and he can fire him.

- **Reward power** derives from an individual's capacity to provide rewards. For example, your boss might offer all the people in your department a paid day off if they work late three nights in a row on an important project. In the film, the mayor relies on reward power: hundreds of local fishermen set out to catch the shark in hopes of winning a monetary reward.

- **Expert power** comes from the information or knowledge that a leader possesses. Expert power is divided in *Jaws*. Faced with any other kind of homicide, Brody's credentials as a former New York City police officer might have given him a fair amount of expert power, but as a newcomer without fishing experience, he gets little respect from the islanders. Matt Hooper, who studies sharks, fares a little bit better. But Quint, who has decades of shark-hunting experience, quickly emerges as the true expert, garnering the respect of his crewmates.

- **Referent power** stems from the admiration, respect, or affection that followers have for a leader. The popular kids in your high school may have had the power to influence other students' style of dress or way of behaving simply because others admired them. In *Jaws*, Quint demonstrates this kind of power: when he relates his story as a survivor of the sinking of the USS *Indianapolis* during World War II, Brody and Hooper gain a new sense of understanding of, and admiration for, his obsession with killing sharks.

It's important to note that these types of power are not exclusive of one another; indeed, most leaders wield several, if not all, of these types of power. Quint, for example, demonstrates legitimate power, as captain of his own vessel, as well as expert and referent power. Note also that individuals gain power only if others grant it to them. That's true to some degree even of coercive power: for example, Brody could have chosen to quit his job early on rather than acquiesce to the mayor. Thus, group members often decide to allow a particular individual to lead them.

Ethics and You

Do you find certain types of power more ethical or appropriate than others? Why or why not?

Shared Leadership

With so many sources of power, it's not surprising that in some groups, several individuals take on leadership roles, each drawing from different sources of power. Thus, leadership is shared by a few members of the group who divvy up the power and take control of specific tasks. For example, imagine that your sorority is planning a trip to Jazz Fest in New Orleans. As chair of the social committee, you take care of organizing the group for the event—publicizing the trip and recording the names of individuals who are interested in going. Another sorority sister, Eva, takes care of booking a block of hotel rooms in the French Quarter and negotiating a group rate. Lily, the chapter president, gets in touch with the sister chapter at Louisiana State University to arrange a meeting. Meanwhile, Keisha, your chapter's community outreach chair, organizes a fundraiser on campus in the hope of raising money for Habitat for Humanity in New Orleans so that your sorority may present the organization with a generous check during your visit.

When the talents and powers of each group member are leveraged through shared leadership, members feel more satisfied with the group process and more motivated to perform (Foels, Driskell, Mullen, & Salas, 2000; Kanter, 2009). As a result, the group is more likely to achieve its goals. Probably for these reasons, many businesses and professional organizations in the United States are moving toward a shared-leadership model, whereby they give people at lower levels of the organization decision-making and leadership responsibilities (Krayer, 2010).

Leadership Styles

What is the best way to lead a group? Should you accept input from the members or rule with an iron fist? Do you focus mainly on the task at hand or help resolve relationship problems? It turns out that there is no one "best" style of leadership. Rather, scholars argue that effective group leaders, whether they're leading alone or sharing power with someone else in the group, adapt their leadership styles to the needs of the group or the situation at hand. Four possible styles are discussed here—directive, participative, supportive, and achievement oriented—each of which works best under different conditions (Gouran, 2003; Pavitt, 1999).

Directive. A **directive leader** controls the group's communication by conveying specific instructions to members. This style works best when members are unsure of what's expected of them or how to carry out the group's tasks. Directive leaders can move their group in the right direction by charting next steps in the group's tasks and clarifying the group's goals, plans, and desired outcomes. For example, an instructor must tell students how to complete an assignment or guide them through an in-class exercise.

Participative. A **participative leader** views group members as equals, welcomes their opinions, summarizes points that have been raised, and identifies problems that need discussion rather than dictating solutions. This style works best when group members are competent and motivated to take on the task at hand. Such leaders typically guide and facilitate rather than give instructions to group members. Many online topic forums and blogs are moderated by participative leaders—they allow discussion among members of the group to take off in many directions, and they contribute right along with everyone else. But when needed, they also step in to remind members who have inappropriately veered away from the purpose of the discussion.

Supportive. A **supportive leader** attends to group members' emotional needs. This style is especially helpful when members feel frustrated with a task or with each other. Supportive leaders might stress the importance of positive relationships in the group, remind members of the group's importance, and express appreciation for members' talents and work ethic. Consider Tim Gunn of *Project Runway*. He acts as a leader and mentor figure to the aspiring designers, helping them visualize their designs and talk through their frustrations, and encouraging team members to communicate with each other, listen to each other, and "make it work." He is always profuse in his praise, and even when a particular design doesn't impress him, he is encouraging and positive in his criticism.

> **Culture and You**
> Consider a leadership position that you currently hold or held in the past. Did you favor a particular leadership style? If so, do you think it had to do with the cultures or co-cultures that you belong to?

Achievement Oriented. An **achievement-oriented leader** sets challenging goals and communicates high expectations and standards to members. This style works best when group members see themselves as competent and are motivated to excel at their tasks. In addition to setting lofty goals, such leaders encourage outside-the-box thinking, compare the group with other high-performing groups, and keep members focused on tangible outcomes. Will Schuester, the leader of the New Directions show choir on *Glee*, has an achievement-oriented leadership style. He sets a clear goal for the club—to qualify for and compete at a national competition—and in preparation, he has members check out competitors and create their own new and unique singing routines.

📍 With Mr. Schuester's achievement-oriented leadership, the New Directions choir gleefully sees one of its goals met: winning regionals.

What About You?

What Type of Leader Are You?

Choose the answer that best describes what you might do in each situation.

1. Your chemistry professor assigned a full-semester group project and has asked you to take the lead in your group because chemistry is your best subject. When it comes down to assigning tasks to other group members and getting the project done, what do you do?
   A. Ask a lot of questions. Who knows, someone else may know just as much as you, but is too shy to act on it.
   B. Get down to business! You know the facts, so you immediately delegate work to each member of the group.
   C. Assume you're working with very smart people and allow everyone a chance to say what direction the group should take.
   D. Because you don't want to hurt anyone's feelings, you ask for input and watch everyone's emotional reactions to ensure they are happy.

2. You organized a study group to prepare for your history final exam and invited a handful of other hardworking students from class. Another classmate, Scott, shows up. Scott is rarely prepared for class and isn't contributing to the group. What do you do?
   A. Start asking Scott questions in areas you think he might be knowledgeable. You hope that by inviting him to participate, he will begin contributing to the group.
   B. Don't really notice if Scott is contributing or not because you're too busy organizing the group's class notes.
   C. Try to get Scott to participate but don't go out of your way too much. If he is to be an equal member of the group, he has to reach out too.
   D. Concerned with Scott's feelings, you move your chair next to his and ask how he's doing. This may slow the group's progress, but at least it includes Scott.

3. Managing a local, casual restaurant has its ups and downs, and today is one of the downs. Customers have been complaining that the waiters and waitresses have not been friendly, so you've decided to call a "worker meeting" to address the problem. What do you do at the meeting?
   A. Tell the workers what the customers said and then sit back and listen to everyone's responses.
   B. Explain the problem and offer possible solutions while delegating particular tasks (such as checking on customers) to specific individuals.
   C. Tell your workers about the complaints and explain that you're shocked—you could never have imagined that this scenario would happen.
   D. Open the group meeting by having each member state what's been on his or her mind lately; you figure personal problems may affect the working environment.

If your answers are mostly A's—you are a participative leader; B's—you are a directive leader; C's—you are an achievement-oriented leader; D's—you are a supportive leader. A mix of answers indicates a diverse leadership style.

Competence and Ethics

An ability to mix and match leadership styles to suit your group's needs is an essential skill for a leader. But competent leadership requires other skills. The most effective leaders remain focused on their group's goals, and they hold both themselves *and* the group accountable for achieving those results. They treat all group members in an ethical manner. They also have credibility with their group. That is, members see them as knowledgeable, experienced, believable, and respectable—even if they don't like their leader personally. Finally, competent leaders use skilled communication techniques, such as describing a compelling vision of success and acknowledging the group's valuable talents, to inspire members to contribute their best.

But not all leaders demonstrate these qualities. Some use unethical tactics to try to acquire and keep control over an entire group or individual members within a group. These tactics can include **bullying** or behaviors such as criticizing harshly, name-calling, gossiping, slandering, attacking personal traits, or threatening safety or job security (Smith, 2005). It can also include gesturing offensively, ignoring, giving withering looks, or using a sarcastic tone of voice. Bullies may try to manipulate group members by withholding needed information, excluding them from meetings, or insisting on unrealistic deadlines or expectations. Unfortunately, such unethical tactics can prove successful for some leaders to some degree. Take the case of chef Gordon Ramsay on the reality TV series *Hell's Kitchen*. Aspiring chefs are split into two teams that are pitted against each other in challenges while also preparing and serving dinner to a roomful of diners. Ramsay is very particular about how he wants the food to taste and look. If something is not up to par, he often screams profanities at the contestant responsible for the mistake, showing no qualms about insulting contestants' appearance, ethnicity, or professional background. While his anger and derogatory statements are usually met with a grim "Yes, chef" and he may gain the respect of some contestants, others tire of being abused on a regular basis and break down or walk out.

THINGS TO TRY

Create a chart that lists the four leadership styles described here (directive, participative, supportive, and achievement oriented). Evaluate the leaders of each of the different groups in which you participate—your boss at work, your professors, the resident assistant of your dorm—in terms of their leadership style. Where do they fall on your chart? Do some fit more than one category? Do some fit none?

⦿ Gordon Ramsay's constant belittlement of *Hell's Kitchen* contestants creates a very hostile work environment. Only the brave and thick-skinned need apply!

Ethics and You

Have you ever experienced bullying from a group leader? How did you resolve the situation? Did the leader succeed in manipulating the group, or did more ethical communication techniques prevail?

LearningCurve
bedfordstmartins.com/commandyou

Culture and Group Leadership

As you'll recall from Chapter 3, culture can strongly shape the way people approach leading a group and the ways in which members respond to a leader. Let's look at three particular factors—gender, high versus low context, and power distance—that prove to be especially powerful when leading a group.

Gender and Leadership

Would you vote for a female presidential candidate? A 2007 Gallup poll found that 88 percent of Americans said they would vote for a well-qualified female president to lead the nation (Kohut, 2007). But why the concern over a leader's biological sex? Is there really a difference between men and women as leaders?

With a few key exceptions, research has provided little support for the popular notion that men and women inherently lead differently, though the idea has nonetheless persisted. In essence, we may assume that men have a masculine style of leadership, emphasizing command and control, while women have a feminine style of leadership, emphasizing more nurturing communication environments. For example, some research has suggested that feminine leaders think of organizations as webs of relationships, with leaders at the center of the web, in contrast to the more traditionally masculine view of organizations as pyramids with a leader at the top. Feminine leaders may also view the boundaries between work and personal life as fluid and may communicate their understanding of employees' need to balance professional and personal obligations (Helgesen, 1990; Mumby, 2000; Rosener, 1990).

Interestingly, a study by Sarah Rutherford (2001) notes that men's and women's leadership styles are often dictated by factors other than sex and gender, such as the general communication style of the group or organization. In the marketing department of an organization Rutherford studied, for example, 47 percent of the managers were women, yet the department had a decidedly masculine style, perhaps due to the competitive and confrontational nature of a business that favored a less nurturing response. You might contrast this with the leadership style of Sun-Joo Kim, the chairperson and chief executive of luxury-goods company MCM Worldwide, who leans on motherhood as a model of leadership and seeks to run her business with her heart (Covel, 2008). Such a style might well work in an organization that values and promotes nurturing, sharing, and other traditionally feminine values.

> **Culture and You**
> Do you feel that men and women manage groups differently? What differences have you noticed, and what led you to notice them? Have you seen examples of behavioral flexibility in leaders too?

However, regardless of the leadership style encouraged by a division or an organization, 84 percent of female respondents in Rutherford's study (2001) believed that women manage differently than men did, while 55 percent of men believed the same—supporting the point that the idea of sex differences can be hard to shake. That said, we encourage you to remember the concept of *behavioral flexibility* discussed in Chapter 3. Leadership is a complicated and messy topic, and it seems clear that men and women—when leading a business or even a student organization—must look for opportunities to use the best skills from both traditional styles of leadership at the right time for ethical purposes, regardless of their biological sex.

{ **With a few key exceptions, research has provided little support for the popular notion that men and women inherently lead differently, though the idea has nonetheless persisted.** }

Context and Power Distance

Two additional leadership factors are context and power distance. For example, you may recall that people from high-context cultures (such as Japan) tend to communicate in indirect ways, whereas those from low-context cultures (like the United States) communicate more directly (Hall, 1976). Imagine, for example, a manager tasked with keeping a team on target to meet a very tight deadline. A leader from a high-context culture might simply present a calendar noting due dates and filled with tasks and competing projects; she would rely on her team to get the point that the deadline is in trouble and expect team members to offer solutions. A leader from a low-context culture, on the other hand, would be more likely to clarify the situation directly: "I'm moving the deadline earlier by two weeks; that means you'll need to accelerate your work accordingly." The ways in which group members respond will also be influenced by culture: group members from a high-context culture might communicate in a similarly indirect way with their leader ("We have some concerns about the new deadline"), while those from a low-context culture would be more direct ("Sorry, we can't make the new deadline").

In addition to high- and low-context cultures, power distance is a cultural difference that affects how groups communicate. As we learned in Chapter 3, *power distance* is the extent to which less powerful members of a group, be it a business organization or a family, accept that power is distributed unequally. This means that a person who is leading a group in a high power distance culture and wants all members to offer their ideas in a meeting might need to make a special effort to encourage everyone to participate in the discussion, whereas in a group with low power distance, members are likely to offer their opinions without much prodding.

LearningCurve
bedfordstmartins.com/commandyou

Decision Making in Groups

Because of the large numbers of exchanges and people involved, decision making in a group differs markedly from decision making by one individual or between just two people. For one thing, in a group, a complex set of forces influences decision making. These forces also influence how a group progresses through the decision-making process. In this section, we examine each of these topics in detail.

📍 In a low power distance culture, meetings might feel like roundtable discussions, where everyone gets a chance to speak. In a high power distance culture, meetings are usually more hierarchical.

Forces That Shape a Group's Decisions

Experts have identified three forces—cognitive, psychological, and social—that strongly affect how groups and their leaders discuss and arrive at decisions (Hirokawa, Gouran, & Martz, 1988). Going back to the devastating *Challenger* example from Chapter 9, let's take a deeper look at these forces.

Cognitive Forces. **Cognitive forces** consist of group members' thoughts and beliefs. These affect how everyone in a particular group perceives, interprets, evaluates, stores, and retrieves information, which in turn influences the group's decisions.

Cognitive forces influenced the NASA officials who made the fateful decision to launch the *Challenger* shuttle, a subject you read about in Chapter 9. The officials discounted the credibility of key information available to them at the time, and they drew incorrect conclusions from the data. They also wrongly believed that the shuttle system was sound, which made them overly confident in their ability to have a successful launch.

Psychological Forces. **Psychological forces** refer to group members' personal motives, emotions, attitudes, and values. In the *Challenger* disaster, lower-level NASA decision makers had initially recommended postponing the launch until the temperature warmed up later in the day. But when higher-ups pressured them to reverse their recommendation, they caved in—perhaps because they were worried about losing their jobs if they didn't go along.

The decision makers also changed their attitudes about which criteria to use for postponing a shuttle launch. Previously, NASA rules dictated that a launch wouldn't take place if anyone doubted its safety. But with the *Challenger*, the rule had changed: the launch would proceed unless someone presented conclusive evidence that it was unsafe. Engineers hesitated to express their inconclusive qualms, and so the launch proceeded.

Social Forces. **Social forces** are group standards for behavior that influence decision making. In the *Challenger* disaster, engineers were unable to persuade their own managers and higher-up NASA officials to postpone the launch. They tried to prove that it was *unsafe* to launch rather than take the opposite (and possibly more effective) tactic: to show that no data existed to prove that the launch was *safe*.

The Problem-Solving Process

To make decisions, groups and their leaders often go through a six-step process (Dewey, 1933). To illustrate these steps, consider EcoCrew, a group of sixteen environmentally active students at a West Coast community college who wish to resolve environmental problems in their community.

Identifying the Problem. The EcoCrew group has scheduled its first meeting in the student union lounge. Susan, the group's founder, is the designated leader. Deciding to adopt a participative leadership style, Susan invites each person to give his or her perception of the problem the group will set out to address before debates or questions occur. Members pipe up with a number of issues and activities they'd like the group to address. One suggests the elimination of plastic bags from campus shops; another wants to address littering on the beaches.

By inviting members to voice their concerns one at a time, Susan is providing an opportunity for the group to identify and define several problems. Once all the members have presented their views, Susan encourages the group to discuss the various proposed definitions of the problem and agree on one that EcoCrew can productively address. The group decides that litter, both on campus and on the nearby beach, is the most immediately troubling environmental issue.

Having defined the problem it wants to address, EcoCrew has gotten off to an effective start. According to researchers, many groups don't spend enough time identifying the problem they want to tackle (Gouran, 2003). Without a clear, agreed-on problem, a group can't work through the rest of the decision-making process in a focused way.

Analyzing the Problem. Having decided to tackle litter cleanup as its primary mission, EcoCrew begins to analyze the problem. Susan suggests that each member carry a diary for a week and note how much litter they see and where. When the group meets again the following week, all members agree that the two biggest litter problems in the area are on the beaches and in the wooded areas surrounding the campus parking lots. Several members note that the trash cans on the beaches are not being emptied often enough by city sanitation workers, causing trash overflow to be blown onto the beach by the ocean wind.

Generating Solutions. Once the EcoCrew team has identified and analyzed the problem, the next step is to come up with a solution. Susan starts asking for ideas from the group and writes them down on a whiteboard, to be evaluated later.

This technique, called *brainstorming*, encourages members of a group to come up with as many ideas as possible without judging the merits of those ideas yet. The intent is to prompt fresh thinking and to generate a larger number of potential solutions than a group might arrive at if members evaluated each idea as it came up. As the EcoCrew members throw out idea after idea, the whiteboard grows dense and colorful with possibilities (see **Figure 10.1**).

Once the members have run out of new ideas, they'll need to narrow down the list. To help them focus on the one or two strongest ideas, Susan invites them to define the criteria that eventual solutions will have to meet. First, Susan reminds them that the primary goal would be to reduce litter on the beach. Another member, Wade, then points out that at this point, the group has no budget, so it needs to limit its initial efforts to tasks that have little or no cost. Another member, Larissa, notes that because the group has a relatively small membership, it should focus on things that either the group can manage on its own or the group could encourage nonmembers to participate in as well. The group

◊ Writing down any ideas that your team has on a whiteboard can be a great way to get the creative juices flowing.

concludes that an acceptable solution must meet these key criteria.

> **Technology and You**
>
> If you were involved with Susan's EcoCrew, would you suggest using technology to assist with problem solving? Why or why not? If so, what technologies would you consider?

Evaluating and Choosing Solutions. Once Eco-Crew has generated its list of possible solutions, group members have to evaluate the pros and cons of each idea to consider how well it meets the criteria the members have defined. For example, one member, Kathryn, points out that the lack of funding makes replacing the garbage cans out of the question and would make an antilitter advertising campaign difficult, if not impossible. Wade notes that organizing a beach cleanup would cost next to nothing; they could all volunteer to get together to pick up garbage

◖ Figure 10.1 **Susan's Whiteboard**

- More trash cans!
  - Can we provide these?
  - Get the city to provide?
- Covered trash cans that keep litter in—wind-resistant?
- Increase city sanitation pickups!
  - Letter writing/e-mail campaign?
  - Contact the mayor?
- Beach cleanup?
  - Massive volunteer beach cleanup event
  - Monthly volunteer beach cleanup?
- Antilitter advertising? "Don't pollute!"
  - Flyers/posters would create more litter.
  - Permanent signs/billboards? $$$$

and clean up the beach. Larissa adds that if they get the word out, they'd also be able to attract additional volunteers—and potential new members—from outside the group to participate. Thus the group decides to launch a monthly beach cleanup: a regular social event to raise awareness of the group, encourage nonmembers to participate and new members to join, and involve little to nothing in terms of cost.

Implementing the Solution. Implementing a solution means putting into action the decision that the group has made. For EcoCrew, this means making plans for the regular beach cleanup. The group focuses first on logistics—setting dates and times. One member, Allison, volunteers to act as a liaison with the county sanitation department to see if it can provide trash bags and picks for the volunteers and to arrange for the sanitation trucks to pick up the trash once it's been bagged.

Larissa adds that with a bit of legwork, the group could turn the cleanup into a large community event; she volunteers to arrange for an end-of-day gathering and to see if she can get her mother's sandwich shop to donate food. Wade notes that he

can probably get his roommate's band to entertain free of charge as well.

Assessing the Results. Once a group has implemented its agreed-on solution, members should evaluate the results. Evaluation can shed light on how effective the solution was and whether the group needs to make further decisions about the problem at hand. For EcoCrew, it will be helpful to assess the first event in terms of how well it met the three key criteria:

- Was the beach cleaner at the end of the day as a result of the group's efforts? Before-and-after photos of the beach reveal a very successful cleanup.

- Did the event wind up costing the members any money? Thanks to the donations of local restaurants and supplies provided by the county sanitation department, the event cost the group absolutely nothing.

- Did the event attract volunteers from outside the group? Fifteen nonmembers participated in the cleanup, among them several schoolchildren who attended with their parents.

◊ After their beach cleanup, the EcoCrew team needs to assess the results. The first question should be: "Was the beach cleaner after our event?"

By revisiting these criteria, the group is able to tweak its plan for the following month's cleanup event. Larissa suggests that the members pitch in a few dollars to place an ad in the local paper thanking the volunteers and donors and announcing the date of the next cleanup. Wade follows up by suggesting that the group make a pitch at the local elementary school to get more kids and their families involved. Kathryn volunteers to submit a brief story about the cleanup, along with photos of the event and the results, to the campus newspaper. And Susan suggests holding a raffle at the next event, with half the proceeds paid out in prizes and half retained by the group, to get a small budget started to cover future ads and expenses.

LearningCurve
bedfordstmartins.com/commandyou

Leadership in Meetings

EcoCrew was able to identify a problem, create a solution, and implement it very successfully. Much of the planning and implementation took place in

meetings. Group leader Susan was able to direct the discussion and manage the deliberations in ways that kept the group focused and invited input from all participants. Indeed, meetings—whether face to face, over the phone, online, or through a combination of media—are an integral part of many group activities. But they are not always successful, and the failure of a meeting often rests on the shoulders of the group leader.

Consider Julia, a freelance Web designer who works from a home office. On Friday, Julia received an e-mail from her biggest client, Jacob, asking her to phone in to a meeting with the sales team to discuss marketing materials related to the launch of the new Web site she's designing for his skateboard manufacturing company. Struggling with several competing deadlines, Julia dreaded spending an hour or two listening to a group of people she'd never met discuss parts of the project with which she had little to do. But she reluctantly confirmed that she could take part in the meeting the following Monday.

After spending the better part of Monday morning reviewing her design for the project and outlining a few ideas for ways it could be teased into the marketing campaign, Julia dutifully dialed in to the conference room at the designated time, only to find herself placed on hold for twenty minutes before the meeting began. What followed was equally frustrating: Jacob spent the better part of an hour describing all aspects of the site to the team of salespeople, who were entirely unfamiliar with the project. Julia—who was responsible only for creating the look and functionality of the Web site and had nothing to do with content or sales—sat miserably watching the clock, grateful that at least the team couldn't see her as she scribbled angry doodles and notes to herself.

Meetings can be integral to group decision making, but they can often be unproductive and frustrating. Ineffective meetings are one of the top time wasters cited by workers: one survey of more than thirty-eight thousand workers worldwide found that people spend more than five working hours per week in meetings, and about 70 percent of the respondents felt that most meetings weren't productive (Microsoft, 2005). In this section, we'll analyze meetings from a communication perspective and consider how they can be best used to arrive at better decisions and solutions. We'll discuss how technology has changed meetings—and how it hasn't. Most important, we'll show that effective leadership is crucial to conducting effective and productive meetings.

Planning Meetings Effectively

Let's consider all the reasons Julia found the meeting we've just described so frustrating. First, it was a bad time: she was struggling to meet deadlines and really didn't want to stop working to sit in on a meeting. Worse, she probably didn't really have to be there either—the client was using the meeting to inform the sales team about the site as a whole, not to discuss Julia's design. Further complicating the issue were the meeting's late start, Julia's unfamiliarity with the sales force, and a medium—speakerphone—that limited Julia's communication with the team. Put simply, the meeting was poorly planned.

Proper planning is crucial for successful meetings. Making a few decisions beforehand and taking steps to clarify goals and logistics for the team can lead to more effective decision making during the meeting itself. There are several steps that group leaders can take to plan meetings more effectively.

Justify the Meeting. Before calling a meeting, a group leader should consider what he or she wants to accomplish and assess whether a meeting is even necessary to meet that goal. If there are no clear goals for a meeting, it's impossible for any goals to be met as a result of it. The leader also needs to ensure that only those whose presence is necessary in order to meet the goals or who would truly benefit from attending are included. While not a typical meeting, a good example of this is when Harry Potter first begins to assemble Dumbledore's Army in

◊ Everyone present at the Dumbledore's Army gatherings is well aware of the goal of these meetings: to learn how to fight and defend themselves against the evil Voldemort.

Harry Potter and the Order of the Phoenix. He determines the goals of the meetings (to teach other students how to defend themselves in the face of Voldemort's return to power) and invites only students who he knows will use the training and won't derail the meeting.

In many cases, meetings can be avoided altogether or made smaller and more efficient by asking team members to contribute information ahead of time or by simply picking up the phone to ask someone a question when one arises (Conlin, 2006).

Clarify the Purpose and the Participants. If a meeting is necessary, it is the responsibility of the leader to clearly articulate the goals of the meeting

> If there are no clear goals for a meeting, it's impossible for any goals to be met as a result of it.

and the roles of everyone who is to attend. Think back to Julia's situation. Her client, Jacob, wants to get his sales force interested and excited about the launch of the Web site. Getting the sales force together to view the beta version and get feedback on it might seem like a good way to brainstorm ideas for marketing. But Jacob failed to clarify what he wanted to accomplish at the meeting and what Julia's role would be. He might have made more efficient use of Julia's time by discussing elements of the design with her prior to the meeting or by asking her to outline a few key features for him to use at the meeting instead of requiring her to attend.

Set an Agenda. President Dwight D. Eisenhower noted, "I have often found that plans are useless, but planning is indispensable." Creating a plan is a valuable phase in decision making, even if the plan itself isn't followed to the letter in the end. Setting an agenda is crucial.

An **agenda** for a meeting should detail the meeting's subject, goal, logistics, and schedule. It should list or include any materials that participants would need to have read or reviewed in advance of the meeting so that everyone arrives with the appropriate background on the issue. Think of your agenda as a checklist—an essential component of meeting success (Gawande, 2009). A sample agenda for Jacob's meeting is provided in **Figure 10.2.**

Managing Meetings Effectively

So you now see that meetings can go well—or they can go horribly off track. During a meeting, it is the responsibility of the leader to manage the discussion in ways that help the group communicate while remaining focused on the meeting's goal. The following steps can help.

Arrive Prepared. In a 2005 interview, veteran businessman and writer Simon Ramo estimated that he had attended forty thousand meetings during his career, so he had a strong sense of what works and what doesn't. When running a meeting, the most important thing for a leader to do, Ramo advised, is to be prepared. If you've planned properly, you are fully aware of your goals for the meeting and familiar with all the background information you'll need.

Keep the Group Focused. It's also important to know who the participants are. You should have a sense beforehand of which participants are likely to be the biggest contributors, as well as who will likely need to be kept on track. When a member brings up a topic that's not on the agenda or goes off on a tangent, Ramo advised, "As tactfully as possible, interrupt to move the discussion along" ("Why Most Meetings Stink," 2005). This might be as simple as saying, "We're getting off the subject here," and bringing the group back to the main topic of the meeting.

Of course, as the meeting progresses, it is likely that the goal may be redefined or new goals may emerge. "Keep the objective of the meeting constantly in your mind so you'll keep moving toward the goal," Ramo advised. "But if the goal changes during or because of the meeting, be prepared to invent Plan B."

Summarize Periodically. As a group explores and settles on decisions, it's important that someone (a leader or any member) regularly summarizes what has happened. Summaries provide members with opportunities to confirm, correct, or clarify what has occurred so far during the conversation. Summaries thus help ensure agreement, delineate the next steps, and direct members on how best to carry out their designated tasks.

Keep an Eye on the Time. Nobody likes wasting time sitting through a long meeting when a short one would do. Group leaders need to be aware of time constraints to keep their meetings running efficiently and to respect the time pressures on the other members. When large groups are involved or when the agenda includes many topics or issues, it can be helpful to impose *time limits* on certain

Meeting with sales team to discuss marketing strategies for new SlickBoards Web site.

Date: March 24, 2014
Time: 10:00 A.M.–12:00 P.M. (EST)
Location: Conference Room 2. Call-in number 555-555-0823.

AGENDA

I. Welcome
    A. Quick introduction of core team working on Web site
    B. Introduce purpose of meeting—to discuss the marketing strategies for the new SlickBoards Web site
II. Why do we need a new SlickBoards Web site?
    A. Overview of our current Web site and its deficiencies
    B. Present the concept of the new Web site, why we needed a revamp, and how it improves on the old site
III. What will be on the new SlickBoards Web site?
    A. Outline all the new information about the products that will be on the Web site and how it will increase sales
    B. Explain how clients will be able to customize their SlickBoard directly on the new Web site
IV. How should we market this new Web site?
    A. Discuss the focus of the marketing campaign: What's the message?
    B. Brainstorm how to get the message out
    C. Distill list of ideas; assign roles
V. Conclusion and follow-up
    A. Take any questions or concerns
    B. Establish next meeting time and what should be accomplished by then

◐ **Figure 10.2** Jacob's **Agenda.** Although Jacob's meeting agenda is very well organized, there is no indication that Julia needs to be present or that she plays a role in this meeting.

components of the discussion. When a decision must be made, taking an informal vote—called a **nonbinding straw poll**—can help move the group forward.

Manage Conflict. As you saw in Chapter 8, the best decisions are usually those that have come from productive conflict (Kuhn & Poole, 2000; Nicotera, 1997).

When group members deal with conflict productively, they ask clarifying questions, respectfully challenge one another's ideas, consider worst-case scenarios, and revise proposals as needed to reflect new information and insights. This process leads to sound decisions because it enables group members to generate the widest possible range of ideas as well as test each idea's pros and cons. An idea that survives this rigorous process has a better chance of succeeding in action.

The other advantage of productive conflict is that the group members who have a hand in exploring and arriving at a decision will feel a greater sense of ownership over that decision, which leads to greater commitment. Thus, decisions made through productive conflict have a greater chance of being implemented. That's a good thing, since even the most brilliant decision is useless unless a group puts it into action.

For this reason, making decisions by consensus is often a better approach than making decisions by majority vote. According to the consensus approach, everyone must agree on the final decision before it can be implemented. It takes more time than deciding by majority vote, but because of its power to enhance feelings of ownership and commitment from group members, consensus should be used whenever time allows.

Follow Up. After the meeting has concluded, group members should implement their decisions and take stock of the results as well as the experience of working together. A simple follow-up e-mail that details the decisions reached at the meeting can ensure that everyone came away with the same perceptions and is aware of what each person must do to keep the group moving toward its goal.

Using Technology in Meetings

Technology has changed the nature of meetings in both positive and negative ways. Obviously, the ability to set up virtual meetings through teleconferencing and Internet videoconferencing makes it possible

◊ Research indicates that group members work better face to face initially, but that individuals who are familiar with each other and established as a team also work productively with videoconferencing technology.

for groups to collaborate over long distances. That's how Julia, the freelance designer, is able to "attend" a meeting with her client and his sales staff without leaving home. Such virtual links can be beneficial for a team that needs to actively communicate about some issue or problem. But it also can be ineffective; the fact that everyone *can* be included doesn't necessarily mean that everyone *must* be included. Julia, for example, did not need to sit in on the meeting with the sales team; she had little to add and gained nothing by being there. Further, the ability to share information with team members quickly and efficiently via e-mail and file sharing has enabled teams to avoid some meetings altogether (Conlin, 2006). Julia and Jacob, for example, might have e-mailed a link to the beta version of the site to the entire sales team rather than meet with them to discuss it in the abstract.

> The other advantage of productive conflict is that the group members who have a hand in exploring and arriving at a decision will feel a greater sense of ownership over the decision, which leads to greater commitment.

Select a city, state, or campus problem that is relevant to the members of your class. Form a group to solve the problem using the six-step decision-making process described in this chapter.

Technology and You

Do you prefer virtual or face-to-face communication in meetings and group work? Can you think of examples of electronic communication making group work easier? Can you think of instances in your life where it made group work more difficult?

But is there a difference between face-to-face meetings and virtual meetings? Research indicates that face-to-face teams perform better initially, but once the group is established, virtual teams actually do better at brainstorming, whereas face-to-face teams perform better on tasks that require negotiation or compromise (Alge, Wiethoff, & Klein, 2003; Salkever, 2003). Savvy team leaders, then, will bring their teams together for face time early in the process, if possible, so that team members can get to know one another and get a sense of the others' styles and personalities. But as the teams develop, electronically mediated communication—especially e-mail—can often take the place of face-to-face group meetings.

LearningCurve
bedfordstmartins.com/commandyou

Evaluating Group Performance

Groups that intend to work together and meet on a regular basis should evaluate their decision-making performance periodically. By assessing how well the group makes decisions, achieves its goals, and solves problems, a group can identify and address areas that need improvement. When evaluating your group's performance, it's helpful to assess its overall effectiveness as well as the performance of individual members and leaders.

Albert Kowitz and Thomas Knutson (1980) have done extensive research evaluating groups as a whole. They recommend assessing three aspects of a group's performance: the informational, the procedural, and the interpersonal.

Informational Considerations

Ask yourself whether your group is working on a task that requires everyone's expertise and insights. If not, the group doesn't actually need to be a group! In this case, it should select a different task or assign just one or two members to deal with the current task.

If the task does require contributions from all members, how well is the group doing on this front? For example, are members conducting needed research and inviting one another to share information during group gatherings? Does the group know when it needs to get more data before making a decision? Does the group analyze problems well? Come up with creative solutions? Offer opinions respectfully? Elaborate on problems, concerns, and solutions?

By regularly assessing these aspects of information management in your group, you can identify where the group is falling short and address the problem promptly. For instance, if you notice that the group rushes to make decisions without getting all the facts first, you could say something like "I think we need to find out more about the problem before we take action."

Procedural Effectiveness

How well does your group coordinate its activities and communication? Key things to evaluate on this front are how the group elicits contributions,

○ Think about whether each group member's expertise is necessary to achieve a goal. If not, those members don't need to be present.

delegates and directs action, summarizes decisions, handles conflict, and manages processes.

For example, do some members talk too much while others give too little input? If so, the group needs someone to improve the balance of contributions. Simply saying something like "Allie, I think we should hear from some other people on this subject" can be very effective.

Or does your group tend to revisit issues it has already made a decision on? If so, you can expect many members to express frustration with this time-wasting habit. A leader or another member can steer the group back toward its current task by saying something like "OK, what we've been talking about is . . ." or "I'm not sure revisiting this

previous decision is helping us deal with our current problem."

Interpersonal Performance

How would you describe the relationships among the members of your group while everyone is working together to accomplish a task? If these relationships are strained, awkward, or prickly, the group probably won't function effectively. Observe how group members behave on the following four fronts:

- Do they provide *positive reinforcement* for one another—for instance, by showing appreciation for each other's contributions and hard work?
- Do members seem to feel a sense of *solidarity* with one another—for example, by sharing responsibility for both successes and failures?
- Do members *cooperate freely* with one another, fulfilling the responsibilities they've agreed to shoulder and pitching in when needed?
- Do members demonstrate *respect* for one another—for example, by keeping disagreements focused on the issues or positions at hand rather than on personal character?

If you answer "yes" to these four questions, your group scores high on interpersonal performance.

LearningCurve
bedfordstmartins.com/commandyou

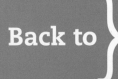

Back to } *Parks and Recreation*

At the beginning of this chapter, we talked about Leslie Knope, a midlevel government bureaucrat in the fictional town of Pawnee, Indiana. Let's take a look at Leslie's leadership and decision-making skills in light of what we've learned in this chapter.

- At Pawnee Town Hall, there is a clear hierarchy of legitimate power. As deputy director, Leslie's power is subordinate to Ron's, but in many ways, their relationship is an example of shared leadership: Ron's commitment to "doing as little as possible," as well as his genuine affection for Leslie and his respect for her work ethic, means that he leaves her in charge of pretty much everything. But although Leslie takes responsibility for the day-to-day running of the department, decision-making power still lies largely with Ron.

- Leslie has an achievement-oriented style of leadership. She identifies a goal and then does everything in her power to reach it. Her commitment, enthusiasm, and optimism are infectious, motivating everyone around her—from her apathetic coworkers to local businesses and other departments—to help pitch in to make it happen.

- In addition to her legitimate power, Leslie has a substantial amount of referent power—she is as committed to behaving ethically as she is to providing services to the people of Pawnee. Her ethics and character inspire the police to work for free during the Harvest Festival.

Your Reference

Describe the types of power that effective leaders employ:

- **Leadership** is the ability to influence others' behaviors and thoughts toward a productive end (p. 212).
- **Legitimate power** ⊙ comes from an individual's role or title (pp. 212–213).
- **Coercive power** ⊙ stems from the ability to threaten or harm others (p. 213).
- **Reward power** ⊙ is derived from the ability to bestow rewards (p. 213).
- **Expert power** ⊙ comes from the information or knowledge an individual possesses (pp. 213–214).
- **Referent power** ⊙ stems from the respect and affection that followers have for a leader (p. 214).
- Most leaders will use more than one type of power, and often leadership is shared by more than one individual (p. 214).

Describe how leadership styles should be adapted to the situation:

- The best leaders adapt their leadership styles to the situation (p. 214).
- A **directive leader** gives specific instructions; this is a good choice when members are unsure of expectations (p. 215).
- A **participative leader** views members as equals, inviting collaboration; this is effective when members are competent and motivated (p. 215).
- A **supportive leader** attends to members' emotional needs; this is helpful when members are frustrated or discouraged (p. 215).
- An **achievement-oriented leader** sets challenging goals and has high expectations; this is useful when members are motivated to excel (p. 215).
- The best leaders behave ethically and avoid **bullying** (p. 217).

Identify how culture affects appropriate leadership behavior:

- Masculine leadership—valuing hierarchy and control—and feminine leadership—valuing nurturance and caring—may stem more from organizational situations and constraints than from deeply entrenched sex differences (p. 218).
- Leaders from high-context cultures tend to make suggestions rather than dictate orders or impose solutions (p. 219).
- Group members in a high power distance culture typically defer to those with higher status (p. 219).

List the forces that shape a group's decisions:

- **Cognitive forces** are members' thoughts, beliefs, and emotions (p. 220).
- **Psychological forces** refer to members' personal motives, goals, attitudes, and values (p. 220).
- **Social forces** are group standards for behavior that influence decision making (p. 220).

Explain the six-step group-decision process:

- Identify and define the problem (pp. 220–221).
- Analyze the problem (p. 221).
- Generate solutions, identifying the criteria that eventual solutions will have to meet (p. 221).
- Evaluate and choose a solution (pp. 221–222).
- Implement the solution (p. 222).
- Assess the results (pp. 222–223).

List behaviors to improve effective leadership in meetings:

- To ensure a well-planned meeting, assess whether the meeting is necessary, ensure that those present are necessary, ask for information in advance, articulate goals, and set an **agenda** (pp. 224–225).
- To manage the meeting, you should arrive prepared; keep the group focused; summarize periodically; keep an eye on the time, perhaps using a **nonbinding straw poll** to help move things along; manage conflict; foster productive conflict; and follow up after the meeting (pp. 225–227).
- Use technology effectively, arranging a face-to-face meeting for the start-up, but as the team develops, allowing mediated communication (pp. 227–228).

Demonstrate three aspects of assessing group performance:

- Informational considerations: Does the group require all its members? Does it need more data? Does it come up with creative solutions? (p. 228)
- Procedural effectiveness: Does the group coordinate activities and communication? Manage problems? (pp. 228–229)
- Interpersonal performance: Do the group members reinforce one another? Feel a sense of solidarity? Cooperate freely? Respect one another? (p. 229)

 Look for LearningCurve throughout the chapter to help you review.
bedfordstmartins.com/commandyou

11 } Preparing and Researching Presentations

Since the early 1980s, Macintosh users have sung Apple's praises with a level of enthusiasm and devotion usually reserved for favored sports teams. The lead cheerleader, however, was always the late Steve Jobs, the company's founder and former CEO. Whenever Apple launched a new product or service, Jobs was there—dressed in his trademark black turtleneck and sneakers—to introduce it.

Jobs was always intimately familiar with the company's products, making him the ideal person to present Apple's latest inventions. Jobs was well known for his effective and appropriate use of presentation aids. In many cases, his topic—the iPhone, iPad, iPod, or iMac—*was* the presentation aid. But because of his familiarity with his subject—and because he was always sure to be prepared for his speaking event—he was never entirely dependent on those aids. For example, when Jobs took the stage in a hall crowded with rabid Mac fans eager to hear about the new iPhone 4 in 2010, the Wi-Fi connection became overwhelmed, and Jobs was unable to connect. But he didn't panic. "He's so well prepared that he knew what was coming next," noted Carmine Gallo, author of *The Presentation Secrets of Steve Jobs* (2009).

After you have finished reading this chapter, you will be able to

Describe the power of public speaking and how preparation eases natural nervousness.

Identify the purpose of your speech.

Conduct audience analysis.

Choose an appropriate topic and develop it.

Support and enliven your speech with effective research.

Cull from among your sources the material that will be most convincing.

Give proper credit to sources and take responsibility for your speech.

public figure is naturally expected to speak well, but few public figures—or people in general—are naturally gifted at public speaking. However, the ability to speak appropriately and effectively in a public environment can be learned, developed, and improved. Steve Jobs may have made the entire process look easy, but think about where he would have been if he had relied entirely on his presentation aids to make a point or if he hadn't spent any time preparing ahead of time.

As you will learn in this chapter, the groundwork of becoming a confident, competent speaker and developing strong presentations lies in preparation—namely, clarifying the purpose of your speech, analyzing your audience, choosing an appropriate topic, conducting research, and taking responsibility for your speech. Yet before we even address these issues, you might be wondering why public speaking matters. Let's take a look at why it is so important.

The Power of Public Speaking

Jack has what his Irish mother called the gift of blarney. He is an eloquent conversationalist who dominates the discourse in business meetings and at cocktail parties. But put him in front of an audience, and he'll panic. Jack's ability to charm friends and colleagues, impress potential dates, and talk his way out of parking tickets disappears completely once the atmosphere changes from informal to formal and his conversational partners are reduced to a more passive audience.

Public speaking always includes a speaker who has a reason for speaking, an audience that gives the speaker attention, and a message that is meant to accomplish a specific purpose ("Public speaking," n.d.). It is an incredibly powerful form of communication that has, in fact, changed the world. From the ancient philosophers, who taught debate skills for use in the courts of ancient Greece, to nineteenth-century American abolitionists, who argued to end slavery in the United States, public speakers continue to chart the course of civilization. Ideally, we should all strive to be informed and conscientious citizens who understand the role of public speaking within a democracy and feel compelled to speak in public on topics that matter to us. Just think about what Jack could do if he used his powers of persuasion on a larger and more formal scale.

Learning how to speak publicly can also play a powerful role in *your* personal and professional life, giving you an edge over less skilled communicators and putting you in a leadership role (Ahlfeldt, 2009; O'Hair & Stewart, 1998). Companies and personnel managers all over the United States have stated that public speaking is one of the most important skills a potential employee can possess (O'Hair, Stewart, & Rubenstein, 2010).

But what if you feel anxious about public speaking? First of all, realize that you are not alone: 75 percent of people experience pounding hearts and sweaty palms when they think about getting up in front of an audience (Richmond & McCroskey, 1998). Second, recognize that through patience and practice, you can counter some of this anxiety, if not conquer it altogether. This chapter and the chapters that follow show you how to approach public speaking calmly and pragmatically. The first step lies in preparation, the focus of this chapter. The next step focuses on organization, which we'll talk about in Chapter 12. Then in Chapter 13, we will discuss the causes of speech anxiety and offer techniques that you can use to manage any concerns you may have. For now, know that being concerned about giving a speech is natural, but preparation and solid effort can make you a successful speaker, for this sort of skill building will enable you to conquer your nervousness (Bodie, 2010; Schroeder, 2002).

LearningCurve
bedfordstmartins.com/commandyou

Clarifying the General Purpose of Your Speech

In the real world, choosing a topic and purpose for a speech are seldom difficult tasks. You speak because you volunteered—or were forced—to speak on a topic for which your expertise is relevant to the situation. For example, you are a public health nurse giving a community presentation on the importance of early screening for breast or prostate cancer, or your candidate for student government president wants you, as campaign manager, to make the nominating speech. Often the parameters for a speech are quite general: a high school valedictorian or keynote speaker, for example, has to write a speech that both honors and inspires a large group. The possibilities for such speeches are endless. This communication class may provide a similar challenge—finding a speech topic and purpose that fit within your instructor's guidelines, which may range from very specific ("give a five-minute speech defending the constitutional right to free speech") to quite vague ("give a persuasive speech").

Speaking assignments usually fit within one of three general purposes: informative, persuasive, and special occasion.

THINGS TO TRY

Think back to a memorable speech you witnessed, either in person or through the media. What kind of speech was it? Was the speaker trying to inform, persuade, or celebrate? Was he or she successful in that endeavor? Did the speech change the way you felt?

Informative Speeches

In our information society, managing and communicating information are keys to success (Berrisford, 2006). *Informative speeches* aim to increase your audience's understanding or knowledge by presenting new, relevant, and useful information. Such speeches can take a variety of forms. They might explain a process or plan, describe particular objects or places, or characterize a particular state of affairs. You can expect to give informative speeches in a variety of professional situations, such as when presenting reports to supervisors or stakeholders, when running training sessions for a company, and when formally educating.

President Franklin D. Roosevelt was able to inform a wide audience about events around the country through his radio broadcasts.

Consider the storied Fireside Chats that President Franklin D. Roosevelt delivered during the 1930s and 1940s. Through the then-emerging medium of radio, Roosevelt was able to reach, inform, and reassure a vast number of Americans suffering through the Great Depression and, later, the Second World War. A brief excerpt from his first such address, delivered shortly after he took office and in the immediate aftermath of widespread bank failures, is offered as Sample Speech 11.1. Note how Roosevelt describes what happened with the banks in clear and simple language.

Fireside Chat on the Bank Crisis

FRANKLIN D. ROOSEVELT

■I want to talk for a few minutes with the people of the United States about banking—with the comparatively few who understand the mechanics of banking but more particularly with the overwhelming majority who use banks for the making of deposits and the drawing of checks. I want to tell you what has been done in the last few days, why it was done, and what the next steps are going to be. I recognize that the many proclamations from State Capitols and from Washington, the legislation, the Treasury regulations, etc., couched for the most part in banking and legal terms, should be explained for the benefit of the average citizen. . . .

■ Clearly states purpose at beginning of speech

First of all let me state the simple fact that when you deposit money in a bank the bank does not put the money into a safe deposit vault. It invests your money in many different forms of credit-bonds, commercial paper, mortgages and many other kinds of loans. . . . In other words the total amount of all the currency in the country is only a small fraction of the total deposits in all of the banks. ■

■ Explains banking in very simple terms for listeners unfamiliar with practices

What, then, happened during the last few days of February and the first few days of March? Because of undermined confidence on the part of the public, there was a general rush by a large portion of our population to turn bank deposits into currency or gold—a rush so great that the soundest banks could not get enough currency to meet the demand. The reason for this was that on the spur of the moment it was, of course, impossible to sell perfectly sound assets of a bank and convert them into cash except at panic prices far below their real value.

By the afternoon of March 3 scarcely a bank in the country was open to do business. Proclamations temporarily closing them in whole or in part had been issued by the Governors in almost all the states.

It was then that I issued the proclamation providing for the nation-wide bank holiday, and this was the first step in the Government's reconstruction of our financial and economic fabric. . . . ■

■ Lays out and explains plan for addressing crisis so listeners feel more comfortable about what's going on

Source: From "On the Bank Crisis," radio address by Franklin Delano Roosevelt delivered March 12, 1933. Retrieved from "Fireside Chats by Franklin D. Roosevelt" at the Franklin D. Roosevelt Presidential Library and Museum, http://www.fdrlibrary.marist.edu/031233.html.

Persuasive Speeches

Persuasive speeches are very common in daily life and are a major focus of public speaking classes (R. Smith, 2004). You may think that persuasion is a dishonest tactic used to coerce someone into doing or believing something, but that is not necessarily the case. Rather, *persuasive speeches* are intended to influence the attitudes, beliefs, and behaviors of the audience. Although they often ask for audiences to *change*, persuasive speeches can also reaffirm existing attitudes, beliefs, and behaviors: for example, a politician speaking at a rally of core constituents

> **You may think that persuasion is a dishonest tactic used to coerce someone into doing or believing something, but that is not necessarily the case.**

probably doesn't need to change their minds about anything, but she uses persuasive speaking nonetheless to get them excited about her platform or energized for her reelection campaign. In other cases, persuasive speech is a more straightforward call to action. In Sample Speech 11.2, for example, the entertainer and human rights activist Ricky Martin urges

---

SAMPLE SPEECH 11.2

Speech at the Vienna Forum

RICKY MARTIN

As a musician, activist, and universal citizen, I thank the United Nations Global Initiative to Fight Human Trafficking for allowing the Ricky Martin Foundation to share our commitment to end this horrible crime. Since this modern-day form of slavery has no geographical boundaries, the truly international reach of this unprecedented forum is an essential platform to combat this global nightmare.

My commitment toward this cause was born from a humbling experience. In my 2002 trip to India I witnessed the horrors of human trafficking as we rescued three trembling girls [who were] living on the streets in plastic bags. Saving these girls from falling prey to exploitation was a personal awakening. ▪

I immediately knew the Foundation had to fiercely battle this scourge.

That was six years ago. . . . Since then the Foundation expanded and launched People for Children, an international initiative that condemns child exploitation. The project's goal is to provide awareness, education, and support for worldwide efforts seeking the elimination of human trafficking—with special emphasis on children.

This unscrupulous market generates anywhere from $12 to $32 billion annually, an amount only surpassed by the trafficking of arms and drugs. . . . My hope is to secure every child the right to be a child through a not-for-profit organization conceived as a vehicle to enforce their basic human rights in partnership with other organizations, socially responsible corporations, and individuals. . . . ▪

I am certain that our voices, together with the power of other organizations that work against this horrible crime, will continue to galvanize efforts to prevent, suppress, and punish human trafficking.

▪ Effectively uses a real-life, personal experience to awaken audience to horror of the situation

▪ Lays out facts and clearly describes persuasive goal for speech

Changing attitudes and human behavior is difficult, but never forget that multiple small triumphs over a long period of time are tantamount to social change.

As a foundation that supports the objectives of this historic forum, which aims to put this crime on the global agenda, be certain that:

We will continue to tell the world that human trafficking exists; we will keep educating the masses; and we will keep working on prevention, protection and prosecution measures in our campaigns to alleviate the factors that make children, women, and men vulnerable to the most vicious violation of human rights.

Human trafficking has no place in our world today. I urge you to join our fight. React. It's time. ■

■ Call to action: hopes to persuade audience to get involved

Source: From "Speech at the Vienna Forum" by Ricky Martin, United Nations Global Initiative to Fight Human Trafficking, February 13, 2008. Retrieved from www.ungift.org/ungift/en/vf /speeches/martin.html.

members of the international community to step up efforts to put an end to human trafficking. A United Nations goodwill ambassador, Martin offers both facts and statistics related to this global crime, outlines efforts to combat it, and calls for support.

Ethics and You

What kind of ethics do you think come into play when giving a persuasive speech? Have you ever been persuaded by a speech that you later determined used unethical practices?

Special-Occasion Speeches

Special-occasion speeches use the principles of both informative and persuasive speaking for occasions such as introducing a speaker, accepting an honor or award, presenting a memorial, or celebrating an achievement. Almost certainly at some point in your life you will be called on to deliver a speech at a wedding, a toast at a retirement party, or a eulogy at a funeral. Special-occasion speeches are frequently delivered on the world stage as well. In 2005, for example, Bruce Springsteen inducted fellow rockers U2 into the Rock and Roll Hall of Fame. An excerpt of his speech is presented in

Sample Speech 11.3. As you'll see, the speech is intended to bring everyone listening to the same conclusion: this band is a true icon of rock and roll that changed the sound and scope of popular music.

LearningCurve
bedfordstmartins.com/commandyou

Analyzing Your Audience

As you will quickly discover, **audience analysis**—a highly systematic process of getting to know your listeners relative to the topic and the speech occasion—is a critical step in the speech preparation process (O'Hair, Stewart, & Rubenstein, 2010; Yook, 2004). Because you are asking audience members to accept your message—to learn new information; to change their attitudes, beliefs, or behaviors; or to recommit themselves to a cause or an organization—it is important for you to know where they are starting from. You must consider not only their expectations but also the unique situational factors affecting them, as well as their demographic backgrounds, while anticipating their reaction to your speech. Gaining this understanding will be crucial to choosing a topic that will resonate with them.

SAMPLE SPEECH 11.3

U2 Rock and Roll Hall of Fame Induction

BRUCE SPRINGSTEEN

Uno, dos, tres, catorce. That translates as *one, two, three, fourteen.* That is the correct math for a rock and roll band. For in art and love and rock and roll, the whole had better equal much more than the sum of its parts, or else you're just rubbing two sticks together searching for fire. A great rock band searches for the same kind of combustible force that fueled the expansion of the universe after the big bang. . . .

It's embarrassing to want so much, and to expect so much from music, except sometimes it happens—the Sun Sessions, *Highway 61, Sgt. Pepper,* The Band, Robert Johnson, *Exile on Main Street, Born to Run*—whoops, I meant to leave that one out [laughter]—the Sex Pistols, Aretha Franklin, the Clash, James Brown . . . the proud and public enemies it takes a nation of millions to hold back. This is music meant to take on not only the powers that be, but on a good day, the universe and God himself—if he was listening. It's man's accountability, and U2 belongs on this list. . . . ◼

■ Compares U2 to other accomplished, well-known artists to show level of their success

They are both a step forward and direct descendants of the great bands who believed rock music could shake things up in the world, who dared to have faith in their audience, who believed if they played their best it would bring out the best in you. They believed in pop stardom and the big time. Now this requires foolishness and a calculating mind. It also requires a deeply held faith in the work you're doing and in its powers to transform. U2 hungered for it all, and built a sound, and they wrote the songs that demanded it. . . .

Now the band's beautiful songwriting—"Pride (In the Name of Love)," "Sunday Bloody Sunday," "I Still Haven't Found What I'm Looking For," "One," "Where the Streets Have No Name," "Beautiful Day"—reminds us of the stakes that the band always plays for. It's an incredible songbook. In their music you hear the spirituality as home and as quest. How do you find God unless he's in your heart? In your desire? In your feet? I believe this is a big part of what's kept their band together all of these years. . . . ◼

■ Lists U2's impressive accomplishments

This band . . . has carried their faith in the great inspirational and resurrective power of rock and roll. It never faltered, only a little bit. They believed in themselves, but more importantly, they believed in "you, too." Thank you Bono, the Edge, Adam, and Larry. Please welcome U2 into the Rock and Roll Hall of Fame.

Source: From "Bruce Springsteen Inducts U2 into the Rock and Roll Hall of Fame, March 17, 2005." Retrieved from http://www.u2station.com/news/archives/2005/03/transcript_bruc .php. Used with permission of Bruce Springsteen.

Considering Audience Expectations and Situational Factors

People naturally bring different sets of expectations and emotions to a speech event (O'Hair, Stewart, & Rubenstein, 2010). And as with other forms of communication discussed in this book, competent public speaking involves understanding and acknowledging the expectations of your communication partners—in this case, your audience.

Audiences are likely to have expectations about your speech based on the speaking situation, the information their culture provides about public speaking, and even their knowledge about you as an individual

📍 The bane of a school presenter's existence? Students who can't pay attention, whether due to lack of interest or lack of sleep.

or as a speaker. For example, think about the types of expectations you bring to a wedding toast or a valedictorian's speech. Would you expect a best man to mention that the bride is untrustworthy because she cheated on her taxes last year? This would clearly defy tradition and cultural expectations. Similarly, as we learned from some Russian colleagues, an American businessperson giving a speech in Moscow might defy audience expectations by coming right to the point when informing them about a particular technology. In Russia, audiences expect speeches to favor storytelling rather than direct fact sharing.

Audiences can also be influenced by a variety of situational factors that you cannot always plan for. Be aware of issues such as the time of day of your speech, events happening in the outside world, or the comfort and attractiveness of the room—because these issues do matter when attempting to hold an audience's attention.

Considering Audience Demographics

Although understanding audience expectations and situational factors is an important component of audience analysis, it is only one of the important steps. You should also examine your audience's demographics. **Demographics** is the systematic study of the quantifiable characteristics of a large group. An audience analysis might focus on co-cultural statistics such as gender, socioeconomic status (including income, occupation, and education), religious and political affiliation, family status (married, single, divorced, partnered, with children, without children), age, and ethnic background. Other statistics that might be relevant include student enrollment status (full-time or part-time), student residential status (on campus or off campus), major area of study, or the geographical regions students hail from.

Understanding such statistics can lead speakers to topics that will be of interest and will carry meaning for specific audiences. For example, one of the most easily quantifiable and useful demographic statistics to consider is the age range of your audience. If you have a good sense of how old most of your audience members are, you'll be able to choose a topic that is relevant to concerns of their generation and ensure that the examples and anecdotes you use in your speech will resonate with the age groups you are addressing.

Culture and You

Have you ever found yourself feeling disconnected from a speaker, whether it was a course instructor or a politician, because he or she failed to consider your age, gender, sexual orientation, or ethnic background? Conversely, have you ever found a speaker very effective because he or she did consider such factors?

As we learned in Chapter 3, some audience characteristics will be more *salient*—or significant—in some speaking situations than in others. For example, if your audience members are mostly Latina women in their fifties who have survived breast cancer, their status as survivors is not likely to be salient if you are informing them about the importance of maximizing their annual contributions to their 401(k) plans before retiring in the next ten years. But if you are persuading a group to contribute money to the American Cancer Society in order to support new research campaigns, their experience fighting cancer should be firmly in your mind as you develop and deliver your speech.

Now, you're probably thinking, "How can I possibly know all the demographics of my audience members?" You're right, of course. You can't necessarily know that the guy who sits three rows back on the left side of the classroom is a heterosexual Libertarian genetics major from a working-class family and a Christian who works part-time at the deli around the corner from his off-campus apartment. But you can look for some general traits and trends. For example, most school Web sites make data available on factors like age, race, gender, and religion and often provide information on the percentage of students receiving financial aid, the number of students living on campus versus those who commute, how many are enrolled full-time versus part-time, and so on.

There are some limitations to using demographic information that deserve mention here. Sometimes speakers—including politicians and advertisers—mistakenly apply stereotypes to demographic groups or overgeneralize about common views of group members. And, in some cases, the results of demographic data collection can be flawed or even downright wrong (Sprague, Stuart, & Bodary, 2010). Because of this, it's important to be mindful of the way you use demographic information. For example, your class may be 75 percent Catholic, but that doesn't *automatically* mean that they'll be interested in a speech related to the church. That's why it's important to anticipate how

Angelina Jolie often dons stylish all-black outfits in her role as an activist, but she alters her image based on the audience and context: formal wear for a press conference and casual clothes for fieldwork.

your audience members might respond to your speech—even before you officially choose your topic and conduct your research.

Anticipating Your Audience's Response

As speech instructors, we openly confess that we get tired of hearing speeches on gun control, abortion, and euthanasia. These topics are surely worthy of thoughtful public discourse, but we've heard the same arguments over and over, and we're interested in learning about new topics. All audience members feel this way from time to time. You may be required to attend meetings at work that have nothing to do with your projects or your job, or you may sit through a religious sermon that doesn't relate to your life experiences. When you are the speaker, it's always useful to remember these experiences and do your best to ensure that you don't cause your audience to feel similarly alienated! Considering a few practical points, and adapting your speech accordingly, can certainly help:

- **Consider audience motivation.** Is your audience choosing to listen to your speech or are they required to attend? Voluntary audiences tend to be motivated to listen because they have *chosen* to hear what you say. The audience members in your class, however, are usually required to listen—and some of them may be entirely unmotivated to do so. Therefore, you must work to choose a relevant, engrossing topic that they will care about and to engage them with your delivery skills (a topic we'll address in Chapter 13).

- **Seek common ground.** Do you and your audience members share certain opinions or experiences with one another? If so, you can capitalize on this **homogeny**—or sameness—by delivering a message that will keep their attention. For example, when his university changed taxation policies for graduate students receiving stipends, Eduardo delivered a speech informing his fellow students of the steps they would need to take to ensure proper tax

withholding. It didn't matter that the students hailed from assorted fields and departments because they were all stuck dealing with the same confusing tax questions.

- **Determine prior exposure.** Audience members' interest in your speech may differ greatly depending on whether or not they have previously been exposed to your ideas and arguments. Having a general sense of what they know about the topic—and how they have reacted to it in the past—will help you prepare. For example, if your informative speech on vegetarian cooking went over well with your classmates, then it's reasonable to think that they might be interested in hearing a persuasive speech on the health and financial benefits of a diet with more produce and less meat.

- **Consider disposition.** Your audience's preexisting attitudes toward a particular message—or even toward you as a speaker—can have an impact on how they receive your speech. If you are a company executive informing employees that they will not be receiving an annual pay raise, you can assume your audience will be angry with the message (and may well dislike you as a speaker). You would be well advised to focus on areas of agreement, seek common ground, and attempt mutual understanding rather than to elicit sweeping changes in attitudes. (We will address how to adjust your speech to receptive, hostile, and neutral audiences in Chapter 15.)

As was the case when gathering demographic information, you may wonder exactly *how* you go about finding information to anticipate your audience's reaction to your speech. Luckily, there are a few steps you can take that may yield incredibly helpful information.

- **Observe people.** People watching is a hobby for some but a must for speakers! You can learn a lot by casually observing those around you. How do they react to topics discussed in class—particularly if the topics are controversial? What types of speakers do they seem to respond to?

- **Get to know people.** This may seem like common sense, but you'd be surprised how often students complete a course without making personal connections. Talk to a few people who sit next to you in class or engage in online chatting with those in your virtual course. Ask questions. Learn more about your classmates' hobbies, life situations, and other factors that might help you develop an effective speech.

- **Survey and interview your audience.** You might also want to assess your audience on a more formal level. After receiving approval from your instructor, you might develop and distribute a short questionnaire to determine your classmates' opinions on a topic you're considering for your speech. Or you might talk with several members of a student organization to get feedback on your topic before you deliver your speech at the next group meeting.

- **Use the Web.** Do a Web search for opinion polls on your topic, especially polls that gauge the views of college students or other key demographic groups in your audience. Examine the kind of attention the issue has been getting on campus or in the local media (such as the school's newspaper or Web site).

All the information you gain about your audience members—from their expectations and situational constraints to their demographics and possible reactions—sets the stage for you to move forward in developing an effective and appropriate speech. The next step is choosing your topic.

LearningCurve
bedfordstmartins.com/commandyou

Choosing Your Topic

Choosing a topic can seem like a daunting task, but it doesn't have to be. As noted, you'll want to consider the audience's expectations for the speech and topics that will interest them, taking their demographics

into account. In this course, you may have some guidance in that your instructor may give you a specific assignment. Be certain of your instructor's expectations, by asking questions if necessary, to ensure that your topic and speech are appropriate. In searching for a good topic, you might try two proven strategies for generating ideas: considering personal interests and brainstorming or clustering.

Finding a Topic That Intrigues You

It's hard to give a persuasive speech about something you don't find particularly inspiring or an informative speech on a topic you know nothing about. Choosing a topic you find interesting will prove useful, making you more motivated to research, refine your ideas, and generate audience enthusiasm.

But when you have a variety of interests, it can be hard to pinpoint one to speak about. One way to get started is to write a thorough and detailed list of topics that interest you (or others), which can be a great tool for stimulating speech ideas.

Brainstorming and Clustering

Once you've determined a very general topic—from your interests or an instructor's assignment—you'll need to start amassing information, thinking creatively, and considering problems and solutions related to your topic. This is a process known as **brainstorming**.

In brainstorming, you might consider using **clustering**, a technique for identifying potential topics (R. E. Smith, 1993). It begins with a core idea from which the writer branches out into a web of related thoughts and ideas. Rather than generating a list of ideas, clustering "spills" ideas onto paper. To begin, simply write a main word or phrase in a circle; then create a web or collection of ideas inspired by the nucleus word or phrase. See **Figure 11.1** for a sample of clustering for the nucleus phrase *country music*. As the process continues, you'll be struck by some concepts that might be suitable topics for your speech. In a sense, it's like googling your own brain, starting out with a word or concept and branching to form a web of links to related thoughts.

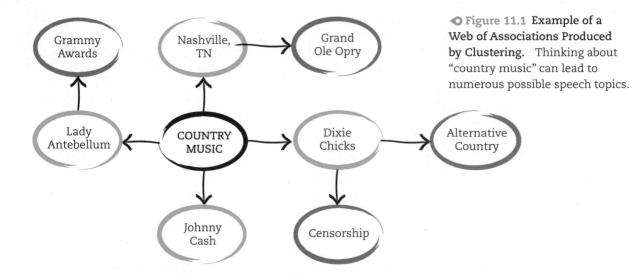

⚬ **Figure 11.1 Example of a Web of Associations Produced by Clustering.** Thinking about "country music" can lead to numerous possible speech topics.

Narrowing Your Topic

Now that you have searched for potential topics, it's time to make a choice. Your goal is to select the topic that best meets the following three criteria:

1. Is it a topic you are interested in and know something about?
2. Does the topic meet the criteria specified in the assignment?
3. Is it a topic that your audience will find worthwhile?

Once you are satisfied that your topic meets these criteria, you can begin to consider how to break down your topic further so that it is more specific and manageable. This will aid you a great deal in your research (which we discuss later in this chapter) since it is considerably easier to find information on a specific topic (such as traditional Jewish foods served for Passover) than on an extremely general one (such as the Jewish faith). One way to narrow down your topic is to break it up into categories. Write your general topic at the top of a list, with each succeeding word a more specific or concrete topic. As illustrated in Figure 11.2, you might begin with the very general topic of cars and trucks and then narrow it down a step at a time until you focus on one particular model (the Chevy

Tahoe hybrid) and decide to persuade your listeners about the advantages of owning a hybrid vehicle with all the SUV amenities.

Determining the Specific Purpose of Your Speech

Once you've narrowed your topic, you'll need to zero in on a specific purpose for your speech. Ask yourself, "What is it about my topic that I want my audience to learn, do, consider, or agree with?" A **specific purpose statement** expresses both the topic and the general speech purpose in action form and in terms of the specific objectives you hope to achieve with your presentation.

Let's consider an example. Imagine you are giving a persuasive speech on volunteerism. Your general purpose and specific purpose might look like this:

> **Topic:** Volunteer reading programs
> **General purpose:** To persuade
> **Specific purpose:** To have audience members realize the importance of reading with local elementary schoolchildren so that they sign up for a volunteer reading program such as Everybody Wins

There is an additional level of specificity to consider when preparing your speech. It is called the *thesis*

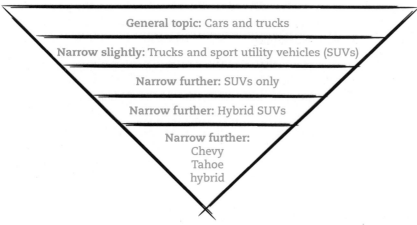

○ Figure 11.2 **Narrowing Your Topic.** Start with a general idea and become increasingly specific until you have a manageable topic for your speech.

statement—you're probably familiar with this term from high school or your college composition course. We help you understand and develop your own thesis in the next section.

Developing a Thesis Statement

Once you have homed in on your topic, general purpose, and specific speech purpose, you can start to encapsulate your speech in the form of a **thesis statement**, a statement that conveys the central idea about your topic. The thesis statement must clearly summarize what you want the audience to get out of your speech, but it is not the same thing as your specific purpose statement; as noted, it is more specific. Revisiting the example about volunteer reading programs, note how your thesis statement works with your general purpose and specific speech purpose and how it expresses the core idea that you want your listeners to walk away with:

> **Thesis statement:** Volunteers who read with local elementary schoolchildren through programs such as Everybody Wins improve young lives by enhancing children's self-esteem and expanding their possibilities for academic success.

Can you see how the thesis statement works? Offering a solid thesis statement your audience will remember long after your visual aids have faded from their minds will help you achieve your general purpose and your specific purpose: to persuade your listeners to get out there and read with local kids. For additional examples of thesis statements, see Table 11.1.

Researching the Topic

Anyone can make a speech. But a good speech should offer listeners something new, some information, insight, perspective, or idea that they didn't have before. Such original thoughts are usually the product of both deep reflection and careful research.

In a speech, research is information that helps support the points that you make, strengthening your message and credibility. For many students, the prospect of researching for a speech or presentation might seem boring, overwhelming, or both—and it can be. But if you are working with a topic that intrigues you and you approach your research in a practical way, the research process can be better than you think.

> { Anyone can make a speech. But a good speech should offer listeners something new, some information, insight, perspective, or idea that they didn't have before. }

Table 11.1 **Generating a Thesis Statement**

Topic	General Purpose	Specific Purpose	Thesis Statement
Low-carbohydrate diets	To inform	To inform listeners about low-carbohydrate diets so that they can make good decisions about their own eating habits	Before choosing to start a low-carbohydrate diet, it is important to have a thorough understanding of how carbohydrates affect your body and what the possible benefits and risks of the diet are so that you can make an informed decision about your health.
Study-abroad programs	To persuade	To have listeners realize that studying abroad is an exciting opportunity and encourage them to consider spending a semester taking classes in another country	Studying abroad is an amazing opportunity to learn about another culture, to enhance your educational experience, and to make yourself more appealing to prospective graduate schools and employers.
My grandparents	To honor an amazing couple on their fiftieth wedding anniversary (special occasion)	To celebrate with my family and my grandparents' friends in light of this happy milestone in their lives	In big and small ways, my grandparents have shared their fifty years of love and commitment with their family, their congregation, and their students, having been dedicated teachers for three decades.

Types of Information to Consider

A variety of types of support materials in your speech, including testimony, scholarship and statistics, anecdotes, quotations, and comparisons and contrasts, will enliven your speech and make it more effective.

Testimony. When you need to prove a point about which you are not an authority, incorporating the voice of an expert into your speech can lend it some validity. **Expert testimony** is the opinion or judgment of an expert, a professional in his or her field. Opinions from doctors, coaches, engineers, and other qualified, licensed professionals serve as expert testimony. In a speech about knee surgery, for example, you might cite an orthopedic surgeon when explaining the

difference between arthroscopy and knee replacement surgery. **Lay testimony** is the opinion of a nonexpert who has personal experience or witnessed an event related to your topic. In a speech on weather disasters, you could provide the testimony from a witness who survived a tornado.

Scholarship and Statistics. If you can bolster testimonies with hard numbers and facts, you'll be more effective as a speaker. **Scientific research findings** carry a lot of weight with audiences, particularly if your topic is related to medicine, health, media, or the environment. For example, in a speech about educational television programs, a speaker might point out that studies have found that children who watched *Sesame Street* as preschoolers were more likely to enjoy elementary school and to achieve higher grades even in high school (Huston & Wright, 1998).

Statistics—information provided in numerical form—can also provide powerful support for a speech, sometimes more than mere words can. Statistics reveal trends, explain the size of something, or illustrate relationships. They can be made more meaningful when paired with or made part of *factual statements*—truthful, realistic accounts based on actual people, places, events, or dates. For example, when speaking about domestic violence, you might use a combination of statistics and factual statements to back your assertion that a person is more likely to be killed by a family member or close acquaintance than by a stranger:

> Out of 13,636 murders studied in the United States, 30.2 percent of the victims were murdered by persons known to them (4,119 victims), 13.6 percent were murdered by family members (1,855 victims), 12.3 percent were murdered by strangers (1,676 victims), and 43.9 percent of the relationships were unknown (investigators were not able to establish any relationship). (U.S. Department of Justice, 2010)

Anecdotes. While facts and statistics are useful for gaining credibility, they can also be boring and easily forgotten. An effective way to breathe life into them—and into your speech in general—is by including personal details that give faces to statistics and facts and make them part of a memorable and cohesive story. **Anecdotes** are brief, personal stories that have a point or punch line. The statistics on murder presented above would be greatly enhanced if they were paired with one or two personal stories that bring them down to a more intimate and relatable level. Anecdotes can be pointed or emotionally moving; they can also be humorous or inspiring. When used well, they add a personal and memorable element to your speech.

Quotations. You can also call on the words of others to lend your speech a sense of history, perspective, and timeless eloquence. *Quotations*, repeating the exact words of another person, are usually most effective when they are brief, to the point, and clearly

related to your topic. You might quote a historical figure, a celebrity, a poet, or a playwright. Your sources do not need to be famous—you may be motivated to quote a friend or family member: "My grandfather always told me, 'An education is never a burden.'" Be sure to point out the source of your quote and, if necessary, explain who the person is or was.

Comparisons and Contrasts. Comparisons and contrasts, used separately or played against each other, have the potential to make your speech more memorable. *Comparisons* measure the similarity of two things. In a comparison, the likeness or resemblance of two ideas or concepts is pointed out. *Contrasts* show dissimilarities between two or more things. By illustrating differences, speakers can make distinctions among ideas they are discussing. A speech on school funding, for example, might call attention to disparities between schools by providing contrasting descriptions of the equipment in their science labs or gyms. You could follow that up by contrasting statistics on their students' average test scores or graduation rates.

Researching Supporting Material

Of course, the facts, statistics, anecdotes, and other supporting material that you want for your speech won't come out of thin air. Now that you've got your list of ingredients for your speech, you'll need to do some shopping—that is, you'll need to go out and find the material. Here's how.

Talk to People. If you're looking for testimony, narratives, real-world examples, and anecdotes, you'll need to start talking to people. You may be looking for experts in a particular field or people who have had firsthand experience with an event or occurrence; finding such individuals can be a challenge. You can try networking with people you know, as well as searching Internet resources.

You can also talk to people through **surveys**, which involve soliciting answers to a question or series of questions related to your topic from a broad range of individuals. Conducting a survey can give you a sense of how a group of people view a particular

⚬ Surveying local farmers about the effects factory farming and mass-produced food have on their livelihood will likely give you some interesting insights and quotations to use in your speech.

event, idea, or phenomenon. For example, if you are giving an informative speech on fear of terrorism in the United States, you might randomly select students on campus and ask them how safe they feel from terrorist attacks. Results from surveys can be discussed to back up your points.

Search the Literature. Published literature lets you reach beyond your own knowledge and experience and can be a valuable resource for supporting material for your speech. If you're giving a speech on hip-hop music, for example, you're likely to find some great material in the pages of a magazine like *Vibe*. If you're looking for studies on mental-health issues affecting rescue workers after Hurricane Katrina, you might search through newspaper archives or scholarly journals such as the *New England Journal of Medicine*.

Most current publications are available in searchable databases in libraries; some can even be accessed via the Internet (though you may have to pay a fee to download complete articles). Such databases give you access to a wealth of stored information. The Internet Movie Database (www.imdb.com), for example, is a

great example of a commonly used database, and its comprehensive information on film, television, and video games is entirely free. Another type of secondary resource is a **directory**. Directories are created and maintained by people rather than automatically generated by computers. Because human editors compile them, directories often return fewer links but higher-quality results. Directories guide you to the main page of a Web site organized within a wider subject category. You can also access useful literature through **library gateways**—collections of databases and information sites arranged by subject, generally reviewed and recommended by experts (usually librarians). These gateway collections assist in your research and reference needs because they identify suitable academic pages on the Web. In addition to scholastic resources, many library gateways include links to specialty search engines for biographies, quotations, atlases, maps, encyclopedias, and trivia. There are also a number of "virtual libraries" that exist only on the Internet. Some well-known library gateways and directories are identified in Table 11.2.

Make the Internet Work for You. Twenty years ago, the first stop on any research mission would have been the library. Today, the Internet puts a multitude of information at your fingertips. Navigating the vast sea of information—not to mention misinformation—available on the Internet can be daunting, and even, without wise searching, a waste of time; solid knowledge of search tools can make your efforts more fruitful and efficient.

An Internet **search engine** is a program that indexes Web content. Search engines such as Google, Yahoo!, and Bing search all over the Web for documents containing specific keywords that you've chosen. Search engines have several advantages—they offer access to a huge number of publicly available Web pages and give you the ability to search through large databases. But they frequently return irrelevant links, and they don't index the "invisible Web"—databases maintained by universities, businesses, the government, or libraries that cannot always be accessed by standard search engines. If a search engine fails to produce useful results, try a

Table 11.2 Useful Internet Search Sites

Library gateways	Digital Librarian *www.digital-librarian.com*
	Internet Public Library *www.ipl.org*
	Living Web Library *www.livingweb.com/library/search.htm*
	New Canaan Library *www.newcanaanlibrary.org*
Directories	Academic Info *www.academicinfo.net*
	LookSmart *www.looksmart.com*
	Open Directory Project or DMOZ *www.dmoz.org*

metasearch engine—a search engine that scans multiple search engines simultaneously. Metasearch technology delivers more relevant and comprehensive results than a search engine.

Technology and You

What are some advantages you've encountered in using the Internet for school or work research? Have you encountered any disadvantages or areas where other methods of searching are still more effective?

Evaluating Supporting Material

Once you've gathered a variety of sources, you must critically evaluate the material and determine which sources to use. After all, your credibility as a speaker largely depends on the accuracy and credibility of your sources, as well as their appropriateness for your topic and your audience.

Credible Sources. In today's media, anyone can put up a blog or a Web page, edit a wiki, or post a video to YouTube. What's more, a large and growing number of opinion-based publications, broadcasting networks, and Web sites provide an outlet for

⭘ We rely heavily on the Internet for our research needs. In fact, *google* has become a legitimate verb in our everyday language!

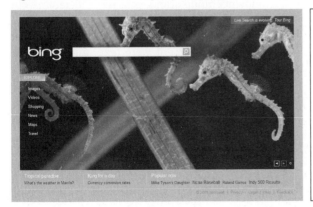

research that is heavily biased. Consequently, it is always worth spending a little time evaluating **credibility**—the quality, authority, and reliability—of each source you use. One simple way to approach this is to evaluate the author's credentials. This means that you should note if the author is a medical doctor, a Ph.D., an attorney, a CPA, or another licensed professional and whether he or she is affiliated with a reputable organization or institution. For example, if you are seeking statistics on the health effects of cigarette smoke, an article written by an M.D. affiliated with the American Lung Association would be more credible than an editorial written by your classmate.

In print and online, a reliable source may show a trail of research by supplying details about where the information came from, such as a thorough list of references. In news writing, source information is integrated into the text. A newspaper or magazine article, for example, will credit information to named sources ("Baseball Commissioner Bud Selig said . . .") or credentialed but unnamed sources ("One high-ranking State Department official said, on condition of anonymity . . .").

The Internet poses special problems when it comes to credibility owing to the ease with which material can be posted online. Check for balanced, impartial information that is not biased, and note the background or credentials of the authors. If references are listed, verify them to confirm their authenticity. Web sites can be quickly assessed for reliability by looking at the domain, or the suffix of the Web site address. Credible Web sites often end with *.edu* (educational institution), *.mil* (military site), or *.gov* (government).

Technology and You

Have you ever run into credibility problems with sources you've found on the Internet? What was the situation, and how did you verify (or refute) their authenticity?

Up-to-Date Sources. In most cases, you'll want to use the most recent information available to keep your speech timely and relevant. Isaiah, for example, is speaking to a group of potential clients about his company's graphic design services. If, during his speech, he makes reference to testimonials from satisfied clients in 2008 and earlier, the audience may wonder if the company has gone downhill since then. For this reason, always determine when your source was written or last updated; sources without dates may indicate that the information is not as timely or relevant as it could be.

Accurate Sources. When compiling support for your speech, it is important to find accurate sources—sources that are true, correct, and exact. A speaker who presents inaccurate information may very well lose the respect and attention of the audience. There are several ways to help ensure that you are studying accurate sources. In addition to being credible and up-to-date, accurate sources are exact—meaning they offer detailed and precise information. A source that notes that more than 33,000 people died as a result of automobile accidents in the United States last year is less accurate than a source that notes that 33,808 people died in such accidents. The more precise your sources, the more credibility you will gain with your audience.

Compelling Sources. Support material that is strong, interesting, and believable is considered *compelling* information. This kind of information helps your audience understand, process, and retain your message. A speaker might note that 65 percent of adults were sending and receiving texts in September 2009 and that 72 percent were texting in May 2010. However, adults do not send nearly the number of texts per day as teenagers (twelve- to seventeen-year-olds), who send and receive, on average, five times more (Lenhart, 2010). Now those are some compelling statistics!

To be compelling, your supporting material should also be *vivid*. Vivid material is clear and vibrant, never vague. For example, in a speech about the 2004 cicada invasion of the Washington, D.C., area, Ana might reference a source describing these bugs as large insects, about one and a half inches long, with red eyes, black bodies, and fragile wings; she might also use a direct quotation from a D.C. resident who noted that "there were so many cicadas that the ground, trees, and streets looked like they were covered by an oil slick." Such vivid (and gross) descriptions of information interest listeners. Look for clear, concrete supporting details that encourage the audience to form visual representations of the object or event you are describing.

LearningCurve
bedfordstmartins.com/commandyou

THINGS TO TRY

Tune in to a few news pundits—for example, Bill O'Reilly, Rachel Maddow, Randi Rhodes, or Rush Limbaugh—on the radio or on television. Listen carefully to what they say, and consider how they back up their statements. Do they provide source material as they speak? Can you link to their sources from their online blogs? How does the way they back up their points or fail to back them up influence your perceptions of what they say?

What About You?

Assessing Your Sources

After you have gathered a variety of sources, critically evaluate the material and determine which sources you should use in your final speech. Here is a checklist of questions to ask yourself regarding your supporting material:

_____ 1. Are my sources credible and reliable?

_____ 2. Are my sources up-to-date?

_____ 3. Are my sources accurate?

_____ 4. Are my sources compelling?

As noted throughout the chapter, if you cannot answer "yes" to these questions, then you will likely benefit from additional research. The more credible, reliable, up-to-date, accurate, and compelling your sources, the more credible and trustworthy you will be as a speaker—and the better you will be able to inform or persuade your audience.

Ethical Speaking: Taking Responsibility for Your Speech

As a responsible public speaker, you must let ethics guide every phase of planning and researching your speech. Being an ethical speaker means being responsible: responsible for ensuring that proper credit is given to other people's ideas, data, and research that you have incorporated into your presentation, as well as being responsible for what you say (and how you say it) to your audience. Let's review, starting with what happens when you plagiarize, or fail to cite your sources properly.

Recognizing Plagiarism

Plagiarism is the crime of presenting someone else's words, ideas, or intellectual property as your own, intentionally or unintentionally. It is a growing problem and is not limited to the written word—or to students (Park, 2003). In March 2011, German defense minister Karl-Theodor zu Guttenberg resigned after it was revealed that he had plagiarized large portions of his doctoral thesis (McGroarty, 2011). Most universities and colleges have clear definitions of plagiarism and enforce strict penalties regarding the issue—your school's plagiarism policy may even be included on your classroom syllabus. If so, *read this document carefully*. The syllabus is like your contract with your professor; by enrolling in the course, you have agreed to follow it.

Despite the problems associated with plagiarism, many students, writers, and speakers remain unsure of how, when, or why they must credit their sources. In fact, many people are shocked to find that they can be guilty of plagiarism with a seemingly unimportant error, like simply failing to include quotation marks or mistakenly deleting one little footnote when completing a paper or speech. To avoid making the same mistake, keep careful track of where all your material comes from and document it properly. In Chapter 12, we explain how to document your sources in your speech; for now, we will focus on the important role of taking accurate and thorough notes during the research phase.

> ### Ethics and You
> How do you feel about the fact that even unintentionally using someone else's words, ideas, or intellectual property is still plagiarism? Is it unfair that you might suffer severe consequences even if you do something without intent? Why or why not?

Taking Accurate Notes

The noted historian Doris Kearns Goodwin was accused of using passages from three other books in her own work without proper attribution. After settling with the wronged authors and making corrections to her book, Goodwin explained that the misrepresentation had been the result of a crucial error she had made during the note-taking phase. "Though my footnotes repeatedly cited [another author's] work, I failed to provide quotation marks for phrases that I had taken verbatim, having assumed that these phrases, drawn from my notes, were my words, not hers" (Goodwin, 2002, para. 3).

As this example shows, keeping track of all your outside material and its sources can be one of the most challenging aspects of conducting research. That's why taking accurate notes is so critical. To stay organized, consider using note cards to keep track of references separately. Or place all your references into an electronic document, such as a word processing file or a note-taking application on your smart phone or computer. Regardless of the format you choose, your entry should contain the quote or material you want to use, along with pertinent information, such as author name, publication information (title, volume, publisher, location, date), and relevant page numbers from the source. In addition, each card or entry should note whether the material is copied *verbatim* (word for word) or *paraphrased* (put into your own words). When your research is complete (or nearly complete), you'll be able to shuffle these individual cards or entries—without losing track of their sources—as you develop your speech. Two sample note cards are shown in **Figure 11.3**.

You'll also need to keep a **running bibliography**—a list of resources you've consulted. There are various styles of organizing these resources (including styles dictated by the Modern Language Association, American Psychological Association, and so on), so make sure to ask your instructor what his or her preference is if you're required to hand this document in. Regardless, all styles generally require you to list the following information:

- The complete name of each author, or origin of the source if no author is named ("National Science Foundation Web site," or "*New York Times* editorial")

◐ Figure 11.3 **Sample Note Cards**

INTELLECTUAL THEFT / Internet Piracy

SOURCE: Scott Turow, Paul Aiken, and James Shapiro: "Would the Bard Have Survived the Web?" Op-ed, in *The New York Times*, February 15, 2011, p. A29. Verbatim:

"The rise of the Internet has led to a view among many users and Web companies that copyright is a relic, suited only to the needs of out-of-step corporate behemoths. Just consider the dedicated 'file-sharers'—actually, traffickers in stolen music, movies, and, increasingly, books—who transmit and receive copyrighted material without the slightest guilt." (p. A29)

INTELLECTUAL THEFT / Internet Piracy

SOURCE: John P. Mello, Jr., "*Avatar* Tops Most Pirated List for 2010." *PCWorld*, December 22, 2010, retrieved from http:// www.pcworld.com /article/214676/avatar_tops_most_pirated_list_for_2010.html. Paraphrased:

Avatar is the most pirated movie of the year, with more than 16.5 million illegal downloads through BitTorrent alone. Runners-up were *Kick-Ass* with 11.4 million illegal downloads and *Inception* with 9.7 million.

- The title and subtitle of the source (article, book chapter, Web page) and of the larger work in which it appears (magazine, newspaper, journal, book, Web site)
- The publication date of the source; for Web sources, date of publication and date of access; for journals, volume and issue numbers
- For books, publisher and city of publication; for Web resources, the complete URL
- Page numbers for the material used and for the entire work being cited

We present an example of a running bibliography in APA style in **Figure 11.4**.

References

Boutin, P. (2010, December). The age of music piracy is officially
over. *Wired*. Retrieved from http://www.wired.com/magazine
/2010/11/st_essay_nofreebird/

Johns, A. (2010). *Piracy: The intellectual property wars from Gutenberg to
Gates*. Chicago, IL: University of Chicago Press.

Mellow, J. P., Jr. (2010, December 22). *Avatar* tops most pirated list
for 2010. *PCWorld*. Retrieved from http://www.pcworld.com
/article/214676/avatar_tops_most_pirated_list_for_2010.html

Turow, S., Aiken, P., & Shapiro, J. (2011, February 15). Would the Bard
have survived the Web? [Op-ed]. *The New York Times*. Retrieved
from http://www.nytimes.com/2011/02/15/opinion/15turow
.html

U.S. Department of Justice, Federal Bureau of Investigation. (n.d.).
Risks of peer-to-peer systems. Retrieved from http://www.fbi
.gov/scams-safety/peertopeer

◔ Figure 11.4 **Sample
Running Bibliography in
APA Style**

Speaking Ethically and Responsibly

Your responsibility as a speaker goes beyond simply giving credit to others' work; you need to take responsibility for what *you* say.[1] If you use inflammatory, hurtful, or hateful language, even quoted and cited from another source, you will bear the brunt of the audience's reactions.

The First Amendment to the U.S. Constitution guarantees every citizen the right to free speech, but not all speech is ethical. As a public speaker,

you are responsible for providing your audience members with all the necessary information for them to make accurate, appropriate decisions about you and your message. The speeches by Chinese leader Deng Xiaoping, who tried to intimidate Chinese citizens into revealing the whereabouts of leaders of the unsuccessful 1989 student uprising in Tiananmen Square in Beijing, were unethical and coercive. In addition, it's important to recognize that the right to free speech in this country is not without limits. As Supreme Court Justice Oliver Wendell Holmes wrote in 1919, the Constitution "would not protect a man falsely shouting fire in a theater and causing a panic" (*Schenck v. United States*, 1919). Speech that endangers people—for

---

[1]Much of this discussion was inspired by the work of Michael Josephson, founder and president of the Joseph and Edna Josephson Institute of Ethics in Marina del Rey, California.

⚪ While the First Amendment allows anyone to step up on a soapbox and say whatever he or she wants to say, it's still important to refrain from unethical or derogatory speech.

example, speech that incites riots, advocates the unlawful overthrowing of the government, or causes unnecessary panic—would not only be ethically questionable but might also be illegal (*Gitlow v. New York*, 1925; *Schenck v. United States*, 1919).

Although everyone has different standards for ethical communication, the qualities of dignity and integrity are universally seen as core to the idea of ethics. *Dignity* is feeling worthy, honored, or respected as a person; *integrity* is incorruptibility—the ability to avoid compromise for the sake of personal gain

Ethics and You

Consider your own personal opinions about ethical speaking. Would you add anything to the four principles noted here? If so, what characteristics would you cite?

(Gudykunst, Ting-Toomey, Sudweeks, & Stewart, 1995). Basic rules for ethical speaking require that we adhere to four principles: we should strive to be trustworthy, respectful, responsible, and fair in our speeches (Day, 1997).

- *Trustworthiness* refers to being honest with your audience about the goal of your message and providing accurate information.
- By treating people right, you are showing *respect*. In public speaking, respect is shown by focusing on issues rather than on personalities, allowing the audience the power of choice, and avoiding excluding the audience in discussions.
- As a *responsible* public speaker, it is your job to consider the topic and purpose of the speech, evidence and reasoning of the arguments, accuracy of your message, and honest use of emotional appeals.
- Ethical public speakers must be *fair* by presenting alternative and opposing views to the audience. A fair speaker will not deny the audience the right to make informed decisions.

 LearningCurve
bedfordstmartins.com/commandyou

Back to } Steve Jobs

At the beginning of this chapter, we talked about how Steve Jobs's careful preparation and intimate knowledge of his projects enabled him to be a powerful public speaker on behalf of his company. Let's take a look at his presentation skills in light of what we've learned in this chapter.

- Clearly, Steve Jobs enjoyed technology. But he also knew the importance of preparation and practice. If he relied entirely on presentation aids, he would have fallen flat during inevitable technical glitches. His research and preparation shined brighter than his presentation technology.

- Jobs also knew his audience. His audience of Apple fans was always eager to hear what he had to say and see what he had to show. He didn't bother talking about competing products because he knew the crowd was more interested in hearing about Apple products.

- Prior exposure played a role in the way Jobs presented his products. The original iPod, launched in 2001 along with the iTunes Store, was a revolutionary device, and Jobs's presentation was full of surprises for his audience. When introducing later iterations of the device, Jobs focused only on new features and options.

- The company also limits prior exposure by maintaining a high level of secrecy about products in development. When Jobs introduced a *new* product, there was little chance that the crowd had already heard anything more than rumors about it beforehand, which affected how Jobs presented information to the audience.

Your Reference }

A Study Tool
Now that you have finished reading this chapter, you can

Describe the power of public speaking and how preparation eases natural nervousness. Identify the purpose of your speech:

- *Informative speeches* aim to increase the audience's understanding and knowledge of a topic (pp. 235–236).
- *Persuasive speeches* are intended to influence the beliefs, attitudes, and behaviors of your audience (pp. 237–238).
- *Special-occasion speeches* are given at common events (like weddings and funerals), and many of us will deliver them at some point in time (pp. 238–239).

Conduct audience analysis—the process of getting to know your audience:

- It is important to understand and appreciate your audience's expectations for the speech as well as key situational factors (p. 240).
- Knowing **demographics**, the quantifiable characteristics of your audience, will help you identify topics that the audience would be interested in learning about (pp. 240–242).
- You will want to anticipate your audience's response by considering their motivation, seeking common ground (**homogeny**), determining prior exposure, and considering disposition (p. 242).
- You can learn about your audience by observing people, getting to know people, conducting interviews, using surveys, and researching their traits by using the Web (pp. 242–243).

Choose an appropriate topic and develop it:

- Speak about something that inspires you (p. 243).
- Use **brainstorming** and **clustering** to amass information, think creatively, and consider problems and solutions related to your topic (p. 243).
- A **specific purpose statement** expresses the topic and the general speech purpose in action form and in terms of the specific objectives you hope to achieve with your presentation (p. 244).
- Narrow your topic and write a **thesis statement** ⓞ, a summary of your central idea (p. 245).

Support and enliven your speech with effective research:

- Include **expert testimony**, the opinion of an authority, or **lay testimony**, opinion based on personal experience (p. 246).
- **Scientific research findings** carry weight in topics on medicine, health, media, and the environment; **statistics**, information in numerical form, can clarify your presentation (pp. 246–247).
- **Anecdotes** ⓞ, relevant personal stories, bring the human experience to the speech (p. 247).
- **Surveys** will add the point of view of a larger range of people (pp. 247–248).
- Use databases to find material, such as **directories**, **library gateways**, **search engines**, and **metasearch engines** (pp. 248–249).

Cull from among your sources the material that will be most convincing:

- Take time to evaluate the **credibility**—the quality, authority, and reliability—of each source you use (pp. 249–250).
- Up-to-date information convinces the audience of its timeliness (p. 250).
- Citing accurate and exact sources gains audience respect (p. 250).
- Compelling information is influential and interesting (pp. 250–251).

Give proper credit to sources and take responsibility for your speech:

- Avoid **plagiarism**, presenting someone else's intellectual property as your own (p. 252).
- Keep accurate track of all your references to avoid unintentional errors (p. 252).
- Keeping a **running bibliography**, the list of resources you've consulted, will free you from having to write the same information over and over (pp. 252–253).
- Honor the basic rules for ethical speaking (pp. 254–255).

Look for **LearningCurve** throughout the chapter to help you review.
bedfordstmartins.com/commandyou

12 } Organizing, Writing, and Outlining Presentations

The Constitution of the United States of America makes a simple demand of the president: "He shall from time to time give to the Congress Information of the State of the Union, and recommend to their Consideration such Measures as he shall judge necessary and expedient" (art. 2, sec. 3).

For much of our nation's history, the State of the Union address was a lengthy letter to Congress read by a clerk. But over time it has evolved into an elaborate and highly politicized annual affair that allows the president to present major ideas and issues directly to the public: the Monroe Doctrine (James Monroe, 1823), the Four Freedoms (Franklin D. Roosevelt, 1941), and the War on Terror (George W. Bush, 2002) were all

detailed for the American people during State of the Union addresses (Longley, 2007).

And so each January, White House speechwriters face the daunting task of addressing both Congress and the nation with a speech that outlines what is going on in foreign and domestic policy in a way that flatters the president and garners support for his agenda for the following year. As if that isn't difficult enough, speechwriters must also navigate a deluge of requests from lobbyists, political consultants, and everyday citizens eager to get their pet project, policy, or idea into the president's speech. "Everybody wants [a] piece of the action," lamented former White House speechwriter Chriss Winston in 2002.

After you have finished reading this chapter, you will be able to

Organize and support your main points.

Choose an appropriate organizational pattern for your speech.

Move smoothly from point to point.

Choose appropriate and powerful language.

Develop a strong introduction, a crucial part of all speeches.

Conclude with as much strength as you had in the introduction.

Prepare an effective outline.

I magine that you are building a bridge, a skyscraper, or even a little house. You might have ambitious blueprints, but before you can build it, you need to form a solid foundation and develop a structurally sound framework. Any architect will tell you that even the most exciting and lofty designs are useless without these two crucial components. Skimp on either one and your structure will crack, shift, or collapse.

Building a speech follows a similar process. Whether you are writing a national address for the president of the United States or a three-minute class presentation, you will be unable to make your point if your speech is not structurally sound. As we discussed in Chapter 11, you begin with your idea and then build your foundation with research and a clear thesis statement. The next step is to develop your framework—the overall structure of your presentation. In this chapter, we'll focus on organizing all your ideas and information into a clear and practical framework and integrating them into a well-written speech. Let's begin by considering the main points of your speech.

Organizing Your Speech Points

You've got your purpose, your research, and your thesis. But before you begin writing, it's best to organize your ideas—to set out the points you want to make, the examples you plan to use to support them, and the basic order in which you want to present them. And you will want to do all of this *before* you write your introduction or conclusion. In this section, we'll focus on identifying your main points and developing your supporting points, in addition to considering useful ways to arrange those points and connect them in your speech.

Identifying Your Main Points

First and foremost, you must determine the **main points** of your speech, which are the central claims that support your specific speech purpose and your thesis statement (which you learned about in Chapter 11). That is, you need to identify and organize key ideas that will lead the audience members to accept or weigh what you are asking them to do, believe, or consider.

Before you begin developing your main points, you may be wondering how many you will need in your speech. Because each speech is unique, there is no easy answer—but the general rule is that audiences have trouble remembering more than three or four main points. This will generally serve you well for the purposes of your human communication course, but always check with your instructor if you have questions.

With this in mind, let's consider how main points work in action. Let's say you're giving a persuasive speech advocating for listeners to vote in favor of removing unhealthy candy and soda vending machines from your local high school in order to combat obesity. What key points do you think will influence your listeners to vote this way? Perhaps they would be motivated to do so if they knew the scope of the problem:

Main Point 1: Obesity in children and adolescents is a growing national health problem in the United States.

You'd likely further your argument by connecting the types of food and beverages in vending machines to the obesity problem:

> **Main Point 2:** Vending machines typically offer food choices and beverages with low nutritional value in addition to excess fats and refined sugars.

Finally, they might want to hear about some success stories to motivate them to take action:

> **Main Point 3:** Several major school districts successfully removed soda machines from their schools with positive benefits.

Note that each main point includes only one major idea. This prevents you from overwhelming your audience with too much information and makes it easier for you to supply the examples, testimonies, statistics, and facts to back up each point. When in doubt about developing your main points, ask yourself, "Does this point prove my thesis? Does it help me achieve my specific purpose?" If you can confidently answer "yes," then you're on the right track.

Supporting Your Main Points

Each main point—as well as your speech as a whole—is fully fleshed out with the use of subpoints that provide support for the main points. **Subpoints** utilize your research to back up your main points in the same way that your main points back up your thesis statement and specific purpose; you can use a similar test to check their usefulness, asking yourself, "Does this bit of information back up my main point?" For example, two subpoints under our main point about obesity as a growing national health threat might be

> The Centers for Disease Control and Prevention notes that 19.6 percent of children and 18.1 percent of adolescents in the United States are obese (Centers for Disease Control, 2010).

> According to the Office of the Surgeon General, type 2 diabetes—which is linked with obesity—has increased dramatically in children and adolescents (U.S. Department of Health & Human Services, 2007).

⬧ Think of your main points and subpoints as Russian *matryoshka* dolls—each sub-subpoint should nest inside a subpoint, which should nest inside your main point.

Like main points, subpoints may—and often should—be backed up with more information, referred to as *sub-subpoints*.

Well-chosen supporting points will naturally fall under your main point in a clear hierarchy of ideas, forming the basic outline of your speech. Each main point should be supported by a number of coordinating subpoints, each carrying equal weight, as well as sub-subpoints that carry less weight. The resulting structure reflects a pyramid-like hierarchy of ideas: a foundation of many sub-subpoints supports a structure of fewer but larger subpoints, which in turn support a few main points, which together support the thesis statement and ultimately your specific purpose. This structural hierarchy of points, depicted in Figure 12.1, ensures that you've presented a coherent and sturdy argument in support of your thesis and specific purpose. Later in the chapter, we'll show you how to use an outline to detail this hierarchy of points in a text format, but next we'll consider helpful ways to arrange your points.

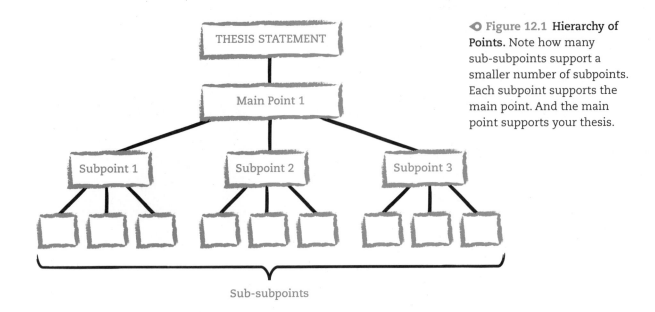

○ Figure 12.1 **Hierarchy of Points.** Note how many sub-subpoints support a smaller number of subpoints. Each subpoint supports the main point. And the main point supports your thesis.

Arranging Your Points

Think for a moment of a family photo album. If you were to put one together that covered your entire life, how would you arrange it? You could work chronologically, simply placing the photos in the order in which they were taken. You might expand on that chronological approach by trying to arrange the photos in a way that tells the story of your family. Alternatively, you might arrange it by topic, with separate sections for certain types of events or individual family members.

You have similar options when preparing a speech. During the process of sorting out your main points and subpoints, you may have taken the initial step of arranging your ideas in some sequence. Here are some common arrangements, or patterns, to consider.

Chronological Pattern. Often it makes sense to organize your points according to time: what happened first, second, and so on. A **chronological pattern** presents the main points of a message forward (or backward) in a systematic, time-related fashion. A chronological organization can be especially useful when analyzing a step-by-step process, such as a presentation on how to use a new computer program.

Topical Pattern. Also known as a *categorical pattern*, the **topical pattern** is based on organization into categories, such as persons, places, things, or processes. Thus you might use it to describe the various departments in an organization, the characteristics of a successful employment interview, or the reasons for giving a charitable contribution to a specific organization.

One key concern when selecting this approach is the sequencing of topics—which topic to offer first, second, and so on. Depending on the circumstances, the best approach is often ascending or descending order—that is, according to the relative importance, familiarity, or complexity of the topics. The **primacy-recency effect** can also offer some guidance in that it notes that audiences are most likely to remember points you raise at the very beginning or very end of a message, indicating that you might place your strongest

> Think for a moment of a family photo album. If you were to put one together that covered your entire life, how would you arrange it?

○ Deciding how to organize your speech, like deciding how to arrange family photos, can be tricky because you have many options to consider: you can do it chronologically, topically, or even spatially.

point first or last so that your audience members keep it in mind long after you end your presentation.

Spatial Pattern. The geographical or **spatial pattern** arranges main points in terms of their physical proximity or position in relation to each other (north to south, east to west, bottom to top, left to right, outside to inside, and so on). As an organizational pattern, it is most useful when describing objects, places, or scenes in terms of their component parts.

Problem-Solution Pattern. If you're trying to call an audience to action to address a particular problem, the **problem-solution pattern** of organization can be especially effective. This pattern involves dramatizing an obstacle and then narrowing alternative remedies down to the one that you recommend. The message is organized to focus on three key points:

1. There is a problem that requires a change in attitude, belief, or behavior.

2. A number of possible solutions might solve this problem.

3. Your solution is the one that will provide the most effective and efficient remedy.

Topics that lend themselves to this pattern include business, social, economic, and political problems for which you can propose a workable solution.

Cause-Effect Pattern. With the **cause-effect pattern**, you attempt to organize the message around cause-to-effect or effect-to-cause relationships. That is, you might move from a discussion of the origins or causes of a phenomenon (for example, rising fuel costs) to the eventual results or effects (increases in the cost of airplane tickets). You can also work in reverse, starting with a description of present conditions and then examining apparent or possible causes. The choice of strategy is often based on which element—cause or effect—is more familiar to the intended audience: if you're talking about fuel prices, for example, it might be best to start with the cost of gasoline—a very familiar expense—and work backward from there. The cause-effect pattern of organization is especially useful when your purpose is to get your audience to agree with or understand your point, rather than to call people to action.

Narrative Pattern. Speakers often tie their points together in a way that presents a vivid story, complete with characters, settings, plot, and imagery. This is called a **narrative pattern**. However, most speeches built largely on a story (or a series of stories) are likely to incorporate elements of other organizational arrangements. For example, you might present a story in a cause-effect design, in which you first reveal why something happened (such as a small aircraft crash) and then describe the events that led up to the accident (the causes).

Motivated Sequence Pattern. The **motivated sequence pattern**, created more than seventy years ago by the noted public speaking scholar Alan Monroe, is a five-step plan for organizing a speech, which can be useful in a variety of contexts. Based on the psychological elements of advertising, the motivated sequence pattern includes five phases, which may be modified to suit the desired outcome of your speech: Attention, Need, Satisfaction, Visualization, and Action. Monroe argued that these five steps motivate listeners; presentations that lend themselves to the motivated sequence include persuasive presentations, inspirational speeches, graduation addresses, and motivational talks. (For a more detailed discussion and examples of Monroe's Motivated Sequence, see pp. 350–351 in Chapter 15.)

Connecting Your Points

When you're pulling together, supporting, and arranging your points, you may find yourself falling

When organizing your speech in a narrative pattern, put your feet in a storyboard artist's shoes. Visualize your outline as a storyboard, and think of your speech points as scenes.

into what we like to call the "grocery list trap." Essentially, this occurs when your speech begins to seem like a thorough list of good but seemingly unrelated ideas. So, how do you move smoothly from one point to another? The key lies in your use of transitions, signposts, and internal previews and summaries.

Transitions. **Transitions** are sentences that connect different points, thoughts, and details in a way that allows them to flow naturally from one to the next. Clear transitions cue the audience on where you're headed with the speech and how your ideas and supporting material are connected. They also alert your audience that you will be making a point. Consider the following examples of transitions:

> I've just described some of the amazing activities you can enjoy in our national parks, so let me tell you about two parks that you can visit within a three-hour drive of our university.

> In addition to the environmental benefits of reducing your energy consumption, there are some fantastic financial benefits that you can enjoy.

Notice how the transitions in both examples also serve to alert your audience that you will be making a point that you want them to remember. Transitions are therefore essential to making your points clear and easy to follow.

Signposts. Effective speakers make regular use of **signposts**, key words or phrases within sentences that signify transitions between points. Think of signposts as links or pivot points at which you either connect one point to another ("similarly," "next," "once again") or move from one point to a related but perhaps opposing or alternative point ("however," "on the other hand"). Table 12.1 details various examples

Table 12.1 **Useful Signposts**

Function	Example
To show comparison	Similarly In the same way In comparison
To contrast ideas, facts, or data	On the other hand Alternatively In spite of
To illustrate cause and effect	It follows, then, that Consequently Therefore Thus
To indicate explanation	For example In other words To clarify
To introduce additional examples	Another way in which Just as Likewise In a similar fashion
To emphasize significance	It's important to remember that Above all Bear in mind
To indicate sequence of time or events	First . . . , Second . . . , Third Finally First and foremost Once Now . . . , Then Until now Before . . . , After Earlier . . . , Later Primarily
To summarize	As we've seen Altogether Finally In conclusion

Source: O'Hair, Stewart, & Rubenstein (2007), p. 181. Adapted with permission.

of signposts and considers how they function effectively to achieve a specific purpose.

Internal Previews and Internal Summaries. Like a good map that shows travelers points along the way to their destination, **internal previews** prime the audience for the content immediately ahead. They often work best in conjunction with **internal summaries**, which allow the speaker to crystallize the points made in one section of a speech before moving to the next section. The following examples have both an internal summary and an internal preview.

> So far, I have presented two reasons why you should enroll your puppy in obedience school. First, it benefits your dog. Second, it benefits your family. Now I will address my third point: taking your dog to obedience school benefits your neighborhood.

> Now that I have explained what asthma is and the two main types of asthma, allergic and nonallergic, I will discuss what you can do to avoid an asthma attack.

⬤ Direct the audience from one point in your speech to the next with signpost words or phrases, such as "similarly" or "on the other hand."

By first summarizing and then previewing, the speakers in these examples have created useful transitions that gracefully move the speech forward while offering audiences an opportunity to synthesize the information already received.

LearningCurve
bedfordstmartins.com/commandyou

Using Language That Works

Now you know quite a bit about identifying, supporting, arranging, and moving between the main points of your speech. But to describe and explain the points themselves, you must make competent language choices that bring your ideas to life right before your audience's eyes. The words that you choose for your speech are clearly powerful, so it's important to think about them *now*, in the preparation and writing stages, so that you can eventually incorporate them into your actual presentation.

Respect Your Audience

As noted earlier, communication involves not only what we say but also how others perceive what we say. Most audiences are composed of both men and women from many different cultures, races, religious backgrounds, lifestyles, and educational levels. Therefore, it is important to use unbiased and appropriate language that makes the entire audience feel included and respected.

Culture and You

Have you ever sat through a speech in which the speaker failed to use language the audience easily understood? Do you remember anything important from this speech—or even its main point? How did you feel during the speech?

Keep It Simple

Albert Einstein once advised, "Make everything as simple as possible, but no simpler." This applies to language: speakers and writers who use unfamiliar or inappropriate language are not as effective as those who speak directly and in terms that their audience can readily understand and interpret. You don't need to "dumb down" your points; just make your points in language that is clear, simple, and unambiguous so that your audience can follow what you are saying. In addition, there is no speaker quite as dreaded as the long-winded one who repeats the same points or uses six examples where one would suffice. If you keep your speech short and to the point, you'll have a better chance of reaching your audience with your intended message.

Use Vivid Language

Language paints a picture for an audience. The more vivid your terms, the more the audience members can use their imaginations and their senses. For example, if you say your father had a car, your listeners hear a common, forgettable fact. If you tell them that your father drove a faded orange 1972 Volkswagen Beetle with a dent in the left fender and a broken taillight, you'll give them a very clear and memorable picture of this vehicle. You may have great, eye-catching slides and props, but remember that words count—often even more than your PowerPoint slides do.

Audience members wouldn't conjure this clear and memorable picture in their minds unless it was painted with vivid language by the speaker.

Incorporate Repetition, Allusion, and Comparisons

In 1851, American abolitionist and women's rights activist Sojourner Truth delivered an effective and memorable speech at the Women's Convention in Akron, Ohio. The speech, now known as "Ain't I a Woman?" is effective not only because of its powerful message about the evils of slavery and the mistreatment of women but also because Truth's passionate use of language helped make a lasting impression on her listeners. Consider, for example, her use of repetition, allusion, and comparisons. (See **Sample Speech 12.1**.)

Repetition. *Repetition*—saying certain terms, phrases, or even entire sentences more than once—can help increase the likelihood that the audience will remember what matters most in your speech. In Truth's speech, she repeats "Ain't I a woman?" several times. This repetition highlights each of the injustices she feels and influences audience members to consider Truth and, by association, all women deserving of the rights and privileges withheld from them.

Allusion. An *allusion* is making a vague or indirect reference to people, historical events, or concepts to give deeper meaning to the message and possibly evoke emotional responses. Allusions can also provide grounded context that goes beyond what you are saying directly. In Truth's "Ain't I a Woman?" speech, for example, she uses an allusion: "If the first woman God ever made was strong enough to turn the world upside down all alone, these women together ought to be able to turn it back, and get it right side up again." She is alluding to the biblical figure Eve, who ate the forbidden fruit from the tree of the knowledge of good and evil and upset the harmonious balance between God and humankind. Truth does not take time to explain this story; she knows that her audience will understand her reference and uses allusion to add power and emotion to her message.

Comparisons: Similes and Metaphors. One of the most common and useful tools in public speaking

◊ Sojourner Truth's "Ain't I a Woman?" speech uses vivid and effective language to persuade.

is the figure of speech known as the *simile*. A simile uses *like* or *as* to compare two things. Truth uses a simile to conjure up the images of her strength and fortitude when she states, "I could work as much and eat as much as a man—when I could get it—and bear the lash as well!"

Like similes, *metaphors* compare one thing to another in a literal way, even though there may be no literal connection between the two. A metaphor presents a comparison as a statement of fact—it does not contain the word *like* or *as*—but it is not expected to be taken as a fact. You might use a metaphor, such as "The fog was a heavy blanket over the city," to add imagery to your speech.

LearningCurve
bedfordstmartins.com/commandyou

Ain't I a Woman?

SOJOURNER TRUTH

Well, children, where there is so much racket there must be something out of kilter. I think that 'twixt the negroes of the South and the women at the North, all talking about rights, the white men will be in a fix pretty soon. But what's all this here talking about?

That man over there says the women need to be helped into carriages, and lifted over ditches, and to have the best place everywhere. Nobody ever helps me into carriages, or over mud-puddles, or gives me any best place! And ain't I a woman? Look at me! Look at my arm! I have ploughed and planted, and gathered into barns, and no man could head me! And ain't I a woman? I could work as much and eat as much as a man—when I could get it—and bear the lash as well! And ain't I a woman? I have borne thirteen children, and seen most all sold off to slavery, and when I cried out with my mother's grief, none but Jesus heard me! And ain't I a woman? ∎

Then they talk about this thing in the head; what's this they call it? [member of the audience whispers "intellect"] That's it, honey. What's that got to do with women's rights or negroes' rights? If my cup won't hold but a pint, and yours holds a quart, wouldn't you be mean not to let me have my little half measure full?

Then that little man in black there, he says women can't have as much rights as men, 'cause Christ wasn't a woman! Where did your Christ come from? Where did your Christ come from? From God and a woman! Man had nothing to do with Him.

If the first woman God ever made was strong enough to turn the world upside down all alone, these women together ought to be able to turn it back, and get it right side up again. And now they is asking to do it, the men better let them. ∎

Obliged to you for hearing me, and now old Sojourner ain't got nothing more to say.

∎ Truth encourages audience to extend belief about women to her, as she too is a woman

∎ Truth invokes religious stories familiar to audience members in effort to persuade them

Source: From Sojourner Truth, "Ain't I a Woman?" speech delivered at the Women's Convention in Akron, Ohio, May 1851. Retrieved from http://www.feminist.com/resources/artspeech/genwom/sojour.htm.

Writing a Strong Introduction

Like a lead paragraph of a news story that hooks readers, the introduction to your speech must accomplish three crucial tasks: it must grab your audience's attention, it must offer a preview of your main points, and it must give your listeners a sense of who you are and why they should want to hear what you have to say. Recall the *primacy effect* discussed earlier in this chapter. Your introduction is the first thing your audience will hear; it therefore sets the tone and the stage for the rest of your speech.

{ **Like a lead paragraph of a news story that hooks readers, the introduction to your speech must accomplish three crucial tasks: it must grab your audience's attention, it must offer a preview of your main points, and it must give your listeners a sense of who you are and why they should want to hear what you have to say.** }

Capture Your Audience's Attention

Finding a creative, attention-grabbing opening can be a struggle, but in the end it will be well worth the effort, for your first words can and do make a big impression on your audience (Hockenbury & Hockenbury, 2002). If you open with something as boring as "Hi, my name is ..." or "Today I'm going to talk about ... ," your audience may conclude that there's nothing more interesting to follow. In many cases, you'll finalize your introduction after the bulk of your speech has been written. This is an advantage because you will be able to approach your introduction armed with your main points and supporting material—and probably a few ideas on how to make it lively! Consider the following suggestions.

Use Surprise. It is likely that while researching your topic, you came across a fact, statistic, quote, or story that truly surprised you. Chances are that such information will likewise come as a surprise to your audience. A startling statement uses unusual or unexpected information to get an audience's attention. For example, in a speech on sleep deprivation, you might begin as follows:

> Did you know that every semester, university students are legally drunk for one week straight? Yet, despite feeling drunk, they never drink a drop of alcohol. During finals week, students at the University of Oklahoma sleep an average of five hours per night. Sleep deprivation—characterized by getting five hours or less of sleep per night—can affect reaction time and mental sharpness. After being awake for seventeen hours straight, a sleep-deprived person has the reaction time and mental sharpness of someone with a blood alcohol concentration of 0.05, which is considered legally drunk throughout most of Europe.

Tell a Story. As discussed in Chapter 11, anecdotes can be useful illustrations for your speech. Real-world stories can be particularly effective when worked into an opening, where they can make audiences feel invested in a speaker before they even know what the thesis of the speech is. For example, Miriam thinks her audience will tune out if she simply informs them that she's going to discuss the secret costs of credit cards. But what if she opens with a story like the following?

> A few months ago, my friend Monica—not her real name—decided that she positively *needed* to own a pair of Jimmy Choo boots. Now, I'll admit, these were some amazing boots: black leather, calf-high, four-inch heels. But they cost—are you sitting down?—$895. Like most of us, she didn't have that kind of cash lying around, so she bought the boots on credit and figured that she would pay them off month by month. Despite the fact that she diligently puts $50 toward her payment each and every month, it's going to take Monica 102 months—more than eight years—to pay for those boots. In addition, she'll pay over $750 in interest, which is almost as much as the boots cost in the first place!

By telling a story, Miriam puts a familiar face on her subject; she's also caught the attention of anyone who's ever had the experience of really wanting something they couldn't afford—which is pretty much everyone!

Start with a Quote. Leading with a quotation is a convenient and interesting speech opening. Quotes can connect you as a speaker to real people and real situations. For example, Kenneth is preparing an informative speech on Alzheimer's disease. In his opening, he uses a quote from former president Ronald

Table 12.2 **Using Quotes Wisely**

Use quotes worth using.	Don't quote something that you could say or explain more effectively in your own words; paraphrase instead, with an attribution to the original source.
Use relevant quotes.	Even the prettiest bit of prose is useless if it doesn't support your points.
Include a clear attribution.	Whether you're quoting Shakespeare or your six-year-old nephew, it's important that audiences know who said what.
Is the quote from a notable source?	Cite not only the author in your speech but also the date and the work in which the quote appeared, if relevant.
Double-check for accuracy.	You do not want to misquote anyone in your speech, so it's important that you proofread your copy against the original. If you've used an online quote source, it is wise to double-check the quote against additional sources known to be reliable because many quote sites fail to provide accurate source information.

Reagan, who passed away in 2004 after a ten-year struggle with the disease:

> "I now begin the journey that will lead me to the sunset of my life." That's how Ronald Reagan, upon learning he would be afflicted with Alzheimer's disease, described the illness that would eventually rob him of the eloquence, wit, and intelligence that had defined him as an actor, a politician, and a president. I'm here today to talk about the tragedy of Alzheimer's disease.

Quotations can come from familiar sources, like Reagan, or from everyday people. Table 12.2 offers tips for using quotes wisely.

Ask a Question. Posing a question is a great way to get the audience's attention and to make people think. Rather than simply presenting some bit of information, posing a question invites listeners to react, in effect making them participants in the speech.[1] For example, when speaking about Internet safety, an engaging opening question might be "Would you leave your child in a room full of anonymous strangers? No? Then why would you allow your child to participate in online chats?" Here again, saying something startling can add to the effect: not only have you gotten your listeners' attention by saying something provocative, but you've also asked them to internalize what you've said and to react to it. As a result, they're likely to be more interested in and open to what you're about to say.

Make Them Laugh. Humor is another effective way to begin your speech. Usually, humor that's brief, that's relevant to your topic, and that makes a point is most effective. For example, consider this opening, which makes the audience laugh but is clearly tied to the main topic of the speech on the effects of multitasking: "I find that the key to multitasking is to lower your expectations. Sure, I can do two things at once—if I do them poorly! Today, I want to talk about the hazards of multitasking."

Culture and You

Can you think of a situation in which you either did modify or should modify your preferred method of introduction based on the perceived makeup of the audience?

---

[1] Asking questions is an effective way of gaining participation in many communication contexts; see O'Hair, O'Rourke, and O'Hair (2000).

Pick a general topic, and try to come up with several different attention getters for it. Here's an example for the topic "dogs":

- Tell a funny story about your dog.
- "Did you know that the human mouth contains more germs than a dog's mouth?"
- "In my hometown, there is a dog that walks upright like a human because he does not have any front legs."
- "Did you know that approximately ten million unwanted dogs are euthanized annually in the United States?"

Try this with a topic such as your favorite food, favorite vacation spot, or some other appealing subject.

💧 You don't have to turn your speech into a stand-up comic performance, but a good opening joke will pique the audience's interest.

Introduce Your Purpose and Topic

As you were capturing your audience's attention with stories, questions, quotations, and so on, it's likely that you gave them a fairly overt introduction to your topic. It is *essential* that your introduction clearly establish what your speech will be about and what you hope to achieve by speaking (your thesis statement). Imagine that you just caught your audience's attention with the description of a fun-filled and active day: kayaking on a pristine lake, hiking in a rain forest, rock climbing on a craggy coastline, and so on. You would then introduce your thesis: "All of these activities—and many more—are available to you in one of our nation's most diverse protected spaces: Olympic National Park. I hope to persuade you to visit and to take advantage of all this park has to offer."

Preview Your Main Points

Another key goal for your introduction is to provide a preview of the main points that will be covered in the body of the speech, in the order that you will talk about them. For example, if you are giving a speech about why students should enroll in an art course, you might say: "There are two reasons why every college student should enroll in an art course. First, it provides students with a creative outlet, and second, it teaches students useful and creative ways of thinking about their own subjects of study." Audiences prefer to listen to speakers who are prepared and have a plan the audience can follow; by previewing, you offer a mental outline that your listeners can follow as they attend to your speech.

Connect with Your Audience

Another goal for your introduction is to establish a relationship with your listeners, providing them with a sense of who you are and why they should listen to what you have to say. Like participants in an interview, the members of your audience will come to your speech with three points in mind. They will be curious about the nature of your speech: will it be boring, interesting, or inspiring? They'll also be wondering what they will get from it: will the speech be worth their time and attention? Finally, they will be curious about you as a speaker: will they like and trust you? Your introduction

271

should provide enough information to allow the audience to make accurate assumptions about your speech and about you.

One way that a speaker can establish a relationship with the audience is to demonstrate why listeners should care about the topic. First, make sure that you verbally link the topic to the audience's interests. You should also try to appeal to your listeners' personal needs—let them know what's in it for them. For example, a college recruiter speaking at a high school might talk about what his school offers prospective students. He might also touch on recent local or national events to show the relevance of the school's curriculum.

LearningCurve
bedfordstmartins.com/commandyou

Writing a Strong Conclusion

There's a reason why courtroom dramas like TV's *Law and Order* almost always include footage of the hero lawyer's closing statements. When a wealth of evidence, testimony, and facts have been presented, it's easy for juries (and television audiences) to get bogged down in the details and lose track of the bigger, more dramatic picture. For any speaker, it is important to end a presentation with a compelling and pointed conclusion. Once again, the *recency effect* reminds us that the conclusion is the *last* thing the audience will hear in your speech, and it is likely what they will remember most. As such, a speech conclusion must address a number of functions.

Signal the End

Your conclusion should alert the audience that the speech is coming to a close. You might do that by using a transitional phrase, such as "In conclusion," "Finally," or "Let me close by saying." Such phrases serve as signposts, telling audiences that you're about to conclude and asking for their full attention

one last time. Remember to keep it brief. Audiences do not like to be overwhelmed with a lot of new information at the end.

Reinforce Your Topic, Purpose, and Main Points

The conclusion of your speech is the last opportunity you'll have to reinforce the topic and purpose of your speech as well as to remind your audience about the key points you want to live on in their memories. In other words, competent speakers should reiterate this essential information so that listeners are able to mentally check off what they have heard and what they should remember. For example, "Today, I discussed the benefits of seeing your physician for an annual physical, even when you're feeling fine. Not only can this simple visit offer peace of mind and help prevent costly medical conditions in the future, but it may also save your life if you have an underlying medical problem that requires early diagnosis and treatment."

Make an Impact

Your conclusion, a culmination of all your efforts to develop your points and share your research, should be memorable and interesting for your audience members. Several techniques discussed in the section on introductions can be useful for memorable conclusions as well.

Quotations. To wrap up a speech, speakers often use quotes from historical figures, writers, philosophers, or celebrities. Take care in choosing a quote

> **Ethics and You**
>
> Have you ever heard a speech in which you felt that the speaker sacrificed ethics in order to make a greater impact at the end of the speech? What was ethically suspect about the speech's conclusion?

so that you leave the audience with something to think about. For example, if you are concluding a speech that illustrates the importance of friendships, you might quote the writer Edna Buchanan: "Friends are the family you choose for yourself." A strong quotation helps make an unforgettable impression.

Statements and Questions. In some types of speeches, it can be especially effective to end with a statement or question that drives home your main point. This rhetorical device is important for conclusions because you want to emphasize the points you made during your speech and have the audience feel connected to your ideas. For example, you might end a speech explaining how to change the oil in your car with a simple statement that sums up your thesis: "Remember, the best way to protect your car is to change the oil every three thousand miles—and it's something you can do yourself."

A Final Story. Stories are also as effective for conclusions as they are for introductions. Stories should always tie in to your speech topic, be relatively short, and make a related point. For example, if you are advocating a college-level foreign-language requirement for your university, you might tell this well-known tale: "Mother Mouse was crossing the street with her three children. She got about halfway across when she saw a cat, ready to pounce on them. The cat and Mother Mouse eyeballed each other for several minutes. Finally, Mother Mouse let out an enormous 'woof!' The cat ran away. Mother Mouse turned to her children and said, 'Now do you see the advantage of a second language?'"

Challenge the Audience to Respond

The point of a speech (whether informative or persuasive) is to learn something new, right? As the speaker, you must also consider what you want your audience to do with the information you are providing. According to O'Hair, Stewart, and Rubenstein (2010), in an informative speech, you should challenge your audience members to make use of the

information. You may extend an invitation to your listeners: "Please join me on Wednesday evening for a town hall meeting on this subject. Our local congressperson will be there to listen to our concerns. I will have the sign-up sheet in the back of the room for you at the end of my presentation."

In most persuasive speeches, the challenge will come through a **call to action** that urges listeners to act in response to the speech, see the problem in a new way, or change their beliefs, actions, and behavior (O'Hair, Stewart, & Rubenstein, 2010). For example, "Sign this petition. In doing so, you will make a difference in someone's life and make our voices heard" or "Don't forget to vote next Tuesday!"

> **Ethics and You**
> Think about some of the potential ethical dangers of crossing the line between an informative and a persuasive speech. When might you be tempted to persuade your audience when you've meant to inform them? How can you keep your speech strictly informative? Do you think that's possible?

LearningCurve
bedfordstmartins.com/commandyou

Outlining Your Speech

At this point, you have all the building blocks for a successful speech. Now you're ready to pull your work together in an **outline**—a structured form of your speech content (Fraleigh & Tuman, 2011). An effective outline helps you confirm that your points are arranged clearly and properly, ensures that you've cited your all-important research, and assists you in your speech delivery. (In fact, many instructors require students to turn in an outline before the presentation. Be sure to check on your instructor's preferences.)

You may already be familiar with the basics of outlining from your high school courses or from your college composition class. We'll refresh that information for you with a discussion of the essentials of outlining before we move on to types of outlines and the heart of this section: preparation and speaking outlines.

Essentials of Outlining

In every phase of outlining, basic guidelines will help you structure and prepare your speech. A solid outline will clearly reveal the structure of your arguments and the hierarchy of your points.

- **Use standard symbols.** What an outline does, essentially, is put the hierarchy of points visualized in Figure 12.1 (p. 262) into text format. To do this, outlines generally use roman numerals, letters, and standard numbers to indicate different levels of importance in the hierarchy.

    I. Main Point
        A. Subpoint
        B. Subpoint
            1. Sub-subpoint
            2. Sub-subpoint

    If you need to break down the sub-subpoints even further, you may use lowercase letters (a, b, etc.) to create sub-sub-subpoints.

- **Use subdivisions properly.** It is basic logic that a whole of anything—a sandwich, a doughnut, or an outline heading—can never be split into fewer than two pieces. Therefore, as you divide your ideas from main points to subpoints, remember that each numbered or lettered entry must come in a series of at least two points: if you have a I, you must have a II; if you have an A, you must have a B; and so on.

- **Separate the parts of your speech.** It is typically helpful to label your introduction, conclusion, and even your transitions to distinguish them from the body of your speech (your main points and supporting subpoints).

- **Call out your specific purpose and thesis.** Many instructors want students to include this pertinent information at the top of the outline, so check with your instructor to determine his or her preference. You may feel that you already know this information by heart, but it can be helpful to see it at the top of your outline page to ensure that all your main points support the purpose and thesis. Also, you may wind up tweaking them a bit as you work your way through the outlining process.

- **Cite your sources.** As discussed in Chapter 11, it is extremely important to give proper citations in your speech. As you work on the outline, you should always mark where a specific point requires credit. Directly after the point, insert either a footnote or a reference in parentheses; once you complete the outline, arrange the references in order on a separate sheet titled "Works Cited," "Notes," or "References." Citations can be presented in a variety of formats, including styles dictated by such organizations as the Modern Language Association (MLA) and the American Psychological Association (APA). See **Figure 12.2** on page 281 for a sample of how you might handle references in APA format. Your instructor may have his or her own preferences about how to handle citations, so when in doubt, ask.

- **Give your speech a title.** Once all your ideas and points are organized on paper, you can give your speech a catchy title that captures its essence. You might also consider using a provocative question as the title or part of a memorable quotation that you will use in the body of the speech.

At every phase of development, you should review your outline for sound organization. When reviewing, you should see a clear hierarchy of points reflected in each tier of your structure. A weak link in the outline—an unsupported argument, an unrelated point—reveals an overall weakness in the way you've presented and defended your thesis. A solid outline shows not only how well you've organized

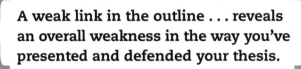

{ **A weak link in the outline . . . reveals an overall weakness in the way you've presented and defended your thesis.** }

your material but also how each point is supported by two or more subpoints, making a stronger case for your thesis statement. It also shows the scope and validity of your research by detailing your evidence with complete citations.

Styles of Outlines

There are three basic approaches you can take to outlining your speech, which vary according to the level of detail. All three formats—sentence outlines, phrase outlines, and key-word outlines—can be valuable tools in developing and eventually delivering your speech. In most cases, you'll move from one format to another as you progress from preparing your speech to actually delivering it.

Sentence Outline. The first type of outline is the **sentence outline**, which offers the full text of what you want to say in your speech. Sentence outlines are generally used as you develop and prepare early drafts because they help you become more comfortable with all aspects of your speech; they are typically not ideal for your actual presentation because you may wind up reading directly from the outline, missing out on valuable eye contact with the audience. Consider the following example from **Sample Speech Outline 12.1** (see p. 278) regarding sleep deprivation:

II. There are many causes of sleep deprivation, according to the Centers for Disease Control and Prevention.
   A. Busy work and family schedules contribute to sleep deprivation.
      1. As college students, many of us are trying to handle full-time course work and full- or part-time jobs to help pay for tuition,

in addition to maintaining relationships with loved ones.
      2. New parents are often incredibly sleep deprived as they attempt to adjust to life with an infant as well as those infamous nighttime feedings.
      3. Shift workers (including police officers, nurses, pilots, and so on) often have trouble establishing good sleep habits because their schedules change frequently and they are sometimes required to work the night shift.
   B. Late-night television and Internet use can also interfere with the ability to fall asleep or can prevent individuals from adhering to a bedtime schedule.
   C. The use of caffeine and alcohol can also make it difficult to fall asleep and stay asleep.
   D. Some medical conditions—including insomnia and obstructive sleep apnea—also make sleeping incredibly difficult.

Phrase Outline. A **phrase outline** takes parts of sentences and uses those phrases as instant reminders of what the point or subpoint means. Consider the following example:

II. Many causes of sleep deprivation (CDC)
   A. Busy work and personal lives
      1. Students struggling with school and work
      2. New parents adjusting to baby schedule
      3. Shift work disrupts sleep
   B. Using TV or computer late at night
   C. Use of caffeine and alcohol
   D. Medical conditions—insomnia and sleep apnea

The phrase outline is often preferred because it offers speakers a clear road map of their presentation, with reminders of key points and phrases, while also allowing speakers to deliver a speech rather than simply to read it.

Read a famous or familiar speech (such as Martin Luther King's "I Have a Dream" speech), and create an outline for it. Can you follow a clear sequence of points? Do the subpoints support the speaker's main points?

Key-Word Outline. A **key-word outline** is the briefest possible outline, consisting of specific "key words" from the sentence outline to jog the speaker's memory. This type of outline allows the speaker to maintain maximum eye contact with the audience, though the speaker must be *extremely* familiar with the content of the speech. An example of a key-word outline is as follows:

II. SD causes (CDC)
    A. Family and work
        1. College students
        2. New parents
        3. Shift workers
    B. Television and Internet
    C. Caffeine and alcohol
    D. Medical conditions—insomnia, apnea

From Preparation Outline to Speaking Outline

In most public speaking situations, you will use the basics you've learned to create two outlines. The first is a **preparation outline** (sometimes called a *working outline*), a draft that you will use, and probably revisit and revise continually, throughout the preparation for your speech. The function of a preparation outline is to firm up your thesis statement, establish and organize your main points, and develop your supporting points. From the preparation outline, you will eventually develop a **speaking outline**, or *delivery outline*, which is your final speech plan, complete with details, delivery tips, and important notes about presentation aids (which we will discuss in Chapter 13).

You may find that a sentence outline works well when you work on your preparation outline; as you move toward a final speaking outline, it's best to switch

◊ As you develop your speech, you'll transition from a more detailed preparation outline to a speaking outline that will equip you for the actual presentation.

to a phrase or key-word approach (or a combination of the two). To do this, look at your full sentences, and pull out key words, phrases, or headers that will jog your memory and serve as guideposts as you speak. Sample Speech Outline 12.1 shows the full progression from preparation outline to speaking outline.

Your speaking outline should also include **delivery cues**, brief reminders about important information related to the delivery of your speech that are for your eyes alone. You'll likely want to include reminders to show a presentation aid or speak slowly at the beginning of the speech, when you are likely to be the most nervous. We'll discuss more about delivery in Chapter 13.

Another important aspect of your speaking outline is that it should contain notes for your **oral citations**, the references to source materials that you mention in the narrative of your speech. After a sentence or phrase in your outline, you might simply place the source in parentheses so that you remember to give credit. For example, the key words "SD—financial costs (Skerritt, HBR)" should prompt you to say: "Sleep deprivation costs businesses more

What About You?

Assessing Your Outline

To ensure that your speech is well organized and that your thesis is soundly supported, use the following checklist as you prepare your outline.

- Is there a clear hierarchy of points in my outline?

- Are my points each supported by at least two subpoints?

- Do I call out the parts of my speech, including the introduction, transitions, and conclusion?

- Have I incorporated my research into my outline effectively?

- Have I worked oral citations into my outline to avoid unintentional plagiarism?

- Does my outline offer a complete list of references for all the research I cite in my speech?

- Does my speaking outline provide important delivery cues that will help me when I present?

- Have I verified the style of my outline with my instructor (for example, a sentence outline for a preparation outline or a phrase outline for a speaking outline)?

If you cannot answer "yes" to each of these questions, then you will likely benefit from additional work on your outline. Remember, the more effort you put into addressing these details, the better prepared and the more confident you will be when it is time to deliver your speech.

than $3,000 per employee annually, in terms of lowered productivity, according to a recent report by Patrick Skerritt in the *Harvard Business Review*." For material quoted word for word from the source, the oral citation must clarify that the material is in fact quoted rather than your own expression ("As Skerritt notes, 'This doesn't include the cost of absenteeism—those with insomnia missed an extra five days a year compared to good sleepers'"). In such instances, you will likely want to use full sentences in your outline, rather than key words or phrases, to ensure that you do not misquote or misrepresent your source.

Finally, you should choose a comfortable format for using your speaking outline in front of your audience. You may transfer the outline to note cards, which will enable you to flip through notes quickly; alternatively, you might create virtual note cards on your smart phone or tablet, or you might prefer to use a standard-size sheet of paper. In many classroom situations, your instructor will indicate the preferred format.

From Preparation Outline to Speaking Outline

Title: Sleep It Off: Understanding the Dangers of Sleep Deprivation
General Purpose: To inform
Specific Speech Purpose: To inform my audience about the dangers of sleep deprivation so that they may take appropriate steps to avoid this troubling medical issue.
Thesis Statement: You must understand the causes and effects of sleep deprivation, as well as simple steps to take to avoid it, to improve your life now and avoid costly personal and social ramifications.

Sample Preparation Outline ▪

▪ Speaker uses sentence outline style throughout preparation outline

Introduction

I. Do you ever feel like you're struggling to juggle relationships, work, and classes? Many of us do, and often enough, the first thing we cut out of our busy daily routine is sleep. ▪

▪ Speaker opens with attention-getting question and offers response audience will likely relate to

II. For better or worse, the human body needs an adequate amount of sleep to function properly, and my research indicates that we simply aren't getting enough of it.

III. You must understand the causes and effects of sleep deprivation, as well as simple steps to take to avoid it, to improve your life now and avoid costly personal and social ramifications. ▪

▪ Thesis statement

IV. Today I will speak about sleep deprivation. I will begin by explaining what it is, before moving on to its causes and effects and examining simple solutions to the problem. ▪

▪ Preview of main points

Transition: So what exactly is sleep deprivation?

Body

I. In a personal communication with Dr. Arkeenah Jones, a family physician, on March 15, 2011, she noted that sleep deprivation is a condition in which a person does not get enough sleep, which can lead to chronic exhaustion. ▪

▪ Main point 1

A. The National Sleep Foundation's 2009 survey notes that 70 percent of adults sleep less than eight hours per night, and 40 percent sleep less than the minimum recommended seven hours per night.

B. The results of the survey I passed out last week reveal that 30 percent of people in this very classroom get less than six hours of sleep on weeknights.

Transition: By a show of hands, how many people in this room *like* to sleep? ▪ I thought so. So, if we enjoy sleeping so much, why are we not getting enough of it?

▪ Speaker keeps audience involved by asking questions

II. There are many causes of sleep deprivation, according to the Centers
for Disease Control and Prevention. ▪
  A. Busy work and family schedules contribute to sleep deprivation.
    1. As college students, many of us are trying to handle full-time
       course work and full- or part-time jobs to help pay for tuition,
       in addition to maintaining relationships with loved ones. ▪
    2. New parents are often incredibly sleep deprived as they
       attempt to adjust to life with an infant as well as those
       infamous nighttime feedings.
    3. Shift workers (including police officers, nurses, pilots, and so
       on) often have trouble establishing good sleep habits because
       their schedules change frequently and they are sometimes
       required to work the night shift.
  B. Late-night television and Internet use can interfere with the
     ability to fall asleep or can prevent individuals from adhering to a
     bedtime schedule.
  C. The use of caffeine and alcohol can also make it difficult to fall
     asleep and stay asleep.
  D. Some medical conditions—including insomnia and obstructive
     sleep apnea—also make sleeping incredibly difficult.

Transition: As we've seen, busy schedules, overuse of media, the intake of
alcohol and caffeine, and medical conditions can all cause sleep deprivation,
▪ but why does sleep deprivation truly matter so much?

III. Sleep deprivation can have negative effects on the health and safety
of individuals and the community at large. ▪
  A. According to Dr. Michael J. Breus, a clinical psychologist and writer
     for WebMD, sleep deprivation decreases performance and alertness.
    1. Sleep deprivation decreases workplace productivity, at a cost of
       more than $3,000 per employee annually, as noted by Patrick
       Skerritt in the *Harvard Business Review*.
    2. Sleep deprivation is a leading cause of automobile accidents,
       especially among adolescent motorists, according to a February
       15, 2010, report by the American Academy of Sleep Medicine. ▪
  B. Dr. Michael J. Breus also notes that sleep deprivation causes
     relational stress.
    1. In my own life, I certainly find that I argue more with friends
       and family when I'm exhausted than I do when I'm well rested. ▪
    2. The results of the survey I conducted indicate that 55 percent
       of the members of this class find that "arguing with a loved
       one" is a problematic outcome of not getting enough sleep.
  C. Dr. Arkeenah Jones notes that sleep deprivation affects memory
     and cognitive ability.
    1. In fact, a Centers for Disease Control and Prevention study
       noted that 23.2 percent of sleep-deprived individuals report

▪ Main point 2

▪ Speaker continually makes topic relevant to audience

▪ Speaker effectively uses internal summary in transition to next main point
▪ Main point 3

▪ Speaker continually uses oral citations to credit sources

▪ Speaker builds credibility, noting she too is prone to effects of sleep deprivation

difficulties with concentration. Similarly, 18.2 percent report difficulty remembering information.

    2. Dr. Pamela Thatcher, a psychology professor at St. Lawrence University, conducted a study in which she discovered that students who pull all-night study sessions typically have lower GPAs than those who do not.

  D. Sleep deprivation can contribute to chronic health conditions, including depression, obesity, and diabetes, according to the Centers for Disease Control and Prevention.

Transition: So far, we've discussed the common causes of sleep deprivation as well as its negative—and potentially tragic—effects. At this point you may be wondering how to avoid sleep deprivation altogether. I will discuss several suggestions now. ■

  IV. You can avoid sleep deprivation with a few simple changes to your daily routine.

    A. Make sleeping a priority in your life, along with your other commitments.

    B. Have consistent sleep and wake-up times, even on weekends.

    C. Don't watch television, play on your laptop, or even study in bed. Try to reserve your bed for sleeping.

    D. Don't drink alcohol or consume caffeine too close to bedtime.

    E. Dr. Arkeenah Jones recommends contacting your primary care physician or a nurse practitioner in the Student Health Center in order to address underlying medical problems that might affect your sleep.

Transition: Regulating your schedule and developing good habits are essential for preventing sleep deprivation.

Conclusion

  I. Sadly, a realization about the dangers of sleep deprivation came too late for Zlatko Glusica, a fatigued pilot whose slow reaction time caused a fatal error in landing an Air India Express flight in 2010. According to a report by Alan Levin in *USA Today*, 158 people—including Mr. Glusica—died. ■

  II. As you've seen today, sleep deprivation is a concerning problem for individuals and communities.

    A. It has many causes, ranging from busy schedules and media use to caffeine and alcohol consumption and medical problems.

    B. Its effects can be devastating, as I've detailed in this speech.

    C. Luckily, many of us can prevent sleep deprivation by making simple changes to our daily routines. ■

  III. Now go get some rest . . . after the remainder of today's speeches are over, that is! ■

Marginal notes:

■ Speaker transitions to final main point with internal summary and internal preview

■ Speaker signals end of speech with tragic story that drives home main points

■ Speaker reiterates main points

■ Speaker uses memorable statement and humor to end speech

◐ Figure 12.2 **References (in APA style)**

References

American Academy of Sleep Medicine. (2010, February 15). Sleep problems and sleepiness increase the risk of motor vehicle accidents in adolescents. *Science Daily*. Retrieved from http://www.sciencedaily.com/-releases/2010/02/100215081728.htm

Breus, M. J. (2004). Sleep habits: More important than you think. In *WebMD: Sleep disorders guide*. Retrieved from http://www.webmd.com/sleep-disorders/guide/important-sleep-habits

Centers for Disease Control and Prevention. (2008, February 28). CDC study reveals adults may not get enough rest or sleep. Retrieved from http://www.cdc.gov/media/pressrel/2008/r080228.htm

Centers for Disease Control and Prevention. (2011). Insufficient sleep is a public health epidemic. Retrieved from http://www.cdc.gov/Features/dsSleep

Levin, A. (2010, November 18). Air India pilot's "sleep inertia" caused crash. *USA Today*. Retrieved from http://www.usatoday.com/news/world/2010-11-18-airindia18_ST_N.htm

National Sleep Foundation. (2009). Sleep in America poll: Summary of findings. Retrieved from http://www.sleepfoundation.org/article/sleep-america-polls/2009-health-and-safety

Skerritt, P. D. (2011, January 12). Your health at work: Sleep deprivation's true workplace costs. *Harvard Business Review*. Retrieved from http://blogs.hbr.org/your-health-at-work/2011/01/sleep-deprivations-true-workpl.htm

St. Lawrence University. (2007, December 1). All-nighters equal lower grades. *Science Daily*. Retrieved from www.sciencedaily.com/releases/2007/11/071130162518.htm

Sample Speaking Outline

Introduction [Speak slowly! Look at audience!]

  I. Juggling commitments? Many give up sleeping.

  II. We need sleep; research = we don't get enough.

  III. Be informed about sleep deprivation (SD) to improve life and prevent negative consequences. ▪

  IV. I will discuss SD: what, causes, effects, prevention. ▪

Transition: What is SD?

Body

  I. SD = not enough sleep; can lead to chronic exhaustion. (Dr. Arkeenah Jones, personal communication, March 15, 2011) ▪

    A. 70% of adults sleep < 8 hours per night, and 40% sleep < 7 hours per night. (National Sleep Foundation's 2009 survey) ▪

    B. 30% of people in class sleep < 6 hours on weeknights. (my survey)

Transition: *Like to sleep? Then why not sleeping?* **[Smile, encourage audience response]**

  II. SD causes (CDC) ▪

    A. Family and work

      1. College students—course work, jobs, relationship

      2. New parents—crying, hungry babies

      3. Shift workers—trouble with inconsistent schedules

    B. Television and Internet

    C. Caffeine and alcohol

    D. Medical conditions—insomnia and obstructive sleep apnea

Transition: Causes: schedules, media, alcohol/caffeine/medical conditions. Who cares?

  III. SD has negative effects for individuals and community. ▪

    A. Decreases performance and alertness (Dr. Michael J. Breus, clinical psychologist & writer for WebMD)

      1. Decreases workplace productivity; costs > $3,000 per employee annually (Patrick D. Skerritt, *Harvard Business Review*)

      2. Causes auto accidents, especially for teens (American Academy of Sleep Medicine, February 15, 2010) ▪

    B. Causes relational stress (Dr. Breus)

      1. True for me!

      2. 55% of class fights with loved ones due to SD. (my survey)

    C. Affects memory and cognitive ability (Dr. Jones)

      1. 23.2% report difficulties with concentration; 18.2% report difficulty remembering info. (CDC)

▪ Thesis statement. Speaker is so familiar with speech purpose and thesis, she only needs brief reminder.

▪ Key-word preview of main points

▪ Main point 1

▪ Speaker retains more detail in this subpoint to keep statistics straight

▪ Main point 2

▪ Main point 3

▪ Speaker makes sure that oral citations are clear throughout speaking outline

   2. All-nighters lead to lower GPA. (Dr. Pamela Thatcher, psychology professor at St. Lawrence University)
   D. Chronic health conditions—depression, obesity, diabetes (CDC)

Transition: Discussed causes and effects. How to prevent SD?

IV. Daily routine changes **[Don't read as list. Look up!]** ▪
   A. Prioritize sleeping
   B. Consistent sleep and wake-up times
   C. No TV/Internet in bed; just sleep
   D. No alcohol/caffeine close to bedtime
   E. Talk to MD or NP at health center about medical concerns. (Dr. Jones)

▪ In practice, speaker noted tendency to read directly from notes, preventing useful interaction with audience

Transition: Changes in routine and good habits prevent SD.

Conclusion

   I. Zlatko Glusica **[Zlat*ko Glue*sick*uh]**, ▪ fatigued pilot, Air India Express, killed 158 people landing plane. (Alan Levin, *USA Today*, 2010) **[Show image of crash]**
   II. SD is concerning problem for individuals and communities.
   A. Causes: busy schedules, media use, alcohol/caffeine/medical problems
   B. Devastating effects
   C. Mostly preventable with simple changes
   III. Get some rest!

▪ Speaker uses effective delivery cues throughout speech: here for a difficult pronunciation

LearningCurve
bedfordstmartins.com/commandyou

Back to } The State of the Union Address

As this chapter shows, organizing, writing, and outlining your speech are crucial steps in eventually delivering an effective presentation. Recall our discussion of White House speechwriters preparing the State of the Union address from the beginning of the chapter. What considerations and challenges will affect their organization and outlines? How will their organization influence their audiences' perceptions of the speech?

- Ideas will come in from every direction, so planning and organization are key. David Frum, a former White House speechwriter, observed that "the planning for the next State of the Union really begins the day after the last State of the Union" (as cited in Jackson, 2006).

- Speechwriters need to bear in mind that they are writing for two different—albeit not mutually exclusive—audiences. Chriss Winston (2002) points out that members of Congress and Washington insiders judge the speech primarily on its policy content, while everyday Americans tend to look for leadership qualities and their own values in the president. The challenge lies in choosing content and language that speak to both groups.

- The key to avoiding what Matthew Scully (2005) refers to as a "tedious grab bag of policy proposals" lies in the skillful use of transitions. Instead of jumping from point to point, speechwriters need to find and build unifying themes among the many policies under discussion. Thus George W. Bush's speechwriters were able to draw connections between such issues as cloning and war by focusing on the overall theme of human dignity and human rights. These connections allowed for natural transitions from one issue to the next (Scully, 2005).

- Creating unified themes is also crucial to keeping the content (and length) of the speech from spiraling out of control. President Bill Clinton was known for long State of the Union speeches that detailed many policy proposals, while President George W. Bush preferred to stick to big ideas.

Your Reference

}

A Study Tool

Now that you have finished reading this chapter, you can

Organize and support your main points:

- Identify your **main points**, the central claims that support your specific speech purpose and your thesis statement (p. 260).
- **Subpoints** support your main points using all the statistics, stories, and other forms of research you discovered on your topic (p. 261).

Choose an appropriate organizational pattern ⊙ for your speech:

- A **chronological pattern** presents main points in a systematic, time-related fashion (p. 262).
- A **topical pattern** is based on categories, such as person, place, thing, or process (p. 262). The **primacy-recency effect** argues that audiences are most likely to remember what comes at the beginning and end of messages (pp. 262–263).
- A **spatial pattern** arranges points according to physical proximity or direction from one to the next (p. 263).
- The **problem-solution pattern** presents an obstacle and then suggestions for overcoming it (p. 263).
- The **cause-effect pattern** moves from the cause of a phenomenon to the results or vice versa (p. 263).
- The **narrative pattern** uses a story line to tie points together (p. 263).
- The **motivated sequence pattern** uses a five-step plan to motivate listeners: attention, need, satisfaction, visualization, and action (pp. 263–264).

Move smoothly from point to point:

- Build strong **transitions** ⊙, sentences that connect the points so that topics flow naturally (p. 264).
- Use **signposts**, key words or phrases that signify transitions (pp. 264–265).
- **Internal previews** prime the audience for the content immediately ahead (p. 265).
- **Internal summaries** crystallize points in one section before moving on (p. 265).

Choose appropriate and powerful language:

- Consider your audience when you choose your words (p. 266).
- Use simple, unambiguous words (p. 266).

- Be concise (p. 266).
- Use vivid language (p. 266).
- Use repetition, allusion, similes, and metaphors to make a lasting impression (p. 267).

Develop a strong introduction, a crucial part of all speeches:

- **Grab listeners' attention** ⊙ with surprise, a good story, a quote, a question, or **humor** ⊙ (pp. 269–270).
- Introduce your purpose and topic (p. 271).
- Preview your main points to provide a mental outline for your audience (p. 271).
- Establish a relationship with the audience (pp. 271–272).

Conclude with as much strength as you had in the introduction:

- Signal the end to ask for listeners' full attention, and wrap up quickly (p. 272).
- Reiterate your topic, purpose, and main points (p. 272).
- Make a final impact with a memorable closing quote, statement, question, or story (pp. 272–273).
- Challenge the audience to respond with a **call to action**—what you hope they will do in response to the speech (p. 273).

Prepare an effective outline:

- The **outline** puts the hierarchy of points into a text format (pp. 273–274).
- The hierarchy of points for a strong outline will show each point supported by two or more subpoints (p. 274).
- There are three essential styles of outlines (from most detailed to most spare): **sentence outline**, **phrase outline**, and **key-word outline** (pp. 275–276).
- Write a **preparation outline** (or working outline) to organize and develop your speech (p. 276).
- The **speaking outline** (or delivery outline) is your final speech plan (p. 276).
- Add **delivery cues**, brief reminders about important information, to your speaking outline (p. 276).
- **Oral citations**, references to source materials to be included in your narrative, should also be in your speaking outline (pp. 276–277).

✓ Look for LearningCurve throughout
the chapter to help you review.
bedfordstmartins.com/commandyou

13 } Delivering Presentations

B efore the film *The King's Speech* won the best picture Oscar in 2011, few Americans knew the story of Britain's King George VI. Born into royalty but never intended for the throne, King George—known as Albert or "Bertie"—lived much of his life in the shadow of his older brother, the dashing Edward. And that was fine with Albert, who suffered from a devastating stutter and tended to shy away from public speaking. But when Edward famously abdicated the British throne, Albert was thrust into a position of leadership that he didn't want but that he was bound by duty and honor to fulfill.

With his country on the brink of World War II, Albert was naturally expected to make a radio address. His speech was not perfect, but he managed to get through it and deliver his message to a frightened public. Colin Firth, who won an Oscar for playing Albert, reviewed audio and video footage of the king delivering his speeches in order to prepare for the role. "It's absolutely heartbreaking," said Firth. "It's very moving because it's not just the struggle. It's the courage with which he deals with the struggle" (as cited in CBS News, 2010).

Albert's story was an inspiration to David Seidler, who had left Britain during the war and who also suffered from what he described as a "profound" stutter. Seidler overcame his stutter as a teenager and went on to become a Hollywood screenwriter. Upon winning the Oscar for *The King's Speech*, Seidler himself gave a moving speech, accepting the award "on behalf of all the stutterers in the world. We have a voice. We have been heard" (Seidler, 2011).

After you have finished reading this chapter, you will be able to

Identify and control your anxieties.

Choose a delivery style best suited to you and your speaking situation.

Employ effective vocal cues.

Employ effective visual cues.

Connect with your audience.

Enhance your words with effective presentation aids.

Make efficient use of your practice time.

M any people feel anxious about delivering speeches—and some manage to avoid it. But consider the nervousness and challenges that King George and David Seidler managed to overcome in the process of finding their voices. As their stories illustrate, with the right tools and plenty of practice, even the most nervous or challenged individuals can become accomplished and engaging speakers. In this chapter, you'll learn the basics of competent speech delivery that will help you connect with your audience and deliver an effective presentation. We begin by acknowledging the nervousness you may naturally experience before moving on to key methods of delivery, guidelines for effective delivery and presentation aids, and tips for practicing your speech.

Understanding and Addressing Anxiety

Jerry Seinfeld once joked, "According to most studies, people's number one fear is public speaking. Number two is death. . . . This means to the average person, if you go to a funeral, you're better off in the casket than doing the eulogy" (as cited in Peck, 2007). Whether Seinfeld's statistics are accurate or not, it's true that speechmaking can cause some level of **public speaking anxiety** (PSA), the nervousness we experience when we know we have to communicate publicly to an audience (Behnke & Sawyer, 1999; Bippus & Daly, 1999). While we might think of PSA as an emotional challenge, it often manifests itself with real physical symptoms, including a rapid heartbeat, erratic breathing, increased sweating, and a general feeling of uneasiness. (To determine your own level of PSA, visit James McCroskey's online quiz at www.jamescmccroskey.com/measures/prpsa.htm.)

For some individuals, however, this nervousness goes far beyond giving a speech and extends to such essential speaking tasks as answering a question in class, meeting new people, or voicing an opinion. Noted communication scholar James McCroskey (1977) calls this **communication apprehension** (CA) because it is a more general "fear or anxiety associated with either real or anticipated communication with another person or persons" (p. 78). Clearly, though, speaking up or speaking out can enhance personal opportunities and career prospects.

But don't despair! Whether you suffer from PSA or even the more general CA, you can learn to control your nervousness. In more severe cases, you might consider meeting with a trained professional at your campus counseling center. For less disruptive symptoms, you might simply find comfort in the fact that nervousness is a natural part of life—and that it can actually spur you on to do your best (in the case of a speech, this may mean preparing more thoroughly and practicing more diligently). You may also benefit from the advice we offer here on identifying your anxiety triggers and building your confidence.

Identifying Anxiety Triggers

Before you can conquer your nervousness, you need to identify it. Just what has you so frightened? Research, as well as our personal experiences, points to several key factors, including upsetting experiences, fear of evaluation, and distaste for attention (Ayres, 2005; Bodie, 2010).

Upsetting Experiences. Anna forgot her line in the second-grade school play, and the audience laughed. They thought it was adorable, but to Anna, the experience was devastating. It's fairly common for a negative experience in our past to shape our expectations for the future, but it's important to remember that it's never too late to learn or improve on personal skills. Anna needs to think about other skills that she has mastered, despite her initial nervousness: she was anxious the first time she drove a car, for example. With practice, she was able to master it—even though she failed her first road test. She needs to approach public speaking with the same kind of "try, try again" attitude.

Fear of Evaluation. Anna's anxiety about public speaking may not be about speaking but about being evaluated on her speaking abilities: graded in class or laughed at in other situations. We all feel this way from time to time, but Anna must remember that her instructor will consider other aspects of her speech preparation, including her organization and research. In addition, she should recall that she's not under the intense scrutiny that she imagines: in most public speaking situations, the audience wants the speaker to succeed. Keeping the presentation in this perspective will help her feel less anxiety.

Distaste for Attention. Alonzo loves to sing in the car, in the shower, and at concerts. But he refuses to sing a solo because being the center of attention makes him feel incredibly uncomfortable. While he may be able to avoid singing a solo, he will likely have to speak publicly at some point. He can minimize his discomfort with being the center of attention by thinking of his speech as an opportunity to communicate with a group rather than to perform. In other words, if he were to give the best-man speech at his brother's wedding, he'd be communicating with a group of family members and close friends (people who share his love for his brother) rather than putting on a performance.

📍 Public speaking anxiety manifests itself both psychologically and physically, but it can be overcome by identifying the triggers of anxiety and by building confidence.

> **Culture and You**
>
> Do you think the culture you were raised in has affected your taste or distaste for attention? Do other members of your family share a similar attitude? Are they comfortable or nervous about public speaking?

Building Your Confidence

Most people can cope effectively with periodic bouts of public speaking anxiety by taking the following advice, which can also be employed for more general cases of communication apprehension.

- **Prepare for the unexpected.** Anxiety has positive effects as well, such as driving you to be more prepared. For example, anxiety over forgetting your speech's main points might cause you to prepare with solid notes. By

Pay attention to how you meet people and the general first impression you receive from them. Ask yourself what makes you feel the way you do about the person. Does the person make you feel comfortable by smiling at you, looking you in the eye, or coming across as sincere? If you can pinpoint the reasons for your own first impressions, you can better understand what an audience expects from a speaker (and adjust your own behaviors in order to make a good impression).

💧 Meditating or practicing yoga can help you learn to relax your muscles and focus your attention.

thinking about what might go wrong, you can come up with simple solutions for just about any scenario.

- **Desensitize yourself.** Sometimes the best way to get over something is to "just do it." You address your fear of public speaking by making attempts to get up in front of a crowd in less threatening situations, like asking a question in class or at a community meeting or singing karaoke with friends.

- **Visualize your success.** Research shows that people with high speech anxiety tend to concentrate on negative thoughts before giving their speeches (Ayres & Hopf, 1993). In order to reduce those thoughts (and their accompanying anxiety), it's important to spend time imagining positive scenarios and personal success, a technique known as **performance visualization** (Ayres, 2005; Ayres & Hopf, 1993). Imagine yourself standing before your audience with confidence and grace—and it just may happen.

- **Take care of yourself.** In order to be productive, remember to take care of yourself in the days leading up to your speech: get enough rest, budget your time effectively to make room for your speech practice sessions, try to eat a light meal before the presentation, and try relaxation techniques (such as deep breathing, yoga, a calming walk, or laughing with friends).

- **Practice, practice, practice.** As we've mentioned—and as we'll discuss throughout this chapter—adequately preparing for your speech will increase the likelihood of success and lessen your apprehension or anxiety (Smith & Frymier, 2006). Research demonstrates that confidence does come through preparation and skill building, which means that conducting thorough research, organizing your points, and preparing a useful outline will help you achieve a positive outcome (Schroeder, 2002).

With a more realistic understanding of the role of anxiety—and with these tips for controlling it in mind—

Technology and You

Would you ever practice a presentation in front of a virtual or simulated audience? Do you think you would find it helpful? Why or why not?

let's move on to the various methods of delivery that you may confront over the course of your life as a student, professional, and citizen.

LearningCurve
bedfordstmartins.com/commandyou

Methods of Delivery

You might think of a great speaker as someone who is eloquent yet also sounds as though he or she is speaking without having prepared a written speech. Although that's possible in certain situations, most speakers spend time preparing in the ways we've already discussed in Chapters 11 and 12—writing a speech and preparing an outline of some sort. Deciding just how to prepare for your speech affects, and is affected by, your choice of delivery style. We'll examine four specific delivery options and the potential benefits and pitfalls of each.

Speaking from Manuscript

If you've watched the president of the United States deliver the annual State of the Union address, you may have noticed that he alternates between two teleprompter screens as he reads his speech. That's because he's delivering a speech from manuscript. When you speak from manuscript, you write your entire speech out and then read it word for word from the written text because your allegiance is to the words that you have prepared. Speaking from manuscript is common for presidential speeches. That's because they are by nature quite long and will likely be quoted and interpreted throughout the world. A mistake in the delivery of such a speech might not merely embarrass the president but might also affect world events. Manuscript delivery is useful in any situation where accuracy, time constraints, or worries about misinterpretation outweigh the need for a casual and natural delivery style.

However, manuscript delivery also has a number of downsides. First, it's time-consuming, involving countless rewrites to get the written message exactly right; this makes it a better fit for a president (who has a team of speechwriters at his disposal) than a typical college student. Second, the static nature of reading from a written speech—whether from a manuscript or a teleprompter—limits your ability to communicate nonverbally with movements, facial expressions, gestures, or eye contact. As you'll learn later in this chapter, planning and rehearsing are crucial for overcoming these tendencies when delivering a speech from manuscript.

Speaking from Memory

Speaking from memory is an ancient public speaking tradition referred to as **oratory**. In this style of

📍 Speaking from manuscript is a fitting method of delivery for TV newscasters such as Brian Williams, for whom accuracy and time constraints are critical.

speaking, you prepare the speech in the manuscript form as just described but then commit the words to memory.

Oratory delivery is fairly uncommon today as a form of public speaking, as it is both time-consuming and risky. A speaker who forgets a word or phrase can easily lose his or her place in the speech, panic, and never recover. But even if every line is delivered perfectly, the very nature of memorization can create a barrier between speaker and audience. Having memorized the speech and rehearsed without an audience, the speaker tends to deliver it as if the audience isn't there. Such a speech can therefore end up feeling more like a performance, a one-man or one-woman show, rather than a communication that engages with the audience.

Speaking Spontaneously

Impromptu speaking refers to situations where you speak to an audience without any warning or preparation. When you are unexpectedly called on to speak in class or suddenly motivated to give a toast at a party, you must speak impromptu. The secret to excelling at impromptu speaking is understanding that it's never entirely spontaneous; if you are always prepared to give a speech unexpectedly, no speech is entirely unexpected. One major aspect of preparation is the ability to think on your feet: when called on to speak unexpectedly, begin by first acknowledging the person who introduced or called on you, and then repeat or rephrase the question or issue. This will give you a moment to focus on the topic and quickly construct a plan. Usually you'll want to choose a simple format easily applied to the topic, such as noting advantages and disadvantages or cause and effect. Another way to prepare for spontaneous public speaking is by listening to others. Determine if you have some personal application of a point or an example that a speaker has made that either substantiates or refutes another speaker. Most audiences enjoy hearing speakers tell a brief story that illustrates a

point that another speaker made or a theme that an event uses.

Speaking Extemporaneously

Have you witnessed those calm, collected speakers who seem to be making it up as they go along in a surprisingly organized manner? This is called **extemporaneous speaking**.

When you speak extemporaneously, you plan the content, organization, and delivery well in advance, but instead of writing the entire speech out word for word, you speak from an outline of key words and phrases or speaking aids such as Power-Point slides. Extemporaneous speaking involves delivering your speech in an impromptu style, even though the speech is neither spontaneous nor unrehearsed. Most speakers favor extemporaneous delivery because they can fully prepare and rehearse their presentations while economizing on time because they need not determine in advance the exact words that they want to use.

One downside to extemporaneous speaking is that it's difficult to use precise timing or wording, and speakers can easily get off track, become wordy or repetitive, or exceed their allotted time.

So what's the secret to succeeding at extemporaneous speaking? You can achieve success and confidence through practice and preparation. Consider the following points:

- **Prepare well in advance.** You can begin preparing for an extemporaneous speech as soon as you decide on a topic. Think about some possible points you want to make and how you might support them.

- **Don't forget the outline!** As mentioned in Chapter 12, your key-word or phrase outline keeps you focused but gives you lots of flexibility with your word choice.

- **Practice truly makes perfect.** Actors or musicians don't always give the exact same performance, but they do practice a lot. When you get really familiar with a script or a musical

 Will Ferrell and his costars ad-libbed much of *Step Brothers*, not unlike what you will do when speaking extemporaneously.

composition (or a speech), you may indeed memorize parts of it, but a little bit of it will change each and every time, allowing for a more natural delivery.

◊ Effective speaking is a crucial skill. Whether you're a sports star giving a press conference or a climbing instructor giving a safety demonstration, you need to know how to deliver your words in an articulate and expressive manner.

Guidelines for Effective Delivery

Everything from selecting a topic and researching information to outlining your presentation is a prerequisite to the big moment: actually delivering your speech. In this section, we'll take a fresh look at a point that we've emphasized throughout this book: how you say something is as important as what you say. That is, audiences receive information not only from the actual words that you speak but also through two channels of nonverbal communication: the vocal and the visual. Let's see how these nonverbal channels play out in your speech.

{ **Everything from selecting a topic and researching information to outlining your presentation is a prerequisite to the big moment: actually delivering your speech.** }

Effective Vocal Delivery

Actor Seth Rogen is the rare comedian who uses a monotone voice to great comic effect—his delivery of zinging punch lines in a flat, unchanging tone adds an extra layer of irony to films like *This Is the End* (2013), *Pineapple Express* (2008), and *Knocked Up* (2007). But listening to him deliver a long speech in the same style would likely lull you to sleep. By using varying aspects of your voice, you can engage your audience as well as convey confidence and trustworthiness. Through practice, you can learn to control the elements of vocal delivery, which include pitch, volume, rate, pauses, pronunciation, and articulation.

Varying Your Pitch. To be an effective public speaker, you must make use of the range of vocal sounds that the human voice is capable of producing. These variations of sound range from high to low—like musical notes—and are known as *pitch*. You speak in a **monotone** (like Seth Rogen) when you do not vary your pitch at all, and a monotonous speaking voice can be painful for listeners. So how do you ensure that you are using your pitch effectively? One way to practice is to record yourself speaking ahead of time to determine if there are places where you need to use more energy and extend your pitch levels.

Adjusting Your Speaking Rate and Volume. Speakers can use vocal cues to signal to the audience what needs their attention. Just as we use boldface and italic type in the pages of this book to emphasize certain words and phrases, as a speaker you can use audible cues to emphasize certain points.

How fast or slow you speak is known as your **speaking rate**, and it can also be a key factor in effective speaking. You want to speak slowly enough that your audience is able to hear and absorb what you say but quickly enough to capture the urgency and importance of what you are saying. Typically, if you speak faster, compared with your rate for surrounding material, you signal enthusiasm for the content, and the audience's interest will follow. When you slow down, your rate signals a degree of seriousness and concern. You would deliver a persuasive call-to-action speech at a faster pace in order to show and elicit enthusiasm. You would deliver a tribute or dedication, such as a eulogy, at a slower pace to demonstrate sincerity and seriousness.

Changes in *volume*—how loudly or quietly you speak—can also be used to emphasize certain points. What do you want to stand out from your speech for the audience to remember? Is it a statistic, a name, or a product? Think about giving one word or phrase in every few sentences some "punch." This differentiates the word or phrase from its context.

Using Pauses for Effect. Because many speakers believe that their entire goal is to talk, they pause too infrequently. But taking a moment between statements, words, or phrases and not saying anything at all is one of the most powerful tools available to speakers; it can add drama by giving the audience time to reflect on what you have said and anticipate what will follow. For example, in Martin Luther King Jr.'s famous "I Have a Dream" speech, King's use of pauses, combined with rhetorical tools like repetition, helped build drama and anticipation as he delivered his address.

Speaking Clearly and Precisely. One of the quickest ways to lose credibility with your audience is to mispronounce a word—especially a word that is specifically related to the subject of your presentation. **Pronunciation** is the correct formation of word sounds. Many words in the English language are frequently mispronounced, to the point that individuals are not even aware that they are saying these words incorrectly. Check print or online dictionaries for pronunciation keys.

During his presidency, George W. Bush was the butt of countless jokes—often self-deprecating ones—for his frequent errors in pronunciation. But even though Bush sometimes made mistakes in pronunciation, he articulated well. **Articulation** is the clarity and forcefulness with which the sounds are made, regardless of whether they are pronounced correctly. To speak clearly, even if incorrectly, is to be articulate. All speakers strive to be articulate, but there are several ways in

Culture and You

How do you react when you hear speakers with an accent that is different from yours? Do you find them difficult to understand, or do you make assumptions about them based on how they speak? How might your own accent be an advantage or a disadvantage in your next speaking situation?

which we routinely sabotage our efforts (O'Hair, Stewart, & Rubenstein, 2007).

When a speaker omits certain sounds in a word, runs words together, and speaks so softly that a listener can hardly hear, the speaker is guilty of **mumbling**. Most people mumble either because they are in a hurry, because they suffer from communication apprehension, or because they are not prepared to speak clearly.

Effective Visual Delivery

In the same way that a monotone can lull an audience to sleep, so can a stale, dull physical presence. This doesn't mean that you need to be doing cartwheels throughout your speech, but it does mean that you should avoid keeping your hands glued to the podium and that you should look up from your note cards once in a while. Otherwise, you'll be little more than a talking head, and your audience will quickly lose interest. What's more, effective visual cues can enhance a presentation, helping you clarify and emphasize your points in an interesting and compelling way.

Dressing for the Occasion. If you're like most people, you probably hop out of bed in the morning, open your closet, and hope that you have something decent and clean to wear to work or class. However, on the day of your speech—just like the day of a job interview or an important date—you don't want to leave your appearance to chance.

On that day you are a speaker, and even though you may be presenting to a group of friends or classmates you see every week, it is imperative that you look the part of someone capable of informing or persuading the audience. While you certainly don't need to have a Hollywood-perfect body, an expensive wardrobe, or a killer hairstyle to inform or persuade anyone, you should attempt to look and feel your personal best. You can signal authority and enhance your credibility by dressing professionally in neat, ironed clothing—like a pair of black pants or a skirt, with a button-down shirt or simple sweater (Cialdini, 2008; Pratkanis & Aronson, 2001). You should certainly avoid looking overly casual (by wearing shorts, cut-off jeans, or sneakers), which can signal that you don't take the audience, your speech topic, or even yourself as a speaker seriously.

Using Effective Eye Behavior. As we noted in Chapter 5, eye behavior is a crucial aspect of nonverbal communication that can be both effective and appropriate when you consider the cultural context in which you are communicating. In Vietnamese culture, for example, it is considered inappropriate and rude to make prolonged, direct eye contact with someone, particularly if that person is of a higher rank or social status. In the culture of the United States and of many other Western countries, conversely, a lack of eye contact can make a speaker seem suspicious or untrustworthy, making direct eye contact one of the most important nonverbal actions in public speaking, signaling respect for and interest in the audience (Axtell, 1991). But how can a speaker make and maintain eye contact with a large group of individuals?

One way is to move your eyes from one person to another (in a small group) or one section of people to another (in a large group), a technique called scanning. **Scanning** allows you to make brief eye contact with almost everyone in an audience, no matter how large. To use it, picture yourself standing in front of the audience, and then divide the room into four imaginary sections. As you move from idea to idea in your speech, move your eye contact into a new section. Select a friendly-looking person in the quadrant, and focus your eye contact directly on that person

Table 13.1 Tips for Scanning Your Audience

Work in sections and avoid the "lighthouse" effect	Do not scan from left to right or right to left. Always work in sections and move randomly from one section to another. If you simply rotate from left to right, looking at no one in particular, you may look like a human lighthouse!
Look people in the eye	Avoid looking at people's foreheads or over their heads; look them in the eye, even if they are not looking back at you.
Focus for a moment	Remember to pause long enough on an individual so that the person can recognize that you are looking directly at him or her.
Don't jump away	If someone is not looking at you, stay with the person anyway until you've finished your thought. Then move on to another.
Divide large groups	If the audience is too large for you to get to everyone, look at small groups of two or three people sitting together.

while completing the idea (just make sure you don't pick a friend who will try to make you laugh!). Then change quadrants, and select a person from the new group. Tips for using the scanning technique are offered in Table 13.1.

Incorporating Facial Expressions and Gestures. Have you ever seen a cartoon in which a character's face contorts, the jaw dropping to the floor or the eyes becoming small white dots? The animator certainly gets the point across—this character is either entirely surprised or seriously confused. Your facial expressions, while not as exaggerated as those of a cartoon character, serve a similar purpose: they let your audience know when your words arouse fear, anger, happiness, joy, frustration, or other emotions. The critical factor is that your expressions must match the verbal message that you are sending in

📍 Without the extremely frustrated and devious looks on Calvin's face, we wouldn't get the feeling that he has some serious plots up his sleeve.

your speech. As a competent communicator, you are unlikely to smile when delivering a eulogy—unless you are recounting a particularly funny or endearing memory about the deceased.

Like facial expressions, gestures amplify the meaning of your speech. Clenching your fist, counting with your fingers, and spreading your hands far apart to indicate distance or size all reinforce or clarify your message. What is most important is that your gestures are appropriate and natural. So if you want to show emotion but you feel awkward putting your hand over your heart, don't do it; your audience will be able to tell that you feel uncomfortable.

Controlling Body Movements. In addition to eye behavior, facial expressions, and gestures, your audience can't help but notice your body. In most speaking situations you encounter, the best way to highlight your speech content is to restrict your body movements so that the audience can focus on your words. Consider, for example, your **posture**, or the position of your arms and legs and how you carry your body. Generally, when a speaker slumps forward or leans on a podium, rocks back and forth, or paces forward and backward, the audience perceives the speaker as unpolished, and listeners' attention shifts from the message to the speaker's body movements.

How do you prevent such movements from happening, particularly if you're someone who fidgets when nervous? One useful technique is called **planting**. Stand with your legs apart at a distance that is equal to your shoulders. Bend your knees slightly so that they do not lock. From this position, you are able to gesture freely, and when you are ready to move, you

can take a few steps, replant, and continue speaking. The key is to plant following every movement that you make.

Connecting with Your Audience

It is through vocal and visual delivery that speakers are able to interact with their audiences—that's what makes public speaking different from just writing a good presentation. When you compose an essay, you write it and it goes off to the reader; it's a linear model of communication (as discussed in Chapter 1). But speaking before an audience is more than just providing information through words; it's an interaction between speaker and audience.

Indeed, gifted speakers—like the late Ronald Reagan and Bill Clinton—are always aware of this and become known for their ability to deliver even the most formal speeches in a style that feels conversational, personal, and connected. That's because they are able to use their words, voices, and gestures to convey the way they

{ **Like facial expressions, gestures amplify the meaning of your speech. Clenching your fist, counting with your fingers, and spreading your hands far apart to indicate distance or size all reinforce or clarify your message.** }

⚬ President Bill Clinton earned his reputation as a gifted public speaker by recognizing the interaction between speaker and audience and presenting himself as approachable and self-assured.

feel about a subject. They also speak directly to their audiences in a way that seems unrehearsed and sincere. Let's now take a look at the way our words converge with our vocal and visual delivery to establish such a connection with the audience. We'll also consider the ways we can adapt our delivery to suit the audience's needs and expectations.

Expressing Emotion.

If you do not feel passion for what you are talking about, you can be sure that your audience will not feel it either. One of your responsibilities is to ensure that throughout your speech, the audience feels the same emotions that you do for your subject matter. Many Americans, for example, felt an intimate connection to New York mayor Rudy Giuliani when he addressed the media in the immediate aftermath of the terrorist attacks on the city on September 11, 2001. Although he remained authoritative and in control, he was also able to express his grief in a way that rang true to everyone watching or listening. When an audience feels that a speaker is simply acting, they may question the sincerity of the message.

Adapting to Your Audience.

One common mistake speakers make is to speak to—or even at—the audience, rather than to speak *with* the audience. As discussed earlier, in Western cultures this generally means making and maintaining eye contact. But it also means listening to audience reactions, paying attention to listeners' body movements, and continually gauging their responses to what you say and do so that you can make adjustments to your speech as you go along. For example, if you observe audience members frowning or squinting, it may be a sign of misunderstanding. You can take this as a cue to slow down or emphasize key points more explicitly. Alternatively, if you notice your audience members responding with smiles, focused eye contact, or even laughter, you probably want to maintain the style of speaking that produced such a positive reaction.

Creating Immediacy with Your Audience.

As you learned in Chapter 5, immediacy is a feeling of closeness, involvement, and warmth between people as communicated by nonverbal behavior (Mehrabian, 1971; Prager, 2000). We often think of immediacy as being an important facet of close interpersonal relationships. This is certainly true—but it is also an important component of building trust in the relationship between the speaker and the audience.

Speakers enhance their immediacy with their audience by following many of the guidelines we have already set forward in this chapter: establishing and maintaining eye contact with audience members, smiling, moving toward the audience, using inclusive gestures and posture, speaking in a relaxed or conversational tone or style, and using humor. However, as is the case with interpersonal relationships, immediacy is a two-way street. Audiences help foster this feeling of closeness and trust by listening actively, responding with eye contact, nodding, and offering nonverbal indications of agreement, surprise, confusion, and so on.

LearningCurve
bedfordstmartins.com/commandyou

Effective Presentation Aids

Bill Gates is a technology buff, to be sure. He is the man behind Microsoft, the company that invented the ubiquitous presentation software, PowerPoint. So when he gives speeches on behalf of the Bill and Melinda Gates Foundation, it's not surprising that he uses PowerPoint slides to graphically display information on changing death rates from malaria in poor countries and the impact of mosquito netting, vaccines, and other preventatives. But Gates also thinks outside the technological box when it comes to presentation aids: "Malaria is, of course, spread by mosquitoes," he tells the crowd. "I've brought some here," he adds, as he opens a jar to let a small fleet of (uninfected) insects fly around the auditorium. "There's no reason only poor people should have the experience" (Gates, 2009). This simple presentation aid got the audience's attention and made the fight against malaria familiar to anyone who has ever swatted a mosquito off their arm on a summer evening.

Like Gates, today's speakers have many tools to create dramatic visual presentations that enhance their words and deepen the audience's understanding of the topic. We'll explore how presentation aids work in this section.

The Function of Presentation Aids

Although presentation aids can be a valuable asset to a speech, heightening an audience's interest and helping you convey technical information, these aids should *supplement* your speech, not substitute for it. Sure, you may have a moving video or shocking image to share with the audience. But if you haven't researched your topic thoroughly, assembled a useful speaking outline, or even looked up from the podium while speaking, who will care? To be truly useful, presentation aids must enhance your speech, accomplishing three goals:

- **Help listeners process and retain information.** Effective presentation aids help the audience see relationships among concepts, variables, or items. Always make a point, refer to the presentation aid, direct the listeners' attention to where you want them to focus, and then restate, reiterate, or rephrase what you have said.

- **Promote interest and motivation.** If you show terms, photographs, statistics, tables, and other items that truly reinforce your spoken message, the audience will be more likely to go along with you.

- **Convey information clearly and concisely.** There is no comparison between the amount of time it would take you to read a series of figures versus showing them on a table, graph, or chart. A good visual can present a lot of information in a clear, concise, and simple manner, saving the speaker's time for interpretation and elaboration.

📍 **Bill Gates was certainly thinking outside the box— or the jar!—when he released mosquitoes into the auditorium to aid a presentation on malaria.**

Types of Presentation Aids

Students often ask, "What type of visual aid should I use for my speech?" The answer to that question is never entirely straightforward because it depends on your topic, the needs of your individual speech, the time constraints, the constraints of the speaking location, and a myriad of additional factors. What we can share, however, is a look at the dominant types of presentation aids and their general purposes for speakers. We begin by considering props and models before moving on to media clips and images, graphs and charts, posters and transparencies, flip charts and marker boards, and presentation software.

Props and Models. Some things, people, places, or processes are difficult to describe with only words and gestures, making visual aids both effective and appropriate. An object, or a **prop**, removes from the audience the burden of having to imagine what something looks like as you speak. For instance, if you are giving an informative speech on the way to tune a guitar, you might find it difficult to explain the process with only words and gestures. Demonstrating the process on an actual guitar would be an effective visual (and audio) aid. You can also be your very own prop! For example, if you're teaching your audience particular moves in Irish dancing, you might do well to display those moves for everyone to see.

⚲ An interesting prop can be a helpful visual aid. This speaker might have trouble illustrating certain muscles and nerves in the human body without his model.

If a prop is too large to bring into the classroom or too small to be easily viewed by your audience members, consider using a **model**, an appropriately scaled object. One of our past students brought in a small-scale model of the Soviet nuclear submarine *Kursk* to demonstrate how the vessel tragically encountered problems, exploded, and sank.

Be mindful and considerate when selecting the objects and models you bring to your presentation. You may be surprised to learn how many speakers have brought their pets in for a demonstration—despite the fact that other students in the classroom may have severe allergies. Along the same lines, avoid objects that may be dangerous or even illegal, such as firearms, knives, chemicals, and so on. Think safety first!

Media Clips and Images. Images, as well as film, television, and Internet video clips, can add another dimension to your speech by providing vivid illustrations or clarifications of topics that are difficult to capture with words alone. A speaker informing an audience about reconstructive surgery for cleft palate, for example, might show a photograph of a child born with the condition, as well as postsurgical photos, rather than try to describe the condition and outcome only in words. When choosing media clips and images, keep a few points in mind:

- Make sure that your classroom has the equipment you need to make your selection viewable to your audience.

- Keep your video clips short (say, one to two minutes maximum, depending on the length of the speech).

- Don't overwhelm your audience with ten illustrations or photographs when two or three would suffice.

- Remember that your visual aids should not be the center of your speech; one hundred beautiful pictures will not make up for a lack of research or a poor delivery.

Graphs and Charts. When you're delivering a speech rich in statistics, data, and facts, visual aids can be indispensable presentation tools. You can actually cut your presentation time drastically and increase your listeners' interest by pointing to some figures on a graph rather than reading them aloud, number by number. Graphs take several different forms. **Bar graphs** show the relationship of two or more sets of figures. A figure comparing a freshman class's average SAT scores by section, for example, is well illustrated with a bar graph. **Pie charts** show percentages of a circle divided proportionately; for example, a university admissions office uses a pie chart to reveal the percentage of freshman students scoring in a particular range on an SAT exam. A pie chart should ideally have from two to five segments; under no circumstances should it have more than eight since it will become difficult for the audience to read: if you have too many categories, you can add the smallest ones up and present them in a single segment identified more broadly, as "other," for example.

> **Ethics and You**
>
> Have you ever seen a speaker present statistics in an unethical manner using graphs or charts? How might you make sure that your use of these visual aids is ethically sound?

Posters and Transparencies. You may find it helpful to have key words or ideas written out or visually displayed for your audience members to see. In such cases, it may make sense to use posters and transparencies. For example, if you're informing your audience about the Kübler-Ross model of the grieving process, you may wish to have the five stages (denial, anger, bargaining, depression, and acceptance) written down on a poster so that you can point to each stage as you begin to discuss it. Similarly, when persuading your audience about the effectiveness of graphic antidrug campaigns on television, you might want to place a poster of such an ad in clear view for everyone to see.

As with posters, transparencies can greatly enhance your ability to present complex information in your speech. They have an additional advantage in that they can often be rendered ahead of time to look more professional through the use of particular fonts and graphics. Verify that your classroom is equipped with a transparency projector, or request one if that is possible. Then purchase low-cost transparency sheets at an office supply store and use a photocopier to duplicate color and black-and-white pages.

When designing posters and transparencies, it's often helpful to keep a few key points in mind:

- Write in large, clear letters or use a typeface that is large and legible so that your audience doesn't have to strain to see your visual aid. For computer-generated transparencies, this means choosing at least a twenty-point font.
- Use vivid colors to make your posters and transparencies more appealing.
- Avoid cramming more than one main idea or main point onto a poster or transparency sheet unless it has a very specific purpose to enhance your meaning (for example, a collage of photos of missing and exploited children in your area might be used to illustrate the scope of the crisis).
- Put the transparency sheets and poster pages in order of use, and number them in case they get shuffled.
- If possible, use a pointer and stand near the poster to limit excessive body movement.
- When using transparencies, try to stand near the screen instead of at the projector with your back to the audience.

Flip Charts and Marker Boards. Flip charts and marker boards (or chalkboards), which are very common in professional settings, have a distinct advantage over posters and transparencies for displaying words and ideas: they can invite and organize audience participation. For example, when presenting a new health insurance plan to a group of managers, a human resources representative might open the speech by asking the managers, "What aspects of health insurance matter most to your employees?" The audience members may respond with comments like "flexibility" or "low copays," which the speaker can jot down on the flip chart or board. He can then refer to each priority as he addresses it in his speech.

Boards and flip charts are also valuable when you wish to "unfold" an idea, step by step, before an audience, such as a coach might use a board to break down a certain defense or offense play. Just remember that your use of flip charts and boards should never be distracting. In other words, your audience may become irritated if you're constantly flipping back and forth between pages or running around to point to multiple diagrams on the board.

Presentation Software. Sitting through hours of slides from your Aunt Sonja's vacation is boring enough. Sitting through a slide show that essentially repeats your speech outline can be positively unbearable. Presentation software (such as Microsoft Power-Point, Apple Keynote, and Google Docs), when used appropriately, allows you to have a one-stop home for lots of different visual aids without having to awkwardly move back and forth between different media.

However, presentation software is frequently misused by speakers who plug meaningless text or pointless visuals into slides without considering how to keep the audience's attention. You may, in fact, be familiar with the phrase "death by PowerPoint" (DuFrene & Lehman, 2004). Too often speakers allow their slides to dominate their presentations, attempting to wow the audience with their technical proficiency rather than focusing on interesting points or

well-researched evidence. We often warn our students that the fancier and more detailed the digital presentation, the more suspicious we are of the information being presented.

If you decide to use presentation software in your speech, here are some tips for developing effective slides:

- Become familiar with all the features and options of your specific software before you begin to plug in your presentation information.

- Use as few slides as possible. Remember, more is not always better!

- Use a minimal amount of text. Research indicates that restrained and very direct use of bullet points can positively affect audience recall of information (Vogel, Dickson, & Lehman, 1986).

- Make sure the font is large enough for easy viewing (we suggest forty-point type for titles and twenty-point type and above for all other text).

- Use only design elements that truly enhance meaning.

📍 Beware the terrible PowerPoint slide! A long bulleted list of all your speaking points on a distracting background is a surefire way to detract from your speech and lose your audience's attention.

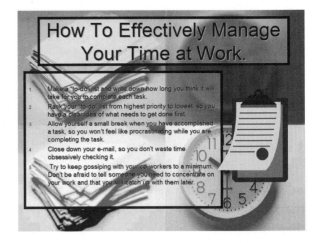

Technology and You

What are your experiences with presentation software like PowerPoint? Have you been in a classroom or at a work presentation where it was used? How do you usually react when you see it will be used?

- Be prepared to give the same speech without slides in case of a technology glitch. In other words, make sure your presentation is effective even without your slides.

- Prepare and practice in advance! As we will discuss in the next section, you need to give yourself enough time to organize, reorganize, edit, and feel comfortable moving between slides.

LearningCurve
bedfordstmartins.com/commandyou

Practicing Your Speech

If there's one key to developing skill as a public speaker, it's practice. Practice transforms nervous public speakers into confident ones and good public speakers into great ones, particularly when speakers pay attention to four important points: remembering the speaking outline, practicing with presentation aids, simulating the speaking situation, and practicing the actual delivery.

Remember Your Speaking Outline

You know the benefits of creating a speaking outline consisting of key words and phrases. Now it's time to practice from it. Review your speaking outline to make sure that all your key words and phrases work as prompts—if you can't remember that "SD" stands for "sleep deprivation," for example, you might need to write that term out.

Practice Using Presentation Aids

Recall our discussion of Steve Jobs's annual keynote presentations in Chapter 11. Clearly, Jobs rehearsed his presentations, including his use of presentation software and other technological aids—in fact, he knew it all well enough to work around the inevitable

technological glitches when they arose. When practicing with your presentation aids, consider the following tips:

- **Eliminate surprises.** If you're using any kind of technology, practice with it long before you deliver your speech. A skipping DVD or an MP3 clip that didn't download properly may stall your presentation.

- **Test the facilities in advance.** Be proactive. Will the classroom PC be able to read files created on your Mac? It should, but you'll rest easier if you test it out beforehand. Likewise, you should do visual and sound checks for video and audio clips to make sure that the entire audience will be able to see and hear them.

- **Write notes to yourself.** In your outline, make sure that you provide delivery cues to let yourself know when to move to the next item or slide or when to show an image or play a clip. This will help you avoid rushing ahead to get to a particular aid, as well as ensure that you don't forget any.

- **Rehearse any demonstrations with a partner.** When your presentation aid is actually a live prop (for example, a student in your class), you'll need to practice with this person in advance of the presentation.

- **Have a backup plan.** What will you do if something malfunctions during your speech? If a video clip won't play, can you present the information as a story? You might have a handout prepared for your audience members, just in case your software doesn't work.

Simulate the Situation

You already know that few people can simply walk up to a podium for the first time and deliver a perfect speech. Seasoned public speakers often look and sound great in large part because they've done it before and done it often. Exposing yourself to some of the more unnerving aspects of public speaking—for example, an audience—through

What About You?

Assessing Your Practice Session

After you have practiced your speech aloud (either alone or in front of a mock audience), critically assess your performance and answer the following questions. *Note:* If you will be practicing in front of a group, you might consider offering your audience members a copy of this quiz so that they can answer the questions as they listen to you.

_____ 1. Does your voice project confidence? Authority?

_____ 2. Are you varying your pitch (to avoid being monotonous)?

_____ 3. Are you varying your speaking rate and volume?

_____ 4. Are you articulating well? Are you mumbling? Can other people understand your words?

_____ 5. Does your speech contain words that might pose pronunciation problems for you?

_____ 6. Are you effectively scanning as you rehearse? (If others are present, are you making eye contact? If not, are you looking at different quadrants of the room you are rehearsing in?)

_____ 7. Do you use occasional gestures to emphasize a point you're making in your speech? Do they feel natural?

_____ 8. Do you animate your facial expressions as you deliver your speech?

_____ 9. Are you able to integrate your presentation aids into your presentation effectively?

_____10. Is your speech within the required time limits for the assignment?

_____11. Are your speaking notes helpful and effective?

As noted throughout the chapter, if you cannot answer "yes" to these questions, then you will likely benefit from additional rehearsal time. Remember, the more you employ effective visual and vocal delivery—and the better prepared you are with effective and helpful notes—the more competent and confident you will be when you attempt to speak before your real audience.

> **Remember, the more you employ effective visual and vocal delivery—and the better prepared you are with effective and helpful notes—the more competent and confident you will be when you attempt to speak before your real audience.**

simulation can help you become more comfortable. A simulation might include some or all of the following elements:

- **Create similar conditions.** Think about the room you'll deliver your speech in: what is its size, space, layout? Keep these things in mind as you rehearse— or even better, arrange to rehearse in the room where you will be speaking. Awareness of these conditions will help you practice eye contact, movement, gestures, and your use of notes.

- **Practice in front of someone.** Try practicing in front of someone or, preferably, a few people. One method for getting over anxiety about speaking in front of an audience is to "practice upward": practice first in front of one friend, then two, then three, and so on, until you are comfortable speaking before a fairly large group.

- **Keep an eye on your time.** Use a stopwatch or a kitchen timer to stay on target with your allotted speech time. You might even keep track of how much time you spend on each point, particularly if you have a tendency to go into a lot of detail early on or to rush at the end.

Practice Your Delivery

In any speech, your objective should be to communicate a message to an audience. If your message is clear, the audience will connect with it; if it's buried in a sea of mumbling or if it's forced to compete with distracting body language, the audience will miss your point. As you practice, you can improve the aspects of delivery you studied in this chapter and concentrate on your message.

- **Focus on your message.** Concentrate on the way that you express an argument, paraphrase a quotation, or explain a statistic. If you focus on your message, the right delivery will usually follow naturally.

- **Use mirrors cautiously.** Conventional wisdom has advocated rehearsing in front of a mirror in order to practice eye contact, maximize facial expressions, and assess gestures and movement. But you won't have mirrors when you deliver the speech; they can also make you feel self-conscious about your appearance, distracting you from your message.

- **Record a practice session.** Before you gasp in horror and skip to the next bullet point, please trust us: this really does help. Even many teachers and professors record themselves to get a sense of their presence in the classroom. Recording your performance will allow you to get a sense of how well you project your voice, articulate your points, and use nonverbal cues.

- **Ask for feedback.** See if you can find a person or two to listen to your speech and give you an honest and constructive critique of your performance. Ask what they remember most about your presentation. Did they focus mostly on your content, or were they distracted by your postures, gestures, or stammering? Were your presentation aids helpful, or were they distracting or confusing?

LearningCurve
bedfordstmartins.com/commandyou

Back to } *The King's Speech*

At the beginning of the chapter, we talked about Britain's king George VI, or Albert, who was thrust into a position that demanded public speaking skills even though he struggled with a challenging stutter. In light of what we've learned in this chapter, let's think about Albert's journey, as well as that of David Seidler, who was inspired by Albert's story and eventually brought it to the screen with *The King's Speech*.

- Given his royal position, Albert knew that public speaking would be a part of his life. As such, part of his preparation was to build confidence and overcome anxiety by addressing his stutter through prolonged, and somewhat experimental, speech therapy. Had he not been a prince (and, later, a king), he might never have addressed his fear.

- As a king in the early twentieth century, Albert had to contend with emerging media—particularly radio—when giving speeches. While he still had to contend with the transactional nature of public speeches (in which he had to interact with and adjust to the audience), radio gave him the opportunity to gain confidence and practice: the radio audience's feedback was limited by its linear model of communication.

- The audience plays a role in the success of any speech, and it is likely that British citizens, facing the uncertainty of world war, *wanted* the king to succeed. As actor Colin Firth noted, "People knew this man was facing his demons just by speaking to them. I think there was a sense that it cost him something. They found it valiant" (CBS News, 2010).

Your Reference

} ## A Study Tool

Now that you have finished reading this chapter, you can

Identify and control your anxieties:

- **Public speaking anxiety** (PSA) is the nervousness we experience when we know we have to communicate publicly to an audience (p. 288).
- **Communication apprehension** (CA), fear or anxiety associated with communication, is a common barrier to effective delivery (p. 288).
- Common anxiety triggers include upsetting past experiences, fear of evaluation, and distaste for attention (pp. 288–289).
- Confidence comes from being prepared, desensitizing yourself, visualizing success (particularly through **performance visualization**), taking care of yourself, and practicing a lot (pp. 289–291).

Choose a delivery style that is best suited to you and your speaking situation:

- Speaking from manuscript is helpful when you need to get the details 100 percent right, but it can be static and dull (p. 291).
- Speaking from memory, referred to as **oratory**, doesn't invite rapport with the audience and is rare today (pp. 291–292).
- Speaking spontaneously—when you're asked to speak with no warning beforehand—is known as **impromptu speaking** (p. 292).
- **Extemporaneous speaking** ⓒ makes the speech look easy and spontaneous, but it's actually based on an outline of key points and practice, practice, practice (pp. 292–293).

Employ effective vocal cues:

- Use *pitch* to vary your sound range and avoid a **monotone** (p. 294).
- Cue the audience as to what's important by adjusting your **speaking rate** and *volume* (p. 294).
- Add drama to the speech by pausing for effect (p. 294).
- Speak clearly and precisely: use proper **pronunciation**, practice careful **articulation**, and avoid **mumbling** (pp. 294–295).

- If you have an accent, be aware of how it might influence your audience (p. 295).

Employ effective visual cues:

- Dress appropriately for the speaking occasion (p. 295).
- Make brief eye contact with almost everyone, using the technique known as **scanning** (pp. 295–296).
- Facial expressions and gestures must match the verbal message of your speech (pp. 296–297).
- Maintain a steady, confident **posture** by positioning your legs at a distance equal to your shoulders, with slightly bent knees, in the stance known as **planting** (p. 297).

Connect with your audience:

- Share your passion for the topic with your audience through effective use of emotion (p. 298).
- Gauge the audience response and adapt to it (p. 298).
- Generate *immediacy* with your audience (p. 298).

Enhance your words with effective presentation aids:

- Effective presentation aids help listeners process and retain information, promote interest and motivation, and convey information clearly and concisely (p. 299).
- Based on the needs of your presentation, you can choose among helpful presentation aid types, including **props** and **models**, media clips and images, graphs and charts (including **bar graphs** and **pie charts**), posters and transparencies, flip charts and marker boards, and presentation software (pp. 299–303).

Make efficient use of your practice time:

- Make sure the key words in your speaking outline are meaningful prompts (p. 303).
- Do a run-through with your presentation aids (particularly the electronic ones), and try to simulate the actual speaking conditions (pp. 303–305).
- Focus on the message (p. 305).

Look for **LearningCurve** throughout the chapter to help you review.
bedfordstmartins.com/commandyou

14 } Informative Speaking

It's not surprising that people enjoy asking astrophysicist and planetarium director Dr. Neil deGrasse Tyson questions: What happens if you get sucked into a black hole? Why was Pluto demoted to "dwarf planet" status? What is surprising, however, is that people recognize who Tyson is. After all, even noted scientists are not often celebrities, and unless you're a fan of the television show *The Big Bang Theory*, astrophysics is a field that seems far removed from everyday life. Yet Tyson has, in many ways, become the face of science today, having written several bestselling books, given lectures around the country, hosted *NOVA Science Now* on PBS, and made appearances on *The Daily Show*, *The Colbert Report*, and *Jeopardy!*, among others. He has more than 36,000 Facebook fans and over 124,000 followers on Twitter.

Tyson's popularity is rooted in both his cosmic expertise and his communication skills: he has a knack for presenting the vast mysteries of the universe in ways that laypeople can understand. During a presentation at the University of Texas, for example, Tyson noted, "We have no evidence to show whether the universe is infinite or finite," before explaining that astrophysicists can only go so far as to calculate a horizon—similar to the horizon line viewed from a ship at sea. He then continued that comparison: "Yet a ship is pretty sure that the ocean goes beyond the horizon of the ship, just as we are pretty sure the universe extends beyond our particular horizon. We just don't know how far" (Tyson, 2009).

Tyson recognizes the challenge of informing the general public about complex scientific ideas that researchers devote decades to understanding: "It was not a priority of mine to communicate science to the public," Tyson says. "What I found was that enough members of the public wanted to know what was going on in the universe that I—decided . . . to get a little better at it so I could satisfy this cosmic curiosity" (cited in Byrd, 2010).

After you have finished reading this chapter, you will be able to

Describe the goals of informative speaking.

List and describe each of the eight categories of informative speeches.

Outline the four major approaches to informative speeches.

Employ strategies to make your audience hungry for information.

Structure your speech to make it easy to listen to.

L ike Neil deGrasse Tyson, the best informative speakers share information, teach us something new, or help us understand an idea. Clearly, Tyson has a talent for informative presentations. He knows how to analyze his audience members and tailor his presentations to engage them quickly. He organizes his information clearly and efficiently so that listeners can learn it with ease. And he presents information in an honest and ethical manner. In this chapter, we'll take a look at how you can use these same techniques to deliver competent informative speeches in any situation.

The Goals of Informative Speaking

As you'll recall from Chapter 11, the purpose of **informative speaking** is to increase the audience's understanding or knowledge; put more simply, the objective is for your audience to learn something. But to be a truly effective informative speaker, you need to make your presentation not only fill your listeners' informational needs but also do so with respect for their opinions, backgrounds, and experiences. In addition, you want to be objective, focusing on informing

(not persuading) your audience, and ethical. In this section, we examine these goals and investigate ways that you can ensure that your speech remains true to them at every phase of development and delivery.

Meeting the Audience's Informational Needs

Effective speakers engage their listeners because they have made the effort to understand the needs of their audience members. This is especially important in informative speaking. You want to avoid delivering a long list of facts that are already common knowledge because the object is for your audience to learn something new. Understanding your listeners' needs also involves choosing an appropriate topic and making that topic relevant to your listeners. Let's take a look at these points using DNA evidence as an example.

- **Gauge what the audience already knows.** Estimating the knowledge level of the audience helps determine where to begin, how much information to share, and at what level of difficulty the audience can understand and still maintain interest. If your goal is to inform an audience of fellow students about DNA evidence, for instance, you should assume that they are not experts on your topic; only a few students may be majoring in fields that would provide them with a detailed background about it. Your tasks involve describing the procedures related to the collection of DNA evidence (such as saliva and skin cells) and explaining why the criminal justice system uses forensic DNA testing. You might even want to ask your listeners if they feel they are familiar with DNA evidence from watching shows like *CSI* or *Bones*.

- **Decide on an appropriate approach to the topic.** Involving your listeners through the appropriate use of language and presentation aids gives them the impression that you have fine-tuned the speech for a particular group of people. You might present the story of a defendant who was convicted based on DNA evidence or of a convict who was later exonerated by it. Be sure to consider the different types of sources at your disposal: visual images, models, artifacts, fingerprints or footprints, and expert testimony. These sorts of things will captivate your audience and help them remember the new information you are teaching them.

- **Make the topic relevant to each member of the audience.** Always specifically connect the subject to the audience by pointing out how it is pertinent and useful to your listeners' lives. For example, you might appeal to your audience members' personal senses of right and wrong when you share stories of elusive criminals being brought to justice with DNA evidence. Similarly, you can draw your audience members in by noting the way that such evidence can come to their aid should they ever be the victims of crime themselves.

Informing, Not Persuading

As you learned in Chapter 11, informative speaking serves as the base for persuasive speaking: in many cases, speakers inform audiences in hopes of persuading them to behave in a certain way. In a similar vein, persuasive speakers must first inform their audiences about certain facts and information before they can attempt to influence them. But while these two types of speaking are naturally related, it's important to recognize that they differ in one very important way: an informative speech is intended to be **objective**—it presents facts and information in a straightforward and evenhanded way, free of influence from the speaker's personal thoughts or opin-

THINGS TO TRY

Locate a persuasive speech that you found particularly compelling. Print it out and edit it, removing any and all material that you feel is persuasive in nature (for example, the speaker's opinions, any notably biased statements, any evidence that is subjective rather than objective). Does the remainder of the speech hold up as an informative speech? How could you change it to make it a purely informative presentation?

ions. A persuasive speech, by contrast, is expected to be **subjective**—it presents facts and information from a particular point of view.

When delivering an informative speech, you must always remain objective; if you find yourself expressing an opinion or choosing only facts, information, or other material that supports your personal view, you are in fact delivering a persuasive speech. So when delivering an informative speech, it's important

📍 When you're speaking to an audience that is knowledgeable about your topic, you don't want to bore them with a long list of facts they already know. Tell them something new!

Ethics and You

Have you ever treated a speech, another assignment, or a work-related task subjectively when it was intended to be as objective as possible? Do you feel that it's possible to stay entirely objective in many situations that call for it?

Table 14.1 **Informative Versus Persuasive Speaking**

	Informative Speeches	Persuasive Speeches
Approach	From a perspective of inquiry or discovery; the speaker researches a topic to find out what information exists and shares that information with an audience.	From a perspective of advocating a position or desired outcome; the speaker researches a topic to find information that supports a particular point of view and then tries to convince an audience to change an attitude or take some action based on that point of view.
Objectivity	The speaker reports information objectively, in the role of a messenger.	The speaker argues a case subjectively and speaks from a particular point of view.
Use of facts and information	The speaker sets out the current facts or state of affairs concerning the topic.	The speaker builds a case that he or she is passionate about and includes information that supports his or her favored position.
Expression of opinions	The speaker may provide others' opinions but refrains from giving his or her own.	The speaker provides others' opinions that support his or her own position or viewpoint; the speaker may mention differing opinions only to rebut or discredit them.

to examine your process at every step to ensure that you are being truly objective. Some of the issues you'll need to evaluate are examined in Table 14.1, above.

Speaking Appropriately and Ethically

Objectivity is not the only ethical consideration you must bear in mind when delivering an informative speech. Because communication is a powerful instrument for influencing people's attitudes, beliefs, and behaviors, we must consider the implications of our actions (Sides, 2000). As we've discussed throughout this book, an ethical speaker has a responsibility to provide an audience with information that is relevant and reliable in a way that is respectful of both the au-

dience and the subject. The types of supporting material you offer (or do not offer) and your motives for speaking on a particular subject reveal quite a bit about you as an ethical speaker. Ethical speakers must also avoid plagiarism by orally citing sources and providing a complete list of references at the end of a speech outline. If your speech misinforms your

Ethics and You

Have you ever misinformed anyone? How did it happen? Was it intentional or unintentional?

audience in any way, you are not offering an appropriate or ethical informative speech.

LearningCurve
bedfordstmartins.com/commandyou

Topics for Informative Presentations

When it comes to choosing a topic for an informative speech, there are countless options. You can speak, for example, about something very concrete, such as a person, a place, a thing, a process, or an event. In many cases, your topic will fit into more than one category: for example, a speech on hip-hop music might include descriptions of the genre (thing) as well as of particular bands (people) and performances (events). You might also talk about the way the music developed over time (process). In the sections that follow, we'll take a look at eight categories for informative speech topics identified by the communication researchers Ron Allen and Ray McKerrow (1985).

People

If there's one subject that fascinates most people, it's other people: think of the interest generated by biographies of historical figures, celebrity news, or family gossip. The life of another person certainly makes for an interesting informative speech topic. You might lean toward giving a speech about someone who is famous (or infamous)—indeed, audiences are usually receptive to learning about someone famous simply because they revere or worship celebrity (Atkinson & Dougherty, 2006). An obscure but interesting person can also be a great speech topic.

> If there's one subject that fascinates most people, it's other people: think of the interest generated by biographies of historical figures, celebrity news, or family gossip.

The key to giving a successful speech about another person is to focus on the person's human qualities as well as his or her achievements, to show not merely what the person did but why and how that person did it. You need to give your audience a real sense of who the person is. To meet this goal, your speech should include anecdotes, quotes, and stories that show the motivations behind his or her actions. Chapter 11 offers help in adding these speech supports.

Places

Like people, places can be interesting and compelling topics for an informative speech. You might focus on an inspired description of a real but perhaps unfamiliar place (the surface of Mars, the Arctic tundra) or even a fictional one (the fires of Mount Doom in *The Lord of the Rings*). Even a very familiar place offers opportunities to provide audiences with some new information. For example, you might investigate the oldest building on your campus or in your town and detail some of its history in your speech. This will allow you not only to describe the place but also to talk about the people who designed and built it and how the building has been changed over the years.

> **Culture and You**
>
> Would you consider preparing an informative speech about the place where you grew up? What details would you emphasize to make it interesting for the audience?

Objects and Phenomena

A third source of ideas for informative speeches consists of objects or phenomena. These speeches explore anything that isn't human, such as living things (like animals, plants, even entire ecosystems), as well as inanimate objects, such as your first car, an iPad, or the *Mona Lisa*. Objects can also be imaginary things (such as

⬧ From legendary movie stars to historic natural disasters, you can develop a compelling informative speech on virtually anything (or anyone!).

light sabers) or hypothetical ones (such as a perpetual motion machine) or even entire phenomena (like the El Niño wind patterns in the western United States).

Events

Noteworthy occurrences (past and present) are good topics for informative speeches. Our understanding of history is shaped by events, and at a more intimate level, events of personal significance can also make interesting and compelling topics for speeches.

You might build an informative speech around important, tragic, funny, or instructive events in your personal life—the day you went skydiving, your bar mitzvah, the death of a close friend, or the birth of your first child. Just remember that these stories of personal events must be ethical and truthful, and exaggeration or fabrication is never ethical.

In addition to helping an audience understand the meaning of personal and historical single events, a speaker can also explore the social significance of *collections* of events. A speaker might, for example, talk about the significance of dances for Native American tribes, of high school football games in a small town, or of the role of weddings and funerals in his or her family.

Processes

A process is a series of actions, changes, or functions that bring about a particular result. Process speeches help an audience understand the stages or steps through which a particular outcome is produced, and such speeches usually fall into one of two categories. The first is speeches that explain how something works or develops. For example, you might give a speech detailing how a hybrid car works, how the human brain's nervous system processes sound, or how lightning forms. The second type of process speech teaches how to do something: how to knit, for example, or how to use a new MP3 player. For this type of speech, it is often helpful to incorporate props, visuals, or hands-on demonstrations into your presentation.

Concepts

Whereas people, places, objects, events, and processes are concrete things that we can readily visualize, concepts are abstract or complex ideas or even theories, like "art," "patriotism," "artificial intelligence," or "free speech," which are much more difficult for us to understand. The challenge of a concept speech, then, is to take a general idea, theory, or thought and make it concrete and meaningful for your audience.

Although the challenge is great, many worthwhile informative speeches focus on the explanation of a concept. The idea of ethnocentrism, the belief that one's cultural ways are superior to those of other cultures, would be an informative speech about a concept (Armstrong & Kaplowitz, 2001). You could then make reference to important historical events that were influenced by ethnocentrism: the

Imagine a process you do every day, such as driving a car. Think about how you would explain the process to someone who's never done it or even seen it done before. List different ways you could make the level of the presentation appropriate for different audiences. Talking to a child, for example, you might simply say that pressing on the gas pedal makes the car go; you might offer more detail when speaking to adults, explaining how the car works.

Holocaust, ethnic cleansing in Bosnia, or responses to the 9/11 terrorist attacks.

Issues

An issue is a problem or matter of dispute that people hope to resolve. Informative speeches about issues provide an overview or a report of problems in order to increase understanding and awareness. Issues include social and personal problems (such as racial profiling, health care, or unemployment) as well as ideas,

Your speech doesn't necessarily have to be about a historical event. The first time you went skydiving can be just as compelling a topic as the first time man walked on the moon.

activities, and circumstances over which opinions vary widely (such as birth control or affirmative action).

Because of the controversial nature of many issues, giving an informative presentation on one can be a challenge, as it can be difficult to keep your own opinions from influencing the speech. But if you keep your focus on delivering a speech that is truly one of discovery, inquiry, and objectivity, then even controversial topics often break down into more manageable components that you can look at objectively. For example, if you were to give an informative speech on stem cell research, you could break all your information down into groups of basic facts: what the current laws are, where stem cells come from, how the research is done, and why such research is being conducted. You should also address the controversy over the issue itself by presenting differing opinions from both inside and outside the scientific community. If, however, you take a look at the research and plot your speech points but still doubt your ability to describe an issue objectively, you probably should save the topic for a persuasive speech.

> ### Culture and You
>
> Would you find it hard to speak in a purely informative manner on certain subjects? Would you be able to speak, for example, in a nonpersuasive way about your religious beliefs? Your favorite film? A musical act that you just can't stand?

Plans and Policies

Allen and McKerrow's final category for informative speeches concerns plans and policies (1985). In such speeches, the speaker tries to help an audience understand the important dimensions of potential courses of action (for example, raising fares on commuter trains in your city or eliminating work-study scholarships at your college). Such speeches do not argue for a particular plan or policy; they simply lay out the facts. Like issue speeches, plan and policy speeches can easily evolve into persuasive addresses, so you

must be very careful to focus on objective facts; if you find yourself unable to keep your opinion from influencing your speech, consider a different topic.

LearningCurve
bedfordstmartins.com/commandyou

Approaches to Conveying Information

Once you have selected a topic for an informative speech, you can develop it in a variety of ways. Here we briefly describe the four major approaches to informative speeches: description, demonstration, definition, and explanation.

Description

Description is a way of verbally expressing things you have experienced with your senses. While most speeches use some type of description, some focus on this task more closely than others. The primary task of a **descriptive presentation** is to paint a mental picture for your audience that portrays places, events, persons, objects, or processes clearly and vividly.

An effective descriptive speech begins with a well-structured idea of what you want to describe and why. As you move through the development process, you emphasize important details and eliminate unimportant ones, all the while considering ways to make your details more vivid for your audience. Descriptive speeches are most effective when the topic is personally connected to the speaker. Consider the following excerpt from President Barack Obama's January 2011 speech at the "Together We Thrive: Tucson and America" memorial held at the University of Arizona to honor those killed and wounded in the Tucson shootings. Many people found Obama's description of the youngest victim, Christina Taylor Green, to be particularly moving:

> And then there is nine-year-old Christina Taylor Green. Christina was an A student; she was a

dancer; she was a gymnast; she was a swimmer. She decided that she wanted to be the first woman to play in the Major Leagues, and as the only girl on her Little League team, no one put it past her.

She showed an appreciation for life uncommon in a girl her age. She'd remind her mother, "We are so blessed. We have the best life." And she'd pay those blessings back by participating in a charity that helped children who were less fortunate (White House, 2011).

From these few vivid lines, audience members learn who Christina was and they can imagine who she might have become.

Demonstration

New York City resident Peggy Paul was offered the opportunity to appear on *The Rachael Ray Show* after informing the celebrity host that she could prepare a four-course gourmet dinner in her tiny apartment with just a toaster oven, a microwave, and a hot plate (Annino, 2007). Sound impossible? But what if she showed you? Rachael Ray (and Peggy Paul) caught on to an important truth: often the best way to explain how something works is to demonstrate it. **Demonstration speeches** answer "how" questions—how to use a smart phone, how to bake a pie crust, how to salsa dance—by showing an audience the way something works. In this case, Peggy used a combination of explanatory narration and physical demonstration to show how she whips up baked apple pork chops, pear and gorgonzola salad, and chocolate hazelnut quesadillas as easily as we make peanut butter and jelly sandwiches, all the while making use of props, models, and other visual aids.

The key to delivering an effective demonstration speech is to begin with a clear statement of purpose and to follow a very straightforward organizational pattern. In most cases, a chronological pattern works best for a demonstration, with the process broken down into a number of steps that are presented in order of completion. Even with a strict chronological format, however, it can be helpful to introduce the completed end product first, before going through the process of creating or finishing it from step one.

Definition

Most informative speeches require that the speaker define a term or an idea at some point; when you define something, you identify its essential qualities and meaning. Although we typically think of definitions as short entries in a dictionary, in fact many speeches are focused entirely on definitions. The main goal of **definitional speeches** is to provide answers to "what" questions. Such questions as "What is torture?" and "What is marriage?" have prompted heated debate in the halls of Congress (and elsewhere) in recent years, making it clear that defining terms is neither simple nor unimportant. As a speaker, you can approach a definitional speech in a variety of ways. A definition in a speech might use one of these approaches; a definitional speech might incorporate more or even all of them.

- An **operational definition** defines something by explaining what it is or what it does. For example, salsa can be defined by what it is: "Salsa is a condiment, usually made of tomatoes, onions, and peppers, common in Spanish and Latin American cuisine." Alternatively, it can be defined by what it does: "Salsas are most commonly used as dipping sauces for fried tortilla chips, but they also work well alongside grilled fish."
- **Definition by negation** defines something by telling what it is not. For example, "Salsa is not the same as taco or piquante sauce."
- **Definition by example** defines something by offering concrete examples of what it is. For example, "Salsas include the basic tomato version you get at your local Mexican restaurant, as well as variants made from mangoes, pineapples, or tomatillos."
- **Definition by synonym** defines something by using words that mean almost the same thing. For example, "Salsa is basically just a chunky sauce, similar to chutney in Indian cuisine."
- **Definition by etymology** defines something by using the origin of a word or phrase. For example, "*Salsa* is the Spanish and Italian word for sauce, derived from the Latin word for 'salty.'"

As noted, definitional speeches can take one or more of these approaches to defining a specific term.

Explanation

The basic purpose of most informative speeches is to create awareness or understanding; **explanatory speeches** answer the question "Why?" or "What does that mean?" Explanatory presentations delve into more complexity than demonstration speeches by providing reasons or causes and demonstrating relationships. To make your points in an explanatory speech, you must use interpretation and analysis. To this end, you should keep three main goals in mind: clarifying concepts, explaining the "big picture," and challenging intuition.

Clarifying Concepts. If an audience's chief difficulty rests with understanding the meaning and use of a certain term, the speaker should provide **elucidating explanations**—details that illuminate the concept's meaning and use. Good elucidating explanations do three things. First, they define a concept by listing each of its critical features. For example, notice in the following sentence how the speaker provides succinct illustrations for the concept of rhetoric: "Aristotle described the canons of rhetoric as consisting of *pathos* (appeal to emotions), *logos* (appeal to logic), and *ethos* (appeal to character)."

Second, elucidating explanations contrast examples of the concept. For instance, a speaker might suggest that the difference between gun control and partial gun control is as distinct as night and day. Finally, elucidating examples present opportunities for audiences to distinguish between contrasting examples by looking for a concept's critical features—for instance, demonstrating that the most important features of a golf swing are keeping the left arm straight and keeping the head still.

Explaining the Big Picture. If an idea is difficult chiefly because its complexity makes its main points—the "big picture"—hard to grasp, speakers should use a quasi-scientific explanation. Just as scientists try to develop models of the world, **quasi-scientific explanations** model or picture the key dimensions of some

⬥ Doctors essentially give explanatory speeches to their patients, describing the causes of a medical condition and how it may be treated.

phenomenon for a typical audience. Speakers presenting complex topics to laypeople—how microchips work, the similarities and differences between levees and dams, or how DNA molecules pass along genetic information—should try to use quasi-scientific explanations. Effective quasi-scientific explanations highlight the main points with such features as titles, organizing analogies, presentation aids, and signposts ("The first key point is . . ."). Good quasi-scientific explanations also connect key points by using transitional phrases (such as "for example"), connectives ("because"), and diagrams depicting relationships among parts.

Challenging Intuition. Sometimes an idea's chief difficulty is that it runs contrary to what intuition tells us. Consider the polio vaccine, which was tested in 1952 and used an injected dose of an inactive (essentially, dead) polio virus. The notion of using something that makes people sick to prevent people from getting sick is counterintuitive. Imagine how difficult this must have been to explain to patients and worried parents at the time.

{ You want to make your audience hungry for the information you are going to present—get them excited about, or at least interested in, your topic. }

If you are giving an informative speech on how vaccines work, you might want to design your talk around transformative explanations. **Transformative explanations**, which help people understand counterintuitive ideas, are designed to help speakers transform "theories" about phenomena into more accepted notions. For your speech on vaccines, you might describe how, by exposing the body to a similar but benign virus (like the dead polio virus), a vaccine essentially teaches the body to defend itself against a specific disease.

LearningCurve
bedfordstmartins.com/commandyou

Guidelines for Informative Speeches

In Chapters 11 through 13, we provided the basics for developing, preparing, writing, and delivering effective presentations. In this section, we take a look at how you can tailor those basic strategies to the needs of an informative speech. Your first goal as a speaker is to get your audience interested in your topic. But you'll also want to make sure that your speech is easy to listen to. It's hard to inform people who are struggling to keep up with you—or wishing they were somewhere else!

Create Information Hunger

You want to make your audience hungry for the information you are going to present—get them excited about, or at least interested in, your topic. As you consider a topic for your informative speech, ask yourself, "How will this audience benefit from this information?" If you can't come up with a compelling reason for each person to pay attention to what you say, you need to rethink your topic. Several strategies help you create information hunger, including arousing curiosity and working your topic.

Arouse People's Curiosity. A few years ago, we watched a student inform the audience about kimonos. A kimono is a long, loose Japanese robe with wide sleeves traditionally worn with a broad sash as an outer garment. The speaker defined a kimono, contrasted different types of kimonos, and then demonstrated how to get into one and wear it properly. Although her speech was interesting and her demonstration was effective, in the end we had no idea why we had listened to it! The problem was that although she competently explained the historical and cultural significance of the kimono and gave a detailed demonstration of the process of designing and wearing one, she did little to make the audience interested in the subject as a whole. She might have fared better had she offered some sort of connection between the kimono and the daily lives of the audience. The following introduction to her topic, for example, might have addressed that issue.

> Think of your favorite article or ensemble of clothing—that one perfect item or outfit that you just hope you have the occasion to wear. Would you have worn it ten years ago? Will it still be stylish ten years from now? Magazine editors and clothing designers like to throw the word *timeless*

around, claiming that some things—the Armani suit, the little black dress—will never go out of fashion. But the truth is that style is a fickle thing, and lapels, hemlines, colors, and waistbands change with the tides. Today, I'm going to talk about an article of clothing that truly is timeless, one that is worn by both men and women and has remained largely unchanged in shape and form for over one thousand years. I'm speaking, of course, about the traditional garment of Japan, the kimono.

Here we've piqued people's interest by asking them first to think about their own experience—about something they own or wish to own. We then draw them into our subject, the kimono, by contrasting it with what Westerners tend to consider "classic" fashion. Such comparisons and personalization of the subject can help keep the audience interested. We might, for example, go on to show ways in which the kimono has influenced Western fashion.

> **Culture and You**
> What elements of your life or experiences do you think would arouse people's curiosity in a speech? Are there any elements of your life that you feel would make a poor choice for a topic?

Work Your Topic. But what if you can't change the topic? Sometimes you may have the luxury of choosing a topic that you find interesting and engaging, but in many real-world situations, you may be asked to explain, define, describe, or demonstrate something that strikes you as boring or irrelevant. A CEO will frequently need to address shareholders with reports of profits and losses, for example, and spokespersons for government agencies are often required to make statements about public policies or current events.

In every one of these cases, the speaker must find the relevance of the subject and establish it for the audience quickly and assertively. If your topic seems somehow disconnected from your audience, it's your job to find the relevance. For example, can you save the audience money or time? Can you help people do

something better or improve quality? Even if the benefit is not for the short term, will listening to your speech help them in some way in the future, once they become parents or graduate students or homeowners? Unless you present a clear benefit that people can derive from listening to you, you will not get or keep their attention.

For example, imagine that you are an office manager and need to deliver a presentation to your colleagues explaining how to fill out the company's new expense reports. One way to get them interested in what they might perceive as an unnecessary presentation is to show them that learning how to do this task will benefit them in some way:

> I know it's hard to get excited about something as mundane as filing expense reports. But the good news is that our new electronic transmittal system will get your reimbursements to you faster and more reliably. As you know, it typically takes four to six weeks for an expense report to be routed, approved, and transmitted to accounts payable and another two weeks for accounts payable to cut the check. With this new system, we'll be able to have funds deposited directly to your bank account in as little as ten business days. So with that in mind, let's take a look at how the new system works.

By clearly connecting the subject with the lives and needs of your listeners, you're more likely to have their attention as you demonstrate the less interesting aspects of the process. If you cannot find the subject's relevance, you may need to refine or revise the topic.

Make It Easy

Creating a good informative speech is hard work; listening to one should not be. Your job as a speaker is to find and distill a lot of information in a way that is easy for your audience to listen to, absorb, and learn. In short, you need to do your listeners' work for them. To this end, there are a number of objectives to bear in mind as you prepare your speech, which we will now discuss.

Choose a Clear Organization and Structure. People have orderly minds. When they are presented with new information, they need to organize it in a

🜂 Bill Nye the Science Guy has made it his job to help kids learn about potentially tricky topics like energy transfer or static electricity by making the information accessible and fun.

way that makes sense to them. You can help them in this endeavor by organizing your speech around a clear and logical structure. Recall from Chapter 12 that there are a number of arrangements for presentations, including chronological, topical, and spatial organizations; problem-solution, cause-effect, and narrative patterns; and arrangements based on motivated sequences. Your choice of organizational pattern will depend on your topic, and every speech will have several organizational options.

For example, if you're planning to deliver a speech on the history of punk rock, you might choose a chronological organization, beginning with mid-1960s garage bands and following through the 1970s peak with bands like the Sex Pistols and the Ramones, through the post-punk era, and ending with modern punk-influenced bands like Green Day and the Libertines. But you might find it more interesting to approach the topic spatially, noting differences between American and British punk, or even causally, demonstrating how the form arose as a reaction to the popular music that preceded it as well as the economic and political climate of the times. Table 14.2, on page 322, offers some ideas for using organizational approaches for different informative topics, in addition to considering the approaches we discussed earlier (definition, description, demonstration, and explanation).

📍 If your speech is on punk rock, you might organize it chronologically, moving from the Ramones to Green Day.

Table 14.2 Types of Informative Speeches, Sample Topics, Informational Strategies, and Organizational Patterns

Subject Matter	Sample Topics	Informational Strategy (definition, description, demonstration, explanation)	Suggested Organizational Patterns
Speeches about objects or phenomena	■ Personal digital assistants ■ Dialects ■ Comparison of weight-loss diets ■ El Niño wind patterns in the western United States	*Define* and *describe* the object or phenomenon in question. Depending on your specific speech purpose, either conclude at that point or continue with an in-depth *explanation* or a *demonstration* of the object or phenomenon.	You might use a *spatial* pattern if you are explaining how a geographic positioning system (GPS) works in cars. Other useful patterns include *topical*, *problem-solution*, and *cause-effect*.
Speeches about people	■ Authors ■ Humanitarians ■ Inventors ■ Athletes ■ Unsung heroes ■ British royalty	Paint a vivid picture of your subject using *description*. Use *explanation* to address the person's or group's significance.	*Narrative* patterns could be useful for speeches about people since stories can include rich details about a person's life. Other useful patterns include *motivated sequence* and *chronological*.
Speeches about events	■ MTV Awards ■ Democratic or Republican National Convention ■ Battle of the Bulge ■ Iraq War ■ Olympic Games	Use *description* to paint a vivid picture. Use *explanation* to analyze the meaning of the event.	You might use a *chronological* pattern for a topic focusing on events if time or sequence is relevant to your purpose. Other useful patterns include *motivated sequence*, *problem-solution*, and *spatial*.
Speeches about processes	■ How tsunamis form ■ How the thyroid regulates metabolism ■ How to practice "power yoga" ■ Using visualization in sports	If physically showing a process, rely on *demonstration*. If explaining a process, vary strategies as needed.	*Cause-effect* patterns of speech organization are helpful in explaining processes of various kinds. Additional patterns of organization could include *spatial*, *problem-solution*, or *chronological*.
Speeches about issues	■ Police brutality ■ Political issues in the Middle East ■ Climate change	Focus on *description* and *explanation*.	*Problem-solution* is a strong choice for organizing speeches about issues. Other helpful patterns for issues include *topical*, *spatial*, and *cause-effect*.

| Speeches about concepts | ■ Artificial intelligence
■ Chaos theory
■ Nanotechnology
■ Free speech
■ Time travel | Focus on clear *definitions* and *explanations*; the more difficult a concept is, the more ways you will want to define and explain it. Vivid *description* can also be useful. | Consider *topical* organizational patterns for speeches about concepts, as well as the *narrative* pattern. Other patterns that might work well include *spatial* and *problem-solution*. |

Source: O'Hair, Stewart, & Rubenstein (2007), p. 23. Adapted with permission.

Emphasize Important Points. Another way to make it easier for your audience to follow and absorb your speech is to clarify what the important parts are. As you learned in Chapter 12, one of the best means to achieve this is by using a preview device and a concluding summary. The preview device tells the audience what you are going to cover ("First, I will discuss X, second, Y, and third, Z"). A concluding summary reviews what the audience heard during the speech ("Today, I talked about X, then showed you Y, and finally, discussed Z").

Careful and deliberate use of phrases like "The key issue here is . . ." and "I have three main points regarding this piece of legislation" can also signal to your audience that you're about to say something important. In some cases, you might actually highlight what is important by saying so, even telling the audience directly when you're discussing something you want them to remember. This not only supports the organization of your speech but also gives people useful tools for organizing the information as they listen. It's important to make certain, however, that you don't contradict yourself. If you say, "I have one key point to make" and then list four points of equal importance, you will likely confuse (and annoy) your audience.

Don't Overwhelm Your Audience. Have you ever sat through a lecture or a presentation in which the speaker seemed to give far too much information? Ironically, too many points can make a speech seem pointless, and an overabundance of facts and statistics can make it difficult to follow and impossible to retain. Research shows that message receivers' attention and interest levels drop significantly due to information overload. Simply put, too much information overwhelms the audience (Van Zandt, 2004).

Your goal, then, is to keep your presentation as simple as possible so that audiences will find it easy to follow. As you review and rehearse your speech, critically evaluate each and every fact, point, example—indeed, every word—to make certain that it makes a real contribution. Eliminate anything redundant or tangential. You want to strike a perfect balance by telling your listeners just what they need to know to understand your topic—nothing more, nothing less.

Build on Prior Knowledge. Another way to make your speech easier to listen to and retain is to introduce new concepts by relating them to familiar ideas. People are more open to new ideas when they understand how they relate to things they already know about. In an informative speech about successful Internet fashion businesses, you might discuss the concept of the "virtual model image." Instead of trying on clothes in a store (a familiar idea), shoppers can see how certain garments would look on their particular body types. By supplying your measurements online, you can visualize what you would look like in outfits by using the virtual model image (new idea).

> { Ironically, too many points can make a speech seem pointless, and an overabundance of facts and statistics can make it difficult to follow and impossible to retain. }

Define Your Terms. Defining your terms is not just for definitional speeches. In any speech, you should choose terms that your audience will know and understand—and provide clear definitions for any words they might not. If at any point in your speech, audience members find themselves wondering what or who you are talking about, you will begin to lose their attention. When a term comes up that requires definition, you must explain it clearly and succinctly before moving on. If you think an audience is familiar with a word but you just want to be sure, you can simply allude to a more common synonym: "People tend to think of rhinoplasties—commonly referred to as 'nose jobs'—as cosmetic in nature, but in fact many are performed to help improve nasal functioning."

Note that definitions are often necessary for proper nouns as well. Audiences may not have a strong background in geography, politics, or world events, so it can be useful to identify organizations and individuals in the same way that you would define a term: "People for the Ethical Treatment of Animals, or PETA, is the largest animal rights organization in the world" or "Colin Powell, a former U.S. Army general and secretary of state under President George W. Bush, noted that . . ." If you can define and identify terms in a way that is smooth and diplomatic, you will enable audience members who are unfamiliar with them to continue to participate in your presentation, while gaining the confidence of audience members who do know the terms and hear you explain them accurately.

Use Interesting and Appropriate Supporting Material. Select examples that are interesting, exciting, and clear, and use them to reinforce your main ideas. Examples not only support your key points but also provide interesting ways for your audience to visualize what you are talking about. If you are giving a speech about the movie career of Clint Eastwood, you would provide examples of some of his most popular films (*Dirty Harry*, *In the Line of Fire*), his early western films (*A Fistful of Dollars*, *Hang 'Em High*), his lesser-known films (*The First Traveling*

Saleslady, *Honkytonk Man*), and his directorial efforts (*Gran Torino*, *Mystic River*, *J. Edgar*). You might also provide quotes from reviews of his films to show the way Eastwood has been perceived at different points in his career.

When you are offering examples to explain a concept, it's important to choose examples that your audience will understand. Some examples may be familiar enough that you can make quick references to them with little explanation. If you are giving a speech on city planning and rebuilding after disasters, you could probably mention New Orleans after Hurricane Katrina or Haiti after the 2010 earthquake and almost any adult member of your audience will understand your reference. But other examples or audiences might require more detail and explanation. For example, if you are giving a speech about conformity, you might wish to use as an example the incident in Jonestown, Guyana, in 1978, when more than nine hundred members of a religious cult committed mass suicide by drinking cyanide-laced punch. As with many aspects of delivering a speech, audience analysis is crucial: if you are speaking to a younger audience, you'll need to offer a good deal of explanation to make this example work. However, an audience consisting mainly of baby boomers, historians, or social psychologists would require little more than a brief reference to "Jonestown" to get the point of the example.

Use Appropriate Presentation Aids. As you will recall from Chapter 13, presentation aids can add value to your speech by helping audiences follow and understand the information you present. Such aids can be especially helpful in informative speeches. For example, in an informative speech about the importance of a person's credit score, the speaker might show (via slides or handouts) sample credit reports. Seeing this information in addition to hearing about it will underscore the importance of your message: everyone has a credit report and a credit score.

Informative speeches also benefit greatly from the use of graphic presentation aids. When describing

◊ An engaging speech on Clint Eastwood's career would include examples that span his many films, from the classic *The Good, the Bad, and the Ugly* to the more recent *Gran Torino*.

a process, for example, a flowchart outlining the steps you cover in your speech can help audiences visualize how the process works. Graphs can also be helpful in conveying numerical or statistical information. The combination of hearing your message (the speech content) and seeing your message (through presentation aids) helps the audience retain the content of your informative speech.

Let's take a look at an informative speech that undergraduate Zachary Dominque gave for his communication course at St. Edward's University (See p. 327). Zachary chose to inform his audience of fellow students about the history and sport of mountain biking, offering them new and interesting information. Zachary himself is a championship cyclist, and his personal experiences and enthusiasm for the topic help him deliver his message effectively.

Zachary organizes the speech in a topical pattern: each of his main points is a subtopic or category of the overall speech topic of mountain biking. This is one of the most frequently used patterns for informative speeches. Zachary's speaking outline and references are included here as well.

◊ Presentation aids are especially appropriate in informative speaking because they enable the audience to not only hear about but also visualize a new topic.

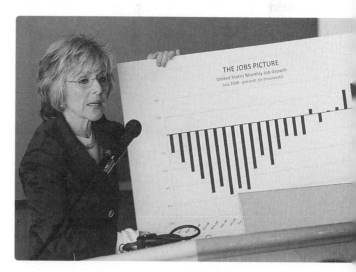

Technology and You
Some presentation aids can include the entire presentation itself as a downloadable file. In your experience, are downloadable presentations as effective as live ones? Can they replace live presentations, or should they just supplement them?

What About You?

}

Assessing Your Informative Speech

As you prepare and rehearse your informative speech, you will do well to remember the main points we developed in this chapter. They will guide you and help you approach your audience competently. Use the following questions to assess your speech honestly. You may also ask your friends, family, or roommates to assess your speech using these questions if you are rehearsing in front of them.

_____ 1. Have you selected an informative topic that will teach your audience members something new?

_____ 2. Are you certain that you can be objective when delivering a speech on this topic, rather than subjective as in a persuasive speech?

_____ 3. Did you select an appropriate approach for your informative speech? Will your audience be able to clearly identify your approach?

_____ 4. Have you presented a clear benefit to learning the information that you are sharing in your speech?

_____ 5. Have you stressed the topic's relevance to your audience?

_____ 6. Does your speech have a clear and logical structure?

_____ 7. Have you defined your terms clearly and related unfamiliar terms to familiar ideas?

_____ 8. Have you selected the most interesting, vivid examples you found in your research?

_____ 9. Are your presentation aids solid, and do they back up your main points (without overwhelming your speech)?

If you cannot answer "yes" to these questions, then you will likely benefit from additional research and rehearsal time. Remember, the more you employ these tips and guidelines, the more successful you will be at informing your audience—and hopefully teaching them something that they will use and apply in their own lives.

The History and Sport of Mountain Biking

ZACHARY DOMINQUE
St. Edward's University

Before I begin, if you'd like, close your eyes for a moment and picture this. You're on a bike, plunging down a steep, rock-strewn mountain, yet fully in control. Adrenaline courses through your body as you hurtle through the air, touch down on pebbled creeks and tangled grasses, and rocket upward again at breakneck speed. You should be scared, but you're not. In fact, you're having the time of your life. ▪

How many of you like to bike? Perhaps you ride to campus, bike for fitness, or cycle just for fun. Some of you might own bikes with lightweight frames and thin wheels and use them to log some serious mileage. Or possibly you ride a comfort bike with a cushy seat and bigger tires.

Good morning, ladies and gentlemen. My name is Zachary Dominque, and I'm a mountain biker. Today, I'm going to take you on a tour of this exciting sport with a rich history. Our stops along the way will include an overview of mountain biking, followed by a brief history of the sport. We'll also investigate the forms and functions of mountain bikes (as compared to road bikes), the different types of mountain biking, and some noteworthy bike courses. ▪ I've been racing since I was eight years old and won the state championship three years ago, so this topic is close to my heart. ▪

To start, let me briefly define mountain biking. ▪

Mountain biking is a sport that can be extreme, recreational, or somewhere in between. The ABC-of-Mountain Biking Web site offers a good basic definition: "Mountain biking is a form of cycling on off-road or unpaved surfaces such as mountain trails and dirt roads; the biker uses a bicycle with a sturdy frame and fat tires." ▪

Mountain bikes are built to tackle rough ground. They feature wide tires with tough tread, straight and wide handlebars, rugged but light frames, and eighteen to twenty-four or more specialized gears. The idea behind mountain biking is to go where other bikes can't take you because they aren't equipped to handle rough terrain. This might mean riding on backcountry roads or on single-track trails winding through fields or forest. It can involve climbing steep hills and racing down them. The focus is on self-reliance because mountain bikers often venture miles from help.

According to the Web site of the National Bicycle Dealers Association, mountain bikes accounted for 28 percent of all bikes sold in the United States in 2009. If you factor in sales of the comfort bike, which is actually a modified mountain bike for purely recreational riders, sales jump to nearly 40 percent of all bikes sold. ▪

So, you see, mountain biking is popular with a lot of people. But the sport itself is fairly new. ▪

▪ By asking audience to visualize, Zachary effectively captures their attention

▪ Previews main points

▪ Pointing to his personal experience with sport lends Zachary credibility

▪ Transitions into speech body

▪ Clearly defines topic for audience

▪ Uses reputable source and informs audience of where information is located

▪ Uses transition to signal change in focus

The man in this picture is Gary Fisher, one of the founders of mountain biking. According to *The Original Mountain Bike Book*, written by pioneering mountain bikers Rob Van der Plas and Charles Kelly, they, along with Fisher and others from the Marin County, California, area, founded the modern sport of mountain biking in the early 1970s.

Early on, these guys decided to take on the adventure of racing down the slopes of Mount Tamalpais, or "Mount Tam," in Corte Madera, California. Back then, they didn't have mountain bikes as we know them, so as you can see, Fisher is riding a modified one-speed Schwinn Cruiser. ■ Cruisers aren't made for off-road use at all; they're just supposed to ferry people around town on their so-called balloon tires. They have hard shocks, and the brakes aren't remotely equipped to handle stops on steep descents. But this is how Fisher and others started out.

■ To add interest and involvement, supplements description with photographs

Very quickly, however, Kelly, Fisher, and other cyclists like Charles Cunningham began to adapt the bikes to their needs. By the mid-1970s, growing numbers of bikers in California were racing one another down the rough slopes of mountains on "fat tire" bikes. This activity led to the famed Repack Downhill Race on Mount Tam, which took place between 1976 and 1979. According to a brief history of mountain biking on the London 2012 Olympics Web site, the race attracted many participants and contributed to putting the sport on the map. Bit by bit, Fisher, Cunningham, Kelly, and others modified their bikes, adding gears, drum brakes, and suspension systems to the frames. As Van der Plas and Kelly noted in *The Original Mountain Bike Book*, it wasn't until 1982, however, that standardized production of these machines began.

To get a better sense of what the mountain bike can and cannot do, consider how they compare to road bikes, the class of bikes that such cyclists as Tour de France winners Alberto Contador and Lance Armstrong use. ■

■ To help foster understanding, compares and contrasts mountain bike with more familiar road bike

Whereas mountain bikes are built to tackle rough ground, road bikes stay on paved, smooth surfaces. And while mountain bikes feature wide tires with tough tread, road bike tires are very thin and the frames are extremely lightweight, letting the cyclist race hard and fast on a road course. This is fine for them, because they're all about productivity. If you take the road bike off-road, however, chances are you'll destroy it. The thinner tires can't provide the stability required, and without the knobby tires found on mountain bikes, road bike tires can't grip the rocks, roots, and other obstacles that cover off-road courses.

The seats—or saddles as we call them—on road and mountain bikes also differ, as do the gears, suspension systems, and handlebar configurations.

Road bike seats are thin and hard to sit on. This suits road cyclists well because they tackle flat, relatively smooth courses. We mountain bikers need a bit more cushion, and as you can see our seats have a split in the middle so they bend with our gluteus maximus. ■

■ Supplements verbal description with visual

Road bikes are geared to go faster than mountain bikes, with higher or harder gears than those on mountain bikes. With mountain bikes, riders can rapidly adjust the gears to match conditions, using lower gears to over-come higher resistance (such as when climbing hills) and higher gears when the cycling is easier. The big gear on a road bike is probably twice the size of my big gear on this mountain bike.

The suspension systems on the two bikes also differ. Many mountain bikes have at least a great front shock-absorbing suspension system; some have rear-suspension systems, and some other bikes have dual suspension systems. Road bikes generally don't have shock absorbers because they're not supposed to hit anything.

A final feature distinguishing mountain from road bikes is the handle-bars. Mountain bikes have flat handlebars. These promote an upright stance, so that cyclists don't flip over when they hit something. The drop handlebars on road bikes require the cyclist to lean far forward to hold on to them. This position suits this type of cycling, which prizes speed.

I hope by now you have a sense of the form and functions of the mountain bike. The exact configurations of these bikes vary according to the type of riding they're designed to handle—downhill, trails, and cross-country. Let's begin with downhill. ▪

> ▪ Internally summarizes speech points and signals shift in gears

Downhill biking is a daredevil sport. These bikers slide down hills at top speeds, and they go off jumps. As described on the Trails.com Web site, downhill racers catch a shuttle going up the mountain, then speed downhill while "chewing up" obstacles. Downhill racing has been com-pared to skiing with a bike, and in fact, in the summer many downhill racers do race on ski slopes.

As far as bikes go, downhill racers need a special downhill bike—one that has fewer gears and is heavier than other types of mountain bikes.

Now let's ride over to trails biking. ▪

> ▪ Transitions serve as critical "traffic signals," alerting audience where they've been and where they will go

Trails bikers hop and jump their bikes over obstacles such as cars, rocks, and large logs. Their goal is not to put their foot down on the ground. In trail biking, the course is set right there in front of you. This is one of the few types of biking where you can watch the entire race, and it's done by time, not with a mass start.

Trails bikes look quite different from other types of mountain bikes. They have very small wheels, measuring either twenty, twenty-four, or twenty-six inches, and they have smaller frames.

A third type of mountain biking, cross-country, is my sport.

Cross-country biking—also called "XC cycling"—is the most common type of mountain biking. It's also the type of mountain biking sponsored by the Olympics. That's right. In 1996, mountain biking became an Olympic sport—just two decades after its inception.

With cross-country biking, you get the best of all worlds. The courses are creative, incorporating hills and valleys and rough to not-so-rough terrain. If done competitively, cross-country biking is like competing in a mara-thon. Done recreationally, it offers you the chance to see the great out-doors while getting, or staying, in great shape.

Cross-country bikes come in two forms: XC bikes are very lightweight, with either full or partial suspension, whereas trail/marathon XC bikes are a bit heavier, with full suspension. These latter bikes are designed for the seriously long ride.

Now that you're familiar with the main types of mountain biking, let's cruise through some notable cross-country courses. ∎

There are many great cross-country courses throughout the United States, some designed for entry-level cyclists and others for the pros. Depending on what state you're in, you may find very technical or very rocky courses. The McKenzie River Trail in Eugene, Oregon, goes on for hours through gorgeous, old-growth forest. In Utah you'll find awesome biking meccas among the incredible canyons and mesas of Moab.

Our own state of Texas draws a lot of riders, with courses running through the desert in the south and flats and mountains in the west and north. My personal favorite is in Colorado. Breckenridge, a ski town in the Rockies, has some of the best courses I've ever ridden. Although I haven't been to Fruita in Colorado, its courses are legendary.

You can find great courses in New York, Vermont, North Carolina, and Puerto Rico; in Ketchum, Idaho, and Downieville, California; and in many other areas nationwide. Trails.com is a good resource for exploring the variety of trails available.

Well, it has been quite a tour. Our course began with an overview of mountain biking and a brief history of the sport. ∎

We also learned about the forms and functions of mountain bikes compared to road bikes, the different types of mountain biking, and noteworthy mountain biking courses around the country.

To me, mountain biking is the perfect sport—fulfilling physical, spiritual, and social needs. It's a great sport to take up recreationally. And if you decide to mountain bike competitively, just remember: ride fast, drive hard, and leave your blood on every trail. ∎

■ Uses "cast-recast" transition, stating what was discussed and previewing what is next

■ Metaphoric language, in which speech becomes tour of biking course, signals close of speech

■ Vivid language makes conclusion memorable and leaves audience with something to think about

References

Cycling—Mountain bike. (n.d.). *London 2012 Olympics*. Retrieved from http://www.london 2012.com/games/Olympic-sports/cycling-mountain-bike.php

National Bicycle Dealers Association. (2009). *Industry overview 2009: A look at the bicycle industry's vital statistics*. Retrieved from http://nbda.com/articles/industry-overview-2009-pg34.htm

Van der Plas, R., Kelly, C., Keyes, P., & Phelan, J. (1998). *The original mountain bike book*. Menasha, WI: Motorbooks International.

Weiss, C. (n.d.). *Types of mountain bikes*. Retrieved from http://www.trails.com/list_3232_types-mountain-bikes.html

What is mountain biking? (n.d.). *ABC-of-mountain biking*. Retrieved from http://www.abc-of-mountainbiking.com/mountain-biking-basics/whatis-mountain-biking.asp

Speaking Outline

The History and Sport of Mountain Biking

ZACHARY DOMINQUE
St. Edward's University

General Purpose: To inform
Specific Purpose: To inform my audience members about mountain biking to increase their knowledge about this sport.
Thesis Statement: Today, I'm going to take you on a tour of mountain biking, an exciting sport with a rich history.

Introduction

 I. **Attention Getter:** Draw mental picture of mountain biking (MB) for audience.
 II. Ask listeners about their biking experience.
 III. Introduce self and personal experience with MB.
 IV. I will discuss MB: overview, history, bikes, types, courses.

Transition: Define MB.

Body

 I. Overview of MB = extreme, recreational, in between.
   A. "Mountain biking is a form of cycling on off-road or unpaved surfaces such as mountain trails and dirt roads; the biker uses a bicycle with a sturdy frame and fat tires." (ABC-of-Mountain Biking)
   B. Bikes = wide tires, tough tread, straight/wide handlebars, rugged/light frames, 18 to 24+ gears.
    1. Go where other bikes won't (backcountry roads, fields, forests, hills).
    2. In 2009, MB bikes = 28 percent of bikes sold in United States. Factor in comfort bikes and sales jump to 40 percent of all bikes. (National Bicycle Dealers Association)

Transition: Popular sport, but fairly new.

 II. History of MB
   A. **[Show photo of GF]** Gary Fisher, one of the founders of MB

   B. *The Original Mountain Bike Book* authors Rob Van der Plas and Charles Kelly (with Fisher) founded MB in Marin County, CA, in early 1970s.
    1. Adventure of racing down Mount Tamalpais **[Tam*el*pie*us]** in Corte Madera, CA.
    2. **[Show photo]** No special bikes; used modified one-speed Schwinn Cruiser.
   C. Sport grows in popularity
    1. Mid-1970s: more bikers racing downhill on "fat tire" bikes.
    2. Repack Downhill Race on Mt. Tam (1976–1979) attracted many participants and put sport on map. (London 2012 Olympics Web site)
    3. Standardized production of bikes begins in 1982. (*The Original Mountain Bike Book*)

Transition: Understand mountain bikes and compare to familiar road bikes (like ones Alberto Contador and Lance Armstrong use).

 III. Form and function of mountain bikes (compare to road bikes) **[Show photos]**
   A. Mountain bikes tackle rough ground. Road bikes stay on smooth surfaces.
   B. Mountain bikes have wide tires/tough tread. Road bikes have thin tires and lightweight frames.
   C. Mountain bikes have cushioned seats. Road bikes have hard seats.
   D. Mountain bikes have versatile gears. Road bikes have higher gears.
   E. Mountain bikes have great front shock-absorbing suspension systems. Road bikes don't need this.
   F. Mountain bikes have flat handlebars for safety. Road bikes have drop handlebars.

Transition/Internal Summary: You should understand form and functions of mountain bikes. Exact configurations depend on the type of riding—downhill, trails, and cross-country.

 IV. Types of MB **[Show photos]**
   A. Downhill
    1. Daredevil sport (slide down hills, top speeds, jumps)

2. Shuttle up the mountain, then speed down "chewing up" obstacles (Trails.com)
3. Compare to skiing
4. Special bike: heavy with fewer gears

B. Trails
1. Hop and jump over obstacles (cars, rocks, logs)
2. Object: don't put foot on ground
3. Done by time
4. Special bike: small wheels and smaller frame

C. Cross-country (my sport)
1. Most common type
2. Became Olympic sport in 1996
3. Creative courses: hills, valleys, rough terrain, easy terrain
4. Competition like marathon; recreational for health and enjoyment
5. Special bikes: XC (lightweight, full or partial suspension) and trail/marathon XC (heavier, full suspension)

Transition: Now you know the main types of MB. Let's look at cross-country courses.

V. Courses
A. McKenzie River Trail, Eugene, OR: old-growth forest
B. UT: canyons and mesas of Moab
C. TX: desert courses in south and flats/mountains in west/north
D. CO: Breckenridge and Fruita
E. Also great courses in NY; VT; NC; PR; Ketchum, ID; Downieville, CA

Conclusion

I. Quite a tour!
II. Looked at overview of MB and history of sport. Learned about forms and functions of bikes, types of mountain biking, various courses.
III. To me, MB is perfect sport: physical, spiritual, social.
IV. If you bike, ride fast, drive hard, leave blood on trails!

LearningCurve
bedfordstmartins.com/commandyou

Back to } **Neil deGrasse Tyson**

At the beginning of this chapter, we read about astrophysicist Neil deGrasse Tyson, who is widely respected not only as one of the foremost researchers on space but also as one of science's most competent and enthusiastic communicators. Let's consider how his informative presentations measure up to the concepts outlined in this chapter.

- Tyson knows his listeners. He understands that while they are not well versed in astrophysics, they are curious about it. He makes abstract topics tangible by using familiar metaphors and examples. When speaking to an audience of fellow astrophysicists, he would not have to take such measures.

- Tyson uses effective nonverbal communication in his presentations. He uses appropriate gestures, laughs heartily at his own jokes, moves around the stage rather than gluing himself to a podium, and uses a tone of voice that generates a casual atmosphere. His trademark vests—embroidered with images of the cosmos—indicate his enthusiasm for the subject.

- Like everyone, Tyson has personal opinions and beliefs. But when he is speaking informatively, he limits his discussions to facts. In his discussion of the universe noted at the beginning of this chapter, for example, Tyson explains, "None of this is about 'belief.' It's about 'what does the evidence show?'" (Tyson, 2009).

Your Reference

} A Study Tool

Now that you have finished reading this chapter, you can

Describe the goals of informative speaking:

- Use **informative speaking** to teach the audience something new (p. 310).
- Gauge what the audience already knows to determine where to begin (p. 310).
- Find an approach that will engage the audience (pp. 310–311).
- Explain the subject's relevance to the audience (p. 311).
- Present facts and information in an **objective**, evenhanded way, unlike in a persuasive speech, which is **subjective**, presenting a point of view (pp. 311–312).
- Speak ethically (pp. 312–313).

List and describe each of the eight categories of informative speeches:

- People: focus on human qualities as well as achievements (p. 313).
- Places: find new aspects of known places, or describe the unfamiliar (p. 313).
- Objects and phenomena: focus on any nonhuman topic (pp. 313–314).
- Events: describe noteworthy events in history, or relate a personal experience (p. 314).
- Processes: show how something works, or teach how to do something (pp. 314–315).
- Concepts: explain an abstract idea (p. 315).
- Issues: remain objective to report on a social or personal problem (pp. 315–316).
- Plans and policies: describe the important dimensions of potential courses of action (p. 316).

Outline the four major approaches to informative speeches:

- The **descriptive presentation** paints a mental picture, portraying places, events, persons, objects, or processes (pp. 316–317).

- **Demonstration speeches** combine explanatory narration and physical demonstration (p. 317).
- There are five categories of **definitional speeches** ⊙: an **operational definition** defines something by explaining what it is or what it does; **definition by negation** defines something by telling what it is not; **definition by example** offers concrete examples; **definition by synonym** defines something with closely related words; **definition by etymology** explains the origin of a word or phrase (pp. 317–318).
- **Explanatory speeches** answer the question "Why?" with **elucidating explanations**, with **quasi-scientific explanations** or models, or with **transformative explanations** that change preconceptions (pp. 318–319).

Employ strategies to make your audience hungry for information:

- Make listeners curious by personalizing the topic and contrasting it with what they know (pp. 319–320).
- Present a clear benefit to learning about the topic and stress the topic's relevance (p. 320).

Structure your speech to make it easy to listen to:

- Devise a clear, logical structure (pp. 320–321).
- Signal your audience when you're about to say something important (p. 323).
- Keep it simple (p. 323).
- Relate new ideas to familiar ideas (p. 323).
- Define terms your audience may not know (p. 324).
- Select interesting examples (p. 324).
- Use strong presentation aids (pp. 324–325).

Look for **LearningCurve** throughout
the chapter to help you review.
bedfordstmartins.com/commandyou

15 } Persuasive Speaking

S uppose you have found a magic lamp with a genie inside. The genie will grant you one wish, but there's a catch: you need to convince him that your wish is worthwhile and that it will have a positive impact on the world. Each year, TED (short for Technology, Entertainment, and Design), an organization devoted to "ideas worth spreading," plays the role of this magic genie. Winners receive $100,000—in addition to the organization's considerable talent and resources—to turn a beneficial and world-changing idea into reality. After months of preparation, TED Prize winners then unveil their wishes and plans at the annual TED conference (TED Prize, 2011).

TED Prize winner and celebrity chef Jamie Oliver presented his wish ("To teach every child about food") at the 2010 conference in Long Beach, California. He opened his speech with a simple statement identifying an important social and medical problem: "In the next 18 minutes when I do our chat, four Americans that are alive will be dead from the food that they eat" (Oliver, 2010, para. 1). Oliver went on to discuss the realities of obesity in the United States and elsewhere, noting the personal health costs as well as the financial costs of caring for people suffering from preventable, diet-related diseases. He then discussed his experiences educating real people whose lives have been shaped by a lack of simple knowledge about food.

Oliver openly considered the causes for the problem he was addressing: a lack of education about healthy food choices at home and in schools; school lunch programs focused on economics rather than on nutrition; a food industry that promotes highly processed, unhealthy foods rather than more costly, healthy options; and confusing or misleading labeling on the foods we buy. But he also proposed solutions, pointing to successful (and nutritious) school lunch programs that could be easily rolled out on a larger scale for a relatively small influx of cash. He also considered and explained how food businesses can—and, indeed, must—be an integral part of the solution.

Oliver ended his speech by reminding his listeners of his personal wish and his goal for speaking that day: to form "a strong sustainable movement to educate every child about food, to inspire families to cook again, and to empower people everywhere to fight obesity" (Oliver, 2010, para. 39).

After you have finished reading this chapter, you will be able to

Define the goals of persuasive speaking.

Develop a persuasive topic and thesis.

Evaluate your listeners and tailor your speech to them.

Explain three forms of rhetorical proof: ethos, logos, and pathos.

Identify the logical fallacies, deceptive forms of reasoning.

Choose an appropriate organizational strategy for your speech.

to eat his peas. In this chapter, we will examine the nature and goals of persuasive speaking while helping you consider your audience, the support for your speech, and helpful organizational patterns.

The Goals of Persuasive Speaking

Persuasive speaking is speech that is intended to influence the attitudes, beliefs, and behavior of your audience. Although these three terms may be familiar to you, let's take a moment to examine them in light of how we will think about them in this chapter.

- **Attitudes** are our general evaluations of people, ideas, objects, or events (Stiff & Mongeau, 2003). When you evaluate something, you judge it as good or bad, important or unimportant, boring or interesting, and so on. For example, you might have a positive attitude toward sports and exercise: "Exercising regularly is good."
- **Beliefs** are the ways in which people perceive reality (Stiff & Mongeau, 2003). They are our feelings about what is true and real and refer to how confident we are about the existence or validity of something: "I believe that exercise is an important component of a healthy lifestyle."
- **Behavior** is the manner in which we act or function. It refers to what we do in response to our attitudes and beliefs (Homer, 2006). For example, if your attitude about exercise is really positive and you believe that it is an important component of a healthy lifestyle, you'll probably be motivated to get out there and walk or jog or lift weights.

What do you think of when you hear the word *persuasion*? When we ask students this question, they often think of sneaky used-car salespeople and dishonest politicians. They also point to *Inception*'s Dom Cobb, a spy who attempts to persuade his targets by manipulating their subconscious minds. The first two examples might involve people attempting to be persuasive, but they certainly involve unethical communication. The final example is a clear-cut description of **coercion**, the act of using manipulation, threats, intimidation, or violence to gain compliance.

Persuasion is none of these things; rather, it is the process of influencing (often changing or reinforcing) others' attitudes, beliefs, and behaviors on a given topic. When done properly and respectfully, it is also an ethical practice. Think of all the important accomplishments that can come from a competent use of persuasion, such as petitioning for money to support victims of natural disasters. Persuasion is also a tool that you use every day, whether you are persuading your roommates to switch from a cable TV subscription to Hulu Plus or convincing your four-year-old

> Persuasion is also a tool that you use every day, whether you are persuading your roommates to switch from a cable TV subscription to Hulu Plus or convincing your four-year-old to eat his peas.

In many ways, speaking to persuade your listeners is similar to speaking for informative purposes. Just look at any presidential campaign. The candidates all want to inform you about their plans and goals for the nation, but they also use organized and well-developed presentations to influence their audience's attitudes and beliefs about their suitability for the presidency. And, of course, they want to influence your behavior by getting you to vote for them.

Influencing your audience does not necessarily mean changing their attitudes, beliefs, or behavior; it can also mean reinforcing them. For example, when a political party attempts to rally its base, it usually focuses candidates' speeches on issues on which the party faithful already agree. To do this, they must first correctly identify an existing attitude or belief among listeners. The key to determining your audience's attitudes—whether your goal is to change or to reinforce those attitudes—lies with audience analysis (discussed in Chapter 11).

LearningCurve
bedfordstmartins.com/commandyou

📍 In the film *Inception*, spy Dom Cobb takes coercion to the next level by manipulating his targets' subconscious minds to extract valuable information.

Developing a Persuasive Topic and Thesis

An effective topic for a persuasive speech must share characteristics with an informative one: it should be something that you're interested in, that you know something about, and that is specific enough that you can find a variety of appropriate sources on the topic but not so specific that you can't possibly develop it. When your general purpose is to persuade, however, you must keep a few other points in mind.

First, your topic should be one that people could have reasonable disagreement about or resistance to. Issues such as stem cell research, campaign finance reform, and mandatory year-round schooling lend themselves to a persuasive purpose because people hold strongly differing opinions about them. Second, the topic must allow the speaker to develop a message intended to cause some degree of change in the audience. For example, the topic of mandatory smoking bans could seek changes from different audiences who hold very different views: encouraging action (a change in behavior) from people who already agree that smoking should be banned in public or seeking a change in the attitudes of smokers who currently see no problem with smoking in public places.

Once you have determined that a particular topic interests you and can be persuasive, it's time to think about developing your thesis statement. In a persuasive speech, thesis statements are often given as a proposition, or a statement about your viewpoint or position on an issue. There are three types of propositions that we will examine: propositions of fact, propositions of value, and propositions of policy.

Propositions of Fact

If you've ever argued on behalf of something you believed to be true, you've made a **proposition of fact**—a claim of what is or what is not. Persuasive speeches built on propositions of fact commonly involve issues that are open to some interpretation and on which there are conflicting beliefs or evidence. The truth of the statement may be debatable, but the goal of the speech is clear: you want to align the audience's perception or opinion of the fact with your own. While it may seem simple to state your belief and back up your points with research that persuades your audience, it can actually be quite challenging. Propositions of fact get at the heart of how you view the world, and your viewpoints may be quite different from how members of your audience perceive reality. Consider the following proposition-of-fact thesis statements:

- "Single people are as capable of raising happy, healthy, well-adjusted children as married couples are."

- "Your auto dealership will lose money on its sales of compact cars if your inventory is too small."

- "HMOs are a sensible choice for less expensive health care coverage."

Each statement is presented as a fact, yet audiences realize that they are really the beliefs of the speaker, presented for the listeners' consideration, and possibly in conflict with their own. It's important to be tolerant and understanding of people's deeply held beliefs, especially if you hope to get others to see your point of view.

Propositions of Value

Some speeches go beyond discussing what is or what is not and make claims about something's worth. Such evaluative claims are called **propositions of value**. In speeches of this type, you seek to convince an audience that something meets or does not meet a specific standard of goodness or quality or right or wrong. Consider the following examples of propositions of value:

- "Torturing prisoners of war is immoral."

- "The Olympics are becoming less relevant as a sporting event."

- "Organized religion has done a great deal of good for the world."

Each statement offers a judgment about the overall value of the person, event, object, way of life, condition, or action discussed. Like propositions of fact, it's clear to the audience that these statements of value

are not absolute truths but rather the opinion of the speaker. And as with propositions of fact, the speaker must present arguments and evidence that will persuade listeners to align their beliefs and attitudes with the speaker's.

Propositions of Policy

The third type of proposition is concerned with what *should* happen. In **propositions of policy**, the speaker makes claims about what goal, policy, or course of action should be pursued. The examples that follow are propositions of policy:

- "Gay people should have the same rights as all other Americans."

- "Colleges and universities should not consider race when making admission decisions."

- "Any vehicle that gets poor gas mileage (say, less than 25 miles per gallon) should be banned in the United States."

In advocating for any of these statements, your task as the speaker would be to persuade the audience that a current policy is not working or that a new policy is needed. Propositions of policy are common during election campaigns as candidates—especially challengers—offer their ideas and plans for what the government should do and how they would do it.

No matter what your topic, and no matter which type of proposition you are advocating, you'll need to know as much as possible about your listeners in order to persuade them effectively. This is the topic of the next section.

LearningCurve
bedfordstmartins.com/commandyou

Persuading Your Audience

A student once told us an interesting story about audience analysis. At a church service the Sunday after Thanksgiving, her pastor preached on the religious meaning of Christmas. He was hoping to persuade his audience to remember the religious meaning of the holiday and to avoid getting caught up in commercialism, present swapping, and credit card debt. "He was passionate about the topic, and his points were right on," the student said, "but the congregation already agreed with him. It almost felt like he was angry with us or something. It was uncomfortable."

As this story shows, it is crucial to know your audience before developing your speech, as this knowledge will help you tailor your organization, research, and supporting points. It will even help you determine your specific purpose—whether to try to change or to reaffirm the audience's attitudes, beliefs, and behavior. This was the mistake of our student's pastor. He would have benefited from thoroughly understanding his listeners' disposition and needs as well as what was most relevant to them.

Understanding Your Audience's Disposition

According to **social judgment theory** (often called *ego involvement*), your ability to successfully persuade your audience depends on the audience's current attitudes or disposition toward your topic (Sherif, Sherif, & Nebergall, 1965). As such, you might think about your audience members as belonging to one of three different categories: the receptive audience, the neutral audience, or the hostile audience.

- A **receptive audience** already agrees with your viewpoints and message and is likely to respond favorably to your speech. When you address the receptive audience, you probably don't need to do too much to get your listeners to like what you're saying—they already concur. You're reaffirming what they believe and strengthening your case.

- A **neutral audience** falls between the receptive audience and the hostile audience: its members neither support you nor oppose you. Their neutrality can be based on several causes: perhaps they are simply uninterested in your topic, or they don't see how the topic affects them

personally. Or they may know very little about the topic and are therefore unable to take a stance until they learn more. They may require more information about the topic at hand.

- A **hostile audience** is one that opposes your message (and perhaps you personally); this is the hardest type of audience to persuade, particularly if you are trying to change people's behavior. A hostile audience will, of course, need some very special consideration. You will want the members of this audience to find you trustworthy and full of goodwill. You also want to avoid making them feel as though you are trying to force them to accept your viewpoint; research shows that such behavior will backfire and make your audience less likely to engage with you (Brehm, 1966). Instead, you want to acknowledge their point of view and look for ways to bridge the gap between your beliefs and their beliefs.

> ### Technology and You
> Do you find it more or less difficult to read an audience's disposition in a virtual or online communication? How might you determine whether your online audience is receptive, neutral, or hostile?

You must also consider what you want your audience to do at the end of your speech. A lot of what listeners will be willing to do is related to their **latitude of acceptance and rejection**, which is the range of positions on a topic that are acceptable or unacceptable to them based on their **anchor position**—or their position on the topic at the outset of the speech (Sherif & Sherif, 1967). You can probably get members of a receptive audience to do quite a bit, including change their behavior. Members of your neutral audience might be willing to sign a petition or to discuss the topic with friends, but they're not going to go out of their way to help you. When it comes to your hostile audience, it's unlikely that you'll see much behavior change. But you might be able to effect some level of

💧 Coretta Scott King found a receptive audience when she spoke to other like-minded individuals at a press conference on ending the Vietnam War.

belief and attitude change, helping them at least see your point of view.

Understanding Your Audience's Needs

If you feel that your child isn't getting sufficient or proper instruction in mathematics, you probably aren't going to be too interested in hearing a speech on the importance of raising money for new school football uniforms. That's because that topic doesn't address your personal *needs*, or deficits that create tension. Helpful to understanding audience needs is the work of Abraham Maslow (1954). Maslow argues that an individual's motivations, priorities, and behavior are influenced primarily by that person's needs. He identifies needs in a hierarchical structure of five categories (see **Figure 15.1** on p. 341), from low (immature) to high (mature), known as the **hierarchy of needs**.[1]

_____
[1]While Maslow's hierarchy of needs has been recently revised (see Kenrick, Griskevicius, Neuberg, & Schaller, 2010), we have elected to offer the original model as advanced by Maslow, given its utility and application to public speaking.

The theory is that the most basic needs must be met before an individual can become concerned with needs farther up in the hierarchy.

1. *Physiological/survival needs.* These are the things you need for basic survival, such as air, water, food, shelter, sleep, clothing, and so on. Even in the short term, if you listen to a speech while you are very hungry, your mind is likely not on the message but rather on getting food.

2. *Safety needs.* These are needs for security, orderliness, protection, and risk avoidance. They include not only actual physical safety but safety from emotional injury as well. When people in a community are concerned with violence and crime, for example, they are less likely to listen to persuasive appeals to increase local arts funding.

3. *Belongingness/social needs.* These needs center around your interactions with others. They include the desire to be accepted and liked by other people and the need for love, affection, and affiliation. These needs are normally met by family ties, friendships, and membership in work and social groups.

4. *Esteem/ego-status needs.* These needs involve validation—being accepted by some group and being recognized for achievement, mastery, competence, and so on. They can be satisfied by special recognition, promotions, power, and achievement. Unlike the previous three categories, esteem needs are not satisfied internally; they require praise and acknowledgment from others.

5. *Self-actualizing needs.* Needs at the highest level focus on personal development and self-fulfillment—becoming what you can become. Instead of looking for recognition of your worth from others, you seek to measure up to your own criteria for personal success.

If you understand your audience's needs, you can determine your strategy for persuading your listeners.

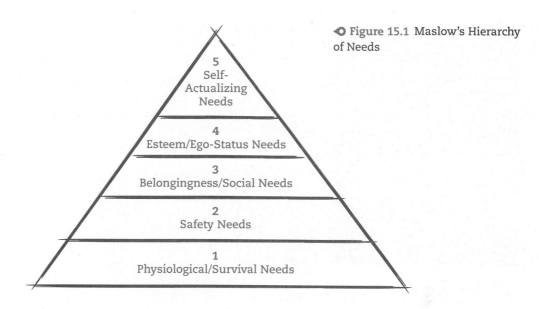

● Figure 15.1 Maslow's Hierarchy of Needs

The message must target the unfulfilled need of the audience. A need that is already met will not move an audience, nor will one that seems too far out of reach in the hierarchy.

Understanding What Is Relevant to Your Audience

Along with appealing to audience needs, you can also persuade listeners—especially neutral listeners—by anticipating their question, "How is this relevant to me?" The **Elaboration Likelihood Model (ELM)**, developed by Richard Petty, John Cacioppo, and their associates, is based on the belief that listeners process persuasive messages by one of two routes, depending on how important—how relevant—the message is to them (Petty & Cacioppo, 1986; Petty & Wegner, 1998;

see also Kruglanski et al., 2006). When they are motivated and personally involved in the content of a message, they engage in **central processing**—they think critically about the speaker's message, question it, and may seriously consider acting on it. When listeners lack motivation to listen critically or are unable to do so, they engage in **peripheral processing** of information, giving little thought to the message or even dismissing it as irrelevant, too complex to follow, or simply unimportant.

Whenever possible, you want your audience to engage in central processing, as it produces deeper, more long-lasting changes in audience perspective than peripheral processing does. Audience members who engage peripherally can certainly be influenced, but they tend to pay attention to things other than the central message, such as the speaker's appearance or reputation or any slogans or emotional manipulation used in the speech (Petty & Cacioppo, 1986), which is less likely to lead to meaningful long-term changes in attitudes or behavior.

{ **Along with appealing to audience needs, you can also persuade listeners—especially neutral listeners—by anticipating their question, "How is this relevant to me?"** }

🔹 Maslow's hierarchy of needs, depicted in the photos above, is helpful in understanding your audience's needs. For example, it might be hard to convince a group of low-income single mothers to enroll their kids in various costly extracurricular activities.

To put the principles of the ELM of persuasion into practice, consider the following points:

- **Make certain that your message is relevant.** Use language and examples to connect your message to your listeners' lives.

- **Be sure to present your message at an appropriate level of understanding.** You can't persuade your audience members if they don't understand the message.

- **Establish credibility with the audience.** Show your research, cite experts, and (if relevant) clearly explain your own credentials and experience.

- **Establish a common bond with your listeners.** Ensure that they see you as trustworthy. Clearly explain why you support this particular message; if you have a specific interest in it, let them know.

These steps will increase the odds that your persuasive appeal will produce lasting, rather than fleeting, changes in the audience's attitudes and behavior (O'Hair, Stewart, & Rubenstein, 2007).

LearningCurve
bedfordstmartins.com/commandyou

Strategies for Persuasive Speaking

It was Aristotle who first named the three means of persuasion or **forms of rhetorical proof** that comprise major persuasive speaking strategies. The first, appeals to ethos, concerns the qualifications and personality of the speaker; the second, appeals to logos, concerns the nature of the message in a speech; the third, appeals to pathos, concerns the nature of the audience's feelings. According to Aristotle—and generations of theorists and practitioners who followed him—you can build an effective persuasive speech by incorporating a combination of these factors. We will examine each of these appeals in turn in addition to considering examples of problematic reasoning that undermine your effective use of ethos, logos, and pathos.

Ethos

If audience members have little or no regard for the speaker, they will not respond positively to persuasive appeals; attitude change in your audience is related to the extent to which you, as the speaker, are perceived to be credible (McCroskey & Teven, 1999; Priester & Petty, 1995). Aristotle believed that speechmaking should emphasize the quality and impact of ideas, but he recognized that the speaker's character and personality also play an important role in how well the audience listens to and accepts the message. He referred to this effect of the speaker as **ethos**, or moral character.

Exactly which elements of a persuasive appeal are based on ethos? The first element is *credibility* or the speaker's knowledge and experience with the subject matter. You can evoke this quality by preparing the speech at all stages (from research to delivery), by demonstrating personal acquaintance with the topic, by revealing familiarity with the work of experts on your topic, and by ensuring that your speech is well organized.

Another element of an ethos-based appeal is the speaker's *character*; the speaker's own ethical standards are central to this element. Research suggests, for example, that a brief disclosure of personal moral standards relevant to the speech or the occasion made in the introduction of a speech will boost audience regard for the speaker (Stewart, 1994). Indeed, you should prepare and present every aspect of your speech with the utmost integrity so that your audience will regard you as *trustworthy*.

A third element of ethos is communicating *goodwill*, the degree to which an audience perceives that the speaker cares for them and has their best interests at heart (Teven & McCroskey, 1997). To show goodwill, you must ensure that you meet your responsibility to help your audience members make informed choices.

By giving listeners all the information they need to make a decision, as well as addressing their needs and expectations relative to the speech, you show that you have their best interests at heart.

Research on the subject indicates there are additional ways a speaker can effectively create credibility. For example, audiences tend to be more easily persuaded by speakers whom they perceive as being similar to them in background, attitudes, interests, and goals, a concept known as *homophily* (Wrench, McCroskey, & Richmond, 2008); research also reveals that we trust (and are more easily persuaded by) speakers we like (Teven, 2008). However, if a speaker is similar to us and very likable but unprepared, uninformed, or disorganized, we probably won't find him or her to be particularly credible. And, as Frymier and Nadler (2010) explain, when liking and credibility come into conflict (for example, when we like a source who has low credibility), credibility outweighs liking and we're unlikely to be moved by the speaker's message.

Logos

Many persuasive speeches focus on issues that require considerable thought, such as "Should the United States adopt a national health care plan?" or "Are certain television programs too violent for children?" When an audience needs to make an important decision or reach a conclusion regarding a complicated issue, appeals to reason and logic are necessary. Aristotle used the term **logos** to refer to persuasive appeals directed at the audience's reasoning on a topic.

Reasoning is the line of thought we use to make judgments based on facts and inferences from the world around us. This basic human capability lies at the heart of logical proof: when we offer our evidence to our audience in hopes that our listeners will reach the same logical conclusions as we have, we are appealing to their reason. There are two types of reasoning: inductive and deductive.

Inductive reasoning occurs when you draw general conclusions based on specific evidence. When you reason inductively, you essentially find and draw on specific examples, incidents, cases, or statistics to

formulate a conclusion that ties them all together. For example, if you work at an animal shelter and have been bitten or snapped at several times by small dogs but never by a large dog, you might conclude inductively that small dogs are more vicious than large dogs. **Deductive reasoning**, by contrast, proceeds from the general to the specific. You begin with a general argument and then apply it to specific cases, incidents, and locations. The most popular way to argue deductively is with a **syllogism**, a three-line deductive argument that draws a specific conclusion from two general premises (a major and a minor premise). Consider this syllogism:

Major premise: All cats are mammals.

Minor premise: Fluffy is a cat.

Conclusion: Therefore, Fluffy is a mammal.

The speaker starts with a proposed conclusion or argument and then tests that argument by gathering facts, observations, and evidence. Applied to a speech, you might use a syllogism in the following ways:

Major premise: Regular cleanings and visits to the dentist will help keep your teeth in excellent condition and reduce your chances of developing costly medical complications.

Minor premise: The proposed student dental insurance plan is affordable and provides for two free cleanings per year and additional coverage on orthodontics and dental procedures.

Conclusion: Therefore, adopting the proposed student dental insurance plan will keep your teeth in excellent condition and help you avoid costly medical complications.

The extent to which your syllogism is persuasive depends on how well the audience accepts the major premise of your case. If the people in your audience do accept your major premise that regular cleanings and visits to the dentist will help keep their teeth in excellent condition and prevent medical complications, then they may believe that the student dental insurance plan that you're advocating is worthwhile and may be inclined to sign up. Hence, your conclusion may be acceptable to them.

Pathos

Another means of persuasion is appealing to the listeners' emotions. The term Aristotle used for this is **pathos**. It requires "creating a certain disposition in the audience," often through emotionally charged language and description. For example, consider this statement: "The sight of fishermen slashing and slicing baby seals should send chills through even the numbest and most stoic capitalists on earth." Makes your skin crawl, doesn't it?

Although emotion is a powerful means of moving an audience, emotional appeals should not be used in isolation—particularly if the emotion you arouse is fear (Rothman, Salovey, Turvey, & Fishkin, 1993; Sutton, 1982). In fact, fear appeals are typically effective only if the speaker can get the audience to see that the threat is serious, that it is likely to happen to them, and that there is a specific action they can take to avoid the threat (Boster & Mongeau, 1984).

Pathos is typically most effective when used alongside logos and ethos, which offer ways of dealing with and addressing the emotions. For example, consider the Montana Meth Project (2007), a campaign to communicate "the risks of methamphetamine to the youth of Montana" and address that state's growing meth problem. The ads are indeed emotional, graphic, and frightening, playing into viewers' love of family and friends, fear of poor health and degenerating appearance, and sense of shame and horror. One print ad depicts a young teenager surrounded by doctors and medical equipment, clinging to life, with text reading, "No one ever thinks they'll wake up here. Meth will change that" (Montana Meth Project,

Culture and You

Think about the last major purchase you made. Now consider the information you had prior to the purchase (advertisements, reviews, advice from others). Did you rely primarily on emotional appeals or logical appeals?

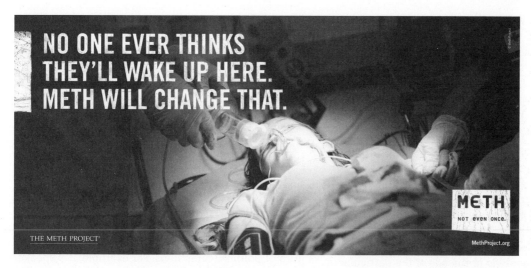

NO ONE EVER THINKS THEY'LL WAKE UP HERE. METH WILL CHANGE THAT.

METH
NOT even once.

THE METH PROJECT

MethProject.org

⬥ The Montana Meth Project persuades with appeals to reason, emotion, and credibility.

2007). The logical appeal is sound—teenagers who become addicted to methamphetamines will destroy themselves and their loved ones—and the ring of truth enhances the persuasiveness of the emotional appeal. The project's follow-up research reveals that the ads have had a significant effect on teens' attitudes toward meth, showing that the ads' credibility is solid as well.

Logical Fallacies

In a predictable scene from any number of movies, TV shows, or actual lives, a teenager argues with her parents that she should be allowed to go to a party because all her friends are going. The exasperated parents roll their eyes and counter, "If your friends were all jumping off a bridge, would you jump too?" In their attempts to persuade, both the parents and the child fail miserably. In the eyes of the parents, "All my friends are going" is not a valid reason their kid should go to party, while comparing going to a party to jumping off a bridge makes no sense to the teenager.

Logical fallacies are invalid or deceptive forms of reasoning. Although they may, at times, be effective

in persuading uncritical listeners, active audience members will reject you as a speaker as well as your argument when they hear a fallacy creep into your speech (Hansen, 2002). So be on the lookout for several types of logical fallacies as you listen to a speaker's arguments and as you craft your own.

Bandwagoning. When our teenager uses "All my friends are going" as an argument, she's guilty of using the **bandwagon fallacy**—accepting a statement as true because it is popular. Unfortunately, bandwagoning can sometimes persuade passive audience members who assume that an argument must be correct if others accept it (Hansen, 2002). But credible speakers and critical audience members must be careful not to confuse consensus with fact. That a large number of people believe in ghosts is not proof that ghosts exist.

Reduction to the Absurd. When the parents counter their daughter's request to go to a party with friends by comparing it to jumping off a bridge with those friends, they are doing little to persuade her. That's because they have extended their argument to

The next time you are in a grocery store or a doctor's waiting room, look through some magazine advertisements (bridal magazines are particularly interesting to search). Page through the advertisements, looking for examples of appeals to ethos, logos, and pathos. Then answer the following questions:

- What magazine and ads did you choose to examine?
- Which form of proof did you find most persuasive? Why?
- Which form of proof did you find least persuasive? Why?
- Is there a form of proof used consistently in the ads of the particular magazine you looked at? Why do you think that is?

the level of absurdity, a fallacy known as **reduction to the absurd**. Pushing an argument beyond its logical limits in this manner can cause it to unravel: the teenager sees no connection between going to a party (which is fun) and jumping off a bridge (which is extremely dangerous).

Red Herring. When a speaker relies on irrelevant information for his or her argument, thereby diverting the direction of the argument, he is guilty of the **red herring fallacy** (so named for a popular myth

Ethics and You

Have you used many logical fallacies in the past, either in the classroom, the workplace, or in personal arguments? Are there particular fallacies you find yourself using repeatedly? How might you avoid them in the future?

about a fish's scent throwing hounds off track of a pursuit). If you say, for example, "I can't believe that police officer gave me a ticket for going 70! Yesterday, I saw a crazy driver cut across three lanes of traffic without signaling while going at least 80. Why aren't cops chasing down these dangerous drivers instead?" you would be using a red herring fallacy. There may well be worse drivers than you, but that doesn't change the fact that you broke the law.

Personal Attacks. A speaker who criticizes a person rather than the issue at hand is guilty of the **ad hominem fallacy**—an attack on the person instead of on the person's arguments. From the Latin meaning "to the man," the ad hominem fallacy is a common feature of political campaigns. For example, if a speaker says, "Terry Malone is the better candidate for district court judge because she is happily married, whereas her opponent just kicked his wife out of their house," the argument is focused on the individual's marriage status, not the person's particular qualifications for the job.

Begging the Question. Speakers who use the fallacy of **begging the question** present arguments that no one can verify because they're not accompanied by valid evidence. For example, if Amanda notes, "People only watch The Vampire Diaries because Twilight is so awesome," she's basing her argument on an unprovable premise (the notion that Twilight is awesome—which is a subjective opinion, rather than a verifiable fact). If you accept Amanda's premise, you must accept her conclusion. For this reason, this fallacy is often referred to as a circular argument.

Either-Or Fallacy. Speakers might try to persuade by using the **either-or fallacy** (sometimes called the false dilemma fallacy), presenting only two alternatives on a subject and failing to acknowledge other alternatives. For example, in a speech about local sports teams, Charlie notes, "In this town, you're either a Bears fan or a Packers fan." He fails to acknowledge that there might be fans of other football teams living in the city or individuals who don't care about football at all.

> **Although audience members may disagree with the evidence and reasoning you use to build your case, your presentation allows for the possibility that they will find the information interesting and plausible.**

your own well-rehearsed presentation to persuade your audience. If you find yourself slipping into logical fallacy to persuade your listeners, you lack solid, compelling evidence in that area of your speech, and you should remedy the situation.

LearningCurve
bedfordstmartins.com/commandyou

Appeal to Tradition. A local community board informs a merchant group that existing "blue laws" preventing them from doing business on Sundays will continue because they have been on the books since the town's founding. This kind of argument is a fallacy known as an **appeal to tradition**—an argument that uses tradition as proof. When speakers appeal to tradition, they are suggesting that listeners should agree with their point because "that's the way it has always been."

The Slippery Slope. The **slippery slope fallacy** is employed when a speaker attests that some event must clearly occur as a result of another event without showing any proof that the second event is caused by the first. For example, "Video surveillance cameras should not be installed in major metropolitan areas. The next thing you know, the government will be spending all of its time and money policing those camera feeds."

Avoiding these logical fallacies goes a long way toward building ethos with your audience—particularly if the audience is hostile toward your speech topic. You want to rely on facts, research, honest emotion, and

Organizing Patterns in Persuasive Speaking

Once you have a topic, audience research, and thoughts about how to deal with logic, emotion, and competence in your presentation, it's time to organize all of this information. As you will recall from Chapter 12, there are a number of organizational strategies available for your speech; the choice you make depends on your objective, your audience, and your available time. When it comes to persuasive speeches, certain organizational strategies can be particularly helpful.

Problem-Solution Pattern

As discussed in Chapter 12, when you use a *problem-solution pattern* for your speech, you establish and prove the existence of a problem and then present a solution. When your objective is to persuade, you also need to add a set of arguments for your proposed solution. This format is valuable because it allows you to establish common ground with your audience about the existence of a problem before moving to more delicate matters (your solution). Although audience members may disagree with the evidence and reasoning you use to build your case, your presentation allows for the possibility that they will find the information interesting and plausible. In some cases, an audience may reject a solution that you present but at least leave convinced that "something has to be done."

> **Culture and You**
> What kinds of logical fallacies do you regularly see used in the media? What is your reaction when advertisers, political campaigns, or pundits try to persuade you using faulty logic?

For example, note in the following outline that the first two main points consider the problem and the third main point offers a solution:

Thesis: Present methods for recycling in our community are inadequate.

Main point 1: The current system for recycling generates low participation by citizens.

Main point 2: Each community in our area has its own recycling plan and system.

Main point 3: Recycling should be a regional, not a local, responsibility.

Some speakers like to use a problem-cause-solution format, making the second point the cause of the problem. This format is often useful because getting your listeners to understand the cause helps them reflect on the problem—making your solution seem plausible or even inevitable. In the following example, the first main point proves the problem, the second main point proves the cause, and the third main point offers a solution:

Thesis: United States presidents should be able to serve more than two terms.

Main point 1: Acceptance of foreign and domestic politics is harmed by changes in administrations.

Main point 2: Historically, our country's greatest periods of weakness have occurred with changes in the presidency.

Main point 3: The American people should choose whether a president is worthy of serving up to four consecutive terms.

This type of format tends to work particularly well when you are presenting a proposition of policy because it often proposes a course of action or a series of steps to achieve resolution.

Refutational Organizational Pattern

If people in your audience have strong objections to a position you are promoting, you will be wise to present, and then refute, their arguments against your main point; it can be an effective way to engage, if not fully persuade, an audience (Allen, 1991; O'Keefe, 1999).

⬙ When speaking about recycling, you might use the problem-solution pattern to clearly establish the problem before persuading your audience with a solution.

In the **refutational organizational pattern**, speakers begin by presenting main points that are opposed to their own position and then follow them with main points that support their own position. Though you can use this pattern when the opposing side has weak arguments that you can easily attack, it is to your advantage to select—and then disprove—the strongest points that support the opposing position (DiSanza & Legge, 2002). This may win over uncertain audience members or even those who initially disagree with your stance.

Culture and You

Have you ever sat through a lecture or class where the instructor offered a lesson affirming a point of view different from your own? Did the instructor acknowledge differing viewpoints? If so, what was your reaction to hearing the instructor's argument against your belief?

In your first main point, you should present the opposing position. Describe that claim and identify at least one key piece of evidence that supports it. In the second main point, you should present the possible effects or implications of that claim. Your third main point should present arguments and evidence for your own position. The final main point should contrast your position with the one that you started with and leave no doubt in the listeners' minds of the superiority of your viewpoint. The following example uses that strategy:

Thesis: Universities are justified in distributing condoms to students free of charge or at reduced prices.

Main point 1: Some parents claim that providing condoms is immoral and encourages casual sex among students.

Main point 2: Making condoms difficult to obtain will result in unwanted pregnancies and the spread of sexually transmitted diseases.

Main point 3: Sexual relations do occur among students at college.

Main point 4: If students will engage in sexual relations regardless of whether condoms are available, it is to everyone's advantage that they have ready access to prophylactics so they can do so safely.

The use of this format with a hostile audience can actually help you build credibility. Having established a sense of respect and goodwill between speaker and audience by acknowledging opposing points, you can then move on to explain the reasons you believe, nonetheless, that your thesis is true.

Comparative Advantage Pattern

Another way to organize speech points is to show that your viewpoint is superior to others on the topic. This arrangement, called the **comparative advantage pattern**, is most effective when your audience is already aware of the issue or problem and agrees that a solution is needed. Because listeners are aware of the issue, you can skip over establishing its existence and

THINGS TO TRY

Check out a persuasive speech video. You can view one of the persuasive speeches available on VideoCentral at this book's accompanying Web site (if you have access), or you can check one out on YouTube. Listen to and watch the speech critically in light of what you have learned about persuasion. Does the speaker use a clear proposition of fact, value, or policy as a thesis statement? What do you feel the speaker is aiming at—influencing your beliefs, attitudes, or behavior? Maybe all three? Is the speaker's use of rhetorical proofs effective? Consider the elements we have discussed: ethos (character), logos (reasoning), and pathos (emotion).

move directly to favorably comparing your position with the alternatives. With this strategy, you are assuming that your audience is open to various alternative solutions.

To maintain your credibility, it is important that you identify alternatives that your audience is familiar with as well as those that are supported by opposing interests. If you omit familiar alternatives, your listeners will wonder if you are fully informed on the topic and become skeptical of your comparative alternative as well as your credibility. The final step in a comparative advantage speech is to drive home the unique advantages of your option relative to competing options with brief but compelling evidence.

> *Thesis:* New members of our hospital's board of directors must be conflict free.
>
> *Main point 1:* Justin Davis is an officer in two other organizations.
>
> *Main point 2:* Vivian Alvarez will spend six months next year in London.
>
> *Main point 3:* Lillian Rosenthal's husband served as our director two years ago.
>
> *Main point 4:* Sam Dhatri has no potential conflicts for service.

Monroe's Motivated Sequence

In Chapter 12, we gave you a brief introduction to Alan Monroe's *motivated sequence pattern* for organizing your speech. It is a time-tested variant of the problem-solution pattern and has proved quite effective for persuasive speaking, particularly when you want your audience to do something—buy a product or donate time or money to a cause, for example. We'll elaborate on Monroe's five-step sequence here:

> *Step 1: Attention.* The attention step gets the audience interested in listening to your speech. It often highlights how the speech will be relevant to them.
>
> > It's two in the morning and you're staring at a blank screen on your computer. You've got a term paper for your history class and a lab report to finish, but these aren't what have you worried right now. It's figuring out your résumé—how to take your work, personal, and educational experiences and cram them all onto one page.
>
> *Step 2: Need.* This step allows you to identify a need or problem that matters to your audience. You want to show that this issue should be addressed.

> > Each person in this room will be applying for internships and jobs; such positions are highly competitive. Your résumé, for better or worse, will make the first impression on your potential employer.
>
> *Step 3: Satisfaction.* The satisfaction step allows you to show your audience the solution that you have identified to meet the problem or need addressed in step 2. This step is crucial as you are offering the audience members a proposal to reinforce or change their attitudes, beliefs, or behavior regarding the problem or need at hand.
>
> > Visiting our college's Office of Career Services is a great way to get help and direction for your résumé. The professionals employed there will be able to help make your job application materials stand out while also making the process seem less overwhelming.
>
> *Step 4: Visualization.* As its name implies, the visualization step helps your audience see how your proposed solution might play out and how they might benefit.
>
> > Instead of sitting at your computer at 2 A.M., you could be sitting with Tamela, a career counselor, at 2 P.M. as she makes suggestions for formatting your résumé or asks you questions about your past work experiences in order to highlight achievements that you had never even thought to mention.
>
> *Step 5: Action.* This final step clarifies what you want your audience members to do. This may involve reconsidering their attitudes, beliefs, or behavior.
>
> > Make an appointment with a career counselor today. Don't wait—you need those early morning hours for that history term paper, not for your résumé!

Now that you've considered organizational patterns and you have a solid grasp on how to handle

What About You?

}

Assessing Your Persuasive Speech

As you prepare and rehearse your persuasive speech, you will do well to remember the main points we developed in this chapter. They will guide you and help you approach your audience competently. Use the following questions to assess your speech honestly. You may also ask your friends, family, or roommates to assess your speech using these questions if you are rehearsing in front of them.

1. Have you selected a topic about which audience members can have a reasonable disagreement? Is it a topic that allows you to influence attitudes, beliefs, or behaviors?

2. Have you developed your thesis statement as a proposition of fact, value, or policy?

3. Have you assessed your audience's disposition and needs? Have you considered what is most relevant to them?

4. Have you worked to ensure that your speech—and your delivery—will help the audience engage in central processing?

5. Do you demonstrate credibility to your audience? Have you effectively worked goodwill, trustworthiness, homophily, and likability into your delivery?

6. Have you used solid reasoning in your argument?

7. Have you effectively made use of emotion in your speech? Is it appropriately supported by logic and credibility?

8. Have you checked (and rechecked) your speech for logical fallacies? Have you addressed and removed any that you've identified?

9. Have you selected an appropriate organizational pattern for your persuasive speech? Is the organization clear and understandable to your listeners during practice sessions?

10. Do you make effective use of presentation aids throughout your speech? Do the aids help you achieve your persuasive goals?

If you cannot answer "yes" to these questions, then you will likely benefit from additional research and rehearsal time. Remember, the more you employ these tips and guidelines, the more successful you will be at persuading your audience—and hopefully teaching them something that they will use and apply in their own lives.

persuasive speaking, let's take a look at a sample speech by Una Chua from Tufts University (see p. 352). In this speech, Una is persuading her audience to recognize the problem of cyberbullying and explaining how listeners can address and prevent it. Organiza-tionally, the speech is arranged along the lines of the problem-cause-solution pattern. Note that Una uses a variety of sources to support her arguments. Be sure to check out Una's reference list as well as her speaking outline, both of which follow the speech sample.

Preventing Cyberbullying

UNA CHUA
Tufts University

On the evening of September 22, 2010, Rutgers University freshman Tyler Clementi updated his Facebook status: "Jumping off the gw [George Washington] Bridge sorry." A few hours later, he did just that. But what would cause Clementi, recognized as a bright student and talented musician with a promising future, to take his own life? The answer, unhappily, involves two bullies and a webcam.

According to a *New York Times* report, Clementi's roommate and a female acquaintance stand accused of invasion of privacy. The charge? Using a webcam to view and transmit private images of Clementi in an intimate encounter with another young man. Tyler Clementi's story is tragic, but it's not an isolated event. You may recall an *ABC News* report on March 29, 2010, regarding the January 2010 suicide of Phoebe Prince. She was a fifteen-year-old high school student from Massachusetts who hanged herself after months of torment from other teens via text messages and social-networking sites. ▪

What is going on here? ▪ In a word—it's cyberbullying.

My name is Una Chua, and I'm here today to confront the growing problem of electronic harassment and to persuade you to fight cyberbullying so that you don't have to endure the kind of pain and humiliation experienced by Tyler Clementi. ▪ I'll start with a look at the various forms cyberbullying takes and describe the scope of the problem. ▪ Next, I'll consider what causes cyberbullies to act as they do and explore the conditions that make this alarming crime so easy to commit. I will also show you how you and your loved ones can stay safe—both by carefully guarding your personal information and by actively thwarting cyberbullies and taking a stand against them. Finally, should you or someone you know become a victim, I want you to be able to respond constructively. All of these steps will make the Internet a safer place for all members of your community to enjoy.

As you can imagine from the heartbreaking stories I've shared about Tyler Clementi and Phoebe Prince, cyberbullying poses serious mental-health risks to the nation's children, teens, and young adults. The Cyberbullying Research Center, a leading resource on the topic, ▪ defines *cyberbullying* as "willful and repeated harm inflicted through the use of computers, cell phones, and other electronic devices." ▪ Cyberbullying can take many forms, including the following: posting or sending harassing messages via Web sites, blogs, or text messages; posting embarrassing or private photos of someone without permission; recording or videotaping someone and sharing it without permission; and creating fake Web sites or social-networking profiles in someone else's name to humiliate them. Often these acts are done anonymously. School psychologists Ted Feinberg and Nicole Robey, writing

▪ Begins speech with several dramatic examples that capture audience's attention

▪ Introduces topic with rhetorical question

▪ Sets up organizational pattern of speech, indicating she will describe problem, review its causes, and offer solutions

▪ Previews main points

▪ Qualifies source and demonstrates its credibility

▪ Begins body of speech by ensuring audience knows what *cyberbullying* means in *Education Digest*, further explain that cyberbullying can involve stalking, threats, harassment, impersonation, humiliation, trickery, and exclusion.

Cyberbullying is a fairly recent social problem, but a substantial body of research has already formed around it. ■ The research paints a chilling picture. According to the Cyberbullying Research Center, about 20 percent of the over 4,400 randomly selected eleven- to eighteen-year-old students surveyed in 2010 said that they were repeatedly picked on by another person or persons online, via e-mail or through text messages. About 10 percent said that in addition to being victims, they had been cyberbullies themselves. Similarly, a 2010 study published in the *American Journal of Orthopsychiatry* found that of the more than two thousand teenagers questioned, 49.5 percent indicated that they had been the victims of cyberbullying, and 33.7 percent confessed to bullying others online.

Whether as victims, victimizers, or both, we see that many young people are touched by the problem of cyberbullying. What does the research say about the causes of cyberbullying? What motivates the cyberbully, and under what conditions is cyberbullying most likely to occur? ■

Sadly enough, one explanation for the motivation behind cyberbullying is that the bully wishes merely to "joke around." The National Crime Prevention Council, a leading anticrime public service organization, ■ reports on its Web site that 81 percent of a nationally representative sample of youths said that others cyberbully because they think it's "funny." In other words, despite the potentially disastrous consequences for victims, the cyberbully's harassing text messages and cruel Facebook wall postings are meant simply as a "joke."

In a lot of cases, underlying this drive to amuse oneself at another's expense is an insecure sense of self. Insecurity, combined with a tendency toward aggressiveness, appears to characterize many cyberbullies, according to researchers Sameer Hinduja and Justin Patchin of the Cyberbullying Research Center. For the bullies, the act of harassing other people serves as an outlet for their aggression and makes them feel at least momentarily powerful.

For many bullies, then, wanting to feel powerful and superior to someone else appears to be a prime motivation to bully. But what are the conditions that allow cyberbullies to act on this drive? ■

According to the research, a lack of parental supervision and the ability to be anonymous provide especially fertile ground. As television talk show host Dr. Phil McGraw notes in his June 24, 2010, congressional testimony—and as many of us have experienced in our own lives—children and teens often know more about texting and social networking than parents and adult guardians. This makes their Internet and cell phone activities difficult for parents to regulate. One study by the National Crime Prevention Council found that a nationally representative sample of 80 percent of youths in the United States do not have enforced rules about Internet use at home, or the rules are easy to get around.

A second, particularly powerful condition enabling cyberbullying is anonymity. Cyberbullies feel emboldened by their ability to do nasty things

■ Transition effectively alerts audience to what's coming next

■ Moves from describing problem to exploring its causes

■ Lends credibility and context to source by noting it is a "leading anticrime public service organization"

■ Transition summarizes previous point and previews next one

with impunity because they believe no one will know they are the culprits. In his book *Girls on the Edge: The Four Factors Driving the New Crisis for Girls*, psychologist and pediatrician Leonard Sax describes it this way:

> Twenty years ago, if a girl wanted to spread rumors about another girl, everybody would know who was doing it. That knowledge constrained what the bully might say. If you got too nasty, your nastiness could reflect badly on you. But now, you can pretend to be a boy who's just received sexual services from Leeanne, then post something about Leeanne online, and nobody will ever know that you are actually a girl who invented the whole story to make Leeanne look bad.

In essence, the anonymity of the Internet makes cyberbullying easy and, in many circumstances, difficult to catch and stop.

By now, you may be feeling that we Internet users are doomed to be victims of cruel torment at the hands of anonymous bullies who will never suffer the consequences of their actions. This is hardly the case, however. You can take steps to protect yourself. ▪

▪ Moves on to solution part of organizational pattern

For one, you can be vigilant about safeguarding your personal information. Our school's information technology office lists the following advice on its Web site. First, never, ever leave your laptops unattended. Second, keep your account passwords and social security numbers totally private. Third, use the highest privacy settings on your social-networking sites. Finally, think carefully about the types of pictures of yourself and your friends that you post online, and restrict views of them to "friends" only. Each of these steps can prevent bullies from having the ability to pose as you in order to harm or embarrass you in some way.

In addition to zealously guarding your personal information, you can help combat cyberbullying by being a voice against it whenever you see it happening.

Don't Stand By, Stand Up! is a student-led organization that was formed soon after Tyler Clementi's suicide and is featured on Facebook. The group urges Internet users to take a stand against cyberbullying by recognizing that bullies—in all forms—rarely succeed in their harassment without the support and attention of bystanders. The National Crime Prevention Council site gives more specific tips on how to thwart a bully's attempts. One is to refuse to pass bullying messages along to others—whether via text or photo messaging, social networking, or e-mailing—and another is to let the original sender know that you find the message offensive or stupid. Remember, if bullies bully because they think their behavior is harmless and funny, then it makes sense to tell them that you find their messages to be quite the opposite.

Despite your best efforts to keep your personal information private and speak out against cyberbullying, you may still become a victim. I don't say this to scare you but rather to advise you on what to do if it does happen to you or to someone you know. In this event, consider the "stop, block, and tell" method of combating cyberbullying.

Online safety expert Parry Aftab, in a July 28, 2009, interview for PBS's *Frontline*, advises victims to use the stop, block, and tell method to respond to bullying behaviors directed against them. While often directed at younger children, this method proves to be useful for victims of any age, as explained on the Don't Stand By, Stand Up! Web site. The site advises that after receiving a bullying message you should first "stop." In other words, do nothing. Take five minutes to cool down, take a walk, breathe deeply, or do whatever helps to calm down the understandable anger you are feeling. Then "block": prevent the cyberbully from having any future communication with you. This may mean anything from removing the person from your social-networking sites' friend lists to having your cell phone service provider block the bully from being able to call or text you. The third step is to "tell" someone about the abuse without embarrassment or shame. For example, you might call campus security or confide in a counselor at the health center. Similarly, parents should encourage their children to report bullying to a trusted adult, whether a parent, teacher, principal, or guidance counselor.

Today, we've ventured into the very real—and very dangerous—world of cyberbullying. ■ We've seen cyberbullying's negative impact on children, teens, and young adults. We've analyzed the insecure and aggressive personality traits that characterize cyberbullies and looked at two key conditions that make it easier for the cyberbully to operate: lack of parental supervision and the ability to be anonymous. We've also seen how you can counter this potentially deadly problem.

■ *Signals conclusion of speech with summary of main points*

Be vigilant about protecting your personal information.

Speak out against cyberbullying.

And if you or someone you know experiences cyberbullying, react constructively with the stop, block, and tell method.

Cyberbullying isn't just someone else's problem. It's very likely something you need to guard against, now or in the future. I urge each of you to make a personal commitment to do your part to combat the problem. Refuse to stay silent in the face of cyberbullying. Resolve that you will never send or pass along cyberbullying messages of any kind, no matter how harmless they might seem. This act alone can make a world of difference in the life of an intended victim. After all, wouldn't you want someone to take this simple step for you? ■ In addition, voice your concerns at the campus and community levels. For example, a student group from our university recently organized a candlelight vigil to remember those who fell victim to bullying and discrimination. Even if you're not interested in becoming a member, you can support events that bring cyberbullying—and its serious consequences—to light.

■ *Issues call to action*

We must never forget Tyler Clementi, Phoebe Prince, and the other young lives cut short by unnecessary bullying. Who knows? Your best friend, your younger brother, or your son could just as easily have been on that bridge that fateful September evening. ■

■ *Stressing personal relevance leaves listeners with something to think about*

References

Ensuring Student Cyber Safety: Hearing before the U.S. House Education Subcommittee to Examine Cyber Safety for Students of the U.S. House of Representatives Education and Labor Committee. (2010, June 24). (Testimony of Dr. Phillip C. McGraw, Ph.D.). Retrieved from http://republicans.edlabor.house.gov/UploadedFiles/06.24.10_mcgraw.pdf

Feinberg, T., & Robey, N. (2009). Cyberbullying. *Education Digest, 74*(7), 26–31.

Foderaro, L. W. (2010, September 29). Private moment made public, then a fatal jump. *New York Times*. Retrieved from http://www.nytimes.com/2010/09/30/nyregion/30suicide.html

Goldman, R. (2010, March 29). Teens indicted after allegedly taunting girl who hanged herself. *ABC News*. Retrieved from http://abcnews.go.com/Technology/TheLaw/teens-charged-bullying-mass-girl-kill/story?id=10231357

Hinduja, S., & Patchin, J. W. (2010a). Cyberbullying: Identification, prevention, and response. *Cyberbullying Research Center Fact Sheet*. Retrieved from http://www.cyberbullying.us/Cyberbullying_Identification_Prevention_Response_Fact_Sheet.pdf

Hinduja, S., & Patchin, J. W. (2010b). Cyberbullying research summary: Cyberbullying and self-esteem. *Cyberbullying Research Center Fact Sheet*. Retrieved from http://www.cyberbullying.us/cyberbullying_and_self_esteem_research_fact_sheet.pdf

Mishna, F., Cook, C., Gadella, T., Daciuk, J., & Solomon, S. (2010). Cyberbullying behaviors among middle and high school students. *American Journal of Orthopsychiatry, 80*(3), 362–374.

Sax, L. (2010). *Girls on the edge: The four factors driving the new crisis for girls.* New York, NY: Basic Books.

Stop, block, and tell. (2009, July 28). *Relationships: Predators and bullies.* Video retrieved from http://www.pbs.org/wgbh/pages/frontline/digitalnation/relationships/predators-bullies/stop-block-and-tell.html?play

Stop cyberbullying. (n.d.). Retrieved from http://www.stopcyberbullying.org/take_action/stop_block_and_tell.html

Stop cyberbullying before it starts. (n.d.). *National Crime Prevention Council.* Retrieved from http://www.ncpc.org/resources/files/pdf/bullying/cyberbullying.pdf

Speaking Outline

Preventing Cyberbullying

UNA CHUA
Tufts University

General Purpose: To persuade

Specific Purpose: To persuade my audience to understand and confront the growing problem of electronic harassment.

Thesis Statement: I'm here today to confront the growing problem of electronic harassment and to persuade you to fight cyberbullying.

Introduction

I. **Attention Getter:** Relate tragic stories of cyberbullying.
   A. 9/22/10: Rutgers U freshman Tyler Clementi (TC) updates Facebook (FB) "Jumping off gw [George Washington] Bridge sorry." He does.
   B. TC's roommate and female friend accused of invasion of privacy. Used webcam to transmit private images. (Foderaro, *NYT*, Sept. 29, 2010)
   C. 15-year-old high school student from MA, Phoebe Prince (PP), commits suicide after text/social-networking torment. (Goldman, *ABC News*, March 29, 2010)

II. Here to confront electronic harassment and fight cyberbullying (CB)

III. Introduce self

IV. Will discuss forms, scope, and causes of CB; conditions allowing it; staying safe from and responding to CB

Body

I. Forms of CB
   A. "Willful and repeated harm inflicted through the use of computers, cell phones, and other electronic devices" (CB Research Center)
   B. Posting/sending harassing messages via Web sites, blogs, texts
   C. Posting embarrassing photos w/o permission
   D. Recording/videotaping someone and sharing w/o permission
   E. Creating fake Web sites/profiles to humiliate
   F. CB involves stalking, threats, harassment, impersonation, humiliation, trickery, exclusion. (Feinberg & Robey, *Education Digest*)

Transition: CB = recent problem with a substantial body of research.

II. Scope of CB
   A. CB Research Center's 2010 study
      1. 20% of 4,400 11–18-year-old students experienced CB.
      2. 10% initiated CB.

   B. *American Journal of Orthopsychiatry* (2010) study
      1. 49.5% of 2,000 teens experienced CB.
      2. 33.7% initiated CB.

Transition: Many lives are touched by CB. But why? What are its causes?

III. Causes of CB
   A. Joking around
      1. 81% of youths said CB is funny. (National Crime Prevention Council)
      2. FB postings and texts are meant as a joke.
   B. Bully insecurity
      1. Insecurity and aggressiveness = CB behavior. (Hinduja & Patchin, CB Research Center)
      2. CB makes bullies feel powerful.

Transition: What conditions allow CB to happen?

IV. Conditions allowing CB
   A. Lack of supervision
      1. Kids know more about texting and social networking than adults do. (McGraw, congressional testimony, June 24, 2010)
      2. Difficult to track kids' Internet and cell phone activities
      3. 80% of youths don't have rules for home Internet use. (National Crime Prevention Council)
   B. Anonymity
      1. Psychologist/pediatrician Leonard Sax: *Girls on the Edge: The Four Factors Driving the New Crisis for Girls* [**Read extended quote from transparency.**]
      2. Makes CB difficult to catch/stop

Transition: Are we doomed to suffer? No. Take steps to protect yourself.

V. Steps for staying safe from CB
   A. Safeguard personal information (school IT office).
      1. Never leave laptop unattended.
      2. Keep passwords and SSN private.
      3. Use privacy settings.
      4. Post photos with caution.

B. Be a voice against CB.
  1. Don't Stand By, Stand Up! (formed in honor of TC on FB): bullies don't succeed without help.
  2. Don't pass on CB messages and inform the senders that their messages are offensive/stupid. (National Crime Prevention Council)

Transition: You may still become a CB victim.

VI. **[Show poster board.]** Responding to CB: use "stop, block, tell." (Parry Aftab, July 28, 2009, *Frontline* interview)
  A. Stop: take 5, cool down, walk, breathe deeply.
  B. Block: prevent communication—remove bully from social-networking lists and block cell #.
  C. Tell: campus security, counselor, etc. Children tell parent, teacher, principal.

Transition/Internal Summary: We've seen CB's negative impact, analyzed causes/conditions, discussed countering CB (privacy, speak out, "stop, block, tell").

Conclusion

I. CB is not someone else's problem.

II. Call to action: make a personal commitment to combat CB.
  A. Refuse to be silent.
  B. Never pass along CB messages.
  C. Voice your concerns at the campus and community levels.

III. Don't forget TC, PP, and other CB victims. Your loved one could be next.

LearningCurve
bedfordstmartins.com/commandyou

Jamie Oliver's TED Prize–Winning Wish

Back to } At the beginning of this chapter, we discussed celebrity chef Jamie Oliver's TED speech, in which he presented his wish to educate children about food (Oliver, 2010). Let's consider his speech in light of what we've learned in this chapter.

- Oliver has done his share of informative speaking: as a celebrity chef and star of *Food Revolution*, he gives regular cooking demonstrations that are designed to teach techniques and provide information about food. But this speech, and much of the speaking he does as an activist, is persuasive in nature—he wants to teach people to use the information he provides to change their lives and improve their health, as well as the health of the public at large.

- Oliver organizes his speech with a problem-cause-solution pattern. First, he identifies the problem, offering startling statistics and compelling personal stories. He then details the causes behind the problem before moving on to solutions, such as giving people the proper information and tools to change their eating behavior and take charge of their lives. He ends with his "wish," his purpose for speaking, hoping to motivate his audience to make it a reality.

- Oliver successfully uses presentation aids during his speech: photos of people who are dying from obesity-related diseases, a graphic detailing deaths from diet-related illnesses like type 2 diabetes and heart disease, and for maximum impact, a wheelbarrow filled with sugar cubes to demonstrate the amount of sugar an average child consumes in five years by drinking just two containers of chocolate milk per day.

- Oliver considers his audience when he speaks. He knows that the crowd at his TED speech is receptive to his message; they gave him the award, after all. His message is therefore directed at broad solutions at the institutional level—changes he knows the TED audience can help enact. When speaking to individuals who are less educated about or interested in food and nutrition, he would likely focus on change at the personal level.

Your Reference

} A Study Tool

Now that you have finished reading this chapter, you can

Define the goals of persuasive speaking:

- **Coercion** involves threats, intimidation, or violence (p. 336).
- **Persuasive speaking** uses the process of **persuasion** to influence **attitudes**, **beliefs**, and **behavior** (pp. 336–337).

Develop a persuasive topic and thesis:

- Choose a topic that is controversial, and aim to create change in the audience (p. 337).
- Thesis statements are often given as a proposition, a statement of your viewpoint on an issue (p. 337).
- A **proposition of fact** is a claim of what is or what is not and addresses how people perceive reality (pp. 337–338).
- A **proposition of value** makes claims about something's worth (p. 338).
- A **proposition of policy** concerns what should happen and makes claims about what goal, policy, or course of action should be pursued (p. 338).

Evaluate your listeners and tailor your speech to them:

- **Social judgment theory** holds that your ability to persuade depends on audience members' attitudes toward your topic (p. 339).
- A **receptive audience** agrees with you (p. 339).
- A **neutral audience** neither supports nor opposes you (p. 339).
- A **hostile audience** opposes your message (p. 339).
- **Latitude of acceptance and rejection** refers to the range of positions on a topic that are acceptable or unacceptable to your audience, influenced by their original or **anchor position** (pp. 339–340).
- Maslow's **hierarchy of needs** holds that our most basic needs must be met before we can worry about needs farther up the hierarchy (pp. 340–341).
- The **Elaboration Likelihood Model (ELM)** highlights the importance of relevance to persuasion and holds that listeners will process persuasive messages by one of two routes: **central processing** (deep, motivated thinking) or **peripheral processing** (unmotivated, less critical thought) (pp. 341–342).

Explain three forms of rhetorical proof:

- The speaker's moral character, or **ethos**, influences the audience's reaction to the message (p. 343).

- **Logos** refers to appeals to the audience's **reasoning** ◎, judgments based on facts and inferences (pp. 343–344).
  - **Inductive reasoning** involves drawing general conclusions from specific evidence; **deductive reasoning** applies general arguments to specific cases (pp. 343–344).
  - A **syllogism** is a three-line deductive argument, drawing a conclusion from two general premises (p. 344).
- **Pathos** appeals to the listeners' emotions (pp. 344–345).

Identify the logical fallacies ◎, deceptive forms of reasoning:

- The **bandwagon fallacy**: a statement is considered true because it is popular (p. 345).
- **Reduction to the absurd**: an argument is pushed beyond its logical limits (pp. 345–346).
- The **red herring fallacy**: irrelevant information is used to divert the direction of the argument (p. 346).
- The *ad hominem* fallacy: a personal attack; the focus is on a person rather than on the issue (p. 346).
- **Begging the question**: advancing an argument that cannot be proved because there is no valid evidence (p. 346).
- **Either-or fallacy**: only two alternatives are presented, omitting other alternatives (p. 346).
- **Appeal to tradition**: "that's the way it has always been" is the only reason given (p. 347).
- The **slippery slope fallacy**: one event is presented as the result of another, without showing proof (p. 347).

Choose an appropriate organizational strategy for your speech:

- The *problem-solution pattern* proves the existence of a problem and then presents a solution (pp. 347–348).
- The **refutational organizational pattern** presents the main points of the opposition to an argument and then refutes them. This works well when the opposing argument is weak (pp. 348–349).
- The **comparative advantage pattern** tells why your viewpoint is superior to other viewpoints on the issue (pp. 349–350).
- Monroe's *motivated sequence pattern* is a five-step process that begins with arousing listeners' attention and ends with calling for action (p. 350).

 Look for **LearningCurve** throughout the appendix to help you review.
bedfordstmartins.com/commandyou

A } Competent Interviewing

J on Stewart interviews plenty of celebrities, politicians, and authors on *The Daily Show*. But some of the show's interviews are conducted by the show's correspondents, with a more satirical or absurd edge. For example, following a series of 2009 business scandals, correspondent John Oliver interviewed a Columbia University School of Business professor as well as MBA candidates at Harvard and MIT about the teaching of ethics in American business schools. Specifically, he wanted to know what future MBAs were learning about ethics and whether they would be willing to commit to a new business ethics oath being circulated by students from the Harvard Business School.

The interviews were presented in the serious tone of a nightly newscast. But the content was

anything but serious: for example, after the professor described the ethics program at Columbia, noting that they've been teaching ethics for decades, Oliver responded with sarcasm: "Would you say you're good at your job?" (*The Daily Show*, 2009). In the early days of *The Daily Show*, interviewees were sometimes taken by surprise when the correspondent pieced together clips that made them, or their cause, look foolish. But today, most interviewees are in on the joke. The MBA students Oliver interviewed were all *Daily Show* fans and were well aware of how their refusal to take the ethics oath might come off after the footage got through the show's editors and producers. "We all knew what we were going into and had fun with it," said one participant, Roy Ben-Ami. "Despite the fact that this is indeed a fake news show, it does talk about real issues and makes a point about them" (Marcott, 2009).

After you have finished reading this appendix, you will be able to

Define the nature of interviews.

Outline the different types of interviews.

Describe the three parts of an interview: opening, questions, and conclusion.

Devise an interview strategy from the interviewer's point of view.

Prepare for the role of interviewee.

Secure job interviews and manage them with confidence.

A lthough *The Daily Show*'s correspondents' "reports" are not serious, they do follow many important rules for interviews. From John Oliver and company, for example, we can learn about the roles of the interviewer and interviewee and the effects of questions and answers. In this appendix, we examine interviews from a communication standpoint—how they relate to other forms of communication, what kinds of factors are at work in an interview situation, and how all people, from recent college graduates to newscasters, can improve their interviewing skills.

The Nature of Interviews

Although interviewing is not exactly like grabbing lunch with one of your friends, the same principles that apply to all forms of communication are also at work in an interview, with some important differences.

An **interview** is an interaction between two parties that is deliberate and purposeful for at least one of the parties involved. By nature, interviews are more structured and goal-driven than other forms of communication, and they are a form of discourse that is planned, dyadic, and interactive (O'Hair, Friedrich, & Dixon, 2007).

- **Interviews are planned.** Interviews have a purpose that goes beyond the establishment and development of a relationship. At least one of the parties has a predetermined reason for initiating the interview (for example, to gather information).

- **Interviews are goal-driven.** Because a goal exists in advance of the interaction, at least one of the participants plans a strategy for initiating, conducting, and concluding the interview.

- **Interviews are structured.** The primary goal of an interview is almost always defined at the beginning of the meeting, something that's rarely true of a conversation with a friend. Interview relationships are more formally structured, and clear status differences often exist. One party usually expects to exert more control than the other.

- **Interviews are dyadic.** Like other forms of interpersonal communication, the interview is dyadic, meaning that it involves two parties. In some instances, a "party" consists of more than one person, as when survey researchers conduct group interviews or when job applicants appear before a panel of interviewers. In such situations, even though a number of individuals are involved, there are only two parties (interviewers and interviewees), each with a role to play.

- **Interviews are interactive.** Interviews involve two-way interactions in which both parties take turns in speaking and listening roles, with a heavy dependence on questions and answers. Although most interviews occur face to face, interactions over the phone or via a videoconference are also considered interactive discourse.

Think back to Jon Stewart and company. The correspondents' interviews are not only dyadic and interactive but also highly planned. They write questions ahead of time, based on the interviewee's views

🔹 All interviews, whether a question-and-answer session with *E!* on the red carpet or a serious job interview, are goal-driven, as well as dyadic and interactive in nature.

and background, and they structure their interviews in a way that helps Stewart and company achieve their goal: a hilarious spoof on key topics.

LearningCurve
bedfordstmartins.com/commandyou

Types of Interviews

What type of scene plays out in your mind when you think of the word *interview*? Maybe you start sweating thinking about an upcoming job interview for a position that you really want or remembering interviews for college. But interviewing encompasses much more than just getting a job or getting into the right school. In this section, we look at the different

types of interviews that play a role in most of our lives (Stewart & Cash, 2011).

The Information-Gathering Interview

In the film *Juno*, sixteen-year-old Juno MacGuff sits in the expensively furnished living room of Mark and Vanessa Loring, a couple interested in adopting Juno's unborn child. Vanessa and her adoption lawyer pepper Juno with questions like "How far along are you?" and "You really think you're going to go ahead with this?" They're trying to obtain *information* from Juno by collecting attitudes, opinions, facts, data, and

{ **Interviewing encompasses much more than just getting a job or getting into the right school.** }

experiences through an **information-gathering interview**. We take part in, or are exposed to, the results of such interviews every day; perhaps you've compiled a survey about experiences with campus parking, or maybe you've initiated information gathering when you asked your communication professor about career possibilities. In all these instances, the information-gathering interview serves to transfer knowledge from one party to the other.

🔻 On the popular A&E documentary series *Hoarders*, counselors work with compulsive hoarders to assess the case and devise a treatment plan.

> ### Culture and You
>
> Have you ever imagined interviewing a particular celebrity, political leader, or historical figure? If you were given such an opportunity, what would your goals be for the interview? What kind of questions would you ask?

The Appraisal Interview

In just about every career—including your academic career—**performance appraisals** are a regular part of reviewing your accomplishments and developing goals for the future. In most corporate environments, a performance appraisal is a highly structured routine dictated by company policies, involving a written appraisal and a one-on-one interview between a supervisor and an employee. But in other less structured performance appraisals, you might meet with your professor to discuss a project or paper or lobby for a change in your grade. Although being evaluated can be stressful, the appraisal can offer insight into strengths as well as weaknesses. In other words, if the appraisal interview offers reassurance about what you're doing well and gives some guidance for improvement or growth, it is less threatening and more useful (Culbert, 2010).

The Problem-Solving Interview

Of course, not every appraisal interview is positive. Sometimes a **problem-solving interview** is needed to

deal with problems, tensions, or conflicts. If you've ever seen an episode of A&E's *Intervention* or *Hoarders*, you've seen this type of interview in action. Typically, friends and family contact a counselor to help them deal with a loved one's addictive behavior, whether it's drug abuse, video game addiction, or an inability to discard personal items. The counselor works with the family, asking questions, gathering information, and formulating a plan or solution before the official intervention, when the counselor, friends, and family all confront the loved one.

Problem-solving interviews can also occur in the workplace or even in medical situations. For example, your primary care physician interviews you about problems or concerns in your life that may affect your physical health; you should prepare ahead of time for the interview and ask questions that will help you and the doctor understand your health better (Dwamena, Mavis, Holmes-Rovner, Walsh, & Loyson, 2009). Of course, during the interview, you should always volunteer information to help solve the problem (Coulehan & Block, 2006).

The Exit Interview

Hiring and training new people is an expensive process in terms of both time and money, so most organizations want to keep good employees. By conducting **exit interviews** with employees who opt to leave the company, employers can identify organizational problems—such as poor management style, noncompetitive salary, or weak employee benefits—that might affect employee retention.

The Persuasive Interview

At times the goal of an interview is not merely to inform or gather information. In a **persuasive interview**, questions are designed to elicit some change in the interviewee's behavior or opinions. Some political surveys, for example, are aimed at securing your support for (or against) a particular candidate or cause. You might also do some persuasive interviewing to convince others to give blood during a campus campaign or to vote for your candidate in a campus, local, or national election.

The Service-Oriented Interview

Did your computer freak out and delete all your programs? Do you have a roach problem? Have you ever found unauthorized charges on your credit card bill? If any of these things have ever happened to you, you are probably intimately familiar with "help desks" or customer service lines. Representatives contacted at these organizations will conduct **service-oriented interviews**, or helping interviews, designed to cull information and provide advice, service, or support based on that information.

The Selection Interview

If you're a fan of *South Park*, you might remember the episode in which Stan, Kyle, and Cartman hold a series of interviews and competitions to fill the open slot in their group left void by Kenny's demise. Silly as it may be, it's an example of a **selection interview**, the primary goal of which is to secure or fill a position within an organization. Selection interviews usually involve recruiting, screening, hiring, and placing new candidates (Baker & Spier, 1990; Joyce, 2008). Members of an organization (such as a university, company, sorority, fraternity, or volunteer organization)

◊ Parodying the format of shows like *The Bachelor*, Cartman and the gang on *South Park* question and screen various secondary characters on the show, hoping to uncover the new Kenny.

and candidates evaluate one another by exchanging information to determine if they'd make a good match. Usually both parties want to make a good impression: the interviewer wants to persuade the interviewee about the value of the position or organization, while the interviewee wants to sell his or her unique qualities and abilities.

Technology and You

Have you ever been a part of an interview conducted virtually? What type of interview was it? Were there advantages to using technology rather than face-to-face interaction? What were the disadvantages?

The **job interview** is one of the most common types of selection interviews in business, government, and military organizations, with the end goal of filling a position of employment (DiSanza & Legge, 2002). Since job interviewing is usually very important to college students, we devote much of this chapter to helping you become more competent in this context.

LearningCurve
bedfordstmartins.com/commandyou

The Format of an Interview

Whether you are interviewing for a job, answering questions for a news reporter, or even watching competitors on a show like *The Apprentice*, you will note the same basic pattern: an opening, the questions, and a conclusion.

The Opening

Jay Leno's interviewees are always welcomed with a grand entrance and the audience clapping and cheering (Babad & Peer, 2010). But if you're not a movie star plugging your latest project, you probably won't have to worry about this. Your interviews will begin in a calmer manner, setting the tone for the discourse to follow. Before or just as the interview begins, you should always think about three interrelated issues:

- The *task*: the nature of this interview and how it will proceed
- The *relationship*: whether you like or trust the other party
- *Motivation*: what you hope to gain by participating in the interview

For example, Eva is doing a telephone survey on student attitudes about parking on campus. The students she calls want to know about the topic of the interview and how long it will take (the task). They want to know something about her and how the information she gathers will be used (the relationship). They want to know how they (or someone else) will benefit from participating in the interview (the motivation). Eva needs to plan what she can say or do at the *start* of the interview that is responsive to these needs (see Table A.1).

Table A.1 **Sample Interview Opening Techniques**

Goal	Description	Example
Clarify the *task*	Orient the interviewee, who may not be well informed about the reason for the interview.	"As you may know, we're looking for ways to increase productivity among our sales associates. I'm hoping you will give me information to jump-start this initiative."
Define the *relationship*	Make a connection to a third party respected by the interviewee if the interviewee doesn't know you and you want to put him or her at ease.	"I was referred to you by Liam Fitzpatrick, who told me that you've done great work for him in the past."
Determine the *motivation*	Request the interviewee's advice or assistance with regard to a problem.	"I'm hoping that you can help me get insight into the way things work between your division and marketing."

The Questions

Once you have set the stage for the interview with an appropriate opening, you need to develop the organizational plan for the body of the interview using questions and answers. The interviewer sets up the structure of the interview (identifying the purpose of the interview) and then solicits a response from the interviewee. This response then prompts reactions from the interviewer, and it just keeps building from there. To have the most effective and most successful interview possible, whether you're the interviewer or interviewee, you need to consider question type, impact, and sequence.

Types of Questions. The path of the interview is largely determined by the types of questions asked. Questions vary in two distinct ways: the amount of freedom the respondent has and how the questions relate to what has happened in the course of the interview.

{ **The path of the interview is largely determined by the types of questions asked.** }

First, questions vary in terms of how much leeway the interviewee has in generating responses. An **open question** gives the interviewee great freedom in terms of how to respond. Questions like "What's it like being a student here?" and "What issues will influence your decision to vote for one of the presidential candidates?" allow the interviewee to determine the amount and depth of information provided. Interviewers often ask open questions when the interviewee knows more about a topic than the interviewer does or to help the interviewee relax (there is no "correct" answer, so no answer is wrong).

In other situations, the interviewer will want a more direct answer. **Closed questions** give less freedom to the interviewee by restricting answer choices. For example, an interviewer conducting a survey of student attitudes toward parking on campus might ask more closed questions ("When do you arrive on campus?" "Where do you park?" "How long do you stay?"). The most closed form of a question is the **bipolar question**, for which there are only two possible responses, "yes" and "no" ("Do you normally eat breakfast?" "Do you own a car?" "Did you vote in the last election?"). Another possibility is to ask interviewees to respond on a scale, as with the question "How would you rate parking availability on campus on a scale of one to five?"

Questions also vary in terms of how they relate to what has happened so far in the interview. **Primary questions** introduce new topics; **secondary questions** seek clarification or elaboration of responses to primary questions. Thus, if you were interviewing an older family member, you might open an area of questioning by asking, "What can you tell me about my family history?" This primary question might then be followed by a number of

📍 Prospective students on a campus tour should ask their student guides open questions ("What's the social scene like?") and closed questions ("Is the dining hall open on the weekends?") to figure out what student life is *really* like.

Table A.2 Secondary Questions

Behavior	Definition	Example
Clarification	Directly requests more information about a response	"Could you tell me a little more about the reasons you chose to join the military after high school?"
Elaboration	Directly requests an extension of a response	"Are there any other specific features that you consider important in your search for a new house?"
Paraphrasing	Puts the response in the questioner's language in an attempt to establish understanding	"So, you're saying that the type of people you work with is more important to you than location?"
Encouragement	Uses brief sounds and phrases that indicate attentiveness to and interest in what the respondent is saying	"Uh-huh," "I see," "That's interesting," "Good," "Yes, I understand."
Summarizing	Summarizes several previous responses and seeks confirmation of the correctness of the summary	"Let's see if I've got it: your ideal job involves an appreciative boss, supportive colleagues, interesting work, and a location in a large metropolitan area?"
Clearinghouse	Asks if you have elicited all the important or available information	"Have I asked everything that I should have asked?"

Source: Labels and definitions from O'Hair, Friedrich, & Dixon (2007).

secondary questions, such as "How did my grand-parents meet?" and "How did they deal with the fact that their parents disapproved of their marriage?" Secondary questions can take a variety of forms. Some of the more common forms are illustrated in **Table A.2**.

Question Impact. In addition to considering question type, interviewers must also consider the likely impact of a question on the interviewee. The way in which a question is constructed can directly influence

the information received in response. A good question is clear, relevant, and unbiased. To create clear questions, consider the following criteria:

- Make questions understandable. Ask the classic and simple news reporter's questions—who, what, when, where, why, and how—before you proceed to more complex ones (Payne, 1951).
- Ensure that the wording of the questions is as direct and simple as possible. For example, asking "For whom did you vote in the last mayoral election?" will get you a more precise answer than asking "How do you vote?"
- Keep the questions short and to the point.

{ **A good question is clear, relevant, and unbiased.** }

- Phrase questions positively and remain civil (Ben-Porath, 2010). For example, asking "Have you ever voted in campus student government elections?" is clear and objective; using negative phrasing ("You haven't ever voted in the campus student government elections, have you?") can be confusing and, in some cases, may be unethical and biased (Doris, 1991).

Speaking of ethics, a question that suggests or implies the answer that is expected is called a **directed question**. Some directed questions are subtle in the direction they provide ("Wouldn't it be so much fun if we all got together to paint my apartment this weekend?"). These subtle directed questions are **leading questions**. Other directed questions are bolder in their biasing effect and are called **loaded questions** ("When was the last time you cheated on an exam?" which assumes, of course, that you *have* cheated). Questions that provide no hint to the interviewee concerning the expected response are **neutral questions**—for example, "What, if anything, is your attitude toward the fraternities and sororities on this campus?"

Ethics and You

Have you ever been asked unethical, biased, or uncivil questions in an interview? Did you ever, knowingly or unknowingly, ask these types of questions yourself? How can you deal with questions like these if you find yourself in that uncomfortable position?

Question Sequence. The order in which the interviewer asks questions can affect both the accomplishment of the interview's goals and the comfort level of the interviewee. There are three main "shapes" that guide the ordering of questions: the funnel, inverted funnel, and tunnel sequences.

THINGS TO TRY

Observe a press conference on television. Who is being interviewed? Who is conducting the interview? What is the goal of the press conference? How is control distributed? List five questions that are asked, and label them according to the types listed in this chapter (open, closed, bipolar, primary, secondary). Did the questioning involve a particular sequence (funnel, inverted funnel, tunnel)? What did you learn about this interview format by answering these questions?

In the **funnel sequence**, the interviewer starts with broad, open-ended questions (picture the big end of a funnel) and moves to narrower, more closed questions. The questions become more personal or more tightly focused as the interview progresses, giving the interviewee a chance to get comfortable with the topic and open up. The funnel sequence works best with respondents who feel comfortable with the topic and the interviewer.

- What do you think about children playing competitive sports? (general)
- So what disadvantages have you witnessed? (specific)

- What constraints would you advocate for young players? (very specific)

The **inverted funnel sequence** starts with narrow, closed questions and moves to more open-ended questions. The inverted funnel works best with interviewees who are emotional, reticent, or need help "warming up."

- Did you perform a Mozart piece for your piano recital in junior high school? (very specific)
- What other classical compositions are you comfortable playing? (specific)
- How did you feel about taking piano lessons as a child? (general)

In the **tunnel sequence**, all the questions are at one level. The tunnel sequence works particularly well in polls and surveys. A large tunnel would involve a series of broad, open-ended questions. A small tunnel (the more common form) would ask a series of narrow, closed questions, as in the following example:

- Have you attended any multicultural events on campus? (specific)
- Have you attended sports games or matches? (specific)
- Have you attended any guest lecturer series on campus? (specific)

The three sequences are depicted visually in **Figure A.1**.

Interviewers can put together the three sequences in various combinations over the course of an interview based on the goals for the interview, the direction the interview takes, and the comfort level of both parties involved.

The Conclusion

Once the purpose of the interview has been achieved, the interaction should come to a comfortable and satisfying close. This closing phase of the interview is especially important because it is likely to determine the impression the interviewee retains of the interview as a whole.

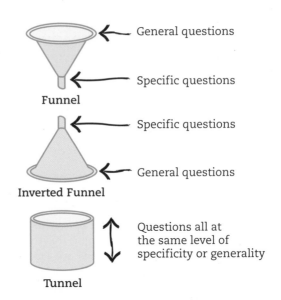

⬥ **Figure A.1** Funnel, Inverted Funnel, and Tunnel Sequences

There are important norms involved when individuals take leave of each other (Knapp, Hart, Friedrich, & Shulman, 1973), so in closing the interview, the interviewer needs to employ both verbal and nonverbal strategies to serve three important functions (Von Raffler-Engel, 1983):

- To *conclude*, or signal the end of the interview
- To *summarize*, or review the substantive conclusions produced by the interview
- To *support*, or express satisfaction with the interaction and project what will happen next

Table A.3 illustrates closing strategies that may help you conclude, summarize, and support. As these sample statements indicate, bringing the interview to a close is largely the responsibility of the interviewer. In the next section, look at how this and other responsibilities and roles are filled in a variety of interviewing situations.

LearningCurve
bedfordstmartins.com/commandyou

Table A.3 **Closing Strategies**

Behavior	Definition	Example
Declare the completion of the purpose or task.	The word *well* probably signals a close more than any other phrase; people automatically assume the end is near and prepare to take their leave.	"Well, I think we've covered a lot of territory today."
Signal that time for the meeting is up.	This is most effective when a time limit has been announced or agreed on in the opening of the interview. Be tactful; avoid being too abrupt or giving the impression that you're moving the interviewee along an assembly line.	"We have just a few minutes left, so . . ."
Explain the reason for the closing.	Be sure the reasons are real; if an interviewee thinks you're giving phony excuses, future interactions will be strained.	"Unfortunately, I've got another meeting in twenty minutes, so we'll have to start wrapping things up."
Express appreciation or satisfaction.	This is a common closing because interviewers have usually received something from the interview (information, help, a sale, a story, a new employee).	"Thank you for your interest in our cause."
Plan for the next meeting.	This reveals what will happen next (date, time, place, topic, content, purpose) or arranges for the next interview.	"I think we should follow up on this next week; my assistant will call you to arrange a time."
Summarize the interview.	This common closing for informational, appraisal, counseling, and sales interviews may repeat important information, stages, or agreements or verify accuracy or agreement.	"We've come to three major agreements here today." (List them briefly.)

Source: Labels from Stewart & Cash (2006).

Understanding Roles and Responsibilities in Interviews

Jan, a thirty-five-year-old high school biology teacher, is seeking a new career. She can approach this job hunt in two ways. First, she could simply answer advertisements for open positions and hope to be called in for an interview. Alternatively, she can identify people or organizations that she thinks she'd like to work for and arrange for information-gathering interviews with them. In the first approach, Jan, the job hunter, fills the role of *interviewee*—she answers questions posed by the interviewer. In the second example, Jan acts as the *interviewer*, asking people in various positions for information about potential career paths in their industry. So how are these roles different? How are they similar? Let's find out.

Roles and Responsibilities of the Interviewer

In any interview situation, there are specific behaviors that competent interviewers share. Specifically, they must identify potential barriers, make the interviewee comfortable, ask ethical and appropriate questions, and effectively listen and respond to the interviewee. In addition, interviewers must be culturally sensitive.

Identify Potential Barriers. Before heading into an interview situation, interviewers should take some time to reflect on potential barriers that might disrupt the interview. For example, is the space where the interview will take place quiet, private, and fairly neat and organized? True story: Val is an academic counselor at a prestigious university who is unfortunate enough to have an office next door to a copy room with an old Xerox machine that causes her wall to shake whenever one of her colleagues makes a photocopy. In order to avoid this distraction, she must take students to a private conference room when interviewing them about their coursework or their career plans.

Make the Interviewee Comfortable. Interviewees, particularly job applicants and medical patients, are often very nervous in interview situations—and understandably so. A good interviewer should adapt to the situational and relational contexts to help the interviewee feel at ease (Ralston, Kirkwood, & Burant, 2003). It would be effective and appropriate, for example, for an interviewer to smile, make eye contact, and offer a handshake. But be sure to keep these behaviors appropriate to the context; imagine if your doctor entered the examining room and gave you a big hug or if a job interviewer told you about his problems with his partner's parents.

Ask Ethical and Appropriate Questions. We've already discussed types of questions and question

sequences that you can use to guide productive, competent interviews that achieve your goals. It's also important to remember that good questions are also ethical and appropriate questions. For example, if Erik is a representative from his school newspaper interviewing a biology professor about her recent grant from the National Institutes of Health (NIH), his questions should stick to her research and her plans to implement a new lab on campus. It would be inappropriate and unethical for him to ask how much money she will be receiving from the NIH or whether she expects to receive a promotion and salary increase from the university after receiving the award.

On a job interview, certain unethical and inappropriate questions are also illegal. We illustrate these later in this appendix.

Listen and Respond Effectively. The role of the interviewer is not limited to structuring an interview and asking questions. After all, an effective interviewer needs to listen to, respond to, and evaluate the information that the answers to those questions reveal. Throughout the interview, the interviewer should keep both immediate and future goals in mind by making notes (written or mental) during the interview. A medical doctor might take notes about your family history and ask follow-up questions or order tests regarding your health based on this discussion.

Roles and Responsibilities of the Interviewee

True, the interviewer is responsible for quite a bit of work in an interview situation, but that doesn't mean that the interviewee is off the hook. If you are the interviewee, you will benefit greatly by clarifying your personal goals, being prepared, listening and responding effectively, and adapting to the interviewer and the situation.

Clarify and Fulfill Personal Goals. One of the most important things that an interviewee can bring to the interview is a clear sense of personal goals. That is, you should have a clear idea of what *you* want to achieve in the interview; this allows you to look for and seek out opportunities to advance those aims, such as looking for specific openings in the conversation (Waldron & Applegate, 1998). A job interviewee—whose goal it might be to impress a hiring manager—can seek out appropriate places to give examples of his or her energy, drive, and willingness to be a team player. An informational interviewee may advance the public relations goals of her organization by selecting information to be shared with the press.

Prepare Yourself Responsibly. Your school's career services office and your previous employment situations have likely prepared you for the fact that you'll need to draft a résumé and a cover letter in advance of a job interview. But all interviews, from job interviews to legal interviews, benefit from some advance planning.

> { One of the most important things that an interviewee can bring to the interview is a clear sense of personal goals. }

For one thing, you'll want to be well rested and alert for the interview. From personal experience, we urge you not to skip meals—more than a few of our students have had growling stomachs during interviews! You'll also want to consider the context and be dressed appropriately for the occasion; this is especially important for official job interviews, where you should match or exceed the dress policy at that place of business. Also remember to plan what you should bring with you to the interview: copies of your résumé to a job interview, for example, or your medical history to an interview with a new doctor.

Listen and Respond Effectively. Just as interviewers must listen and respond effectively, so

---

♀ The kind of job you're interviewing for dictates your dress. For an interview in the typically more conservative finance industry, you will need a suit. For an interview at an art gallery, you *might* wear a more casual outfit.

must the interviewee. For example, in a performance appraisal, carefully consider your answers to your boss's questions. If she asks you to assess what you have accomplished and excelled at, honestly highlight your individual achievements or your contributions to the team you work with—without exaggerating.

Adapt to the Interviewer and the Situation. It is the interviewee's responsibility to adapt to the interviewer and the interview situation appropriately—particularly with verbal and nonverbal communication. If a professor in your department is interviewing you to see if you would be a good fit for your college's honors program, you should plan on looking at the interview quite formally. For example, you would use professional, formal address when speaking to the professor ("Professor Arisetty" or "Dr. Edmunds"). But if you have known this professor for three years, you babysit her children, and she insists that you call her Emilia, you can adapt, feeling free to use her first name and a less strict, more personal style of conversation.

Culture also plays a profound role in job interview situations (Gardner, Reithel, Foley, Cogliser, & Walumbwa, 2009). As an interviewee or as an interviewer, you should expect to adapt to the culture of your communication partner. For example, many people from various ethnic and religious backgrounds find it difficult to brag about their accomplishments at a job interview because their culture frowns on such boastful behavior. Research shows that rather than clearly state a strength ("I have extremely strong organizational skills"), African American interviewees often tell stories about themselves to illustrate their strengths (Hecht, Jackson, & Ribeau, 2003). Researchers also note that European American interviewers often judge storytelling candidates to be "unfocused." Thus, African Americans who adapt by directly listing their strengths for a job are perceived more positively in interviews (Hecht, Jackson, & Ribeau, 2003); conversely, a European American interviewer who looks for the message behind the story an interviewee tells has competently adapted as well.

LearningCurve
bedfordstmartins.com/commandyou

The Job Interview

In the film *The Devil Wears Prada*, young Andy (Anne Hathaway) goes to an interview at *Runway*, a fictional fashion magazine. She is dressed in a plain and simple, yet respectable, outfit suitable for an aspiring young journalist. But when she arrives at *Runway*, she encounters an office full of sleek, stylish people dressed in expensive designer clothes, and when she finally has the opportunity to interview with editor-in-chief Miranda Priestly (Meryl Streep), Priestly insults

Not all bosses are like Miranda Priestly, and not all offices are like *Runway*'s. So don't worry that your interviewer will make fun of your cerulean polyester-blend sweater!

her for not reading *Runway*, for not being familiar with the editor's reputation, and for having no interest in fashion.

While such scenes make for great entertainment, in truth, most job interviews are polite and diplomatic affairs. In the remaining pages of this chapter, we describe how job interviews usually occur and offer solid advice on how to prepare for, engage in, and follow up on the process (Muir, 2008).

Getting the Interview

The first step involves actually getting the interview. This important phase involves three interrelated tasks: locating jobs and doing homework on the organizations, preparing materials to be used in the process (the résumé and cover letter), and building realistic expectations about the interviewing process.

The Job Search. The first element of preinterview preparation involves identifying potential jobs and then researching the field and the organizations. Although there are many strategies for locating jobs, your three best sources are likely to be people you know or manage to meet, placement centers, and discipline-specific job sites.

A great place to start is with family, friends, professors, former employers, and individuals working in your field of interest. You should also plan to network (Brazeel, 2009). **Networking** is the process of using interconnected groups or associations of persons you know to develop relationships with their connections that you don't know. Contact everyone you know who works in your field or who might know someone who does, let these individuals know the kind of job you are looking for, and ask for suggestions. You can also make new contacts via social-networking services like Facebook and LinkedIn or through an organization for professionals in your chosen field (many offer student memberships).

Placement centers are another source of jobs. Most college campuses have a centralized placement center where recruiters from major companies come to interview potential employees.

Finally, start looking for specific job openings. While general employment Web sites (like Monster .com) can be starting places, they may not yield significant results simply because they attract a large number of applicants (J. O'Loughlin, personal communication, July 23, 2010). A more productive search uses sites that cater to specific industries or even an organization's site (Pearce & Tuten, 2001; Young & Foot, 2005). For example, mediabistro.com and EntertainmentCareers.net focus on jobs in the media and entertainment industries. You can also find job postings on the Web sites for most major companies and organizations (look for links to "Careers" or "Employment"). Consider using job information and posting aggregators (such as LexisNexis) that will let you set criteria or parameters for the types or even geographic locations of positions you want. Doing so will put you in touch with sites that have less traffic and give you a better chance of being noticed.

Prepare Your Materials. Once you've identified potential jobs, you'll need to make contact with the people in a position to hire you. As a job applicant, the crucial first impression you make on a potential employer will likely be via your written materials—a formal cover letter and résumé. In this section, we show you how to prepare these materials so that they communicate the right message about you.

But first, a cautionary note: *before* you send off these written materials, make sure you have cleaned up any searchable information that does not portray you in a favorable light (Brandenburg, 2008; Holson, 2010). If you use social-networking sites, adjust your privacy settings to ensure that you have not been,

---

Technology and You

Do you have an account with Facebook, Twitter, or some other social-networking site? Think objectively about the impression, if any, your public page conveys about you. Would you hire you?

and cannot be, tagged in any photographs that you wouldn't want a potential employer to see and that your wall is not visible to anyone other than your approved friends. Perform searches for your name and e-mail address to make sure that any comments you've left on public forums or chat rooms don't come back to haunt you.

The résumé. Begin by pulling together a **résumé**—a printed summary of your education, work experiences, and accomplishments. It is a vehicle for making a positive first impression on potential employers. An effective résumé tells just enough about you to make employers believe they may need your skills and experience.

No two résumés look exactly alike, but most résumés should contain the following general information:

- **Contact information.** Include both campus and home addresses if necessary, phone numbers, and your e-mail address. Make sure that your voice mail greets callers with a clear, professional message, and check it often. If you have an odd or a cute address for your regular e-mail (partygirl@provider.com, numberonedad @provider.net), consider opening another account with a more serious name for your professional communication.

- **Employment objective.** Be concise and specific about what you're looking for in a position and your career goals. If you are applying for several types of jobs, you should create multiple résumés tailored to specific positions.

- **Education.** List the institutions you have attended, their locations, and the dates of attendance. List degrees received (or dates to be received), academic majors, and areas of concentration. Awards and GPA can be listed if they enhance your marketability.

- **Work experience.** If your work experiences are all in the same area, list them in reverse chronological order, focusing on concrete examples of achievement or skills that you have mastered. Explain job functions as well as titles. If, like many students, you have had a variety of

jobs (for example, waiting tables and being a camp counselor), reverse chronological order may not be very practical. Consider grouping actual employment and volunteer activities together in a way that best matches the job responsibilities you are seeking. Remember that prospective employers read this section carefully to discover how your experience, abilities, and achievements relate to their organization's needs.

- **Activities.** For employers, participation in a variety of academic, extracurricular, or social activities indicates that you are motivated and get involved. Include activities that are relevant to your career objective, emphasizing accomplishments and leadership roles—and link them clearly together.

- **Special skills.** Do you speak fluent Spanish? Are you skilled in a particular programming language? Did you climb Mount Everest? Don't be shy—let potential employers know this information. Your skills may be useful to the organization, and your accomplishments show dedication and determination.

- **References.** Your references are typically professors, previous supervisors, or anyone else who can confirm your employment history and attest to your work ethic and character. You are not necessarily required to include your references as part of your résumé, but be sure to have their current contact information handy in case a hiring manager requests them. Be sure to include only people who have agreed to serve as references for you.

A sample résumé appears in Figure A.2.

Once your résumé is complete, take some time to prepare it for electronic submission. You can avoid translation issues by saving it as a PDF document, so that employers can read it regardless of what type of computer they have. You should also name the file carefully, so that employers will be able to identify it easily. Include your name (or just your last name) in the file title, along with the word *resume* and perhaps a date. For example, *MartinezResumeJan2012.pdf* is a title preferable to *MyResume.pdf*.

Ellen Ng
111 A Street, Apt. 2C, San Marcos, TX 78666
(555) 375-7111 • ellen.ng@serviceprovider.com

OBJECTIVE

To obtain an entry-level editorial position where I can use my strong writing and editing skills while expanding my knowledge of the publishing process.

EDUCATION

Texas State University, *San Marcos, TX*   2012–2014
    Bachelor of Arts, English, May 2011   GPA: 3.7/4.0
    Honors: Recipient of the Lorin D. Parkin scholarship (2010); Member of the Sigma Tau Delta honor society
Northwest Vista College, *San Antonio, TX*   2010–2012
    Associate of Arts, Liberal and Media Arts (General), May 2009

RELATED WORK EXPERIENCE

Intern, Chronicle Books, *San Francisco, CA*   *Summer 2012*
    Wrote reports on the marketability and publication potential of cookbook proposals and manuscripts submitted to publisher. Drafted rejection letters, letters to authors, and letters requesting outstanding permissions fees. Created cost and sales figure spreadsheets. Prepared manuscripts and artwork for production.
Writing Counselor, Writing Center, *Texas State University*   *Fall 2011–Spring 2013*
    Aided students with their academic research papers, résumés, and cover letters. Developed exercises and writing samples to aid with college-level writing.
Writer/Editor, MyWay in Education, *Hong Kong*   *Summer 2011*
    Created and edited reading comprehension articles and over 300 grammar questions per week for ten different grade levels in accordance with Hong Kong public school standards for company's Web site.
Volunteer, San Antonio Public Library, *San Antonio, TX*   *Fall 2007–Spring 2011*
    Created themed book displays for special events, such as Hispanic Heritage Month and various national and international holidays. Read to children ages 3–5 weekly and created arts-and-crafts activities or games structured around the stories.

OTHER WORK EXPERIENCE AND ACTIVITIES

Waitress/Hostess, Applebee's, *San Marcos, TX*   *Fall 2011–Present*
    Waited tables three nights a week. Took food orders, brought meals to tables, and cleared tables. Promoted to hostess in 2010. Take names at host station, greet guests, and show them to their tables.
Cheerleader, Texas State Spirit Program, *Texas State University*   *Fall 2012–Spring 2014*
Cashier, Home Depot, *San Antonio, TX*   *Fall 2008–Fall 2009*
    Rang up customer purchases three nights a week. Assisted in closing up store at the end of each shift.

ADDITIONAL SKILLS

Languages: Fluent in English, proficient in written and conversational Mandarin and Cantonese, conversational Spanish
Computer: Word, Excel, PowerPoint, FileMaker Pro, Internet research

○ **Figure A.2 Sample Résumé**

Assess your goals for employment, and then design (or revise) a résumé for the job you are most interested in. Use the guidelines in this chapter to make it clear and action oriented. Prepare additional résumés for other positions, highlighting the aspects of your training and experience most relevant to each particular position. Discuss your résumé with other students in the class; ask them if your goals are clear. Can they tell what job you are seeking based on the different résumés you show them?

Technology and You

Have you sent out more résumés electronically or on paper, or have you sent out both versions in equal numbers? Do you format your résumé differently when you are sending it electronically?

The cover letter. Whenever you send your résumé to a potential employer, it should be accompanied by a formal **cover letter**, a one-page missive indicating your interest in a specific position. The cover letter gives you the opportunity to express how you learned of the position and the organization, how your skills and interests can benefit the organization, and why you are interested in applying for this particular job. The cover letter also serves as a means by which you can demonstrate your written communication skills, so make sure that you use correct grammar, punctuation, and spelling—and proofread carefully! Figure A.3 shows a strong cover letter.

In many cases, prospective employers accept e-mails as cover letters. So when you e-mail a hiring manager or a human resources representative at an organization, your e-mail should contain the same information as your cover letter. If you are unsure of the protocol, it's always best to be more formal and include an official cover letter with your e-mail. Be sure to include a subject line and to proofread your e-mail carefully before you press Send.

Build Realistic Expectations. The final component of job hunting involves developing realistic expectations about the process. Because only a few résumés will make it through the screening process and you will not be the only candidate who gets called for an interview, you will likely face rejection at least once during the course of a job search—either because there was a better-qualified applicant or because an equally qualified candidate had some advantage (such as a personal contact in the company). Remember that rejection is not uncommon and that it is the inevitable result of a tight job market and a less-than-perfect selection process (Fisk, 2010; Hershatter & Epstein, 2010; Lebo, 2009; Luo, 2010). Persistence pays. If you approach the job search intelligently and persistently, you will eventually get a job.

During the Interview

After a diligent job search, you've finally been called for an interview. Now what? Well, now you impress the socks off your interviewer by making your best

111 A Street, Apt. 2C
San Marcos, TX 78666

May 31, 2014

Jane Smith
Director of Human Resources
Roaring Brook Press
A Division of Macmillan
175 Fifth Avenue
New York, NY 10010

Dear Ms. Smith:

I was extremely excited to see a posting for an editorial assistant position with Roaring Brook Press. I greatly admire your organization's dedication to children and youth, and I would be honored to interview for a position that would allow me to develop my interests in publishing while working on the creative editorial projects that Roaring Brook Press supports.

My publishing experience coupled with my understanding of children's education makes me well suited for an editorial assistant position with your company. I worked as an editorial intern at Chronicle Books in San Francisco, where I maintained author and permissions databases and collated manuscripts and artwork for review and production. I also honed my writing skills through critiquing cookbook proposals and manuscripts based on analysis of the cookbook market.

I have also worked with children in an educational setting. As a volunteer at the San Antonio Public Library, I organized and created various informational displays aimed at getting children interested in subjects or cultures unfamiliar to them. I also created games and activities for children based on the books I read to them during story hour. Through this position, I learned to communicate with children in a creative yet educational way.

I have included my résumé as requested in the job posting, and I can provide references as required. I look forward to discussing my experiences and perspectives with you in person. I can be contacted at ellen.ng@serviceprovider.com or by phone at (555) 375-7111. Thank you for your kind consideration.

Sincerely,

Ellen Ng

Ellen Ng

○ Figure A.3 **Sample Cover Letter**

first impression, preparing for and anticipating different types of questions, preparing questions of your own, and following up after your interview.

Making a Good First Impression. Salina, who works in the nonprofit world, interviewed a candidate who came forty-five minutes late to the interview. To make matters worse, he explained his tardiness by noting that he had to "run home" to get his mom to help him with his tie. Later, Salina had a phone interview with a young woman who didn't bother to ensure that she had adequate cell phone reception, meaning that the question "What did you say?" dominated the conversation. What these candidates forgot is that the interview begins with the very first impression, even before the questions are asked.

In any interview, both verbal and nonverbal behaviors contribute to a good first impression. Thus, control the things you can at the outset. Give yourself plenty of extra time to get there, so that if something comes up (traffic, a stalled train) you'll still make it on time. Have your clothing ready ahead of time. If it's a phone interview, find a quiet place where you can talk undisturbed.

During the interview, do your best to control your nervousness so that you don't appear hesitant, halting, unsure, or jittery (Ayers, Keereetaweep, Chen, & Edwards, 1998; Tsa, Chen, & Chiu, 2005). As with all competent communication, you should adapt your behavior to be both effective and appropriate. Specifically, sit or stand as the other person directs; lower or raise your voice tone, rate, and pitch to fit in with the tone and pacing of the other person (DeGroot & Gooty, 2009). Also, limit gestures so that you don't distract the interviewer from your words—and relax enough to express genuine smiles (Krumhuber, Manstead, Cosker, Marshall, & Rosin, 2009; Woodzicka, 2008). If you practice with an understanding friend (or even record yourself), you can identify your positive behaviors and minimize any distracting behavior before you go into the interview situation.

Anticipating Common Questions. To discover whether there is a potential match between an applicant and a position, an interviewer typically explores

five areas of information as they relate to the specific job:

- **Ability.** First, based on the résumé and the interview, questions will assess your experience, education, training, intelligence, and ability to do what the job requires.

- **Desire.** Second, questions will focus on your desire or motivation to use your abilities to do a good job by exploring such things as your record of changes in jobs, schools, and majors; reasons for wanting this job; knowledge of the company; and concrete examples of prior success that indicate your drive to achieve.

- **Personality.** The third area involves an assessment of your personality and how well you are likely to fit into the position and the organization. Questions are designed to discover your personal goals, degree of independence and self-reliance, imagination and creativity, and ability to manage or lead.

- **Character.** A fourth area of judgment is that of character, learning about your personal behavior, honesty, responsibility, and accuracy and objectivity in reports.

- **Health.** This is a sensitive topic in interviews; certain questions about your health and medical background are illegal. But if a health issue directly affects your ability to do the job in question, the interviewer may ask. For example, if you are applying for a position at a candy factory, the interviewer may ask if you have a peanut allergy because you would be unable to work in a plant where peanuts are processed.

Some examples of frequently asked interview questions are offered in **Table A.4.**

Dealing with Difficult or Unethical Questions. "What fictional character most clearly reflects your outlook on life?" This is an actual question that an interviewer asked a colleague of ours some years ago when she was applying to college. To this day, she remembers the question because she panicked—not because she lacked an answer, but because she wasn't expecting the question. An interviewer might

Table A.4 Common Interview Questions

- Tell me about yourself. What led you to choose your particular field (or your academic major)? Describe your level of satisfaction with your choice.
- Describe what you understand is required in the position you are applying for. Summarize your qualifications in light of this description.
- Why do you want to leave your current employer? *or* Why did you leave your last employer?
- Describe the place/city/surroundings that would be your ideal working environment.
- Tell me what you know about our organization that led you to be interested in us.
- Give me a specific example of something you learned from a previous work experience.
- Describe your ideal working day.
- Describe the job you'd like to be doing five years from now.
- Describe a time when you demonstrated initiative in your employment (or volunteer) position.
- Tell me about a time when your willingness to work was demonstrated to your supervisors.
- Describe your strongest attribute with an example of how it paid off.
- Tell me about a recent project that didn't turn out the way you wanted. What did you do to try to make it work?
- Describe a time when you worked through a difficult coworker situation.
- If I gave you this job, what would you accomplish in the first three months?
- Are there any questions that you want to ask?

Source: Greco (1977). Used with permission.

use such unexpected questions to seek insights into the way candidates view themselves or to judge how well they think on their feet. Some questions are simply tricky—they offer a challenge to the interviewee but also a great opportunity to show one's strengths.

Other questions are more than just difficult; they are unethical and sometimes even illegal. Questions that have no direct bearing on job performance and have the potential to lead to discrimination on the basis of race, color, religion, national origin, sex, age, disability, and marital or family status are illegal in the United States. Although an organization whose employees ask illegal questions during employment interviews can be subject to a variety of penalties imposed by the federal government's Equal Employment Opportunity Commission (EEOC), such questions continue to be asked, and applicants must consider

how to answer them. Stewart and Cash (2011) suggest five tactics you can use to respond to illegal questions. By answering briefly but directly, tactfully refusing to answer, or neutralizing the question, you respond without giving too much information or inviting further inquiry. You can also consider posing a tactful inquiry—that is, asking another question in response—or using the question as an opportunity to present some positive information about yourself. These five strategies are outlined in **Table A.5**.

Asking Questions of Your Own. Of course, the interviewer should not be the only person asking questions in a job interview. A candidate for any job should arrive at an interview prepared to ask thoughtful questions about the position and related career paths within the organization, as well as about the

Table A.5 **Tactics for Responding to Illegal Questions**

Tactic	Sample Illegal Question	Sample Answer
Answer directly but briefly	"Do you attend church regularly?"	"Yes, I do."
Pose a tactful inquiry	"What does your husband do?"	"Why do you ask?" (in a nondefensive tone of voice)
Tactfully refuse to answer the question	"Do you have children?"	"My family plans will not interfere with my ability to perform in this position."
Neutralize	"What happens if your partner needs to relocate?"	"My partner and I would discuss locational moves that either of us might have to consider in the future."
Take advantage of the question	"Where were you born?"	"I am quite proud that my background is Egyptian because it has helped me deal effectively with people of various ethnic backgrounds."

Source: Stewart & Cash (2011). Used with permission.

organization itself (Johnson, 2010). These questions should indicate that the applicant has done solid homework (your preinterview research and preparation can shine here) and is able and willing to do a good job for the company.

Avoid saying things like "I really don't have any questions right now" (even if you don't have any questions), which might imply disinterest. Likewise, try not to focus on questions about your own compensation and benefits, such as "How much vacation will I get?"—at least not at the first interview. Instead, try to pose thoughtful questions that show your interest while enhancing your understanding of the position and the potential for your future. Be prepared to ask such questions as "I noticed in your annual report that you are developing a new training program. If I were hired, would I be in it?" and "If you were sitting on my side of this desk, what would you say are the most attractive features of the job?" And when the interview is ending, be sure to ask what to expect next, such as "What is your time frame for filling this position?"

Following Up After the Interview. You should continue to demonstrate good manners once the interview is over. Thank the interviewer, as well as anyone else you have met within the organization, as you leave. Follow up immediately with a written or e-mailed note of appreciation. Thank the interviewer not only for the interview but also for the chance to expand your knowledge of the organization and the industry. Put in writing how excited you are about the chance to work with such a dynamic organization. Send along any support materials that you discussed during the interview (perhaps a writing sample). Since few interviewees remember to send additional materials and thank-yous, you will certainly stand out.

LearningCurve
bedfordstmartins.com/commandyou

What About You? }

Your Career Preparation

Use the following grid as a starting point to assess your career strengths and goals as you prepare for job interviews. Write three descriptions of your skills, career goals, and life goals. Next, score the organizations that you plan on applying to from 1 to 5 (5 being the highest) as to how they match up with your skills and goals.

My Skills	Organization A	Organization B	Organization C
(Examples: strong writing skills, foreign-language proficiency, computer programming skills)			
1.			
2.			
3.			

My Career Goals

(Examples: become a marketing executive, work in the Dallas area, have a job with little mandatory travel)

1.

2.

3.

My Life Goals

(Examples: have children, live near siblings, retire at age sixty)

1.

2.

3.

Now assess your results. Is there one organization that best supports your goals and skills? If not, consider which goals and skills are *most* important to you. Which organization might be the best fit?

Back to }

The Daily Show **Interview**

At the beginning of this appendix, we talked about the special "reports" filed by *Daily Show* correspondents. Let's examine the nature of those interviews in the context of what we've discussed throughout this appendix.

- Like all interviews, these *Daily Show* interviews are planned, but the process of editing them down to a few minutes makes them less interactive than a real-time interview. Comments and reaction shots are taken out of context, and during editing, the correspondent is able to integrate alternative footage that was not part of the actual interview. This gives the correspondent an unusual amount of control at the expense of the interviewee.

- John Oliver makes comic use of questioning, offering the Columbia University professor a loaded question. It's clear that Oliver doesn't want or expect an answer—the question itself is the joke.

- The format and structure of the interview are also clear to both parties: interviewees are familiar with the show and are essentially in on the joke.

Participants are well aware that their comments can and will be heavily edited and that much of what they say will be taken out of context.

- The goals of the interviewee and interviewer are at once similar and quite different. As satire, *The Daily Show* seeks to illuminate real issues by poking fun at them. The students who participated appreciated that goal: "I am extremely happy with the clip in the sense that it did what it's supposed to do—make people laugh and give them a little something to think about," said Samantha Joseph. "Did it fully express our opinions? No. Were our words twisted? Yes . . . but again, anyone who goes on *The Daily Show* would be nuts to think that wouldn't happen!" (Marcott, 2009).

Your Reference

A Study Tool
Now that you have finished reading this appendix, you can

Define the nature of interviews:

- An **interview** is an interaction between two parties that is deliberate and purposeful (p. 362).
- Interviews are planned, goal-driven, structured, dyadic (involving two parties), and interactive (pp. 362–363).

Outline the different types of interviews:

- The **information-gathering interview** serves to transfer knowledge from one party to the other (pp. 363–364).
- **Performance appraisals** allow you to review your accomplishments and plan your goals (p. 364).
- A **problem-solving interview** deals with problems, tensions, or conflicts (p. 364).
- In **exit interviews**, employers seek to identify organizational problems (pp. 364–365).
- **Persuasive interviews**, are designed to change behavior or opinions (p. 365).
- **Service-oriented interviews** are designed to cull information and provide advice or support (p. 365).
- In a **selection interview**, the primary goal is to fill a position in an organization (pp. 365–366).

Describe the three parts of an interview: opening, questions, and conclusion:

- An interview should open with the three things interviewees will want to know: the topic and length (the task), something about the interviewer and how the information will be used (the relationship), and who will benefit (the motivation) (p. 366).
- Questions and answers accomplish the goals of the interview (p. 367).
- An **open question** gives the interviewee freedom in how to respond (p. 367).
- **Closed questions** restrict answer choices; **bipolar questions** can be answered with only "yes" or "no" (p. 367).
- **Primary questions** introduce new topics; **secondary questions** seek clarification (pp. 367–368).
- **Neutral questions** do not hint at a preferred answer, whereas **directed questions**, **leading questions**, or **loaded questions** may subtly or even blatantly influence the answer (p. 369).

- There are three main structures for ordering interview questions: the **funnel sequence**, the **inverted funnel sequence**, or the **tunnel sequence**, each varying in its level of specificity (pp. 369–370).
- Interviewers use verbal and nonverbal strategies to conclude, summarize, and support the interview (pp. 370–371).

Devise an interview strategy from the interviewer's point of view:

- Consider barriers that might be disruptive (p. 372).
- Find ways to put the interviewee at ease (p. 372).
- Make sure the questions are ethical (p. 372).
- Remember to listen well and take notes (p. 372).

Prepare for the role of interviewee:

- Have a clear idea of your personal goals (pp. 372–373).
- Don't arrive tired or hungry. Dress appropriately, and bring any documents you may need (p. 373).
- Listen and respond effectively (pp. 373–374).
- Adapt to the situation, being particularly sensitive to cultural differences (p. 374).

Secure job interviews and manage them with confidence:

- **Networking** involves meeting new people through people you already know (p. 375).
- Write an effective **résumé** and **cover letter** (pp. 375–379).
- Nonverbal cues are as important as what you say to make a good first impression (p. 380).
- Come prepared to answer standard questions about your abilities, desire, personality, character, and health (p. 380).
- Answer difficult questions honestly to show that you know how to evaluate your own weaknesses and improve on them, but be brief; decline to answer a question that is unethical (pp. 380–381).
- Ask thoughtful questions about the position and the organization (pp. 381–382).
- Follow up with a note of thanks (p. 382).

✔ Look for **LearningCurve** throughout the appendix to help you review.
bedfordstmartins.com/commandyou

Understanding Mass and Mediated Communication

S andie and Chris fell in love during the 1980s, while spending late evenings together watching *Late Night with David Letterman* on NBC. About twenty years later, their teenage daughter, Alice, sits in front of a laptop on a Saturday morning, watching streaming clips of Jimmy Fallon sitting behind Letterman's old desk. She's also monitoring her Facebook page to see if anyone has commented on the picture she created of herself with actor Joseph Gordon-Levitt. She's also rereading the *Hunger Games* series on her Kindle and posting on her blog about the movie versions. Later, she texts her friends to make plans to go to the movies but not before checking out a few trailers online. During dinner, she DVRs a History Channel documentary on the Roman Empire for a school project. After dinner, she's off to the movies and conscientiously turns off her cell phone—it's the first time she's been disconnected all day. By the time Alice goes to sleep, she's seen more media than her parents did in a week when they were her age. Meanwhile, Chris and Sandie pull up Thursday night's episode of *Late Night with Jimmy Fallon* on DVR, grateful that they no longer have to stay up until 1:30 A.M. to finish watching it.

After you have finished reading this appendix, you will be able to

Define mass and mediated communication.

Describe how the business of media and the principle of free speech shape the kinds of media content you encounter.

Define two explanations for the effects of mass media.

Articulate how media exert influence on your attitudes and behaviors.

Describe how the convergence of media technologies can enhance or hinder your participation in the social and political process.

Practice five skills for becoming a more mindful and media-literate consumer.

ost of us, like Alice and her family, spend a great deal of time with these interconnected media technologies, often using two or more simultaneously (Kaiser Family Foundation, 2010). In this appendix, we look at mass and mediated communication and discuss the blurred lines between the two. We explore the forces that shape how media messages are made, such as the economics of the media industries and the attempts at government influence, and we discuss the potential effects that media have on us as audience members. Finally, we examine the benefits and difficulties that the ever-expanding array of media technologies presents for American society, as well as what we can do to cope effectively with our media experience.

Culture and You

How did you spend your time yesterday? How much of your personal, social, collegiate, or professional life revolves around smart phones, iPods, Internet connections, and television sets?

The Nature of Media

While we talk about "the media" all the time, media are not actually one unified entity. They take many different forms and have many different uses and effects, as we see with Alice and her family. Some media communicate messages very broadly (such as television), while others have more narrowly targeted audiences (ranging from special-interest magazines all the way down to Twitter updates targeting a specific list of followers). But different media also have several qualities in common that distinguish them from face-to-face communication, such as interpersonal or small group interaction.

Defining Mass and Mediated Communication

As we learned in Chapter 1 and have discussed throughout this book, **mediated communication** occurs when there is some technology that is used to deliver messages between sources and receivers. Media may be print (such as newspapers or magazines) or electronic (such as television, radio, or the Internet). But just having our messages mediated does not make communication "mass," since we use many forms of media (phone, e-mail, Facebook, blogs) to communicate in interpersonal, small group, organizational, public, and intercultural contexts. When mediated communication occurs on a very broad scale, we refer to it as **mass communication**. Before the advent of the Internet and social networking, mass communication was characterized by several factors:

- First, the types of media that we considered to be mass media had extremely large audiences, typically described in millions (of viewers, readers, listeners, etc.).
- Second, the sources of messages tended to be professional communicators. These are people whose livelihoods depend on the success of communication—publishers, actors, writers, reporters, advertising executives, or even the guard at the film studio's gate.

- Third, traditional mass media outlets have less interactivity and opportunity for feedback than other forms of communication, which has made it more difficult for those sources to know their audience.

These features still apply to many traditional mass media rooted in the publishing, broadcasting, and entertainment industries—but they've also been challenged over the past decade by the increasingly participatory nature of digital communication.

In addition, although traditional mass media are distinct in many ways from the more clearly interpersonal uses of media (such as telephone and e-mail), the changing digital media environment has increasingly blurred the difference between these types of communication. For example, when Alice posts a status update on Facebook for her friends or forwards a joke over e-mail, her message could potentially wind up being seen by thousands of people—thereby adding a "mass" element to communication that is otherwise mainly interpersonal. Similarly, individual audience members may provide immediate feedback to professional news organizations and TV show creators by posting comments on political and fan blogs—adding interactivity and feedback to what was once a linear form of mass communication.

This merging of traditional mass communication with digital computing and telecommunication technologies is called **media convergence**. Convergence is a critical part of living in a digital media environment, and it affects how mass media content is shaped as well as how mass media messages can influence audiences (Pavlik & McIntosh, 2011).

The Pervasiveness of Media

With global satellite technology and 24/7 news and entertainment content, many of us have mass media content available to us at all times. The average adult spends about 5 hours per day watching TV and about 3 hours per day on the Internet. Recent data suggest that on a typical day children and teens now spend about 7.5 hours devoted to entertainment media, including TV, movies, computers, cell phone enter-

tainment, video games, music/audio, and print—an increase of more than an hour per day in just five years (Kaiser Family Foundation, 2010). Much of this time is spent **media multitasking**—using more than one media type at the same time—and that overlapping usage allows kids to pack nearly 11 hours of content into those 7.5 hours of daily use. The increased availability and decreased costs of portable media devices have contributed greatly to the rise in media use among all ages. In fact, in today's digital media environment, it is almost impossible to *escape* media (Pavlik & McIntosh, 2011).

LearningCurve
bedfordstmartins.com/commandyou

Understanding Mass Media Messages

There are several important factors that help shape the kinds of mass media messages that are made and delivered. In this section, we discuss these key influences, including the economics of a high-risk media industry, the principle of free speech and government regulation, and the role of media bias.

The Business of Media

Media organizations range from tiny production companies to huge international conglomerates (such as Sony) that are parent companies to a number of other large organizations (such as Sony Pictures, which itself is the parent company of Columbia Pictures and Screen Gems, among others). Some companies form just for the purpose of making one movie or television show, while others, such as Universal and Disney, oversee, purchase, or distribute hundreds of movies and TV programs each year. But all of these companies are businesses—they need to make money to stay in business.

Sources of Revenue. There are two main sources of revenue for the mass media: consumer purchases and advertising. Consumers pay directly for some media messages, such as going to the movies, subscribing to cable or satellite services, and buying magazines, e-books, or DVDs and Blu-ray discs. Advertising dollars also support many of the same media that consumers purchase (magazines, newspapers, cable TV) because purchases alone are not enough to keep these industries afloat. Advertising is also the *sole* support for several other media, including broadcast TV and radio and much of the World Wide Web. Advertising rates are determined mainly by how many people are in the audience (and for how long). For print media, this means circulation size (the number of people who buy or subscribe to newspapers and magazines); for TV and radio, this primarily means ratings (the number of households that are in the viewing or listening audience for a given time slot). For Web sites, usage data gets more complicated, but everything gets measured—from unique hits (that is, individual visitors to a site) and the amount of time people spend browsing to people's patterns of click-through behavior with links.

Big box office and high ratings are keys to mass media success because mass communication messages

{ **A half-hour TV sitcom can range from several hundred thousand dollars per episode to several million.** }

are expensive to make and deliver. A half-hour TV sitcom can range from several hundred thousand dollars per episode to several million. Such high investment costs mean that profit can be elusive. In fact, most new TV shows are canceled, few movies become blockbusters, most novels do not become bestsellers, and few albums sell strongly (Vogel, 2011). How, then, do the media ever make money? The few blockbuster movies, bestselling books, and hit television shows or albums must make up for all the rest. In economics, this is called **exponentiality**: relatively few items bring most of the income, while the rest add only a little (Vogel, 2011). Across the media industries, about 80 to 90 percent of mass media revenue comes from only 10 to 20 percent of the products made.

Broad Versus Narrow Appeal. For the biggest of the mass media, network television, messages must have very broad appeal to attract the millions of

---

⦿ Following the economic principle of exponentiality, blockbusters such as *Fast Five* bring in most of the film industry's profits and pick up the slack of box office bombs, such as *Battleship*.

viewers that are needed in order to sell profitable advertising time. The Super Bowl is such a widely popular event that the cost of advertising is extremely expensive: in 2012, a thirty-second commercial during the Super Bowl cost around $3.5 million. But prime-time network TV (ABC, CBS, NBC, Fox, and The CW) requires programming that attracts a very large audience on a regular basis. The traditional way for networks to capture broad audiences has been to rely on content that is often described as **low culture**—entertainment that appeals to most people's baser instincts, typified by lurid, sensational images and stories charged with sex, violence, scandal, and abuse (Berger, 2007). In addition, the networks have relied on programming that doesn't require a great deal of thought or cultural sophistication, leading critics to echo the sentiments of former FCC chairman Newton Minow when, in 1961, he first called commercial television a "vast wasteland" (Minow, 1961; Minow & Cate, 2003).

But, wait, you say: there are a lot of popular shows on television right now that are intellectually stimulating, well written, and impressively produced. Scholars agree. Jason Mittel (2006), for example, makes the case that the landscape of television during the last twenty years has actually gotten "smarter." He notes that, while there is much popular content on TV that remains highly conventional, the past two decades have seen a huge increase in critically acclaimed and popular TV shows with **narrative complexity**—complicated plots and connections between characters, a blurring of reality and fantasy, and time that is not always linear or chronological. Beginning with hits like *The X-Files* (1993–2002) and *Buffy the Vampire Slayer* (1997–2003) and continuing with shows like *Lost* (2004–2010) and *The Good Wife* (since 2009), intricate plots, subplots, and "story arcs" weave between stand-alone episodes and continuous serial storytelling (Mittel, 2006). Many of these shows give you a cognitive "workout" because you must think carefully to make sense of what is happening (Johnson, 2005).

This trend did not likely emerge out of any charity on the part of the entertainment industry. Rather, it is because audiences themselves have gotten more

cognitively demanding, and there is money to be made in meeting that demand (Johnson, 2005). Many of these are *hit* shows, after all. But even without major hits, uniquely appealing shows are possible because of another major industry trend. **Narrowcasting** (also called *niche marketing*) is the process of targeting smaller, specific audiences. Beginning with cable television in the 1980s and continuing today with satellite television and a diverse array of specialty media outlets, including the Web, media industries can tap into multiple smaller, but loyal and often passionate, audiences (Mittel, 2006). Thus, while it's not surprising that a megahit like CBS's *NCIS* averaging close to twenty million viewers each week) pulls in solid advertising revenue (Rice, 2011), shows with smaller audiences (like FX's *Justified*, with just under four million weekly viewers) can still be profitable—particularly if the audience watching them represents a key demographic group that advertisers want to target (Gorman, 2011).

Although the most popular cable/satellite shows have not yet attracted anywhere near the size of prime-time network audiences, they are increasingly taking viewers away from the networks and spreading audiences across a much wider spectrum of more specialized entertainment choices (Gorman, 2010; Stelter, 2011). Of course, narrowcasting doesn't necessarily result in more intellectually demanding or sophisticated content. But popular cable programming (and creative Internet content) provides competition that can lead to more innovative network programming. The media industries must adapt to the challenges and opportunities presented by digital technologies in order to remain profitable in an increasingly fragmented media landscape.

Minimizing Risk. The desire for a large audience often means minimizing risk wherever possible. The TV networks do this in part by promoting content that they believe reflects the cultural and moral values of their audiences. They do extensive audience research, attempting to understand the passions, commitments, values, and relational bonds of viewers and listeners. They also engage in **self-censorship**, carefully monitoring their own content and eliminating messages that might offend their viewers or sponsors. If network executives believe a show's script is too explicit or its message is too morally risky, they may insist on rewrites or prevent the show from airing altogether.

The fear of offending viewers or advertisers does not mean that the media avoid controversy. Indeed, controversy can be used to increase ratings. We discussed earlier that lurid, sensational coverage is common across news media outlets, whether about celebrity sex scandals and drug overdoses or political corruption and gruesome murder cases. Entertainment programming can also benefit from controversy—the already highly rated and popular *Two and a Half Men* saw a jump in viewers (even in repeats) during Charlie Sheen's much-publicized meltdown in 2011 (Oldenburg, 2011). But controversy doesn't always translate into high ratings or long-term success.

Perhaps the most prominent way media industries try to minimize risk is to repeat what has already been proven to work. Although they do aim to discover some fresh new idea that will lead to the next big blockbuster or hit TV show, that kind of success is difficult to predict in advance. So media professionals often count on the sure thing, the products or ideas that have *already been* successful. Thus, hit films—from *Iron Man* to *Saw*—are usually followed by a sequel (or two, or three ad infinitum). Popular films are also frequently derived from successful novels (such as *The Girl with the Dragon Tattoo*), graphic novels and comic book franchises (like *The Avengers*), foreign films (*The Grudge*, for example), or existing films or television programs (for instance, *Dark Shadows*) that bring with them built-in audiences. For television, this means copycat shows (as is the case with the hugely successful *American Idol*, an Americanized version of the British hit *Pop Idol*) and spin-offs (*Family Guy* begat *The Cleveland Show*). While some such offerings are failures, studios continue to mine familiar stories and characters that they believe audiences already enjoy.

Free Speech and Media Bias

The infamous 2004 Super Bowl halftime show featured a moment that entered the cultural lexicon as a "wardrobe malfunction" when performer Justin Timberlake pulled off a cover, exposing Janet Jackson's breast. CBS stations around the country faced major fines for indecency, as well as an extended series of court battles over those fines. The debate over whether the government has the right to fine networks or censor objectionable messages is rooted in competing interpretations of constitutional law.

The First Amendment. The First Amendment to the U.S. Constitution states, "Congress shall make no law . . . abridging the freedom of speech, or of the press." The principle here is that news media and individual citizens of a well-functioning republic need to be free to criticize their government and speak their views. This means that, even when speech is offensive, the government cannot ban it, punish it, or restrict it, except under very rare circumstances. Interestingly, this doesn't mean that the U.S. government hasn't *tried* to exercise control over media content. But its attempts at regulation are often struck down by the courts as unconstitutional (such as bans on pornography and heavy regulation of political campaign speech). The regulations that U.S. courts allow mostly involve rules about technical issues, such as broadcast signals or ownership of stations and copyright laws. In effect, the U.S. government actually has little direct influence on media *content* compared to the governments of other countries.

Do all American media benefit from this protection? The courts have generally held that creative expression *is* protected speech, whether in print, on TV, in movies, or on the Internet. However, the courts have also upheld some content regulations for some kinds of media, particularly broadcasting, as we'll see in the next section.

Electronic Media Regulation. There is an important legal difference between broadcast signals and cable or satellite channels. **Broadcasting** refers to signals carried over the airwaves from a station transmitter to a receiver. For radio, these are the AM/FM stations you might listen to in your car. For television, they are the major networks (ABC, CBS, NBC, FOX, and The CW) and independent local stations. Most cable and satellite companies now carry these signals to you, so the broadcast TV channels today look just like every other channel on TV.

However, because broadcasting frequencies are limited and because the airwaves themselves are essentially a public resource, the government—through the Federal Communications Commission (FCC)—can regulate which private companies may broadcast over them. In order to keep their broadcasting licenses, broadcasters must agree to serve the public interest. Cable and satellite providers, on the other hand, do not use publicly owned resources to deliver their signals, so they have not been subject to the same kinds of regulations.

While the First Amendment right to free speech and press do apply to broadcasters, broadcast television networks and radio stations are subject to some speech restrictions. The courts have held that the government can impose restrictions that serve a "compelling government interest" (that is, the government has a really good reason for doing it, such as to protect children) and only when the regulation is the "least restrictive" way to serve that interest (that is, the government cannot ban all adult TV content just to protect kids from seeing it) (*Action for Children's Television v. FCC*, 1991).

Recall the Janet Jackson Super Bowl incident discussed earlier. CBS stations were fined because the FCC said that the dance number violated a ban on broadcast **indecency**. *Indecency* legally means "patently offensive . . . sexual or excretory activities or organs" (*FCC v. Pacifica Foundation*, 1978), but in practice it means talking about or showing sexual or other bodily functions in a very lewd or vulgar way. This is a very subjective evaluation, of course, which is why broadcasters frequently end up fighting over their fines in court.

The Supreme Court has upheld the government's expressed interest in protecting children from indecent content (*FCC v. Pacifica Foundation*, 1978). However, the courts have also said that the ban must be limited only to specific times of day (such as 6 A.M. to 10 P.M.) when children are likely to be in the audience (*Action for Children's Television v. FCC*, 1995). Remember that this ban does not apply to cable and

◊ When *Saturday Night Live* premiered on broadcast network NBC in 1975, the original cast of "Not Ready for Prime Time Players" was relegated to a late-night airtime to allow for its often boundary-pushing sketch comedy.

satellite channels—so MTV and Comedy Central, for example, may choose to air nudity or use bad language at any time, based solely on their sense of what their audiences will tolerate.

Although indecency rules are what you may hear most about, there are also other important areas of media regulation. Much FCC action is directed at how the media corporations conduct their business, such as approving or denying mergers. The FCC has also recently expanded its influence over the Internet, including controversial attempts to limit the control that Internet service providers have over the online traffic that flows through their services.

Media Bias. As you'll recall from Chapters 1 and 2, our own thoughts, opinions, and experiences influence the messages we send as well as the way we interpret the messages we receive. These communication biases are also at work when it comes to mass media. Most scholars agree that media sources—both

Compare the news coverage for a political controversy on the Web sites of Fox News, CNN, MSNBC, NPR, and the wire services (AP and Reuters). What are the similarities? What are the differences? Then check the Web sites for both Media Matters for America and Media Research Center (or its offshoot, NewsBusters), and see how each of these media watchdogs criticizes the coverage. Do these watchdogs themselves seem to hold biases too?

news and entertainment—express some degree of bias in their viewpoints and in their content. News coverage of the Tea Party movement, for example, can be quite different, depending on the political leanings of the network or news organization doing the reporting as well as the personal ideologies of individual reporters, editors, and producers.

The trend toward more partisan news has increased since the 1990s (Coe et al., 2008; Iyengar & Hahn, 2009). In the latter half of the twentieth century, news organizations across the entire mass media generally expressed commitment to the goal of objectivity—that is, they were primarily concerned with facts and uninfluenced by personal or political bias, prejudice, or interpretation. Although traditionally embraced as a laudable goal, both consumers and journalists over the years have questioned whether this goal has been (or even can be) met (Duffy, Thorson, & Vultee, 2009; Figdor, 2010). Today's media, in any case, appear more willing to embrace the economic advantages of partisanship, as cable news networks in particular tend to narrowcast to one viewpoint or another in search of higher ratings. The Internet also supports a wide range of political news and analysis, from the *Breitbart* series of Web sites on the right to the *Huffington Post* on the left, not to mention the "blogosphere" of individual writers and commentators online. Thus the variety of ideologies represented by mass media today makes it difficult to pin any particular bias on "mainstream" media as a whole.

That does not mean, however, that bias is unimportant. Studies suggest that when presented with coverage of any given issue, strong partisans of both

⦿ Liberal commentator Rachel Maddow and conservative Sean Hannity hail from opposite ends of the spectrum of politicized news coverage, and they are not subtle in their partisanship.

parties, especially those who discuss media bias with like-minded partisans, perceive the news to be biased against their own side (Eveland & Shah, 2003). In a nutshell, that means we tend to see those we agree with as less biased than those we disagree with.

Critics on the right *and* the left agree that bias in the media is also a function of the economics and constraints of the news-gathering process itself (Farnsworth & Lichter, 2010). The 24/7 news cycle with multiple technological outlets to fill may lead to overreliance on easy sources—particularly spokespersons for government or interest groups. The focus on breaking news rather than ongoing issues may lead to a lack of depth, and the need to frame issues in ways that increase drama encourages coverage of politics as a horse race between conflicting parties rather than as the complex process that it is.

LearningCurve
bedfordstmartins.com/commandyou

Effects of Mass Media

James gets in trouble at school for trying to kickbox his classmates as he sees characters do in his video games. Abigail watches a lot of televised high school dramas and worries that appearing too "smart" will make the boys not like her. Are media messages influencing the attitudes and behaviors of these kids? We have already seen how audiences and other factors shape media messages. In this section, we will explore the research and theories on how mass media messages might actually shape *us*.

In the early years of mass media research (from about the 1920s to the 1940s), audiences were thought to be extremely vulnerable to media messages. Given the effective political impact of propaganda during the First World War and the rise of Nazism, it was believed that media effects were powerful, direct, and uniform and that audiences had no ability to resist them. But empirical research on media effects

simply did not support the idea that mass media could have total control of people. So, although this view still exists today in some popular criticism of media, communication researchers have outlined several more empirically supported theories about media effects.

Selectivity and the Active Audience

Do you remember all the commercials you saw last night? Did you read every status update that every one of your friends posted on Facebook? As we discussed in Chapter 6, we make specific choices about which messages we will select and attend to. This selectivity means that audiences are not passive sponges that absorb everything media throws at them. Rather, many communication scholars argue, audiences, even those made up of children, are instead active cognitive processors of information (Huston, Bickham, Lee, & Wright, 2007). Being active does not mean, however, that we critically evaluate the messages we see (although we can certainly do that); it means that we look for cues that tell us whether something on TV (or in other media) is interesting, relevant, or otherwise worth noticing (Valkenburg & Vroone, 2004). It also refers to the idea that different people have different reactions and interpretations of media messages (Morley, 2006). The concepts of selectivity and an active audience suggest that media effects are much more limited than we might otherwise believe.

Uses and Gratifications. Rather than looking at what media do *to us*, the **uses and gratifications perspective** focuses on what *we do* with media—that is, the way we make media choices (uses) in order to satisfy our needs and goals (gratifications) (Blumler & Katz, 1974). We might watch comedies or fantasy to escape our troubles at work, or we might search the Internet for updated information on local tornado warnings. In fact, media are competing with ways to meet our needs—when we are feeling lonely, we can get together with friends or phone a family member. Media are also competing with each other—we can check Facebook, watch a beloved TV character, or tune in to our favorite sports commentator (Dimmick, Chen, & Li, 2004).

Of course, what solves loneliness for *you* might just be escapism or entertainment for *me*. It's all in the individual's perceptions of the media choices available. For example, studies of gender and video game use find that male college students play for far more hours than do females. Both men and women report that they are motivated to play by the desire to beat the game, but men are more motivated by the value of the game for competition and social interaction with other guys (Lucas & Sherry, 2004). Women presumably prefer other options for social interaction.

When we come to *expect* that media will serve certain needs, it can lead to **media dependence** (Ball-Rokeach, 1998). Certainly in times of crisis, such as after the 9/11 attacks or during local emergencies (such as earthquakes, tornadoes, or blizzards), most of us become dependent on media for information and connection to the world. But even without crisis, many people find that they depend on media for specific needs. One national survey found that one-third to one-half of respondents said that they depend on the Internet for in-depth information about health, science, or business issues on a weekly basis (Riffe, Lacy, & Varouhakis, 2008). Another study found that some college students even label themselves "addicted" to television, particularly those who are easily bored and more introverted (McIlwraith, 1998). All of these studies suggest that what the viewer or listener *brings* to the media experience is important.

Reinforcing Existing Attitudes. One important way in which selectivity limits the effects of media is our tendency to select and evaluate media in a way that confirms our existing views. For example, we often choose our news sources based on whether we anticipate that they will agree with us. In an experimental study of the effects of perceived agreement on news choices, Democrats and liberals preferred CNN and NPR and avoided Fox News, whereas Republicans and conservatives did the opposite (Iyengar & Hahn, 2009).

Increasingly, diverse media outlets make it easier than ever to select and attend to only the entertainment and news messages that already agree with us—political blogs, fan forums, TV and radio analysts, partisan cable and online news. Some critics lament the fact that we can so easily insulate ourselves from opposing views, arguing that it polarizes us as citizens and is unhealthy for democracy (Sunstein, 2007). But the case can also be made that the ability of audiences to self-filter messages is empowering and is at least better than having others (such as professional media editors or the government) do all the filtering *for* us.

The Third-Person Effect. Another way that selectivity may limit media effects is that we tend to overestimate how much influence media actually have on people. The **third-person effect** is a well-documented tendency we have to assume that negative media messages and bias have a much greater influence on *other people* than on ourselves or people we think are like us (Davison, 1983; Sun, Pan, & Shen, 2008). The third-person effect can lead to censorship when we believe it will protect "other" people who we (or our government or religious community) don't think are able to handle certain media messages. A recent study finds that the effect is particularly strong for social networking—we think others are more influenced by Facebook than we ourselves are (Zhang & Daugherty, 2009). With all media, you need to be aware that you may be overestimating the effect on others or underestimating the effect on yourself (or both).

> **Culture and You**
>
> Do you recall ever using third-person effect, assuming that others will be influenced by negative media influences but you will not? What was the medium and message? Why didn't you think it would affect you?

Influences on Attitudes and Behaviors

Although selectivity may give audiences some power and make them resistant to being influenced by media, there are several areas where media do have more substantial influences on audiences. These include encouraging people to imitate behavior, cultivating cultural attitudes, and setting the political issue agenda.

Social Cognitive Theory. According to **social cognitive theory**, we learn behavior by watching the behaviors of those whom we have identified as models (Bandura, 2001). We must first attend to the modeled behavior, then remember it, and then have the ability and motivation to imitate it. We are particularly likely to imitate modeled behaviors when we see that the models are rewarded for what they do—when your big brother gets lots of praise for playing the guitar, you then try to play the guitar! How does this apply to media effects? Media provide many modeled behaviors for children and adults to learn from and imitate, both positive (like sharing or giving to charity) and negative (such as acting violently). Decades of experimental studies looking at the effects of television violence on children's behavior have found that children are more likely to be aggressive after viewing rewarded rather than punished TV violence (see Bushman & Huesmann, 2001, for a review). Most studies are limited to examining short-term effects (behavior right after viewing), so it is unclear whether children would make long-term behavior changes after a one-time viewing experience, especially if they later get in trouble at home or school for being aggressive.

There are several factors besides rewards and punishments that can increase the likelihood of imitating behaviors we witness on television (violent or otherwise). Children are more likely to imitate behavior that is realistic (as opposed to fantasy), justified (the character has a good reason for doing it), and committed by characters the children identify with (the hero). In addition, younger children have more difficulty understanding characters' motives and distinguishing fantasy from reality and are therefore more likely to be influenced by TV models. The good news is that providing strong, likable, and realistic positive role models for children can promote good behavior.

Cultivation Theory. If you watch a lot of reality TV about cosmetic surgery, are you more likely to believe that plastic surgery is normal and acceptable? George Gerbner's **cultivation theory** indeed argues that a steady, long-term diet of heavy television viewing results in perceptions of reality that match the (distorted) view of reality presented on television (Gerbner, Gross, Morgan, & Signorielli, 1994). Originally developed in the 1970s, the theory did not distinguish between different kinds of programs; it treated the entire TV world as basically the same—dominated by messages about crime and violence. The theory proposed that the more TV you watch, the more you will develop a perception of the world as a scary, violent place. Studies showed that individuals who watch a lot of television were indeed more likely to be afraid of crime or of walking alone at night, to estimate greater police activity, and to mistrust other people (Gerbner, Gross, Morgan, & Signorielli, 1994).

However, the explosion of television channels, genres, and new media has led to criticism of the idea that all television messages are the same, and research during the past two decades has largely shifted toward looking at correlations between attitudes and heavy viewing of certain types of media messages—young girls who consume a lot of "thin media" messages having poorer body images, for example (Harrison & Cantor, 1997; Tiggeman, 2005). But critics of cultivation theory argue not only that the effects are pretty small but also that it is impossible to determine whether any of the correlations that cultivation studies find are actually media effects (Nabi, 2009). This is because the causal direction could arguably be going the other way: girls who have a poor body image or low self-esteem are likely to seek out messages that confirm their views (that is, by finding thin models to compare themselves to). Similarly, people who are already accepting of plastic surgery are the very people most likely to watch shows about it. Still, it is important to be aware of our media "diet," as this may well be connected to the kinds of stereotypes, attitudes, and perceptions we are developing or reinforcing.

Agenda Setting. Whether or not media have the ability to cultivate our attitudes about issues, there is evidence that media *do* have an impact on what issues we think about in the first place. **Agenda setting** is the idea that extensive media coverage of a particular issue, such as an oil spill in the Gulf of Mexico or health care reform in Washington, will "set the agenda" for what issues people are thinking and talking about (see McCombs, 2005). Issues that do not get much coverage will not seem very important.

Agenda setting is important because we use the issues we are thinking about to evaluate political leaders and potential policy decisions. For example, when the BP oil spill was getting nonstop cable news coverage in May and June of 2010, people tended to evaluate President Obama based on how they thought he was handling the oil spill (as opposed to how he might have been dealing with other issues). Indeed, when his ratings on leadership and the handling of the crisis dropped, his overall approval ratings also dropped (Allen, 2010). Obama's decision to ban offshore oil drilling was a huge concern among audiences—applauded by those with long-standing concerns about oil and the environment and heavily criticized by those concerned about the Gulf's economy. But in either case, the importance of that decision was likely a function of the heavy press scrutiny at the time, along with continuing coverage of the oil pouring into the Gulf. Once the oil leak had been repaired and the news shifted to other topics, the moratorium on oil drilling seemed to also fade from people's concerns, despite its continuing effects on the Gulf's economy. As news coverage of oil issues rises or falls in the future, the concern about domestic drilling may resurface or fade as an important political battle.

With a diverse range of media news outlets available online, we might predict that media would no longer provide *an* agenda but would instead offer differing levels of coverage. But there is evidence that, even on the Internet, audiences still seem to

> Whether or not media have the ability to cultivate our attitudes about issues, there is evidence that media *do* have an impact on what issues we think about in the first place.

have their agendas influenced. Discussions on electronic bulletin boards, for example, have been found to correspond with the topics that had been covered

⎯⎯⎯⎯⎯⎯⎯⎯⎯⎯⎯⎯⎯⎯⎯⎯⎯

○ Due in great part to vanity-focused TV programs and reality stars, plastic surgery—even in extreme forms—is perceived as almost routine, particularly among females.

days beforehand in the mainstream news (Marilyn, Wanta, & Dzwo, 2002).

LearningCurve
bedfordstmartins.com/commandyou

Converging Media Technologies

Earlier in this chapter, we argued that today's media are converging—the lines between traditional mass communication and digital computing and telecommunication technologies are increasingly blurry (Pavlik & McIntosh, 2011). In this section, we explore the benefits and challenges for society of the increased interactivity and selectivity that media convergence allows.

> ### Technology and You
>
> Can you think of some examples of convergence in your daily life? Were these examples present five or ten years ago? How have these changes affected you?

Democratic and Social Participation

One benefit of converging media is the great potential for individuals and groups to participate more actively in the political process and contribute more directly to the culture. With traditional media, only the professionals (news organizations, television networks, studios, and so on) act as **gatekeepers**, controlling the creation and distribution of information and entertainment. Those outlets require enormous capital investment as well as highly technical production skills and capability. Internet use, on the other hand, doesn't require the same degree of skill, money, or access. This means that individuals online

have the opportunity to discover and provide voices competing with those of traditional media; they also have a means to connect with others locally and globally.

Connecting Marginalized Voices. How did revolts in Tunisia and Egypt so quickly escalate to thousands of citizens in the streets, eventually resulting in their governments toppling despite efforts to squelch Internet access and limit news media coverage? How did friends, relatives, rescue workers, and relief organizations make connections in the wake of a massive earthquake and tsunami in Japan? And how do fans of quirky shows, people dealing with rare illnesses, and individuals seeking specific goals even find each other? The use of the Web, e-mail, texting, and social networking (in combination with traditional modes of communication) allows groups that would not get much media coverage or whose members are not centralized geographically to better connect, provide alternative sources of information, and spread the word about their causes. They may also build **social capital**, which refers to the valuable resources (such as information and support) that come from having connections and relationships among people (Williams, 2006). Social networking via Facebook in particular has been shown to increase the strength of what would otherwise be weak ties among acquaintances or friends who have moved to different geographic locations (Ellison, Steinfeld, & Lampe, 2007). Although we would probably prefer that some groups or individuals *not* have such connectedness—such as hate groups, terrorists, and sexual predators—remember that open access means facilitating the participation of many different voices, not just the ones we like.

Empowering Individuals. Even artist Andy Warhol, who once predicted that eventually everyone would have the opportunity to be famous for fifteen minutes, might have been surprised by the ease with which anyone can put themselves into media today. Blogs, YouTube, and even professional news organizations offer opportunities for **citizen journalists** to report and comment on events in their communities.

Individuals can also contribute their own entertainment messages online.

Many forms of **user-generated content** have emerged, ranging from simple home videos uploaded to YouTube to elaborate mash-ups of popular songs or artworks (Pavlik & McIntosh, 2011). Content that manages to break into mass media culture is said to have "gone viral"—that is, spread from user to user (like an infection) via a link or Web post. Teen idol Justin Bieber first rose to fame in this manner, and in 2011, Rebecca Black's heavily autotuned song "Friday" went viral after comic Daniel Tosh joked about it on his *Tosh 2.0* blog (Shultz, 2011). Tosh himself felt the negative effects of viral content when outrage over a distasteful joke he made in a small comedy club became viral news in 2012. Social networking on Facebook or Twitter has also allowed individuals to elevate their everyday personal lives to public ones. Our status updates and photos can alert everyone we know (and friends of friends of people we know) as to what we are doing, feeling, and thinking. We even use social networking to feel more connected to the personal thoughts and feelings of celebrities, limited of course to the thoughts they purposely release to us via Twitter.

In short, media convergence enables individual voices to contribute to news, politics, and culture. While the quality of their messages varies greatly, there is some sense that allowing more voices to contribute to what has become known as the **marketplace of ideas**—the open forum in which ideas compete—is beneficial for society as a whole (*Abrams v. United States*, 1919).

Barriers to Participation

Media convergence may open up access to social, political, and cultural participation but only for those people who are willing and able to take advantage of these technologies. Although Internet use is widespread, much exposure is still confined to traditional mass media, especially television (Stelter, 2011). There are also several groups whose access to computers or high-speed Internet is limited or who are reluctant to use technology. And even among those who actively use converging media, effective participation may be limited by the ways they use media.

Digital Divide. Back in 1995, a mere 3 percent of Americans had used the Internet; by 2012, almost 80 percent had. Compared to any other technology of the last century, that is quite a rapid penetration into the population. Although the numbers of Internet users continue to grow across all demographic groups, there is still a **digital divide** between the haves and have-nots in terms of regular access, especially to broadband connections. This gap is primarily tied to income levels: in households with incomes above $30,000, Internet use ranges from 84 to 95 percent; it is used by only 63 percent of households earning less than $30,000 (Pew Research Center, 2010). As the cost of technology continues to decline, the income divide will most likely continue to close, and lower-income groups will gain opportunities for participation (Hanson, Thackeray, Barnes, Neiger, & McIntyre, 2008). Beyond the income barrier, a difficulty for some reluctant users is a lack of confidence when it comes to using technology, though increasingly user-friendly and affordable Web connections and applications can continue to increase self-efficacy.

> **Technology and You**
>
> Do you feel that you are able to participate fully and effectively in new areas of converged media? What barriers have you experienced using mass communication technology?

Ineffective Participation. When Amy's twin girls were born almost three months prematurely, her husband Vern got online right away to find out everything he could about "preemies." But his search quickly became overwhelming: for every opinion in one direction, there seemed to be someone else giving the opposite advice. The sheer volume of messages made available by converging media can lead to **information overload**, the difficulty in sorting through and making sense of vast amounts of information. Pavlik and McIntosh (2011) argue that, apart from the difficulty for individuals, information overload can also hinder the ability of government agencies to act on shared information and make it difficult for employees to share information effectively within their companies. Media multitasking can exacerbate the problem, as we may not be able to focus on the information we most need if we are texting or e-mailing during meetings or presentations.

It can also be difficult to evaluate the quality of information in converging media. Some information online is edited by professional journalists, some is user contributed and edited (such as on Wikipedia), and some is unedited information posted on forums, blogs, or personal Web sites. Rumors, hoaxes, and conspiracy theories abound (cataloged and investigated at Snopes.com). The potential for effective citizen participation is limited when users create or distribute false or other dangerous kinds of information online.

Participation is also ineffective when users fail to think critically about the information they find on the Internet. Much as with the traditional media,

a site that *looks* credible, with professional design and impressive depth of content, may be given higher credence even if it might otherwise be suspect given its origins or sponsorship. To make good on the promises of digital media for social and political participation, we need to devote our attention to the *quality* of our own and others' mediated communication.

LearningCurve
bedfordstmartins.com/commandyou

Becoming a More Mindful Media Consumer

Media scholars argue that the way to avoid or counteract negative media effects is by becoming **media literate** (Potter, 2008; Potter & Byrne, 2009). This means developing an understanding of your own media habits and critically evaluating and analyzing media sources and messages. To become media literate, you should practice the following skills.

Monitor Your Media Use and Exposure

Like counting calories or carbohydrates, being aware of what you consume can end up making you consume less or at least make wiser choices about your media diet. Parents often find that if they limit the hours per day or week of their children's "screen time" (TV, video games, Internet use), children tend to be much more selective in their media choices. Monitoring your own media use—including what you read or watch intentionally as well as the peripheral messages you are exposed to along the way—encourages you to take more responsibility for your exposure to media messages.

Consider the Source of Media Messages

Remember that every message you receive has a source, and it's your job to question its credibility. If

📍 Our information age may well be considered the "Too Much Information Age," as converging media deliver more content than we can process.

you understand the biases and goals of media sources—from advertisers and journalists to filmmakers and bloggers—you will be in a better position to know whether to resist or accept their messages. Bear in mind the economics of media, and think about how the business of mass communication might affect the messages you receive. And remember to be just as critical with material that supports your views as you are with material that does not.

Be Aware of Media Effects

Bear in mind how the media effects we discussed earlier in the chapter influence the way you receive, interpret, and react to media messages. Which media messages do you choose to attend to, and which do you tend to ignore? Do the messages you choose tend to change or reinforce your opinions on specific issues? Do you think that you are more immune to media effects than other people are?

Understand the Grammar of Media

Media each have a **grammar**—a set of rules and conventions that dictates how they operate. When you grow up with a medium, you often take for granted some of this grammar: you learned pretty early that the television screen going wavy is a sign of a flashback or dream sequence. But it is also useful to pay attention to other forms of television grammar, such as how news media arrange their visuals to maximize emotional impact. Understanding media conventions helps you recognize the limitations of media, so that you can better separate, for example, TV sitcom logic from real-life situations. You can also

better appreciate the genres you love, distinguish the good from the poor versions of these forms, and recognize the value of parodies of these conventions (such as *The Colbert Report*'s satire of news and talk shows). With digital media technology, there are many more grammars that you have to learn: Twitter has developed its own vernacular and symbols, for example. With emerging media, you may need to take time just to figure out the basics before you can engage in deeper levels of literacy and competence.

Actively Evaluate Media Messages

When you put together all the above skills, you can critically evaluate media messages and become a more competent participant in mass communication. Ask yourself what was great about a television episode (was it insightful, clever, funny, or moving?) and what was poor (unbelievable, unrealistic, or clichéd?). Consider carefully what underlying themes or values are being presented in your entertainment and news content. Are these consistent with your own values? *Should* they be? Might these images be suggesting that you should compromise your morals or engage in unhealthy behavior?

Take time to think critically about the messages you send as well as those you receive. Be mindful when posting on Facebook or Twitter: Are you respecting the privacy of others when you tag them in photos? Are the messages in your status updates appropriate? Is it fair to retweet an embarrassing post that the author might regret having written? Remember, as both a consumer and a producer of media messages, it's up to you to communicate competently and ethically.

Ethics and You

How does your awareness of media effects influence how you spread information and content by sharing it on Facebook, Twitter, or other social media? Are there some stories or media clips that would be irresponsible to share without knowing more about them?

What About You?

Your Media Diet

How much of your life is experienced through media convergence? Consider the following activities, and estimate the average number of minutes per day you spend using different media types for each activity. Also, indicate the main reasons for using that media type (to escape, for entertainment, for information, or to maintain relationships, for example).

Activity	Minutes per Day	Reasons for Use
Reading		
Printed hard copy (books, newspapers, magazines)		
Web pages (news, research articles)		
E-readers (Kindle)		
Watching television programming		
Live (as aired on broadcast, cable, or satellite)		
Streamed online (whole shows or clips)		
Recorded (podcasts, DVR)		
Engaging with user-generated content		
Other people's uploaded videos or artwork		
Creating and uploading your own content		
Listening to music		
Streamed online (Pandora)		
Recorded (iPod, MP3 player, CD)		
Live (radio station)		
Interacting with other people		
Mobile phone text messaging		
Talking on the phone (cell or landline)		
Social networking (Facebook, Twitter)		
E-mail		
Instant messaging (online)		
Other media/technology use		

LearningCurve
bedfordstmartins.com/commandyou

Back to } Alice's Multimedia Family

At the beginning of this appendix, we talked about teenager Alice and the many types of mass and mediated communication that she and her family use in a single day, much of it at the same time. Consider Alice's media experiences in light of what you've learned in this appendix.

- Alice is experiencing media convergence. She combines traditional forms of mass media—television and books—with more interactive computer technology as she streams her favorite shows on the Internet and comments on fan blogs. Traditional media are still prominent, but these media interact with her use of texting and social networking. Even her "family time" with her brother is connected to media (video games and television), as is her schoolwork.

- Because of the different forms of media that Alice has access to, she can be very selective about what she uses and why. She is not likely to bother with content that she doesn't like or want. Thus, media content creators (filmmakers, television producers, and so on) must be sure to include messages that appeal to her and others in her demographic group.

- Alice uses Facebook not only to make connections with her peers but also to contribute her own comments and feelings about cultural phenomena, such as the *Hunger Games* trilogy and the actor Joseph Gordon-Levitt. This cultural bonding may build social capital among her network of friends.

Your Reference

} A Study Tool

Now that you have finished reading this appendix, you can

Define mass and mediated communication:

- **Mediated communication** occurs when there is some technology that is used to deliver messages; when it occurs on a very broad scale, we refer to it as **mass communication** (pp. 388–389).
- **Media convergence** means that we often engage in **media multitasking** (p. 389).

Describe how the business of media and the principle of free speech shape the kinds of media content you encounter:

- Most media are businesses that must attract audiences and advertising dollars to remain profitable. **Exponentiality** means that relatively few items bring in most of the income (p. 390).
- Media often cater to **low culture** in order to attract broad audiences, but they have also found success in programs with **narrative complexity**. They target niche audiences through **narrowcasting** (pp. 390–391).
- Media producers minimize risk by conducting extensive audience research and engaging in **self-censorship**, as well as by relying on proven formulas for success (pp. 391–392).
- The courts have allowed some restrictions on First Amendment freedoms when it comes to **broadcasting** (there are limitations on broadcasting **indecency**, for example) (pp. 392–393).
- Like all forms of communication, mass communication can be biased (pp. 393–395).

Provide two explanations for the effects of mass media:

- The **uses and gratifications perspective** argues that we make media choices in order to satisfy our needs and goals. The expectation that media can satisfy all these needs can lead to **media dependence** (pp. 395–396).
- We often make media choices in order to reinforce our existing attitudes and tend to think that media messages have more of an affect on others than they do on us, a phenomenon known as the **third-person effect** (p. 396).

Articulate how media exert influence on your attitudes and behaviors:

- **Social cognitive theory** argues that we learn behavior by watching how media models behave (p. 397).
- In **cultivation theory**, the belief is that a steady, long-term diet of TV viewing can distort our perceptions of the world (p. 397).
- News coverage can have an **agenda setting** ⊙ effect— we tend to judge the importance of issues by the amount of news coverage they get (pp. 398–399).

Describe how the convergence of media technologies can enhance or hinder your participation in the social and political process:

- A benefit of converging media is that traditional media no longer serve as the sole **gatekeeper** of information and creative content (p. 399).
- Media connections allow marginalized or geographically dispersed groups to build **social capital**—valuable resources like information and support that come from having connections and relationships among people (p. 399).
- Modern media also empower individuals to become **citizen journalists** ⊙ and to create other kinds of **user-generated content** ⊙, creating greater competition in the **marketplace of ideas** (pp. 399–400).
- A **digital divide** persists between those who have media access (and use it) and those who do not (p. 400).
- Ineffective participation in the digital world can be the result of **information overload**. A failure to think critically about media also hinders participation (pp. 400–401).

Practice five skills for becoming a more mindful and media-literate consumer:

- Monitor your media use and exposure (p. 401).
- Consider the source of media messages (pp. 401–402).
- Be aware of media effects (p. 402).
- Understand the grammar of media (p. 402).
- Actively evaluate media messages (p. 402).

GLOSSARY

abstraction ladder: A model that ranks communication from specific, which ensures clarity, to general and vague.

accent: A pattern of pronunciation that is specific to a certain upbringing, geographical region, or culture.

accenting: Nonverbal behavior that clarifies and emphasizes specific information in a verbal message.

accommodation: Adapting and adjusting one's language and nonverbal behaviors for other people or cultures.

achievement-oriented leader: A leader who sets challenging goals and communicates high expectations and standards to members.

active listening: Being an active participant in making choices about selecting, attending, and the other steps in the listening process.

active strategies: In relationship management, strategies that allow one to obtain information about a person more directly, by seeking information from a third party.

adaptors: Body movements that satisfy some physical or psychological need, such as rubbing your eyes when you're tired or twisting your hair when you're nervous or bored.

ad hominem **fallacy:** A logical fallacy that entails attacking a person instead of the person's arguments.

adjourning: The stage of group development in which members reflect on their accomplishments and failures as well as determine whether the group will disassemble or take on another project.

affect displays: Body movements that convey feelings, moods, and reactions; they are often unintentional, reflecting the sender's emotions.

affiliation: The affect, or feelings, we have for others.

agenda: A plan for a meeting that details the subject and goal, logistics, and a schedule.

agenda setting: The idea that extensive media coverage of a particular issue will "set the agenda" for what issues people are thinking and talking about.

all-channel network: A network in which all members are an equal distance from one another and all members interact with each other.

anchor position: An audience's position on a topic at the outset of the speech.

anecdotes: Brief, personal stories that have a point or punch line.

antigroup roles: Roles that create problems because they serve individual members' priorities at the expense of overall group needs.

appeal to tradition: A logical fallacy in which the speaker uses tradition as proof, suggesting that listeners should agree with his or her point because "that's the way it has always been."

appreciative listening: Listening with the simple goal of taking pleasure in the sounds that one receives.

articulation: The clarity and forcefulness with which sounds are made, regardless of whether they are pronounced correctly.

artifacts: Accessories carried or used on the body for decoration or identification.

attending: The step in the listening process of focusing attention on both the presence and communication of someone else.

attitudes: Our general evaluations of people, ideas, objects, or events.

attraction-similarity hypothesis: The belief that the extent to which we project ourselves onto another person is the direct result of the attraction we feel for that person.

attributions: Personal characteristics that are used to explain other people's behavior.

audience analysis: A highly systematic process of getting to know one's listeners relative to the topic and speech occasion.

back-channel cues: Vocalizations that signal when we want to talk versus when we are just encouraging others to continue their talking.

G-1

bandwagon fallacy: Accepting a statement as true because it is popular.

bar graph: A presentation aid that shows the relationship of two or more sets of figures.

begging the question: A logical fallacy in which the speaker presents arguments that no one can verify because they are not accompanied by valid evidence.

behavior: Observable communication, including both verbal and nonverbal messages; the manner in which we act or function in response to our attitudes and beliefs.

behavioral affirmation: Seeing or hearing what one wants to see or hear in the communication of assorted group members.

behavioral confirmation: Acting in a way that makes one's expectations about a group come true.

behavioral flexibility: The ability to have a number of communication behaviors at one's disposal and the willingness to use different behaviors in different situations.

beliefs: The ways in which people perceive reality; our feelings about what is true and real and how confident we are about the existence or validity of something.

biased language: Words that are infused with subtle meanings that influence our perceptions about the subject.

bipolar question: The most closed form of a question, for which there are only two possible responses, "yes" and "no."

bonding: The process of relational partners sharing formal symbolic messages with the world that their relationship is important and cherished.

boundary turbulence: Readjusting the need for privacy against the need for self-disclosure and connection when there is a threat to one's privacy boundaries.

brainstorming: A process that entails focusing on a general area of interest, amassing information, thinking creatively, and considering problems and solutions related to the topic.

broadcasting: Signals carried over the airwaves from a station transmitter to a receiver.

bullying: Behaviors such as harsh criticism, name-calling, gossip, slander, personal attacks, or threats to safety or job security, used to try to acquire and keep control over an entire group or individual members within a group.

call to action: In a persuasive speech, a challenge to listeners to act in response to the speech, see the problem in a new way, or change their beliefs, actions, and behavior.

cause-effect pattern: A pattern of speech arrangement that organizes the message around cause-to-effect or effect-to-cause relationships.

central processing: Thinking critically about the speaker's message, questioning it, and seriously considering acting on it; occurs when listeners are motivated and personally involved in the content of a message.

chain network: A network in which information is passed from one member to the next rather than shared among members.

challenging strategies: Strategies that promote the objectives of the individual who uses them, rather than the desires of the other person or the relationship.

channel: The method through which communication occurs.

channel discrepancy: When one set of behaviors says one thing, and another set says something different.

chronological pattern: A pattern of speech arrangement that presents the main points of a message forward (or backward) in a systematic, time-related fashion.

citizen journalism: Reporting and commenting on local events by nonprofessional, nonjournalist citizens.

civility: The social norm for appropriate behavior.

clique: A small subgroup of individuals who have bonded together within a group; also called *coalitions*.

closed question: A type of interview question that gives less freedom to the interviewee by restricting answer choices.

clustering: A technique for identifying potential speech topics whereby the writer begins with a core idea and branches out into a web of related thoughts and ideas.

co-culture: A smaller group of people within a culture who are distinguished by features such as race, religion, age, generation, political affiliation, gender, sexual orientation, economic status, educational level, occupation, and a host of other factors.

code: A set of symbols that are joined to create a meaningful message.

code switching: A type of accommodation in which communicators change their regular language and slang to fit into a particular group.

coercion: The act of using manipulation, threats, intimidation, or violence to gain compliance.

cognitions: Thoughts that communicators have about themselves and others.

cognitive forces: Group members' thoughts and beliefs, which affect how members perceive, interpret, evaluate, store, and retrieve information and, in turn, influence the group's decisions.

cognitive language: The specific system of symbols that one uses to describe people, things, and situations in one's mind.

cohesion: The degree to which group members have bonded, like each other, and consider themselves to be one entity.

collectivist culture: A culture in which individuals perceive themselves first and foremost as members of a group and communicate from that perspective.

communication: The process by which individuals use symbols, signs, and behaviors to exchange information.

communication acquisition: The process of learning individual words in a language and learning to use that language appropriately and effectively in the context of the situation.

communication apprehension (CA): Fear or anxiety associated with communication, which is often a common barrier to effective delivery.

communication boundary management: Reluctance to discuss certain topics with particular people.

communication climate: The dominant temper, attitudes, and outlook of relational partners.

communication privacy management theory (CPM): An explanation of how people perceive the information they hold about themselves and whether they will disclose or protect it.

communication processing: The means by which we gather, organize, and evaluate the information we receive.

communication skills: Behaviors based on social understandings that help communicators achieve their goals.

comparative advantage pattern: An organizing pattern for persuasive speaking in which the speaker shows that his or her viewpoint is superior to other viewpoints on the topic.

competent communication: Communication that is effective and appropriate for a given situation, in which the communicators continually evaluate and reassess their own communication process.

competent communication model: A transactional model of communication in which communicators send and receive messages simultaneously within a relational, situational, and cultural context.

complementing: Nonverbal behavior that matches (without actually mirroring) the verbal message it accompanies.

compromise: A way to resolve conflict in which both parties must give up something to gain something.

conflict: A negative interaction between two or more interdependent people, rooted in some actual or perceived disagreement.

conflict management: The way we engage in conflict and address disagreements with relational partners.

connotative meaning: The emotional or attitudinal response people have to a word.

contact cultures: Cultures that depend on touch as an important form of communication.

contradicting: Nonverbal behavior that conveys meaning opposite of the verbal message.

control: The ability of one person, group, or organization to influence others, and the manner in which their relationships are conducted.

convergence: When speakers shift their language or nonverbal behaviors toward each other's way of communicating.

cooperative strategies: Strategies that benefit a relationship, serve mutual rather than individual goals, and strive to produce solutions that benefit both parties.

costs: The negative elements of a relationship.

countercoalitions: Subgroups that are positioned against other subgroups.

cover letter: A one-page letter indicating interest in a specific position.

credibility: The quality, authority, and reliability of a source of information.

critical listening: Evaluating or analyzing information, evidence, ideas, or opinions; also known as *evaluative listening.*

cultivation theory: The argument that a steady, long-term diet of heavy television viewing results in perceptions of reality that match the (distorted) view of reality presented on television.

cultural myopia: A form of cultural nearsightedness grounded in the belief that one's own culture is appropriate and relevant in all situations and to all people.

culture: A learned system of thought and behavior that belongs to and typifies a relatively large group of people;

the composite of their shared beliefs, values, and practices.

cyberbullying: Multiple abusive attacks on individual targets conducted through electronic channels.

deception: The attempt to convince others of something that is false.

declining stage: The stage at which a relationship begins to come apart.

decoding: The process of receiving a message by interpreting and assigning meaning to it.

deductive reasoning: The line of thought that occurs when one draws specific conclusions from a general argument.

defensive climate: A communication climate in which the people involved feel threatened.

defensive listening: Responding with aggression and arguing with the speaker without fully listening to the message.

definitional speech: A presentation whose main goal is to provide answers to "what" questions by explaining to an audience what something is.

definition by etymology: Defining something by using the origin of a word or phrase.

definition by example: Defining something by offering concrete examples of what it is.

definition by negation: Defining something by telling what it is not.

definition by synonym: Defining something by using words that mean almost the same thing.

delivery cues: In a speech outline, brief reminders about important information related to the delivery of the speech.

demographics: The systematic study of the quantifiable characteristics of a large group.

demonstration speech: A speech that answers "how" questions by showing an audience the way something works.

denotative meaning: The basic, consistently accepted definition of a word.

descriptive presentation: An approach to conveying information that involves painting a mental picture for the audience.

devil's advocate: A role that involves pointing out worst-case scenarios.

dialectical tensions: Tensions that arise when opposing or conflicting goals exist in a relationship; can be external or internal.

digital divide: The gap between the haves and have-nots in terms of regular access to modern technology, especially broadband connections.

directed question: A type of interview question that suggests or implies the answer that is expected.

directive leader: A leader who controls the group's communication by conveying specific instructions to members.

directory: A type of secondary resource that is created and maintained by people rather than automatically by computers; guides visitors to the main page of a Web site organized within a wider subject category.

discrimination: Behavior toward a person or group based solely on their membership in a particular group, class, or category.

dyad: A pair of people.

either-or fallacy: A fallacy in which the speaker presents only two alternatives on a subject and fails to acknowledge other alternatives; also known as the *false dilemma fallacy*.

Elaboration Likelihood Model (ELM): A model that highlights the importance of relevance to persuasion and holds that listeners process persuasive messages by one of two routes, depending on how important the message is to them.

elucidating explanation: An explanation that illuminates a concept's meaning and use.

empathic listening: Listening to people with openness, sensitivity, and caring; attempting to know how another person feels.

encoding: The process of mentally constructing a message for production.

equivocation: Using words that have unclear or misleading definitions.

escapist strategies: Strategies that people use to try to prevent or avoid direct conflict.

ethics: The study of morals, specifically the moral choices individuals make in their relationships with others.

ethnocentrism: A belief in the superiority of one's own culture or group and a tendency to view other cultures through the lens of one's own.

ethos: A form of rhetorical proof that appeals to ethics and concerns the qualifications and personality of the speaker.

euphemism: An inoffensive word or phrase that substitutes for terms that might be perceived as upsetting.

evasion: Intentionally failing to provide specific details.

exit interview: An interview that employers hold with employees who opt to leave the company, to identify organizational problems that might affect future employee retention.

expert power: Power that comes from the information or knowledge that a leader possesses.

expert testimony: The opinion or judgment of an expert, a professional in his or her field.

explanatory speech: A speech that answers the question "Why" or "What does that mean?" by offering thorough explanations of meaning.

exploratory stage: The stage of a relationship in which one seeks relatively superficial information from one's partner.

exponentiality: The economic principle that relatively few items bring most of the income to a particular industry, while the rest add only a little.

extemporaneous speaking: A style of public speaking that involves delivery with few or no notes, but for which the speaker carefully prepares in advance.

family: A small social group bound by ties of blood, civil contract (such as marriage, civil union, or adoption), and a commitment to care for and be responsible for one another, usually in a shared household.

feeling: The use of language to express emotion; one of the five functional communication competencies.

flaming: The posting of online messages that are deliberately hostile or insulting toward a particular individual.

forming: The stage of group development in which group members try to negotiate who will be in charge and what the group's goals will be.

forms of rhetorical proof: Means of persuasion that include *ethos*, *logos*, and *pathos*; first named by Aristotle.

friendship: A close and caring relationship between two people that is perceived as mutually satisfying and beneficial.

functional perspective: An examination of how communication behaviors work to accomplish goals in personal, group, organizational, or public situations.

fundamental attribution error: The tendency to overemphasize the internal and underestimate the external causes of behaviors we observe in others.

funnel sequence: A pattern of questioning that progresses from broad, open-ended questions to narrower, more closed questions.

gatekeepers: Those organizations and individuals who control the creation and distribution of information and entertainment.

gender: The behavioral and cultural traits assigned to one's sex; determined by the way members of a particular culture define notions of masculinity and femininity.

generation: A group of people who were born into a specific time frame, along with its events and social changes that shape attitudes and behavior.

genetic-similarity hypothesis: The theory that two individuals who hail from the same ethnic group are more genetically similar than two individuals from different ethnic groups.

goal achievement: Relying on communication to accomplish particular objectives.

grammar of media: For each form of media, a set of rules and conventions that dictate how it operates.

group: A collection of more than two people who share some kind of relationship, communicate in an interdependent fashion, and collaborate toward some shared purpose.

groupthink: A situation in which group members strive to maintain cohesiveness and minimize conflict by refusing to critically examine ideas, analyze proposals, or test solutions.

haptics: The study of touch as a form of communication.

hearing: The physiological process of perceiving sound; the process through which sound waves are picked up by the ears and transmitted to the brain.

hierarchy of needs: A hierarchical structure that identifies needs in five categories, from low (immature) to high (mature).

high-context culture: A culture that relies on contextual cues—such as time, place, relationship, and situation—to both interpret meaning and send subtle messages.

high language: A more formal, polite, or "mainstream" language, used in business contexts, in the classroom, and at formal social gatherings.

homogeny: Sameness, as applied to a public speaker and his or her audience.

hostile audience: An audience that opposes the speaker's message and perhaps the speaker personally; the hardest type of audience to persuade.

hyperbole: Vivid, colorful language with great emotional intensity and often exaggeration.

hyperpersonal communication: A phenomenon surrounding online communication in which a lack of proximity, visual contact, or nonverbal cues results in exaggerated perceptions.

illustrators: Body movements that reinforce verbal messages and visually help explain what is being said.

imagining: The ability to think, play, and be creative in communication; one of the five functional communication competencies.

immediacy: The feeling of closeness, involvement, and warmth between people as communicated by nonverbal behavior.

impromptu speaking: A style of public speaking that is spontaneous, without any warning or preparation.

inclusion: To involve others in our lives and to be involved in the lives of others.

indecency: Discussing or showing sexual or other bodily functions in a very lewd or vulgar way.

individualist culture: A culture whose members place value on autonomy and privacy, with relatively little attention to status and hierarchy based on age or family connections.

inductive reasoning: The line of thought that occurs when one draws general conclusions based on specific evidence.

informal-formal dimension: A psychological aspect of the situational context of communication, dealing with our perceptions of personal versus impersonal situations.

informational listening: Processing and accurately understanding a message; also known as *comprehensive listening.*

information-gathering interview: An interview that serves to transfer knowledge from one party to another by collecting attitudes, opinions, facts, data, and experiences.

information overload: The difficulty in sorting through and making sense of vast amounts of information, created by the volume of messages made available by converging media.

informative speaking: A form of public speaking intended to increase the audience's understanding or knowledge.

informing: The use of language to both give and receive information; one of the five functional communication competencies.

ingroup: The group with which one identifies and to which one feels one belongs.

initiating stage: The stage of a relationship in which one makes contact with another person.

insensitive listening: Listening that occurs when we fail to pay attention to the emotional content of someone's message, instead taking it at face value.

integrating: The process of relational partners "becoming one."

intensification stage: The stage of a relationship in which relational partners become increasingly intimate and move their communication toward more personal self-disclosures.

interaction appearance theory: The argument that people change their opinion about the attributions of someone, particularly their physical attractiveness, the more they interact with that person.

interaction model: Communication between a sender and a receiver that incorporates feedback.

interactive strategies: Speaking directly with a relational partner rather than observing him or her passively or asking others for information.

intercultural communication: The communication between people from different cultures who have different worldviews.

intercultural sensitivity: Mindfulness of behaviors that may offend others.

interdependence: Mutual dependence where the actions of each partner affect the other(s).

intergroup communication: A branch of the communication discipline that focuses on how communication within and between groups affects relationships.

intergroup contact theory: The argument that interaction between members of different social groups generates a possibility for more positive attitudes to emerge.

internal preview: In public speaking, an extended transition that primes the audience for the content immediately ahead.

internal summary: An extended transition that allows the speaker to crystallize the points made in one section of a speech before moving to the next section.

interpersonal communication: The exchange of verbal and nonverbal messages between two people who have a relationship and are influenced by the partner's messages.

interpersonal relationships: The interconnections and interdependence between two individuals.

interview: An interaction between two parties that is deliberate and purposeful for at least one of the parties involved.

intimacy: Closeness and understanding of a relational partner.

inverted funnel sequence: A pattern of questioning that progresses from narrow, closed questions to more open-ended questions.

jargon: Technical language that is specific to members of a particular profession, interest group, or hobby.

job interview: A type of selection interview, with the end goal of filling a position of employment.

key-word outline: The briefest type of outline, consisting of specific "key words" from the sentence outline to jog the speaker's memory.

kinesics: The way gestures and body movements communicate meaning.

language: The system of symbols (words) that we use to think about and communicate experiences and feelings.

latitude of acceptance and rejection: The range of positions on a topic that are acceptable or unacceptable to an audience based on their *anchor position*.

lay testimony: The opinion of a nonexpert who has personal experience of or has witnessed an event related to the speaker's topic.

leadership: The ability to direct or influence others' behaviors and thoughts toward a productive end.

leading question: A type of directed question that subtly suggests or implies the answer that is expected.

legitimate power: Power that comes from an individual's role or title.

library gateway: A collection of databases and information sites arranged by subject, generally reviewed and recommended by experts (usually librarians).

linear model (of communication): Communication in which a sender originates a message, which is carried through a channel—perhaps interfered with by noise— to the receiver.

linguistic determinism: The idea that language influences how we see the world around us.

linguistic relativity: The belief that speakers of different languages have different views of the world.

listening: The process of recognizing, understanding, accurately interpreting, and responding effectively to the messages communicated by others.

listening apprehension: A state of uneasiness, anxiety, fear, or dread associated with a listening opportunity; also known as *receiver apprehension*.

listening barrier: A factor that interferes with the ability to accurately comprehend information and respond appropriately.

listening fidelity: The degree to which the thoughts of the listener and the thoughts and intentions of the message producer match following their communication.

loaded question: A type of directed question that boldly suggests the answer that is expected.

logical fallacy: An invalid or deceptive form of reasoning.

logos: A form of rhetorical proof that appeals to logic and is directed at the audience's reasoning on a topic.

love: A deep affection for and attachment to another person involving emotional ties, with varying degrees of passion, commitment, and intimacy.

low-context culture: A culture that uses very direct language and relies less on situational factors to communicate.

low culture: Entertainment that appeals to most people's baser instincts, typified by lurid, sensational images and stories charged with sex, violence, scandal, and abuse.

low language: A more informal, easygoing language, used in informal and comfortable environments.

main points: In public speaking, the central claims that support the specific speech purpose and thesis statement.

marketplace of ideas: The open forum in which ideas compete.

masculine culture: A culture that places value on assertiveness, achievement, ambition, and competitiveness; sometimes referred to as an *achievement culture*.

masking: A facial management technique in which an expression that shows true feeling is replaced with an expression that shows appropriate feeling for a given interaction.

mass communication: The occurrence of mediated communication on a very broad scale.

matching hypothesis: The theory that we seek relationships with others who have comparable levels of attractiveness.

media convergence: The merging of traditional mass communication with digital computing and telecommunication technologies.

media dependence: The expectation that media will serve certain needs.

media literacy: Having an understanding of one's own media habits and critically evaluating and analyzing media sources and messages.

media multitasking: Using more than one media type at the same time.

mediated communication: The use of technology to deliver messages between sources and receivers.

message: The words or actions originated by a sender.

metasearch engine: A search engine that scans multiple search engines simultaneously.

mimicry: The synchronized and usually unconscious pattern of imitating or matching gestures, body position, tone, and facial expressions to create social connections between people.

mindfulness: The process of being focused on the task at hand; necessary for competent communication.

mindlessness: A passive state in which the communicator is a less critical processor of information, characterized by reduced cognitive activity, inaccurate recall, and uncritical evaluation.

model: A presentation aid—an appropriately scaled object.

monochronic culture: A culture that treats time as a limited resource, as a commodity that can be saved or wasted.

monopolistic listening: Listening in order to control the communication interaction.

monotone: A way of speaking in which the speaker does not vary his or her vocal pitch.

motivated sequence pattern: A pattern of speech arrangement that entails five phases based on the psychological elements of advertising: attention, need, satisfaction, visualization, and action.

mumbling: Omitting certain sounds in a word, running words together, or speaking so softly that listeners can hardly hear.

narrative complexity: In mass media, complicated plots and connections between characters, a blurring of reality and fantasy, and time that is not always linear or chronological.

narrative pattern: A pattern of speech arrangement that ties points together in a way that presents a vivid story, complete with characters, settings, plot, and imagery.

narrowcasting: In mass media, the process of targeting smaller, specific audiences; also known as *niche marketing.*

network: A pattern of interaction that governs who speaks with whom in a group and about what.

networking: The process of using interconnected groups or associations of persons one knows to develop relationships with their connections whom one does not know.

neutral audience: An audience that falls between the receptive audience and the hostile audience; neither supports nor opposes the speaker.

neutral question: A type of interview question that provides no hint to the interviewee concerning the expected response.

noise: Interference with a message that makes its final form different from the original.

nonbinding straw poll: An informal vote on a decision that can help a group move forward when time is an issue.

noncontact culture: A culture that is less touch sensitive or even tends to avoid touch.

nonverbal codes: Symbols we use to send messages without, or in addition to, words.

nonverbal communication: The process of intentionally or unintentionally signaling meaning through behavior other than words.

norming: The stage of group development in which members establish agreed-upon norms that govern expected behavior.

norms: Recurring patterns of behavior or thinking that come to be accepted in a group as the "usual" way of doing things.

objectivity: Presenting facts and information in a straightforward and evenhanded way, free of influence from the speaker's personal thoughts and opinions.

oculesics: The study of the use of eyes to communicate.

open question: A type of interview question that gives the interviewee great freedom in terms of how to respond.

operational definition: Defining something by explaining what it is or what it does.

oral citation: A reference to source materials that the speaker mentions in the narrative of a speech.

oratory: A form of public speaking in which a speech is committed to memory.

outcome: The product of an interchange.

outgroups: Those groups one defines as "others."

outline: A structured form of a speech's content.

overaccommodation: Going too far in changing one's language or nonverbal behavior, based on an incorrect or stereotypical notion of another group.

paralanguage: The vocalized sounds that accompany words.

paraphrasing: A part of listening empathetically that involves guessing at feelings and rephrasing what one thinks the speaker has said.

participative leader: A leader who views group members as equals, welcomes their opinions, summarizes points that have been raised, and identifies problems that need discussion rather than dictating solutions.

passive listening: Failing to make active choices in the listening process.

pathos: A form of rhetorical proof that concerns the nature of the audience's feelings and appeals to their emotions.

perception: A cognitive process through which one interprets one's experiences and comes to one's own unique understandings.

performance appraisal: An interview designed to review an individual or party's accomplishments and develop goals for the future; used in corporate and academic environments.

performance visualization: Spending time imagining positive scenarios and personal success in order to reduce negative thoughts and their accompanying anxiety.

performing: The stage of group development in which members combine their skills and knowledge to work toward the group's goals and overcome hurdles.

peripheral processing: Giving little thought to a message or even dismissing it as irrelevant, too complex to follow, or simply unimportant; occurs when listeners lack motivation to listen critically or are unable to do so.

persuasion: The process of influencing others' attitudes, beliefs, and behaviors on a given topic.

persuasive interview: An interview in which questions are designed to elicit some change in the interviewee's behavior or opinions.

persuasive speaking: Speech that is intended to influence the attitudes, beliefs, and behaviors of an audience.

phrase outline: A type of outline that takes parts of sentences and uses those phrases as instant reminders of what the point or subpoint means.

pie chart: A presentation aid that shows percentages of a circle divided proportionately.

pitch: Variations in the voice that give prominence to certain words or syllables.

plagiarism: The crime of presenting someone else's words, ideas, or intellectual property as one's own, intentionally or unintentionally.

planting: A technique for limiting and controlling body movements during speech delivery by keeping the legs firmly set apart at a shoulder-width distance.

politically correct language: Language that replaces exclusive or negative words with more neutral terms.

polychronic culture: A culture whose members are comfortable dealing with multiple people and tasks at the same time.

posture: The position of one's arms and legs and how one carries the body.

power distance: The way in which a culture accepts and expects the division of power among individuals.

pragmatics: The ability to use the symbol systems of a culture appropriately.

prejudice: A deep-seated feeling of unkindness and ill will toward particular groups, usually based on negative stereotypes and feelings of superiority over those groups.

preparation outline: A draft outline the speaker will use, and probably revisit and revise continually, throughout the preparation for a speech; also known as a *working outline*.

primacy-recency effect: In public speaking, the tendency for audiences to remember points the speaker raises at the very beginning, or at the very end, of a message.

primary group: A long-lasting group that forms around the relationships that mean the most to its members.

primary question: A type of interview question that introduces new topics.

probing: Asking questions that encourage specific and precise answers.

problem-solution pattern: A pattern of speech arrangement that involves dramatizing an obstacle and then narrowing alternative remedies down to the one the speaker wants to recommend.

problem-solving group: A group with a specific mission.

problem-solving interview: An interview that is used to deal with problems, tensions, or conflicts.

process: The methods by which an outcome is accomplished.

productive conflict: Conflict that is managed effectively.

profanity: Words or expressions considered insulting, rude, vulgar, or disrespectful.

pronunciation: The correct formation of word sounds.

prop: A presentation aid—an object that removes the burden from the audience of having to imagine what something looks like as the speaker is presenting.

proposition of fact: A claim of what is or what is not.

proposition of policy: A claim about what goal, policy, or course of action should be pursued.

proposition of value: A claim about something's worth.

proxemics: The study of the way we use and communicate with space.

proximity: A state of physical nearness.

pseudolistening: Pretending to listen when one is actually not paying attention at all.

psychological forces: Group members' personal motives, emotions, attitudes, and values.

public-private dimension: An aspect of the situational context of communication dealing with the physical space that affects our nonverbal communication.

public speaking: A powerful form of communication that includes a speaker who has a reason for speaking, an audience that gives the speaker attention, and a message that is meant to accomplish a specific purpose.

public speaking anxiety (PSA): The nervousness one experiences when one knows one has to communicate publicly to an audience.

quasi-scientific explanation: An explanation that models or pictures the key dimensions of some phenomenon for a typical audience.

random selection: A way to reach compromise that entails choosing one of two options at random, such as by a coin toss.

reasoning: The line of thought we use to make judgments based on facts and inferences from the world around us.

receiver: The target of a message.

receptive audience: An audience that already agrees with the speaker's viewpoints and message and is likely to respond favorably to the speech.

reconciliation: A repair strategy for rekindling an extinguished relationship.

red herring fallacy: A fallacy in which the speaker relies on irrelevant information for his or her argument, thereby diverting the direction of the argument.

reduction to the absurd: A logical fallacy that entails extending an argument beyond its logical limits to the level of absurdity; also known as *reductio ad absurdum*.

referent power: Power that stems from the admiration, respect, or affection that followers have for a leader.

refutational organizational pattern: An organizing pattern for persuasive speaking in which the speaker begins by presenting main points that are opposed to his or her own position and then follows them with main points that support his or her own position.

regulating: Using nonverbal cues to aid in the coordination of verbal interaction.

regulators: Body movements that help us manage our interactions.

relational dialectics theory: The theory that *dialectical tensions* are contradictory feelings that tug at us in every relationship.

relational history: The sum of shared experiences of the individuals involved in a relationship.

relational network: A web of relationships that connects individuals to one another.

relationships: The interconnection or interdependence between two or more people required to achieve goals.

remembering: The step in the listening process of recalling information.

repair tactics: Ways to save or repair a relationship.

repeating: Nonverbal behavior that offers a clear nonverbal cue that repeats and mirrors the verbal message.

responding: The step in the listening process of generating some kind of feedback or reaction that confirms to others that one has received and understood their messages.

résumé: A printed summary of one's education, work experiences, and accomplishments.

reward power: Power that derives from an individual's capacity to provide rewards.

rewards: The beneficial elements of a relationship.

ritualizing: Learning the rules for managing conversations and relationships; one of the five functional communication competencies.

role conflict: A situation that arises in a group whenever expectations for members' behavior are incompatible.

running bibliography: A list of resources the speaker has consulted, to which he or she can refer on note cards.

salient: Brought to mind in the moment; one's social identity and communication shift depending on which of one's multiple group memberships is salient in a given moment.

Sapir-Whorf hypothesis: The claim that the words a culture uses or doesn't use influence its members' thinking.

scanning: A technique for making brief eye contact with almost everyone in an audience by moving one's eyes from one person or section of people to another.

scientific research findings: Hard numbers and facts that are particularly useful for public speeches on medicine, health, media, or the environment.

search engine: A program that indexes Web content and searches all over the Web for documents containing specific keywords that the researcher has chosen.

secondary questions: A type of interview question that seeks clarification or an elaboration of responses to primary questions.

selecting: The step in the listening process of choosing one sound over another when faced with competing stimuli.

selection interview: An interview whose primary goal is to secure or fill a position within an organization.

selective listening: Listening that involves zeroing in only on bits of information that interest the listener, disregarding other messages or parts of messages.

selective perception: Active, critical thought resulting in a communicator succumbing to the biased nature of perception.

self-actualization: The feelings and thoughts one experiences when one knows that one has negotiated a communication situation as well as possible.

self-adequacy: The feelings one experiences when one assesses one's own communication competence as sufficient or acceptable; less positive than *self-actualization*.

self-censorship: In mass media, carefully monitoring content and eliminating messages that might offend viewers or sponsors.

self-concept: One's awareness and understanding of who one is, as interpreted and influenced by one's thoughts, actions, abilities, values, goals, and ideals.

self-denigration: A negative assessment about a communication experience that involves criticizing or attacking oneself.

self-directed work team: A group of skilled workers who take responsibility for producing high-quality finished work.

self-disclosure: Revealing oneself to others by sharing information about oneself.

self-efficacy: The ability to predict, based on self-concept and self-esteem, one's effectiveness in a communication situation.

self-esteem: How one feels about oneself, usually in a particular situation.

self-fulfilling prophecy: A prediction that causes an individual to alter his or her behavior in a way that makes the prediction more likely to occur.

self-monitoring: The ability to watch one's environment and others in it for cues as to how to present oneself in particular situations.

self-presentation: Intentional communication designed to show elements of self for strategic purposes; how one lets others know about oneself.

self-serving bias: The idea that we usually attribute our own successes to internal factors while explaining our failures by attributing them to situational or external effects.

semantics: The study of the relationship among symbols, objects, people, and concepts; refers to the meaning that words have for people, either because of their definitions or because of their placement in a sentence's structure (syntax).

sender: The individual who originates communication, with words or action.

sentence outline: A type of outline that offers the full text of a speech, often the exact words that the speaker wants to say to the audience.

separation: Removing oneself from a conflicted situation or relationship.

service-oriented interview: An interview that is designed to cull information and provide advice, service, or support based on that information; used, for example, by customer service representatives.

signposts: Key words or phrases within sentences that signify transitions between main points.

situational context: The social environment, physical place, and specific events that affect a situation.

slang: Language that is informal, nonstandard, and usually particular to a specific group.

slippery slope fallacy: A logical fallacy that is employed when a speaker attests that some event must clearly occur as a result of another event without showing any proof that the second event is caused by the first.

social capital: The valuable resources, such as information and support, that come from having connections and relationships among people.

social cognitive theory: The theory that we learn behavior by watching the behaviors of those whom we have identified as models.

social comparison theory: A theory that explains our tendency to compare ourselves to others, such as friends and acquaintances or popular figures in the media, as we develop our ideas about ourselves.

social exchange theory: A theory that explains the process of balancing the advantages and disadvantages of a relationship.

social forces: Group standards for behavior that influence decision making.

social group: A group in which membership offers opportunities to form relationships with others.

social identity theory: The theory that we each have a *personal identity*, which is our sense of our unique individual personality, and a *social identity*, the part of our self-concept that comes from group memberships.

social information processing theory: The theory that communicators use unique language and stylistic cues in their online messages to develop relationships that are just as close as those that grow from face-to-face content; because using text takes time, it takes longer to become intimate.

social judgment theory: The theory that a speaker's ability to successfully persuade an audience depends on the audience's current attitudes or disposition toward the topic.

social loafing: Failure to invest the same level of effort in the group that people would put in if they were working alone or with one other person.

social penetration theory (SPT): The theory that partners move from superficial levels to greater intimacy.

social roles: Group roles that evolve to reflect individual members' personality traits and interests.

spatial pattern: A pattern of speech arrangement that arranges main points in terms of their physical proximity or position in relation to each other (north to south, east to west, bottom to top, left to right, outside to inside, and so on).

speaking outline: The final speech plan, complete with details, delivery tips, and important notes about presentation aids; also known as the *delivery outline*.

speaking rate: How fast or slow one speaks.

specific purpose statement: A statement that expresses both the topic and the general speech purpose in action form and in terms of the specific objectives the speaker hopes to achieve with his or her presentation.

speech repertoire: A set of complex language behaviors or language possibilities that one calls on to most effectively and appropriately meet the demands of a given relationship, situation, or cultural environment.

stable stage: The stage of a relationship in which it is no longer volatile or temporary; both partners have a great deal of knowledge about one another, their expectations are accurate and realistic, and they feel comfortable with their motives for being in the relationship.

statistics: Information provided in numerical form.

stereotyping: The act of organizing information about groups of people into categories so that we can generalize about their attitudes, behaviors, skills, morals, and habits.

storming: The stage of group development in which members inevitably begin experiencing conflicts over issues such as who will lead the group and what roles members will play.

strategic topic avoidance: When one or both relational partners maneuver the conversation away from undesirable topics because of the potential for embarrassment, vulnerability, or relational decline.

study groups: Groups that are formed for the specific purpose of helping students prepare for exams.

style switching: A type of accommodation in which communicators change their tonality, pitch, rhythm, and inflection to fit into a particular group.

subjectivity: Presenting facts and information from a particular point of view.

subpoints: In public speaking, points that provide support for the main points.

substituting: Replacing words with nonverbal cues.

support group: A set of individuals who come together to address personal problems while benefiting from the support of others with similar issues.

supportive climate: A communication climate that offers communicators a chance to honestly and considerately explore the issues involved in the conflict situation.

supportive leader: A leader who attends to group members' emotional needs.

survey: To solicit answers to a question or series of questions related to one's speech topic from a broad range of individuals.

syllogism: A three-line deductive argument that draws a specific conclusion from two general premises (a major and a minor premise).

symbols: Arbitrary constructions (usually in the form of language or behaviors) that refer to people, things, and concepts.

task roles: Roles that are concerned with the accomplishment of the group's goals.

team: A group that works together to carry out a project or specific endeavor or to compete against other teams.

termination stage: The end of a relationship; may come about by a gradual decline in the relationship or by sudden-death.

territoriality: The claiming of an area, with or without legal basis, through continuous occupation of that area.

thesis statement: A statement that conveys the central idea or core assumption about the speaker's topic.

third-person effect: The tendency to assume that negative media messages and bias have a much greater influence on other people than on oneself or people one thinks are like oneself.

time orientation: The way cultures communicate about and with time.

tone: A modulation of the voice, usually expressing a particular feeling or mood.

topical pattern: A pattern of speech arrangement that is based on organization into categories, such as persons, places, things, or processes.

trading: A way to reach compromise whereby one partner offers something of equal value in return for something he or she wants.

transactional: Involving two or more people acting in both sender and receiver roles whose messages are dependent on and influenced by those of their communication partner.

transformative explanation: An explanation that helps people understand ideas that are counterintuitive and is designed to help speakers transform "theories" about phenomena into more accepted notions.

transitions: Sentences that connect different points, thoughts, and details in a way that allows them to flow naturally from one to the next.

trolling: The posting of provocative or offensive messages to whole forums or discussion boards to elicit some type of general reaction.

tunnel sequence: A pattern of questioning in which all questions are at the same level, either broad and open-ended or narrow and closed; commonly used in polls and surveys.

uncertain climate: A communication climate in which at least one of the people involved is unclear, vague, tentative, and awkward about the goals, expectations, and potential outcomes of the conflict situation.

uncertainty avoidance: The process of adapting behaviors to reduce uncertainty and risk.

uncertainty event: An event or behavioral pattern that causes uncertainty in a relationship.

uncertainty reduction theory: The theory that when two people meet, their main focus is on decreasing the uncertainty about each other.

understanding: The step in the listening process of interpreting and making sense of messages.

understatement: Language that downplays the emotional intensity or importance of events, often with euphemisms.

undue influence: Giving greater credibility or importance to something shown or said than should be the case.

unproductive conflict: Conflict that is managed poorly and has a negative impact on the individuals and relationships involved.

user-generated content: Songs, videos, and other content that individuals create and share publicly through mass media.

uses and gratifications perspective: A perspective that focuses not on what media does to us, but on what we do with media—that is, the way we make media choices (uses) to satisfy our needs and goals (gratifications).

verbal aggressiveness: Attacks on individuals, rather than on issues.

vocalizations: Paralinguistic cues that give information about the speaker's emotional or physical state, for example, laughing, crying, or sighing.

volume: How loud or soft the voice is.

wheel network: A network in which all group members share their information with one central individual, who then shares the information with the rest of the group.

worldview: The framework through which one interprets the world and the people in it.

REFERENCES

Aakhus, M., & Rumsey, E. (2010). Crafting supportive communication online: A communication design analysis of conflict in an online support group. *Journal of Applied Communication Research, 38*(1), 65–84.

Abrams v. United States, 250 U.S. 616 (1919).

Action for Children's Television v. Federal Communications Commission, 932 F.2d 1504 (ACT II) (D.C. Cir. 1991).

Adkins, M., & Brashers, D. E. (1995). The power of language in computer-mediated groups. *Management Communication Quarterly, 8,* 289–322.

Afifi, T. D., McManus, T., Hutchinson, S., & Baker, B. (2007). Parental divorce disclosures, the factors that prompt them, and their impact on parents' and adolescents' well-being. *Communication Monographs, 74,* 78–103.

Afifi, T. D., McManus, T., Steuber, K., & Coho, A. (2009). Verbal avoidance and dissatisfaction in intimate conflict situations. *Human Communication Research, 35*(3), 357–383.

Ahlfeldt, S. L. (2009). Serving our communities with public speaking skills. *Communication Teacher, 23*(4), 158–161.

Albada, K. F., Knapp, M. L., & Theune, K. E. (2002). Interaction appearance theory: Changing perceptions of physical attractiveness through social interaction. *Communication Theory, 12,* 8–40.

Alexander, A. L. (2008). Relationship resources for coping with unfulfilled standards in dating relationships: Commitment, satisfaction, and closeness. *Journal of Social & Personal Relationships, 25*(5), 725–747.

Alge, B. J., Wiethoff, C., & Klein, H. J. (2003). When does the medium matter? Knowledge-building experiences and opportunities in decision-making teams. *Organizational Behavior and Human Decision Processes, 91,* 26–37.

Allen, J. A. (2010, June 23). Poll: Obama's ratings fall amid Gulf oil spill. Reuters. Retrieved from http://www.reuters.com/article/2010/06/24/us-obama-poll-idUSTRE-65N0AB2010624

Allen, M. (1991). Comparing the persuasiveness of one-sided and two-sided messages using meta-analysis. *Western Journal of Speech Communication, 55,* 390–404.

Allen, R. R., & McKerrow, R. E. (1985). *The pragmatics of public communication* (3rd ed.). Dubuque, IA: Kendall/Hunt.

Allport, G. W. (1954). *The nature of prejudice.* Cambridge, MA: Addison-Wesley.

Altman, I., & Taylor, D. A. (1973). *Social penetration: The development of interpersonal relationships.* New York: Holt, Rinehart & Winston.

Amodio, D. M., & Showers, C. J. (2005). "Similarity breeds liking" revisited: The moderating role of commitment. *Journal of Social and Personal Relationships, 22,* 817–836.

Andersen, P. A., & Blackburn, T. R. (2004). An experimental study of language intensity and response rate in e-mail surveys. *Communication Reports, 17,* 73–84.

Anderson, C. M., & Martin, M. M. (1999). The relationship of argumentativeness and verbal aggressiveness to cohesion, consensus, and satisfaction in small groups. *Communication Reports, 12,* 21–31.

Anderson, C. M., Riddle, B. L., & Martin, M. M. (1999). Socialization in groups. In L. Frey, D. Gouran, & M. Poole (Eds.), *Handbook of group communication theory and research* (pp. 139–163). Thousand Oaks, CA: Sage Publications.

Anderson, T., & Emmers-Sommer, T. (2006). Predictors of relationship satisfaction in online romantic relationships. *Communication Studies, 57*(2), 153–172.

Annino, J. (Executive producer). (2007, July 5). Cooking in cramped quarters [Television series episode]. In *The Rachael Ray Show.* Video retrieved from http://www.rachaelrayshow.com/show/segments/view/cooking-in-cramped-quarters

Antheunis, M. L., Valkenburg, P. M., & Peter, J. (2010). Getting acquainted through social network sites: Testing a model of online uncertainty reduction and social attraction. *Computers in Human Behavior, 26*(1), 100–109.

Antonijevic, S. (2008). From text to gesture online: A microethnographic analysis of nonverbal communication in the *Second Life* virtual environment. *Information, Communication & Society, 11*(2), 221–238.

Appleby, C. (1996, December). Getting doctors to listen to patients. *Managed Care Magazine.* Retrieved from http://www.managedcaremag.com/archives/9612/MC9612.listening.shtml

Arasaratnam, L. (2007). Research in intercultural communication competence. *Journal of International Communication, 13*, 66–73.

Araton, H. (2010, April 26). The understated elegance of the Yankees' Rivera. *The New York Times*, p. D1.

Armstrong, B., & Kaplowitz, S. A. (2001). Sociolinguistic interference and intercultural coordination: A Bayesian model of communication competence in intercultural communication. *Human Communication Research, 27*, 350–381.

Atkinson, J., & Dougherty, D. S. (2006). Alternative media and social justice movements: The development of a resistance performance paradigm of audience analysis. *Journal of Western Communication, 70*, 64–89.

Avtgis, T. A., & Rancer, A. S. (2003). Comparing touch apprehension and affective orientation between Asian-American and European-American siblings. *Journal of Intercultural Communication Research, 32*(2), 67–74.

Avtgis, T. A., West, D. V., & Anderson, T. L. (1998). Relationship stages: An inductive analysis identifying cognitive, affective, and behavioral dimensions of Knapp's relational stages model. *Communication Research Reports, 15*, 280–287.

Axtell, R. E. (1991). *Gestures: The do's and taboos of body language around the world.* New York: Wiley.

Ayres, J. (2005). Performance visualization and behavioral disruption: A clarification. *Communication Reports, 18*, 55–63.

Ayres, J., & Hopf, T. (1993). *Coping with speech anxiety.* Norwood, NJ: Ablex.

Ayres, J., Keereetaweep, T., Chen, P., & Edwards, P. (1998). Communication apprehension and employment interviews. *Communication Education, 47*, 1–17.

Ayres, J., Wilcox, A. K., & Ayres, D. M. (1995). Receiver apprehension: An explanatory model and accompanying research. *Communication Education, 44*, 223–235.

Babad, E., & Peer, E. (2010). Media bias in interviewers' nonverbal behavior: Potential remedies, attitude similarity and meta-analysis. *Journal of Nonverbal Behavior, 34*(1), 57–78.

Baird, J. E., Jr. (1986). Sex differences in group communication: A review of relevant research. *Quarterly Journal of Speech, 62*, 179–192.

Baker, H. G., & Spier, M. S. (1990). The employment interview: Guaranteed improvement in reliability. *Public Personnel Management, 19*, 85–90.

Bakke, E. (2010). A model and measure of mobile communication competence. *Human Communication Research, 36*(3), 348–371.

Balaji, M., & Worawongs, T. (2010). The new Suzie Wong: Normative assumptions of white male and Asian female relationships. *Communication, Culture & Critique, 3*(2), 224–241.

Baldwin, M. W., & Keelan, J. P. R. (1999). Interpersonal expectations as a function of self-esteem and sex. *Journal of Social and Personal Relationships, 16*, 822–833.

Ball-Rokeach, S. J. (1998). A theory of media power and a theory of media use: Different stories, questions, and ways of thinking. *Mass Communication and Society, 1*, 5–40.

Bandura, A. (1982). Self-efficacy mechanism in human agency. *American Psychologist, 37*, 122.

Bandura, A. (2001). Social cognitive theory of mass communication. *Media Psychology, 3*, 265–299.

Barker, L. L., & Watson, K. W. (2000). *Listen up: How to improve relationships, reduce stress, and be more productive by using the power of listening.* New York: St. Martin's Press.

Barstow, D., Dodd, L., Glanz, J., Saul, S., & Urbina, I. (2010, June 21). Regulators failed to address risks in oil rig fail-safe device. *The New York Times*, p. A1.

Bates, B. (1988). *Communication and the sexes.* New York: Harper & Row.

Bavelous, A. (1950). Communication patterns in task-oriented groups. *Journal of the Acoustical Society of America, 22*, 725–730.

Baxter, L. A., Braithwaite, D. O., Bryant, L., & Wagner, A. (2004). Stepchildren's perceptions of the contradictions in communication with stepparents. *Journal of Social and Personal Relationships, 21*, 447–467.

Baxter, L. A., & Erbert, L. (1999). Perceptions of dialectical contradictions in turning points of development in heterosexual romantic relationships. *Journal of Social and Personal Relationships, 16*, 547–569.

Baxter, L. A., Foley, M., & Thatcher, M. (2008). Marginalizing difference in personal relationships: How partners talk about their differences. *Journal of Communication Studies, 1*(1), 33–55.

Baxter, L. A., & Simon, E. P. (1993). Relationship maintenance strategies and dialectical contradictions in personal relationships. *Journal of Social and Personal Relationships, 10*, 225–242.

Baxter, L. A., & Wilmot, W. W. (1985). Taboo topics in close relationships. *Journal of Social and Personal Relationships, 2*, 253–269.

Bayly, S. (1999). Caste, society and politics in India from the eighteenth century to the modern age. Cambridge: Cambridge University Press.

Beall, M. L. (2006). Contributions of a listening legend. *International Journal of Listening, 20*, 27–28.

Beard, D. (2009). A broader understanding of the ethics of listening: Philosophy, cultural studies, media studies and the ethical listening subject. *International Journal of Listening*, 23(1), 7–20.

Beatty, M. J., & Payne, S. K. (1984). Effects of social facilitation on listening comprehension. *Communication Quarterly*, 32, 37–40.

Behnke, R. R., & Sawyer, C. R. (1999). Milestones of anticipatory public speaking anxiety. *Communication Education*, 48, 164–172.

Bellis, T. J., & Wilber, L. A. (2001). Effects of aging and gender on interhemispheric function. *Journal of Speech, Language, and Hearing Research*, 44, 246–264.

Benne, K. D., & Sheats, P. (1948). Functional roles in group members. *Journal of Social Issues*, 4, 41–49.

Bennett, J. M., & Bennett, M. J. (2004). Developing intercultural sensitivity: An integrative approach to global and domestic diversity. In D. Landis, J. M. Bennett, & M. J. Bennett (Eds.), *Handbook of intercultural training*, 3rd ed. (pp. 147–165). Thousand Oaks, CA: Sage Publications.

Ben-Porath, E. (2010). Interview effects: Theory and evidence for the impact of televised political interviews on viewer attitudes. *Communication Theory*, 20(3), 323–347.

Bentley, S. C. (2000). Listening in the twenty-first century. *International Journal of Listening*, 14, 129–142.

Bergen, K. M. (2010). Accounting for difference: Commuter wives and the master narrative of marriage. *Journal of Applied Communication Research*, 38(1), 47–64.

Berger, A. (2007). *Media and society: A critical perspective.* Lanham, MD: Rowman & Littlefield.

Berger, C., & Calabrese, R. (1975). Some explorations in initial interaction and beyond: Toward a developmental theory of interpersonal communication. *Human Communication Research*, 1, 99–112.

Berrisford, S. (2006). How will you respond to the information crisis? *Strategic Communication Management*, 10, 26–29.

Berscheid, E. (1985). Interpersonal attraction. In G. Lindzey & E. Aronson (Eds.), *Handbook of social psychology: Vol. 2. Special fields and applications* (3rd ed., pp. 413–484). New York: Random House.

Biever, C. (2004, August). Language may shape human thought. *New Scientist.* Retrieved from http://www.newscientist.com

Bippus, A. M., & Daly, J. A. (1999). What do people think causes stage fright? Native attributions about the reasons for public speaking anxiety. *Communication Education*, 48, 63–72.

Bishop, G. (2010, February 20). On and off the ice, Ohno is positioned for success. *The New York Times*, p. D3.

Bishop, R. (2000). More than meets the eye: An explanation of literature related to the mass media's role in encouraging changes in body image. In M. E. Roloff (Ed.), *Communication yearbook* (Vol. 23, pp. 271–304). Thousand Oaks, CA: Sage Publications.

Blumler, J., & Katz, E. (1974). *The uses of mass communications.* Beverly Hills, CA: Sage Publications.

Blumstein, P., & Schwartz, P. (1983). *American couples: Money, work, sex.* New York: Morrow.

Bodie, G. D. (2010). A racing heart, rattling knees, and ruminative thoughts: Defining, explaining, and treating public speaking anxiety. *Communication Education*, 59(1), 70–105.

Bommelje, R., Houston, J. M., & Smither, R. (2003). Personality characteristics of effective listeners: A five factor perspective. *International Journal of Listening*, 17, 32–46.

Boonzaier, F. (2008). "If the man says you must sit, then you must sit": The relational construction of woman abuse: Gender, subjectivity and violence. *Feminism & Psychology*, 18(2), 183–206.

Boster, F. J., & Mongeau, P. (1984). Fear-arousing persuasive messages. In R. N. Bostrom (Ed.), *Communication yearbook 8* (pp. 330–375). Beverly Hills, CA: Sage Publications.

Bourhis, R. Y. (1985). The sequential nature of language choice in cross-cultural communication. In R. L. Street Jr. & J. N. Cappella (Eds.), *Sequence and pattern in communicative behaviour* (pp. 120–141). London: Arnold.

Boyd, D. (2010). Social network sites as networked publics: Affordances, dynamics, and implications. In Z. Papacharissi (Ed.), *A networked self: Identity, community, and culture on social network sites* (pp. 39–58). New York: Routledge.

Bradac, J. J. (1983). The language of lovers, flovers, and friends: Communicating in social and personal relationships. *Journal of Language and Social Psychology*, 2, 234.

Bradac, J. J., & Giles, H. (2005). Language and social psychology: Conceptual niceties, complexities, curiosities, monstrosities, and how it all works. In K. L. Fitch & R. E. Sanders (Eds.), *The new handbook of language and social psychology* (pp. 201–230). Mahwah, NJ: Erlbaum.

Brandau-Brown, F. E., & Ragsdale, J. D.(2008). Personal, moral, and structural commitment and the repair of marital relationships. *Southern Communication Journal*, 73(1), 68–83.

Brandenburg, C. (2008). The newest way to screen job applicants: A social networker's nightmare. *Federal Communications Law Journal*, 60(3), 597–626.

Brazeel, S. (2009). Networking to top talent or networking your way to top talent. *POWERGRID International*, 14(10), 2.

Brehm, J. W. (1966). *A theory of psychological reactance.* New York: Academic Press.

Brenneis, D. (1990). Shared and solitary sentiments: The discourse of friendship, play, and anger in Bhatgaon. In C. A. Lutz & L. Abu-Lughod (Eds.), *Language and the politics of emotion* (pp. 113–125). Cambridge: Cambridge University Press.

Brilhart, J. K., & Galanes, G. J. (1992). *Effective group discussion* (7th ed.). Dubuque, IA: Brown.

Brody, L. R. (2000). The socialization of gender differences in emotional expression: Display rules, infant temperament, and differentiation. In A. H. Fischer (Ed.), *Gender and emotion: Social psychological perspectives* (pp. 24–47). Cambridge: Cambridge University Press.

Brooks, J., & Groening, M. (Producers). (2006, April 30). Girls just want to have sums. [Television series episode]. In *The Simpsons*. Culver City, CA: Gracie Films.

Brown, S. L. (2000). The effect of union type on psychological well-being: Depression among cohabitors versus marrieds. *Journal of Health and Social Behavior, 41,* 241–255.

Buck, R. (1988). Emotional education and mass media: A new view of the global village. In R. P. Hawkins, J. M. Wiemann, & S. Pingree (Eds.), *Advancing communication science: Merging mass and interpersonal processes* (pp. 44–76). Beverly Hills, CA: Sage Publications.

Burgoon, J. K., & Bacue, A. E. (2003). Nonverbal communication skills. In J. O. Greene & B. R. Burleson (Eds.), *Handbook of communication and social interaction skills* (pp. 179–219). Mahwah, NJ: Erlbaum.

Burgoon, J. K., Buller, D. B., & Woodall, W. G. (1989). *Nonverbal communication: The unspoken dialogue*. New York: Harper & Row.

Burgoon, J. K., & Hoobler, G. D. (2002). Nonverbal signals. In M. L. Knapp & J. A. Daly (Eds.), *Handbook of interpersonal communication* (pp. 240–299). Thousand Oaks, CA: Sage Publications.

Burleson, B. R. (1994). Comforting messages: Features, functions, and outcomes. In J. A. Daly & J. M. Wiemann (Eds.), *Strategic interpersonal communication* (pp. 135–161). Hillsdale, NJ: Erlbaum.

Burleson, B. R., Holmstrom, A. J., & Gilstrap, C. M. (2005). "Guys can't say that to guys": Four experiments assessing the normative motivation account for deficiencies in the emotional support provided by men. *Communication Monographs, 72,* 468–501.

Busch, D. (2009). What kind of intercultural competence will contribute to students' future job employability? *Intercultural Education, 20*(5), 429–438.

Bushman, B. J., & Huesmann, L. R. (2001). Effects of televised violence on aggression. In D. G. Singer & J. L. Singer (Eds.), *Handbook of children and the media* (pp. 223–254). Thousand Oaks, CA: Sage Publications.

Byrd, D. (2010, January 16). *Neil deGrasse Tyson: "Learning how to think is empowerment."* Retrieved from http://earthsky .org/human-world/neil-degrasse-tyson

Byrne, D. (1971). *The attraction paradigm*. New York: Academic Press.

Calhoun, B. (Producer). (2010, September 12). Right to remain silent [Show 414] [Audio podcast]. In *This American Life*. Retrieved from http://www.thisamericanlife.org/radio -archives/episode/414/right-to-remain-silent

Campbell, J. D. (1990). Self-esteem and clarity of the self-concept. *Journal of Personality and Social Psychology, 59,* 538–549.

Canary, D. J. (2003). Managing interpersonal conflict: A model of events related to strategic choices. In J. O. Greene & B. R. Burleson (Eds.), *Handbook of communication and social interaction skills* (pp. 515–550). Mahwah, NJ: Erlbaum.

Canary, D. J., & Cody, M. J. (1993). *Interpersonal communication: A goals-based approach*. New York: St. Martin's Press.

Canary, D. J., Cody, M. J., & Manusov, V. (2003). *Interpersonal communication: A goals-based approach* (3rd ed.). New York: Bedford/St. Martin's.

Canary, D. J., Cody, M. J., & Manusov, V. (2008). *Interpersonal communication: A goals-based approach* (4th ed.). New York: Bedford/St. Martin's.

Canary, D. J., Cody, M. J., & Smith, S. (1994). Compliance-gaining goals: An inductive analysis of actors' goal types, strategies, and successes. In J. A. Daly & J. M. Wiemann (Eds.), *Strategic interpersonal communication* (pp. 33–90). Hillsdale, NJ: Erlbaum.

Canary, D. J., Cunningham, E. M., & Cody, M. J. (1988). Goal types, gender, and locus of control in managing interpersonal conflict. *Communication Research, 15,* 426–446.

Canary, D. J., & Dainton, M. (Eds.). (2003). *Maintaining relationships through communication: Relational, contextual, and cultural variations*. Mahwah, NJ: Lawrence Erlbaum Associates.

Canary, D. J., & Spitzberg, B. H. (1993). Loneliness and media gratifications. *Communication Research, 20,* 800–821.

Caplan, S. (2001). Challenging the mass-interpersonal communication dichotomy: Are we witnessing the emergence of an entirely new communication system? *Electronic Journal of Communication, 11.* Retrieved March 24, 2003, from http://www.cios.org/getfile/CAPLAN_v11n101

Carey, B. (2008, February 12). You remind me of me. *The New York Times*. Retrieved from http://www.nytimes .com/2008/02/12/health/12mimic.html

Carey, B. (2010, April 6). Seeking emotional clues without facial cues. *The New York Times*, p. D1.

Cargile, A. C., & Giles, H. (1996). Intercultural communication training: Review, critique, and a new theoretical framework. In B. R. Burleson (Ed.), *Communication yearbook 19* (pp. 3335–3423). Newbury Park, CA: Sage Publications.

Carless, S. A., & DePaola, C. (2000). The measurement of cohesion in work teams. *Small Group Research, 31,* 71–88.

Casmir, F. L. (Ed.). (1997). *Ethics in intercultural and international communication.* Mahwah, NJ: Erlbaum.

Cassell, J., Huffaker, D., Tversky, D., & Ferriman, K. (2006). The language of online leadership: Gender and youth engagement on the Internet. *Developmental Psychology, 42*(3), 436–449.

Caughlin, J. (2003). Family communication standards: What counts as excellent family communication, and how are such standards associated with family satisfaction? *Human Communication Research, 29,* 5–40.

CBS News. (2010, November 28). Colin Firth on playing King George VI: Katie Couric talks with *The King's Speech* star about the monarch's battle against a debilitating stutter. Retrieved from http://www.cbsnews.com/stories/2010/11/28/sunday/main7096682.shtml

Cegala, D. (1981). Interaction involvement: A cognitive dimension of communicative competence. *Communication Education, 30,* 109–121.

Census seen lax on diversity. (2010, February 25). *The Washington Times.* Retrieved from http://www.washingtontimes.com/news/2010/feb/25/census-seen-lax-on-diversity/

Centers for Disease Control and Prevention. (2010). *Childhood obesity.* Retrieved from http://www.cdc.gov/healthyyouth/obesity

Chen, G., & Starosta, W. J. (1996). Intercultural communication competence: A synthesis. In B. R. Burleson (Ed.), *Communication yearbook* (Vol. 19, pp. 353–383). Thousand Oaks, CA: Sage Publications.

Chen, Y., & Nakazawa, M. (2009). Influences of culture on self-disclosure as relationally situated in intercultural and interracial friendships from a social penetration perspective. *Journal of Intercultural Communication Research, 38*(2), 77–98.

Childs, C. (2009). Perfect quiet. *Miller-McCune, 2*(4), 58–67.

Christenson, P. (1994). Childhood patterns of music uses and preferences. *Communication Reports, 7,* 136–144.

Christians, C., & Traber, C. (Eds.). (1997). *Communication ethics and universal values.* Thousand Oaks, CA: Sage Publications.

Cialdini, R. (2008). *Influence: Science and practice* (5th ed.). Englewood Cliffs, NJ: Prentice Hall.

Clark, A. J. (1989). Communication confidence and listening competence: An investigation of the relationships of willingness to communicate, communication apprehension, and receiver apprehension to comprehension of content and emotional meaning in spoken messages. *Communication Education, 38,* 237–248.

Clarke, I., Flaherty, T. B., Wright, N. D., & McMillen, R. M. (2009). Student intercultural proficiency from study abroad programs. *Journal of Marketing Education, 31*(2), 173–181.

Coe, K., Tewksbury, D., Bond, B. J., Drogos, K. L., Porter, R. W., Yahn, A., & Zhang, Y. (2008). Hostile news: Partisan use and perceptions of cable news programming. *Journal of Communication, 58,* 201–219.

Comer, D. R. (1998). A model of social loafing in real work groups. *Human Relations, 48,* 647–667.

Conlin, M. (2006, December 11). Online extra: How to kill meetings. *Business Week.* Retrieved from http://www.businessweek.com

Connelly, S. (2009, December 3). Rupert Everett: Coming out of the closet ruined my career in Hollywood. *Daily News.* Retrieved from http://articles.nydailynews.com/2009-12-03/gossip/17940844_1_gay-best-friend-closet-major-stars

Conville, R. L. (1991). *Relational transitions: The evolution of personal relationships.* Westport, CT: Praeger.

Cook, G. (2002, February 14). Debate opens anew on language and its effect on cognition. *The Boston Globe,* p. A10.

Cook, K. S. (1987). *Social exchange theory.* Beverly Hills, CA: Sage Publications.

Cooper, L. O. (1997). Listening competency in the workplace: A model for training. *Business Communication Quarterly, 60*(4), 74–84.

Costa, M. (2010). Interpersonal distances in group walking. *Journal of Nonverbal Behavior, 34*(1), 15–26.

Coulehan, J. L., & Block, M. L. (2006). *The medical interview: Mastering skills for clinical practice.* Philadelphia: Davis.

Covel, S. (2008, June 9). The benefits of a "feminine" leadership style. *The Wall Street Journal.* Retrieved from http://www.wsj.com

Crane, D. (2000). *Fashion and its social agendas: Class, gender, and identity in clothing.* Chicago: University of Chicago Press.

Culbert, S. A. (2010). *Get rid of the performance review! How companies can stop intimidating, start managing—and focus on what really matters.* New York: Business Plus/Hachette Book Group.

Cupach, W. R., & Spitzberg, B. H. (Eds.) (2011). *The dark side of close relationships II.* New York: Routledge.

Dailey, R. M., & Palomares, N. A. (2004). Strategic topic avoidance: An investigation of topic avoidance frequency, strategies used, and relational correlates. *Communication Monographs, 71,* 471–496.

The Daily Show with Jon Stewart. (2009, August 12). Oliver-MBA ethics oath. Video retrieved from http://www.thedailyshow.com/watch/wed-august-12-2009/mba-ethics-oath

Dainton, M., & Gross, J. (2008). The use of negative behaviors to maintain relationships. *Communication Research Reports, 25,* 179–191.

Daniel, E. (2008). *Stealth germs in your body.* New York: Union Square Press.

Davies, P. T., Sturge-Apple, M. L., Cicchetti, D., & Cummings, E. M. (2008). Adrenocortical underpinnings of children's psychological reactivity to interparental conflict. *Child Development, 79,* 1693–1706.

Davis, M. S. (1973). *Intimate relations.* New York: Free Press.

Davison, W. P. (1983). The third-person effect in communication. *Public Opinion Quarterly, 40,* 1–15.

Day, L. A. (1997). *Ethics in Media Communications: Cases and Controversies.* Belmont, CA: Wadsworth.

DeGroot, T., & Gooty, J. (2009). Can nonverbal cues be used to make meaningful personality attributions in employment interviews? *Journal of Business and Psychology, 24*(2), 179–192.

DeKay, S. H. (2009). The communication functions of business attire. *Business Communication Quarterly, 72*(3), 349–350.

Derks, D., Bos, A. E. R., & von Grumbkow, J. (2008). Emoticons and online message interpretation. *Social Science Computer Review, 26*(3), 379–388.

Derlega, V. J., Winstead, B. A., Mathews, A., & Braitman, A. L. (2008). Why does someone reveal highly personal information? Attributions for and against self-disclosure in close relationships. *Communication Research Reports, 25*(2), 115–130.

Dewey, J. (1933). *How we think.* Lexington, MA: Heath.

Diener, E., & Diener, M. (1995). Cross-cultural correlates of life satisfaction and self-esteem. *Journal of Personality and Social Psychology, 68,* 653–663.

Dillard, J. P., Solomon, D. H., & Palmer, M. T. (1999). Structuring the concept of relational communication. *Communication Monographs, 66,* 49–65.

Dillon, R. K., & McKenzie, N. J. (1998). The influence of ethnicity on listening, communication competence, approach, and avoidance. *International Journal of Listening, 12,* 106–121.

Dimmick, J., Chen, Y., & Li, Z. (2004). Competition between the Internet and traditional news media: The gratification-opportunities niche dimension. *Journal of Media Economics, 17,* 19–33.

Dindi, K., & Timmerman, L. (2003). Accomplishing romantic relationships. In J. O. Greene & B. R. Burleson (Eds.), *Handbook of communication and social interaction skills* (pp. 685–722). Mahwah, NJ: Erlbaum.

Dipper, L., Black, M., & Bryan, K. (2005). Thinking for speaking and thinking for listening: The interaction of thought and language in typical and non-fluent comprehension and production. *Language and Cognitive Processes, 20,* 417–441.

DiSanza, J. R., & Legge, N. J. (2002). *Business and professional communication: Plans, processes, and performance* (2nd ed.). Boston: Allyn & Bacon.

Dixon, J. A., & Foster, D. H. (1998). Gender, social context, and backchannel responses. *Journal of Social Psychology, 138,* 134–136.

Docter, P., & Peterson, B. (Directors). (2009). *Up* [motion picture]. United States: Pixar Walt Disney Studios.

Doll, B. (1996). Children without friends: Implications for practice and policy. *School Psychology Review, 25,* 165–183.

Doris, J. (Ed.). (1991). *The suggestibility of children's recollections.* Washington, DC: American Psychological Association.

Doshi, A. (with Drvaid, S., Giri, R., & David, S.). (2005, June 20). Sweep stake: Technology, television and the fast pace of modern life have dramatically altered the rules of the dating game. *India Today.* Retrieved from http://proquest/umi.com

Douglas, C. (2002). The effects of managerial influence behavior on the transition to self-directed work teams. *Journal of Managerial Psychology, 17,* 628–635.

Douglass, J., Jr. (2005, January 23). Some Norwegians thought Bush was saluting Satan. *The Standard-Times,* p. B3.

Ducharme, J., Doyle, A., & Markiewicz, D. (2002). Attachment security with mother and father: Associations with adolescents' reports of interpersonal behavior with parents and peers. *Journal of Social and Personal Relationships, 19,* 203–231.

Duck, S. W. (1984). A perspective on the repair of personal relationships: Repair of what, when? In S. W. Duck (Ed.), *Personal relationships: Vol. 5. Repairing personal relationships.* New York: Macmillan.

Dues, M., & Brown, M. (2004). *Boxing Plato's shadow: An introduction to the study of human communication.* New York: McGraw-Hill.

Duffy, M., Thorson, E., & Vultee, F. (2009). Advocating advocacy: Acknowledging and teaching journalism as persuasion. Paper presented at the annual meeting of the Association for Education in Journalism and Mass Communication, Sheraton Boston, Boston, MA. Retrieved from http://www.allacademic.com/meta/p375952_index.html

DuFrene, D., & Lehman, C. (2004). Concept, content, construction and contingencies: Getting the horse before the PowerPoint cart. *Business Communication Quarterly, 67*(1), 84–88.

Dunbar, N. E., & Burgoon, J. K. (2005). Perceptions of power and interactional dominance in interpersonal relationships. *Journal of Social & Personal Relationships, 22*(2), 207–233.

Duncan, S., & Fiske, D. (1977). *Face-to-face interaction.* Hillsdale, NJ: Erlbaum.

Dwamena, F., Mavis, B., Holmes-Rovner, M., Walsh, K., & Loyson, A. (2009). Teaching medical interviewing to patients: The other side of the encounter. *Patient Education and Counseling, 76*(3), 380–384.

Dwyer, K. M., Fredstrom, B. K., Rubin, K. H., Booth-LaForce, C., Rose-Krasnor, L., & Burgess, K. B. (2010). Attachment, social information processing, and friendship quality of early adolescent girls and boys. *Journal of Social & Personal Relationships, 27*(1), 91–116.

Eckholm, E. (2010, May 10). What's in a name? A lot, as it turns out. *The New York Times,* p. A12.

Edwards, C., & Edwards, A. (2009). Communication skills training for elementary school students. *Communication Currents, 4*(4), 1–2.

Edwards, R. (1990). Sensitivity to feedback and the development of self. *Communication Quarterly, 28,* 101–111.

Efran, M. G. (1974). The effect of physical appearance on the judgment of guilt, interpersonal attraction, and severity of recommended punishment in a simulated jury task. *Journal of Research in Personality, 8,* 45–54.

Eibl-Eibesfeldt, I. (1973). The expressive behavior of the deaf-and-blind-born. In M. von Cranach & I. Vine (Eds.), *Social communication and movement: Studies of interaction and expression in man and chimpanzee* (pp. 163–194). New York: Academic Press.

Ekman, P., & Friesen, W. V. (1969). The repertoire of nonverbal behavior: Categories, origins, usage, and coding. *Semiotica, 1,* 49–98.

Ekman, P., & Friesen, W. V. (1971). Constants across cultures in the face and emotion. *Journal of Personality and Social Psychology, 17,* 124–129.

Ekman, P., Friesen, W. V., & Ellsworth, P. (1972). *Emotion in the human face: Guidelines for research and an integration of findings.* New York: Pergamon Press.

Endo, Y., Heine, S. J., & Lehman, D. R. (2000). Culture and positive illusions in close relationships: How my relationships are better than yours. *Personality and Social Psychology Bulletin, 26,* 1571–1586.

Erdur-Baker, O. (2010). Cyberbullying and its correlation to traditional bullying, gender and frequent and risky usage of Internet-mediated communication tools. *New Media and Society, 12,* 109–125.

Etcoff, N. (1999). *Survival of the prettiest: The science of beauty.* New York: Anchor Books.

Eveland, W. P., & Shah, D. V. (2003). The impact of individual and interpersonal factors on perceived news media bias. *Political Psychology, 24,* 101–117.

Ewald, J. (2010). "Do you know where X is?": Direction-giving and male/female direction-givers. *Journal of Pragmatics, 42*(9), 2549–2561.

Ewalt, D. (2005, September 17). Jane Goodall on why words hurt. *Forbes.* Retrieved from http://www.forbes.com

Faiola, A. (2005, September 22). Men in land of samurai find their feminine side. *Washington Post Foreign Service.* Retrieved from http://www.washingtonpost.com/wp-dyn/content/article/2005/09/21/AR2005092102434.html

Farnsworth, S. J., & Lichter, S. R. (2010). *The nightly news nightmare: Media coverage of U.S. presidential elections, 1988–2008* (3rd ed.). Lanham, MD: Rowman & Littlefield.

Farroni, T., Csibra, G., Simion, F., & Johnson, M. (2002, July 9). Eye contact detection in humans from birth. *Proceedings of the National Academy of Sciences of the United States of America, 99,* 9602–9605. Retrieved from http://www.pnas.org/cgi/doi/10.1073/pnas.152159999

Federal Communications Commission v. Pacifica Foundation, 438 U.S. 726 (1978).

Fehr, B. (2001). The life cycle of friendship. In C. Hendrick & S. S. Hendrick (Eds.), *Close relationships: A sourcebook* (pp. 71–82). Thousand Oaks, CA: Sage Publications.

Fent, B., & MacGeorge, E. L. (2006). Predicting receptiveness to advice: Characteristics of the problem, the advice-giver, and the recipient. *Southern Communication Journal, 71,* 67–85.

Festinger, L. (1954). A theory of social comparison processes. *Human Relations, 7,* 117–140.

Figdor, C. (2010). Objectivity in the news: Finding a way forward. *Journal of Mass Media Ethics, 25,* 19–33.

Fisk, G. M. (2010). "I want it all and I want it now!" An examination of the etiology, expression, and escalation of excessive employee entitlement. *Human Resource Management Review, 20*(2), 102–114.

Fiske, S. T., & Taylor, S. E. (1991). *Social cognition.* New York: McGraw-Hill.

Fitch-Hauser, M., Powers, W. G., O'Brien, K., & Hanson, S. (2007). Extending the conceptualization of listening fidelity. *International Journal of Listening, 21*(2), 81–91.

Flecha-García, M. (2010). Eyebrow raises in dialogue and their relation to discourse structure, utterance function and pitch accents in English. *Speech Communication, 52*(6), 542–554.

Fletcher, C. (1999). Listening to narratives: The dynamics of capturing police experience. *International Journal of Listening, 13*, 46–61.

Floyd, J. J. (2006). Ralph G. Nichols: Prophet, pioneer, and visionary. *International Journal of Listening, 20*, 18–19.

Folger, J. P., Poole, M. S., & Stutman, R. K. (1997). *Working through conflict* (3rd ed.). New York: Longman.

Folger, J. P., Poole, M. S., & Stutman, R. K. (2001). *Working through conflict: Strategies for relationships, groups, and organizations* (4th ed.). New York: Longman.

Ford, W. S. Z. (1999). Communication and customer service. In M. E. Roloff (Ed.), *Communication yearbook* (Vol. 22, pp. 341–375). Thousand Oaks, CA: Sage Publications.

Fowers, B. J., Fışıloğlu, H., & Procacci, E. K. (2008). Positive marital illusions and culture: American and Turkish spouses' perceptions of their marriages. *Journal of Social & Personal Relationships, 25*(2), 267–285.

Fraleigh, D. M., & Tuman, J. S. (2011). *Speak up! An illustrated guide to public speaking* (2nd ed.). New York: Bedford/ St. Martin's.

French, J. R. P., & Raven, B. (1959). The bases for power. In D. Cartwright (Ed.), *Studies in social power* (pp. 150–167). Ann Arbor, MI: Institute for Social Research.

Friedman, T. L. (2007). *The world is flat: A brief history of the twenty-first century.* New York: Farrar, Straus & Giroux.

Frum, D. (2000). *How we got here: The '70s.* New York: Basic Books.

Frymier, A. B., & Nadler, M. K. (2010). *Persuasion: Integrating theory, research, and practice.* Dubuque, IA: Kendall Hunt.

Gabriel, T. (2010, November 4). Learning in dorm, because class is on the Web. *The New York Times.* Retrieved from http://www.nytimes.com/2010/11/05/us/05college.html

Gagnon, M., Gosselin, P., Hudon-ven der Buhs, I., Larocque, K., & Milliard, K. (2010). Children's recognition and discrimination of fear and disgust facial expressions. *Journal of Nonverbal Behavior, 34*(1), 27–42.

Gallois, C., Franklyn-Stokes, A., Giles, H., & Coupland, N. (1988). Communication accommodation in intercultural encounters. In Y. Y. Kim & W. B. Gudykunst (Eds.), *Theories in intercultural communication* (pp. 157–185). Newbury Park, CA: Sage Publications.

Gardner, W. L., Reithel, B. J., Foley, R. T., Cogliser, C. C., & Walumbwa, F. O. (2009). Attraction to organizational culture profiles: Effects of realistic recruitment and vertical and horizontal individualism–collectivism. *Management Communication Quarterly, 22*(3), 437–472.

Garner, J. T., & Poole, M. S. (2009). Opposites attract: Leadership endorsement as a function of interaction between a leader and a foil. *Western Journal of Communication, 73*(3), 227–247.

Gates, B. (2009, February). TED Talks: Bill Gates on Mosquitoes, Malaria, and Education. Retrieved from http://www.ted.com/talks/lang/eng/bill_gates_unplugged.html

Gawande, A. (2009). *The checklist manifesto: How to get things right.* New York: Metropolitan Books.

Gerbner, G., Gross, L., Morgan, M., & Signorielli, N. (1994). Growing up with television: The cultivation perspective. In J. Bryant & D. Zillmann (Eds.), *Media effects: Advances in theory and research* (pp. 17–41). Hillsdale, NJ: Lawrence Erlbaum.

Gettleman, J. (2008, October 18). Rape victims' words help jolt Congo into change. *The New York Times*, p. A1.

Gibb, J. (1961). Defensive communication. *Journal of Communication, 2*, 141–148.

Gilbertson, J., Dindi, K., & Allen, M. (1998). Relational continuity constructional units and the maintenance of relationships. *Journal of Social and Personal Relationships, 15*, 774–790.

Giles, H., Fortman, J., Dailey, R. M., Barker, V., Hajek, C., Anderson, M. C., & Rule, N. O. (2006). Communication accommodation: Law enforcement and the public. In R. M. Dailey and B. A. LePoire (Eds.), *Applied interpersonal communication matters: Family, health, and community relations* (pp. 241–269). New York: Peter Lang.

Giles, H., Reid, S., & Harwood, J. (Eds.) (2010). *The dynamics of intergroup communication.* New York: Peter Lang.

Giles, H., & Smith, P. M. (1979). Accommodation theory: Optimal levels of convergence. In H. Giles & R. N. Saint Clair (Eds.), *Language and social psychology* (pp. 45–65). Oxford: Blackwell.

Giles, H., & Wiemann, J. M. (1987). Language, social comparison, and power. In C. R. Berger & S. H. Chaffee (Eds.), *Handbook of communication science* (pp. 350–384). Newbury Park, CA: Sage Publications.

Gillath, O., McCall, C., Shaver, P. R., & Blascovich, J. (2008). What can virtual reality teach us about prosocial tendencies in real and virtual environments? *Media Psychology, 11*(2), 259–282.

Gitlow v. New York, 268 U.S. 652 (1925).

Goffman, E. (1967). *Interaction ritual: Essays on face-to-face behavior.* Garden City, NY: Doubleday.

Goffman, E. (1971). *Relations in public: Microstudies of the public order.* New York: Harper & Row.

Goodrich, A. (2007, March 28). Anxiety about study abroad. *The Georgetown Independent.* Retrieved from http://travel.georgetown.edu/51469.html

Goodwin, D. K. (2002, January 27). How I caused that story. *Time*. Retrieved from http://www.time.com/time/nation/article/0,8599,197614,00.html#ixzz1FMvG5yK9

Gordon, P. (2004, October 15). Numerical cognition without words: Evidence from Amazonia [Supplementary online materials]. *Science Online*. Retrieved March 25, 2008, from http://www.sciencemag.org/cgi/content/full/sci;1094492/DC1

Gore, J. (2009). The interaction of sex, verbal, and nonverbal cues in same-sex first encounters. *Journal of Nonverbal Behavior, 33*(4), 279–299.

Gorman, B. (2010, April 12). Where did the primetime broadcast TV audience go? TV by the Numbers, Zap2it.com. Retrieved from http://tvbythenumbers.zap2it.com/2010/04/12/where-did-the-primetime-broadcast-tv-audience-go/47976/

Gorman, B. (2011, March 29). FX's critically acclaimed hit drama *Justified* gets third season pickup [Press Release]. Retrieved from http://tvbythenumbers.zap2it.com

Goss, B., & O'Hair, D. (1988). *Communicating in interpersonal relationships*. New York: Macmillan.

Gottman, J. M. (1994). *What predicts divorce? The relationship between marital processes and marital outcomes*. Hillsdale, NJ: Erlbaum.

Gottman, J. M., & Silver, N. (1999). *The seven principles for making marriages work: A practical guide from the country's foremost relationship expert*. New York: Three Rivers Press.

Gouran, D. S. (2003). Communication skills for group decision making. In J. O. Greene & B. R. Burleson (Eds.), *Handbook of communication and social interaction skills* (pp. 835–870). Mahwah, NJ: Erlbaum.

Grahe, J. E., & Bernieri, F. J. (1999). The importance of nonverbal cues in judging rapport. *Journal of Nonverbal Behavior, 23*, 253–269.

Gray, F. E. (2010). Specific oral communication skills desired in new accountancy graduates. *Business Communication Quarterly, 73*(1), 40–67.

Greco, B. (1977). Recruiting and retaining high achievers. *Journal of College Placement, 37*(2), 34–40.

Greenhouse, S. (2006, September 3). Now bringing home the leaner bacon: Borrowers we be. *The New York Times*. Retrieved from http://www.nytimes.com

Greenwalk, A. G., Bellezza, F. S., & Banaji, M. R. (1988). Is self-esteem a central ingredient of self-concept? *Personality and Social Psychology Bulletin, 14*, 34–45.

Greulich, M. (2005, Fall). Are you a feminist? E-Quality. Retrieved March 25, 2008, from http://www.cbeinternational.org/new/E-Journal/2005/05fall/05fallsurvey.html

Grossman, R. B., & Kegl, J. (2007). Moving faces: Categorization of dynamic facial expressions in American Sign Language by deaf and hearing participants. *Journal of Nonverbal Behavior, 31*, 23–28.

Gudykunst, W. B. (1993). Toward a theory of effective interpersonal and intergroup communication: An anxiety/uncertainty management (AUM) perspective. In R. L. Wiseman & J. Koester (Eds.), *Intercultural communication competence* (pp. 33–71). Newbury Park, CA: Sage Publications.

Gudykunst, W. B. (2004). *Bridging differences: Effective intergroup communication* (4th ed.). Thousand Oaks, CA: Sage Publications.

Gudykunst, W. B., & Ting-Toomey, S. (1988). *Culture and interpersonal communication*. Newbury Park, CA: Sage Publications.

Gudykunst, W. B., Ting-Toomey, S., Sudweeks, S., & Stewart, L. P. (1995). *Building bridges: Interpersonal skills for a changing world*. Boston: Houghton Mifflin Company.

Guerrero, L. K., & Afifi, W. A. (1995). Some things are better left unsaid: Topic avoidance in family relationships. *Communication Quarterly, 43*, 276–296.

Guerrero, L. K., Andersen, P. A., & Afifi, W. A. (2007). *Close encounters: Communication in relationships*. Los Angeles, CA: Sage Publications.

Guerrero, L. K., Farinelli, L., & McEwan, B. (2009). Attachment and relational satisfaction: The mediating effect of emotional communication. *Communication Monographs, 76*(4), 487–514.

Guerrero, L. K., & Floyd, K. (2006). *Nonverbal communication in close relationships*. Mahwah, NJ: Erlbaum.

Guerrero, L. K., La Valley, A. G., & Farinelli, L. (2008). The experience and expression of anger, guilt, and sadness in marriage: An equity theory explanation. *Journal of Social & Personal Relationships, 25*(5), 699–724.

Hall, E. T. (1959). *The silent language*. New York: Doubleday.

Hall, E. T. (1976). *Beyond culture*. New York: Anchor/Doubleday.

Hall, E. T., & Hall, M. R. (1990). *Understanding cultural differences: Germans, French, and Americans*. Yarmouth, Maine: Intercultural Press.

Hall, J. A. (1998). How big are nonverbal sex differences? The case of smiling and sensitivity to nonverbal cues. In D. J. Canary & K. Dindia (Eds.), *Sex differences and similarities in communication: Critical essays and empirical investigations of sex and gender in interaction* (pp. 155–178). Mahwah, NJ: Erlbaum.

Hall, J. A., Carter, J. D., & Hogan, T. G. (2000). Gender differences in nonverbal communication of emotion. In A. H. Fischer (Ed.), *Gender and emotion: Social psychological perspectives* (pp. 97–117). Cambridge: Cambridge University Press.

Hample, D. (1987). Communication and the unconscious. In B. Dervin & M. J. Voight (Eds.), *Progress in communication sciences* (Vol. 8, pp. 83–121). Norwood, NJ: Ablex.

Han, B., & Cai, D. (2010). Face goals in apology: A cross-cultural comparison of Chinese and U.S. Americans. *Journal of Asian Pacific Communication, 20*(1), 101–123.

Hansen, H. V. (2002). The straw thing of fallacy theory: The standard definition of "fallacy." *Argumentation, 16,* 133–155.

Hanson, C., Thackeray, R., Barnes, M., Neiger, B., & McIntyre, E. (2008). Integrating Web 2.0 in health education preparation and practice. *American Journal of Health Education, 39,* 157–166.

Hare, B. (2010, March 2). Roger Ebert debuts his "new voice" on "Oprah." *CNN.com.* Retrieved from http://articles.cnn.com/2010-03-02/entertainment/roger.ebert.oprah_1_roger-ebert-text-to-speech-software-voice?_s=PM:SHOWBIZ

Harrigan, J. A., & Taing, K. T. (1997). Fooled by a smile: Detecting anxiety in others. *Journal of Nonverbal Behavior, 21,* 203–221.

Harrison, K., & Cantor, J. (1997). The relationship between media consumption and eating disorders. *Journal of Communication, 47,* 40–66.

Hartnett, S. J. (2010). Communication, social justice, and joyful commitment. *Western Journal of Communication, 74*(1), 68–93.

Hartup, W. W., & Stevens, N. (1997). Friendships and adaptation in the life course. *Psychological Bulletin, 121,* 355–370.

Harvey, J. H., Weber, A. L., & Orbuch, T. L. (1990). *Interpersonal accounts: A social psychological perspective.* Cambridge, MA: Blackwell.

Harwood, J. (2000). Communication media use in the grandparent-grandchild relationship. *Journal of Communication, 50*(4), 56–78.

Harwood, J., & Giles, H. (Eds.) (2005). *Intergroup communication: Multiple perspectives.* New York: Peter Lang.

Hayakawa, S. I. (1964). *Language in thought and action.* New York: Harcourt Brace Jovanovich.

Hazel, M., Wongprasert, T. K., & Ayres, J. (2006). Twins: How similar are fraternal and identical twins across four communication variables? *Journal of the Northwest Communication Association, 35,* 46–59.

Hecht, M. L., Jackson, R. L., II, & Ribeau, S. A. (2003). *African American communication: Exploring identity and culture.* Mahwah, NJ: Erlbaum.

Helgesen, S. (1990). *The female advantage: Women's ways of leadership.* Garden City, NY: Doubleday.

Hendrick, S. S., & Hendrick, C. (1992). *Liking, loving, and relating.* Pacific Grove, CA: Brooks/Cole.

Hendriks, A. (2002). Examining the effects of hegemonic depictions of female bodies on television: A call for theory and programmatic research. *Critical Studies in Media Communication, 19,* 106–123.

Hershatter, A., & Epstein, M. (2010). Millennials and the world of work: An organization and management perspective. *Journal of Business and Psychology, 25*(2), 211–223.

Heslin, R. (1974). *Steps toward a taxonomy of touching.* Paper presented at the Western Psychological Association Convention, Chicago.

Hinckley, D. (2010, March 14). The price of beauty. *NYDailyNews.com.* Retrieved from http://www.nydailynews.com/entertainment/tv/2010/03/14/2010-03-14_vh1s_price_of_beauty_hosted_by_jessica_simpson_is_ditzy_look_at_international_be.html

Hinkle, L. L. (1999). Nonverbal immediacy communication behaviors and liking in marital relationships. *Communication Research Reports, 16,* 81–90.

Hirokawa, R. Y., Gouran, D. S., & Martz, A. E. (1988). Understanding the sources of faulty group decision-making: A lesson from the *Challenger* disaster. *Small Group Behavior, 19,* 411–433.

Hockenbury, D. H., & Hockenbury, S. E. (2002). *Psychology* (3rd ed.). New York: Worth.

Hoeken, H., Van den Brandt, C., Crijns, R., Domínguez, N., Hendriks, B., Planken, B., & Starren, M. (2003). International advertising in Western Europe: Should differences in uncertainty avoidance be considered when advertising in Belgium, France, the Netherlands and Spain? *Journal of Business Communication, 40*(3), 195–218.

Hofstede, G. (1984). *Culture's consequences: International differences in work-related values.* Beverly Hills, CA: Sage Publications.

Hofstede, G. (2001). *Culture's consequences: Comparing values, behaviors, institutions, and organizations across nations.* Thousand Oaks, CA: Sage Publications.

Holson, L. M. (2008, March 9). Text generation gap: U r 2 old (jk). *The New York Times.* Retrieved from http://www.nytimes.com/2008/03/09/business/09cell.html

Holson, L. M. (2010, May 8). Tell-all generation learns to keep things offline. *The New York Times,* p. A1.

Homer, P. M. (2006). Relationships among ad-induced affect, beliefs, and attitudes: Another look. *Journal of Advertising, 35,* 35–51.

Horwitz, A. V., & White, H. R. (1998). The relationship of cohabitation and mental health: A study of a young adult cohort. *Journal of Marriage and the Family, 60,* 505–514.

Howe, N., & Strauss, W. (1992). *Generations: The history of America's future, 1584 to 2069.* New York: Quill.

Husband, C. (2009). Between listening and understanding. *Continuum: Journal of Media & Cultural Studies, 23*(4), 441–443.

Huston, A. C., Bickham, D. S., Lee, J. H., & Wright, J. C. (2007). From attention to comprehension: How children watch and learn from television. In N. Pecora, J. P. Murray, & E. A. Wartella (Eds.), *Children and television: Fifty years of research* (pp. 41–63). Mahwah, NJ: Lawrence Erlbaum.

Huston, A., & Wright, J. C. (1998). Television and the informational and educational needs of children. *The Annals of the American Academy of Political and Social Science, 557*(1), 9–23.

Iedema, R., Jorm, C., Wakefield, J., Ryan, C., & Sorensen, R. (2009). A new structure of attention? Open disclosure of adverse events to patients and their families. *Journal of Language & Social Psychology, 28*(2), 139–157.

Infante, D. A. (1988). *Arguing constructively.* Prospect Heights, IL: Waveland Press.

Ivy, D., & Backlund, P. (2004). *Gender speak: Personal effectiveness in gender communication* (3rd ed.). New York: McGraw-Hill.

Iyengar, S., & Hahn, K. S. (2009). Red media, blue media: Evidence of ideological selectivity in media use. *Journal of Communication, 59,* 19–39.

Jackson, D. (2006, January 29). State of the Union address: A meshing of many ideas. *USA Today.* Retrieved from http://www.usatoday.com/news/washington/2006-01-29-sotu-speech_x.htm?POE=click-refer

James, C. H., and Minnis, W. C. (2004, July–August). Organizational storytelling: It makes sense. *Business Horizons,* 23–32.

Janis, I. L. (1982). *Groupthink: Psychological studies of policy decisions and fiascoes* (2nd ed.). Boston: Houghton Mifflin.

Janusik, L. (2005). Conversational listening span: A proposed measure of conversational listening. *International Journal of Listening, 19,* 12–28.

Janusik, L. A., & Wolvin, A. D. (2009). 24 hours in a day: A listening update to the time studies. *International Journal of Listening, 23*(2), 104–120.

Jay, T., & Janschewitz, K. (2008). The pragmatics of swearing. *Journal of Politeness Research: Language, Behavior, Culture, 4*(2), 267–288.

Jin, B., & Oh, S. (2010). Cultural differences of social network influence on romantic relationships: A comparison of the United States and South Korea. *Communication Studies, 61*(2), 156–171.

Johannesen, R. L. (1996). *Ethics in human communication.* Prospect Heights, IL: Waveland Press.

Johnson, I. W., Pearce, C. G., Tuten, T. L., & Sinclair, L. (2003). Self-imposed silence and perceived listening effectiveness. *Business Communication Quarterly, 66*(2), 23–45.

Johnson, S. (2005, April 24). Watching TV makes you smarter. *The New York Times.* Retrieved from http://www.nytimes.com/2005/04/24/magazine/24TV.html

Johnson, T. (2010, April 19). Land that job: What interviewers really want you to ask them. *Good Morning America.* Retrieved from http://abcnews.go.com/GMA/JobClub/questions-job-interview/story?id=10409243

John-Steiner, V. (1997). *Notebooks of the mind: Explorations of thinking.* New York: Oxford University Press.

Johnston, M. K., Weaver, J. B., Watson, K. W., & Barker, L. B. (2000). Listening styles: Biological or psychological differences? *International Journal of Listening, 14,* 32–46.

Jones, C. (2005, May 16). Gay marriage debate still fierce one year later. *USA Today.* Retrieved from http://www.usatoday.com/news/nation/2005-05-16-gay-marriage_x.htm

Jones, E. E. (1990). *Interpersonal perception.* New York: Freeman.

Joyce, M. P. (2008). Interviewing techniques used in selected organizations today. *Business Communication Quarterly, 71*(3), 376–380.

Kaiser Family Foundation. (2010, January 20). Daily media use among children and teens up dramatically from five years ago. In *Generation M2: Media in the lives of 8- to 18-year-olds.* Retrieved from http://www.kff.org/entmedia/8010.cfm.

Kanter, R. M. (2009). *Supercorp: How vanguard companies create innovation, profits, growth, and social good.* New York: Crown Business.

Kato, S., Kato, Y., & Scott, D. (2009). Relationships between emotional states and emoticons in mobile phone email communication in Japan. *International Journal on E-Learning, 8*(3), 385–401.

Katzenbach, J. R., & Smith, D. K. (1993). *The wisdom of teams.* Boston: Harvard Business School Press.

Keaten, J. A., & Kelly, L. (2008). "Re: We really need to talk": Affect for communication channels, competence, and fear of negative evaluation. *Communication Quarterly, 56*(4), 407–426.

Kenrick, D. T., Griskevicius, V., Neuberg, S. L., & Schaller, M. (2010). Renovating the pyramid of needs: Contemporary extensions built upon ancient foundations. *Perspectives on Psychological Science, 5*(3), 292–314.

Kiesling, S. F. (1998). Men's identities and sociolinguistic variation: The case of fraternity men. *Journal of Sociolinguistics, 2*(1), 69–99.

Kline, S., Horton, B., & Zhang, S. (2005). *How we think, feel, and express love: A cross-cultural comparison between American and East Asian cultures.* Paper presented at the annual meeting of the International Communication Association, New York.

Klocke, U. (2007). How to improve decision making in small groups: Effects of dissent and training interventions. *Small Group Research, 38,* 437–468.

Knapp, M. L., & Hall, J. A. (2010). *Nonverbal communication in human interaction.* Boston, MA: Wadsworth, Cengage Learning.

Knapp, M. L., Hart, R. P., Friedrich, G. W., & Shulman, G. M. (1973). The rhetoric of goodbye: Verbal and nonverbal correlates of human leave-taking. *Communication Monographs, 40,* 182–198.

Knapp, M. L., & Vangelisti, A. (2000). *Interpersonal communication and human relationships* (4th ed.). Newton, MA: Allyn & Bacon.

Knapp, M. L., & Vangelisti, A. L. (2008). *Interpersonal communication and human relationships* (6th ed.). Boston: Allyn and Bacon.

Knobloch, L. K., & Solomon, D. H. (2002). Information seeking beyond initial interaction: Negotiating relational uncertainty within close relationships. *Human Communication Research, 28,* 243–257.

Kohut, A. (2007, May 9). Are Americans ready to elect a female president? *Pew Research Center Publications.* Retrieved from http://pewresearch.org/pubs/474/female-president

Kowitz, A. C., & Knutson, T. J. (1980). *Decision making in small groups: The search for alternatives.* Needham Heights, MA: Allyn & Bacon.

Kramer, M. W., & Pier, P. M. (1999). Students' perceptions of effective and ineffective communication by college teachers. *Southern Communication Journal, 65,* 16–33.

Kraybill, D. B. (2007, October 6). Shunning: It's tough love for the Amish. *Winston-Salem Journal.* Retrieved from http://www.journalnow.com

Krayer, K. (2010). *Influencing skills for effective leadership.* Dallas: University of Dallas College of Business.

Krcmar, M., & Greene, K. (1999). Predicting exposure to and uses of television violence. *Journal of Communication, 49,* 24–46.

Krumhuber, E., Manstead, A., Cosker, D., Marshall, D., & Rosin, P. (2009). Effects of dynamic attributes of smiles in human and synthetic faces: A simulated job interview setting. *Journal of Nonverbal Behavior, 33*(1), 1–15.

Kuhn, T., & Poole, M. S. (2000). Do conflict management styles affect group decision making? Evidence from a longitudinal field study. *Human Communication Research, 26,* 558–590.

Kurdek, L. (1989). Relationship quality of gay and lesbian cohabiting couples. *Journal of Homosexuality, 15*(3–4), 93–118.

La Ferla, R. (2009, August 6). An everywoman as beauty queen. *The New York Times,* p. E1.

Landis, D., Bennett, J. M., and Bennett, M. J. (Eds.). (2004). *Handbook of intercultural training.* Thousand Oaks, CA: Sage Publications.

Landsford, J. E., Antonucci, T. C., Akiyama, H., & Takahashi, K. (2005). A quantitative and qualitative approach to social relationships and well-being in the United States and Japan. *Journal of Comparative Family Studies, 36,* 1–22.

Larkey, L., & Hecht, M. (2010). A model of effects of narrative as culture-centric health promotion. *Journal of Health Communication, 15*(2), 114–135.

Lawson, A. E., & Daniel, E. S. (2010). Inferences of clinical diagnostic reasoning and diagnostic error. *Journal of Biomedical Informatics, 43*(5), 563–574.

Leal, S., & Vrij, A. (2008). Blinking during and after lying. *Journal of Nonverbal Behavior, 32*(4), 187–194.

Leathers, D. (1986). *Successful nonverbal communication: Principles and applications.* New York: Macmillan.

Leavitt, H. J. (1951). Some effects of certain communication patterns on group performance. *Journal of Abnormal and Social Psychology, 46,* 38–50.

Lebo, B. (2009). Employing millennials: Challenges and opportunities. *New Hampshire Business Review, 31*(26), 21.

Lee, E-J. (2007). Effects of gendered language on gender stereotyping in computer-mediated communication: The moderating role of depersonalization and gender-role orientation. *Human Communication Research, 33*(4), 515–535.

Lee, J. A. (1973). *The colors of love: An exploration of the ways of loving.* Don Mills, Ontario, Canada: New Press.

Leland, J. (2008, October 7). In "sweetie" and "dear," a hurt for the elderly. *The New York Times,* p. A1.

Lenhart, A. (2010, Sept. 2). Cell phones and American adults. *Pew Internet & American Life Project.* Retrieved from http://www.pewinternet.org

Lewis, T., & Manusov, V. (2009). Listening to another's distress in everyday relationships. *Communication Quarterly, 57*(3), 282–301.

Lim, G. Y., & Roloff, M. E. (1999). Attributing sexual consent. *Journal of Applied Communication Research, 27,* 1–23.

Lindsley, S. L. (1999). Communication and "the Mexican way": Stability and trust as core symbols in *maquiladoras. Western Journal of Communication, 63,* 1–31.

Lipari, L. (2009). Listening otherwise: The voice of ethics. *International Journal of Listening, 23*(1), 44–59.

Lipman, A. (1986). Homosexual relationships. *Generations, 10* (4), 51–54.

Loden, M., & Rosener, J. B. (1991). *Workforce America! Managing employee diversity as a vital resource.* Chicago: Business One Irwin.

Longley, R. (2007). From time to time: The State of the Union. *About.com: U.S. government info.* Retrieved December 31, 2007, from http://usgovinfo.about.com/od/thepresidentandcabinet/a/souhistory.htm

Lucas, K., & Sherry, J. L. (2004). Sex differences in video game play: A communication-based explanation. *Communication Research, 31,* 499–523.

Luo, M. (2010, March 29). Overqualified? Yes, but happy to have a job. *The New York Times,* p. A1.

Lustig, M. W., & Koester, J. (1993). *Intercultural competence: Interpersonal communication across cultures.* New York: HarperCollins.

Lustig, M. W., & Koester, J. (2006). *Intercultural competence: Interpersonal communication across cultures* (5th ed.). Boston: Allyn & Bacon.

Lyall, S. (2009, April 17). Unlikely singer is YouTube sensation. *The New York Times.* Retrieved from http://www.nytimes.com/2009/04/18/arts/television/18boyle.html

Maag, C. (2007a, November 28). A hoax turned fatal draws anger but no charges. *The New York Times.* Retrieved from http://www.nytimes.com

Maag, C. (2007b, December 16). When the bullies turned faceless. *The New York Times.* Retrieved from http://www.nytimes.com

Madden, M., & Smith, A. (2010, May 26). Reputation management and social media. *Pew Internet & American Life Project.* Retrieved from http://www.pewinternet.org/Reports/2010/Reputation-Management.aspx

Madlock, P. E., & Kennedy-Lightsey, C. (2010). The effects of supervisors' verbal aggressiveness and mentoring on their subordinates. *Journal of Business Communication, 47*(1), 42–62.

Maguire, K. C. (2007). "Will it ever end?": A (re)examination of uncertainty in college student long-distance dating relationships. *Communication Quarterly, 55*(4), 415–432.

Maguire, K. C., & Kinney, T. A. (2010). When distance is problematic: Communication, coping, and relational satisfaction in female college students' long-distance dating relationships. *Journal of Applied Communication Research, 38*(1), 27–46.

Mansson, D. H., Myers, S. A., & Turner, L. H. (2010). Relational maintenance behaviors in the grandchild-grandparent relationship. *Communication Research Reports, 27*(1), 68–79.

Manusov, V., & Patterson, M. L. (2006). *The Sage handbook of nonverbal communication.* Thousand Oaks, CA: Sage Publications.

Marcott, A. (2009, August 14). Four Sloanies take on a *Daily Show* correspondent. *Slice of M.I.T.* Retrieved from http://alum.mit.edu/pages/sliceofmit/2009/08/14/sloanies-on-daily-show/

Marilyn, R., Wanta, W., & Dzwo, T. H. (2002). Agenda setting and issue salience online. *Communication Research, 29,* 452–465.

Martinez, E. (2010, March 26). Alexis Pilkington brutally cyber bullied, even after her suicide. *CBS News.* Retrieved from http://www.cbsnews.com/8301-504083_162-20001181-504083.html

Maslow, A. (1954). *Motivation and personality.* New York: Harper & Row.

Mast, M. S. (2002). Dominance as expressed and inferred through speaking time. *Human Communication Research, 28,* 420–450.

Matsumoto, D. (1989). Cultural influences on the perception of emotion. *Journal of Cross-Cultural Psychology, 20*(1), 92–105.

McCain, J. S. (2008, January 28). John McCain, prisoner of war: A first person account. *U.S. News & World Report.* Retrieved from http://politics.usnews.com/news/articles/2008/01/28/john-mccain-prisoner-of-war-a-first-person-account.html

McClanahan, A. (2006, March 9). What does a feminist "look" like? *Pocono Record.* Retrieved April 8, 2008, from http://www.poconorecord.com

McClintock, E. A. (2010). When does race matter? Race, sex, and dating at an elite university. *Journal of Marriage & Family, 72*(1), 45–72.

McCombs, M. (2005). The agenda-setting function of the press. In G. Overholser & K. H. Jamieson (Eds.), *The press* (pp. 156–168). New York: Oxford University Press.

McConnell, M. (1987). *Challenger: A major malfunction.* Garden City, NY: Doubleday.

McCroskey, J. C. (1977). Oral communication apprehension: A summary of recent theory and research. *Human Communication Research, 4,* 78–96.

McCroskey, J. C. (1982). *An introduction to rhetorical communication* (4th ed.). Englewood Cliffs, NJ: Prentice Hall.

McCroskey, J. C. (1997). The communication apprehension perspective. In J. A. Daly & J. C. McCroskey (Eds.), *Avoiding communication: Shyness, reticence, and communication apprehension* (pp. 13–38). Cresskill, NJ: Hampton Press.

McCroskey, J. C., & Teven, J. J. (1999). Goodwill: A reexamination of the construct and its measurement. *Communication Monographs, 66,* 90–103.

McDaniel, E., & Andersen, P. A. (1998). International patterns of interpersonal tactile communication: A field study. *Journal of Nonverbal Behavior, 22,* 59–75.

McGroarty, P. (2011, March 1). German minister resigns over plagiarism scandal. *The Wall Street Journal Online*. Retrieved from http://online.wsj.com/article/SB10001424052748704506004576173970765020528.html

McIlwraith, R. D. (1998). "I, addicted to television": The personality, imagination, and TV watching patterns of self-identified TV addicts. *Journal of Broadcasting and Electronic Media, 42*, 371–386.

McLean, C. (2011, January 24). *Glee*: The making of a musical phenomenon. *The Telegraph*. Retrieved from http://www.telegraph.co.uk/culture/8271318/Glee-the-making-of-a-musical-phenomenon.html

McLeod, D. N., Detenber, B. H., & Eveland, W. P., Jr. (2001). Behind the third-person effect: Differentiating perceptual processes for self and other. *Journal of Communication, 51*, 678–695.

Mehrabian, A. (1971). *Silent messages*. Belmont, CA: Wadsworth.

Mello, B. (2009). For K-12 educators: Speaking, listening, and media literacy standards. *Spectra, 45*(3), 11.

Merkin, R. S. (2009). Cross-cultural communication patterns—Korean and American communication. *Journal of Intercultural Communication, 20*, 5.

Merolla, A. J. (2010a). Relational maintenance and noncopresence reconsidered: Conceptualizing geographic separation in close relationships. *Communication Theory, 20*(2), 169–193.

Merolla, A. J. (2010b). Relational maintenance during military deployment: Perspectives of wives of deployed U.S. soldiers. *Journal of Applied Communication Research, 38*(1), 4–26.

Microsoft, Inc. (2005, March 15). Survey finds workers average only three productive days per week [Press release]. Retrieved April 30, 2008, from http://www.microsoft.com

Miczo, N. (2008). Dependence and independence power, conflict tactics and appraisals in romantic relationships. *Journal of Communication Studies, 1*(1), 56–82.

Miller, C. W., & Roloff, M. E. (2007). The effect of face loss on willingness to confront hurtful messages from romantic partners. *Southern Communication Journal, 72*(3), 247–263.

Miller, D. T., & Morrison, K. R. (2009). Expressing deviant opinions: Believing you are in the majority helps. *Journal of Experimental Social Psychology, 45*(4), 740–747.

Miller, L. C., Cooke, K. K., Tsang, J., & Morgan, F. (1992). Should I brag? Nature and impact of positive boastful disclosures for women and men. *Human Communication Research, 18*, 364–399.

Minow, N. N. (1961, May 9). Television and the public interest. Speech presented at the meeting of the National Association of Broadcasters, Washington, DC.

Minow, N. N., & Cate, F. H. (2003). Revisiting the vast wasteland. *Federal Communications Law Journal, 55*, 407–434.

Mittel, J. (2006). Narrative complexity in contemporary American television. *The Velvet Light Trap, 58*, 29–40.

Moeller, S., Crocker, J., & Bushman, B. J. (2009). Creating hostility and conflict: Effects of entitlement and self-image goals. *Journal of Experimental Social Psychology, 45*(2), 448–452.

Molloy, J. T. (1983). *Molloy's live for success*. New York: Bantam Books.

Money is the top subject for marital spats. (2006, March 20). *Webindia123.com*. Retrieved May 1, 2006, from http://news.webindia123.com/news/ar_showdetails.asp?id=603200038&cat=&n_date=20060320

Montana Meth Project. (2007). Retrieved August 1, 2007, from http://www.montanameth.com

Montepare, J., Koff, E., Zaitchik, D., & Alberet, M. (1999). The use of body movements and gestures as cues to emotions in younger and older adults. *Journal of Nonverbal Behavior, 23*, 133–152.

Moran, B. (2003, November 18). She explores the world of language and thought. *The Boston Globe*, p. C2.

Moreland, R. L., & Levine, J. M., (1994). *Understanding small groups*. Boston: Allyn & Bacon.

Morley, D. (2006). Unanswered questions in audience research. *The Communication Review, 9*, 101–121

Morris, D. (1977). *Manwatching*. New York: Abrams.

Morry, M. M. (2005). Relationship satisfaction as a predictor of similarity ratings: A test of the attraction-similarity hypothesis. *Journal of Social and Personal Relationships, 22*, 561–584.

Morzy, M. (2009). On mining and social role discovery in Internet forums. *Social Informatics, 74*–79. Retrieved from http://www.cs.put.poznan.pl/mmorzy/papers/socinfo09.pdf

Motley, M. T. (1990). On whether one can(not) communicate: An examination via traditional communication postulates. *Western Journal of Speech Communication, 56*, 1–20.

Motley, M. T., & Reeder, H. M. (1995). Unwanted escalation of sexual intimacy: Male and female perceptions of connotations and relational consequences of resistance messages. *Communication Monographs, 62*, 355–382.

Mouawad, J., & Krauss, C. (2010, June 4). Another torrent BP works to stem: Its CEO. *The New York Times*, p. A1.

Muir, C. (2008). Job interviewing. *Business Communication Quarterly, 71*(3), 374–376.

Mulac, A. J., Wiemann, J. M., Widenmann, S. J., & Gibson, T. W. (1988). Male-female language differences and effects in same-sex and mixed-sex dyads: The gender-linked language effect. *Communication Monographs, 55*, 315–335.

Mulanax, A., & Powers, W. (2001). Listening fidelity development and relationship to receiver apprehension and locus of control. *International Journal of Listening, 15,* 69–78.

Mumby, D. (2000). Communication, organization, and the public sphere: A feminist perspective. In P. Buzzanell (Ed.), *Rethinking organizational and managerial communication from feminist perspectives* (pp. 3–23). Thousand Oaks, CA: Sage Publications.

Mungazi, F. (2009, June 19). In defense of the vuvuzela. *BBC Sport.* Retrieved from http://news.bbc.co.uk/sport2/hi/football/africa/8108691.stm

Muntigl, P., & Choi, K. T. (2010). Not remembering as a practical epistemic resource in couples therapy. *Discourse Studies,* 12(3), 331–356.

Murphy, D. R., Daneman, M., & Schneider, B. A. (2006). Do older adults have difficulty following conversations? *Psychology and Aging, 21,* 49–61.

Nabi, R. L. (2009). Cosmetic surgery makeover programs and intentions to undergo cosmetic enhancements: A consideration of three models of media effects. *Human Communication Research, 35,* 1–27.

Newcomb, A. F., & Bagwell, C. L. (1995). Children's friendship relations: A meta-analytic review. *Psychological Bulletin, 117,* 306–347.

Newman, M. L., Groom, C. J., Handelman, L. D., & Pennebaker, J. W. (2008). Gender differences in language use: An analysis of 14,000 text samples. *Discourse Processes, 45(3),* 211–236.

Nicholas, S. (2009). "I live Hopi, I just don't speak it"—The critical intersection of language, culture, and identity in the lives of contemporary Hopi youth. *Journal of Language, Identity & Education,* 8(5), 321–334.

Nichols, R. G. (2006). The struggle to be human: Keynote address to first International Listening Association convention, February 17, 1980. *International Journal of Listening, 20,* 4–12.

Nichols, R. G., Brown, J. I., & Keller, R. J. (2006). Measurement of communication skills. *International Journal of Listening,* 20, 13–17.

Nicotera, A. M. (1997). Managing conflict communication groups. In L. R. Frey & J. K. Barge (Eds.), *Managing group life: Communicating in decision-making groups* (pp. 104–130). Boston: Houghton Mifflin.

Nierenberg, R. (2009). *Maestro: A surprising story about leadership by listening.* New York: Portfolio.

Nomani, A. Q. (2005, December 14). Tapping Islam's feminist roots. *The Washington Post.* Retrieved March 7, 2008, from http://www.seattletimes.nwsource.com

O'Brian, L. (2010, September 30). Facebook fakery: The alternate reality of Aaron Sorkin's *The Social Network.* Retrieved from http://www.slate.com

Oetzel, J. G., & Ting-Toomey, S. (Eds.). (2006). *The Sage handbook of conflict communication: Integrating theory, research, and practice.* Thousand Oaks, CA: Sage Publications.

O'Hair, D., & Cody, M. (1994). Deception. In W. R. Cupach & B. H. Spitzberg (Eds.), *The dark side of interpersonal communication* (pp. 181–213). Hillsdale, NJ: Erlbaum.

O'Hair, D., Friedrich, G. W., & Dixon, L. D. (2002). *Strategic communication in business and the professions* (4th ed.). Boston: Houghton Mifflin.

O'Hair, D., Friedrich, G. W., & Dixon, L. D. (2007). *Strategic communication in business and the professions* (6th ed.). Boston: Houghton Mifflin.

O'Hair, D., & Krayer, K. (1987). A conversational analysis of reconciliation strategies. Paper presented at the Western Speech Communication Association, Salt Lake City.

O'Hair, D., O'Rourke, J., & O'Hair, M. J. (2000). *Business communication: A framework for success.* Cincinnati, OH: South-Western.

O'Hair, D., & Stewart, R. (1998). *Public speaking: Challenges and choices.* New York: Bedford/St. Martin's.

O'Hair, D., Stewart, R., & Rubenstein, H. (2007). *A speaker's guidebook* (3rd ed.). New York: Bedford/St. Martin's.

O'Hair, D., Stewart, R., & Rubenstein, H. (2010). *A speaker's guidebook: Text and reference* (4th ed.). New York: Bedford/St. Martin's.

O'Keefe, D. J. (1999). How to handle opposing arguments in persuasive messages: A meta-analytic review of the effects of one-sided and two-sided messages. In M. E. Roloff (Ed.), *Communication yearbook 22* (pp. 209–249). Thousand Oaks, CA: Sage Publications.

Oldenburg, A. (2011, March 1). Charlie Sheen saga boosts *Two and a Half Men* ratings. *USA Today.* Retrieved from http://content.usatoday.com/communities/entertainment/post/2011/03/charlie-sheen-saga-boosts-two-and-a-half-men-ratings-/1.

Oliver, J. (2010, February). Jamie Oliver's TED Prize wish: Teach every child about food. Video retrieved from http://www.ted.com/talks/jamie_oliver.html

Olson, L. (2004). The role of voice in the (re)construction of a battered woman's identity: An autoethnography of one woman's experiences of abuse. *Women's Studies in Communication, 27(1),* 1–33.

Oprah.com. (2008). *Oprah's debt diet.* Retrieved from http://www.oprah.com/packages/oprahs-debt-diet.html

O'Sullivan, P. B. (2000). What you don't know won't hurt me: Impression management functions of communication channels in relationships. *Human Communication Research, 26,* 403–431.

O'Sullivan, P. B., Hunt, S. K., & Lippert, L. R. (2004). Mediated immediacy: A language of affiliation in a technological age. *Journal of Language and Social Psychology, 23,* 464–490.

Pagotto, L., Voci, A., & Maculan, V. (2010). The effectiveness of intergroup contact at work: Mediators and moderators of hospital workers' prejudice towards immigrants. *Journal of Community & Applied Social Psychology, 20*(4), 317–330.

Palomares, N. A. (2008). Explaining gender-based language use: Effects of gender identity salience on references to emotion and tentative language in intra- and intergroup contexts. *Human Communication Research, 34*(2), 263–286.

Palomares, N. A. (2009). Women are sort of more tentative than men, aren't they?: How men and women use tentative language differently, similarly, and counterstereotypically as a function of gender salience. *Communication Research, 36*(4), 538–560.

Palomares, N. A., & Lee, E-J. (2010). Virtual gender identity: The linguistic assimilation to gendered avatars in computer-mediated communication. *Journal of Language & Social Psychology, 29*(1), 5–23.

Paolini, S., Harwood, J., & Rubin, M. (2010). Negative intergroup contact makes group members salient: Explaining why intergroup conflict endures. *Personality and Social Psychology Bulletin, 36,* 1723–1738.

Park, C. (2003). In other (people's) words: Plagiarism by university students—literature and lessons. *Assessment and Evaluation in Higher Education, 28,* 471–488.

Park, W. (2000). A comprehensive empirical investigation of the relationships among variables of the groupthink model. *Journal of Organizational Behavior, 21,* 874–887.

Parker-Pope, T. (2010a, April 18). Is marriage good for your health? *The New York Times,* p. MM46.

Parker-Pope, T. (2010b, May 11). The science of a happy marriage. *The New York Times,* p. D1.

Parks, M., & Roberts, L. (1998). "Making MOOsic": The development of personal relationships on line and a comparison of their off-line counterparts. *Journal of Social and Personal Relationships, 15,* 517–537.

Patry, M. W. (2008). Attractive but guilty: Deliberation and the physical attractiveness bias. *Psychological Reports, 102*(3), 727–733.

Patterson, B. R., & O'Hair, D. (1992). Relational reconciliation: Toward a more comprehensive model of relational development. *Communication Research Reports, 9,* 119–127.

Pauley, P. M., & Emmers-Sommer, T. M. (2007). The impact of Internet technologies on primary and secondary romantic relationship development. *Communication Studies, 58*(4), 411–427.

Pavitt, C. (1999). Theorizing about the group communication-leadership relationship. In L. R. Frey, D. S. Gouran, & M. Poole (Eds.), *Handbook of group communication theory and research* (pp. 313–334). Thousand Oaks, CA: Sage Publications.

Pavlik, J. V., & McIntosh, S. (2011). *Converging media: A new introduction to mass communication* (2nd ed.). New York: Oxford University Press.

Pawlowski, D. (1998). Dialectical tensions in marital partners' accounts of their relationships. *Communication Quarterly, 46,* 396–416.

Payne, S. L. (1951). *The art of asking questions.* Princeton, NJ: Princeton University Press.

Pearce, C., & Tuten, T. (2001). Internet recruiting in the banking industry. *Business Communication Quarterly, 64*(1), 9–18.

Pearson, J. C., & Spitzberg, B. H. (1990). *Interpersonal communication: Concepts, components, and contexts* (2nd ed.). Dubuque, IA: Brown.

Pearson, J. C., Turner, L. H., & Todd-Mancillas, W. R. (1991). *Gender and communication* (2nd ed.). Dubuque, IA: Brown.

Peck, J. (2007, December 29). *Top 7 tips for conquering public speaking fear.* Retrieved January 9, 2008, from http://ezinearticles.com/?expert=Jason_Peck

Petronio, S. (2000). The boundaries of privacy: Praxis of everyday life. In S. Petronio (Ed.), *Balancing the secrets of private disclosures* (pp. 37–50). Mahwah, NJ: Erlbaum.

Petronio, S. (2002). *The boundaries of privacy: Dialectics of disclosure.* Albany: State University of New York Press.

Petronio, S. (2004). Road to developing communication privacy management theory: Narrative in progress, please stand by. *Journal of Family Communication, 4,* 193–207.

Pettigrew, T. F., & Tropp, L. R. (2006). A meta-analytical test of the intergroup contact theory. *Journal of Personality and Social Psychology, 90,* 751–783.

Petty, R. E., & Cacioppo, J. T. (1986). The Elaboration Likelihood Model of persuasion. In L. Berkowitz (Ed.), *Advances in experimental social psychology* (Vol. 19, pp. 123–205). San Diego, CA: Academic Press.

Petty, R. E., & Wegner, D. T. (1998). Matching versus mismatching attitude functions: Implications for scrutiny of persuasive messages. *Personality and Social Psychology Bulletin, 24*(3), 227–240.

Pew Research Center. (2010, April 5). Demographics of Internet users. *Pew Internet and American Life Project Tracking Survey.* Retrieved from http://www.pewinternet.org/Trend-Data /Whos-Online.aspx

Phanor-Faury, A. (2010, June 24). "Nude" doesn't translate in fashion. *Essence*. Retrieved from http://www.essence.com/fashion_beauty/fashion/nude_dresses_racial_bias_fashion_world.php

Pines, M. (1997). The civilizing of Genie. In L. F. Kasper (Ed.), *Teaching English through the disciplines: Psychology* (2nd ed.). New York: Whittier.

Planalp, S., & Honeycutt, J. (1985). Events that increase uncertainty in personal relationships. *Human Communication Research, 11,* 593–604.

Potter, W. J. (2008). *Media literacy* (4th ed.). Thousand Oaks, CA: Sage Publications.

Potter, W. J., & Byrne, S. (2009). Media literacy. In R. L. Nabi & M. B. Oliver (Eds.), *The Sage Handbook of Media Processes and Effects* (pp. 345–360). Thousand Oaks, CA: Sage Publications.

Prager, K. J. (2000). Intimacy in personal relationships. In C. Hendrick & S. S. Hendrick (Eds.), *Close relationships: A sourcebook* (pp. 229–242). Thousand Oaks, CA: Sage Publications.

Pratkanis, A. R., & Aronson, E. (2001). *Age of propaganda: The everyday use and abuse of persuasion.* New York: W. H. Freeman.

Priester, J. R., & Petty, R. E. (1995). Source attributions and persuasion: Perceived honesty as a determinant of message scrutiny. *Personality and Social Psychology Bulletin, 21,* 637–654.

Public speaking. (n.d.). *Compton's online encyclopedia.* Retrieved June 10, 2000, from http://www.comptons.com/encyclopedia

Punyanunt-Carter, N. M. (2005). Father and daughter motives and satisfaction. *Communication Research Reports, 22,* 293–301.

Purdy, M. (2006). Ralph Nichols: A leader in and of his time. *International Journal of Listening, 20,* 20–21.

Quenqua, D. (2010, March 18). I need to vent. Hello, Facebook. *The New York Times,* p. E1.

Quinn, A. (2008, July 18). Review: WALL-E: Out of this world. *The Independent.* Retrieved from http://www.independent.co.uk/arts-entertainment/films/reviews/walle-u-870497.html

Ralston, S. M., Kirkwood, W. G., & Burant, P. A. (2003). Helping interviewees tell their stories. *Business Communication Quarterly, 66,* 8–22.

Ramirez, A., Sunnafrank, M., & Goei, R. (2010). Predicted outcome value theory in ongoing relationships. *Communication Monographs, 77*(1), 27–50.

Rappaport, S. D. (2010). Putting listening to work: The essentials of listening. *Journal of Advertising Research, 50*(1), 30–41.

Rawlins, W. K. (1992). *Friendship matters: Communication, dialectics, and the life course.* Piscataway, NJ: Aldine Transaction.

Rawlins, W. K. (1994). Being there and growing apart: Sustaining friendships during adulthood. In D. J. Canary & L. Stafford (Eds.), *Communication and relational maintenance* (pp. 275–294). New York: Academic Press.

Rawlins, W. K. (2008). *The compass of friendship: Narratives, identities, and dialogues.* Thousand Oaks, CA: Sage Publications.

Reaction to the president's speech. (2009, September 9). *CNN Larry King Live.* [Television program]. Retrieved from http://transcripts.cnn.com/TRANSCRIPTS/0909/09/lkl.01.htm

Rehling, D. L. (2008). Compassionate listening: A framework for listening to the seriously ill. *International Journal of Listening, 22*(1), 83–89.

Reis, H. T. (1998). Gender differences in intimacy and related behaviors: Context and process. In D. J. Canary & K. Dindia (Eds.), *Sex differences and similarities in communication: Critical essays and empirical investigations of sex and gender in interaction* (pp. 203–231). Hillsdale, NJ: Erlbaum.

Rempel, J., Holmes, J., & Zanna, M. (1985). Trust in close relationships. *Journal of Personality and Social Psychology, 49,* 95–112.

Rheingold, H. (2002). *Smart mobs: The next social revolution.* New York: Basic Books.

Rice, L. (2011, March 30). Ratings alert: What you're watching if you're 11, 50 or 34 years old (the results may surprise you!). *Entertainment Weekly,* Inside TV. Retrieved from http://insidetv.ew.com/2011/03/15/ratings-by-age/

Richmond, V., & McCroskey, J. C. (1998). *Communication apprehension, avoidance, and effectiveness* (5th ed.). Boston: Allyn & Bacon.

Richmond, V. P., McCroskey, J. C., & Payne, S. K. (1991). *Nonverbal behavior in interpersonal relations.* Englewood Cliffs, NJ: Prentice Hall.

Richmond, V. P., Smith, R. S., Jr., Heisel, A. D., & McCroskey, J. C. (2001). Nonverbal immediacy in the physician-patient relationship. *Communication Research Reports, 18,* 211–216.

Riffe, D., Lacy, S., & Varouhakis, M. (2008). Media system dependency theory and using the Internet for in-depth, specialized information. *Web Journal of Mass Communication Research, 11.* Retrieved from http://www.scripps.ohiou.edu/wjmcr/vol11/11-b.html

Rill, L., Balocchi, E., Hopper, M., Denker, K., & Olson, L. N. (2009). Exploration of the relationship between self-esteem, commitment, and verbal aggressiveness in romantic dating relationships. *Communication Reports, 22*(2), 102–113.

Riordan, M. A., & Kreuz, R. J. (2010). Cues in computer-mediated communication: A corpus analysis. *Computers in Human Behavior, 26,* 1806–1817.

Robbins, L. (2010, June 20). BP chief draws outrage for attending yacht race. *The New York Times,* p. A20.

Roberto, A., Carlyle, K. E., Goodall, C. E., & Castle, J. D. (2009). The relationship between parents' verbal aggressiveness and responsiveness and young adult children's attachment style and relational satisfaction with parents. *Journal of Family Communication, 9*(2), 90–106.

Rogers Commission. (1986, June 6). *Report of the presidential commission on the space shuttle Challenger accident.* Retrieved from http://science.ksc.nasa.gov/shuttle /missions/51-l/docs/rogers-commission/Chapter-5.txt

Roloff, M. E. (1980). Self-awareness and the persuasion process: Do we really know what we are doing? In M. E. Roloff & G. Miller (Eds.), *Persuasion: New directions in theory and research* (pp. 29–66). Beverly Hills, CA: Sage Publications.

Rose, G., Evaristo, R., & Staub, D. (2003). Culture and consumer responses to Web download time: A four-continent study of mono- and polychronism. *IEEE Transaction on Engineering Management, 50*(1), 31–44.

Rosener, J. (1990). Ways women lead. *Harvard Business Review, 68,* 119–125.

Rosenthal, M. J. (2001). High-performance teams. *Executive Excellence, 18,* 6.

Ross, L., & Nisbett, R. E. (1991). *The person and the situation: Perspectives of social psychology.* Philadelphia: Temple University Press.

Rothman, A. J., Salovey, P., Turvey, C., & Fishkin, S. A. (1993). Attributions or responsibility and persuasion: Increasing mammography utilization among women over 40 with an internally oriented message. *Health Psychology, 12,* 39–47.

Roup, C. M., & Chiasson, K. E. (2010). Effect of dichotic listening on self-reported state anxiety. *International Journal of Audiology, 49*(2), 88–94.

Ruben, B. D. (2005). Linking communication scholarship and professional practice in colleges and universities. *Journal of Applied Communication Research, 33,* 294–304.

Rubin, A. M. (1981). An examination of television viewing motives. *Communication Research, 8,* 141–165.

Rubin, A. M., Perse, E. M., & Powell, R. A. (1985). Loneliness, parasocial interaction, and local television news viewing. *Human Communication Research, 12,* 155–180.

Rubin, D. L., Hafer, T., & Arata, K. (2000). Reading and listening to oral-based versus literate-based discourse. *Communication Education, 49,* 121–133.

Rushton, J. P. (1980). *Altruism, socialization, and society.* Englewood Cliffs, NJ: Prentice Hall.

Rushton, J. P. (1990). Sir Francis Galton, epigenetic rules, genetic similarity theory, and human life-history analysis. *Journal of Personality, 58,* 117–140.

Rutherford, S. (2001). Any difference? An analysis of gender and divisional management styles in a large airline. *Gender, Work and Organization, 8*(3), 326–345.

Sahlstein, E., Maguire, K. C., & Timmerman, L. (2009). Contradictions and praxis contextualized by wartime deployment: Wives' perspectives revealed through relational dialectics. *Communication Monographs, 76*(4), 421–442.

Salkever, A. (2003, April 24). Home truths about meetings. *Business Week.* Retrieved from http://www.businessweek.com

Samovar, L. A., Porter, R. E., & McDaniel, E. R. (Eds.). (2009). *Intercultural communication: A reader.* Belmont, CA: Wadsworth Cengage Learning.

Samovar, L. A., Porter, R. E., & Stefani, L. A. (1998). *Communication between cultures.* Belmont, CA: Wadsworth.

Samter, W. (2003). Friendship interaction skills across the life span. In J. O. Greene & B. R. Burleson (Eds.), *Handbook of communication and social interaction skills* (pp. 637–684). Mahwah, NJ: Erlbaum.

Sanford, K. (2010). Perceived threat and perceived neglect: Couples' underlying concerns during conflict. *Psychological Assessment, 22,* 288–297.

Sapir, E., & Whorf, B. L. (1956). The relation of habitual thought and behavior to language. In J. B. Carroll (Ed.), *Language, thought, and reality: Selected writings of Benjamin Lee Whorf* (pp. 134–159). Cambridge, MA: MIT Press.

Sarich, V., & Miele, F. (2004). *Race: The reality of human differences.* Boulder, CO: Westview Press.

Scheerhorn, D., & Geist, P. (1997). Social dynamics in groups. In L. R. Frey & J. K. Barge (Eds.), *Managing group life: Communicating in decision-making groups* (pp. 81–103). Boston: Houghton Mifflin.

Schelbert, L. (2009). Pathways of human understanding: An inquiry into Western and North American Indian worldview structures. In L. A. Samovar, R. E. Porter, & E. R. McDaniel (Eds.), *Intercultural communication: A reader* (pp. 48–58). Belmont, CA: Wadsworth Cengage Learning.

Schenck v. United States, 249 U.S. 47 (1919).

Schofield, T., Parke, R., Castañeda, E., & Coltrane, S. (2008). Patterns of gaze between parents and children in European American and Mexican American families. *Journal of Nonverbal Behavior, 32*(3), 171–186.

Schrodt, P. (2009). Family strength and satisfaction as functions of family communication. *Communication Quarterly, 57*(2), 171–186.

Schrodt, P., & Wheeless, L. R. (2001). Aggressive communication and informational reception apprehension: The influence of listening anxiety and intellectual inflexibility on trait argumentativeness and verbal aggressiveness. *Communication Quarterly, 49*, 53–69.

Schrodt, P., Wheeless, L. R., & Ptacek, K. M. (2000). Informational reception apprehension, educational motivation, and achievement. *Communication Quarterly, 48*, 60–73.

Schroeder, L. (2002). The effects of skills training on communication satisfaction and communication anxiety in the basic speech course. *Communication Research Reports, 19*, 380–388.

Schullery, N. M., & Gibson, M. K. (2001). Working in groups: Identification and treatment of students' perceived weaknesses. *Business Communication Quarterly, 64*, 9–30.

Scott, W. R. (1981). *Organizations: Rational, natural, and open systems.* Englewood Cliffs, NJ: Prentice Hall.

Scully, M. (2005, February 2). Building a better State of the Union address. *The New York Times.* Retrieved from http://www.nytimes.com

Secret of the wild child [Transcript]. (1997, March 4). *Nova.* Public Broadcasting System. Retrieved March 25, 2008, from http://www.pbs.org/wgbh/nova/transcripts/2112gchild.html

Segrin, C., Hanzal, A., & Domschke, T. J. (2009). Accuracy and bias in newlywed couples' perceptions of conflict styles and the association with marital satisfaction. *Communication Monographs, 76*, 207–233.

Segrin, C., & Passalacqua, S. A. (2010). Functions of loneliness, social support, health behaviors, and stress in association with poor health. *Health Communication, 25*(4), 312–322.

Seidler, D. (2011, February 27). Acceptance speech presented at the 83rd Annual Academy of Motion Picture Arts and Sciences Awards, Hollywood, CA.

Shachaf, P., & Hara, N. (2010). Beyond vandalism: Wikipedia trolls. *Journal of Information Science, 36*(3), 357–370.

Shannon, C. E., & Weaver, W. (1949). *The mathematical theory of communication.* Urbana: University of Illinois Press.

Shannon, M., & Stark, C. (2003). The influence of physical appearance on personnel selection. *Social Behavior & Personality: An International Journal, 31*(6), 613.

Sherif, C. W., Sherif, M. S., & Nebergall, R. E. (1965). *Attitude and attitude change.* Philadelphia: W. B. Saunders.

Sherif, M., & Sherif, C. W. (1967). Attitude as the individual's own categories: The social judgment-involvement approach to attitude and attitude change. In C. W. Sherif & M. Sherif (Eds.), *Attitude, ego-involvement, and change* (pp. 105–139). New York: Wiley.

Shotter, J. (2009). Listening in a way that recognizes/realizes the world of "the other." *International Journal of Listening, 23*(1), 21–43.

Shuangyue, Z., & Merolla, A. J. (2006). Communicating dislike of close friends' romantic partners. *Communication Research Reports, 23*(3), 179–186.

Shultz, B. G. (1999). Improving group communication performance: An overview of diagnosis and intervention. In L. Frey, D. Gouran, & M. Poole (Eds.), *Handbook of group communication theory and research* (pp. 371–394). Thousand Oaks, CA: Sage Publications.

Shultz, C. L. (2011, March 17). Rebecca Black takes back the Internet from Charlie Sheen. *People.* Retrieved from http://www.people.com/people/article/0,,20474201,00.html

Sides, C. H. (2000). Ethics and technical communication: The past quarter century. *Journal of Technical Writing and Communication, 30*, 27–30.

Smith, A. (2010a, August 11). Home broadband 2010. *Pew Research Center Internet & American Life Project Report.* Retrieved from http://www.pewinternet.org/Reports/2010/Home-Broadband-2010.aspx.

Smith, A. (2010b, July 7). Mobile access 2010. *Pew Research Center Internet & American Life Project Report.* Retrieved from http://www.pewinternet.org/Reports/2010/Mobile-Access-2010.aspx

Smith, P. (2005, February 11). Bullies incorporated. *Sydney Morning Herald.* Retrieved from http://www.smh.com.au

Smith, R., Jr. (2004). Recruit the student: Adapting persuasion to audiences. *Communication Teacher, 18*, 53–56.

Smith, R. E. (1993). Clustering: A way to discover speech topics. *The Speech Teacher, 7*(2), 6–7.

Smith, T. E., & Frymier, A. B. (2006). Get "real": Does practicing speeches before an audience improve performance? *Communication Quarterly, 54*, 111–125.

Snyder, M. (1974). Self-monitoring of expressive behavior. *Journal of Personality and Social Psychology, 30*, 526–537.

Snyder, M. (1979). Self-monitoring processes. In L. Berkowitz (Ed.), *Advances in social psychology* (Vol. 12, pp. 86–128). New York: Academic Press.

Snyder, M., & Klein, O. (2005). Construing and constructing others: On the reality and the generality of the behavioral confirmation scenario. *Interaction Studies, 6*, 53–67.

Sokol, R. I., Webster, K. L., Thompson, N. S., & Stevens, D. A. (2005). Whining as mother-directed speech. *Infant and Child Development, 14*, 478–486.

Sprague, J., Stuart, D., and Bodary, D. (2012). *The Speaker's Handbook.* Boston: Cengage Learning.

Stafford, L. (2003). Summarizing and questioning Canary and Stafford's model of relational maintenance. In D. Danary & M. Dainton (Eds.), *Maintaining relationships through communication* (pp. 51–77). Mahwah, NJ: Erlbaum.

Stafford, L. (2005). *Maintaining long-distance and cross-residential relationships.* Mahway, NJ: Laurence Erlbaum Associates.

Stafford, L. (2010). Geographic distance and communication during courtship. *Communication Research, 37*(2), 275–297.

Steil, L. K., Barker, L. L., & Watson, K. W. (1983). *Effective listening: Key to success.* Reading, MA: Addison-Wesley.

Steil, L. K., Summerfield, J., & de Mare, G. (1983). *Listening: It can change your life.* New York: Wiley.

Steinberg, B. (2010). Swearing during family hour? Who gives a $#*! *Advertising Age, 81*(22), 2–20.

Stelter, B. (2011, January 2). TV viewing continues to edge up. *The New York Times.* Retrieved from http://www.nytimes.com/2011/01/03/business/media/03ratings.html

Stephens, K. K., & Davis, J. (2009). The social influences on electronic multitasking in organizational meetings. *Management Communication Quarterly, 23*(1), 63–83.

Sternberg, R. J. (1988). *The triangle of love: Intimacy, passion, commitment.* New York: Basic Books.

Stewart, C. J., & Cash, W. B., Jr. (2006). *Interviewing: Principles and practices* (11th ed.). New York: McGraw-Hill.

Stewart, C. J., & Cash, W. B., Jr. (2011). *Interviewing: Principles and practices* (12th ed.). New York: McGraw-Hill.

Stewart, L. P., Cooper, P. J., & Steward, A. D. (2003). *Communication and gender.* Boston: Pearson Education.

Stewart, R. A. (1994). Perceptions of a speaker's initial credibility as a function of religious involvement and religious disclosiveness. *Communication Research Reports, 11*, 169–176.

Stiff, J. B., & Mongeau, P. (2003). *Persuasive communication.* New York: Guilford Press.

Stillion Southard, B. F., & Wolvin, A. D. (2009). Jimmy Carter: A case study in listening leadership. *International Journal of Listening, 23*(2), 141–152.

Stollen, J., & White, C. (2004). The link between labels and experience in romantic relationships among young adults. Paper presented at the International Communication Association, New Orleans Sheraton, New Orleans, LA, LA Online.

Stommel, W., & Koole, T. (2010). The online support group as a community: A micro-analysis of the interaction with a new member. *Discourse Studies, 12*(3), 357–378.

Sugitani, Y. (2007). Why is it easier to communicate by e-mail? CMC contributes to the self-presentation efficacy. *The Japanese Journal of Social Psychology, 22*(3), 234–244.

Sullivan, L. (2006, July 26). In U.S. prisons, thousands spend years in isolation [Audio podcast]. In *All Things Considered.* Retrieved from http://www.npr.org/templates/story/story.php?storyId=5582144

Sun, Y., Pan, Z., & Shen, L. (2008). Understanding the third-person perception: Evidence from a meta-analysis. *Journal of Communication, 58*, 280–300.

Sunstein, C. (2007). *Republic.com 2.0.* Princeton, NJ: Princeton University Press.

Susan G. Komen 3-Day for the Cure (2011). *Thank you* [Informational video]. Retrieved from http://www.the3day.org

Sutton, S. R. (1982). Fear arousal and communication: A critical examination of theories and research. In J. Eiser (Ed.), *Social psychology and behavioral medicine* (pp. 303–337). Chichester, UK: Wiley.

Suzuki, B. H. (2002). Revisiting the model minority stereotype: Implications for student affairs practice and higher education. *New Directions for Student Services, 97*, 21.

Sybers, R., & Roach, M. E. (1962). Clothing and human behavior. *Journal of Home Economics, 54*, 184–187.

Tajfel, H., & Turner, J. C. (1986). An integrative theory of intergroup conflict. In S. Worchel & W. Austin (Eds.), *Psychology of intergroup relations* (pp. 2–24). Chicago: Nelson-Hall.

Tannen, D. (1992). *You just don't understand: Women and men in conversation.* London: Virago Press.

Tannen, D. (2009). Framing and face: The relevance of the presentation of self to linguistic discourse analysis. *Social Psychology Quarterly, 72*(4), 300–305.

Tannen, D. (2010). Abduction and identity in family interaction: Ventriloquizing as indirectness. *Journal of Pragmatics, 42*(2), 307–316.

Tannen, D., Kendall, S., & Gorgon, C. (Eds.). (2007). *Family talk: Discourse and identity in four American families.* New York: Oxford University Press.

Taylor, P., Morin, R., Cohn, D., & Wang, W. (2008, December 29). Who moves? Who stays put? Where's home? *PewResearch.* Retrieved from http://pewresearch.org/movers-and-stayers.pdf

TEDPrize. (2011). About the TED Prize. *TEDPrize: Wishes big enough to change the world.* Retrieved from http://www.tedprize.org/about-tedprize/

Teven, J. J. (2008). An examination of perceived credibility of the 2008 presidential candidates: Relationships with believability, likeability, and deceptiveness. *Human Communication, 11*, 383–400.

Teven, J. J., & McCroskey, J. C. (1997). The relationship of perceived teacher caring with student learning and teacher evaluation. *Communication Education, 46*, 1–9.

Theiss, J. A., Knobloch, L. K., Checton, M. G., & Magsamen-Conrad, K. (2009). Relationship characteristics associated with the experience of hurt in romantic relationships: A test of the relational turbulence model. *Human Communication Research, 35*(4), 588–615.

Thomas, L. T., & Levine, T. R. (1994). Disentangling listening and verbal recall: Related but separate constructs? *Human Communication Research, 21*, 103–127.

Tidwell, L. C., & Walther, J. B. (2002). Computer-mediated communication effects on disclosure, impressions, and interpersonal evaluations: Getting to know one another a bit at a time. *Human Communication Research, 28*(3), 317–348.

Tierney, J. (2007, July 31). The whys of mating: 237 reasons and counting. *The New York Times*, p. F1.

Tiggemann, M. (2005). Television and adolescent body image: The role of program content and viewing motivation. *Journal of Social & Clinical Psychology, 24*, 361–381.

Todd, T. L., & Levine, T. R. (1996). Further thoughts on recall, memory, and the measurement of listening: A rejoinder to Bostrom. *Human Communication Research, 23*, 306–308.

Tong, S. T., Van Der Heide, B., Langwell, L., & Walther, J. B. (2008). Too much of a good thing? The relationship between number of friends and interpersonal impressions on Facebook. *Journal of Computer-Mediated Communication, 13*(3), 531–549.

Torregrosa, L. L. (2010, August 31). Palin woos women and stirs up foes. *The New York Times*. Retrieved from http://www.nytimes.com/2010/09/01/us/01iht-letter.html

Tracy, J. L., & Robins, R. W. (2008). The nonverbal expression of pride: Evidence for cross-cultural recognition. *Journal of Personality & Social Psychology, 94*(3), 516–530.

Tracy, K. (2008). "Reasonable hostility": Situation-appropriate face-attack. *Journal of Politeness Research: Language, Behavior, Culture, 4*(2), 169–191.

Triandis, H. C. (1986). Collectivism vs. individualism: A reconceptualization of a basic concept in cross-cultural psychology. In C. Bagley & G. Verma (Eds.), *Personality, cognition, and values: Cross-cultural perspectives of childhood and adolescence*. London: Macmillan.

Triandis, H. C. (1988). Collectivism vs. individualism. In G. Verma & C. Bagley (Eds.), *Cross-cultural studies of personality, attitudes, and cognition*. London: Macmillan.

Triandis, H. C. (2000). Culture and conflict. *The International Journal of Psychology, 35*(2), 1435–1452.

Triandis, H. C., Brislin, R., & Hul, C. H. (1988). Cross-cultural training across the individualism-collectivism divide. *International Journal of Intercultural Relations, 12*, 269–289.

Tripathy, J. (2010). How gendered is gender and development? Culture, masculinity, and gender difference. *Development in Practice, 20*(1), 113–121.

Troester, R. L., & Mester, C. S. (2007). *Civility in business and professional communication*. New York: Peter Lang Publishing.

Tsa, W. C., Chen, C. C., & Chiu, S. F. (2005). Exploring boundaries of the effects of applicant impression management tactics in job interviews. *Journal of Management, 31*(1), 108–125.

Tuckman, B. (1965). Developmental sequences in small groups. *Psychological Bulletin, 63*, 384–399.

Tyson, N. D. (2009, February 17). *Is the universe infinite?* Speech presented at the University of Texas, Arlington. Retrieved from http://www.youtube.com/watch?v=yD1qAEeyets&feature=related

U.S. Department of Health & Human Services, Office of the Surgeon General. (2007). *Overweight in children and adolescents*. Retrieved from http://www.surgeongeneral.gov/topics/obesity/calltoaction/fact_adolescents.htm

Valkenburg, P. M., & Vroone, M. (2004). Developmental changes in infants' and toddlers' attention to television entertainment. *Communication Research, 31*, 288–311.

Vangelisti, A., & Banski, M. (1993). Couples' debriefing conversations: The impact of gender, occupation, and demographic characteristics. In *Family relations* (Vol. 42, pp. 149–157).

Van Zandt, T. (2004). Information overload and a network of targeted communication. *RAND Journal of Economics, 35*, 542–561.

Victor, D. A. (1992). *International business communication*. New York: HarperCollins.

Villaume, W. A., & Brown, M. H. (1999). The development and validation of the vocalic sensitivity test. *International Journal of Listening, 13*, 24–45.

Vogel, D. R., Dickson, G. W., & Lehman, J. A. (1986). Persuasion and the role of visual presentation support: The UM/3M study (MISRC-WP-86-11), Minneapolis, MN: University of Minnesota, Management Information Systems Research Center.

Vogel, H. L. (2011). *Entertainment industry economics: A guide for financial analysis* (8th ed.). New York: Cambridge University Press.

Von Raffler-Engel, W. (1983). *The perception of nonverbal behavior in the career interview*. Philadelphia: Benjamin.

Voss, B. (2010, December 22). Sibling revelry. *TheAdvocate.com*. Retrieved from http://www.advocate.com/Arts_and_Entertainment/Television/Sibling_Revelry/

Wade, N. (2010, January 12). Deciphering the chatter of monkeys and chimps. *The New York Times*, p. D1.

Waldron, V. R., & Applegate, J. A. (1998). Effects of tactic similarity on social attraction and persuasiveness in dyadic verbal disagreements. *Communication Reports, 11,* 155–166.

Walker, A. (1982). *The color purple.* New York: Harcourt Brace Jovanovich.

Wallis, C. (2006, March 27). The multitasking generation. *Time,* 48–55.

Walther, J. B. (1996). Computer-mediated communication: Impersonal, interpersonal, and hyperpersonal interaction. *Communication Research, 23,* 3–43.

Walther, J. B. (2004). Language and communication technology: Introduction to the special issue. *Journal of Language and Social Psychology, 23,* 384–396.

Walther, J. B., & Parks, M. R. (2002). Cues filtered out, cues filtered in: Computer-mediated communication and relationships. In M. L. Knapp & J. A. Daly (Eds.), *Handbook of interpersonal communication* (pp. 529–563). Thousand Oaks, CA: Sage Publications.

Walther, J. B., & Ramirez, A., Jr. (2009). New technologies and new directions in online relating. In S. W. Smith & S. R. Wilson (Eds.), *New directions in interpersonal communication research* (pp. 264–284). Newbury Park, CA: Sage Publications.

Walther, J. B., Van Der Heide, B., Kim, S-Y., Westerman, D., & Tong, S. T. (2008). The role of friends' appearance and behavior on evaluations of individuals on Facebook: Are we known by the company we keep? *Human Communication Research, 34*(1), 28–49.

Walther, J. B., Van Der Heide, B., Tong, S. T., Carr, C. T., & Atkin, C. K. (2010). Effects of interpersonal goals on inadvertent intrapersonal influence in computer-mediated communication. *Human Communication Research, 36*(3), 323–347.

Wang, G., & Liu, Z. (2010). What collective? Collectivism and relationalism from a Chinese perspective. *Chinese Journal of Communication, 3*(1), 42–63.

Wasserman, B., & Weseley, A. (2009). ¿Qué? Quoi? Do languages with grammatical gender promote sexist attitudes? *Sex Roles, 61*(9/10), 634–643.

Watson, K., Barker, L., & Weaver, J. (1995). The listening styles profile (LSP-16): Development and validation of an instrument to assess four listening styles. *International Journal of Listening, 9,* 1–13.

Weger, H., Jr., Castle, G. R., & Emmett, M. C. (2010). Active listening in peer interviews: The influence of message paraphrasing on perceptions of listening skill. *International Journal of Listening, 24*(1), 34–49.

Weisz, C., & Wood, L. F. (2005). Social identity support and friendship outcomes: A longitudinal study predicting who will be friends and best friends 4 years later. *Journal of Social and Personal Relationships, 22,* 416–432.

Westmyer, S., DiCioccio, R., & Rubin, R. (1998). Appropriateness and effectiveness of communication channels in competent interpersonal communication. *Journal of Communication, 48,* 27–48.

Wheelan, S. (1994). *Group process: A developmental perspective.* Boston: Allyn & Bacon.

Wheeless, L. R. (1975). An investigation of receiver apprehension and social context dimensions of communication apprehension. *Speech Teacher, 24*(3), 261–268.

White House, Office of the Press Secretary. (2011, January 12). Remarks by the president at a memorial service for the victims of the shooting in Tucson, Arizona [Press release]. Retrieved from http://www.whitehouse.gov/the-press-office/2011/01/12/remarks-president-barack-obama-memorial-service-victims-shooting-tucson

Why most meetings stink. (2005, October 31). *Business Week.* Retrieved from http://www.businessweek.com

Wiemann, J. M. (1977). Explication and test of a model of communication competence. *Human Communication Research, 3,* 195–213.

Wiemann, J. M., & Backlund, P. M. (1980). Current theory and research in communication competence. *Review of Educational Research, 50,* 185–189.

Wiemann, J. M., & Knapp, M. L. (1999). Turn-taking in conversations. In L. K. Guerrero, J. A. DeVito, & M. L. Hecht (Eds.), *The nonverbal communication reader: Classic and contemporary readings* (pp. 406–414). Prospect Heights, IL: Waveland Press.

Wiemann, J. M., & Krueger, D. L. (1980). The language of relationships. In H. Giles, W. P. Robinson, & P. M. Smith (Eds.), *Language: Social psychological perspectives* (pp. 55–62). Oxford: Pergamon Press.

Wiemann, J. M., Takai, J., Ota, H., & Wiemann, M. O. (1997). A relational model of communication competence. In B. Kovčaić (Ed.), *Emerging theories of human communication* (pp. 25–44). Albany, NY: State University of New York Press.

Wiemann, J. M., & Wiemann, M. O. (1992). *Interpersonal communicative competence: Listening and perceiving.* Unpublished manuscript, University of California–Santa Barbara.

Wiemann, M. O. (2009). *Love you/hate you: Negotiating intimate relationships.* Barcelona, Spain: Editorial Aresta.

Wierzbicka, A. (2006). *English: Meaning and culture.* New York: Oxford.

Wiesenfeld, D., Bush, K., & Sikdar, R. (2010). The value of listening: Heeding the call of the Snuggie. *Journal of Advertising Research, 50*(1), 16–20.

Willard, G., & Gramzow, R. (2008). Exaggeration in memory: Systematic distortion of self-evaluative information under reduced accessibility. *Journal of Experimental Social Psychology, 44*(2), 246–259.

Williams, D. (2006). On and off the 'net: Scales for social capital in an online era. *Journal of Computer Mediated Communication, 11*, 593–628.

Williams, D. E., & Hughes, P. C. (2005). Nonverbal communication in Italy: An analysis of interpersonal touch, body position, eye contact, and seating behaviors. *North Dakota Journal of Speech & Theatre, 18*, 17–24.

Williams, K. N., Herman, R., Gajewski, B., & Wilson, K. (2009). Elderspeak communication: Impact on dementia care. *American Journal of Alzheimer's Disease & Other Dementias, 24*(1), 11–20.

Wilmot, W. W. (1987). *Dyadic communication* (3rd ed.). New York: Random House.

Winston, C. (2002, January 28). State of the Union stew. *The Christian Science Monitor.* Retrieved from http://www.csmonitor.com

Winter, J., & Pauwels, A. (2006). Men staying at home looking after their children: Feminist linguistic reform and social change. *International Journal of Applied Linguistics, 16*(1), 16–36.

Wolvin, A. D. (2006). Modeling listening scholarship: Ralph G. Nichols. *International Journal of Listening, 20*, 22–26.

Wolvin, A. D., & Coakley, C. G. (1991). A survey of the status of listening training in some *Fortune* 500 corporations. *Communication Education, 40*, 151–164.

Wood, B. (1982). *Children and communication: Verbal and nonverbal language development* (2nd ed.). Englewood Cliffs, NJ: Prentice Hall.

Wood, J. T. (2008). Gender, communication, and culture. In L. A. Samovar, R. E. Porter, and E. R. McDaniel (Eds.), *Intercultural communication: A reader* (pp. 170–180). Belmont, CA: Wadsworth Cengage.

Wood, J. T. (2009). *Gendered lives: Communication, gender, and culture* (8th ed.). Boston, MA: Wadsworth Publishing.

Wood, J. T. (2011). *Gendered lives: Communication, gender, and culture* (9th ed.). Boston, MA: Wadsworth Publishing.

Woodzicka, J. (2008). Sex differences in self-awareness of smiling during a mock job interview. *Journal of Nonverbal Behavior, 32*(2), 109–121.

Wrench, J. S., McCroskey, J. C., & Richmond, V. P. (2008). *Human communication in everyday life: Explanations and applications.* Boston: Allyn & Bacon.

Wright, C. N., Holloway, A., & Roloff, M. E. (2007). The dark side of self-monitoring: How high self-monitors view their romantic relationships. *Communication Reports, 20*(2), 101–114.

Wright, J. W., & Ross, S. (1997). Trial by media? Media reliance, knowledge of crime and perception of criminal defendants. *Communication Law & Policy, 2*(4), 397–416.

Wyatt, E. (2009, November 14). More than ever, you can say that on television. *The New York Times,* p. A1.

Yaguchi, M., Iyeiri, Y., & Baba, Y. (2010). Speech style and gender distinctions in the use of *very* and *real/really*: An analysis of the Corpus of Spoken Professional American English. *Journal of Pragmatics, 42*(3), 585–597.

Yasui, E. (2009, May). Collaborative idea construction: The repetition of gestures and talk during brainstorming. A paper presented at the 59th meeting of the International Communication Association, Chicago, IL.

Yook, E. (2004). Any questions? Knowing the audience through question types. *Communication Teacher, 18*, 91–93.

Young, J., & Foot, K. (2005). Corporate e-cruiting: The construction of work in *Fortune* 500 recruiting Web sites. *Journal of Computer-Mediated Communication, 11*(1), 44–71.

Zacchilli, T. L., Hendrick, C., & Hendrick, S. S. (2009). The romantic partner conflict scale: A new scale to measure relationship conflict. *Journal of Social and Personal Relationships, 26*(8), 1073–1096.

Zeller, T., Jr. (2010, June 18). Drill ban means hard time for rig workers. *The New York Times,* p. B1.

Zhang, J., & Daugherty, T. (2009). Third-person effect and social networking: Implications for online marketing and word-of-mouth communication. *American Journal of Business, 24*, 54–63.

Zimbushka (2008, May 27). *Mike Caro's 10 ultimate poker cues.* Retrieved from http://www.youtube.com/watch?v=QqF8m12JSDE

ACKNOWLEDGMENTS

Text Credits

Box 1.2: The National Communication Association, "Credo for Ethical Communication." Copyright © 1999 by the National Communication Association. Reprinted by permission. **Figure 2.4:** Dan O'Hair, et al., "Assessing Our Perceptions of Self." From *Competent Communication*, Second Edition. Copyright © 2007 by Bedford/St. Martin's. Used by permission of Bedford/St. Martin's. **Page 46:** Mark Snyder, "Self-Monitoring Test" adapted from "Self-monitoring and expressive behavior" in *Journal of Personality and Social Psychology* 30 (1974): 526–537. Reprinted by permission. **Figure 4.1:** Dan O'Hair et al., "The Abstraction Ladder." Adapted from Dan O'Hair et al., *Competent Communication*, 2/e. Copyright © 1997. Adapted with the permission of Bedford/St. Martin's. **Table 5.1:** Dale Leathers, "The Power of Eye Contact" from *Successful Nonverbal Communication: Principles and Applications*, 3/e, by Dale Leathers, copyright © 1997. Adapted by permission of Pearson Education, Inc., Upper Saddle River, NJ. **Figure 5.2:** Dan O'Hair et al., "Zones of Personal Space." From *Competent Communication*, 2/e, copyright © 1997 by Bedford/St. Martin's. Adapted with the permission of Bedford/St. Martin's. **Table 6.1:** Dan O'Hair et al., "Listening Goals" from *Competent Communication*, second edition. Copyright © 1997 by Bedford/St. Martin's. Adapted with the permission of Bedford/St. Martin's. **Page 132:** Lawrence R. Wheeless. "An investigation of receiver apprehension and social context dimensions of communication apprehension." *Communication Education*, January 9, 1975: 261–268. Copyright © 1975. Adapted with permission of Taylor & Francis, Ltd., www.informaworld.com. **Table 7.1:** John Caughlin, excerpt from "Family Communication Standards: What counts as excellent family communication, and how are such standards associated with family satisfaction?" from *Human Communication Research* 29 (2003): 5–40. Reprinted with the permission of John Wiley and Sons. **Table 7.4:** D. J. Canary and M. J. Cody, "Romantic Relational Termination Strategies." From *Interpersonal Communication: A Goals-Based Approach*. Copyright © 1994 by Bedford/St. Martin's Press. Adapted with the permission of Bedford/St. Martin's. **Page 182:** Dominic A. Infante, "Self-Assessment: Hitting Above and Below the Belt" from *Arguing Constructively* (Long Grove, IL: Waveland Press, 1988). Reprinted by permission of Waveland Press. All rights reserved. **Figure 9.1:** Dan O'Hair et al., "Complexity of Group Relationships." From *Competent Communication*, Second Edition. Copyright © 2007 by Bedford/St. Martin's. Used by permission of Bedford/St. Martin's. **Figure 9.2:** "Group Communication Networks" from *Organizations: Rational, Natural, and Open Systems* by W. Richard Scott, copyright © 1981. Adapted by permission of Pearson Education, Inc., Upper Saddle River, NJ. **Page 206:** James McCroskey, "How Well Do You Interact in a Group Setting?" from *An Introduction to Rhetorical Communication*, 9/e, by James C. McCroskey, copyright © 2006. Adapted by permission of Pearson Education, Inc., Upper Saddle River, NJ. **Page 237:** Ricky Martin, Speech presented at the Vienna Forum. Used by permission of Ricky Martin, President and Founder of Ricky Martin Foundation. **Figure 11.1:** Dan O'Hair et al., "An Example of the Web of Associations Produced by Clustering." Adapted from D. O'Hair, R. Stewart, and H. Rubenstein, *Competent Communication*, 2/e. Copyright © 1997 by Bedford/St. Martin's. Adapted with the permission of Bedford/St. Martin's. **Table 12.1:** Dan O'Hair et al., "Useful Signposts." From D. O'Hair, R. Stewart, and H. Rubenstein, *A Speaker's Guidebook*, Third Edition. Copyright © 2007 by Bedford/St. Martin's Press. Reprinted with the permission of Bedford/St. Martin's. **Table 14.2:** Dan O'Hair et al., "Types of Informative Speeches, Sample Topics, Informational Strategies, and Organizational Patterns." From D. O'Hair, R. Stewart, and H. Rubenstein, *A Speaker's Guidebook*, Third Edition. Copyright © 2007 by Bedford/St. Martin's Press. Adapted with the permission of Bedford/St. Martin's.

Photo Credits

Cover: Young couple in photo booth, photo by Siri Stafford, © Getty Images; mixed breed dog, close-up, photo by Chris Whitehead, © Getty Images; couple laughing and pulling faces, photo by Ken Fisher, © Getty Images; young man in photo booth, photo by Siri Stafford, © Getty Images; couple in photo booth, photo by Jessica Peterson, © Getty

Images; **Page 2:** John Moore/Getty Images; **6:** (grid, L-R) © JoeFoxNewYork/Alamy, Carin Baer/© AMC/Courtesy: Everett Collection, © Focus Features/Courtesy Everett Collection, Kevin Mazur/WireImage/Getty Images; **7:** © 20th Century Fox Film Corp./Photofest; **9:** (top) © David Grossman/The Image Works, (bot) © imagebroker/Alamy; **13:** (top) © 20th Century Fox Film Corp/Courtesy Everett Collection. All rights reserved, (bot) Chip Somodevilla/Getty Images; **15:** Greg Gayne/ © FOX/Courtesy Everett Collection; **16:** AP Photo/Jason DeCrow, File; **Figure 1.1:** Asia Images/Superstock; **Figure 1.2:** (L) iStockphoto, (R) © Fancy/Alamy; **Figure 1.3:** © PhotoAlto sas/Alamy; **22:** (L) © Mango Productions/Corbis, (R) © Robert Fried/Alamy; **28:** Photo by Ken McKay/Rex USA, courtesy Everett Collection; **32:** David Young-Wolff/PhotoEdit; **33:** THE BUCKETS copyright 2003 Greg Cravens. Reprinted with permission of Universal Uclick for UFS. All rights reserved.; **36:** © 20th Century Fox/courtesy Everett Collection; **38:** (top) AP Photo/Pablo Martinez Monsivais, (bot) Photo by Paul Drinkwater/NBC/NBCU Photo Bank via Getty Images; **39:** Patrick McElhenney/© FX/Courtesy: Everett Collection; **Figure 2.5:** © Image Source/Alamy; **45:** Wathiq Khuzaie/Getty Images; **51:** Matthias Clamer/© Fox Television/Courtesy Everett Collection; **55:** Yellow Dog Productions/Getty Images; **59:** © Mervyn Rees/Alamy; **62:** AP Photo/Warner Bros., Michael Rozman; **65:** KEVIN DIETSCH/UPI/Landov; **66:** Chu Yang/Xinhua/Photoshot/Newscom; **71:** (grid, L-R) AP Photo/ Charles Dharapak, File, PhotoAlto/Eric Audras/Getty Images, Clarissa Leahy/Getty Images; **74:** (grid, L-R) Quinn Rooney/ Getty Images, ABC/Photofest, Getty Images, © Martin Norris/Alamy, © Photofusion Picture Library/Alamy, Stockbyte/Getty Images; **77:** (L) Index Stock/Jupiter Images/, (R) Comstock/Jupiter Images; **79:** © Ian Middleton/Alamy; **83:** PEDRO ARMESTRE/AFP/Getty Images; **85:** (L) © Beathan/Corbis; © Stephanie Sinclair/VII Photo Agency; **89:** Ronnie Kaufman/ Larry Hirshowitz/Blend Images/Getty Images; **93:** Blend Images/Alamy; **96:** (top-bot) © Walt Disney Co./courtesy Everett Collection, © Walt Disney Co./courtesy Everett Collection, © Walt Disney Co./courtesy Everett Collection; **99:** (L) Simon Baker/Getty Images, (R) AP Photo/Al Behrman; **100:** REUTERS/Las Vegas Sun/Steve Marcus/Landov; **103:** Hiroko Masuike/Getty Images; **Figure 5.1:** (grid, L-R) iStockphoto, © INSADCO Photography/Alamy, © RubberBall/ Alamy, iStockphoto, iStockphoto, © FRANCK CAMHI/Alamy, © Fancy/Alamy; **108:** Patrick Jube/Getty Images; **110:** SONJA FLEMMING/CBS/Landov; **115:** AP Photo/The Advocate Messenger, Clay Jackson; **118:** Blend Images/Punchstock; **121:** (L) Blend Images/Punchstock, (R) Blend Images/Punchstock; **124:** ABC/Photofest; **126:** Sonja Flemming/CBS via Getty Images; **127:** Juice Images/Punchstock; **129:** © Vikki Martin /Alamy; **130:** Imagestate/Photolibrary/Getty Images; **131:** © Warner Brothers/Courtesy Everett Collection; **135:** Fox/ Photofest; **137:** © 20th Century Fox Film Corp. All rights reserved/courtesy The Everett Collection; **140:** Harry How/ Getty Images; **143:** TLC/Photofest; **145:** Alexandra Wyman/ WireImage/Getty Images; **147:** (grid, L-R) Getty Images, The Image Works, Landov, Getty Images; **150:** © Bettmann/ Corbis; **151:** Jonathan Wenk/© Columbia Pictures/Courtesy Everett Collection; **154:** CBS/Photofest; **156:** © Warner Bros./ Courtesy Everett Collection; **160:** BENOIT TESSIER/Reuters/ Landov; **166:** Merrick Morton/© Columbia Pictures/Courtesy Everett Collection; **169:** DK Stock/Donn Thompson; **170:** © Deborah Jaffe/FoodPix/Getty Images; **176:** THE KOBAL COLLECTION/Art Resource, NY; **178:** © Rick Friedman/ Corbis; **180:** Jennifer Durham/Jupiter Images/Getty Images; **181:** Creatas/Jupiter Images/Getty Images; **185:** John Lund/ Drew Kelly/Getty Images; **188:** AP Photo/J. Scott Applewhite; **191:** © David Atlas/Retna; **193:** David Furst/AFP/Getty Images; **194:** (L) © Bob Mahoney/The Image Works, (R) AP Photo/ Damian Dovarganes; **196:** ROBERT VOETS/CBS/Landov; **198:** AP Photo/Herbert Knosowski; **201:** Bruce Bennett/Getty Images; **203:** © Bettmann/Corbis; **206:** Fox/Photofest; **207:** © Buena Vista Pictures/courtesy Everett Collection; **210:** Mitchell Haaseth/© NBC/Photofest; **213:** © Universal Pictures/ courtesy Everett Collection; **215:** Carin Baer/© FOX/courtesy Everett Collection; **217:** © 20th Century Fox Film Corp. All rights reserved, Courtesy: Everett Collection; **219:** (L) Image 100/Punchstock, (R) Blend Images/Punchstock; **221:** Punchstock; **223:** © Jeff Greenberg/Alamy; **224:** © Warner Bros./ courtesy Everett Collection; **227:** B. Busco/Getty Images; **229:** © Wavebreak Media ltd/Alamy; **232:** Justin Sullivan/ Getty Images; **235:** Marie Hansen/Time Life Pictures/Getty Images; **240:** Doug Menuez/Getty Images; **241:** (L) ROGER L. WOLLENBERG/UPI/Landov, (R) AP Photo/Boris Heger, UNHCR; **248:** Lauren Gordon/The Breeze/James Madison University; **249:** (L) Used with permission from Microsoft, (R) Courtesy of Google, Inc. Reprinted with permission; **255:** © NMPFT/ DHA/SSPL/The Image Works; **258:** Photo by Pete Souza/ The White House via Getty Images; **261:** Comstock/Jupiter Images; **263:** © Caro/Alamy; **264:** THE KOBAL COLLECTION/ BOLAND, JASIN/Art Resource, NY; **265:** Jonathan Larsen/ Veer; **266:** © ilbusca/istockphoto.com; **267:** MPI/Getty Images; **271:** Digital Vision/Getty Images; **276:** Michael Newman/PhotoEdit Inc.; **286:** © The Weinstein Company/Courtesy Everett Collection; **289:** © Roger Ressmeyer/Corbis; **290:** © Blend Images/Alamy; **291:** BILL GREENBLATT/UPI/Landov; **293:** (grid, L-R) © Columbia Pictures/courtesy Everett Collection, Streeter Lecka/Getty Images, Jim Jordan Photography/ Getty Images, © Jeff Morgan education/Alamy, © Chris

INDEX

More Media. Integrated. }

bedfordstmartins.com/commandyou

The *Communication and You* companion Web site includes videos from *VideoCentral: Human Communication* that complement the material in the text, offering examples and explanations of key concepts. Here is a quick list of the videos and where their concepts appear in the text.